'This book is imaginative, ambitious, state of the art, interdisciplinary and international and has futuristic reflections on justice for victims.'
Dr Pamela Davies, *Teaching Fellow and Director of Criminology, Northumbria University, UK*

'*Justice for Victims* is an anthology that should be in university libraries across the world. It provides an impressive smorgasbord of writings from some known scholars, but also many new scholars whose contributions to Victimology can now be easily accessed. It covers rights for victims, justice in countries in transition, and issues of reconciliation between oppressors and oppressed.'
Irvin Waller, *President, International Organization for Victim Assistance and Professor, University of Ottawa, Canada*

Justice for Victims

Justice for Victims brings together the world's leading scholars in the fields of study surrounding victimization in a pioneering international collection. This book focuses on the current study of victims of crime, combining both legal and social-scientific perspectives, articulating both in new directions and questioning whether victims really do have more rights in our modern world.

This book offers an interdisciplinary approach, covering large-scale (political) victimization, terrorist victimization, sexual victimization and routine victimization. Split into three sections, this book provides in-depth coverage of: victims' rights, transitional justice and victims' perspectives, and trauma, resilience and justice. Victims' rights are conceptualized in the human rights framework and discussed in relation to supranational, international and regional policies. The transitional justice section covers victims of war from the point of view of those caught between peace and justice, as well as post-conflict justice. The final section focuses on post-traumatic stress, connecting psychological and anthropological perceptions in analysing collective violence, mass victimization and trauma.

This book addresses challenging and new issues in the field of victimology and the study of transitional and restorative justice. It will be of interest to researchers, practitioners and students interested in the fields of victimology, transitional justice, restorative justice and trauma work.

Inge Vanfraechem, PhD, is Manager of the European FP7 ALTERNATIVE project and works at the KU Leuven, where she received her BA, MA and PhD in criminology (2006).

Dr Vanfraechem is the editor of *Restorative Justice: an International Journal*, the only peer-reviewed, high standard, academic and international journal in the field of restorative justice. Dr Vanfraechem is also a key member of the Working Group on Victimology of the European Society of Criminology (ESC).

Antony Pemberton, PhD, is Associate Professor and Director of Studies at the International Victimology Institute Tilburg (INTERVICT) in the Netherlands. He has published more than 60 articles, books and book chapters on victimological subjects, with a particular emphasis on victims in justice processes.

Felix Mukwiza Ndahinda, PhD, is an Assistant Professor at Tilburg Law School's International Victimology Institute Tilburg (INTERVICT, Tilburg University, the Netherlands) and he is also the coordinator for the Masters in Victimology and Criminal Justice at Tilburg Law School. He holds a PhD from Tilburg University (2009); an LLM from the Raoul Wallenberg Institute of Human Rights (Sweden-2006) and a Bachelor's degree (LLB) from the National University of Rwanda (2003).

Justice for Victims

Perspectives on rights, transition and reconciliation

Inge Vanfraechem, Antony Pemberton and Felix Mukwiza Ndahinda
With Ivo Aertsen, Victor Jammers, Sonja Leferink, Rianne Letschert and Stephan Parmentier

Routledge
Taylor & Francis Group
LONDON AND NEW YORK

First published 2014
by Routledge

2 Park Square, Milton Park, Abingdon, Oxon OX14 4RN
711 Third Avenue, New York, NY 10017, USA

Routledge is an imprint of the Taylor & Francis Group, an informa business

First issued in paperback 2016

Copyright © 2014 selection and editorial material, Inge Vanfraechem, Antony Pemberton and Felix Mukwiza Ndahinda; individual chapters, the contributors.

The right of Inge Vanfraechem, Antony Pemberton and Felix Mukwiza Ndahinda to be identified as author of this work has been asserted by them in accordance with sections 77 and 78 of the Copyright, Designs and Patents Act 1988.

All rights reserved. No part of this book may be reprinted or reproduced or utilised in any form or by any electronic, mechanical, or other means, now known or hereafter invented, including photocopying and recording, or in any information storage or retrieval system, without permission in writing from the publishers.

Notices:

Product or corporate names may be trademarks or registered trademarks, and are used only for identification and explanation without intent to infringe.

British Library Cataloguing in Publication Data
A catalogue record for this book is available from the British Library

Library of Congress Cataloging-in-Publication Data
Justice for victims: perspectives on rights, transition and reconciliation / edited by Inge Vanfraechem, Antony Pemberton and Felix Mukwiza Ndahinda.
　pages cm
　1. Victims of crimes. 2. Restorative justice. I. Vanfraechem, Inge. II. Pemberton, Antony. III. Ndahinda, Felix Mukwiza.
　HV6250.25.J87 2014
　362.88–dc23
　2013048744

ISBN 978-1-138-66610-8 (pbk)
ISBN 978-0-415-63433-5 (hbk)
ISBN 978-0-203-09453-2 (ebk)

Typeset in Times New Roman
by Sunrise Setting Ltd, Paignton, UK

Contents

List of figures x
List of tables xi
List of contributors xii
Acknowledgements xvii

General introduction 1
FELIX MUKWIZA NDAHINDA, ANTONY PEMBERTON AND
INGE VANFRAECHEM

PART I
Victims' rights 9

1 Victims' rights 11
   PAUL ROCK

2 Respecting victims of crime: key distinctions
   in a theory of victims' rights 32
   ANTONY PEMBERTON

3 Recognition of victims' rights through EU
   action: latest developments and challenges 51
   HELGA EZENDAM AND FRIDA WHELDON

4 Implementing victim rights in newly industrialized
   countries: reflections on major challenges
   and recommendations for the future 66
   K. JAISHANKAR

5 Should reparations for massive human rights abuses perpetrated on African victims during colonial times be given? 89
JEREMY SARKIN

6 State compensation for victims of violent crime 105
DAVID MIERS

7 Legal protection and assistance for victims of human trafficking in the United States: a harm reduction approach 140
XIN REN

PART II
Transitional justice 159

8 Victims, transitional justice and social reconstruction: who is setting the agenda? 161
HARVEY WEINSTEIN

9 Integral justice for victims 183
RAMA MANI

10 Repairing the impossible: victimological approaches to international crimes 210
RIANNE LETSCHERT AND STEPHAN PARMENTIER

11 Transitional justice and the victims: a special focus on the case of Chile 228
JOSÉ ZALAQUETT

12 The Transitional Justice Imaginary: Uncle San, Aunty Yan and victim participation at the Khmer Rouge Tribunal 247
ALEXANDER LABAN HINTON

PART III
Trauma, resilience and justice 263

13 Perceived control over traumatic events: is it always adaptive? 265
PATRICIA FRAZIER

14 Procedural justice for victims of crime: are victim impact statements and victim–offender mediation rising to the challenge? 277
TINNEKE VAN CAMP AND VICKY DE MESMAECKER

15 Delivering justice to child victims of crime: navigating the support and criminal justice systems 300
ILSE VANDE WALLE

16 ETA terrorism victims' experience with restorative encounters in Spain 322
GEMA VARONA

17 Victims of corruption: a conceptual framework 355
QINGLI MENG AND PAUL C. FRIDAY

18 Reconceptualizing sexual victimization and justice 378
KATHLEEN DALY

Index 396

Figures

7.1	The legal elements in identifying a crime of trafficking in persons	144
7.2	Polaris Project (2013): 2013 State ratings on human trafficking laws	147
9.1	Dimensions of Integral Justice	191
16.1	ETA killings without condemned main offender	333

Tables

1.1	Cases received by the Parliamentary Ombudsman under the Victims' Code 2009–2011	22
2.1	Comparing key characteristics of sympathy and empathy	39
7.1	Human trafficking cases investigated by HSI in 2011 and 2012	143
16.1a	Numbers of ETA fatal victims over time (total 829 fatalities)	323
16.1b	ETA fatalities by status, gender and location of victimization	324
16.2	Recovery and restorative factors in the process of de-victimization for terrorism in Spain	335
17.1	Relationship of corruption manifestation and level of victimization – for illustrative purposes	366
18.1	Sexual violence and justice matrix, A and C country contexts (B country contexts, developing country at peace, excluded)	385

Contributors

Kathleen Daly is Professor of Criminology and Criminal Justice, Griffith University (Brisbane). She writes on restorative justice, indigenous justice, and innovative justice responses to partner, family, and sexual violence. Her book, Redressing Institutional Abuse of Children, is forthcoming (Palgrave). She is a Fellow of the Academy of the Social Sciences in Australia, and past President of the Australian and New Zealand Society of Criminology (2005–9).

Vicky De Mesmaecker obtained a PhD in Criminology at the University of Leuven, Belgium. She worked as a doctoral researcher and postdoctoral researcher at the Leuven Institute of Criminology (University of Leuven) and has been a visiting researcher at Yale University in the United States and at the Netherlands Institute for the Study of Crime and Law Enforcement in the Netherlands. Her main fields of study include theories of procedural justice, the legitimacy of criminal justice, victimology and restorative justice.

Helga Ezendam studied criminal law at Leiden University. She started working at the public prosecutor's office both in practice and in the development of policy. Now she works as a senior policy officer for the Ministry of Security and Justice. Her earlier volunteer work in the field of victim support is a source of inspiration for her current work in the field of policy for victims of crime.

Patricia Frazier, PhD, is a distinguished McKnight University Professor of Psychology and Associate Chair for Research in the Department of Psychology at the University of Minnesota, Minneapolis, MN, USA. Her research examines the effects of traumatic life events, including victimization. She is a Fellow of the American Psychological Association and has published numerous articles on the effects of victimization.

Paul C. Friday is Professor of Criminal Justice and Director, International Center for China Studies at the University of North Carolina-Charlotte. He has published eight books and numerous articles on international criminal justice, victimology and juvenile justice. He served twenty-four years as Treasurer and Executive Board member of the World Society of Victimology and in 2012 he received a Certificate of Appreciation for his work in Victimology and for the World Society.

Alexander Laban Hinton is Director of the Center for the Study of Genocide and Human Rights, Professor of Anthropology, and UNESCO Chair on Genocide Prevention at Rutgers University. He is the author of the award-winning *Why Did They Kill? Cambodia in the Shadow of Genocide* (California, 2005) and nine edited or co-edited collections. In recognition of his work on genocide, the American Anthropological Association selected him as the recipient of the 2009 Robert B. Textor and Family Prize for Excellence in Anticipatory Anthropology. He is also the immediate past President of the International Association of Genocide Scholars (2011–13) and was a Member/Visitor at the Institute for Advanced Study at Princeton (2011–13).

K. Jaishankar, PhD, is a Senior Assistant Professor in the Department of Criminology and Criminal Justice, MSU and Member of Syndicate (Board of Management), Manonmaniam Sundaranar University (MSU), Tirunelveli, Tamil Nadu, India. He has published more than 100 publications, including articles, editorials, book chapters and books. He is the recipient of the prestigious National Academy of Sciences, India (NASI) – SCOPUS Young Scientist Award 2012 – Social Sciences.

Rianne Letschert is Professor of Victimology and International Law and Deputy Director at the International Victimology Institute Tilburg (INTERVICT). At INTERVICT she works on issues such as victims' rights and human security issues, in particular on international lawmaking in the field of victims' rights and victims of international crimes, especially reparations. She is member of the Board of Governance of the Dutch Victim Support Organization, and expert consultant for the Special Tribunal for Lebanon on victim issues. In 2013, she was appointed to the Dutch Royal Young Academy of Sciences.

Rama Mani is Senior Research Associate, Centre for International Studies at University of Oxford; Councillor, World Future Council; Co-Convenor, 'Agents of Transformation'; formerly Executive Director of ICES, Sri Lanka; Director of Global Peace and Security Course, GCSP-Geneva; and Strategy Manager on African conflicts at OXFAM-GB. She authored *Beyond Retribution: Seeking Justice in the Shadows of War* (Polity/Blackwell 2002/ 2007) and co-edited *Responsibility to Protect: Cultural Perspectives from the Global South* with Thomas Weiss (Routledge 2011). Her PhD is from the University of Cambridge.

Qingli Meng is Associate Director, International Center for China Studies, University of North Carolina-Charlotte. Her PhD is in Public Policy from UNC Charlotte. She is the author of *Corruption in Transitional China: A 33 Year Study* (Wolf Legal Publishers, 2013). She is also a Post-Doctoral Fellow at the School of Political Science and Public Administration, Beihang University, Beijing, China.

Dr David Miers is an Emeritus Professor and has a long-standing research interest in the criminal justice system's responses to victims of crime, in particular in arrangements for their compensation by offenders and by the state. He has written extensively on and given many conference presentations on these matters. He is now retired, but still contactable at miers@cf.ac.uk

Stephan Parmentier studied law and sociology at the KU Leuven (Belgium) and sociology and conflict resolution at the Humphrey Institute for Public Affairs, University of Minnesota-Twin Cities (USA). He currently teaches sociology of crime, law, and human rights at the Faculty of Law of the KU. Leuven, and has served as the head of the Department of Criminal Law and Criminology (2005–9). In July 2010 he was appointed Secretary-General of the International Society for Criminology and he also serves on the Advisory Board of the Oxford Centre of Criminology and on the Board of the International Institute for Sociology of Law (Oñati).

Antony Pemberton, PhD, is Associate Professor and Director of Studies at the International Victimology Institute Tilburg (INTERVICT) in the Netherlands. He has published more than sixty articles, books and book chapters on victimological subjects, with a particular emphasis on victims in justice processes. He co-authored a book on victims of terrorism (*Assisting Victims of Terrorism: Towards a European Standard of Justice*, Springer, 2010), co-edited a volume on victims of international crimes (*Victimological Approaches to International Crimes*, Africa, 2011) and has published a series of articles applying concepts from social and clinical psychology to victimology (included in *The Cross-over: An Interdisciplinary Approach to the Study of Victims of Crime*, Maklu, 2010). More information can be found at http://www.tilburguniversity.edu/webwijs/show/?uid=a.pemberton

Xin Ren, PhD, has been Professor of Criminal Justice at the California State University, Sacramento, USA since 1990. She is also Adjunct Professor of L.L.D. Program at the Institute of International Studies, Ramkhanhaeng University, Bangkok, Thailand. Previously, she was elected two-term member of the Executive Committee of World Society of Victimology and the Chairperson for both Victim Service and membership Committees. Her research interests include comparative studies of juvenile justice system, human trafficking and prostitution in Asia and China.

Paul Rock is an Emeritus Professor of Sociology at the London School of Economics. He has been a Visiting Professor at a number of institutions, including the Australian National University, the Center for Advanced Studies in the Behavioral Sciences, Princeton University and the University of Pennsylvania. He is a Fellow of the British Academy and the Royal Society of Arts, and is the author of a number of studies on criminological theory and criminal justice policy-making. He is currently working on the official history of criminal justice.

Jeremy Sarkin has undergraduate and postgraduate law degrees from South Africa, a Master of Laws from Harvard Law School and a Doctor of Laws degree on comparative and international law. He is admitted to practice as attorney in the USA and South Africa. He is an Extraordinary Professor of Law at the University of South Africa (UNISA). He is a member, and was Chairperson-Rapporteur (2009–12), of the United Nations Working Group on Enforced or Involuntary Disappearances.

Tinneke Van Camp has worked as a research assistant at the Catholic University of Leuven and the National Institute for Criminalistics and Criminology (Belgium). In 2011, she obtained a PhD in criminology from the University of Montreal (Canada). In 2013, she joined the School of Law at the University of Sheffield. Her main interests lie in victim experiences with restorative justice and judicial proceedings.

Ilse Vande Walle is a qualified Social Worker and works as a trainer and consultant for different Victim Support organizations in Europe. Since the start of her work for Victim Support in 1995 she has specialized in support for young victims of crime. She devised different methodologies to work with children and youngsters and worked out training for VS workers. She developed a framework and training for improving the assessment of victims' needs, particularly the needs of young victims. Ilse trained people in several European countries to be aware of young victims and to learn how to support them. In 2012 her second book, *Ik krijg het moeilijk uit mijn hoofd*, containing testimonies of child victims and their parents, was published in Belgium and the Netherlands.

Gema Varona is a Lecturer in Criminology and Victimology at the University of the Basque Country (Spain) and Senior Researcher at the Basque Institute of Criminology. Among her books in Spanish are: *Irregular Migration: Human Rights and Duties* (1994); *Reparative Mediation as Social Control Strategy: A Criminological Perspective* (1998); *Juries and the Architecture of Juridical Criminal Truth* (2000); *Restorative Justice Through Public Penal Mediation Services in the Basque Country: An external Evaluation* (2009); *Local Analysis of Safety From the Standpoint of Criminology* (2012); *Brief Dictionary of Restorative Justice. An Interdisciplinary Invitation* (2012, co-authored with Idoia Igartua and Alberto Olalde), and in English: *Restorative Justice: New Social Rites within the Criminal Justice System?* (1996).

Harvey M. Weinstein, MD, MPH is Senior Research Fellow at the Human Rights Center of the University of California, Berkeley and a retired Clinical Professor in the School of Public Health. As Associate Director of the Human Rights Center from 1998–2005, he directed the Forced Migration and Health Project and was Co-Principal Investigator on three other projects – 'Communities in

Crisis; Justice, Accountability and Social Reconstruction in Rwanda and Former Yugoslavia', 'Intrastate Conflict and Social Reconstruction', and 'Education for Reconciliation in Rwanda: Creating a History Curriculum After Genocide'.

Frida Wheldon is the Director of Policy for Victim Support Europe, providing policy guidance, recommendations and expert advice on victim issues and practical implications of European legislation. She also serves as the Senior Policy and Research Officer for Victim Support Scotland, where she is developing an internal victimology capacity while advocating to ensure that new Scottish legislation and public policy reflects the needs of people affected by crime. Originally from Sweden where she received her first Masters Degree in law, she moved to Scotland in 2005 to study an LLM in International Law at Edinburgh University.

José Zalaquett is a Professor of Human Rights at the University of Chile. He was involved in the defence of human rights during the 1973–90 military dictatorship in Chile. Following his country's return to democracy he was appointed to the Chilean Truth and Reconciliation Commission. Subsequently he has worked in the field of transitional justice in many countries.

Acknowledgements

The main editors would like to formulate a special word of thanks to the editing committee of this book: Ivo Aertsen, Victor Jammers, Sonja Leferink, Rianne Letschert and Stephan Parmentier.

The *14th Symposium of the World Society of Victimology* which was the occasion that inspired this book, was made possible thanks to the World Society of Victimology, in cooperation with INTERVICT (University of Tilburg, the Netherlands), Leuven Institute of Criminology (KU Leuven, Belgium) and Victim Support Europe, represented by Slachtofferhulp Nederland (Victim Support the Netherlands), with the contribution of the following additional sponsors: Ministry of Security and Justice; City of The Hague; Ministry of Foreign Affairs; Dutch Victim Support Fund; Tilburg Law School; Wolf Legal Publishers; The Hague Global Justice Institute; Achmea Foundation for Victims and Society; and CZ Zorgverzekeringen.

The Symposium Organizing Committee consisted of the following people: Chair Victor Jammers, Vice-chair Rianne Letschert, Vice-chair Stephan Parmentier; Symposium manager Barbara van Gorp; Assistant Anneke Overbosch; members Ivo Aertsen, Sonja Leferink, Antony Pemberton, Inge Vanfraechem, Miriam Sessink, Danique Gudders and Birgit Vanderstraeten; Communication officers Kathelijn van Heeswijk and Debbie Rovers; student assistant Sylvia Hazenbroek; and Financial administrators Jacqueline Nahon, Lenie Herrema and Evelien van Rijt.

Birgit Vanderstraeten and Danique Gudders were of great help in setting up the conference programme, and the INTERVICT team composed of Barbara van Gorp, Kathelijn van Heeswijk, Anneke Overbosch, Debbie Rovers and a number of Tilburg University students took care of the practical organization.

A special word of thanks goes to the editorial team at Routledge for their efficient work in preparing and finalizing this book.

General introduction

Felix Mukwiza Ndahinda, Antony Pemberton and Inge Vanfraechem

This book is the result of the *14th International Symposium of Victimology*, held by the World Society of Victimology in cooperation with INTERVICT (University of Tilburg, the Netherlands), Leuven Institute of Criminology (KU Leuven, Belgium) and Victim Support Europe, represented by Slachtofferhulp Nederland (Victim Support the Netherlands) in the Hague, May 2012. Looking at justice for victims, the conference focused on three themes that are important for victimology as it stands today: victim rights, transitional justice, and trauma, resilience and justice. These themes come to the fore in victimological writings and theorizing as seminal in current thinking: after years of bringing the forgotten party into the picture, can we speak of 'victim rights' or are we rather providing standards for victims when confronted with the criminal justice system? When looking at societies in transition in Eastern Europe, Latin America and Africa, what is the position of the victim? The relatively new field of transitional justice covers this latter question as well as related questions dealing with accountability, reparations and the rebuilding of society after gross atrocities. Lastly, the broad theme of trauma, resilience and justice looks at more psychological findings that are not always connected to the victimological field, as well as reflections on the possibilities of restorative justice in offering the victim a more central role in the criminal handling of the case.

Both 'victims' and 'rights' are elastic concepts (Joutsen, 2013) and therefore 'victim rights' may mean different things. Paul Rock in his contribution asserts that at first sight victim rights seem to be self-evident at the beginning of the twenty-first century: (inter)national provisions such as the 2012 European Council Directive (see also the contribution from Ezendam and Wheldon, this volume) put forward certain (procedural) rights, such as the right to information, to being heard and to be treated with respect. Nevertheless, Rock argues that victim rights are met with resistance and are therefore, at least in the common law world, reduced to service standards which cannot always be enforced. Rights then can be deemed to be 'aspirational'.

Antony Pemberton departs from the assessment that the introduction of victims' rights into criminal justice has not been informed by a systematic rationale. His contribution calls for more conceptual clarity in understanding what is owed to victims and why. To this end he analyses three key distinctions between closely related constructs, which he finds to be confused within thinking about victims' rights. First he distinguishes two different forms of respect. *Recognition* respect entails giving the fact of victimization appropriate consideration in one's actions, while failing to do so amounts to a failure to meet a moral standard. *Appraisal* respect instead is closer to admiration: it consists in the attitude itself and does not require any subsequent action. He argues that while recognition rather than appraisal respect is an appropriate base for victims' rights, the latter frequently does play a role. Second, he juxtaposes empathy and sympathy. Empathy offers room for viewing the victim as an equal agent, while sympathy instead will lead to paternalizing action. Rights grounded in sympathy rather than empathy fail to sufficiently recognize victims' own agency. Finally, the author considers harmfulness and wrongfulness: the harm experienced by victims of crime is in part constituted by its character as a public wrong. This contribution and victims' own unique perspective on the extent of harm suffered often leads to an understanding that this also applies to the features of the wrongfulness of crime, to which the victims' own experience does not admit. Pemberton considers this to be mistaken, both on empirical grounds and as it is grounded in the wrong form of respect.

Helga Ezendam and Frida Wheldon describe the origins of the 2012 EU Directive concerning minimum standards on the rights, support and protection of victims of crime. They explain how the evaluation of the preceding Framework Decision in the same area found this legal instrument to be too vague to secure harmonious transposition into the legislation of EU member states. With the Directive, the hope is that the downsides of the Framework Decision can be avoided. Rights which are provided within the Directive include the right to information and protection, legal assistance, translation and support. In view of the authors' backgrounds, the right to support is further elaborated. The EU Directive is binding and could therefore have a high impact in practice but as Ezendam and Wheldon point out, the actual implementation within the member states may vary widely and it remains to be seen whether one can really talk about 'rights' rather than standards. It is interesting to note that the EU Directive is entitled 'minimum standards', which could be linked to the finding in common law countries (as stated by Rock) that rights are mostly translated into standards.

K. Jaishankar starts from the UN Declaration of Basic Principles of Justice for Victims of Crime and Abuse of Power (1985) to study nine newly industrialized countries (NICs), namely Brazil, China, India, Malaysia, Mexico, Philippines, South Africa, Thailand and Turkey. The author concludes that there is still some work to be done when it comes to implementing victim rights in legislation, although some countries have undertaken steps in that direction. The author 'would rank Thailand as the top NIC which guarantees the rights of victims by specific legal procedures and a separate law for victim compensation. (…) Except Thailand, all NIC countries analysed in this chapter need to revamp their criminal justice system focusing on the rights of victims of crime (…)'.

Jeremy Sarkin in his contribution evaluates to what extent victims of human right abuses in African colonial times have a right to reparation. He argues that at the time when the atrocities took place, victims already had rights and that 'international law has recognized the right of the individual to claim human rights' for a long time. The author shows some examples of reparations for atrocities committed in the eighteenth and nineteenth centuries and concludes that since rights existed then, victims and antecedents can claim a right for reparation for abuses committed in the past, especially since the consequences of these abuses affect contemporary generations through, for example, the loss of natural resources. Sarkin explains that reparations should not be merely financial, but they may include 'damages, redress, restitution, compensation, rehabilitation and satisfaction'. Rather than individual compensation, he believes 'group or collective reparations are a better alternative' – an element which probably needs some further reflection although some work on this has been done in the field of transitional justice (the theme of Part II of this volume; see also e.g. Aertsen *et al.*, 2008).

David Miers looks more in depth at the specific right to compensation. He describes the provisions in the EU and US, and in addition compares Australia, Canada and Great Britain, looking at three defining characteristics: the scope of a criminal injury, the approach to undeserving victims, and the injuries and losses that are covered. The underlying argument for state compensation tends to be that it is a recognition for the suffering, but it cannot be seen as taking up responsibility for not being able to protect citizens from victimization. Thus, victims generally have a right to compensation by the offender, but Miers concludes that when it comes to state compensation, this right does not amount to much.

Xin Ren studies the legal provisions regarding legal protection and assistance for victims of human trafficking in the US. According to Ren, human trafficking is an emerging human rights issue. She points out that beside federal and state level legislation in the US, the UN Protocol to prevent, suppress and punish trafficking in persons, especially women and children (2000) and the UN Protocol against the smuggling of immigrants by land, sea and air (2003) are important tools in the combat against human trafficking. US provisions contain immigration relief, benefits and services, civil remedies, and legal aid and assistance. The Equal Employment Opportunity Commission investigates claims of discrimination and represents victims against abusive employers in labour trafficking cases.

Since the end of World War II, societies confronted with gross violations of human rights committed or tolerated by the state have struggled to come to terms with the tragic legacy successor governments are confronted with. Since the end of the 1980s and early 1990s, the various mechanisms and processes aimed at addressing the legacy of violations as societies struggle to move forward have been captured under the concept of transitional justice.

Harvey Weinstein provides a compelling and critical analysis of dominant narratives in the transitional justice literature. He places the victim at the centre of an exploration of the tensions between societal reconstruction and the quest for accountability in the aftermath of a conflict that resulted in gross human rights violations. The chapter cautions against dogmatic prescriptions from a variety of global actors involved in transitional processes that do not always account for the actual needs and voices of the real victims who bear the scars of the committed atrocities. The author argues that in spite of a multiplicity of transitional justice mechanisms, they are still prominently dominated by a retributive paradigm, regardless of the otherwise relevant contexts of applicability. Furthermore, he argues that not only do dominant transitional justice processes 'reinforce a sense of victimhood and entitlement that rarely is satisfied' but also that those who suffered at the hands of an abusive regime can end up 'lost in the politics of victimhood, discipline boundaries and political power plays'. In addition to an elaboration on the disempowering dimension of the 'victim' label, Weinstein further argues that the dominant emphasis in litigation of human rights' abuse may hamper rather than reinforce the goal of social reconstruction after the conflict. The author emphasizes the necessity of responses of conflict and human rights violations that build on contextual realities and needs.

Rani Mani somewhat complements Weinstein when she introduces the notion of integral justice, whereby victims are treated as 'incipient heroes' instead of remaining trapped in their status as victims. In an effort to enable victims to make the transition from victimhood to 'hero-hood', the author argues that integral justice capitalizes on developments and findings in going beyond dominant victimology and transitional justice by capturing dimensions not covered by these fields such as culture, ecology and spirituality. Integral justice is presented as a form of justice that 'transcends borders, penetrates and understands cultures, and combines disciplines to provide satisfactory responses to the injustice suffered by victims and the wounds inflicted upon society as a whole as a consequence'. It is presented as a holistic form of justice that integrates politico-legal, societal, cultural, ecological and spiritual dimensions. Mani argues that taking these dimensions into consideration in responses to victimization might lead to victim transformation. Integral justice would not only provide justice to the victims but also aim at social reintegration of perpetrators.

Rianne Letschert and Stephan Parmentier take a victimological approach in examining what they deem to be an impossible task of providing full individual reparations to victims in contexts of mass victimization. In an attempt to apply victimological theory to situations of mass victimization, the chapter uses empirical data from three different contexts of mass victimization in examining the contemporary practice in some forms of reparations for victims of mass atrocities. The authors acknowledge that owing to the contextual difference but also to the fact that the data from Bosnia and Serbia, Northern Uganda and Cambodia were gathered using different methodologies, it is not an easy task to systematically compare these situations. In spite of differences in individual attitudes and needs, the authors find that victims are strongly interested in individual or collective forms of reparations, be they material, financial, symbolic or social services.

It is widely documented that the concept of transitional justice was coined in reference to the transition from military rule in a number of Latin American countries from the 1980s. José Zalaquett draws on his academic and practical experience as an activist and practitioner in reflecting on the role of victims in transitional processes in Latin America, with a particular focus on his native Chile. His examination shows that victims were the central focus and key players in the transitional processes aimed at bringing accountability for human rights violations committed in a number of countries on the sub-continent. Reflecting on the dilemmas and lessons of transitional justice processes in the studied context, the author argues that all aspects of transitional justice, namely truth telling, memory preservation, acknowledgement, reparations, criminal justice and national reconciliation can be and should be examined from the standpoint of the victims' needs.

Alex Hinton examines the imagery of transitional justice in Cambodia through the narrative of Uncle San and Aunty Yan. These two fictional characters are portrayed in a booklet aimed at sensitizing the Cambodian population on the benefits of participating in the proceedings before the Extraordinary Chambers in the Courts of Cambodia. The Chambers, also known as the Khmer Rouge Tribunal, were set up to try dignitaries of the Khmer Rouge regime for atrocities committed during their reign of terror between April 1975 and January 1979. By transitional justice imagery, the author unpacks 'a set of interrelated discourses, practices, and institutional forms that help generate a sense of shared belonging among a group of people'. The imagery carries an idea of 'transformation of post-conflict societies from a negatively marked spatio-temporal modality of being to a positively valued future, with the transitional justice mechanism serving as the vehicle of change'.

Victimology is an interdisciplinary field. Academics and practitioners with a wide variety of backgrounds embark on studies of the experience of victims of crime. This offers opportunities for disciplinary integration and learning from the insights of other perspectives, but also entails the risk of fragmentation, reinventing the wheel and construct drift, where the correct meaning of concepts and research findings is lost in translation. Under the heading *Trauma, Resilience and Justice* the *14th International Symposium of the World Society of Victimology* specifically sought to bridge disciplinary divides and enhance interdisciplinary understanding, simultaneously challenging notions of passivity, helplessness and vindictiveness in victims of crime.

Patricia Frazier's contribution summarizes her extensive work on the effects of different attributions on victims' coping with the effect of crime and in particular the extent to which perceptions of control lead to or more or less distress. Her research has revealed that it is crucial to distinguish forms of control along a temporal dimension. Believing that one could have prevented the event from occurring or had control over the fact that the event occurred (past control) is related to more distress, which is also true for dwelling upon other attributions – for instance blaming the offender – for the occurrence of the event. Focusing on the question of future control – can I keep it from happening again? – also leads to poorer outcomes. Instead better adjustment is linked to what we *can* actually control in the present: how we react to the event, and how we think and feel about the event. Stimulating this present control is therefore an important avenue for improving victims' recovery after traumatic events and Frazier shows the application of this in the online tool she has developed.

Control is also an important theme in the procedural justice literature. As Tinneke Van Camp and Vicky De Mesmaecker emphasize, a certain degree of process control or 'voice' is an important determinant of the experience of participants in a wide of justice processes, much of which also applies to victims in criminal justice processes. Voice is one of three elements – with quality of treatment and fairness of decision making – which are commonly regarded as the antecedents of perceptions of procedural fairness. Van Camp and De Mesmaecker use these three categories as a guide to analysing the extent to which victim impact statements (VIS) and victim–offender mediation (VOM) meet victims' needs in justice processes. A VIS is a written or oral statement in which the victim of a crime describes the physical, material, psychological and social harm suffered as a result of the crime, while VOM is a form of restorative justice, bringing together victims and offenders with an impartial mediator to collectively resolve how to deal with the aftermath of the offence and its implications for the future. According to Van Camp and De Mesmaecker VIS is not yet fulfilling its potential for delivery of procedural justice, while they find VOM to more fully apply the procedural justice model, with its attention to the parties' voices, interactional quality and transparency.

Notions of procedural justice have been instrumental in the development of the position of victims of crime from their unwelcome status as the forgotten party of criminal justice. This is not equally true for children who fall victim to crime, as Ilse Vande Walle's work reveals. Vande Walle challenges many presumptions in the way child victims are approached: that they are by definition more vulnerable and less resilient, should be completely shielded from what has happened and/or should be repetitively encouraged to emote about their experiences. She shows that many of the needs young victims have are similar to those of adults: the need to voice their concerns, to receive information about what happened, to be taken seriously and given space and time to recover – while others are idiosyncratic about their situation, emphasizing the importance of their pets, school and parents.

Where VOM is increasingly a regular feature of criminal justice systems across the world, there are areas in which its application remains a point of controversy. A case in point is restorative justice encounters in the aftermath of terrorist victimization. Gema Varona's contribution analyses the complexities of bringing victims and offenders of ETA-terrorism in the Basque Country together. Over the course of the past decades ETA has been responsible for more than eight hundred fatalities, as well as more low level but also more widespread and pervasive threatening behaviour. In 2011 it declared a definitive cessation of its activities and called for an end to the conflict. Varona brings out much of the dilemmas currently facing the Basque Country and calls for a multi-polar and flexible approach to justice: there are no easy answers. Just to mention two examples: on the one hand, victims may fear the recasting of the years of terror as political conflict, which retrospectively casts their losses in a different and in many ways unfavourable light and associate restorative justice with this perspective. Any reframing at the societal level will place pressure on the victims' narratives of events. On the other hand, victims may welcome the opportunity to meet their offender or another member of ETA and be able to express their views and feelings, while societal parties frown upon these encounters.

The importance of understanding the different societal levels impacted by crime is also a key issue in Qingli Meng and Paul Friday's conceptual framework concerning victims of corruption. The negative impact of this form of crime is difficult to quantify exactly, but estimates invariably point to astronomical figures of tens or hundreds of billions of dollars. As Meng and Friday emphasize, it is not a private matter between corrupted and corruptor, but something that may destroy and degrade whole economies and cultures. This is particularly true of systemic/endemic forms of corruption, which they distinguish from sporadic (sectoral) and individual forms of corruption. A similar threefold distinction is made between individual damage, institutional damage, and social or societal damage. Distinguishing these dimensions is an important element in recognizing the different needs of victims of corruption.

Kathleen Daly's chapter finally brings together many of the threads under the heading of trauma, resilience and justice and in fact of the whole symposium. Her Victimization and Justice model provides a roadmap for future victimological research, in which she interweaves justice mechanisms, victimization contexts and victims' justice interests. As to the former: instead of juxtaposing different paradigms of justice, Daly calls for a view of justice mechanisms on a continuum ranging from *conventional* to *innovative*, which can be combined in a variety of ways and does not a priori privilege one form of innovation over other possibly equally rewarding potentialities. In reviewing justice mechanisms, she calls for a renewed attention to conceptual clarity, instead of the loose use of terms which is common in the field. The different contexts of victimization are set out in Daly's Sexual Violence and Justice Matrix. Here she points to the fact that much victimological evidence is likely to be context specific and to this end the matrix offers two key dimensions: different country contexts (developed, developing, at peace or conflict/post-conflict) and what Daly calls the offending-victimization contexts (individual, organizational, institutional and collective). Finally Daly draws attention to the problem of the lack of adequate methods to determine the effectiveness of justice mechanisms, with both satisfaction surveys and therapeutic approaches coming up short. She calls for a reorientation on the key question of effectiveness towards the mechanisms' capacity to address victims' justice interests and the extent they do so. These justice interests can then be categorized as participation, voice, validation, vindication and offender accountability.

Bibliography

Aertsen, I., Arsovska, J., Rohne, H.-C., Valiñas, M. and Vanspauwen, K., eds, 2008. Restoring justice after large-scale violent conflicts. Kosovo, DR Congo and the Israeli-Palestinian case. Cullompton: Willan Publishing.

Joutsen, M., 2013. Trends in victims' rights. Unpublished paper.

Shoham, S.G., Knepper, P. and Kett, M., eds, 2010. International handbook of victimology. Boca Raton: CRC Press.

Walklate, S., ed., 2007. Handbook of victims and victimology. Cullompton: Willan Publishing.

Part I

Victims' rights

Chapter 1

Victims' rights

Paul Rock[1]

Introduction

At first blush, the proposition that the victims of crime should have rights is unexceptionable and a number of States assert that they have now ceded them. After all, it had long been complained that victims were marginal, the 'forgotten party', treated only as potential witnesses, complainants and 'alleged victims' until a conviction had been secured and, in very exceptional cases, as claimants to criminal injuries compensation. Victims were denied property in their own crimes (Christie 1977); denied information about the progress of 'their' cases (see Shapland *et al.* 1985); found it difficult to retrieve stolen possessions; experienced delays and discomfort waiting for trial (if trials ever materialized); and were subjected to the possibility of aggressive cross-examination at trial itself. In 1987, Lois Herrington (1987, p. 141), the former Assistant Attorney General of the United States and the chairwoman of the 1982 Presidential Task Force on Victims of Crime, claimed that:

> The system served the judges, lawyers, and defendants, while ignoring, blaming, and mistreating the victims. Once they survive the initial impact of a crime, the victims are drawn into a system that treats them with indifference at best and abuse at worst.

An increasing number of victims cried out for what they called recognition and respect.

During and after the 1970s, a concatenation of events began to remedy that neglect: the emergence, first, of a renewed, 'second generation' feminism deploring the treatment of the female victims of rape (see, for example, Brownmiller 1977) and domestic violence as 'secondary victimisation' and bringing about the founding of rape crisis centres and women's refuges (see Pizzey 1977; Dobash and Dobash 1979). Later other activist organizations came into being, claiming greater rights to acknowledgement and participation in procedure, claims that were accompanied by the establishment of self-help and campaigning groups that agitated for change; the apprehension that the criminal justice system needed its witnesses, and companion fears that victims might desert the criminal justice system, refuse to report crime and refuse to testify (see Knudten et al. 1978). All this led to prosecutor- and police-initiated programmes for victims and witnesses; the maturing of the new discipline of victimology, founded in the 1940s and 1950s (see von Hentig 1948; Wertham 1949; Mendelsohn 1963) and dedicated to the analysis and, in many cases, the amelioration of the standing of victims; the work, in England and Wales and elsewhere, of Victim Support; the revelations of crime surveys about the incidence and impact of crime, and much else. It is now hard to deny victims. Their demands, it has even been said, are being used to give legitimacy to the actions of states whose moral authority has been weakened (see Allen et al. 2000; Boutellier 2000), drowning out the voices of experts and practitioners.

Yet on inspection, both words, 'victim' and 'right', have proved, partly by design, to be ambiguous and elusive, politically freighted and practically contested. What has been conceded and to whom it has been given is not at all transparent. In exploring these matters, I shall perforce concentrate on what I know best, the role of the victim in common law countries, and in England and Wales above all.

Who are the victims?

Let me begin with the meaning of the term *victim*. The definition offered by *The New Shorter Oxford English Dictionary* (1993) talks not only about what might seem to be the straightforward case of victims of crime conventionally understood, but also those killed and offered as sacrifices; those who are tortured or killed by another; 'a person subjected to cruelty, oppression, or other harsh or unfair treatment or suffering death, injury, ruin, etc., as a result of an event, circumstances, or oppressive or adverse agency'; or a person who is taken advantage of or a dupe. A *victim* may then be other than one who suffers as a result of a simple criminal act. And lest it is imagined that such a catholic description has been favoured simply by outsiders – those who are not lawyers, politicians, practitioners or criminologists – recall the busy agitation that has continually taken place within the criminal justice system to extend the elasticity of the term. Although the term *victim* connotes loss, weakness, submission, subjugation and pain; although some reject its associations with passivity and defeat, disown victim status and, following those who endured the Holocaust, prefer instead to employ the word 'survivor'; the word also carries with it the promise of rewards. In what often takes the form of a binary system, the victim is the man or woman who has been vindicated, not the wrongdoer but the wronged; the innocent, not the guilty; one who deserves compassion and support, not condemnation; compensation and vindication; retribution and reparation. There are gains to be made in being so classified and individuals and groups have striven to achieve them.

Recall the jostling that attended the framing of the 1985 United Nations Declaration of Basic Principles of Justice for Victims of Crime and Abuse of Power, a jostling that ultimately furnished a somewhat baggy description of quite who it is who should be recognized as a victim for political and practical purposes. Matti Joutsen (1987, p. 23), then of HEUNI, an organization affiliated to the United Nations, who was one of the architects of the Declaration, remarked that the task of definition lay

> at the heart of one of the greatest drafting difficulties in preparing the... Declaration... According to the broader perspective, victims are to be understood as those who suffer as a result of acts that a) are a violation of national criminal laws, b) are a violation of international criminal law, c) are a violation of internationally recognized human rights, or d) otherwise involve an abuse of political or economic power. This is the view that was taken... by some of the drafters of the United Nations Declaration.

The result was that victims were defined conservatively enough under paragraph 1 as 'persons who, individually or collectively, have suffered harm, including physical or mental injury, emotional suffering, economic loss or substantial impairment of their fundamental rights, through acts or omissions that are in violation of criminal laws operative within Member States...', but also, much more loosely (see Bassiouni 1999, p. 48), and not unlike an earlier totalitarian model of crimes by analogy, under paragraph 18 as

> persons who, individually or collectively, have suffered harm, including physical or mental injury, emotional suffering, economic loss or substantial impairment of their fundamental rights, through acts or omissions that do not yet constitute violations of national criminal laws but of internationally recognized norms relating to human rights.[2]

In Canada, at much the same time, the Federal-Provincial Task Force on Justice for Victims chiefly attended to the victimization of women, native Canadians, the elderly and the handicapped, but excluded young men and those who were gay – and its decisions were political. Feminism had awarded women a strong political presence in the Ottawa of the 1980s, but young and gay men, it was thought, lacked public sympathy and, in the words of one federal official, 'they were nobody's favourite victim' (Rock 1986, pp. 310–311). Recall too the moves being made in the 1990s by those who wished to be acknowledged as members of an ever-expanding circle of victims: those identified as victims of the new and increasingly well-populated category of hate crime (Jacobs and Potter 1998); the alleged victims of abuse made known through what was called 'recovered memory' (Pendergrast 1995); the secondary and tertiary victims of crime, including, importantly, the families of homicide victims; those who may have been distressed by having witnessed and attended atrocious crimes; the families of serious offenders who have on occasion claimed to be 'the other victims of crime' (Rock 2000); and even offenders themselves. Even *within* victim groups there has sometimes been a sifting and ranking process organized by what the traumatically bereaved labelled 'competitive grief'. Rather luridly perhaps, one of the outcomes of such a contest for recognition, some like Charles Sykes (1992) would say, is that a country like the United States has been turned into 'a nation of victims'.

It is in this sense that a description of who is or is not a victim implicates a certain view of politics, an ordering of identity, status and reward, a model of causality and a framework for blame and explanation. It presents an iconography of who it is who may be said to have suffered at whose hands with what consequences and in what sort of social, moral and economic system (see Pitch 1985). Holstein and Miller (1990, p. 107) once remarked that: 'As an act of interpretive reality construction, victimization unobtrusively advises others in how they should understand persons, circumstances, and behaviours under consideration.' How else is one to read the conclusions of the Task Force on Victims' Rights and the Justice System (1991, p. 337): 'The issues of economic and environmental victimization are of EXTREME URGENCY, transcending national boundaries?' [emphasis in the original]. How else, too, is one to read the manifesto of a feminist 'international tribunal' that was convened in California in the mid-1970s: 'the women present completely rejected patriarchal definitions of crime; all man-made forms of women's oppression were seen as crimes. Most of the crimes testified about are not recognized as such by patriarchal nations...'? (Russell and Van de Ven 1976, p. xv). Radical criminology and critical victimology have had their preferred victims as well. In the empirically innocent days before crime surveys began to make their full mark, and some on the left realized that crime hurts the poor as well as the rich (see Lea and Young 1985), minority ethnic groups as well as members of the majority population, women as well as men (see Jones *et al.* 1986), there were those who would have had us concentrate not on those who suffer from or commit volume crime – that, it was argued, was a source of ideological irrelevance, mystification and distraction – but almost solely (if victims were to be considered at all) on those who experienced racism, imperialism, sexism, corporate crime and crimes and abuses of human rights inflicted by the State (see Kauzlarich *et al.* 2001).

But even if one restricts the conception of 'victim' to the notion of one who has suffered from a crime narrowly defined, there are still difficulties in identifying and ratifying the potential bearer of rights.

Who deserves rights?

According to estimates based on the British Crime Survey,[3] there were some nine and a half million crimes committed in England and Wales in 2010–2011, and the figure of recorded police crime was 4.2 million. Just under a quarter (23 per cent) of the incidents reported to the British Crime Survey were crimes of violence, including robbery; a fifth (22 per cent) incidents of vandalism; about half (47 per cent) were thefts, of which vehicle-related theft was the most common[4] and one-twelfth (8 per cent) burglaries. There were 642 homicides, leaving behind perhaps some three or four thousand immediately bereaved people. We know too that, because of repeat victimization, the experience of crime can be especially concentrated and intense for some: 44 per cent of the victims of domestic violence, 27 per cent of the victims of vandalism, and 19 per cent of the victims of acquaintance violence were repeat victims (and, as a counterweight, individual crimes may well have multiple victims). Overall, more than two-fifths of reported crime in England and Wales was said in the mid-1990s to have been experienced by 4 per cent of victims (National Board for Crime Prevention 1994).

We still understand rather too little about the phenomenology of victimization and victim identity (Rock 2002), but it may be conjectured that, distressing as an incident of theft and burglary can be (Maguire 1982), it need not necessarily form the basis of an indelible master status. To embark on a moral career self-consciously as a victim is an unusual venture: being victimized and assuming an enduring social role of victim are not at all the same. There are contingencies and chief amongst them is the presence of an uncommonly distressing trauma or trauma-like experience or succession of linked experiences that seems to signal, if only for a while, an irreversible existential turning-point, a ready-made narrative or set of narratives and an organized response to ratify and make sense of what has been undergone. The victims who make political demands, who campaign and who seek rights, are unlikely to have been recruited from the great mass of people who have experienced volume crime. Those who have mobilized themselves *as* victims and come prominently before the mass media, the politicians and the policy-makers, the men and women who have seized the popular and political imagination, tend not to be the victims of burglary or theft or isolated incidents of petty vandalism. They are not those who might be called victims *an sich*, but victims *für sich*, the victims at first hand of sexual abuse, prolonged violence, stalking, abuse, hate crime, rape and arson and, at second hand, of murder and manslaughter. Politicized or activist victims are exceptional figures, secondary victims in the sense that Edwin Lemert might have recognized, people who have acquired a self-conscious victim identity, but it is they who have chiefly made their mark on representations of victims and on the politics of victims' rights. That has certainly been the case in Australia (Rock 2006), Canada (Rock 1986), the United States and, latterly, after the partial political eclipse of Victim Support, England and Wales (but not, it seems, Scotland). About a third of those witnesses who elected to come forward or were nominated by NOVA, the American National Organization for Victim Assistance, to testify before the influential 1982 *President's Task Force on Victims of Crime* were said to be victims and the very few I could identify were all relatives of murder victims. None, it seems, was a victim of a misdemeanour.[5] Such victims have a compelling intensity. They make an impression. The President's Task Force report (1982, p.vii) subsequently reflected that:

> You must know what it is to have your life wrenched and broken, to realize that you will never really be the same. ... We who have served on this Task Force have been forever changed by the victims we have met, by the

experiences they have shared, by the wisdom sprung from suffering that they imparted.

So it was too with the Victims Advisory Panel that was set up in England and Wales in 2004 to allow politicians to confer with victims: six of the initial twelve members were homicide survivors, one a victim of a stalker, one a victim of an aggravated burglary, one a victim of sexual assault and another a victim of rape. The then Lord Chancellor, Lord Falconer, reflected that:

> They are a vocal – and for us – challenging group that ask pointed questions on our commitment to deliver and meet the needs of people like them. We see the panel as a key part of our drive to ensure a victim-centred approach to Criminal Justice.[6]

The rights and services of which such people speak are of immediate moment to the seriously afflicted (the one major victim assistance organization that cannot be thus described, the British body, Victim Support, was set up by a group of penal reformers, not by victims themselves (Rock 1990); it caters for the victims of volume crime as well as those of traumatic crime, and it was long wary of demanding rights at all). In England and Wales, members of the Victims Advisory Panel talked about the right to obtain trial transcripts (although no more than 18 per cent of crimes go to trial, and even fewer to courts of record where such transcripts are prepared, a mere 6 per cent of total proceedings in 2010[7]); a review of the Coroners' Service (responsible for inquests in cases of unnatural death); legal support; and counselling in the management of post-traumatic stress disorder, the condition peculiarly associated with grave crime and sudden bereavement.

The victim's eligibility for rights

How victims and victimization come into view has been shaped accordingly: in many jurisdictions victims are represented as blame-free, harrowed and traumatized people who have experienced major crimes and require significant psychological or psychiatric support. *Rebuilding Lives: Supporting Victims of Crime*, a 2005 White Paper issued by the three Departments of State administering the criminal justice system of England and Wales, recorded a drift to that view when it reported that:

> Even relatively minor crimes can be traumatic, but the most serious cause enormous emotional and physical harm. ... There is scope for more use of specialist staff in delivering services to victims with particular needs, for example in the most serious cases such as sexual offences, domestic violence, serious violent offences and racial offences.
> (Secretary of State for the Home Department, the Secretary of State for Constitutional Affairs and the Attorney General 2005, p. 3, 31)

And even then, further interpretive work must be done to refine the depiction of victims. Only a few will actually be deemed worthy of rights.

First, it must be said that eligibility is usually linked to the management of encounters with criminal justice agencies and many rights are on offer to victims only when a crime has been reported and an offender has been identified. People who remain outside the criminal justice system (and some 60 per cent of offences are not reported to the police) may be comparatively benighted (see Reeves and Dunn 2010, p. 66).

Second, it is not victims, warts and all, who receive immediate recognition (Christie 1986). David Downes once said informally that victims are both saints and pariahs, and some victims' groups, politicians and victimologists have not found that dissonance comfortable. The very idea that victims may have been complicit in what befell them; that they may have some responsibility for their suffering; that they may offend as well as being offended against; that a useful predictor of who will become a victim is his or her criminal record; that victims may be morally tainted; that, in short, and borrowing Inkeri Antilla's words (1964, p. 5), one should not think as victimologists of blacks and whites but of greys; has at times been dismissed as an unconscionable 'victim-blaming' (see Clark and Lewis 1977; Lamb 1996). Images of victims have often been sanitized by campaigners, particularly in the cases of domestic violence and rape, and even more particularly still in cases of homicide, so that it is rare that one will encounter a description of a victim of murder or manslaughter that is other than eulogistic. Victim impact statements, obituaries and newspaper reports generally (but not always) seek to construct an unblemished, bowdlerized memory by lauding the dead. The dead are supposed always to be irreproachable. *De mortuis nil nisi bonum.*

Those filtrations may be formalized and reinforced in law and its adversarial system. Defendants at trial cannot receive grey verdicts: they are supposed to be found unambiguously guilty or not guilty (at least in English and Welsh law, if not in Scots law). One cannot be just a little guilty. The Criminal Injuries Compensation Authority of England and Wales makes awards only to the 'blameless victims of violent crime' (2011, p. 1). Politicians will not besmirch victims when they talk about law and order. Proclaiming the first Victims of Crime Week in April 1987, President Reagan opened by saying that: 'Nearly thirty-five million Americans became victims of crime in 1986. Six million of them were victims of serious, violent crimes. Crime – of any kind – can have a devastating impact on innocent victims and their families.'[8] Note the president's instant recourse to the vocabulary of a juxtaposed innocent victim and violent crime.

Invisible in much of the politics of victims, at least (for the time being) outside the United Kingdom, then, is the commonplace, not infrequently flawed, man or woman who has suffered a burglary, theft or vandalism, the most abundant – three quarters – of all crimes in England and Wales and the United States.[9] The rights and services which that man or woman seeks (and only sporadically receives) may not have been overwhelmingly affected in every particular (after all, they too would have advice, support, protection and information), but they are often overlooked rhetorically and sometimes excluded practically, and the rights and services which *are* awarded have often been significantly skewed (and in the United Kingdom are becoming more skewed) to favour a small and unrepresentative, although no doubt very needy and distressed, minority of victims. The emphasis has been on long-term psychological distress to the neglect of those experiencing other kinds of need (Winkel and Vrij 1998).

The nature of rights

Let me now consider *rights*. They too are elusive and multivocal. *The New Shorter Oxford English Dictionary* says that a right is:

> That which is consonant with justice, goodness, or reason; that which is morally or socially correct; just or equitable treatment; fairness in decision; justice. ... Entitlement or justiciable claim, on legal or moral grounds, to have or obtain something, or to act in a certain way. A legal, equitable, or moral title or claim to the possession of property or authority, the enjoyment of privileges or immunities.

Rights may be laid out as a spectrum, from the aspirational and the moral claim, at the one pole, to the demand that is clearly enforceable at law, at the other – a demand that, in Campbell's words (2008, p. 1025), serves as 'an entitlement authorizing a person to do or to have something'. One imagines that many activist victims seek a combination of moral claims (victimization is, above all else, a matter of moral slight) and legal entitlements, if only because of the strong propensity continually to compare and contrast what is imagined to be the offender's favoured lot with that of the victim. In an urgent effort to restore order, meaning and purpose to a disturbed symbolic universe, a universe where conventional moral assumptions about behaviour and reward have been turned upside down (see Lerner 1980), the activist may well pitch the irreprehensible victim against a demonized offender; a life lost against a life still lived; the absence of legal aid for the bereaved with the provision of legal representation for the defendant; an impact statement with a mitigation speech; the paucity of victims' rights with what is commonly taken to be an abundance of rights for the defendant; and the creation of a Ministry of Victims to parry a Ministry of Justice (Rock 1998). The very public worth of the victim is gauged by how he or she is treated in a point-by-point comparison with the State's response to the offender. If the offender has rights in law, they say, so should the victim, and some have argued that the rise of the American victims' movement may be understood as a dialectical response to the campaign for prisoners' rights waged in the 1970s (Gottschalk 2006).

In practice, however, and with a few apparent exceptions, almost all victims' rights fall at the aspirational pole and they take the form of affirmations of principle and statements about standards of good practice, rather than of justiciable entitlements (although language is prone to slip back and forth between the one vocabulary and the other). And those declarations of rights tend to follow a common pattern which has been conveyed and standardized through a succession of conferences, symposia and meetings;[10] one jurisdiction after another following templates supplied by governments, nongovernmental organizations[11] and transnational bodies; and mediated by such instruments as the 1985 United Nations Declaration, the European Forum for Victims Services' 1996 *Statements of Victims' Rights in the Process of Criminal Justice*, the Council of the European Union's 2001 Framework Decision and the proposed *Directive of the European Parliament and of the Council Establishing Minimum Standards on the Rights, Support and Protection of Victims of Crime* of 2011 (European Commission 2011; see also Ezendam and Wheldon, this volume). Documents in Europe, North America and Australasia tend to recite almost identical sentiments, talking about the right of the victim to be treated with dignity, to be informed and to confer with the prosecution.

Some of those demands and principles emanate directly from activist victims who were prominent and persuasive enough to be heard by politicians and policy-makers. Some were propounded by Victim Support, APAV (Unidade de Apoio à Vítima Imigrante e de Discriminação Racial ou Étnica) and their sister organizations in Victim Support Europe, that had a powerful influence on, say, the drafting of the European Commission's 2001 Framework Decision. Some, like victim witness assistance programmes, were installed by agencies anxious about a loss of cooperation with the criminal justice system. A number were simply projected onto victims by benign or fearful governments who claimed to know what must have been in their best interests. Criminal injuries compensation, for example, was mooted as a form of *Danegeld* in England and Wales in the late 1950s and early 1960s by reformers apprehensive about what they believed to be the vengefulness of the angry victim of violence who might obstruct or reverse liberal reforms (Rolph 1958). No one at the time thought that victims should be consulted about what they actually wanted – it never occurred to them (Rock 1990) – and pecuniary compensation may, in fact, be little more than an extremely expensive way of offering victims something that they might not otherwise have strongly demanded or needed.[12]

In other cases, the general population of victims have been the indirect beneficiaries of policies and problems largely tangential to them. The victims of volume crime have tended to lack a mouthpiece (apart, significantly, from the weakened Victim Support in England and Wales and its counterparts elsewhere). Even organized, activist victims lack the influence of the big battalions of the criminal justice system – the police, courts and prisons – and their voice has been easily drowned. Helen Reeves, the erstwhile Chief Executive Officer, and Peter Dunn, the former head of research, of Victim Support, would claim that it has been a consequence that policies and programmes for victims in England and Wales have long been complicated by their entanglement with, and subordination to, other more pressing goals.

Yet it may only be as a result of a connection with those other priorities, emerging in more pressing political domains, that the victim's position will change at all. The Canadian Federal-Provincial Task Force on Justice for Victims rode to influence in the early 1980s on the back of a consequential feminist politics of domestic violence. The rights embedded in the English and Welsh 2004 Domestic Violence, Victims and Crime Act, Chapter 28, were a rough, late synthesis of measures that had emerged outside the realm of victims proper to protect vulnerable and intimidated witnesses, measures that had been catalysed by the scandal of the notorious treatment in court of a rape victim, and *they* embodied a pressing politics of gender; changes in the management of policing after an inquiry into the ineffectual investigation of the murder of a young Afro-Caribbean man, Stephen Lawrence, an inquiry that encapsulated the explosive politics of race (Macpherson of Cluny 1999); the transformation of victims into consumers of criminal justice services that flowed out of a wholesale application of business models to public administration; and the 1998 Human Rights Act, c.42 – none of which was supposed directly to benefit the victim of everyday crime at all. To be sure, it characteristically takes the dramatization of a particular incident to award victims political prominence – criminal justice reform is often driven by apparent crises seized on by those waiting in the wings – and it is difficult much of the time to excite the same interest in the general lot of victims abstractly conceived, but there are consequences. None of those policies had initially been devised to aid victims *qua* victims, but their political mandate was markedly more authoritative than anything victims could have secured under their own flag and it was largely as an unintended consequence that victims at large acquired some rights or quasi-rights at all (Rock 2004).

The *realpolitik* of victims' rights

Given the frequent political injunction to 'put victims at the heart of criminal justice', echoed, *inter alia*, in the speeches and papers of the European Commission,[13] Government Ministers in the United Kingdom (see Home Office 2002)[14] and the Victims' Commissioner for England and Wales[15] and given that the Crown Prosecution Service of England and Wales[16] proclaims that 'Championing justice and defending the rights of victims, fairly, firmly and effectively is at the heart of all we do', one should mark that the promise to confer rights has in most (but possibly not all) jurisdictions been hedged about with qualifications, ambiguities, disclaimers and procedural complexities. The notion of rights has in practice met with substantial resistance from lawyers, practitioners and politicians.

To be sure, there *has* been a significant increase in the number and quality of services available to victims in England and Wales and elsewhere. But the State in common law jurisdictions has been chary always of treating those provisions as *rights*. It might be perfectly proper to ask whether their translation into rights would indeed make a difference and whether victims of crime in those countries do actually seek rights in any numbers, but rights is my theme, and it is certainly not rights that the victims and witnesses of most jurisdictions have typically achieved. In practice, the remedy for the discontented victim in many places, including England and Wales, is not to go to law but to make complaints which may or may not be investigated by bodies which may or may not report back to the victim. And it appears that recourse to the mechanism of complaint is actually quite uncommon.

Under section 32 of the Domestic Violence, Crime and Victims Act 2004, the governing instrument in such cases in England and Wales is *The Code of Practice for Victims of Crime* of 2006. Statements about the rights conferred by the Code sometimes place the word in apostrophes, as if to emphasize their tentativeness and it is a tentativeness that is confirmed elsewhere. The Code itself does not actually invoke the word *rights* but refers instead to 'the precise standards of care and support that [victims] can expect to receive from criminal justice agencies'. Even then it is guarded. Section 1.3 recites that 'Where a person fails to comply with this Code, that does not, of itself, make him or her liable to any legal proceedings' and the annual report of the Crown Prosecution Service for 2010 echoes that precept: 'Failure to comply with the Code does not of itself give rise to any legal proceedings but can be taken into account in determining any question in any proceedings.'[17] Policy staff of the Office of the Victims' Commissioner told me that they did not call what was embodied in the Code a series of *rights*: 'They're a customer services charter.'

Those who are dissatisfied with the level of service provided by the criminal justice system are told to complain first to the agency which was thought to have failed them. It is a procedure that is not evenly transparent. The Office of the Victims' Commissioner has no tally of the total number of complaints made. The Independent Police Complaints Commission is not aware of how many complaints the police received: in 2009–10, the police forces of England and Wales forwarded to the Commission the 2,746 most serious complaints they had received and all cases involving deaths 'following direct or indirect contact with a police officer'[18], but we do not know how many of those cases fell under the Victim's Code.[19] The Metropolitan Police Service, the largest force in the country, covering a population of approximately 7.2 million people with some 32,000 officers dealing with just under 900,000 recorded crimes a year, reported that it received six Victims' Code allegations in 2009, 7 in 2010 and none in 2011 up to late August. Despite some formal criticism of its treatment of victims and witnesses, the Crown Prosecution Service does not know nationally or regionally, and refused to say locally,[20] how many complaints it receives under the Code.[21] The Courts Service of the Ministry of Justice knew only the aggregate number of complaints the Ministry as a whole received where the party was the victim (there were 191 complaints in the financial year 2008–09, 64 relating to non-payment of awards by the defendant; seven in 2009–10; and none at all thereafter). Even if complete data *were* available, it is evident that the numbers involved are very small and it would be difficult to interpret their meaning. Small numbers could signify high levels of satisfaction with a service, or alienation from the complaints procedure; large numbers could signify discontent or confidence in the procedure.

Victims not satisfied with the outcome of that first stage may then complain to their Member of Parliament who may look into the matter or simply refer it

22 Paul Rock

Table 1.1 Cases received by the Parliamentary Ombudsman under the Victims' Code 2009–2011[a]

Victims' Code cases	Received 2009/2010	2010/2011	Total
Crown Prosecution Service	4	5	9
Cumbria Probation Trust		1	1
Greater Manchester Police	1		1
Her Majesty's Courts and Tribunals Service		3	3
Kent Police		1	1
Metropolitan Police Service	1	1	2
National Probation Service	1	1	2
Police	8	3	11
West Yorkshire Police		1	1
Witness Care Units		2	2
Grand Total	15	18	33

Note
a   I am grateful to the office of the Victims Commissioner for supplying this information.

directly to the Parliamentary Commissioner, who has a limited authority to undertake investigations and make recommendations, but not compel action, about cases breaching the Code. Between 2009 and 2011, at a time when the police recorded a total of some eight and a half million offences and the ombudsman dealt with a total of some 48,000 complaints from all quarters,[22] 33 complaints[23] were made under the Victims' Code, see Table 1.1.

In total, the Ombudsman has considered 58 complaints concerning the Code since its foundation in 2006, of which only two were investigated, the others failing to qualify because they fell outside the Ombudsman's remit or outside the correct process. Only one complaint has been upheld since 2006.[24]

It is clear that, in England and Wales, victims make almost no recourse to the Ombudsman when they believe their rights or expectations have been breached; and that the outcome of any such recourse is more than somewhat paltry. It is intriguing to enquire why this should be so, and, in pursuing the question, I shall remain largely with the case of England and Wales, not only for simplicity's sake but because it is with those countries that I am most familiar. I write, it should also be emphasized, not as a lawyer, but as a sociologist.

The first and most obvious reason why victims have been denied substantial and uncluttered rights is that they would be expensive to introduce. A bad precedent was thought in Government to have been created by the establishment of the criminal injuries compensation scheme which had been initially costed by Leslie Wilkins, then a government statistician, at £150,000 per annum. Now, and despite attempts to trim costs by replacing common law damages by a tariff scheme and by raising the threshold of eligibility, criminal injuries compensation amounts annually to £280 million. It is in effect what the financially-prudent civil servant detests above all, a politically sensitive, open-ended, uncontrolled and demand-led scheme, having had to be supported in 2010–11 by an additional grant of £70 million made available by the Ministry of Justice (Criminal Injuries Compensation Authority 2011). At a time of radical economic cuts, when funding has been withdrawn from some victims' groups altogether, when criminal injuries compensation itself has been reduced,[25] no government department in England and Wales would countenance the proposition that victims should be accorded a new right freely to go to law and, in the process, seek an indefinitely large number of sums in monetary compensation for a breach of an entitlement. It would not only be costly but, as important, it might also be taken to support the disturbing proposal that the State accepted legal liability for the crimes committed against its citizens. The State, emphasized an internal Home Office paper in 1999, 'is not liable for injuries caused to people by acts of others' (in Rock 2004, p. 267).

It was precisely for that reason that the somewhat elliptical method of placing a statutory obligation on criminal justice agencies to provide a standard of service to victims of crime was introduced by the 2004 Act. One of a number of internal draft papers that anticipated the Act's introduction argued in 2000 that:

> There is some hesitation about using the language of rights in a specific way because of the increasing expectation of litigation or financial compensation if those rights are not met... The Government is not convinced that legally enforceable rights, with attendant rights to take civil action; to sue and to receive compensation if they are not met, is the route to take.

And, the then Lord Chancellor commented:

> We should not set up a new comprehensive tier of legally enforceable rights for victims. This would establish a new category of litigation calling for legal aid [and] highly attractive to civil rights lawyers who would be enthused by opportunities to assert deficiencies in the criminal trial process....
> (in Rock 2004, pp. 534–535)

The second, and entirely familiar, reason for baulking at the idea of legal rights flows from the State's assertion of ownership in crime and criminal procedure in common law jurisdictions. Ever since the consolidation of the nation state in the sixteenth century, crime has been deemed to be an affront to the community or society metaphysically conceived (Jeudwine 1917). Paraphrasing William Blackstone (1769, pp. 5–7), Lindsay Farmer, Professor of Law at the University of Glasgow (2008, p. 263) describes crimes as 'violations of rights or duties owed to the whole *community*...' [emphasis in the original]. Trials are joined between the Queen and the defendant; justice rests on the tripod of judge, prosecutor and defence counsel (Burger 1971), and the role of the alleged victim is merely to attest to what he or she claims may have happened, as if he or she were no more than the vessel on which an assault on the collectivity was waged. Although some would have it otherwise, victims are *not* a party to proceedings in common law jurisdictions, nor does the State act for the victim. *The Code for Crown Prosecutors* lays down under Section 4.19 that 'the prosecution service does not act for victims or their families in the same way as solicitors act for their clients, and prosecutors must form an overall view of the public interest'.[26] Victims can have no privileged interest or claim. Neither can they have a reasonable expectation of any such claim in the future. The bestowing of more generous legal rights and recognition on victims is thought dangerously to place in jeopardy the proper allocation of rules, roles and relations of the criminal justice system (see Ashworth 2000).

It is a perception of danger that is deeply entrenched in the structure and occupational culture of the legal profession of England and Wales. Solicitors with a criminal practice are wholly engaged in working for the suspect and defendant. Members of the Bar are free-lance advocates who, although they do specialize, may work for defence or prosecution. It is a consequence of that bipartisan division of labour that lawyers are acutely and continually exercised by the problem of balance, of what they call the 'equality of arms' and of protections for the accused. Conservative, liberal and radical barristers, solicitors and judges and their collective bodies, such as the Bar Council, Law Society, Liberty and JUSTICE, are doughty in shielding what they conceive to be the rights of defendants. There is little of the crusading district attorney in the prosecutions mounted in the Crown Court, but there is a presupposition – valid or invalid – held by prosecutors and defence counsel that according victims' rights would almost certainly infringe on the rights of the defendant.

The perception of danger stems from another source as well. Although I have observed in practitioners no absence of compassion or, indeed, admiration, for the victim, there are yet traces of an ineffaceable distrust in the legal and official mind. Victims retain vestiges of David Downes' pariah about them and they are vestiges with old roots. Before the creation of the office of Director of Public Prosecutions in 1879, although crime was still defined metaphysically as an injury to the community, victims were obliged to confront defendants as private prosecutors in what could be unmediated antagonism and there was a marked propensity by professional lawyers at the time to characterize them as malicious, venal, frivolous, self-interested and vengeful. Victims might resort to blackmail and extortion. The system opened the 'door to bribery, collusion and illegal compromises' (Her Majesty's Commissioners on Criminal Law 1845, p. 14). The utilitarian reformer, Henry Brougham, called private prosecution a 'perversion of the criminal law for personal and guilty purposes' (in Select Committee on Prosecutors 1855, p. iii).

We know almost nothing about the transmission of such typifications within legal circles over the generations. There may well be no continuity at all. But there *are* those who seem even now to relay disturbing echoes of those passions. Victims are from time to time still tainted by that imagery of the harpy bent (despite some contradictory evidence (Hough and Roberts 1999)) on what Jan van Dijk once called 'victimagogic programmes' (1988, p. 117).[27] Their allegedly malign presence has been the subject of peculiar condemnation in North America, where memories of lynching and popular justice remain in force (see Garland 2005).

As a result many politicians, practitioners, lawyers and academics are more than a little nervous about empowering the victim. Indeed, they consider it to be a vital duty of a professional criminal justice system to insulate itself and protect the defendant from what the American scholar, Marie Gottschalk, called the 'public's passion for revenge'.[28] Whilst defendants tend to be regulated in the trial process (Ericson and Baranek 1982), and judges, police, court staff and lawyers are under formal and informal discipline, victims are seen as potentially rogue elements – members of a fluid, shifting and relatively anonymous public, assumed to be lay people who are foreign to the ways of criminal justice and the courthouse, locked uncontrollably into the conflicts of the adversarial system, vindictive, untrustworthy, unreliable and volatile, prone to emotional displays and unguarded outbursts, speaking a language which is not forensic, rational or dispassionate, and liable to upset the expressive order and proper workings of criminal justice (Doak 2005, p. 298). It is perhaps not so remarkable that those typifications should have emerged in that fashion because victims will almost invariably be seen by practitioners just at the moment when they are exposed to the greatest tension: in the immediate aftermath of a crime or in the courtroom. In the 1980s, Home Office civil servants sought to protect their Ministers from activists, known internally as the 'angry victims', lest they be exposed to outbreaks of 'pushing' reinforced by unseemly barracking. After the breaching of that wall and the establishment of the Victims Advisory Panel, victims do now shout at politicians and officials.

It has followed that, although police family liaison officers and other practitioners may develop an acquaintance, even a warm acquaintance, with victims and their families, there is a propensity in the criminal justice circles of England and Wales ever to stay wary, to keep victims at bay and in check, the police, prosecutors and staff of the Witness Service coming in effect to play the sheepdog. Victims are outsiders not insiders, partisans not noncombatants, and they cannot, it is believed, always be trusted to behave responsibly or to police themselves. Alignment with them could be compromising. Court staff have long been anxious not to undermine their neutrality in their dealings with them. Until recently, prosecuting counsel would not even speak to them.

In England and Wales, moreover, there may be a lingering element of class disdain in that process of distancing: insiders will tell one that judges and counsel tend to be upper or upper middle class, solicitors middle class, the police 'respectable' working class or lower middle-class, and victims quite frequently proletarian, members of the *mobile vulgus*. Robert Reiner (2000, p. 138) remarked that 'people at the base of the social hierarchy... are disproportionately the complainants, victims or offenders processed by the police'. How else is one to interpret the Bar Council's response to a government consultation paper floating the idea of victim impact statements?

> The proposal that victims should have a say in decisions as to whether prosecutions are started, terminated, and what charges are brought is potentially inimical to justice... Victims by definition will be emotionally vulnerable. A proportion come from disadvantaged sections of society and will be of modest intellectual and educational attainment.

Judges, including a former and then current Lord Chief Justice, were also reported to be uneasy about possible intrusion: 'They say that the courtroom would become an emotional arena; that it would falsely raise victims' expectations of being able to influence the sentence; and that it would extend rights of audience in the courts beyond the legal profession' (*The Times* 24 December 2005). The scheme's abandonment, despite the initial enthusiasm of Ministers, signified that there is a Rubicon that still may not be crossed. Victims are not to be trusted as full participants in the criminal justice system of England and Wales. They may not have a voice in decisions to charge, in sentencing or parole. What claims they may have are not enforceable. Staved off, corralled and feared, it may well be some time before victims are granted anything that smacks of legal rights.

Notes

1 I am most grateful to Sarah Kincaid and Rod Hill of the Office of the Victims' Commissioner for general advice and to Peter Dunn, Meg Garvin, Marie Manikis, Heather Strang and Tim Newburn for their advice and comments on earlier drafts of the paper on which this chapter is based.
2 A/RES/40/34; www.un.org/documents/ga/res/40/a40r034.htm [Accessed on 2 September 2011].
3 www.homeoffice.gov.uk/publications/science-research-statistics/research-statistics/crime-research/hosb1011/hosb1011snr?view=Binary [Accessed on 4 September 2011].
4 www.statistics.gov.uk/downloads/theme_social/Social_Trends36/ST36_Ch09.pdf [Accessed on 4 September 2011].
5 Marie Manikis told me by email on 6 September 2011 that: 'Lois Haight who chaired the Presidential Task Force on Victims of Crime just informed me that most victims the Task Force spoke to were victims of violent crimes. However, they also had quite a few burglary victims and parents of murdered children and parents of children who suffered sexual abuse. They also heard from victims of rape, robbery, domestic violence and kidnapping. She does not recall any victims of misdemeanours.'

6 www.auditcommission.gov.uk/nationalstudies/communitysafety/Pages/victimsandwitnesses.aspx [Accessed on 29 June 2008].
7 www.justice.gov.uk/downloads/publications/statistics-and-data/criminal-justice-stats/criminal-stats-quarterly-dec10.pdf [Accessed on 30 August 2011].
8 www.presidency.ucsb.edu/ws/index.php?pid=34171#axzz1UfXAR0g0 [Accessed on 4 September 2011].
9 Where that figure of 77 per cent also obtains. See *Criminal Victimization in the United States 2008 Statistical Tables, National Crime Victimization Survey*, Office of Justice Programs, Bureau of Justice Statistics, Washington D.C., March 2010, NCJ 227669.
10 Sometimes, that succession is described as if it should be read as a powerful and irresistible motor of change in its own right. See International Study Institute on Victimology (1976).
11 See the European Forum for Victims Services; *Statements of Victims' Rights in the Process of Criminal Justice; The Social Rights of Victims of Crime*; and *Statement of Victims' Rights to Standards of Service*.
12 Joanna Shapland (1984, p. 144) argued that: 'If the money was regarded as compensation... then it was not the actual receipt of the money that was important, but the judgment which that award represented about the suffering and position of the victim.' Some fourteen years later, an Australian Capital Territory Victim Support Working Party concluded that 'for some victims, personal support and practical help may be far more important and appropriate than financial compensation' (Victim Support Working Party 1998, p. 18).
13 http://ec.europa.eu/commission_2010–2014/reding/victims/index_en.htm [Accessed on 6 September 2011].
14 www.cjsonline.gov.uk/downloads/application/pdf/CJS%20White%20Paper%20-%20Justice%20For%20All.pdf [Accessed on 8 September 2011].
15 www.thersa.org/events/video/vision-videos/louise-casey-putting-the-victim-at-the-heart-of-the-criminal-justice-system [Accessed on 6 September 2011].
16 www.cps.gov.uk/victims_witnesses/ [Accessed on 6 September 2011].
17 www.cps.gov.uk/legal/v_to_z/victims_code_operational_guidance/#a01 [Accessed on 6 September 2011].
18 www.official-documents.gov.uk/document/hc1011/hc01/0144/0144.pdf [Accessed on 6 September 2011].
20 Rather enigmatically, I was told that: 'Unfortunately we do not hold a reliable set of data on complaints received under the Code of Practice for Victims. The reason for this is because the data greatly underestimates the actual number of complaints received which apply to the Victims Code and for that reason we would not be able to release this information.' Email from a research officer at the IPCC received on 18 August 2011.
21 None of the six local CPS branch offices in London replied to my query about complaints received under the code.
22 I received an email on 15 August 2011 from the Correspondence Unit, Crown Prosecution Service, to the effect that: 'The CPS has no central records of the total number of complaints under the Victims' Code. Complaints can be sent directly to any of our regional offices across England and Wales and we do not currently have any mechanisms in place to record the number of complaints that specifically mention the Victims' Code.' When I wrote to one such regional office, CPS London, I received an identical reply dated 22 August 2011.
23 www.ombudsman.org.uk/annualreport/ [Accessed on 6 September 2011].
24 I am grateful to Jane Stephenson of the Public Affairs Department, Parliamentary and Health Service Ombudsman, for compiling this table (email of 4 August 2011). She added: 'We reported on one investigation involving the Victims' Code last year, which

involved complaints again HM Prison Service and the National Probation Service. We upheld the complaints against both those organisations.'
25 Based on an email from Rod Hill of the Office for Victims and Witnesses dated 13 September 2011.
26 www.bbc.co.uk/news/uk-14949226 [Accessed on 22 September 2011].
27 www.cps.gov.uk/publications/docs/code2010english.pdf [Accessed on 1 September 2011].
28 For examples of those fears, see Fattah (1986), Jackson (2003), Matravers (2010) and Tonry (2010).
29 www.barcouncil.org.uk/document.asp?documentid=3437&languageid=1 [Accessed on 3 September 2011], www.tnr.com/book/review/peculiar-institution-david-garland [Accessed on 5 September 2011].

Bibliography

Allen, J., Livingstone, S. and Reiner, R., 2000. No More Happy Endings? The Media and Popular Concern About Crime Since the Second World War. In: T. Hope and R. Sparks, eds, Crime, Risk and Insecurity: Law and Order in Everyday Life and Political Discourse. London: Routledge, pp. 107–125.

Antilla, I., 1964. Victimology – A New Territory in Criminology. In: N. Christie, ed., Scandinavian Studies in Criminology. London: Tavistock, pp. 3–7.

Ashworth, A., 2000. Victims' Rights, Defendants' Rights and Criminal Procedure. In: A. Crawford and J. Goodey, eds, Integrating a Victim Perspective within Criminal Justice. Aldershot: Ashgate, pp. 185–204.

Bassiouni, M., 1999. Crimes Against Humanity. The Hague: Kluwer Law International.

Blackstone, W., 1769. Commentaries on the Laws of England. Book 4. Oxford: Clarendon Press.

Boutellier, H., 2000. Crime and Morality: The Significance of Criminal Justice in Post-Modern Culture. Dordrecht: Kluwer Academic.

Brownmiller, S., 1977. Against our Will: Men, Women and Rape. Harmondsworth: Penguin.

Burger, W., 1971. Address. Second Plenary Session. American Bar Association Annual Meeting.

Campbell, T., 2008. Rights and Duties. In: P. Cane and J. Conaghan, eds, The New Oxford Companion to Law. Oxford: Oxford University Press, pp. 1025–1026.

Christie, N., 1977. Conflicts as Property. British Journal of Criminology, 17(1), pp. 1–15.

Christie, N., 1986. The Ideal Victim. In: E. Fattah, ed., From Crime Policy to Victim Policy. Basingstoke: Macmillan, pp. 17–30.

Clark, L. and Lewis, D., 1977. Rape: The Price of Coercive Sexuality. Toronto: The Women's Press.

Council of the European Community, 2001. Council Framework Decision of 15 March 2001 on the Standing of Victims in Criminal Proceedings (2001/220/JHA) Official Journal of the European Communities L 82/1, Brussels.

Criminal Injuries Compensation Authority, 2011. Fifteenth Report. HC1246. London: The Stationery Office.

Doak, J., 2005. Victims' Rights in Criminal Trials: Prospects for Participation. Journal of Law and Society, 32(2), pp. 294–316.

Dobash, R. and Dobash, R., 1979. Violence Against Wives: A Case against the Patriarchy. New York: Free Press.

Ericson, R. and Baranek, P., 1982. The Ordering of Justice: A Study of Accused Persons as Dependants in the Criminal Process. Toronto: University of Toronto Press.

European Commission, 2011. Proposal for a Directive of the European Parliament and of the Council Establishing Minimum Standards on the Rights, Support and Protection of Victims of Crime. Com(2011) 275 Final, 2011/0129 (Cod), Brussels, 18th May 2011.

Farmer, L., 2008. Crime, Definitions of. In: P. Cane and J. Conaghan, eds, The New Oxford Companion to Law. Oxford: Oxford University Press, pp. 263–264.

Fattah, E., 1986. On Some Visible and Hidden Dangers of Victim Movements. In: E. Fattah, ed., From Crime Policy to Victim Policy. Basingstoke: Macmillan, pp. 1–16.

Garland, D., 2005. Penal Excess and Surplus Meaning: Public Torture Lynchings in Twentieth-Century America. Law and Society Review, 39(4), pp. 793–833.

Gottschalk, M., 2006. The Prison and the Gallows: The Politics of Mass Incarceration in America. Cambridge: Cambridge University Press.

Her Majesty's Commissioners on Criminal Law, 1845. Eighth Report. London: HMSO.

Herrington, L., 1987. Victim Rights and Criminal Justice Reform. Annals of the American Academy of Political Science. November. pp. 139–144.

Holstein, J. and Miller, G., 1990. Rethinking Victimization: An Interactional Approach to Victimology. Symbolic Interaction, 13(1), pp. 103–122.

Home Office, 2002. Justice For All. Cm 5563. London: Home Office.

Hough, M. and Roberts, J., 1999. Sentencing Trends in Britain: Public Knowledge and Public Opinion. Punishment & Society, 1(1), pp. 11–26.

International Study Institute on Victimology, 1976. Conclusions and Recommendations. In: E. Viano ed., Victims and Society. Washington: Visage Press.

Jackson, J., 2003. Justice for All: Putting Victims at the Heart of Criminal Justice? Journal of Law and Society, 30(2), pp. 309–326.

Jacobs, J. and Potter, K., 1998. Hate Crimes: Criminal Law & Identity Politics. Oxford: Oxford University Press.

Jeudwine, J., 1917. Tort, Crime and the Police in Medieval England. London: Williams and Norgate.

Jones, T., MacLean, B. and Young, J., 1986. The Islington Crime Survey: Victimization and Policing in Inner-City London. Aldershot: Gower.

Joutsen, M., 1987. The Role of the Victim of Crime in European Criminal Justice Systems. Helsinki: HEUNI.

Kauzlarich, D., Matthews, R. and Miller, W., 2001. Toward a Victimology of State Crime. Critical Criminology, 10, pp. 173–194.

Knudten, M., Knudten, R. and Meade, A., 1978. Will Anyone be Left to Testify? Disenchantment with the Criminal Justice System. Washington: LEAA US Department of Justice.

Lamb, S., 1996. The Trouble with Blame: Victims, Perpetrators, and Responsibility. Cambridge: Harvard University Press.

Lea, J. and Young, J., 1985. What is to be Done about Law and Order? London: Penguin.

Lerner, M., 1980. The Belief in a Just World: A Fundamental Delusion. New York: Plenum Press.

Macpherson of Cluny, 1999. The Stephen Lawrence Inquiry (Cm 4262-I), Report of an Inquiry by Sir William Macpherson of Cluny, Presented to Parliament by the Home Secretary. London.

Maguire, M., 1982. Burglary in a Dwelling: The Offence, the Offender and the Victim. London: Heinemann.

Matravers, M., 2010. The Victim, the State, and Civil Society. In: A. Bottoms and J. Roberts, eds, Hearing the Victim: Adversarial Justice, Crime Victims and the State. Cullompton: Willan, pp. 1–16.

Mendelsohn, B., 1963. The Origin of the Doctrine of Victimology. Excerpta Criminologica, 3, pp. 239–245.

National Board for Crime Prevention, 1994. Wise After the Event: Tackling Repeat Victimisation. London: Home Office.

The New Shorter Oxford English Dictionary. 1993. Oxford: Clarendon Press.

Pendergrast, M., 1995. Victims of Memory: Incest Accusations and Shattered Lives. Hinesburg, Vermont: Upper Access Books.

Pitch, T., 1985. Critical Criminology, the Construction of Social Problems, and the Question of Rape. International Journal of the Sociology of Law, 13(1), pp. 35–46.

Pizzey, E., 1977. Scream Quietly or the Neighbours will Hear. Harmondsworth: Penguin.

President's Task Force on Victims of Crime, Final Report, 1982. Washington D.C.: US Government Printing Office.

Reeves, H. and Dunn, P., 2010. The Status of Crime Victims and Witnesses in the Twenty-First Century. In: A. Bottoms and J. Roberts, eds, Hearing the Victim: Adversarial Justice, Crime Victims and the State. Cullompton: Willan, pp. 46–71.

Reiner, R., 2000. The Politics of the Police. Oxford: Oxford University Press.

Rock, P., 1986. A View from the Shadows: The Ministry of the Solicitor General of Canada and the Justice for Victims of Crime Initiative. Oxford: Clarendon Press.

Rock, P., 1990. Helping Victims of Crime: The Home Office and the Rise of Victim Support in England and Wales. Oxford: Clarendon Press.

Rock, P., 1998. After Homicide: Practical and Political Responses to Bereavement. Oxford: Clarendon Press.

Rock, P., 2000. Aftermath and the Construction of Victimisation: 'The Other Victims of Crime'. Howard Journal, 39(1), pp. 58–77.

Rock, P., 2002. On Becoming a Victim. In: C. Hoyle and R. Wilson, eds, New Visions of Crime Victims. Oxford: Hart Publishing, pp. 1–22.

Rock, P., 2004. Constructing Victims' Rights: The Home Office, New Labour and Victims. Oxford: Clarendon Press.

Rock, P., 2006. Aspects of the Social Construction of Crime Victims in Australia. Victims and Offenders, 1(3), 289–321.

Rock, P., 2010. Hearing Victims of Crime: The Delivery of Impact Statements as Ritual Behaviour in Four London Trials for Murder and Manslaughter. In: A. Bottoms and J. Roberts, eds, Hearing the Victim: Adversarial Justice, Crime Victims and the State. Cullompton: Willan, pp. 200–231.

Rolph, C.H., 1958. Wild Justice. New Statesman. 18th January, pp. 65–66.

Russell, D. and Van de Ven, N., eds., 1976. Crimes Against Women: Proceedings of the International Tribunal. Millbrae, California: Les Femmes.

Secretary of State for the Home Department, the Secretary of State for Constitutional Affairs and the Attorney General, 2005. Rebuilding Lives – Supporting Victims of Crime. Presented to Parliament. Cm 6705.

Select Committee on Prosecutors, 1855. Report. London: House of Commons.

Shapland, J., 1984. Victims, the Criminal Justice System and Compensation. British Journal of Criminology, 24(2), pp. 131–149.

Shapland, J., Willmore, J. and Duff, P., 1985. Victims in the Criminal Justice System. Aldershot: Gower.

Sykes, C., 1992. A Nation of Victims. New York: St. Martin's Press.

Task Force on Victims' Rights and the Justice System, 1991. In: E. Viano, ed. Oñati Proceedings: Victim's Rights and Legal Reforms. Oñati: The Oñati International Institute for the Sociology of Law, pp. 335–343.

Tonry, M., 2010. 'Rebalancing the Criminal Justice System in favour of the victim': the costly consequences of populist rhetoric. In: A. Bottoms and J. Roberts, eds, Hearing the Victim: Adversarial Justice, Crime Victims and the State. Cullompton: Willan, pp. 72–103.

van Dijk. J., 1988. Ideological Trends Within the Victims' Movement: An International Perspective. In: M. Maguire and J. Pointing, eds, Victims of Crime: A New Deal? Milton Keynes: Open University Press, pp. 115–126.

Victim Support Working Party, 1998. Victim Support in the ACT: Options for a Comprehensive Response, Report of the Victim Support Working Party. ACT: Victim Support.

Von Hentig, H., 1948. The Criminal and his Victim. Hamden: Archon Books.

Wertham, F., 1949. The Show of Violence. New York: Vintage.

Winkel, F. and Vrij, A., 1998. Who is in Need of Victim Support?: The Issue of Accountable, Empirically Validated Selection and Victim Referral. Expert Evidence, 6, pp. 23–41.

Chapter 2

Respecting victims of crime
Key distinctions in a theory of victims' rights

Antony Pemberton

Introduction

Recent decades have seen an increasing role for victims of crime in the criminal justice procedure (Groenhuijsen and Letschert 2008). This is evident in legislation and practice, in adversarial and inquisitorial systems and at the national and international level. Where in the 1970s the victim may have been correctly viewed as the forgotten party of the criminal justice process, this is no longer an accurate description in many jurisdictions. The 'emancipation' of victims of crime (Van Dijk 2009) has been felt far beyond the criminal justice system. In sociological and philosophical analyses of Western society at the dawn of the twenty-first century the victim is often considered to be a central figure (Nolan 1998; Boutellier 2002; Furedi 2004). Richard Rorty (1989), for instance, is well known for finding 'Are you suffering?' to be the central moral question of our times.

The upsurge of the victim is not always welcomed. In fact, in most societal analyses the perceived central position of victimization (processes) is viewed with concern, linked to passivity, overuse of therapeutic measures and irrational 'moral panics' (e.g. Best 1999; Furedi 2004). The role of victims within the criminal justice system has had its fair share of criticism as well (Elias 1993; Sarat 1997; Ashworth 2000). Instruments granting victims participation rights in the criminal justice procedure, rather than increased access to information or compensation, have regularly been the subject of vigorous debate (e.g. Pemberton and Reynaers 2011).

The introduction of victims' rights in the criminal justice process has not, as a rule, been informed by a systematic rationale. Initially pragmatic criminal justice concerns – for instance maintaining public support for criminal justice agencies or increasing/maintaining reporting rates – were the main driver (see Wemmers 1996). Where reference is made to notions underlying victims' rights, it is argued on the basis of the importance of respect for the victims' dignity and/or a specific instance of the general sympathetic reaction to the harm suffered by victims of crime (Groenhuijsen and Letschert 2008; Groenhuijsen and Pemberton 2009).

However these rationales do not offer much guidance in the development of a theory of victims' rights, nor do they provide much clarity in the debate between proponents and opponents of victims' rights. Key is that neither 'respect', nor 'sympathy, nor 'harm' are straightforward and/or unproblematic when viewed in connection to the rights of victims of crime in the criminal justice system.

The implicit assumption that the term 'respect' is self-evident contributes to a loose use of the term, which in turn hampers a meaningful discussion of its meaning and function within the canon of victims' rights.[1] Instead further examination of respect as a construct is in order. Following the illuminating observation of Darwall (1977), there are two relevantly different forms of respect: *recognition respect* and *appraisal respect*. This chapter will argue that the respect due to victims of crime is a clear instance of the former, rather than the latter, while confusing the two forms is a regular feature of both observers and victims' own views of an appropriate role in the criminal justice system.

Similarly, viewing sympathy with the harm done to victims as a (sufficient) reason for offering them rights in a justice procedure, is also based upon an implicit assumption, which should be further scrutinized. Here a key distinction lies between *sympathy* and *empathy* (Wispé 1986). These concepts are similar but distinct, with the former being a vital element of the urge to alleviate another person's suffering, while the latter grounds what Bottoms (2010) called the *duty to understand* the victims' perspective.

Finally there is the distinction between *harmfulness* and *wrongfulness* (e.g. Duff 2001a, 2003). Suffering victimization by crime involves harm, but wrong as well. As these co-occur it is no sinecure to untangle them. Nevertheless I will argue that their role in victims' participation in criminal justice is different. I will argue that the experience of wrongfulness is intimately linked to the justification of involving victims within criminal justice, as a *qualifier*, while the experienced harm is a better base for shaping the manner and the extent of involvement, i.e. as a *quantifier*.

Each of these distinctions is examined in turn. Throughout the chapter the connection with the practice of victims' rights is made, to illuminate the relevance to current debates concerning victims' rights.

Recognition and appraisal respect

Distinguishing recognition and appraisal respect

Darwall (1977) distinguished two different ways in which persons may be the object of respect. The respectful behaviour expected from each of us when we offer our seat in the bus to a senior citizen, step aside when a blind person is making his/her way through a crowded railway station, or follow the instructions of a police officer in traffic are all instance of respect of a qualitatively different order than the feelings of respect we have for substantial achievements, like those by artists, athletes and academics.[2]

In Darwall's terms the former is *recognition respect*, while the latter is *appraisal respect*. In general terms recognition respect for people consists of a disposition to weigh appropriately in one's deliberations some fact about a person – it can apply to persons as a whole, but also to different aspects of the person – and *act* accordingly. The latter point is important: recognition respect carries with it a duty that constricts the range of (morally) appropriate behaviour. Without this behaviour respect for the (feature of the) person is lacking. Importantly: to have recognition respect for a person as such is not giving him credit for anything in particular, recognition respect is not based on merit.

Recognition respect's object is at its core, a *fact*, which factors in deliberations of how to act. Inappropriate consideration of that fact amounts to a failure to meet a moral standard. Recognition respect therefore restricts the scope of behaviour.[3] In contrast, appraisal respect's exclusive objects are (features of) persons which are held to manifest their excellence as persons, engaged in a specific pursuit (Darwall 1977, p. 38). Appropriate grounds for appraisal respect are that the person has manifested characteristics which have made him deserving of such positive appraisal and that these characteristics can be attributed to a person's *character*.[4] This respect does not necessarily imply any action on the part of the person respecting the other: the *attitude* of positive appraisal of that person constitutes the respect. Achievement will not automatically lead to appraisal respect. High achievement sportspersons might achieve a lot, but may not be respected due to other aspects of their behaviour.[5]

Not every positive attitude amounts to respect. This is particularly true if positive attitudes towards another person are conditional on that person serving a function in some self-serving pursuit. As a matter of definition, respecting a person does not include valuing someone for the use they have for our own ends.

The degrees of respect involved in recognition and appraisal differ. One's appraisal respect for *a person* may be higher or lower than for another, or it may be absent altogether, while in the case of recognition respect it is instead the weight that the *fact* ought to have in one's deliberations of what to do that matters. All persons as such should be treated equally and accordingly to the extent this fact can be said to be true about them.

Respecting victims as recognition respect: a straightforward matter?

Viewed through Darwall's lens it is not difficult to conclude that the respect owed to victims of crime is a form of recognition respect. Key is respecting the *fact* that someone was victimized and *acting* upon that fact. Becoming a victim of crime cannot plausibly be viewed as an achievement, while respecting victims of crime involves something more manifest than a positive attitude. Respecting victims involves a moral duty to give appropriate weight to the fact that someone has been victimized in our behaviour towards them, rather than in the experience of respect itself. If victims' rights in the criminal justice process are grounded in respect, it is recognition respect that is intended.

However, respect for victimization by crime has confusing elements related to the nature of the appraisal of *the fact* of victimization. The fact of victimization by crime involves an appraisal itself. I am not referring here to theories of the social construction of crime and victimization (e.g. Walklate 2006), but to the necessity, given existing definitions of these concepts, to assess whether or not a given situation meets the criteria to fall into these categories. This is true of other forms of recognition respect as well. If someone's blindness should play a role in our behaviour towards a person, an assessment of blindness is in order. This will be less or more extensive depending on whether we are merely stepping aside to let the other pass on a busy street or are reviewing their eligibility for a large insurance payment.

There are practical difficulties in determining the fact of victimization. By definition it happened in the past and often does not leave any visible traces in the present, and as most observers will not have witnessed the fact of victimization itself, they will have to rely on other sources than their own perception to ascertain this fact. This is further complicated by the fact that for a variety of reasons victims may not want to share the fact that they are victims themselves (see for instance Brewin *et al.* 2000) while the (psychological) effects of victimization often diminish with time (e.g. Bonanno *et al.* 2011).

Respecting the consequences of disrespect

Aside from these practical difficulties, the assessment of the fact of victimization by crime and the consideration of its bearing on moral behaviour becomes more complicated, due to the fact that it is defined by *(im)moral behaviour* itself. Respecting the fact of victimization means offering respect for the fact that someone else did not do so. Criminal victimization involves a strong form of disrespect: the offender's disrespect of the victims' rights as a person. As I will argue, the wrongfulness, the immorality of the behaviour of the offender is a defining characteristic (Duff 2001a, 2003; Simester and Von Hirsch 2011). This is one of the reasons why respect in the treatment of victims of crime is so significant: while offering respect to a blind person does not contribute to his or her capability to see, offering respect to a victim may impact the effects of victimization. Social acknowledgement and support serve as protective factors in the development of psychological ailments in the aftermath of victimization (Brewin *et al.* 2000).

However, not only the offender's behaviour is a factor; the victim's moral or immoral behaviour plays a role as well (Simester and Von Hirsch 2011). This is apparent in cases in which self-defence is used as a justification (e.g. Chan and Simester 2005), which may in effect lead to a reassessment of the roles of victim and offender, but it will often be necessary to review the victims' own behaviour to establish whether or not a crime has been committed, whether or not the victim substantially contributed to his or her own victimization, while – probably more so in the latter than in the former – a victim's own moral conduct will factor in these assessments. More generally, the evidence surrounding the *just world theory* shows that when faced with an instance of injustice observers will review the conduct of the person suffering the injustice to see whether he or she is – in whole or in part – to blame for the occurrence of injustice (Lerner 1980; Hafer and Begue 2005).

Confounding recognition and appraisal respect in reaction to victimization

What is key in the current discussion is that *assessing the fact* of victimization includes an *appraisal* of the victims' conduct: a victim must be sufficiently blameless for what happened to him or her, for the fact of victimization by crime to be true. Although this appraisal of the victim's behaviour is, in essence, irrelevant beyond what is necessary to ascertain the fact of victimization, it appears that in both observers' and the victim's own views this appraisal is easily confused with something akin to *appraisal respect*.

I can introduce one aspect of this confusion with an anecdote which I personally witnessed at the World Society of Victimology Symposium in Stellenbosch in South Africa in 2003. The speaker at one of the plenary sessions asked the victims in the audience to stand up, after which he called upon the rest of the audience to applaud them, because in his view their victimhood made them '*the true heroes*'. Both history and fiction abound with instances of people showing almost superhuman resilience in the face of extreme adversity, from Homer to Terry Waite, from Snow White to Nelson Mandela. The hero-victim is a true iconic figure, with the trial by fire being one of the main tests by which his or her heroic character comes to the fore.

The point is, however, that in these cases the resilience shown and accompanying actions *following victimization* should be distinguished from the *victimization itself*. One can admire the perseverance and the hardiness in the aftermath of victimization, but this is relevantly different from offering respect for the fact of victimization. The victimization here is better understood as a factor that increases the achievement and strengthens the feeling of admiration. A parallel scenario is the role poverty plays in the life of the central figure in 'from rags to riches' narratives. The poverty-stricken person, due to his or her own ingenuity, capacities and entrepreneurship manages to amass a fortune. The similarity extends to the observation that the actions following victimization imply that the hero-victim is in fact no longer a victim at all, like the from rags to riches-actor is no longer poor.

These observations can hardly lead to problems for the hero-victims themselves, but may have more troubling consequences for others. The expectation that victimization may ennoble those who experience it can easily morph into a normative demand. The epithet 'true hero' then sets a standard which many victims may not reach, and the resulting lack of appraisal respect may bode poorly for the extent to which recognition respect is forthcoming. Indeed the paradoxical situation may emerge that respect – for victims – is given to the hero-victims who do not need it, while it is withheld from those who do.

This is eminently clear in the situations where negative appraisal of unrelated features of the victims' character may lead to a withholding of recognition respect towards victims of crime altogether. Not only are the actions of victims after victimization subjected to scrutiny, but also aspects of their life-story before they were victimized. An example of the latter is the treatment of victims who have been criminals in the past. For instance: the UK bars former felons from receiving compensation for victimization by violent crime, even if their own criminal behaviour is unrelated to the crime visited on themselves (Miers 2007). As I will note below, this is particularly misguided, for it entails using (the lack of) appraisal, rather than recognition respect, as a base for granting or withholding a person rights.

Academic discourse is also not immune. It is a regular feature of victimological literature to find examples, sometimes anecdotes, but also more fully fledged research results, of victims displaying – at least in the eyes of the authors – praiseworthy characteristics such as extending forgiveness, emphasizing conciliation and the like. Subsequently these are held up to be an example of what all victims can and should aspire to; and of which victims should be convinced.[6]

Confusing recognition and appraisal respect is not restricted to observers of victimization. It is also visible in the behaviour and demands of victims themselves. It has been well documented that the experience of victimization may bring about a sense of entitlement in those who experience it (Zitek *et al.* 2010), which is connected to the positive relationship between previous victimization and future wrongdoing (Zitek *et al.* 2010).[7] To be true, this does not apply to all (or even most) victims (see Van Dijk 2006; Vollhardt 2009 for evidence of 'posttraumatic altruism'), but the point here is that for many victims the victimization experience itself becomes an achievement worthy of appraisal respect.

In sum then, the importance of distinguishing between recognition respect and appraisal respect in the experience of victims of crime is that the respect due to victims is an example of the former, while the two are easily and regularly confused. Both the determination of the fact of victimization and the distinction between victimization itself *and* one's reaction to victimization have features that contribute to this confusion. Moreover, respect for the fact of victimization has the intriguing quality that it is due to the fact that someone disrespected the victim, which in turn contributes to the importance of respect in these cases. Not only is respect a necessary component of the rights offered to victims, but it also independently impacts the experience of (recovery) after victimization.

Sympathy for victims' plights; empathy for victims' rights

Distinguishing sympathy and empathy

A concept closely related to respect is empathy (Darwall 2006). Indeed the golden rule 'Do not unto others, as you would have not done on yourself' is intimately connected to empathy, which can be defined as 'the attempt of one self-aware to understand the subjective experiences of another self' (Wispé 1986, p. 318).[8] It involves the recognition of another world of experience, acknowledging another's reality and humanity and the awareness that the self is not exempt – at least in principle – from finding oneself in the same position (Nussbaum 2001).[9] This implies the necessity to understand without judgement the positive and negative experiences of another self and the acknowledgement of the fact that these emotions and reactions are often unclearly understood. One important element of empathy is therefore a process of attempting empathic accuracy.

Sympathy is similar to empathy, as it also concerns the heightened awareness of another person, while both sympathy and empathy are generally taken to imply a benevolent stance towards a person.[10] However sympathy and empathy can be relevantly distinguished from each other. Wispé (1986, p. 318) considers sympathy to refer to 'the heightened awareness of the suffering of another person as something to be alleviated'. It therefore includes an increased sensitivity to the emotions – but emotions of a particular kind! – of the other person and the urge to take whatever mitigating actions are necessary. It is hard to envision sympathy without a measure of empathy: one can only reasonably be assumed to be moved by another's suffering if one can at least partially understand the other's plight.

Table 2.1 provides an overview of the key characteristics of sympathy and empathy (drawn from Wispé 1986).[11] Crucial is the fact that empathy is concerned with (understanding) the point of view of the other, while sympathy is concerned with increasing the well-being – from a negative point of departure – of the other, *irrespective* of the other's own view. The motivating emotion in sympathy is the sympathizer's own experience, the extent to which someone is moved by the other's suffering, while in empathy the locus is the subjective experience of the other.

Whereas sympathy recognizes another's well-being as a relevant consideration, empathy recognizes others as worthy of equal respect. The latter will often be motivated by well-being as well, but not primarily what is for someone's good, but rather for what he/she values and holds good from *his/her point of view as an equal independent agent*. Sympathy on the other hand refers to a care response, which may include doing what's best for a person, even against his/her will.[12]

Sympathy in the aftermath of victimization

If not by definition, than at least in a very large majority of cases, victimization by crime involves a form of suffering, in an emotional, physical and/or financial sense. Sympathy for this suffering plays a large role in the care-response to victims. Offering 'tea and sympathy' has been a staple element of victim support, although it is regularly used as a derogatory classification (for instance Fattah 1999). In turn, the sympathy involved in this care response is an important beneficial, even protective factor in victims' experiences (Brewin *et al.* 2000). The fact that the surroundings are often not as sympathetic as victims may have expected is a prominent source of so-called secondary victimization. This reaction may also be due to the complexities involved in reacting to victimization: a large body of

Table 2.1 Comparing key characteristics of sympathy and empathy

Sympathy	Empathy
Sympathiser is moved by	Empathiser reaches out
To substitute another for oneself	To substitute oneself for another
To know what it would be like to be the other person	To know what it would be like if I were the other person
I am the other person	I act as if I were the other person
Duty to help other's well-being, defined by me	Duty to understand
Relating	Empathic accuracy
Care	Respect

Source: Based on Wispé (1986).

literature illustrates that the aversion that observers feel at the injustice suffered by victims is at odds with the urge to relieve the suffering that was caused by the injustice (Loewenstein and Small 2007).

But sympathy has its own 'dark side' as well. It involves a degree of paternalism (Feinberg 1984). The observer places his/her own view of what should be done above the views the victim may have, and uses his/her own feelings as a guide to action, rather than trying to accurately ascertain what the victim's feelings and views on his or her needs may be. Although sympathy is caused by the perception of another person's suffering, it is driven by the *distress felt by the observer*, upon viewing this suffering, rather than the perspective of the person suffering him or herself.

Sympathy, moreover, pre-determines the focus and direction of the victim's perspective. Wispé (1986, p. 319) notes:

> It is exactly the psychological process that involves the painful awareness of someone else's affliction as something that needs to be relieved. This precludes sympathizing with someone's happiness, because why, except for malicious reasons would one want to terminate someone's happiness?

This means that approaching victims through sympathy restricts victims and actions to the benefit of victims in terms of their suffering, neglecting the fact that victims may have needs and wishes that are either not directly rooted in their suffering, or are not related to coping with or relieving this suffering. For all sympathy's graces, therefore, in supporting and assisting victims it needs to be harnessed: its deployment should recognize and preferably minimize its inherent paternalistic impulses.

Empathy, rather than sympathy in victims' rights

That is particularly true of victim participation in criminal justice process. Sympathetic concern plays a role in the kind of rights made available to victims in the criminal process, and/or in the way these rights are implemented. Many victims' rights across jurisdictions propose to contribute to victims' therapeutic well-being, as a victim-focused branch of *'therapeutic jurisprudence'* (Wexler and Winick 1996; Erez *et al.* 2011). As I have argued previously, this can be to the benefit of victims, where the proposed therapeutic goals mesh well with victims' interests in criminal justice and where the proposed mode of participation is realistically connected to psychological processes.[13] In addition the modes of participation often include measures taken to prevent forms of secondary victimization (e.g. Laxminarayan 2012) and to increase the experience of benefits. An example is the support victims may receive in the Netherlands when submitting a victim impact statement (Lens *et al.* 2010).

However, it is important that both choice and use of rights is underpinned by empathic respect: the victims own standpoint, including the values that hold good from his/her point of view as an equal independent agent, should remain the central focus. If, to the contrary, sympathy was allowed to play a determining role in the use of existing rights, it would diminish the extent to which they *actually amount to rights at all*. Instead of allowing the victim to choose whatever course of action they find best, for whatever goal they deem fit, given the available possibilities, both goal and action would be determined by someone else.

This paternalist approach can then be compounded by the mistake of viewing every choice and action in a victim's life as a function of coping with his or her suffering, while there is no reason why coping with suffering would be the sole or the main reason for participation in a criminal justice procedure (see also Daly 2014, this volume).[14] Indeed, the pursuit of justice after victimization is surely a worthy end in itself, rather than a means that needs its justification in the extent to which it reaches therapeutic goals?

What is lost when this mistake is made can be exemplified by the following quote. In an (otherwise exemplary) review of restorative justice (RJ) practices, Sherman and Strang (2007, p. 62) consider the restrictions of RJ for victims of crime, of which they find one to be: 'And even when offenders are willing to engage in RJ, some victims (or their families) will prefer not to. RJ cannot help those who will not help themselves.' This does more than just misrepresent the evidence on RJ, as any positive therapeutic effect depends upon the self-selection, the choice, of victims participating (e.g. Winkel 2007), while simultaneously misconstruing RJ as a means for victims to 'help themselves' and equating non-participation in RJ with unwillingness to do so (Pemberton *et al.* 2007). But more importantly in the current discussion, it forgets that an intangible benefit of a right lies exactly in the value of being able to *opt out* (see also Van Camp and De Mesmaecker 2014, this volume). Declining to participate in a procedure is a beast of a fundamentally different nature from not being offered to participate at all. It might not amount to 'helping themselves' but in this sense (the offer of) RJ can be of value to non-participants as well.

Wrongfulness and harmfulness, elaborating the *fact* of victimization by crime

Wrongfulness as the key distinguishing element of victimization by crime

The notion that respecting victims of crime involves offering recognition respect for the fact of victimization of crime needs further elaboration. What does the *fact of victimization by crime* entail? In my view the full answer to this question involves understanding the complex way in which the wrongfulness and harmfulness of the experience of victimization by crime are entwined. As Antony Duff (2003, p. 47) summarizes: 'The wrong done to the victim of rape, or wounding, or burglary, is in part constituted by, but also part constitutes the harm that she suffers: to understand such harm, we must understand it as a criminal harm – as a harm that consists in being wrongfully injured.' Indeed it is hard or even impossible to identify the harm independently from the wrong, the crime, that caused it.

The key distinguishing element of victimization by *crime* is thus that it is caused by a wrong,[15] and indeed a public wrong, not in the sense that it is a wrong against the public *rather* than the victim but that it transgresses the values *by which the political community defines itself as a law governed polity* (Duff 2003, p. 48; see also Duff 2001b). It is therefore up to the public to provide an appropriate reaction.[16]

Given this understanding, respecting the fact of victimization by crime requires inclusion of (public) wrongfulness. Importantly, this is not only so because of its inclusion in the definition of crime as such, but also because it is a key component of the experience of crime victims. Being on the receiving end of wrongdoing is a qualitatively different experience from wrongful-*less* harm, which has a particular bearing on the requirements of justice in the aftermath of victimization (Darley and Pittman 2003; Robinson and Darley 2007; Darley 2009). The Oliver Wendell-Holmes aphorism, that *even a dog knows when it is being kicked rather than stumbled over*, summarizes this distinction well.[17]

A key issue is that the conception of repair for wrongful injury necessitates the involvement of the offender: it is his/her apology, not someone else's, that matters (Strang 2002); and any censure or punishment that follows wrongdoing should have him/her as the subject. Indeed any possibility of transferring censure and punishment for wrongdoing to someone else negates the extent to which it in effect can effectively function as censure/punishment for wrongdoing (see more extensively Pemberton 2012b). In addition, the nature of crime as *public* wrongdoing signals the importance of sufficient acknowledgement of victimization by (representatives of) the public (e.g. Orth 2003; Wenzel *et al.* 2008).

The yardstick of harm

As can be understood from Duff's summary above, the relationship between harmfulness and wrongfulness is twofold. Harmfulness first comes in as a constitutive element of what defines crime as such. In other words one of the necessary components of criminalizing behaviour is because it harms or at least is sufficiently likely to harm (Feinberg 1984). The extent of wrongfulness of a given act is correlated with the harm it produces, could have produced or is likely to produce.

However this correlation is not absolute: minor wrongdoing can lead to the experience of great harm, for instance when a momentary lapse of concentration leads to vehicular manslaughter, while attempted murder is a wrong of considerable magnitude, irrespective of the harm it causes. The difference is due to the fact that although harm is a necessary element of wrongdoing, it does not have sole province in determining the extent of wrongdoing in general, nor in individual cases.

In a second sense the wrongfulness of crime is an element of the victims' experience of harm. What is important is to recognize the veracity of Duff's conclusion that a correct interpretation of victims' experience involves understanding that it is *a criminal harm, a harm that consists in being wrongfully injured*. The experience therefore involves a qualitatively different form of harm, but of *harm nonetheless*. Understanding the impact of victimization, its magnitude, is thus appropriately measured along a *yardstick of harm*, to which the victims experience of wrongfulness has contributed.

Harmfulness and wrongfulness and the victim's contribution concerning sentencing

Where the victim's experience is best measured on a yardstick of harm, the extent of censure and indeed punishment due to the offender is a function of his/her wrongdoing. This is something of a mirror image of the victim's experience, for the harm caused by the offender in part constitutes his/her act's wrongfulness, which in turn in part constitutes the harm he/she caused. Where the victim experiences a magnitude of criminal harm, the offender is judged on the extent of his/her harmful wrongdoing. Measurement of these phenomena shares a kernel of common ground, but also includes distinct features. It is beyond the scope of this chapter to extensively explore this distinction, but in general terms, where the victim has to come to terms with the harm that actually emerged from the crime, the issue in a criminal justice process includes whether or not the offender could foresee or had intended these consequences to happen.

In my view appreciating the importance of this distinction provides a key insight into the nature of victim involvement in criminal justice, where it has or can have direct bearing on the sentence of the offender, such as in victim impact statements or victim statements of opinion (Roberts 2009). This understanding will also incorporate the insights gleaned from the previous sections: the differences between recognition and appraisal respect on the one hand and empathy and sympathy on the other.

Respecting the fact of victimization involves respecting the fact that someone suffered criminal harm, a harm that consists in being wrongfully injured. What bearing should this have, in principle, on the sentencing of the offender, for whom the matter at stake is how wrongful his/her behaviour has been? The victim surely has a unique and relevant perspective on his/her own experience of harm; there is no one else who can offer the same insight into his/her experience of this harm as he/she can. Knowing what the victim experiences and has experienced – a key element of the notion of empathy and in particular of empathic accuracy – cannot do without the victim's input. If we would subsequently agree that this 'duty to understand' is a constitutive element of the recognition respect we owe victims due to the fact of their victimization, it seems apparent that respecting victims includes allowing them the opportunity to express their experience of harm (see also Pemberton and Reynaers 2011; Pemberton 2012a).

This experience of harm has bearing on the wrongfulness of the offender's behaviour: as noted, it is part of what constitutes wrongfulness. But does the same apply to the victim's *opinion* of the *extent* of this wrongfulness? In other words, does respecting the fact of victimization and empathy for the victims position imply that the victim should be allowed to offer his/her views on the sentence, which subsequently should be taken into account as an independent source of evidence to determine the sentence of the offender (Sarat 1997)?

I think it does not. Beyond the expression of harm and the evidence the victim has had to offer during the trial, there is no good reason to place added value on the victim's views on the wrongfulness of the offender's behaviour. The part of the victim's experience that can be relevant to this matter concerns the extent to which the victim was harmed; the constituent elements of the extent of wrongfulness that are not covered by this fall outside the range of victims' experience.

A direct translation of the harm the victim experienced into a measure of wrongfulness results in blurring the boundaries between retribution and revenge (e.g. Sarat 1997). In Nozick's (1981) view a key element of this distinction is that retribution is done for a wrong, while revenge may also occur for a harm or a slight. It has been cogently argued on both philosophical (Zaibert 2006) and empirical grounds (Gollwitzer 2009) that this distinction is overstated: from the perspective of the avenger, revenge is also connected to a wrongful act. However, if Nozick's distinction refers to the *yardstick* for this response, it becomes apparent that although both retribution and revenge are 'for wrongs', the extent of revenge is measured along the yardstick of harm, while retribution is measured along the yardstick of wrongfulness, including the extent of intent or culpability of the offender.[18]

The question then is whether the victim's own experience contributes to understanding the extent of intent or culpability of the offender, beyond what is covered by the victim's own yardstick of harm. This can only be answered in the affirmative when the victim's own experience is expected to simultaneously increase his/her insight into the other *non-harm* factors that determine the extent of an offender's wrongfulness. But why would that be a reasonable expectation? Why would we contend that victims are more able than others to estimate the offender's intent, culpability and the like? Indeed, there is good empirical reason to expect victims' assessments of the extent of wrongfulness to be predictably biased (Baumeister 1997; Pinker 2011). The research demonstrating the *moralization gap* reveals that victims have a tendency to exaggerate the offender's intent, to underplay the role of contextual factors and to focus on indicators of malice, while the offender tends to the opposite.[19]

Of course some victims do demonstrate an increased understanding of moral questions, including those relevant to the assessment of wrongfulness, in the aftermath of their victimization (see Van Dijk 2009; Vollhardt 2009). However, using this as a base for victims' rights not only errs as a matter of empirical fact – as current evidence suggests this is more likely to be the exception than the rule – but is also grounded in the wrong form of respect, i.e. appraisal respect rather than recognition respect. As with the *hero-victims* we should take care to distinguish our appraisal respect of certain victims' increased insight from our recognition respect for the fact of victimization, which forms the basis for our (moral) duties towards victims and the grounding of victims' rights.

Conclusion

This chapter has sought to clarify the idea that our duties to victims of crime and the rights that are on offer to them can be grounded in a 'meta-duty' of respect. I have argued that this respect should be seen as *recognition respect* for the *fact of victimization*, which should be distinguished from *appraisal respect* for the *victims' stance following victimization*. The respect that grounds victims' rights is not the respect for the *hero-victim*, nor should it be made contingent on a victim's capability to display praiseworthy characteristics.

The *fact* of victimization crucially includes the understanding that the victim has suffered criminal harm, a harm that consists in being *wrongfully* injured. The harm part constitutes the wrong experienced by the victim, which in turn, part constitutes the experience of harm. However, where the extent of victims' injuries are considered, the *yardstick of harm*, rather than wrongfulness, is appropriate. Wrongfulness instead acts as a *qualifier* in victims' experience. Victims have a unique perspective on the harm they have experienced, to which the wrongfulness of crime contributes. Beyond the extent to which the wrongfulness of crime contributes to victims' experience of harm, however, concerning the other *non-harm* factors that determine the extent of an offender's wrongfulness, it is not apparent what merits the expectation that the victim will have additional insights to offer. This is dubious on empirical grounds, but in my understanding it is also based upon the wrong kind of respect, i.e. appraisal rather than recognition respect.

A close corollary of the meta-duty to respect is a *duty to understand*. Respect is in large part contingent on empathy, which includes the necessity to understand what the object of respect values and holds good from *his/her point of view as an equal independent agent*, while acknowledging the fact that these emotions and reactions are often unclearly understood.

This chapter has stressed the distinction between empathy and sympathy. The two terms are often used interchangeably and the latter is a key emotional component of the care-response focused on relieving victims' suffering: fully understanding a victim's experience and an urge to alleviate the anguish that the victim experiences are intimately connected. Nevertheless, within victims' rights, sympathy can lead us astray. We should not lose sight of sympathy's primary concern with alleviating the distress felt by *the observer* on viewing the victim's suffering, with its pre-arranged choice to solely focus on actions to the benefit of victims in terms of their suffering, neglecting the fact that victims may have needs and wishes that are either not directly rooted in their suffering, or are not related to coping with or relieving this suffering. Indeed the paternalism involved in sympathy can jeopardize the extent to which victims' rights actually amount to rights, rather than preordained avenues to achieve a measure of coping in the aftermath of victimization.

In summary, this chapter hopes to have contributed to a deeper insight into the underlying rationales of victims' rights in the criminal process, which might also alleviate some of the misgivings that have been voiced about victims' rights. Adopting the position taken in this chapter will restrict the extent to which therapeutic rationales can serve as an argument for victims' rights and offers a victim-focused objection to the inclusion of victim statements of opinion about the punishment of the offender.

Nevertheless, further elaboration and discussion of the key concepts in victims' rights might result in unearthing irreducible conflict with other crucial criminal justice values. We should be alive to the possibility that successful integration of victims' rights in the criminal justice system without placing undue pressure on other values we hold dear, might not be feasible.[20] But at least following this line of inquiry will allow us to ascertain what elements of victims' rights conflict by necessity and on principle, rather than by the happenstance of their current implementation.

Notes

1 See for a comparable analysis in the field of human rights, Donnelly (2009) and Rosen (2012).
2 I confess that in the case of the last group some wishful thinking is involved here.
3 In an extended sense, recognition respect may also entail prudential rather than moral restrictions on how to act. The fact that someone obeys a police officer may be due to the moral respect one has for the fact that someone else is a police officer; however, it

46 Antony Pemberton

may also be merely due to the fact that one fears the possible consequences of neglecting a police officer's instructions. This illustrates that moral recognition respect, in the way it implies a duty how to act, is not easily discernible from prudential recognition respect.

4 In a similar but slightly different vein, not all appraisals are attributed to character, but to circumstance and/or nature, although just-world bias (Lerner 1980) and the fundamental attribution error (Ross 1977) make it likely that appraisal respect will be forthcoming in many circumstances that do not objectively merit it. People have a bias to finding character, rather than chance or nature, to be the cause of outcomes (Knobe 2006).

5 There are many examples of this, but maybe a well-known footballing duo that will make this most point clear are Barcelona's Lionel Messi and Real Madrid's Cristiano Ronaldo. The former is not only one of the best soccer players of all time but is also the object of high appraisal respect, due to a great extent to his sportsmanship and his humility, while the latter, for all his talents, is not widely respected due to his arrogance and his many *schwalbes* (dives). My sincerest apologies for offending any Real Madrid supporters by this assessment.

6 This quote from Braithwaite (2003, p. 406) illustrates this phenomenon well (Robinson and Darley 2007 use it to make a similar point): 'However, the restorativist's hope is that the conversation about the urge for retribution will result in it being transcended so that people can move on. The reason restorativists think this way is that they believe peoples' natural retributive urges are not healthy things to perseverate upon. Moreover, in the conditions of contemporary societies, as opposed to the conditions of our biological inheritance, retribution is now a danger to our survival and flourishing. It fuels cycles of hurt begetting hurt. It is hoped that conversations that allow a space for the consideration of healing will help people to see this more clearly.'

7 Zitek *et al.* (2010, p. 246) summarize this phenomenon as follows: 'Wronged individuals feel that they have already done their fair share of suffering – as if there were a maximum amount of victimhood that a person can reasonably be expected to endure – and consequently, they feel entitled to spare themselves some of life's inconveniences, such as being attentive to the needs of others.'

8 This is by no means the only way of defining empathy; the literature is rife with definitions of this phenomenon, and the same is true of the distinction between empathy and sympathy (e.g. Batson 2011). The distinction Wispé (1986) employs is particularly illuminating for the current discussion.

9 Acorn (2004, p. 10) quotes Rousseau as summarizing: 'Why are kings without pity for their subjects? Because they count upon never being mere men.'

10 As I will show, this statement may be qualified, in different ways, for both sympathy and empathy.

11 I should note that there are other ways of defining and distinguishing sympathy and empathy: for the current discussion Wispé's definition seems to be the most helpful.

12 I should note that this not the same as the ethics of care; see for instance Held (2007).

13 Respectively 'criminal justice correspondence' and 'therapeutic coherence'; see Pemberton and Reynaers (2011).

14 We should also note that the extent to which justice processes impact coping is marginal at best (e.g. Pemberton and Reynaers 2011).

15 I am aware that this position is not without its critics, see for instance Christie (1977); Hulsman (1986). See Duff (2001b, pp. 60–64) and Robinson and Darley (2007) for convincing rebuttals.

16 This does not mean that there cannot be other reasons for a public response. The experience of harm of a fellow member of the public can itself be sufficient, however that would then not amount to a response to victimization by *crime*.

17 The way Holmes phrased it himself in *The Common Law* (1881/2011, p. 6) is 'even a dog distinguishes between being kicked and being stumbled over'.
18 In Pemberton (2012b) I also note that retribution entails an exact quantification of the response warranted, while revenge solely sets out an appropriate sphere of response. It appears to me that this is related to the fact that retribution is measured along the yardstick of wrongfulness, while in revenge wrongfulness solely functions as a qualifier, not as a quantification of the amount of revenge.
19 This is not the same as saying that victims are particularly vengeful (Pemberton 2012a). Instead it changes the victims' perspective on factors *that determine wrongfulness in his or her particular case*.
20 See more generally Gray (2000).

Bibliography

Acorn, A., 2004. Compulsory compassion. A critique of restorative justice. Vancouver: UBC Press.
Ashworth, A., 2000. Victims' rights, defendants' rights and criminal procedure. In: A. Crawford and J. Goodey, eds, Integrating a victim perspective within criminal justice. Aldershot: Dartmouth Publishing, pp. 185–206.
Batson, C.D., 2011. Altruism in humans. Oxford: Oxford University Press.
Baumeister, R.F., 1997. Evil. Inside human violence and cruelty. New York: Henry Holt and Company.
Best, J., 1999. Random violence. How we talk about new crimes and new victims. Berkeley: University of California Press.
Bonanno, G.A., Mancini, M. and Westphal, G.A., 2011. Resilience to loss and potential trauma. Annual Review of Clinical Psychology, 7(1), pp. 1–25.
Bottoms, A., 2010. The 'duty to understand' what consequences for victims participation. In: A. Bottoms and J.V. Roberts, eds, Hearing the crime victim. Adverserial justice, crime victims and the state. Cullumpton: Willan Pubblishing, pp. 17–46.
Boutellier, H., 2002. The safety utopia. contemporary discontent and desire as to crime and punishment. Houten: Springer.
Braithwaite, J., 2003. Holism, justice and atonement. Utah Law Review, pp. 389–412.
Brewin, C.R., Andrews, B. and Valentine, J.D., 2000. Meta-analysis of risk factors for posttraumatic stress disorder. Journal of Consulting and Clinical Psychology, 68(5), pp. 748–766.
Chan, W. and Simester, A.P., 2005. Duress, necessity: how many defences? King's College Law Journal, 121, pp. 123–127.
Christie, N., 1977. Conflicts as property. British Journal of Criminology, 17(1), pp. 1–17.
Daly, K., 2014. Reconceptualizing sexual victimization and justice. In: I. Vanfraechem, A. Pemberton and F.N. Ndahinda, eds, Routledge international handbook of victimology. London: Routledge.
Darley, J.M., 2009. Morality in the law: the psychological foundations of citizens desires to punish transgressions. Annual Review of Law and Social Science, (5), pp. 1–23.
Darley, J.M. and Pittman, T.S., 2003. The psychology of compensatory and retributive justice. Personality and Social Psychology Review, 7, pp. 324–336.
Darwall, S.L., 1977. Two kinds of respect. Ethics, 88(1), pp. 36–49.
Darwall, S. L., 2006. The second-personal standpoint. Cambridge: Harvard University Press.

Donnelly, J., 2009. Human dignity and human rights. Geneva. Geneva Academy of International Humanitarian Law and Human Rights.
Duff, R.A., 2001a. Harms and wrongs. Buffalo Criminal Law Review, 5, pp. 13–45.
Duff, R.A., 2001b. Punishment, communication and community. Oxford: Oxford University Press.
Duff, R.A., 2003. Restoration and retribution. In: A. Von Hirsch, J.V. Roberts, A. Bottoms, K. Roach, and M. Schiff, eds, Restorative and criminal justice: competing or reconcilable paradigms. Oxford: Hart Publishing, pp. 43–61.
Elias, R., 1993. Victims still. the political manipulation of crime victims. London: Sage.
Erez, E., Kilchling, M. and Wemmers, J.-A., eds, 2011. Therapeutic jurisprudence and victim participation in criminal justice: international perspectives. Durham: Carolina Academic Press.
Fattah, E., 1999. From a handful of dollars to tea and sympathy. The sad history of victim assistance. In: J.J.M. Van Dijk, R. van Kaam and J.J.M. Wemmers, eds, Caring for crime victims. Monsey: Criminal Justice Press, pp. 187–206.
Feinberg, J., 1984. Harm to others. Oxford: Oxford University Press.
Furedi, F., 2004. Therapy culture. London: Routledge.
Gollwitzer, M., 2009. Justice and revenge. In: M.E. Oswald, S. Bieneck and J. Hupfeld-Heinemann, eds, Social psychology of punishment of crime. Hoboken: Wiley, pp. 137–156.
Gray, J., 2000. Two faces of liberalism. Cambridge: Polity Press.
Groenhuijsen, M.S. and Letschert, R.M., eds, 2008. Compilation of International victims' rights instruments, 2nd (revised) edition. Nijmegen: Wolf Publishing.
Groenhuijsen, M.S. and Pemberton, A. 2009. The EU Framework Decision for victims of crime: does hard law make a difference? European Journal of Crime, Criminal Law and Criminal Justice, 17(3), pp. 43–59.
Hafer, C.L. and Begue, L., 2005. Experimental research on just-world theory. Problems, developments and future challenges. Psychological Bulletin, 131(1), pp. 128–167.
Held, V., 2007. The ethics of care. In: D. Copp, ed., The Oxford handbook of ethical theory. Oxford: Oxford University Press, pp. 537–567.
Holmes, O.W., 1881/2011. The Common Law. Toronto. University of Toronto Law School, Typographical society.
Hulsman, L.H.C., 1986. Critical criminology and the concept of crime. Crime, Law and Social Change, 10(1), pp. 63–80.
Knobe, J., 2006. The concept of intentional action. A case study in the use of folk psychology. Philosophical Studies, 130, pp. 203–231.
Laxminarayan, M.S., 2012. The heterogeneity of crime victims: Variations in procedural and outcome preferences. Nijmegen: Wolf Legal Publishers.
Lens, K., Pemberton, A. and Groenhuijsen, M., 2010. Het spreekrecht in Nederland: een bijdrage aan het emotioneel herstel van slachtoffers? Tilburg: INTERVICT/PrismaPrint Tilburg.
Lerner, M.J., 1980. The belief in a just world. A fundamental delusion. New York: Plenum Press.
Loewenstein, G. and Small, D.A., 2007. The scarecrow and the tinman: the vicissitudes of human sympathy and caring. Review of General Psychology, 11, pp. 112–126.

Miers, D., 2007. Looking beyond Great Britain: the development of criminal injuries compensation. In: S. Walklate, ed., Handbook of victims and victimology. Cullumpton: Willan Publishing, pp. 337–363.
Nolan, J., 1998. The therapeutic state:justifying government at century's end. New York: NYU Press.
Nozick, R.,1981. Philosophical explanations. Cambridge: Harvard University Press.
Nussbaum, M.C., 2001. Upheavals of thought. The intelligence of emotions. Cambridge: Cambridge University Press.
Orth, U., 2003. Punishment goals of crime victims. Law and Human Behavior, 27(2), pp. 173–186.
Pemberton, A., 2012a. Too readily dismissed? A victimological perspective on penal populism. In: H. Nelen and J.C.Claessen, eds, Beyond the death penalty. Antwerpen/Portland: Intersentia, pp. 105–121.
Pemberton, A., 2012b. Occupy victimology. The relevance of David Graeber to the study of victims of crime. In: M.S. Groenhuijsen, R.M. Letschert and S. Hazenbroek, eds, KLM Van Dijk. Liber amoricum J.J.M. Van Dijk. Nijmegen: Wolf Legal Publishers, pp. 297–309.
Pemberton, A., Winkel, F.W. and Groenhuijsen, M.S., 2007. Taking victims seriously in restorative justice. International Perspectives in Victimology, 3(1), pp. 4–14.
Pemberton, A. and Reynaers, S., 2011. The controversial nature of victim participation: the case of the victim impact statements. In: E. Erez, M. Kilchling and J.-A. Wemmers, eds, Therapeutic jurisprudence and victim participation in criminal justice: international perspectives. Durham: Carolina Academic Press, pp. 229–248.
Pinker, S., 2011. The better angels of our nature: the decline of violence in history and its causes. London: Allen Lane.
Roberts, J.V., 2009. Listening to the crime victim. Evaluating victim input at sentencing and parole. In: M. Tonry, ed., Crime, punishment, and politics in comparative perspective. Crime and justice: A review of research, 38, pp. 347–412.
Robinson, P.H. and Darley, J.M., 2007. Intuitions of justice: implications for criminal law and criminal policy. Southern California Law Review, 81, pp. 1–68.
Rorty, R., 1989. Contingency, irony, and solidarity. Cambridge: Cambridge University Press.
Rosen, M., 2012. Dignity: its history and meaning. Cambridge: Harvard University Press.
Ross, L., 1977. The intuitive psychologist and his shortcomings: distortions in the attribution process. In: L. Berkowitz, ed., Advances in Experimental Social Psychology, 10, pp. 173–220.
Sarat, A., 1997. Vengeance, victims and the identities of law. Social and Legal Studies, 6(2), pp. 163–189.
Sherman, L.W. and Strang, H., 2007. Restorative justice. The evidence. London: The Smith Institute.
Simester, A.P. and Von Hirsch, A., 2011. Crimes, harms and wrongs: On the principles of criminalisation. Oxford: Hart Publishing.
Strang, H., 2002. Repair or revenge: Victims and restorative justice. Oxford: Oxford University Press.

Van Camp, T. and De Mesmaecker, V. 2014. Procedural justice for victims of crime – Are victim impact statements and victim–offender mediation rising to the challenge? In: I. Vanfraechem, A. Pemberton and F.N. Ndahinda, eds, Routledge international handbook of victimology. London: Routledge.

Van Dijk, J.J.M., 2006. The mark of Abel. Reflecting on the social labelling of victims of crime. Inaugural lecture Tilburg University. Tilburg: Intervict.

Van Dijk J.J.M., 2009. Free the victim. A critique of the Western conception of victimhood. International review of Victimology, 16, pp. 1–33.

Vollhardt, J., 2009. Altruism born of suffering and prosocial behaviour following adverse life events: a review and conceptualization. Social Justice Research, 22(1), pp. 53–97.

Walklate, S. 2006. Imagining the victim of crime. Maidenhead: Open University Press.

Wemmers, J.A., 1996. Victims in the criminal justice system. The Hague: Kugler.

Wenzel, M., Okimoto, T.G., Feather, N.T. and Platow, M.J., 2008. Retributive and restorative justice. Law and Human Behavior, 32(5), pp. 375–389.

Wexler, D.B. and Winick, B.J., eds, 1996. Law in a therapeutic key: Developments in therapeutic jurisprudence. Durham: Carolina Academic Press.

Winkel, F.W., 2007. Post-traumatic anger. Missing link in the wheel of misfortune. Inaugural lecture, Tilburg University. Tilburg: INTERVICT.

Wispé, L., 1986. The distinction between sympathy and empathy: To call forth a concept, a word is needed. Journal of Personality and Social Psychology, 50, pp. 314–321.

Zaibert, L., 2006. Punishment and revenge. Law and Philosophy, 25, pp. 81–118.

Zitek, E.M., Jordan, A.H., Monin, B. and Leach, F.R., 2010. Victim entitlement to behave selfishly. Journal of Personality and Social Psychology, 98, pp. 245–255.

Chapter 3

Recognition of victims' rights through EU action
Latest developments and challenges

Helga Ezendam and Frida Wheldon[1]

Introduction

In May 2011 the negotiations in the Council of the European Union on the proposal from the European Commission for a Directive containing minimum standards for victims of crime started. Ten years after the enforcement of the Framework Decision on the Standing of Victims in Criminal Proceedings, twenty-seven member states gathered again to discuss rights for victims. Apparently the Framework Decision did not meet the expectations in raising the standards for victims in criminal justice.

Instead of focusing on better implementation of the existing rights, the member states and the European Commission chose to work on a new legislative proposal, the argument being that the wording in the Framework Decision was too vague. In new legislation this could be altered. Also, under the Lisbon Treaty the legal instruments changed. For new legislation with regard to justice topics only a majority is needed in the Council instead of unanimity. The European Parliament has a lot more influence since the regime of co-decision procedure is now valid for topics in the justice area. The role of the European Commission in enforcing the implementation of the legal instrument became larger. These are all valid reasons for creating a Directive to replace the Framework Decision. Is the lack of proper implementation and execution of victims' rights a result from the vague wording of the Framework Decision or is something else needed? Will the Directive be able to meet expectations and really improve the situation for victims all over Europe? The APAV report[2] shows big differences between member states in compliance rates; no member state seems to fully comply with the Framework Decision.

On 1 January 2011 in the Netherlands a law came into force giving victims rights in criminal proceedings, for the first time independent of their status as a witness or injured party, thus implementing the rights from the Framework Decision in hard law, instead of in guidelines. This law was implemented in practice by adapting processes and automation. But even today victims in the Netherlands do not always receive the respectful treatment, the information and compensation they are entitled to by law, despite the efforts of a many professionals working in the criminal justice system. Effective remedies are lacking, so it is impossible for victims to enforce their rights. Will the Directive be able to change this?

In this chapter we will take a closer look at the Directive establishing minimum standards for victims:[3] what rights do victims get and will member states be able to meet expectations? First we will take a short look back at the Framework Decision. To avoid the traps from the Framework Decision it is necessary to take a closer look at this instrument and its results.

Framework Decision 2001

On 15 March 2001 the Council of the European Union unanimously adopted the Framework Decision on the standing of victims in criminal proceedings. This Framework Decision is a binding instrument, to be implemented in the legal order of the member states. It contains rules about the legal position of victims in criminal procedure and the right to support. The Framework Decision is one of the first 'hard law' instruments in the field of criminal justice in the EU. This is in itself remarkable since legislation and policy in the field of criminal justice was hardly ever about victims. Most articles had to be implemented by 22 March 2002. Member states had to send information on the implementation to the European Commission. The European Commission evaluated the implementation and came in 2009 to the conclusion that hardly any country had implemented the Framework Decision fully, eight years after its adoption.

The report of the European Commission[4] stated:

> The implementation of this Framework Decision is not satisfactory. The national legislation sent to the Commission contains numerous omissions. Moreover, it largely reflects existing practice prior to adoption of the Framework Decision. The aim of harmonising legislation in this field has not been achieved owing to the wide disparity in national laws. Many provisions have been implemented by way of non-binding guidelines, charters and recommendations. The Commission cannot assess whether these are adhered to in practice.

Some remarkable issues from the evaluation are pointed out here, since they are relevant for the expectations towards the new Directive. Firstly, the manner in which the Framework Decision should be implemented was left to the member states. But in the evaluation reports from the European Commission formal legislation was the main criterion. For example, guidelines from the public prosecutor, in the Netherlands published and binding, were not regarded as enough for a solid implementation. Putting rights in hard law is thus assumed to lead to better execution.

The European Commission also mentioned in the report that no member state had implemented the Framework Decision in one single piece of national legislation. But looking at the wide range of measures in the Framework Decision and given that no member state started from scratch, this was to be expected. Parts of victims' rights are about the rights of victims in the criminal justice system, usually to be put down in a code of criminal procedure.

Further, the evaluation shows that there is no shared vision between member states on the position of victims. The role of the victim in the criminal justice system differs greatly among member states. The interpretation of the rights mentioned in the Framework Decision followed the existing legislation in member states. The same articles lead to different outcomes for victims.

Lastly, the wording of the Framework Decision was on many points very vague, and with good reason because it had to suit every criminal justice system in the member states. But this is also believed to be the reason for the lack of implementation.

From these findings we can deduce the following expectations with regard to any future instrument. First, implementation of European rules by hard/formal law leads to better execution. This point of view reflects also in the reasoning regarding the need for a new instrument: a Directive is believed to be more enforceable than a Framework Decision and thus lead to better implementation in the member states.

Second, victims' rights are best secured through one single piece of legislation. This is shown in the EU regulations themselves where there is one single piece of legislation for victims about the whole of criminal proceedings and support outside the criminal justice system.[5] By comparison, to lay down the right to information of a suspect an entire Directive was needed.

The third expectation is that the implementation of EU legislation will lead to the same outcome for victims in every member state, even without an agreement or shared vision on the position of victims in criminal proceedings. Finally, the less vague the wording the better the uniformity of implementation will be.

Negotiations on the Directive

During the negotiations on the Directive of the European Parliament and of the Council establishing minimum standards on the rights, support and protection of victims of crime, it became clear that many different and sometimes conflicting expectations surrounded this instrument.

The European Commission seemed dedicated to writing a proposal for a Directive for victims that would really benefit them. They researched the needs of victims and built on those needs a solid proposal for measures that would indeed improve the situation in many member states. An impact assessment gave an indication of costs and the European Commission took those into account when choosing the measures. They expected that common minimum rules should lead to increased confidence in the criminal justice systems of all member states, which in turn should lead to more efficient judicial cooperation in a climate of mutual trust as well as to the promotion of a fundamental rights culture in the EU.

Twenty-seven member states[6] are involved in this process and needed to agree on a package of measures for all victims. Although since the Treaty of Lisbon unanimity is not necessary to reach an agreement, efforts are made to meet boundary conditions of every member state. Since the criminal justice systems in the member states differ so much it is not easy to find a wording of rights that is acceptable to all. A major difference is to be found between the common law and the continental law systems. The more concrete the wording, the greater chances are that some member states oppose the text because it will lead to problems with their existing legislation.

The differences between the systems in the member states led for instance to an important new recital (10c) in the Directive regarding the role of the victim in the criminal justice system. Due to differences in the criminal justice systems, the Directive does not prescribe whether the victim should be a party to criminal proceedings. Certain elementary rights in the Directive will depend upon the role of the victim as determined by each member state separately, such as the right to receive information about the case and the right to interpretation. One thing most member states seem to have in common regarding this Directive is that the Directive should not lead to costly measures. The financial crisis is felt by every member state, although not to the same degree.

The role of the European Parliament regarding the Directive is, as a consequence of the Treaty of Lisbon, bigger than its role was in 2001 with regard to the Framework Decision. In co-decision on this Directive with the twenty-seven member states in the Council they have their own wishes and expectations with regard to rights of victims. High expectations and a strong desire to improve the position of victims were evidenced through the over 500 amendments they made to the text proposed by the European Commission. Looking at the span of control of the amendments, cost seems not to be an issue to the European Parliament. The involvement of FEMM – a committee of the European Parliament[7] – led to quite a few proposals regarding victims of gender-based violence, singling them out. This led to an intense debate about which categories of victims are most in need of special attention and limiting the horizontal character of the instrument.

A very important group of stakeholders of the Directive are the people working in the criminal justice system and in victim support in the member states. Although the negotiations in Brussels seem to be far away from their daily work, when it comes to implementation they are the first to criticise a new instrument if it complicates procedures: they expect the new Directive to be effective and easy to carry out in practice in connection with existing procedures.

But the most interested parties are the victims themselves. Victims demand more rights nowadays. The criminal justice system cannot limit itself to the rights of a suspect any more or it will lose the faith of citizens and victims. The International Crime Victim Survey (van Dijk *et al.* 2007) shows that victims in countries who have relatively high standards for victim support are less satisfied with their police than in countries where standards are lower. One explanation could be found in the expectations of victims: the higher the standards, the higher the expectations might be and the more disappointed victims are if their expectations are not met. So if member states use the future Directive to promise better support and more rights for victims, expectations of citizens will rise. When their expectations when they become a victim are not met, confidence will disappear quickly. The trust of citizens and victims in the criminal justice system is at stake.

The consequence is that we have to be clear about the rights victims have, the services they can expect from the government, organisations in the criminal justices system and victim support organisations. Although the Framework Decision has been a great step in improving rights of victims, it left more to be desired. In order not to make the same mistakes, the text of the Directive should contain clear obligations for member states as far as possible considering the differences between countries. One way to realise this would be to focus more on the output and outcome and leave procedures to member states. But most of all we have to live up to our promises. To be able to practice what we preach it is necessary that the Directive is clear, easy to carry out in practice, not costly and meets the needs of victims.

First of all it is victims' expectations we have to keep in mind. Justified expectations should be met. Sometimes expectations of victims are too high and then we have to give victims clear information on what they can expect. This means also that during negotiations on the Directive we have to be clear to other stakeholders what is realistic in practice and what is not. Looking at all the expectations surrounding the new Directive we have a very demanding challenge at hand and the stakes are high.

Impact of the Directive on victims of crime

For victims, the Directive aims to strengthen their rights to access protection, support, information and a range of other rights in the aftermath of crime.

Objective (Article 1)

The Directive has a clearly stated objective, which highlights its horizontal nature. It aims to ensure that *all* victims of crime:

- receive appropriate information, support and protection;
- are able to participate in criminal proceedings;
- are recognised and treated in a respectful, sensitive, tailored, professional and non-discriminatory manner.

In practice, the objective clarifies that the rights and services contained in the Directive must be available to all victims of crime and cannot be limited to, for instance, only victims of domestic violence, terrorism victims or young victims of crime. While these groups are important and should be able to access rights, services and protection, so should all other victims of crime. It is also clear that this objective should be met in all EU member states – these are minimum standards that all countries must fulfil. To meet this objective, the Directive provides rights for victims throughout the criminal justice process. Below follows a description of victim's journey through the criminal justice system in order to highlight where the individual rights arise for victims.

A crime has been committed

Immediately following the crime, the Directive grants victims a range of rights, such as the right to receive information; the right to understand and to be understood; the right to interpretation/translation; and the right to access support services. These rights are also available for victims of unreported crime, so there is no need to report a crime in order to access these rights. For victims who choose to report the crime, there are additional rights available, such as for instance the right to review a decision not to prosecute.

The case goes to trial

The Directive provides a wide range of rights to victims taking part in the criminal justice process; this is where the vast majority of rights focus. Rights for victims taking part in the criminal justice process include the right to be heard; the right to legal aid; the right to reimbursement of expenses; the right to compensation from the offender; the right to protection (generic right to protection from retaliation, intimidation, repeat and further victimisation, including psychological and emotional harm); the right to avoid contact between victim and offender; the right to protection of privacy; the right to individual assessment to identify specific protection needs; and the right to special measures for victims with specific protection needs.

Beyond the trial

Even beyond the trial, the Directive provides certain rights for the victim, namely the right to receive information (for instance regarding the release of the offender); the right to access support services; the right to safeguards in restorative justice services; and the prevention of re-victimisation – professionals working with victims should be trained to deal with victims in a respectful manner. Their training should include the ability to identify and prevent intimidation and re-victimisation. Unless provided by other public or private services, victim support services should also provide advice relating to the risk and prevention of retaliation, intimidation and repeat or further victimisation.

Cross-border cases

The Directive also clarifies and strengthens the rights for cross-border victims. For instance, it highlights that a victim should be able to make a complaint to the competent authority of the member state of residence if they are unable to do so in the member state where the crime took place or in case of a serious offence, if they do not wish to do so. A victim should also be allowed to report a crime in a language that the victim understands.

Regarding provision of assistance in cross-border cases, the Directive states that:

> if the victim has left the territory of the member state where the criminal offence was committed, that member State should no longer be obliged to provide assistance, support and protection except for what is directly related to any criminal proceedings it is conducting regarding the criminal offence concerned, such as special protection measures during court proceedings. The Member State of the victim's residence should provide assistance, support and protection required for the victim's need to recover.

As described, the Directive provides rights for victims at every stage of the process; immediately following the crime, during any criminal justice proceedings and beyond. It includes rights for victims of unreported crime, although this is an area where further focus should be put to ensure the rights of victims of unreported crime are fully met and as strong as they could be. Finally, the Directive strengthens and clarifies the rights for victims of cross-border crime.

Victim support services

The EU Commission has estimated that, every year, around 75 million people fall direct victims to crime in the EU. If we include family members, partners and other relevant groups, the real number of people adversely impacted by crime in the EU is more likely around 200–300 million people. Not all of these people will need support in the aftermath of crime, but many will and today many victims in Europe are not able to access support services. The European Crime and Safety Survey (EU ICS) 2005 calculated that, on average, only around 16 per cent of victims in Europe are able to access support services. Some 42 per cent of victims who did not receive support would have liked to access support (van Dijk *et al.* 2005, p.77). There is clearly a big gap between supply and demand of victim support services in the EU today.

Right to support requires victim support services

Right to support

Victims have had rights in relation to support for many years. The 1985 United Nation Declaration on Basic Principles of Justice for Victims of Crime and Abuse of Power states that 'victims should receive the necessary material, medical, psychological and social assistance through governmental, voluntary, community-based and indigenous means'. Clearly the right to support is not new; as early as 1985 victims across the world, not just Europe, were given a right to support. The language is, however, quite vague and there is no clarification on who is responsible for establishing or providing support services.

In Europe, the 2001 Framework Decision on the Standing of Victims in Criminal Proceedings established for the first time legally binding rights for victims of crime. This strengthened victims' rights to support and along with it, the status of victim support services, with article 13 requiring member states to 'promote the involvement of victim support' and 'encourage action taken' by victim support organisations. However, these are very vague wordings and member states can claim to be 'encouraging' and to 'promote the involvement' of victim support without actually setting up independent victim support services.

The Council of Europe Recommendation (2006) 8 on assistance to crime victims calls on states to 'provide or promote dedicated services for the support of victims and encourage the work of non governmental organisations in assisting victims'. Similar to many international treaties, the wording is vague and ambiguous without any real accountability or enforcement provisions. However, the Recommendation goes slightly further than the Framework Decision and lists a range of minimum standards for victim support services, stating that they should: be easily accessible; provide victims with free emotional, social and material support before, during and after the investigation and legal proceedings; be fully competent to deal with the problems faced by the victims they serve; provide victims with information on their rights and on the services available; refer victims to other services when necessary; and respect confidentiality when providing services.

The Recommendation also includes calls on states to 'coordinate services for victims' and set up 'free help lines'. As a Recommendation, these calls are not legally binding and many member states did still not develop separate support services following its adoption.

The EU Directive

Where these previous treaties have failed to achieve their desired outcomes, we hope that the new EU Directive establishing minimum standards on the rights, support and protection of victims of crime will be more successful. The Directive aims to ensure that the same level of minimum rules will apply to victims of crime regardless of where they live or where in the EU the crime takes place. The strengthening of rights also relates to support services. The Directive includes a strong right to support:

> Member States shall ensure that victims, in accordance with their needs, have access to confidential victim support services, free of charge, acting in the interest of the victims before, during and for an appropriate time after criminal proceedings.

> Family members shall have access to victim support services in accordance with their needs and the degree of harm suffered as a result of the criminal offence committed against the victim.

Member States shall take measures to establish free of charge and confidential specialist support services in addition to, or as an integrated part of, general victim support services, or to enable victim support organisations to call on existing specialised entities providing such specialist support.

The right to support contained in the EU Directive has clearer wording and provides a more extensive call on member states to set up victim support services (generic and specific) and give access to support services to both victims and family members. The recital (37) clarifies that support should be available from the moment the competent authorities are aware of the victim, throughout any criminal proceedings as well as after any proceeding in accordance with the needs of the victim: 'Support should be provided through a variety of means, without excessive formalities and through a sufficient geographical distribution across the member states to allow all victims the opportunity to access such services.' Given the strong wording of the right to support in the Directive and the clear accountability for member states to ensure access to support, we hope that the implementation of the Directive will lead to the set-up of independent victim support services in every EU member state.

Impact of the Directive on victim support providers

In addition to requiring member states to ensure the provision of victim support services, there are many other rights in the new EU Directive that are likely to impact on victim support service providers. Below follows a summary of these rights and their likely impact.

1. *Access to support for all victims/referrals*: The Directive highlights that member states shall facilitate the referral of victims, by the authority receiving the complaint (police) or by other relevant entities, to a victim support service. If this right to be referred is implemented properly, it has the potential to quickly increase the number of victims who can access support services.
2. *Minimum services provided*: The Directive lists the minimum range of services that victim support should provide to victims. This may expand the range of services that some victim support services currently offer. The Directive highlights that victim support services should deliver, as a minimum:
    - information, advice and support in relation to compensation, victims' rights, their role in the criminal justice proceedings and preparation for attending trial;
    - emotional and, where available, psychological support;
    - advice relating to financial and practical issues arising from the crime;
    - advice relating to the risk and prevention of secondary and repeat victimisation, intimidation and retaliation.

The Directive highlights that specialised services should, as a minimum, provide shelters and any other appropriate interim accommodation, as well as targeted and integrated support for victims with specific needs, such a victims of sexual violence, victims of gender-based violence and victims of violence in close relationships, including trauma support and counselling.

3   *Information*: The Directive strengthens victims' right to receive information, compared to previous legislation. It clarifies that from the first contact with the competent authority, victims have the right to receive a range of information, such as where and how to report a crime; where and how to access support; how and under what conditions they can access protection, legal aid, compensation, translation, interpretation etc.; any cross-border arrangements required for the case; contact details for communications about their case; and available restorative justice services.

    Once the judicial process has started, victims have a right to also receive any decision ending the criminal proceedings, including reasons for that decision; ongoing information regarding the state of the case throughout the criminal justice proceedings; the time and place of the trial; the final judgement in a trial, including any sentence, and including reasons for that decision; and the release of the offender from detention.

    Victim support services in many European countries are likely to be key players in providing this extended amount of information, both in the initial stages and throughout the criminal justice process. As such, the extended information right is likely to have an impact on the information delivered by victim support services and the timings of the interaction between victims and support services.

4   *Individual assessments*: The Directive requires member states to conduct an individual assessment of victims' needs to identify specific protection needs and requirements for protection measures. Victim support services have extensive experience in identifying and meeting the needs of victims of crime, so this is an area where victim support professionals are able to play an important role in conducting the assessments and/or providing recommendations regarding the development of special protective measures.

5   *Training of professionals*: As is already the case in many member states, victim support services are often very well placed to take part in developing and delivering training to criminal justice professionals working with victims of crime.

6   *Identity best practice and assist implementation*: Victim support services are often well placed to provide information on best practice and can give recommendations on (and options for) how the individual rights in the Directive can be implemented in practice.

7   *Monitor implementation, member states' fulfilment of implementation and victims' ability to access their rights*: In addition to providing support services and assistance in implementation, victim support services are often ideally placed to also monitor the implementation of the Directive and victims' ability to access their right in practice.

As highlighted in this chapter, if implemented properly, the EU Directive is likely to have an impact on victim support service providers with respect to both the number of victims they will work with and the operational activities and support services they deliver.

Future challenges and gaps

The Directive is an important step forward in the protection and promotion of victims' rights in the EU. It contains many of the rights that are of vital importance to victims in the aftermath of crime. As highlighted, it has much potential in strengthening victims' access to rights in the aftermath of crime and will also hopefully strengthen the role of victim support services. Having said all that, are there any vital rights that the Directive does not include? Are there any particular challenges in the ability of the Directive to deliver the rights for victims in practice? There are four main points we would like to highlight in this area.

1 *The right to an impartial, independent and timely investigation*: Looking at the content of the Directive, there are in particular two areas that have been overlooked in the list of rights. The first one relates to the initial police investigation.[8] Given the delicate nature of forensic evidence, it is important to secure evidence as soon as possible after an event. If an investigation is delayed it is sometimes very difficult to secure sufficient evidence which will impact on the ability for victims to access justice. Common concerns raised by victims and victims' families (in particular families bereaved by murder) are that the police investigation has been insufficient, prejudiced by the police having an interest in the case or that the investigation was delayed or did not take place at all. Insufficient or prejudiced investigations is a great concern to many victims and without the proper investigation, victims will not be able to access justice through the criminal justice process. The right to an impartial, independent and timely investigation is a vital right, but has not been included in the Directive.
2 *Right to a fair trial within a reasonable time*: There are many time restrictions regarding how long an accused person should have to wait before having the allegation again him/her tried in court, in particular when the accused is on remand. No such restrictions are generally in place regarding victims. Many victims have to wait months if not years until their case is dealt with in court, which in some ways prevents the victim from completely putting the event behind them and starting to rebuild their lives. Victims suffer many of the same effects from the delay as accused persons do; insecurity, anxiety, stress, apprehension etc. In addition, this is a period where the risk of threat and intimidation are higher for victims and witnesses. The inclusion of a right for victims to a fair trial within a reasonable time would have given an incentive to member states to start looking at how justice can be delivered as soon as possible for victims. As the saying

goes 'justice delayed is justice denied'; an available legal redress that is not forthcoming in a timely fashion is effectively the same as having no redress at all. Alas, this right is also absent from the Directive.

3   *Ambiguous wording*: It is to be expected that a treaty covering all EU member states with their different judicial systems and available resources will include vague wording and compromise agreements. In the Directive there are, however, some wordings in particular that are threatening the impact of those rights in practice. Below follow two examples:

   i   Special protection measures: The Directive calls on member states to ensure that victims with specific protection needs are able to access protection measures. However, the article clarifies that '[a] special measure envisaged following the individual assessment shall not be made available if operational or practical constraints make this impossible'. For member states that do not currently provide special measures, there will undoubtedly be many operational and/or practical constraints to implement this right in practice, for instance by establishing appropriate premises, training of professionals, installing CCTV facilities, etc. However, the wording of this caveat offers an opportunity for member states to refrain from delivering the measures in practice by claiming it would be too expensive. No details are given in relation to what steps member states must take to demonstrate their attempts to implement the measures in practice.

   ii Training: The final wording of the article relating to training of professionals is not as strong as Victim Support Europe would have hoped. Although the Directive clarifies that member states shall ensure that police offers and court staff are trained, training should only be made available for judges, prosecutors and lawyers. There is no requirement that they must attend. Regardless of whether or not a range of courses are made available, the training will only have an impact in practice if professionals working with victims actually attend it and take the new learning into account in their contacts with victims of crime.

4   *Implementation*: The Directive is adopted; the main challenge to the success of the Directive now hinges on national implementation. The 2001 EU Framework Decision on the Standing of Victims in Criminal Proceedings did not fulfil its full potential due to lack of implementation: no member state fully implemented all articles and gave victims access to the contained rights. The failure in the implementation of the Framework Decision demonstrated that if member states are not interested or willing to allocate the required resources, the rights will not be fulfilled in practice. In these situations, it is the role and responsibility of the Commission to consider taking actions against the states that are not fulfilling the demands accordingly. This could hopefully be one way of providing an incentive to member states to allocate sufficient time and resources to the implementation.

Implementation in the Netherlands

It took the Netherlands ten years to implement the Framework Decision in formal/hard law. On the first of January 2011 the Netherlands enforced a law giving rights to victims in the criminal justice system, for the first time independent from their role as witness or injured party. Victims are mentioned for the first time in the criminal procedure code.

One of the reasons it took so long is related to culture, namely the importance perceived in practice of victims' rights in the criminal justice system. Implementation of victims' rights through binding guidelines seemed enough to ensure a good practice. In 2004 a broad and thorough examination of the Dutch criminal procedure code was completed. One of the many resulting recommendations was the incorporation of victims' rights in the law. But this was not considered the first priority in the overall plan of bringing the criminal procedure code up to date. In this particular case it took an exceptionally long time to pass the bill on victims' rights through parliament, due to an amendment regarding the position of parents of youth suspects. In between the passing of the bill and the law coming into force, the Dutch Ministry of Security and Justice, along with the organisations working in the criminal justice system, had one year to get it properly implemented. This time appeared too short (even though the implementation preparations started during the discussion in parliament) to change processes and automation fundamentally for a number of organisations working in the criminal justice system. Organisations involved in the implementation were the police, public prosecutor, Victim Support Netherlands, courts, Custodial Institutions, the Violent Offences Compensation Fund and the Central Fine Collection Agency.

It is true that in the recent decennium many victims in the Netherlands were treated with respect, received information and were able to collect compensation through the criminal justice system, just as the Framework Decision and our own guidelines prescribed, but also many were not treated with respect, did not receive the right information in time or were not able to gain compensation. Victims' rights were not and are not executed as properly as rights of defendants. Although processes and automation were adjusted to execute victims' rights, they still are built around the centre and main focus of the criminal justice system, namely defendants' rights. Processes and automation are not built to do justice to victims, they are built to do justice to defendants. No fundamental changes have been made to really meet the needs of victims. For instance, in the Netherlands police and public prosecutor have a huge database with information on suspects/offenders, each with a unique identification number, accessible to every organisation in the criminal justices system. For information about victims no such database is available and relevant information (such as a telephone number or special needs requirements) are not passed on from the police to the public prosecutor. If the obligations in the new Directive are to be met, a solid registration of data of victims is essential and a basic condition to meet the needs of victims.

The impact of the Framework Decision and the EU Directive on the criminal justice system and victim policy is huge, or at least it should be. Just treatment of victims influences the whole criminal justice system, from reporting a crime or even prevention at the start, to the end where the offender is released unconditionally. It also leads to obligations outside the criminal justice system. In the past the general idea seemed to be 'we add some measures to the current suspect-oriented system. No real changes are necessary'. But the implementation of rights for victims is highly underestimated. For a proper execution of victims' rights we have to start rebuilding the processes and automation from scratch, laying a new foundation to build a solid criminal procedure for both victim and offender.

The outcome of a discussion in the Netherlands between all organisations having part in the criminal justice system where victims are concerned is that the Ministry of Security and Justice together with these organisations should work towards a redesign of the criminal justice procedure. The processes in the criminal justice system, including automation, have to be redesigned from a victim's perspective and unrestricted by current organisational constraints.

The Ministry and the organisations in the criminal justice system will redesign the process of information to victims, so that timely information will always be given, from the moment of reporting a crime until the release of an offender. Options for a digital file that victims can consult through the internet will be studied. Also the procedure to claim compensation will be adjusted and organised from a victim's point of view. In the stage of the execution, the needs of victims should be taken into account also, for instance with regard to the decision where the offender will be imprisoned or when an offender is due for leave.

Conclusions

The EU Directive on minimum standards for victims has become a document with extensive rights for victims with regard to the criminal justice procedure and victim support. The debate surrounding the Directive and the process of implementation has brought increased expectations from victims of crime. Meeting their expectations requires more than a Directive containing holistic, clearly worded rights that can be implemented without undue financial burdens on the member states. To (re)build the trust of victims in the criminal justice systems in Europe we must also be able to deliver these new, stronger rights in practice. The adoption of the Directive is only the first step; to ensure victims are able to access their rights in practice, adoption must be followed by effective and coordinated implementation and if required, enforcement. Otherwise we fall into the same trap as with the Framework Decision: much is promised but not accomplished. We simply cannot afford that.

Notes

1 This contribution is a combination of two presentations on the Directive containing minimum standards for victims, representing the perspectives of a service provider and a member state. This contribution does not necessarily reflect the official point of view of the Dutch government.
2 Project Victims in Europe, 2009.
3 Directive 2012/29/EU of the European Parliament and of the Council of 25 October 2012 establishing minimum standards on the rights, support and protection of victims of crime, and replacing Council Framework Decision 2001/220/JHA.
4 SEC (2009) 476.
5 More recently a few Directives were adopted (e.g. on human trafficking) where victims' rights are part of the whole approach of the topic. But up till then the rights of suspects and victims were described in separate instruments.
6 To be more precise; Denmark, the United Kingdom and Ireland have a special status during the negotiations. Denmark is not a party to this Directive. The United Kingdom and Ireland have opted in.
7 Women's Rights and Gender Equality (FEMM). Available at: www.europarl.europa.eu/committees/en/femm/home.html [Accessed 9 July 2013].
8 Victim Support Europe and their national member organisations come into regular contact with victims who have not been able to access an impartial, independent investigation immediately following a crime.

Bibliography

van Dijk, J., Manchin, R., van Kesteren, J., Nevala, S. and Hideg, G., 2005. The Burden of Crime in the EU – Research Analysis: A Comparative Analysis of the European Crime and Safety Survey (EU ICS). Available at: www.europeansafetyobservatory.eu/downloads/EUICS%20-%20The%20Burden%20of%20Crime%20in%20the%20EU.pdf [Accessed 22 April 2013].

van Dijk, J., van Kesteren, J. and Smit, P., 2007. Criminal Victimisation in International Perspective, Key Findings from the 2004–2005 ICVS and EU ICS. Den Haag: WODC.

Chapter 4

Implementing victim rights in newly industrialized countries
Reflections on major challenges and recommendations for the future

K. Jaishankar

Introduction

In ancient times, when people led a nomadic life, the rights of persons were more individual in nature. However, when they settled near rivers with new civilizations and formed various groups, the rights of persons became more communal in nature. The group leaders formed certain rules with the consent of the groups and rights were provided to individuals in a collective manner. When there were rival attacks of groups or individual attacks within groups, the leaders of the group ensured the rights of victims with specific unwritten rules and predominantly justice for the victims was revenge-based (Jaishankar et al. 2008). Though retributive justice was the norm in various ancient laws[1] there was an element of restorative justice which ensured the rights of the victims of crime:

> These ancient codes require offenders' repayment in kind or extent to those suffering criminal victimization in addition to or instead of prescribed retributive sanctions. The goals of these early legal systems were: seeing the victim as a whole and to minimize private revenge.
> (Tobolowsky 1999, p. 23)

Restitution was found to be common in these laws. The Kings of the ancient times ensured justice to the victims of crime and provided adequate compensation to the victims as well. The ancient time period, considered to be a golden age of victims and the victim centred approach, continued 'until approximately eleventh century'(Tobolowsky 1999, p. 23).

During the Anglo-Saxon period, the European society started viewing crimes as private matters, and individuals and groups started settling issues based on revenge (Doak 2008). In European societies, 'the Criminal law was enforced through the payment of compensation to victims and their kin ('bot' and 'wer') and fines were paid to the King ('wite')' (Office of Crime Statistics 1988, p. 6; Doak 2008). Later in the Middle Ages, when the modern states were formed, the rights of victims became more a subject of the state. The state started viewing crime as a 'social harm' and started protecting the rights of the victims by codified and traditional laws (Meloy 2010). When the state's perception towards crime changed to 'social harm' and when the state started posing as victims, it converted the real victim to a mere witness with no role in the justice process. This period 'marked the beginning of an era when the state gradually usurped the role of the victim' (Doak 2008, p. 2). The victim's problem became secondary and restoring social order became the priority of the state (Meloy 2010). 'The state assumed complete responsibility for arresting, prosecuting, and punishing the criminal offender. Crime victims no longer had a part in the decision process; they were just pieces of evidence' (Jerin 2009, p. 109). There are two notions related to the Middle Ages. Schafer (1968) calls this era a 'golden age for the victims' as the system still had restitution provisions and Jerin (2009) calls it a 'dark age for the victims' as the system weaned away the rights of crime victims by replacing them with new justice processes which gave lesser solace to the crime victims. Similar to the Middle Ages in Europe, during the medieval period countries such as India had a system of restitution and the Mughal Kings protected the rights of the victims based on 'Islamic Justice'.

Until the early twentieth century, many countries did not develop adequate laws or rules to protect the rights of the victims of crime. During this period, 'it was the impact of capitalism and social forces driven by a free market economy that contributed to the demise of the victim justice system' (Doerner and Lab 2005, pp. 1–3; Tolbert 2009, p. 111). In the 1940s, it was Hans Von Hentig's efforts to bring the victim to the forefront that made various states think about the 'forgotten entity' of the criminal justice system (Tolbert 2009). In the early 1960s, many countries woke up and started to create victim compensation legislations. In 1963 New Zealand became the first country to develop a victim compensation law, followed by Great Britain in 1964 and the USA (California) in 1965 (Office of Crime Statistics 1988; Walklate 2007). Even though victim compensation laws were created in the early 1960s, it was the British Magistrate Margery Fry's vision on victim compensation, which she envisaged in the 1950s, that assisted in the creation of the compensation laws in various countries (Samuels 1967; Walklate 2007; Maratea 2009). In the 1970s, USA became more conscious of victim rights because of the rise of various victim rights' movements to protect the rights of women, children and minorities (Crowley 2009). Furthermore, 'the efforts to re-establish a greater role for crime victims in the criminal justice process received a major boost when President Ronald Reagan established the President's Task Force on Victims of Crime in 1982' (Tobolowsky 1999, p. 22). Subsequently, the USA became a leading country in ensuring the rights of victims of crime, along with other developed countries such as Great Britain, Australia and New Zealand.

The Magna Carta for Victims[2] of Crime, the 1985 'UN Declaration of the Basic Principle of Justice for the Victims of Crime and Abuse of Power', gave the member states a new direction. 'This document, although not a legally binding treaty, sets out the minimum standard for the treatment of crime victims' (Sarkar 2010, p. 16). Because of the UN Declaration both the developed and the developing nations got a focus on the rights to victims of crime. The UN Declaration also created awareness and mandate among various developing nations which had ignored the rights of crime victims for a long time. Even though this very declaration describes the crime victims' rights holistically, victims' rights can be divided into three segments: industrial victims' rights, crime victims' rights and civil rights of individuals. The term 'industrial victim' includes victims of industrial accidents and victims of industrial financial setbacks and related harassment by the employers. Crime victims' rights include rights against crime and abuse of power by the government authorities as well as private entities. Civil rights ensure individual's rights to the basic necessities which every government has to provide to its citizens. The primary aim of the constitution of every democratic country is to safeguard these rights.

In light of the above, in this chapter I will address the rights of the victims of crime that have been enshrined in the UN Declaration of Basic Principles of Justice for Victims of Crime and Abuse of Power 1985. This declaration divided the concept of victims into two: victims of crime and victims of abuse of power.[3] While for the second group of victims, the Declaration lays down a three part guideline towards the duties of the State,[4] for the first group of victims, the Declaration has four sets of rights, grouped under four heads: (i) access to justice and fair treatment; (ii) restitution; (iii) compensation; and (iv) assistance including material benefits, legal, psychological and medical help. I will carry forward the discussions on the crime victims' rights in nine selected countries, which are grouped under the term newly industrialized countries (NICs): Brazil, China, India, Malaysia, Mexico, Philippines, South Africa, Thailand and Turkey, under the rights provided in the UN Declaration of Basic Principles of Justice for Victims of Crime and Abuse of Power and based on the Constitutions of those countries and other legal provisions. I will also examine the challenges in the implementation of the victims' rights and provide recommendations for their effective implementation.

Victim rights in the newly industrialized countries

NICs, countries based on a new classification, are poised between the developed and developing nations. Though there are many NICs in various classifications, I have chosen nine: Brazil, China, India, Malaysia, Mexico, Philippines, South Africa, Thailand and Turkey. An important feature of the NICs is increased social freedoms and civil rights, which is a sure sign that victim rights are not being ignored. NICs show a potential not only for economic growth but also for revamping the existing criminal justice system which favours offenders instead of victims. There is a remarkable change in the mindset of the officials of the criminal justice system of NICs: most of the countries have started viewing victims as the fulcrum of the criminal justice process. In the following section, I will provide a detailed analysis of the rights of victims of crime in each NIC.

Brazil

Brazil is one of the Latin American countries where the rates of criminal victimization are high. Homicide victimization is particularly high in Brazil, with annual homicide rates above 20 per 100,000 inhabitants – the fourth-highest in Latin America and the Caribbean (Morrison and van Bronkhorst 2006). In addition, 'according to data from victimisation surveys, Brazil in the mid-1990s had the highest rate of victimization for robbery and sexual assault; intimate partner violence affects one in three Brazilian women' (Morrison and van Bronkhorst 2006, p. i). Apart from general crimes, ethnic issues, prison violence, human rights violations and youth violence are very common. Since Brazil was earlier under the Military rule (1964–85) victims of abuse of power are abundant, torture victims especially are ubiquitous. Although there are no adequate statutory laws for the victims, in cases of 'disappearances' during the Military rule, compensation has been paid 'to the next of kin of "disappeared" persons and victims of torture' (David 2006, p. 100) based on a new law (Hamber 2009). Ironically, the compensation provided was highly criticized by victim support groups as a being a way of buying off the victims rather than punishing those involved in the abuse of power. The victim support groups wanted only 'truth' and not compensation, and unfortunately this aspect has made the groups unpopular (Hamber 2009).

Apart from the law for the compensation for the 'disappeared', the constitution of Brazil provides the rights of the victims of crimes (Human Rights Watch 2012a). Chapter I of the Brazilian constitution, which addresses collective rights and duties under article 5, clearly lays down certain basic legal rights for victims of crimes. The constitution guarantees equality before the law and equal rights regarding life, liberty, privacy, free speech, free movement, right to property, etc. It includes a guarantee to access to justice and fair treatment (clause XXXIV):

> all persons are ensured, without the payment of fees: (a) the right to petition the public authorities in defending the rights or against illegal acts or abuse of power; (b) the obtaining of certificates from government departments, in order to defend the rights and clarify situations of personal interest.

Apart from these rights, the judiciary has the right to review any violation of or threat to a right and the state cannot make any law against this right. The constitution also guarantees the rights against impairing a vested right and the principle of *res judicata*; the constitution further states that the penal law shall not be retroactive, except for the benefit of the defendant.

The constitution guarantees rights against crimes and punishments given in view of ex-post facto law and it recognizes the due process of laws in regard to deprivation of assets or basic freedoms. It also recognizes the institution of juries with the organization attributed to it by the law; it also guarantees, among other things, the right to self defence, the sovereignty of the verdicts and jurisdiction to adjudicate intentional crimes against life.

The constitution highlights the victim's rights by declaring certain offences as non-bailable. It clarifies two sets of crimes as non-bailable: the practice of torture, unlawful traffic of narcotics and similar drugs, terrorism and crimes defined as heinous crimes; and the acts of civilian or military armed groups against the constitutional and democratic order. The constitution states that the law would neither consider the first set of offences to mercy or amnesty, nor shall the principals, the accessories and those who, although able to avoid them, abstain from doing so, be held liable. Further, the constitution also guarantees that the right to habeas corpus[5] is granted if someone suffers or believes he or she is threatened by violence or coercion in his or her freedom of movement, by illegal act, or abuse of power. A writ of mandamus is guaranteed to protect a clear legal right which is not protected by habeas corpus or habeas data, when the party responsible for the illegal act or abuse of power is a public authority or an agent of a legal entity performing government duties.

The constitution also speaks about the victim's right to compensation which may be effected from the liability for damages and a decree of loss of assets of the offender. It also recognizes the need to pass on the liability of the offender to his/her successor under the terms of the law up to the limit of the value of the assets transferred. With regard to victim assistance, the constitution lays down in clause LV that 'litigants in court or administrative proceedings and defendants in general are assured of the use of the adversary system and of full defence, with the means and remedies inherent thereto'; however, the constitution favours offenders more than victims. As such, the constitution prohibits the creation of an extraordinary court or tribunal. It also guarantees rights against crimes and punishments given in view of ex post facto law and it recognizes the due process of laws in regard to deprivation of assets or basic freedoms.

The constitution highlights the offenders' rights and lays down certain prescribed forms of punishments which may include deprivation or restriction of freedom; loss of assets; fines; the alternative social obligation;[6] suspension or prohibition of rights. At the same time, it prohibits certain forms of traditional punishments such as the death penalty;[7] life imprisonment; hard labour; banishment; and anything which is cruel. The offender's rights also include the right to be informed about the grounds of arrest, to defence and to consult a legal practitioner. Female convicts have the right to have their children with them, especially when they are nursing and breastfeeding them.

For victims of abuse of power, the constitution provides relatively stronger rights for military through clause LXI which states that 'no one may be arrested except in *flagrante delicto* or by written and substantiated order of a proper judicial authority, except in the case of a military offense or a strictly military crime, as defined by law'. However, the constitution also safeguards the individual's rights against abuse of political power and oppression by the government through the guarantee of writs of mandamus and habeas corpus in general; and highlighting the duties of the State through the three sectors, namely the legislative, the executive and the judiciary.[8]

China

China, one of the few communist nations in the world, is both conventional and modern in its outlook. China's traditional outlook echoes on its legal system and restitution is favoured over the state compensation mechanisms for the victims of crime (Jin 2006). The Chinese legal system is more an inquisitorial system which includes some elements of the adversarial system in 1996, by an amendment. This change in the legal system brought victims of crimes to the forefront as 'parties' and it provided certain procedural rights to the victims of crime (Zheng 2008). In particular, victims became active participants in the criminal justice process (Jin 2006).

The Criminal Procedure Code (1996) and Criminal Law (1997) of China provide the following rights to the victims of crime (Jin 2006, p. 145):

> A victim has the right to entrust agents *ad litem*;[9] a victim may initiate a private prosecution;[10] civil compensation to the victim prior to a fine or confiscation of property;[11] the legitimate property of the victims shall be promptly returned to them.[12]

Restorative processes (including mediation) are newly introduced in China and have proved to be successful. There are specific provisions related to restitution from the offenders[13] and restitution is very speedy in China. Currently, the prosecutors' office is only giving compensation, which is actually the restitution by the offender (Qihui and Yinan 2012). Also, restitution is considered a form of punishment (Jin 2006, p. 147). However, Jin (2006) laments that the state has no mechanism to provide compensation, though there is a form of compensation for the mental injury caused by the offender. The Chinese criminal procedure code also provides provisions for the protection of witnesses (Zheng 2008). China further forbids abuse of power and takes strong steps to protect its citizens from abuse of power (Jin 2006).

Voices for the compensation from the state to the victims of crime have recently been raised (Qihui and Yinan 2012). Zheng (2008, p. 494) asserts that 'although victims' rights can be systematically and comprehensively written into the statute, those rights shall mean little for victims without a supporting structure in state authority and judicial process'. Also Jin (2006, p. 154) feels that though China is doing better with the rights of the victims of crime, 'compared with the requirements of the United Nations Declaration the protection and redress of victims in China still have a long way to go'.

India

The Indian subcontinent is one of the regions with an older history of victim rights. In ancient India, victim offender mediation was a common aspect, based on revenge (Jaishankar *et al.* 2008). Tribal courts ensured justice to the victims of crime. Later, Manusmriti,[14] one of the oldest laws in the world, was promulgated, and the rights of victims of crime were ensured. However, Manusmriti was discriminatory in its legal provisions, because it posed different sets of punishments to people based on the Varna system (caste hierarchy), which is a derogatory system (Jaishankar and Haldar 2004). Also, Artha Sastra,[15] one of the oldest treatises on the state, includes references to provisions for funds for victim compensation. The Tamil legend Thiruvalluvar in his famous couplets 'Thirukurral'[16] emphasized equal justice for everyone and provided verses for victim offender mediation (Periyar and Jaishankar 2004). As mentioned earlier, during the medieval period the Mughal Emperors provided justice to the victims of crime based on Islamic Justice. Restitution was common during the Mughal period (Jaishankar et al. 2008).

Unfortunately, when the British colonized India, the substantial and procedural laws created by them did not consider the rights of victims of crime. Though India is still following the same laws provided by the British, even after independence, some changes have been made in the substantial and procedural laws over the years to provide solace to the victims of crime. The Indian constitution, through parts III and IV, ensures victim's right for justice and fair trial. The right is further ensured through specific provisions of the criminal procedure code and other laws.[17] Apart from some provisions, the judiciary ensured the rights of victims of crimes by various landmark judgements.[18]

Even though a specific victim law is not available, some contemporary developments related to the rights of victims provide hope to the victims of crime in India. Of these developments, the Malimath committee recommendations (2003) are the most laudable[19] (Jaishankar et al. 2008). The Malimath Committee especially has given extraordinary recommendations in the areas of victim participation in the trial and investigation, and rights of the victims and victim compensation in line with the UN declaration. Even though most of the recommendations were not implemented, some were, especially in the criminal procedure amendment (2009).

Based on some of the recommendations of the Malimath Committee, the recommendations of the Law Commission of India and Supreme Court Guidelines, the Criminal Procedure Code of India (CrPC) was amended and put into effect on 31 December 2009. The most important component of the amendments is perhaps the introduction of the definition of 'victim'. This is the first ever time any Indian law has had an appropriate definition of victim. Clause (w) has been inserted in section 2 of the CrPC:

> 'victim' meaning a person who has suffered any loss or injury caused by reason of the act or omission for which the accused person has been charged and the expression 'victim' includes his or her guardian or legal heir.

This definition is closer to the definition provided by the 1985 UN Declaration of the Basic Principle of Justice for the Victims of Crime and Abuse of Power, except for the inclusion of bystanders who assisted in preventing victimization, as 'victims'. However, considering the contemporary unfortunate status of crime victims in India, the inclusion of the definition of 'victim' should be hailed as a positive step in the recognition of victims' rights.

The following are some of the other major amendments which will further assist the victims of crime in India: Clause (1) of Section 357 A deals with the preparation of a scheme for providing funds for the purpose of compensation of victims or his/her dependents who have suffered loss or injury as a result of the crime and who require rehabilitation (Lawteacher.net 2011). In this context of new provisions for the victim assistance fund, it should be noted that in 1995 Tamil Nadu was the first state in India ever to establish a 'Victim Assistance Fund', of 10 million (1 core) rupees. The Victim Assistance Fund is for the grant of financial assistance to the legal heir of the victims of murder and the victims of grievous injury and rape (Rufus and Ramdoss 2008; Chockalingam 2009). Furthermore, a scheme for providing restorative justice to victims of rape through financial assistance as well as support services has been formulated by the Ministry of Women and Child Development, Government of India. Under this scheme, NGO's are given funding to provide assistance to victims of rape for an amount of 300,000 (3 lakhs) rupees.

Clause (2) states that whenever a recommendation is made by the Court for compensation the District Legal Service Authority or the State Legal Service Authority, as the case may be, shall decide the quantum of compensation to be awarded under the above-mentioned scheme (Government of India 2009; Lawteacher.net 2011).

In clause (3) the trial court has been empowered to make recommendations for compensation in cases where either the quantum of compensation fixed by the Legal Services Authority is found to be inadequate, or where the case ends in acquittal or discharge and the victim has to be rehabilitated (Government of India 2009; Lawteacher.net 2011).

Clause (4) states that even when the offender is not traced or identified, but the victim is identified, and when no trial takes place, the victim or his/her dependents may make an application to the state or the District Legal Services Authority for award of compensation (Government of India 2009; Lawteacher.net 2011).

Clause (5) says that on receipt of such recommendations or on the application under clause (4), the state or the District Legal Services Authority shall, after due enquiry, award adequate compensation by completing the enquiry within two months (Government of India 2009; Lawteacher.net 2011).

Further, Clause (6) of the newly introduced section states that the state or the District Legal Services Authority, as the case may be, to alleviate the suffering of the victim, may order for immediate first-aid facility or medical benefits to be made available free of cost on the certificate of the police officer not below the rank of the officer in charge of the police station or a Magistrate of the area concerned, or any other interim relief as the appropriate authority deems fit (Government of India 2009; Lawteacher.net 2011).

The most significant amendment apart from the definition of 'victim' is Section 372, which speaks of a general right to appeal and restricts the right to only those situations as provided for in the CrPC or any other applicable law. This section now provides a victim a specific right of appeal in the following circumstances: acquittal of the accused, conviction for a lesser offence and inadequate compensation (Government of India 2009; Lawteacher.net 2011). A landmark judgement related to Section 372 provided by the Bombay High Court strongly emphasized the amendment with a change in the provisions: 'The Bombay high court has ruled that such victims or their legal heirs do not require permission from the court to file an appeal in order to challenge a trial court verdict' (earlier the victim had to seek permission from the court) (Thomas 2012).

In spite of the fact that a law on victims' rights is not promulgated, the CrPC amendments of 2009 are a positive sign as this shows that the Indian Criminal Justice system is trying to change its perception towards victims. However, the discretion of judges in relation to compensation is still emphasized and there is no statutory right for victim compensation (Lawteacher.net 2011). Still, the judiciary has to play a leading role in implementing these laws in various forms of judgements and guidelines. The implementation of these laws has to be regarded over a period of time (Sarkar 2010). It is all too likely that if current judicial attitudes towards crime victims do not change, the above amendments will become a farce.

Malaysia

Malaysia, a nation in the South East, is a colonized nation like India. Its laws are similar to those of all colonized nations, except for the constitutional provision of a dual justice system of secular and sharia laws, which is unique in nature. Punitive justice is still followed in Malaysia. There is a rise of criminal victimization over the years and the legal system is struggling hard to provide justice to the victims of crime: 'In Malaysia, more specific protection for the rights of victims is provided for victims of domestic violence and child abuse. However, there is no such specific legislation that protects the rights of victims of other crimes' (Hussin 2010, p. 39).

Even though the constitution of Malaysia guarantees basic freedoms including equality, life, liberty, privacy, speech, etc., the question of victims' rights still needs to be addressed properly. Hussin (2010) has pointed out that the basic right of crime victims is enshrined in Article 8 of the constitution which guarantees equality. But at the same time, bringing the offender to trial under specific provisions in cases other than domestic violence and child abuse cases depends largely on the prosecutors and the police and hence the victims may be deprived of actual restitution.

Even though the Malaysian constitution under article 98 mentions that compensation must be charged from the consolidated fund, the concept of compensation is holistically seen from the perspective of 'general' victims and not from the crime victims' perspectives. Crime victim's compensation is largely dealt with by the Malaysian criminal procedure code (Hussin 2010). 'Section 426 (1) of the Criminal Procedure Code gives power to the court to order compensation to victims of offences and costs of prosecution' (Ismail 2011, p. 179). The judge will decide on the beneficiary of victim compensation according to Section 426 (Amin 2000). Apart from this single provision, most of the provisions of criminal procedure code award imprisonment and fines, thereby making fewer attempts to compensate the victim and punishing the offender more through the process of imprisonment. Similar to the South African victim's charter, Malaysia provides for opportunities for a civil suit for victims against offenders for claiming compensation. Hussin (2010) further points out that victims of crime in Malaysia retain the right to assistance only under specific laws under which the offenders would be booked. The right to assistance, especially for female victims in cases of rapes, domestic violence and child abuse is specifically established in the Malaysian criminal procedure code (Devi 2006; Ismail 2011).

Apart from the constitutional provisions for the victims of crime in Malaysia, new provisions are also made in the Malaysian Criminal Procedure Code for the benefit of the victims of crime. Hussin (2011) examined some of the new provisions of the Criminal Procedure code of Malaysia and felt that they have given some voice to the victims of crime in Malaysia. In particular the victim is given a chance to speak and for the first time the right to make a Victim Impact Statement (S.183A) is allowed, the statement to be considered during the pronouncement of judgement (Hussin 2011). A new provision of victim compensation is introduced which is actually restitution by the offender (S.426 1A). While lauding the above new provisions for the victims of crime, Hussin (2011, p. 2403) cautions that: 'these provisions are insufficient and limited. Most of the victim-related legislations in Malaysia focus on the physical protection of victims. Nevertheless, emotional and psychological protections as well as financial compensation are not sufficiently provided.' Ghafar's study (University of Leicester 2010) on victim policy in Malaysia endorses the views of Hussin (2011) and suggests that 'Malaysia's policy is underdeveloped and it lacks a specialised agency to prepare victims for court proceedings' (University of Leicester 2010, para. 3).

Mexico

Mexico is a country which is on the verge of transition in providing rights for victims of crime. Plagued by organized crime, especially the drug mafia, it is the country that perhaps most needed the required law for victim compensation. On 30 April 2012, the Mexican Congress approved a bill for the creation of a separate law for victim compensation, especially for organized crime victims (BBC 2012). This law was made possible because of the persistent efforts of activists Javier Sicilia and Teresa Carmona, who themselves were victims of organized crime. 'This law covers the dead, wounded, kidnapped or missing. It also would cover victims of other crimes, like extortion. The law will establish a national registry of victims and set aside funds to compensate them' (Associate Press 2012, paras. 2, 4).

As well as this new law, the Mexican constitution guarantees basic fundamental rights including the right to equality, life, liberty, property, speech, education, home, privacy, etc. The constitution also guarantees access to justice and fair treatment by law through Articles 17 and 20 (Vazquez 2005). Article 17 specifically emphasizes that judicial services shall be free of charge for victims and defendants. Parker (2002, para. 3) says:

> In 2001, Mexico amended Article 20 of the constitution to guarantee the victims the right to: legal assistance, information about developments in the case, assistance from the prosecutor's office, all information requested, medical and psychological assistance, reparation from the offender.

Article 20 of the Mexican constitution recognizes and guarantees the rights of the victims for restitution (Parker 2002; Vazquez 2005). Even though the provision specifically mentions granting bails to the offenders, it also lays down guidelines whereby the law can deny this right to the offender in view of the security and restitutive interest of the victim. In its second part, Article 20 also guarantees victims' right to legal assistance, medical-psychological-legal help, and assistance from the prosecutor's office, assistance for security and compensation. The provision highlights that 'convicted felons' will not be exempted from paying compensation towards the victims. The provision also highlights the rights to privacy for minor victims who have been subjected to offences such as rape and kidnapping, and states that underage victims cannot be compelled to see the offenders or the accused persons for recording their statements. As Shirk (2011, p. 210) puts it:

> Under Article 20, crime victims can file a criminal motion before a judge in certain cases, which will exert pressure on public prosecutors to investigate cases. Also privacy protection and a system for the redressal of grievance through mediation are provided.

In Mexico, there are many instances of child abuse cases, especially of children being used for drug dealing. Even though the Mexican constitution has addressed a child's right to education, home, nutrition and family, it has not yet addressed these critical issues properly, when children are involved in crimes and are turned into victims themselves. The constitution has addressed only the right of the underage victims with regard to rape or kidnapping. Even though Article 16 of the Mexican constitution lays down strict rules prohibiting unnecessary infringement of privacy by the government agencies on civilians,[20] the report by Human Rights Watch pointed out that there are several cases of torture, killings and 'enforced disappearances' by the military and the police (Human Rights Watch 2011). The report further stated that there are gross instances of violating the norms of Article 20 in regard to forced extraction of statements and fair trial (Human Rights Watch 2011).

Philippines

Philippines is yet another colonized nation: it was colonized by USA and Spain. Philippines has modelled its law based on the US legal system and this respect is similar to all colonized nations. Many of the legal provisions from the US model that are helpful to the victims are in place, and Philippines is one of the nations with progressive legislations supporting victims of crime. The Constitution of Philippines guarantees basic fundamental rights to every citizen. Articles 11 and 12 guarantee the right to access to courts and fair trial and the constitution prohibits any discrimination on grounds of poverty. The constitution also guarantees the right to access information about prosecution proceedings. The constitution (article 12) further guarantees assistance and compensation for crime victims. It also establishes laws with regard to victim's rehabilitation in cases of violent crimes. Apart from the above provisions, victims of crime have several procedural rights under Article 203 of the revised penal code. Victims of crime have the right to counsel, to secure witnesses and to subpoena records and documents. Also, victims of rape have special rights such as free legal assistance and medical examination. The rights provided to rape victims under the anti-rape law are impressive. Apart from the victims, witnesses also 'enjoy rights and benefits under the Witness Protection, Security and Benefits Programme implemented by the Department of Justice' (Redress 2003, p. 9). According to Article 2 of Republic Act No. 6981 24 April 1991, known as the Witness Protection, Security and Benefits Act, witnesses enjoy many rights, such as, 'right to a secure housing facility, assistance in obtaining a means of livelihood, securing his or her employment, provision of travel expenses and subsistence, free medical treatment for any injury incurred or suffered as a result of witness duty' (Redress 2003, p. 9).

Notably, in 2010 a victim bill which was conceptualized in 1998, modelled on the lines US Victim Law, titled 'An Act defining the rights of victims of crime, establishing the Office of Victims of Crime under the Department of Justice and for other purposes' or the 'Victims of Crimes Act' was tabled in the Congress of Philippines for approval (Congress of Philippines 2010). However, for reasons that are not clear the bill failed to attain the status of law. Section 4 gives detailed rights of the victims:

> crime victims will have the right to be given information about victim services, to receive information about the status of the police investigation, prosecution, court case etc, timely disposition of case, the opportunity to attend court proceedings, reasonable protection from the accused.
> (Congress of Philippines 2010, p. 3)

This bill also created a crime victims fund for the payment of compensation. Victims can claim compensation and also a right to restitution under specific laws. It may be pointed out that victims and witnesses enjoy special protection and rights, including the right to material, medical and legal assistance under the proposed law (Congress of Philippines 2010). It is to be hoped that Philippines makes the effort to give this progressive legislation the status of law.

South Africa

South Africa is a unique nation with both a modern and a tribal culture. It was ruled by Holland and Great Britain for a long time before it attained its independence. Hence the influence of colonization can be seen, influencing the development of laws, and also related to the rights of the victims of crime. Criminal victimization in the form of rape, sexual assault, domestic violence and violence in other forms is common in South Africa and the country is struggling to provide adequate justice to victims of crime. There are significant provisions that exist within the legal[21] and policy[22] framework in the South African context which seek to empower victims of crime (Victim Empowerment South Africa 2005). Even though 'the Constitution (1996) does not make specific mention of crime victims' (Frank 2007, p. 16), it guarantees basic freedoms to every resident. This basic right includes the right to access to justice and fair trial. The service charter for victims of crimes in South Africa, popularly known as the Victim's Charter, was created in accordance with section 234 of the constitution, specifically highlighting the right to a fair trial and access to justice for every victim (clause 1). The right includes privacy during trial and aims to minimize secondary victimization at the hands of the criminal justice machinery. The right also includes the right of the victim to be part of the criminal prosecution for accessing information or contributing information.

The victim's charter further highlights the right to restitution in case of damage or grabbing of property and assets by the offender; assures protection against any risk of physical danger to the victim from the offender; and guarantees assistance from the police, prosecutors, courts and court officials. The charter also guarantees compensation to the victim in the case of criminal offences. The victim can proceed with a civil suit against the offender if the criminal court does not award compensation: the compensation has to be provided by the offender as prescribed by law, in other words, restitution.[23] In another development on these lines, Dianne Kohler Barnard, a Member of Parliament, has initiated a fund for a victims of violent crimes bill, which promises easy access to rightful compensation for victims of violent crimes (Democratic Alliance 2012).

Even though the constitution and the charter of victims' rights assures rights against secondary victimization, abuse of power by police for cases of alleged civil disobedience are not ruled out by Human Rights Watch (2012b). Also, various NGOs and activists make the criticism that the South African victim policy is merely on paper without any solace to the victims in reality (Democratic Alliance 2007). 'Many victims of crime complain that they are victimised twice, first by the criminals and then by the criminal justice system, which emphasises crime as an offence against the state and displays insufficient concern for the plight of victims' (Democratic Alliance 2007, p. 3; De-Villiers 2006). Democratic Alliance (2007) feels that the rights provided for in the Victims Charter are quite vague and limited and do not have provisions for a victim assistance fund. Also, there is no coherence of various victim policies (Democratic Alliance 2007; Frank 2007). Notwithstanding these criticisms, South Africa has made strides in ensuring the rights of the victims of crime. Frank (2007, p.vi) asserts that 'the advent of victim policy in South Africa is a critical step towards harnessing both the human rights and crime prevention benefits that services to victims may offer'. However, Frank (2007, p.vi) also cautions that mere access to services will not help; rather it will be the quality of the services that will determine the level of assistance given to the victims of crime.

Thailand

Thailand, a Constitutional Monarchy, has shown promise in providing effective victim services and has significant provisions and laws in place related to the victims of crime. 'Although the new Constitution was made in 2007, it was the 1997 version that first integrated the two main concepts for victim's compensation namely: the rights of crime victims and the miscarriage of justice' (Mahidol 2009, p. 6). Mahidol (2009) feels that the constitutional provisions paved the way for a new law for victims in 2001, the 'Victim Compensation Act of 2001', which provides compensation to victims of crime, covering most expenses (Watanavanich 2006). Part 4 (section 40) of the constitution of Thailand ensures several rights of crime victims.[24] Individuals have the right to access the judicial process easily and without any discrimination; the right to be part of the prosecution procedure, contributing to and accessing relevant information; and protection of witnesses as well as victims is guaranteed. While the criminal justice system largely supports restitution for female victims of domestic violence (Kittayarak 2005), the ordinary victims of crimes are guaranteed the right to compensation under section 245 of the constitution. However, a victim is generally not allowed to carry forward civil suit against the offender and the compensation is disbursed from the state fund (Kittayarak 2005).

Apart from the constitutional provisions and the Victim Compensation Act 2001, victims are provided rights in the criminal procedure code and there is a victim assistance fund (Watanavanich 2006; Mahidol 2009). Furthermore, Thailand is a progressive nation in implementing restorative justice processes in selected areas such as juvenile justice, domestic violence, probation, and for adults who are in prison serving sentences of less than five years' duration (Kittayarak 2005). While being highly positive about the current situation of victims of crime in Thailand, Mahidol (2009, p. 7) was also open in being cautious on the implementation issues. She opines: 'In practice, some shortcomings involving the implementation of these laws are, for example, the delay in processing compensation claims, the lack of public understanding of their rights to remedy, or even of the existence of the laws.'

Turkey

Turkey, a European nation which is yet to be a part of the European Union, has some provisions related to the rights of victims of crime in its constitution and criminal procedure code. But there is no separate law for victims of crime. The constitution of Turkey guarantees basic freedoms and right to access the judiciary and a fair trial under article 19 and also under article 36 which states that everyone has the right of litigation either as plaintiff or defendant and the right to a fair trial before the courts through lawful means and procedures. No court shall refuse to hear a case within its jurisdiction. The constitution through article 19 and article 36 assures the right to restitution and compensation. Individuals have the right to own property under article 35 and in case of infringement of this right the constitution assures restitution through article 36. However, article 38 mentions that criminal responsibility should be personal and article 19 highlights that compensation has to be paid by the state in cases of damages suffered by individuals in the way of treatment by criminal justice machinery. The constitution takes stern action against abuse of power. In cases of rape or torture and any other cases involving abuse of human rights by persons belonging to government agencies, the constitution prescribes immediate action by higher authorities and the courts.

Apart from the constitution some rights of the victims of crime are ensured in articles 233–237 of the Turkey criminal procedure code and a mediation regulation is available (Yenisey 2009). The rights provided in the criminal procedure code only include rights of participation of victims during the investigation and prosecution stage: the victims are eligible for pecuniary compensation, although this is not appropriately regulated (Yenisey 2009). Another significant problem of rights implementation in Turkey is that the police are less aware of the rights of the victims and lack training on the rights of victims of crime. This makes the victims in Turkey more vulnerable. In this context, it is perhaps appropriate for Turkey to enact a new law for victims of crime or, if they join the European Union in the future, the EU Framework Decision on Victims (now Directive, see contribution from Ezendam and Wheldon, this volume).

Major challenges in the implementation of victim rights in the newly industrialized countries

Some of the major challenges faced by NICs in implementing victims' rights include the following.

1 Too much focus on restitution of social order and not enough on the personal injuries of the victims.
2 Usage of judicial discretionary power in deciding the rights of the victims.
3 During the prosecution stage there is more focus on the custodial rights of the offenders than on the rights of the victims.

4 There are almost no separate law emphasizing victims' rights, unlike in the developed countries.
5 Problem of police apathy towards victims.
6 Corruption in the criminal justice system; this prevents victims from getting justice when the offender is more influential.
7 Witness protection rules are poorly implemented.
8 There is a lack of proper coordination between the prosecution and the police.
9 Judges are overburdened with huge numbers of cases.
10 Colonial penal laws still exert an heavy influence on the legal system.

Recommendations for the future

The following recommendations can be formulated to help NICs better implement victims' rights:

1 Victim rights laws should be restructured based on the domestic ancient legal manuals in light of modern victim right treatises, discarding colonial laws.
2 The jury system should be introduced for effective implementation of victim rights.
3 Pecuniary punishments should be favoured more than prison sentences.
4 Overburdening the judges with many cases should be discouraged.
5 Victim supportive laws should be created in preventing victims turning into offenders.
6 Therapeutic advocacy by legal practitioners should be encouraged.
7 Petty crimes should be settled outside the courts and compoundable offences should be mediated.
8 Stronger domestic laws and international regulations should be developed to tackle cross-border crimes and victimization.
9 NGOs working for the welfare of the victims should be involved in assisting the police and other wings of criminal justice system, for specific types of crimes such as cybercrime.
10 Victim provisions should be blended with the elements of both inquisitorial and accusatorial systems.

Conclusion

Of the nine NICs analysed, only a few show great promise in the implementation of the rights of victims of crime. Many countries have a long way to go in the successful implementation of the rights of the victims of crime. Except for Thailand and Latin American countries such as Mexico and Brazil, no NIC has separate legislation for victim compensation. Though Philippines has a bill on victim compensation, this has not got the status of law. Philippines can act fast in implementing its victim compensation bill which will surely ameliorate the problems of the victims. In light of the above, Thailand probably ranks as the top NIC, guaranteeing the rights of victims by specific legal procedures and having a separate law for victim compensation. South Africa also shows some promise in ensuring the rights of crime victims. The 2009 amendments of the Indian Criminal procedure code show some light at the end of that country's tunnel. The Chinese blend of inquisitorial and accusatorial system and its restorative processes are quite commendable. Malaysia also shows some promise in the implementation of victim rights. But except for Thailand, all NIC countries analysed in this chapter need to revamp their criminal justice system to focus more on the rights of victims of crime. I hope the recommendations provided above will be helpful to a certain extent.

Acknowledgements

I sincerely thank Assoc. Professor Dr Nasimah Hussin, Ahmad Ibrahim Kulliyyah of Laws (Law Faculty), International Islamic University, Malaysia, for providing her articles on Malaysian rights of victims of crimes, which were very useful. From the bottom of my heart, I thank Dr Debarati Halder, Advocate and Managing Director, Centre for Cyber Victim Counselling (CCVC), India, for assisting me in the legal analysis.

Notes

1 Cuneiform law (2350–1400 BC), Code of Urukagina (2380–2360 BC), Code of Ur-Nammu, (ca. 2050 BC), Laws of Eshnunna (ca. 1930 BC), Codex of Lipit-Ishtar of Isin (ca. 1870 BC), Code of Hammurabi (ca. 1790 BC), Code of the Nesilim (c. 1650–1500 BC), Hittite laws (ca. 1650–1100 BCE), Hebraic law / Hebrew Bible / Old Testament (Mosaic Law) (ninth–fifth century BC), The Draconian constitution (seventh century BC), Gortyn code (fifth century BC), Twelve Tables of Roman Law (451 BC) and Manusmriti (second or third century AD, India).
2 The UN Declaration of Basic Principles of Justice for Victims of Crime and Abuse of Power 1985, defined the term 'victims' as 'persons who, individually or collectively, have suffered harm, including physical or mental injury, emotional suffering, economic loss or substantial impairment of their fundamental rights, through acts or omissions that are in violation of criminal laws operative within member states, including those laws proscribing criminal abuse of power'.
3 Ibid see clause A and B.
4 Under clause B, the Declaration states as follows:
Art.19. States should consider incorporating into the national law norms proscribing abuses of power and providing remedies to victims of such abuses. In particular, such remedies should include restitution and/or compensation, and necessary material, medical, psychological and social assistance and support.
Art.20. States should consider negotiating multilateral international treaties relating to victims, as defined in paragraph 18.
Art.21. States should periodically review existing legislation and practices to ensure their responsiveness to changing circumstances, should enact and enforce, if necessary, legislation proscribing acts that constitute serious abuses of political or

Rights in Newly Industrialized Countries 83

economic power, as well as promoting policies and mechanisms for the prevention of such acts, and should develop and make readily available appropriate rights and remedies for victims of such acts.

5 Latin for *you have the body*. Prisoners often seek release by filing a petition for a writ of habeas corpus. A writ of habeas corpus is a judicial mandate to a prison official ordering that an inmate be brought to the court so it can be determined whether or not that person is imprisoned lawfully and whether or not he should be released from custody. A habeas corpus petition is a petition filed with a court by a person who objects to his own or another's detention or imprisonment. The petition must show that the court ordering the detention or imprisonment made a legal or factual error.
6 Alternative social obligation is an ethical theory that an entity, be it an organization or individual, has an obligation to act to benefit society at large. For example, a judge may order an offender to serve in a school to clean its premises for fifteen days or more.
7 However, clause XLVII (a) of Article 5 further clarifies that the death penalty can be awarded in the event of declared war, according to Article 84 XIX.
8 See title II, Chapters IV, VII, Title IV, chapters I, II and III of the Brazilian constitution.
9 Article 40, 41 of Criminal Procedure Law.
10 Article 170 of Criminal Procedure Law.
11 Article 36 of Criminal Law.
12 Article 64 of Criminal Law.
13 Articles 36, 64, 88 of the Criminal Law; Articles 77, 78 of the Criminal Procedure Law (Chapter VII Incidental Civil Action); A Regulation on Incidental Civil Action in the Supreme People's Court of China.
14 About the second or third century AD, *Manu*, an important Hindu jurist, drew up the *Dharmasastra* code, which was called as *Manusmriti*. The code recognized assault and other bodily injuries and property offences such as theft and robbery (Griffith 1971; Pillai 1983; Thapar 1990; Raghavan 2002). 'Manusmriti dealt with the duties of a king, the mixed castes, the rules of occupation in relation to caste, occupations in times of distress, expiations of sins, and the rules governing specific forms of rebirth. Though a theoretical textbook, *Manusmriti* dealt with the practicalities of life and was largely a textbook of human conduct' (Jaishankar and Haldar 2004, para 2).
15 An ancient book on the principles of state, written by Kautilya some time in the period 321–296 BC.
16 The Thirukkural, a book of Justice and code of ethics and the most popular, most widely esteemed Tamil classic of all time. The word 'Thiru' denotes sanctity, and 'Kural' means the short verses (couplets). Thiruvalluvar, a poet and philosopher of India, wrote the Thirukkural 2000 years ago in the first century BC. It consists of 133 chapters on different aspects of life, and each chapter consists of ten couplets. It is global in perspective and has universal applicability.
17 The legal provisions with regard to the compensation to the victims of crime in contemporary India are found in the Code of Criminal Procedure 1973 under Sections 357, 358 and 359 (for a detailed analysis see Srinivasan and Mathew 2007) and under Section 5 of the Probation of Offenders Act 1958 and some other statutes, for example Section 22 of the Cattle Trespass Act 1872, Sections 42 and 76 of the Forest Act 1972, and Section 1 of the Public Gambling Act 1967 (Srinivasan and Mathew 2007; Das 2008; Rufus and Ramdoss 2008). Though these provisions have the connotation of 'compensation', actually it is restitution (Chockalingam 1993, 2009). This is because the compensation is provided by the courts from the fine levied on the offender.

18 See generally Hari Kishan and State of Haryana v. Sukhbir Singh; Mrs. Cardino v Union of India; Nilabati Behera v. State of Orissa; Chairman, Railway Board v. Chandrima Das; Palaniappa Gounder v. State of Tamil Nadu; Sarwan Singh v. State of Punjab; Rachhpal Singh v. State of Punjab; Guruswamy v. State of Tamil Nadu; Bipin Bihari v. State of Madhya Pradesh; Mangilal v. State of Madhya Pradesh; Bhaskaran v. Sankaran Vaidhyan Balan; Sarup Singh v. State of Haryana; Manjappa v. State of Karnataka, and Vishaka v. State of Rajasthan. (for a detailed analysis of these case laws, see Srinivasan and Mathew 2007).
19 For a detailed analysis on the Malimath Committee Recommendations on Victims of Crime, see Jaishankar *et al.* (2008).
20 See Article 16 of Mexican constitution.
21 The existing legislative framework governing victim empowerment, specifically, comprises the Domestic Violence Act No. 116 of 1998; the Criminal Law (Sexual Offences and Related Matters) Act 32 of 2007; the Judicial Matters Second Amendment Act No. 55 of 2003; the Older Persons Act 2006 (Act No. 13 of 2006); The Children's Act No 38 of 2005; and the Child Justice Act No. 75 of 2008, amongst others.
22 Some of the policy provisions are: The National Crime Prevention Strategy (1996); the Service Charter for Victims of Crime in South Africa (2004); the National Victim Empowerment Programme (1999); and the National Prosecuting Authority's draft Uniform Protocol on Victim Management (2005).
23 See p. 3 of the service charter for victims of crimes in South Africa.
24 See section 40 of the Thailand constitution.

Bibliography

Amin, G.B.H.M., 2000. Participation of the Public and Victims for More Fair and Effective Criminal Justice Administration. Japan: Resource Material Series. Available at: United Nations Asia and Far East Institute for the Prevention of Crime and Treatment of Offenders website www.unafei.or.jp/english/pdf/RS_No56/No56_22PA_Amin.pdf [Accessed 15 February 2012].

Associate Press, 2012. Mexico Passes Law to Compensate Crime Victims. Available at: www.cbsnews.com/8301-505245_162-57424864/mexico-passes-law-to-compensate-crime-victims/ [Accessed 2 May 2012].

BBC, 2012. Mexico Passes Law to Compensate Victims of Crime. Available at: www.bbc.co.uk/news/world-latin-america-17902965 [Accessed 2 May 2012].

Chockalingam, K., 1993. Restitution to Victims of Crime in India – Recent Developments. Indian Journal of Criminology, 21(2), pp. 72–81.

Chockalingam, K., 2009. Measures for Crime Victims in the Indian Criminal Justice System. The United Nations Asia and Far East Institute for the Prevention of Crime and the Treatment of Offenders (UNAFEI), The 144th International Senior Seminar Visiting Experts' Papers. Japan. Available at: www.unafei.or.jp/english/pdf/RS_No81/No81_11VE_Chockalingam.pdf [Accessed 15 March 2011].

Congress of Philippines, 2010. An Act Defining the Rights of Victims of Crime, Establishing the Office of Victims of Crime under the Department of Justice and for other purposes. Available at: www.congress.gov.ph/download/basic_15/HB00199.pdf [Accessed 15 February 2012].

Crowley, J., 2009. History of Victimology, 1970s. In: J.K. Wilson, ed., The Praeger Handbook of Victimology. Santa Barbara, California: ABC-CLIO, LLC, pp. 119–121.

Das, B.B., 2008. Restorative Justice and Victims: Right to Compensation. In: P. Madhava Soma Sundaram, K. Jaishankar and S. Ramdoss, eds, Crime Victims and Justice: An Introduction to Restorative Principles. New Delhi: Serial Publications, pp. 44–55.

David, P.R., 2006. Measures to Protect Victims of Crime and the Abuse of Power in the Criminal Justice Process. The United Nations Asia and Far East Institute for the Prevention of Crime and the Treatment of Offenders (UNAFEI), The 131st International Training Course Visiting Experts' Papers. Japan. Available at: www.unafei.or.jp/english/pdf/RS_No70/No70_10VE_David1.pdf [Accessed 15 March 2012].

De-Villiers, D., 2006. The Needs and Rights of Victims of Crime. Sandton, Johannesburg: Presentation made to DA Victims of Crime Conference in November 2006.

Democratic Alliance, 2007. Discussion Document on the Rights of Victims of Crime. Available at: www.da.org.za/docs/635/Victims%20of%20Crime_document.pdf [Accessed 15 March 2012].

Democratic Alliance, 2012. Fund for Victims of Violent Crime Bill. Available at: www.da.org.za/docs/635/Victims%20of%20Crime_PMB.pdf [Accessed 15 March 2012].

Devi, P.S.D.S.N.S., 2006. Protection of Victims, particularly Women and Children, against Domestic Violence, Sexual Offences and Human Trafficking. Bangkok, Thailand: Paper presented at 9th General Assembly of the ASEAN Law Association. Available at: www.aseanlawassociation.org/9GAdocs/w5_Malaysia.pdf [Accessed 1 May 2012].

Doak, J., 2008. Victims' Rights, Human Rights and Criminal Justice: Reconceiving the Role of Third Parties. Portland: Hart Publishing.

Doerner, W.G and Lab, S.P., 2005. Victimology. Fifth edition. Newark: LexisNexis Matthew Bender.

Frank, C., 2007. Quality Services Guaranteed? A Review of Victim Policy in South Africa. ISS Monograph Series. Available at: www.iss.co.za/uploads/M137FULL.pdf [Accessed 15 March 2012].

Government of India, 2009. The Code of Criminal Procedure (Amendment) Act, 2008.

Griffith, P., 1971. To Guard My People: The History of the Indian Police. Bombay: Allied Publishers.

Hamber, 2009. Living With The Legacy of Impunity: Lessons for South Africa about Truth, Justice and Crime in Brazil. UNISA Online. University of South Africa. Available at: www.unisa.ac.za/default.asp?Cmd=ViewContentandContentID=7321 [Accessed 15 March 2012].

Human Rights Watch, 2011. Neither Rights Nor Security Killings, Torture, and Disappearances in Mexico's War on Drugs. Available at: www.hrw.org/sites/default/files/reports/mexico1111webwcover_0.pdf [Accessed 15 March 2012].

Human Rights Watch, 2012a. World Report 2012: Brazil. Available at: www.hrw.org/sites/default/files/related_material/brazil_2012.pdf [Accessed 19 March 2012].

Human Rights Watch, 2012b. World Report 2012: South Africa. Available at: www.hrw.org/world-report-2012/world-report-2012-south-africa/pdf [Accessed 15 March 2012].

Hussin, N., 2010. The Rights of Victims of Crime under Malaysian Law: Legal Framework and Prospect for Reforms. International Journal of Interdisciplinary Social Sciences, 5(4), pp. 35–44.

Hussin, N., 2011. Punitive Justice in the Malaysian Criminal Law: Balancing the Rights of Offenders with those of the Victims. Journal of Applied Sciences Research, 7(13), pp. 2399–2404.

Ismail, S.Z., 2011. Constructing Some Possibilities for Compensation as Part of Legal Remedies for Rape Survivors: The Case of Malaysia. European Journal of Social Sciences, 26(2), pp. 176–184.

Jaishankar, K. and Haldar, D., 2004. Manusmriti: A Critique of the Criminal Justice Tenets in the Ancient Indian Hindu Code. ERCES Online Quarterly Review. Available at: www.erces.com/journal/articles/archives/v03/v03_05.htm [Accessed 23 January 2012].

Jaishankar, K., Madhava Soma Sundaram, P. and Halder, D., 2008. Malimath Committee and Crime Victims: Resurrecting the Forgotten Voices of the Indian Criminal Justice System. In: N. Ronel., K. Jaishankar and M. Bensimon, eds, Trends and Issues in Victimology. Newcastle upon Tyne: Cambridge Scholars publishing, pp. 112–127.

Jerin, R. A., 2009. History of Victimology, Pre-1940s. In: J.K. Wilson, ed., The Praeger Handbook of Victimology. Santa Barbara: ABC-CLIO, LLC, pp. 108–111.

Jin, G.F., 2006. The Protection and Remedies for Victims of Crime and Abuse of Power in China. The United Nations Asia and Far East Institute for the Prevention of Crime and the Treatment of Offenders (UNAFEI). 131st International Training Course Participants' Papers. Available at: Resource Material Series website www.unafei.or.jp/english/pdf/RS_No70/No70_15PA_Jin.pdf [Accessed 15 March 2012].

Kittayarak, K., 2005. Restorative Justice in Thailand. Presentation at the Eleventh United Nations Congress on Crime Prevention and Criminal Justice Bangkok, Thailand. Available at: www.icclr.law.ubc.ca/Publications/Reports/11_un/Kittipong%20final%20paper.pdf [Accessed 25 April 2005].

Lawteacher.net, 2011. Our Judges Discretion: Flogging A Dead Horse? – An Analysis of the Vanishing Point of Indian Victim Compensation Law. Available at: www.lawteacher.net/judicial-law/essays/flogging-a-dead-horse.php [Accessed 15 March 2011].

Mahidol, B., 2009. Securing the Lives and Rights of Victims of Crime. Keynote Address on the Occasion of the Opening Ceremony of the 13th International Symposium on Victimology at Tokiwa University, Mito, Japan, 23 August 2009.

Maratea, R., 2009. Compensation Programs. In: J.K. Wilson, ed., The Praeger Handbook of Victimology. Santa Barbara: ABC-CLIO, LLC, pp. 47–49.

Meloy, M. L., 2010. ABC's of Victimology. Available at: www.slideworld.com/slideshows.aspx/ABCs-of-Victimology-ppt-566247 [Accessed 15 March 2012].

Morrison, A. and van Bronkhorst, B., 2006. Crime, Violence and Economic Development in Brazil: Elements for Effective Public Policy. Report No. 36525. World Bank: Poverty Reduction and Economic Management Sector Unit, Latin America and the Caribbean Region. Available at: http://pdba.georgetown.edu/Security/citizensecurity/brazil/documents/docworldbank.pdf [Accessed 15 August 2012].

Office of Crime Statistics, 1988. Victims of Crime: An Overview of Research and Policy. Australian Attorney General's Department, Series C.

Parker, L., 2002. Introducing Restorative Practices to Mexico. Restorative Justice Online. Available at: www.restorativejustice.org/editions/2002/August02/mexico1 [Accessed 15 August 2012].

Periyar, E.E. and Jaishankar, K., 2004. Administration of Justice: Thirukkural's Criminal Justice Outlook. Crime and Justice Perspective, 1(3), p. 2.

Pillai, A., 1983. Criminal Law. Bombay: N. M. Tripathi.

Qihui, G. and Yinan, Z., 2012. Aid Proposed For Crime Victims. China Daily. Available at: www.chinadaily.com.cn/china/201203/16/content_14845752.htm

Raghavan, R.K., 2002. World Factbook of Criminal Justice Systems: India. US Department of Justice, Bureau of Justice Statistics. Available at: www.ojp.usdoj.gov/bjs/pub/ascii/wfbcjind.txt [Accessed 15 August 2012].

Redress, 2003. Reparation for Torture: A Survey of Law and Practice in Thirty Selected Countries – Philippines. Available at: www.redress.org/downloads/country-reports/Philippines.pdf [Accessed 15 February 2012].

Rufus, D. and Ramdoss, S., 2008. The Beneficiaries of the State Victim Assistance Fund in Tirunelveli District of Tamil Nadu – An Empirical Analysis. In: P. Madhava Soma Sundaram, K. Jaishankar and S. Ramdoss, eds, Crime Victims and Justice: An Introduction to Restorative Principles. New Delhi: Serial Publications, pp. 409–421.

Samuels, A., 1967. Compensation for Criminal Injuries in Britain. University of Toronto Law Journal, 17(1), pp. 20–50.

Sarkar, S., 2010. The Quest for Victims' Justice in India. Human Rights Brief. Centre for Human Rights Law and Humanitarian Law American, University Washington College of Law, 17(2), pp. 16–20. Available at: www.wcl.american.edu/hrbrief/17/2sarkar.pdf?rd=1 [Accessed 16 March 2012].

Schafer, S., 1968. The Victim and His Criminal. New York: Random House.

Shirk, D.A., 2011. Criminal Justice Reform in Mexico: An Overview. Mexican Law Review, Nueva Serie, III(2), 189–228. Available at: http://info8.juridicas.unam.mx/pdf/mlawrns/cont/6/arc/arc1.pdf [Accessed 15 February 2012].

Srinivasan, M. and Mathew, J.E., 2007. Victims and the Criminal Justice System in India: Need for a Paradigm Shift in the Justice System. Temida, 4, pp. 51–62.

Thapar, R., 1990. A History of India, Volume I. London: Penguin.

Thomas, S., 2012. Crime Victims Don't Need Court's Nod to Appeal: HC. Available at: http://articles.timesofindia.indiatimes.com/2012-04-28/mumbai/31451413_1_crime-victims-appeal-trial-court [Accessed 1 May 2012].

Tobolowsky, P.M., 1999. Victim Participation in the Criminal Justice Process: Fifteen Years after the President's Task Force on Victims of Crime. Criminal and Civil Confinement, 25, pp. 21–105.

Tolbert, T.F., 2009. History of Victimology, 1940s. In: J.K. Wilson, ed., The Praeger Handbook of Victimology. Santa Barbara: ABC-CLIO, LLC, pp. 111–113.

University of Leicester, 2010. Who Fights for Their Rights? University of Leicester Research Calls for Better Way of Protecting Victims. Available at: www2.le.ac.uk/ebulletin/news/press-releases/2010-2019/2010/06/nparticle.2010-06-10.0028615281 [Accessed 1 May 2012].

Vazquez, C.P., 2005. The Political Constitution of the Mexican United States. Universidad Nacional Autonoma de Mexico. Available at: www.juridicas.unam.mx/infjur/leg/const-mex/pdf/consting.pdf [Accessed 15 February 2012].

Victim Empowerment South Africa, 2005. Existing Legislation Addressing Victim Empowerment, South Africa, Desktop Review. Available at: http://victimempowermentsa.files.wordpress.com/2010/07/exisiting-legislation-and-policy-affecting-victims-of-crime-first-draft-desktop-review.pdf [Accessed 15 February 2012].

Walklate, S., 2007. Imagining the Victim of Crime. Berkshire: Open University Press, McGraw-Hill Education.

Watanavanich, P., 2006. Emergence of Victim's Rights in Thailand: Twenty Years after the U.N. Declaration of Basic Principles of Justice for Victims of Crime and Abuse. Work product of the 131st International Training Course on The Use and Application of the

United Nations Declaration of Basic Principles of Justice for Victims of Crime and Abuse of Power – Twenty Years after Its Adoption. The United Nations Asia and Far East Institute for the Prevention of Crime and the Treatment of Offenders (UNAFEI). Available at: www.unafei.or.jp/english/pdf/RS_No70/No70_05VE_Watanavanich.pdf [Accessed 15 March 2012].

Yenisey, F., 2009. Turkish Criminal Procedure Code. Istanbul: Beta Publishing House.

Zheng, G.G., 2008. Which Kind of Party? The Role of Crime Victims in Chinese Criminal Procedure. Hong Kong Law Journal, 38, p. 493.

Chapter 5

Should reparations for massive human rights abuses perpetrated on African victims during colonial times be given?

Jeremy Sarkin

Introduction

The issue of the rights of African victims of the colonial period is an understudied and under-researched area (Ulrich and Boserup 2001). However, the inhabitants of Africa even during the colonial period had rights and are attempting to claim reparations today based on those rights (Sarkin 2004a). For this reason, dealing with the issues that occurred during colonial times in Africa is highly controversial (Spitzer 2002, p. 1). There are many who argue that such rights do not exist and that such claims should not be supported, even though the effects on Africa and its inhabitants of what occurred many years ago are still being felt today (Howard-Hassmann and Lombardo 2008).[1] Those opposed to Africans having such rights argue that for legal, political, cultural, economic and practical reasons, those rights never existed and reparations to Africans are not justified, not legally due and ought not to be paid.[2] These issues are contentious (Brooks 1999; Osabu-Kle 2000; Wareham 2003, p. 228) partly because it is agreed that genocides, crimes against humanity, exterminations, ethnic cleansing, disappearances, land expropriation, forced labour, the use of comfort women, experimentations and other gross human rights violations were committed by colonial governments and multinational corporations. The question that is raised, however, is whether states and corporations had legal duties to those upon whom the violations were committed. Those who do not support claims by Africans argue that what occurred were not crimes or human rights violations when they occurred as international law at the time did not prohibit such conduct, that anyway too long has passed and that the victims of these atrocities are no longer alive. Thus, the argument made is that rights did not exist and even if they did the passage of time has made them extinct. It is also argued that the former colonizers recognize their responsibilities[3] and give development aid to the countries they once occupied, and this is just compensation for what occurred.

Thus, should inhabitants of former colonized states, even if not directly affected by the events during those times, be able to get reparations, in all of its various forms, from the states who committed such abuses? Or if the state is no longer in existence, should they be able to get reparations from the states that succeeded them, or from the multinational corporations who aided and abetted these violations at the time?

In this context in recent years the reparations issue for atrocities committed during the colonial era has pressed its way to the fore of international legal debate (Thompson 2002). For violations from a long time ago individuals cannot be punished as they are no longer alive and states cannot be held criminally accountable according to criminal law, only civilly liable. Even holding a state liable is extremely difficult as it is difficult to sue states.

Dealing with events from many years ago remains ignored in many parts of the world, and where they are a focus of attention they are extremely marginalized (Biondi 2003, pp. 5–18). The issues are contentious. Intellectual debates on the issues concerning reparations for Africa are, however, of critical importance (Lanham 2003). While there are some that argue that reparations are not due for violations that occurred during colonial times, what is apparent is that there are various positions on these questions. The position adopted is often dependent on where those who take a particular stance come from in the world. Broadly speaking, those in the Global South, including Africa, Latin America and Asia, support reparations. Again, generally speaking, those in the Global North, in other words (but with some exceptions), people in Europe and North America besides African-Americans do not often support such claims. Again, divided by region, those in the Global South argue that this is an issue whose time has arrived, while those in the North argue that this is still a weak issue, which has not gained a great deal of traction.

In this chapter, I argue that such claims are valid and payable legally and otherwise, even if still not widely accepted. The landscape in the countries where the atrocities were committed, because of the legacy of the past, at least in part, presents a picture of extreme hardship. However, the perspective on the causes of the major economic, social and cultural (Bhargava 2007) problems that exist in at least some of these countries is contested. Some blame the effects of mismanagement in the post-independence period. But at least some of the guilt rests with those who caused massive human rights abuses during colonial times. Underdevelopment, which occurred in colonial Africa, has had a major effect on the lack of infrastructure in many parts of the continent today.[4] Those in the developed world benefitted unjustly then and do so still today from the resources, both human and other, that were removed during the colonial era. While many of the direct victims of colonial abuse are no longer alive, their descendants have lost much as a result, including their inheritances and a great deal of land and livestock. Colonial atrocities have other political effects today, especially on some minority groups in former colonized states. Some are minorities today because of what was done to them during the colonial era. This has had massive political effects. The rights of African victims today, the effect of colonial violations on victims today and whether apologies ought to be given are the focus of this chapter. Some of the issues to be addressed include why these matters are still relevant today, sometimes more than a hundred years since they occurred, whether there are precedents for such reparations, whether the time is ripe for such claims, whether international law during colonial times forbade the conduct that occurred and whether such claims are void because of the passage of time.

These issues must also be understood in the context of the rights of victims. While most argue that human rights and victims' rights specifically began only after World War II, it is clear that victims had rights long before this, as will be examined. Victims were in fact able to go before various courts to claim those rights. Victims have been able for at least a century to claim theoretically, and in practice, reparations where their rights were violated. The issues of victims' rights to information, reparation, and their difficulties in obtaining assistance will be addressed, as well as some of the developments and strategies used to overcome obstacles.

Atrocities during Colonialism

The colonial period was filled with massive human rights abuse, including crimes against humanity, war crimes, genocide (before the term was even conceived), extermination, disappearances, torture, forced removals, slavery, racial discrimination, cruel, inhuman, or degrading treatment, and more (Sarkin 2004b). As has been noted:

> Colonialists routinely practiced torture, cruel and inhuman treatment on the African people. They committed crimes against humanity such as sexual assault on African women. They plundered wealth, expropriated and privatized African land and domestic animals; they decimated African wildlife and plants; and they destroyed and looted Africa's cultural property. A large proportion of African cultural heritage is to be found in private and public collections in Europe and North America.
>
> (Gutto 1993, p. 34)

Africa suffered immensely during the colonial years (BBC News 1999). About eighteen million Africans were traded as slaves and millions of Africans died during the attempts to capture them or cross the seas with them (Lovejoy 2000, pp. 65–66, 142). Consequently, while in the sixteenth century Africans constituted twenty per cent of the world population, by the nineteenth century they only represented twelve per cent (Blaut 1993, p. 184). In specific parts of Africa the death toll was particularly severe. Under King Leopold II between five and ten million people were massacred in the Belgian Congo. Yet, it was not only the Belgians and Germans that exacted a high toll – other colonial powers also committed gross human rights abuses. Thus, cases could be brought against Britain, Holland, France, Germany, Belgium, Italy, Spain and Portugal (Gutto 1993, pp. 58–59). The effects of these violations are still felt today. On 26 March 2012, the President of the 66th United Nations General Assembly, Mr. Nassir Abdulaziz Al-Nasser, in remarks delivered to commemorate the International Day of Remembrance of the Victims of Slavery and the Transatlantic Slave Trade, noted with respect to slavery and the slave trade that: 'The terrible impacts of slavery and the slave trade are still felt to this day. They have devastated continents and countries. They have led to profound social and economic inequalities, and have given rise to hatred, racism and prejudice.'[5]

The day of commemoration is important, as it signifies the meaning that the United Nations accords those events. Because of the consequences of having approximately twenty-eight million people, mainly Africans (Thipanyane 2003, p. 32) forced into slavery, this day of commemoration was declared in 2007. Beyond the atrocities committed against Africa's inhabitants,[6] colonialists also extracted and decimated the continent's rich natural resources. The removal of such resources represents just one aspect of the reparations that Africa deserves. As has been noted by Michael Bayzler (quoted in Shelton 2004, p. 259; see also Shelton 2003):

> Not seeking financial restitution, in the face of documented proof that financial giants worldwide are sitting on billions of dollars in funds made on the backs of ... victims, which they then invested and reinvested many times over ..., amounts to an injustice that cannot be ignored.

As far as the legal issues are concerned there is also growing acceptance that colonial abuses may have belated legal implications and that some of the colonizers' actions do not merely retrospectively qualify as violations. There is a growing acceptance that what occurred were already violations of international and domestic law at the time. While it is commonly believed that international protections against human rights violations began from the World War II era, they actually existed much earlier. Legal history shows that a system for protecting groups' and individual's human rights in international law, never mind domestic law, was available from at least the nineteenth century.

Recent developments

A reason why the issue of reparations is now so topical (see De Feyter *et al.* 2005) is the fact that the matter of reparations for slavery and colonialism was a major, and highly contested, agenda item at the World Conference against Racism, Racial Discrimination, Xenophobia and Related Intolerance (WCAR), held in Durban (South Africa) from 31 August until 8 September 2001 (Bossuyt and Vandeginste 2001). Quite a considerable part of the World Conference was devoted to these themes. The issue is also more relevant now because a number of countries, for example Australia, New Zealand, Canada and South Africa, have been finding ways of dealing with such issues from the distant past. Recently there have been a number of developments which have seen the inhabitants of former colonized countries seeking and in some cases receiving reparations from their former colonial masters. In 2009, Italy agreed to pay Libya US$10 billion for atrocities committed during the colonization period (Israely 2008). Court cases have been filed against Britain, Germany and other countries for the human rights violations that are alleged to have been committed during their colonial periods. South Africans have filed cases in the USA, under the Alien Torts Claims Act, against a variety of corporations for their alleged complicit role in the apartheid system. In February 2012 US company General Motors (GM) agreed to settle and pay damages to victims. Armenians still want Turkey to apologize and compensate them for the genocide committed around World War I. A number of other communities are attempting to sue multinational corporations for their role in the commission of such atrocities during colonization. These groups include the Herero of Namibia who have sued various corporations including Deutsche Bank (Anderson 2005). Other groups that want to sue and have sued include Tanzanians, Kenyans, Ugandans, African-Americans in the USA and comfort women in various Asian countries who seek reparations from Japan and others. In the USA the question of reparations to African-Americans for the slave trade remains a controversial matter, with many in favour and many against. Since World War II, Germany[7] has spent more than $100 billion dollars on reparations for violations committed by Nazi Germany to Israel and individual victims. It still pays out about US$1 billion each year. Germany (Schwerin 1972) and other states, including Belgium, France, Britain, the Netherlands and others have not, however, been willing to pay out for human rights violations committed before World War II (Howard-Hassmann 2007).

Various processes designed to obtain apologies and acknowledgements have occurred in various places. In the United Sates there have been processes in 2009 and 2010 in Congress to adopt a resolution calling what occurred to Armenians, around World War I, 'genocide'. Armenians have attempted for years to get Turkey to apologize and compensate them for those events. In Spain there are tremendous demands today to deal with the violations that occurred during the Spanish civil war that took place between 1936 and 1939. Families of the more than 110,000 victims who disappeared seek to have the mass graves that have been found forensically examined. So controversial is this process that Spanish Judge Baltasar Garzón, who attempted to prosecute Chilean dictator General Augusto Pinochet and wanted to investigate these matters, faced charges in Spain for attempting to do so.

The fact is that such old matters do not end with the passage of time. This can be seen from issues relating to World War II. There are still criminal trials being held and a number of legal claims are still being litigated in a number of countries today, more than sixty-five years after the end of the war. Thus, in April 2010, the Duma, the Russian lower house of parliament, passed an amnesty law for World War II crimes. Included were those who survived imprisonment in German concentration camps, workers in munitions factories and survivors of the Leningrad siege. Individuals who committed crimes during World War II are still being prosecuted in various countries. A recent claim occurred in France against the French railways for the role they played in the transport of Jews, political prisoners, homosexuals and gypsies to Nazi death camps. In 2010 Polish victims from World War II mounted claims against German railway companies for the profits made from charging those they transported to the death camps. Thus, issues from a long time ago still resonate in many parts of the world. The only real difference between these claims and colonial claims is the ability of the claimants to have their claims dealt with. This can be seen in the cases brought in the United States against Swiss banks and other corporations in the 1990s. These cases were settled for huge sums of money. Victims in former colonial states, however, do not have the resources and political clout to achieve these results. Some have argued that the fact that such cases are resolved, but colonial ones are not, is racism at work.

A number of former colonial communities are attempting to sue various role players for the atrocities committed during colonization (Sarkin 2009). These groups include the Herero of Namibia who have sued various corporations, including Deutsche Bank in the United States. Another case has seen 228 Samburu and Maasai farmers in Kenya receive £4.5 million in damages from the UK's Ministry of Defence after their family members were killed or maimed over the past fifty years by British Army explosives left behind on military ranges in that country (Sarkin 2009). A further case concerns rape allegedly perpetrated by British soldiers. The case against the British Ministry of Defence (MoD) by more than 650 Kenyan women is for rape cases allegedly carried out by British soldiers in Kenya (OCHA 2003). The MoD is being sued for negligence in that it failed to take steps to prevent the rapes. Another case concerns a challenge to a British court decision made in 1913 to force some 10,000 Maasai off their land in Laikipia and into a new area on the Tanzanian border, where they were affected by malaria (Redfern 2004). The Nandi people of Uganda are to sue Britain for killing their prophet Koitalel arap Samoei in 1905 during a military campaign to suppress Nandi resistance. The king of the Bunyoro in Uganda is also reported to be preparing to take Britain to court for war crimes committed in the 1890s. Former Mau Mau freedom fighters from Kenya will be in a British court in July 2012 claiming reparations for human rights abuses, including torture, committed during colonial times (The Standard 2012). They are seeking compensation from the British government for atrocities committed against the Mau Mau before Kenya's independence (The Nation 2006). Another case relates to the massacres in German East Africa (now Tanzania) between 1905 and 1907 in what was known as the 'Maji Maji rebellion'. It is believed that about 250,000 Ngoni, Matumbi, Waluguru, Makua, Yao and Makonde people were killed (The East African 2006).

As can be seen, there are many cases. This indicates the extent to which people in the former colonial territories want to have these matters dealt with (Sarkin 2009). This is so despite the massive difficulties that victims have in bringing such cases and the lack of funding at their disposal to do so. It is true though that until recently claiming reparations for historical violations has been extremely difficult. This was due in part to the limited number of rights afforded to individuals and a lack of specific means to obtain damages or reparations within the international legal system dealing with human rights law or humanitarian law violations. While the rapid growth of the reparations' movement certainly has assisted potential claimants to bring claims arising from colonial abuses, this does not discount the fact that such claims were available in international law earlier. It is true, however, that these victims could not practically bring such cases, for a number of reasons. Certainly, obstacles still remain. These include issues such as statutes of limitation which state that an individual has to file a claim within a certain period. Courts are willing, at times, to forgo time periods that claims are meant to be lodged if it can be shown that victims were unable to file claims earlier than they did. Certainly, in such cases victims can show that filing such cases earlier than they have done were impossible for a variety of reasons. There are many other groups that want to bring such cases.

The development of the right to reparation

Reparation claims are not a recent phenomenon (Posner and Vermeule 2003). In fact, at least since the end of the twentieth century, reparations processes are not new at all. International law, never mind domestic law, has recognized the right of the individual to claim human rights violations for at least a hundred years (Bassiouni 2006, p. 203).

In 1796 the United States Supreme Court found in *Ware v. Hylton* that private individuals had the right to compensation for acts that occurred during the American Revolution. The Court held that this was the case as rights were 'fully acquired by private persons during the war, more especially if derived from the laws of war only against the enemy and in that case the individual might have been entitled to compensation from the public...' (United States Supreme Court 1796).

Claiming reparations for damages suffered is not a recent practice. In fact, at the conclusion of warfare, agreements were often reached in terms of which a payment or a forfeit of land followed. For example, after the Franco–Prussian War of 1872, France paid Germany reparations (Posner and Vermeule 2003).

There are a number of treaties and instruments that provide for special international tribunals or procedures to address violations of individual rights or obligations arising within these instruments (Sohn and Buergenthal 1973). The rights of individuals in international law and their right to claim compensation or reparation received further recognition in 1907 when individuals were even given standing before the International Prize Court in terms of the Convention on an International Prize Court of 18 October 1907. Individuals were to be able to approach the Court in relation to property. However, insufficient ratifications occurred and the treaty did not come into force. Also in 1907, a Central American Court of Justice was established by Costa Rica, El Salvador, Guatemala, Honduras and Nicaragua. The Court operated from 1908 to 1918 and permitted a range of actors, including individuals, to bring complaints against states other than their own country (Randelzhofer 1999). This was no aberration in granting rights and providing procedures to individuals to claim reparations from states in international law. Article 304 of the Treaty of Versailles provided for the establishment of a Mixed Arbitral Tribunals to hear private claims arising from the payments of German debts to Allied nationals and for the restitution of Allied property. Under the treaty, individuals were permitted direct access to these tribunals. The German-Polish Convention of 1922 created the

Upper-Silesian Arbitral Tribunal for the purpose of protecting minorities and their property rights (Sohn and Buergenthal 1973). Article 87(b) of the Charter granted the General Assembly and Trusteeship Council the authority to accept petitions from inhabitants of the Trusteeship Territories. Other examples include the Polish-Danzig Treaty, the minority treaties in the interwar years, and indirectly, the Mandates Commission of the League of Nations (Forsythe 1991). The International Labour Organization permitted individuals to file private petitions for violations of human rights embedded in labour law (Forsythe 1991). An individual right to compensation is also found in Article III of the Hague Convention of 1907. Thus, international law has permitted individual claims from colonial times. Certainly it is true that the notion that victims of human rights abuses are entitled to an effective remedy has gained considerable international acceptance more recently, but this does not negate the fact that claims were permitted a long time ago.

While the recent and rapid growth of the reparations movement has without a doubt assisted potential claimants to bring claims arising from colonial abuses this does not discount the fact that such claims were available under international law earlier. It is true however, that many victims could not practically bring such cases at the time, for a number of reasons. Even today, obstacles remain, including hurdles such as statute of limitations, among others. But such hurdles are not insurmountable, as evidenced by the recent success of various claims.

Should reparations be paid?

What is clear is that there is massive inequality in the world today. Many agree that development aid ought to be given to the parts of the world where colonialism occurred and where massive poverty exists. Part of the reason that such aid is given is the sense of guilt about the gross human rights' violations that happened. It is recognized, albeit not always publically, that those who benefitted from the colonial era have duties to those who suffered and still suffer today. Reparation is about restitution and other types of reparations, including acknowledgement and the restoration of dignity. More ought to be done to reconcile those who live in different parts of the world. The fact that there is so much anger and unhappiness directed by the Global South to the Global North is to some degree because of the past. Finding ways of dealing with the past and repairing the fractured relationships can only be beneficial for everyone in all regions.

There are many who argue that claims for reparations to Africa should not be supported. They argue that, for legal, political and practical reasons, collective financial reparations to Africa are not a good strategy. While some base their opposition to reparations for colonial atrocities on the fact that financial reparations ought not to be paid partly on the cost involved,[8] reparations do not have to be monetary or monetary only. It is certainly problematic to agree that reparations are owed, but then argue that only certain types of reparations should be paid. Nevertheless, there are many different types of reparations. Reparations can encompass a variety of concepts including damages, redress, restitution, compensation, rehabilitation and satisfaction. Each of these concepts has a unique meaning although they are often used as general terms to encompass all the different types of remedies available to a victim. 'Compensation' or 'damages' typically signify an amount of money awarded by a court or other body for harm suffered. 'Restitution' signifies a return to the situation before the harm occurred, 'rehabilitation' denotes provision of medical or other types of treatment, and 'satisfaction' indicates acknowledgements, apologies and the like. Critically, reparations do not have to be solely or mainly about money (Junk and Miner 2004). There are a range of alternatives.

Some argue that any processes to deal with Africa's ills ought to reflect distributive, rather than restorative, justice. Some believe that there ought to be wealth redistribution and that claims should not be dealt with on the basis of rights. It has also been argued that the 'West' has a duty to assist Africa for historical reasons, but that Africans do not have rights to such claims (Howard-Hassmann and Lombardo 2008). These assertions ignore the direct effects that historical events continue to have on the people who live in these places. While specific and directly quantifiable financial reparations are difficult to assess against the backdrop of what has occurred since the end of colonialism, colonialism must bear at least part of the blame for the situation that many African groups, countries, and in fact, Africa as a whole, are in today.

There are many types of reparations and many ways for reparations to be provided. While individual payouts are one option, community benefits may be more appropriate, especially for events that occurred many years ago. Increased educational funding may be the most appropriate option in certain cases. A number of other processes should be on the table. The healing of the wounds of the past must include the healing of the psyche; thus, reconciliation processes are important (see Daly and Sarkin 2007). Truth and fact-finding efforts could help the healing begin (see Sarkin 1999). Also important is the analysis and documentation of the colonial ravages and their continuing effects (Roper and Barria 2009). But such analyses should also consider and examine the extent to which 'post-independence governments' human rights abuses have contributed to the continuing social and economic marginalization of their populations, because external governments should be held responsible only for deprivation due to their own conduct' (Human Rights Watch 2001).

There are other types of reparations that should also occur. These could include the building of museums and monuments, as well as, more generally, development that benefits communities. Underdevelopment has significantly impacted the quality of the infrastructure in many parts of the continent. Thus, assistance in this area should be forthcoming. Community development facilities, especially those that encourage victim participation, are also important. Proper apologies are also necessary.

The payment of reparations is not only a legal issue. It is relevant for many other disciplines. As far as these issues are concerned there is growing acceptance that colonial abuses may have belated legal implications and that some of the colonizers' actions do not merely retrospectively qualify as violations. There is a growing acceptance that what occurred were already violations of international and domestic law at the time they were committed. It is this point which needs greater research. While some argue that reparations have not been something which individuals could claim until recently and that it is only in the last twenty years or so that there was international law on reparations, particularly for individuals, reparations were in fact a longstanding norm of customary international law for many years. There are a number of treaties and instruments that provide special international tribunals or procedures for individual rights or obligations arising under these instruments.

Why reparations ought to be paid

Colonialism hit Africa hard (see Sarkin 2007). Beyond the atrocities committed against Africa's inhabitants, colonialists also extracted and decimated the continent's rich natural resources. The removal of such resources represents just one aspect of the reparations that Africa deserves. Certainly, at the minimum this plundering qualifies as unjust enrichment. The typical argument is that unjust enrichment has occurred when one party benefits unjustifiably in the absence of a contract. If a contract existed, there would be no need to apply principles of unjustified enrichment, as the contract would be the basis of the claim. It is clear that the colonial powers took what they were not entitled to. They were, in the ordinary meaning of the term, 'unjustly enriched'. As a result, African countries and African people, at least to some degree, were deprived of those assets, and continue to suffer the consequences of not having had the benefit of those resources, both human and otherwise. This legacy is still relevant today.

The 'Martens Clause', contained in the 1899 and 1907 Hague Conventions, plays a significant role in the applicable legal framework because it extended the protections of international law to groups and individuals. Accordingly, there is considerable recognition today that a number of historical occurrences are actionable.

The Martens Clause (Cassese 2000) appeared in the preamble to the 1899 and 1907 Hague Conventions. It states:

> Until a more complete code of the laws of war is issued, the High Contracting Parties think it right to declare that in cases not included in the Regulations adopted by them, populations and belligerents remain under the protection and empire of the principles of international law, as they result from the usages established between civilized nations, from the laws of humanity and the requirements of the public conscience.[9]

The Martens Clause has been frequently reiterated by states in treaties, cited by international and national courts, and invoked by organizations and individuals (Sarkin 2009). This is important because this disposition is a vital link in determining whether at least by the early twentieth century a customary norm existed that prohibited a state from committing gross human rights violations. The use of the terms contained in this clause may, however, have even earlier vintages. Regardless of when the principles became international law, the Martens Clause and customary international law represented a climate of recognition that states were no longer free to treat people in any manner they chose, but that they were subject to basic humanitarian principles. These principles were applicable to the laws of armed conflict, but also to the international legal regime as a whole. They were integral to forming customary international law that recognized humanitarian principles. Among these principles was a prohibition against acts that constituted crimes against humanity. This has been confirmed by the International Criminal Tribunal for the Former Yugoslavia (ICTY), in a *Tadić* ruling in 1995 (ICTY 1995). Thus, the principles of the laws of humanity and the dictates of public conscience have developed over centuries and spanned many societies. They were not inventions of the Martens Clause. They were pre-existing principles of national and international legal regimes. Each usage and agreement reinforced the values and strengthened the norms and rules of preceding usages and agreements.

What is specifically important about the Martens Clause is that it serves either as an interpretative guideline, a general instruction on how to interpret international customary or treaty rules, or else it serves to codify two new sources of international law: the 'laws of humanity' and the 'dictates of public conscience' (Sarkin 2009). Thus, attempts to seek reparations for past gross human rights violations that occurred more than a century ago can rely on this Clause as evidence of a customary norm prohibiting the commission of those mass atrocities at the time.

Crimes against humanity and genocide already constituted crimes at the time although they were not known by those names (Anderson 2005). While the word 'genocide' entered usage in the 1940s, the concept of this crime dates back thousands of years and was certainly an internationally accepted violation by the turn of the twentieth century. The legal principles from which these crimes emerged existed in international law, were acknowledged by the international community and were called upon periodically by 1900. This does not mean that the law only applies retrospectively (although it can) but that these laws were applicable at the time. It is true that some who support historical reparations argue that some legal rules ensure that retrospective liability is a possibility as well. Excluding reparations in other forms beyond symbolic from this duty disregards the reality of what occurred, and the legacy of those events today. This duty has corresponding rights. As has been noted: 'Not seeking financial restitution … amounts to an injustice that cannot be ignored' (Shelton 2004).

Some suggest that the potential legal problems attendant to making claims for generations-old human rights abuses can be avoided if the focus is instead shifted to the contemporary effects of past abuses and to seeking out practical solutions to directly improve the quality of life of the people.

Various other treaties provide evidence that international law recognized and protected indigenous Africans during the late nineteenth century. One such treaty was the 1878 Treaty of Berlin, which provided rights for indigenous peoples. The Treaty has been hailed as the 'most important international body concerned with minority rights prior to 1919' (MacArtney 1968, p. 166). It was particularly important from a human rights standpoint, as it permitted states to intervene in cases of non-compliance (Claude 1955, pp. 8–9). The acceptance of minority rights at this time also coincided with the evolving notion of sovereignty, which, while historically vested in the ruler, was shifting towards the people (Preece 1997, pp. 75–95). Thus, the conceptualization of and belief in the notions of protection that international law provided to groups and individuals at this time were on the rise.

Conclusion

Some reparations, regardless of what type they constitute, ought to be given by the states that were responsible for what occurred (Sarkin 2004a). The enduring legacy of what occurred during those times should not be underestimated. The lasting effects of population decimation, land dispossession, as well as other effects continue to haunt many groups. It impedes their economic, social and political progress.

Former colonizing powers and others must acknowledge, by providing reparations, the untold pain and misery that they caused (Shelton 2004). However, I believe that reparations should not be paid directly to individuals, unless there is a clear connection between the harm caused and a specific victim or his or her direct family. Group or collective reparations are a better alternative in these types of situations. They need not involve specific payouts to individuals but rather can be offered in the form of debt relief or other similar offerings, such as projects that benefit the community as a whole. Finally, that reparations or development assistance occurs is far more important than the name that is used to describe the process. Using the term "reparations" might, however, help to reduce the anger that exists towards the 'West'.[10] As recent events have shown, reconciliation in some form is sorely needed.

Notes

1. See further Abdullahi (1997).
2. See further Bossuyt and Vandeginste (2001, p. 343).
3. On responsibilities of states see Dimitrijevic (2011).
4. This has been extensively debated. See an early treatise Rodney (1972).
5. www.un.org/en/ga/president/66/statements/slavetrade260312.shtml.
6. See further du Plessis (2003), Posner and Vermeule (2003, p. 689).
7. See generally Langbehn and Salama (2011) and Honig (1954).
8. See however (Adejor, n.d.).
9. Hague Convention II with Respect to the Laws of Armed Conflict on Land (1899); Hague Convention IV Respecting the Laws of Armed Conflict on Land (1907).
10. See generally Gloppen (2001).

Bibliography

Abdulaziz Al-Nasser, N., 2012. Speech of the President of the 66th UN General Assembly, on the Occasion of the Commemoration of International Day of Remembrance of the Victims of Slavery and the Transatlantic Slave Trade. New York. Avaliable at: www.un.org/en/ga/president/66/statements/slavetrade260312.shtml [Accessed 12 November 2011].

Abdullahi, A.N.M., 1997. Human Rights Protection in Africa: Towards Effective Mechanisms. East African Journal of Peace and Human Rights, 5(3), pp. 1–31.

Adejor, A., n.d. Reparation to Africa: An Argument for Equity and Alternative Financing Strategy in a Competitive World. Available at: www.codesria.org/links/conferences/Nepad/Adejo Armstrong.pdf

Anderson, R., 2005. Redressing Colonial Genocide Under International Law: The Hereros' Cause of Action Against Germany. California Law Review, pp. 1155–1189.

Barkan, E., 2001. The Guilt of Nations: Restitution and Negotiating Historical Injustices. Baltimore: Johns Hopkins University Press.

Bassiouni, C.M., 2006. International Recognition of Victims' Rights. Human Rights Law Review, (6), pp. 203–279.

BBC News, 1999. Trillions demanded in slavery reparations. Available at: http://news.bbc.co.uk/1/hi/world/africa/424984.stm [Accessed 11 October 2012].

Bhargava, R., 2007. How Should We Respond to the Cultural Injustices of Colonialism? In: J. Miller and R. Kumar, eds, Reparations: Interdisciplinary Inquiries. New York: Oxford University Press, pp. 215–251.

Biondi, M., 2003. The Rise of the Reparations Movement. Radical History Review, 87, pp. 5–18.

Blaut, J.M., 1993. The Colonizer's Model of the World: Geographical Diffusionism and Eurocentric History. New York: Guilford Press.

Bossuyt, M. and Vandeginste, S., 2001. The Issue of Reparation for Slavery and Colonialism and the Durban World Conference against Racism. Human Rights Law Journal, 22(9-12), pp. 341–350.

Brooks, R.L., ed., 1999. When Sorry Isn't Enough: The Controversy Over Apologies and Reparations for Human Injustice. New York: New York University Press.

Cassese, A., 2000. The Martens Clause. Half a Loaf or Simply Pie in the Sky?, 11 EJIL (1), pp. 187–188.

Claude, I., 1955. National Minorities: An International Problem. Cambridge: Harvard University Press.

Daly, E. and Sarkin, J., 2007. Reconciliation in Divided Societies: Finding Common Ground. Pennsylvania: Pennsylvania University Press.

De Feyter, K., Parmentier, S., Bossuyt, M. and Lemmens, P., eds, 2005. Out of the Ashes. Reparation for Victims of Gross and Systematic Human Rights Violations. Oxford: Intersentia Publishers.

Dimitrijevic, N., 2011. Duty to Respond: Mass Crime, Denial, and Collective Responsibility. Budapest: Central European University Press.

du Plessis, M., 2003. Historical Injustice and International Law: An Exploratory Discussion of Reparation for Slavery. Human Rights Quarterly, 25(3), p. 235.

Forsythe, D.P., 1991. The Internalization of Human Rights. Lexington, Massachusetts: Lexington Books.

Gloppen, S., 2001. Review Essay: Reparatory Justice – a road to reconciliation? On the Role of Reparations in Transitional Justice Theory. Theory in George Ulrich and Louise Krabbe Boserup, eds, Human Rights in Development Yearbook 2001. The Hague: Kluwer Law International, pp. 385–401.

Gutto, S., 1993. Human and Peoples' Rights for the Oppressed: Critical Essays on Theory and Practice from Sociology of Law Perspective. Lund: Lund University Press.

Honig, F., 1954. The Reparations Agreement between Israel and the Federal Republic of Germany. American Journal of International Law, 48(4), pp. 564–578.

Howard-Hassmann, R.E., 2007. Framing Reparations Claims: Differences between African and Jewish Movements for Reparations. African Studies Review, 50(1), pp. 27–48.

Howard-Hassmann, R.E. and Lombardo, A.P., 2008. Reparations to Africa. Philadelphia: University of Pennsylvania Press.

Human Rights Watch, 2001. An Approach to Reparations.

International Criminal Tribunal for the Former Yugoslavia. Prosecutor v. Tadić, Appeal on Jurisdiction, 2 October 1995, 35 ILM 32 para. 141.

Israely, J., Time World, 2008. Italy pays reparations to Libya. Available at: www.time.com/time/world/article/0,8599,1838014,00.html [Accessed 11 October 2011].

Junk, J. and Miner, J.M., 2004. Compensating Historical Injustice: More than Just Money. Humanity in Action (6). Reports of the 2004 Fellows in Denmark, Germany and the Netherlands. New York, pp. 43–47.

Langbehn, V. and Salama, M., 2011. German Colonialism: Race, the Holocaust, and Postwar Germany. New York: Columbia University Press.

Lanham, J., 2003. Politics and the Past: On Repairing Historical Injustices. Blue Ridge Summit: Rowman and Littlefield Publishers.

Lovejoy, P., 2000. Transformation in Slavery: A History of Slavery in Africa, 2nd edition. Cambridge: Cambridge University Press.

MacArtney, C.A., 1968. National States and National Minorities. New York: Russell & Russell.

Osabu-Kle, D.T., 2000. The African Reparations Cry: Rationale, Estimate, Prospects, and Strategies, Journal of Black Studies, 30(3), pp. 331–350.

Posner, E.A. and Vermeule, A., 2003. Reparations for Slavery and Other Historical Injustices. Columbia Law Review, 103, pp. 689–748.

Preece, J., 1997. Minority Rights in Europe: from Westphalia to Helsinki. Review of International Studies, 23, pp. 75–95.

Randelzhofer, A., 1999. The Legal Position of the Individual under Present International Law. In: A. Randelzhofer and C. Tomuschat, eds, State Responsibility and the Individual: Reparations in Instances of Grave Violations of Human Rights. The Hague: Martinus Nijhoff, pp. 231–243.

Redfern, P., 2004. Colonialism: Britain Faces Lawsuits. The East African (Nairobi). Available at: http://allafrica.com/stories/200401270639.html [Accessed 18 November 2012].

Rodney, W., 1972. How Europe Underdeveloped Africa. London: Bogle-L'Ouverture Publications.

Roper, S.D. and Barria, L.A., 2009. Why Do States Commission the Truth? Political Considerations in the Establishment of African Truth and Reconciliation Commissions. Human Rights Review, 10(3), pp. 373–391.

Sarkin, J., 1999. The Necessity and Challenges of a Truth and Reconciliation Commission in Rwanda. Human Rights Quarterly, 21, pp. 767–823.

Sarkin, J., 2004a. Reparation for Past Wrongs: Using Domestic Courts Around the World, Especially the United States, to Pursue African Human Rights Claims. International Journal of Legal Information, 32(2), pp. 339–372.

Sarkin, J., 2004b. Pursuing Private Actors for Reparations for Human Rights Abuses Committed in Africa in the Courts of the United States of America. In: E. Doxtader and C. Villa-Vicencio, eds, To Repair the Irreparable: Reparation and Reconstruction in South Africa. Cape Town: David Philip, pp. 271–321.

Sarkin, J., 2007. Reparations for Gross Human Rights Violations in Africa: The Great Lakes. In: S. Pete and M. du Plessis, eds, Repairing the Past – International Perspectives on Reparations for Gross Human Rights Abuses. Antwerp: Intersentia, pp. 199–231.

Sarkin, J., 2008. Colonial Genocide and Reparations Claims in the 21st Century: The Socio-Legal Context of Claims Under International Law by the Herero Against Germany for Genocide in Namibia 1904–1908. Westport: Praeger.

Sarkin, J., 2009. The Origins of International Criminal Law: Its Connection to and Convergence with other Branches of International Law. Hague Justice Journal (4), pp. 15–41.

Schwerin, K., 1972. German Compensation for Victims of Nazi Persecution. Northwestern University Law Review, 67(4), pp. 479–527.

Shelton, D., 2003. The World of Atonement: Reparations For Historical Injustices, Netherlands International Law Review, pp. 289–325.

Shelton, D., 2004. The World of Atonement Reparations for Historical Injustices. Miskolc Journal of International Law, 1(2), pp. 259–289.

Shelton, D., 2005. Remedies in International Human Rights Law, 2nd edition. Oxford: Oxford University Press.

Sohn, L.B. and Buergenthal, T., 1973. International Protection of Human Rights. Indianapolis: Bobbs-Merrill.

Spitzer, R.M., 2002. The African Holocaust: Should Europe Pay Reparations to Africa for Colonialism and Slavery? Vanderbilt Journal of Transnational Law, 35, p. 1.

The Nation (Nairobi), 2006. Kenya: Ex-Mau Mau Set Date to File Case Against UK.

The Standard (Kenya), 2012. Mau Mau Case Filed Against Britain to be Heard in July.

The East African (Nairobi). Mande M. and Edwin, E., 2006. Justice for Maji Maji.

The Monitor. Mukisa, L., 2005. Court Clears UK on Bunyoro Killings.

Thipanyane, T., 2003. Current Claims, Regional Experiences, Pressing Problems: Identification of the Salient Issues and Pressing Problems in an African Post-Colonial Perspective. In: G. Ulrich and L. Krabbe Boserup, eds, Human Rights in Development: Reparations; Redressing Past Wrongs. The Hague: Kluwer Law International, pp. 33–56.

Thompson, J., 2002. Taking Responsibility for the Past: Reparation and Historical Injustice. Cambridge: Polity Press.

Torpey, J., 2003. Politics and the Past: On Repairing Historical Injustices. Lanham: Rowman and Littlefield Publishers.

Ulrich, G. and Krabbe Boserup, L., ed., 2001. Reparations: Redressing Past Wrongs, Human Rights in Development Yearbook. The Hague: Kluwer Law International.

United Nations Office for the Coordination of Humanitarian Affairs (OCHA) Integrated Regional Information Network IRIN Africa English reports, 7/2/2003.

United States Supreme Court of Justice, 1796. Ware v Hylton, 3 US (3 Dall.) 199, 279.

Wareham, R., 2003. The Popularization of the International Demand for Reparations for African People. In: R.A. Winbush, ed., 2003. Should America Pay? Slavery and the Raging Debate in Reparations. New York: Harper Collins, pp. 226–236.

Chapter 6

State compensation for victims of violent crime

David Miers[1]

Introduction

Almost all western liberal democracies make financial provision for the compensation of victims of violent crime. Largely the product of initiatives taken during the 1960s and 1970s, such arrangements now exist in Australia, Canada, the United States of America, and throughout the European Union.[2] Those initiatives were particular to their jurisdictions but they display some common originating features, and, as will be discussed below, common defining features. Many derived from their governments' desire to respond to an increasingly vocal victims' lobby that repeatedly drew attention to the perceived secondary victimization that victims suffered at the hands of criminal justice systems whose objectives and values were focused upon offenders. This critical response to the liberal ideology that informed criminal justice policy during the 1960s and 1970s politicized the experience of personal victimization as a means of questioning that policy's integrity and credibility. The perceived discrepancies between the state's treatment of offenders and of victims was, and continues to be, a powerful and persistent strand in the politics of criminal justice reform, a rhetoric which demands that it be 'rebalanced' in favour of the victim. This demand does not inevitably constitute a zero-sum game, though many of its most vocal supporters have also sought to curtail offenders' rights while arguing for an increase in victims' entitlements, for example, to be routinely informed about the investigation of the offence or to be heard at the trial via a victim impact statement. Many jurisdictions do now incorporate these and other rights for victims, though their scope and implementation remain controversial or incomplete. The allocation of public funds to compensate victims of crime thus constitutes one of the principal means by which governments can demonstrate their commitment to the amelioration of the victim's experience of crime and of contact with the criminal justice system. Of more recent significance are the responses of national and international agencies to provide or recommend the provision of compensation for the victims of terrorist violence.

This chapter falls into four sections. The first provides a broad overview of the existing provision of victim compensation within the European Union and the United States of America for criminal injuries sustained within the victim's home state and, more specifically, for injuries sustained as a result of an act of terrorism at home or abroad. The second section comments on the justifications underlying the introduction of crime victim compensation schemes while the third analyses the similarities and differences between a sample of national schemes in terms of their scope, eligibility rules and compensation function. This section draws particular attention to shifts in the compensation function of schemes in Australia, Canada and Great Britain, before the concluding section comments on the notion of a victim's 'right' to compensation. It will be recognized that in a short chapter it is not possible to do full justice to the many schemes now in operation in common and civil law countries, nor to the subtleties of the extensive literature concerning victims' rights. Also in the interests of space, and of narrative flow, I do not, when remarking on particular states' schemes, fully reference their legislative or other legal provisions. I have instead provided a list of these texts in an Annex to the chapter. Nor, unless indicated, are the schemes I identify intended to be exhaustive of any general point, but are for illustrative purposes only.

Overview

The European Union

Supranational European attention to crime victim compensation first took substantial shape in the Convention on the Compensation of Victims of Violent Crime (Council of Europe 1983a). Article 3 required the ratifying parties to compensate other member states' nationals who were injured in their territories; but the Convention achieved little (Greer 1996). Following the European Union Council conclusion in Tampere in 1999, which called for minimum standards on crime victims' access to justice and their legal protection in criminal proceedings,[3] the European Commission published a consultation paper on compensation arrangements within the member states (Commission of the European Communities 2001). Taking into consideration the findings of Mikaelsson and Wergens' (2001) comprehensive study, this consultation addressed the possible objectives of victim compensation in the European Union. The result was Council Directive 2004/80/EC relating to compensation to crime victims (European Union 2004).

In an echo of the Council of Europe's Convention, the 2004 Directive required member states to create a 'compensation mechanism' for cross-border compensation; that is, to enable nationals criminally injured in one member state to obtain compensation from that state by arrangements established in the member state in which they normally resided. By article 1:

> Member States shall ensure that where a violent intentional crime has been committed in a Member State other than the Member State where the applicant for compensation is habitually resident, the applicant shall have the right to submit the application to an authority or any other body in the latter Member State.

The Directive provided that 'access to compensation in cross-border situations' would operate on the basis of member states' existing schemes for the compensation of victims of violent crime. Where they had not established them, article 12 required member states to ensure that 'their national rules provide for the existence of a scheme on compensation to victims of violent intentional crimes committed in their respective territories, which guarantees fair and appropriate compensation to victims'. It will be seen that the Directive did not directly require every member state to establish, if they did not already exist, arrangements to compensate *their own* nationals; but this was its inevitable result.

The Directive set a compliance date of 1 July 2005, by which time member states should have set up their 'compensation mechanism' for cross-border applications,[4] and by implication their compensation schemes. Noting that most member states had already established such schemes (some in fulfilment of their obligations under the 1983 Convention), many would in this respect already be compliant at the date of the Directive; by contrast, the obligation would pose considerable difficulties for the ten accession states that had become members of the European Union on 1 May 2004. For them, crime victim compensation was only one issue within a much broader agenda concerning their criminal justice systems' compliance with European Union standards.[5] In compliance with its own obligation under article 19, the European Commission reported in early 2009 on the Directive's application. It noted that all member states except Greece had transposed the Directive and that there was a substantial degree of compliance with the requirements of article 12 (European Commission 2009, para.3.4.2). Given that the research was conducted only 12–18 months after the compliance date,[6] the Report's 'main conclusion' on the effectiveness of the cross-border compensation arrangements is hardly surprising: 'there have been very few cases to date' (European Commission 2009, para.3.3). The total of cases dealt with by both assisting and deciding authorities was 335, of which nearly a third had been handled by the British Criminal Injuries Compensation Authority. By way of comparison, that Authority receives some 60,000 applications a year arising from offences of violence in Great Britain (CICA 2012).

In 2010, under the Stockholm Programme and its Action Plan, the Commission presented a package of proposals to reinforce existing national measures aimed at ensuring that victims of crime are given non-discriminatory maximum rights across the EU, irrespective of their nationality or country of residence (European Commission 2011). In addition to the 2012 Directive replacing the 2001 Framework Decision, this 'roadmap' included a second review of the 2004 Directive (European Union 2011). The *Preparatory study for an impact assessment on future EU measures relating to compensation to crime victims* was commissioned in 2011 and reported in 2013 (GHK 2013). Its purpose is to identify (a) ways in which the implementation of the compensation Directive could be improved; (b) minimum standards for what constitutes 'fair and appropriate' compensation; and (c) legislative and non-legislative instruments appropriate for establishing such standards.[7]

Whatever the shortcomings of these cross-border arrangements there is one clear consequence of the 2004 Directive: all of the twenty-seven member states now operate schemes that compensate their residents who are victims of violent crime committed in their territory. By comparison, in December 2005, six months after its compliance date, of the then twenty-five member states only thirteen, consisting entirely of existing members,[8] had established such schemes. However, merely to count the number of schemes currently operating in Europe says nothing of their scope or operation. There continue to be important differences of detail between them in respect of such matters as the range of victimizing events, compensable persons and injuries, heads of damage and their financial limits. The fundamental point is that whatever these differences, each scheme constitutes an answer to the same set of basic questions for the design of *any* scheme: what victims are to be compensated to what level of compensation for what injuries arising from what crimes, and under what conditions can their eligibility be lawfully limited or denied? I return to these questions in section 4.

The United States of America

California created the first compensation programme in 1965 (on this and other early schemes see Edelhertz and Geis 1974). Over the next two decades most of the other states followed suit, establishing the eligibility and payment criteria that for the most part remain standard. Reporting in 1982, the President's Task Force on Victims of Crime noted that thirty-six states and the District of Columbia administered such schemes and, noting also that they were all vulnerable to budgetary pressures, recommended that 'Congress should enact legislation to provide federal funding' to assist them (United States 1982, p. 37). Enacted in 1984, the Victims of Crime Act (VOCA) sought to ensure that states had sufficient funding, but only where they were themselves willing to bear the primary financial burden; from 1986 to 2003 VOCA supplemental funding provided about a quarter of the funding for the states' schemes; now about a third. Administered by the Office for Victims of Crime (OVC) within the US Department of Justice, the Crime Victims Fund supports a range of victim services,[9] and as we shall see, imposes a number of obligations on states as conditions of its contribution to their schemes. In an interesting precursor to the European Union's cross-border arrangements, VOCA required every funded state to cover violent crime within its borders regardless of the state in which the victim was normally resident, and where the home state managed a VOCA funded scheme it was required to compensate the victim if the state in which the injury was sustained had no scheme. The federal government's role in the development of compensation schemes in the United States was therefore principally to commend and to recognize the arrangements introduced by these state-based initiatives, and to provide a small but significant amount of supplemental funding. This was at the time seen as a kind of quid pro quo for the states to cover federal crimes so that the federal government did not have to make its own arrangements. VOCA intervention was no doubt welcome to the existing schemes, but it was not until 1992 that the remaining dozen states joined the club.

In marked contrast to the position in the member states of the European Union,[10] the revenue base for the states' schemes is not 'tax dollars' but the fees and fines that their criminal justice systems impose on offenders, supplemented by the grants made by the Crime Victims Fund, itself financed by fines and penalties paid by convicted federal offenders.[11] A combined total of US$920,872,902 was paid from federal and state revenues during the two fiscal years 2009 and 2010 by way of compensation to victims, of which about a third (US$380,006,000) comprised contributions made under the Fund (Office for Victims of Crime 2011, p. 8). Each state administers its own scheme, but to be funded under VOCA it must meet certain minimum standards; schemes must, for example, reimburse the costs of the victim's medical treatment and mental health counselling, and in the cases of homicide, funeral and burial costs. Because of these conditions many of the fifty-three schemes have very similar eligibility requirements and offer comparable benefits. This convergence is accentuated by their collective membership of the *National Association of Crime Victim Compensation Boards.*[12] While emphasizing the importance of checking the exact eligibility requirements of the state scheme in question, its nationally available leaflet, *Compensation for Crime Victims*, comments that although each is slightly different, it is able to provide some general information about all of them. This would not be so easily accomplished in the case of the national schemes within the European Union.[13]

Compensation for violent acts of terrorism

Where they are sustained within the territory of a state that operates a crime victim compensation scheme, the injuries that are caused by an act of violence that might for legal reasons be treated as an act of terrorism[14] may simply fall to be compensated under its terms. This was so in the case of the bombings on the London Underground on 7 July 2005 (Miers 2006). While the Criminal Injuries Compensation Authority sought to pre-empt the inevitable pressure to resolve 7 July claims quickly by announcing that it would fast-track them and by issuing a Guide giving advice about the application procedure, the levels of compensation available to the injured victims or where they were killed, to their dependants, were the same as would apply to any crime of violence. By contrast, other countries with a history of terrorist violence may enact specific arrangements to compensate their victims, though their initial and current scope may well diverge. In Northern Ireland, where sectarian violence prompted the enactment in the mid-1950s of a sequence of compensation schemes limited to riotous behaviour, the most recent extend to injuries caused by any criminal act of violence.[15] In Spain the history of violence committed by ETA led to legislation initially in the 1980s and later in 1999,[16] though unlike Northern Ireland this jurisdiction is separate from the general system of public assistance to the victims of violent crime and sexual offences. Israel has similarly devised comprehensive legislative responses to two of the primary issues arising in the context of compensation for harm caused by terrorism. The Victims of Hostile Action (Pensions) Law 1970 provides compensation for bodily injuries suffered in terrorist attacks, as well as compensation to family members of deceased victims of terrorism, while the Property Tax and Compensation Fund Law 1961 provides compensation for property damage caused by hostile (terrorist) acts. As Sommer (2003, p. 335) notes in a comprehensive review: 'the original legislative scheme was limited to compensation for harm caused by war. When terrorism emerged as a permanent feature of the Middle East conflict, compensation was extended to civilian victims of terrorism.'[17] While there remains no state scheme for compensating victims who survive violent (non-terrorist) or personal crime (Yanay and Gal 2010), in 2009 the Israeli government introduced limited arrangements under which the dependants of a homicide victim may receive a small lump sum to cover their immediate expenses. These arrangements have not been enacted into law, and nor do they imply any rights for the dependants, but they do mark a change in the state's recognition and treatment of indirect victims (Yanay 2004).[18]

Following the 1995 Oklahoma City bombing in the United States, in 1996 Congress gave the OVC authority to use the VOCA emergency reserve fund to supplement existing grants to state crime victim compensation to cover victims of terrorism and mass violence. Some of the victims of 9/11 were compensated under their state schemes but, as is typical of them, the New York scheme makes no provision for 'non-economic loss' and imposes limits on economic loss; the compensation payable in respect of those killed or injured that day would therefore have been a small fraction of what could have been recovered in a civil action. The relevance of this comparison is that the airlines might have been liable for any negligence on their part in not sufficiently vetting those of their passengers who were instrumental in causing the injuries and loss of life had it not been for federal Public Law 107-42 Title IV: 'The purpose of this title is to provide compensation to any individual (or relatives of a deceased individual) who was physically injured or killed as a result of the terrorist-related aircraft crashes of September 11 2001.'[19] The literature analysing the genesis and implementation of the 'September 11th Victim Compensation Fund of 2001' is far too substantial even to be summarized here.[20] Concluding his comprehensive review of this unique response to those events Shapo (2005, p. 262) notes, 'in our rage, we wanted to do something – at least something *for* someone if we could not then do something *against* someone'. Apart from the individualized determination of the survivors' losses, the non-economic losses of those who died were presumed to be US$250,000, plus US$100,000 for the spouse and each dependant: no state scheme approaches these figures in cases of homicide.[21]

By definition none of the arrangements described above can apply where the state's citizens are injured by terrorist acts committed abroad, such as the Australian and British tourists who were injured in the Bali nightclub bombing in October 2002. Exceptionally, the South Australian crime victim compensation scheme is not so limited, but for all other Australian residents the federal government has in the past provided *ex gratia* payments to victims of terrorist attacks.[22] Following debates over a number of years, legislation enacted in 2012 provides statutory compensation for Australian victims of overseas terrorism events, to a maximum payment of AUS$75,000. The Act covers primary victims, that is victims who were in the place where a declared overseas terrorist act occurred and were harmed as a direct result of that act, and secondary victims, defined as a primary victim's close family members. The British government has maintained the *ex gratia* scheme it introduced after the Bali bombings to cover victims having an 'ongoing disability' arising from any other violent terrorist act occurring after that date (Ministry of Justice 2012a), the last event being the attack on the Taj Mahal Palace in Mumbai in November 2008. In future British visitors sustaining injuries in a 'designated' terrorist incident abroad will be compensable under new arrangements which will be based on the domestic scheme current at the time (Ministry of Justice 2012b).

As the United Nations' review observed, 'cross-border issues relating to acts of terrorist violence abroad may add a layer of complexity to the measures required to protect victims' access to justice and/or compensation' (United Nations 2011, para.10). Besides such matters as establishing to the home state's satisfaction the extent of the victim's injuries, not the least of these difficulties is the validation of the act as one of 'terrorism', a label that neither the home state nor the affected state might be willing to acknowledge. It is for this reason that the United States' arrangements, which reimburse expenses related directly to recovery from the terrorism event to a limit of US$150,000, require, in common with those in Australia and Great Britain, the government so to designate the act. While there is no specific compensation scheme for Canadian victims of acts of terrorism, whether committed in Canada or abroad, the federal Victims Fund provides financial assistance to Canadians victimized abroad, though this is largely limited to the reimbursement of travel expenses to return to Canada.[23] Whether directed to injuries sustained in acts of terrorist violence at home or abroad, it is clear that national compensation schemes vary substantially in scope and levels of payment. In its international review, *The Criminal Justice Response to Support Victims of Acts of Terrorism*, the United Nations Office on Drugs and Crime commented (United Nations 2011, para.296):

> based on the principle of equality, victims of acts of terrorism are not ontologically more deserving of compensation than victims of other crimes in proportion to the harm suffered. However, it must be recognized that the reality of certain criminal acts causing large-scale victimization requires a differentiated approach. Through relevant national procedures, financial compensation may be sought from the offender or other available sources, including, where applicable, national funds of compensation to victims.

Justifying state compensation for victims of crime

When national victim compensation schemes were introduced throughout common law jurisdictions in the 1960s and 1970s their promoters were at pains to justify this novel allocation of public funds to meet the gap between the victim's theoretical civil remedy against the offender and the unreality of its enforcement: 'in an ideal world, it should be the offender who compensates the victim' (Home Office 2005, p. 14). The President's Task Force on Victims of Crime commented (United States 1982, p. 39):

> the philosophical basis for these programs varies from a legal tort theory, whereby the state is seen to have failed to protect its citizens adequately, to a humanitarian rationale through which all citizens should receive assistance for their compelling needs, to a by-products theory that recognizes victim satisfaction as a benefit to the criminal justice system. In reality, most programs represent a mixture of these rationales.

See discussion in Miers (2007), and Elias (1983) for a critical contemporary account of the justifications that were offered by the schemes' promoters. Later, the European Commission's Green Paper argued that in the absence of known offenders with means or of private insurance, victims of personal violence could be considered 'as being in a worse situation than other groups who suffer injury or losses of various kind, for example, due to illness, accidents, or unemployment'.[24] The function of state compensation schemes can be considered, it concluded, 'as providing a safety net for victims' (Commission of the European Communities 2001, para.4.1). Although the state has always rejected the notion that it is vicariously liable for the acts of offenders, the simple and repeated justification for the introduction, for example, of the British scheme in 1964, that 'it is right to do so', continues to underpin the present arrangements. 'Compensation is given to victims of violent crime in recognition of a sense of public sympathy for the pain and suffering of the victim' (Ministry of Justice 2012c, para.149). Sympathy (identifying with another's loss) is reflected in the ethical value, empathy (understanding of another's loss), which also strongly underpinned the Council of Europe's 1983 thinking, that compensation was a matter of social solidarity (Council of Europe 1983a, Preamble; Buck 2005, pp. 150–154). This is also evident in its Guidelines for the protection of victims of terrorism: 'Recalling the necessity for states, notably for reasons of equity and social solidarity, to ensure that victims of terrorist acts can obtain compensation' (Council of Europe 2005, Preamble, (g)).

Underlying these ethical assertions is an argument from social justice that draws on elements of the doctrinal arguments summarized by the President's Task Force. This is that we can construe the assumption of a responsibility to compensate crime victims to be a concomitant of the notion of 'civic trust': 'Justice depends on the public having trust in the system' (Ministry of Justice 2012c, para.22). To experience violent crime is to experience a failure in a condition of social justice which citizens are encouraged to hold, that the state can reliably meet their reasonable expectations for the prevention and prosecution of crime (de Greiff 2006, pp. 461–464; Matravers 2010). This failure requires not only the mobilization of the criminal justice system against offenders, and their denunciation, but also monetary recognition of that experience. Although not explicit, state compensation may also recognize that, unlike those that are accidentally or even negligently caused, the crime victim's injuries are, paradigmatically in the case of intentional conduct, *personal:* the offender's intention was, typically, to hurt *this* victim. This also differentiates them from the victims of property crime precisely because the offender's ill will is in those cases (primarily) directed against an inanimate object. It is this feature of *personal* animus that makes the offender's behaviour morally objectionable and that justifies treating the offence as a public wrong and as the occasion for public censure. It is, additionally, the *individuation* of the offence as reflected in the pain and suffering of *being* a victim of violent crime, and not just of a serious injury, that arguably characterizes the state's unique response to these particular injuries.[25]

A rather different justification underlies the European Union's 2004 Directive requiring member states to establish a 'compensation mechanism' to deal with cross-border applications. Stemming from the decision of the Court of Justice in *Cowan v Le Tresor Public*,[26] the objective is to remove obstacles to the free movement of persons and services. Tourists (such as Cowan), employees of companies located across the Community and other 'natural persons' should be protected from harm in the member state that they are visiting on the same basis as anyone else residing there. The Court held that 'Measures to facilitate compensation to victims of crimes should form part of the realization of this objective' (European Union 2004, Preamble, para.2). Whatever their justification, their legal base will reflect the particular state's juridical characteristics, as the United Nations commented in its review of victim compensation schemes. 'The observation of national legislation and practice on the treatment of victims in the criminal justice system is obviously not an abstract exercise and must respect the specificities of national systems. The choice of predominantly adversarial or inquisitorial procedural models, for example, may determine the form of victim participation and, more generally, the role of victims in the criminal trial. Equally, the scope of application of the right to compensation varies considerably, taking into account the relationship with insurance law' (United Nations 2011, para.52). In the following section I aim to address the variations in the provision of compensation.

Defining characteristics of national crime victim compensation schemes

It is clearly impossible in a single chapter to review the details of all of the schemes that have been touched on so far, let alone the many others now operating across the common and civil law worlds. But it is possible to remark on the three defining characteristics of *any* scheme and to illustrate important similarities and differences between particular schemes' understanding of those characteristics. They are: the scope of 'a criminal injury', their approach to undeserving victims, and the injuries and losses that they cover. These similarities and differences in turn reflect each state's conception of its scheme's compensation function. Broadly speaking this has been located at a point along a continuum between a welfare function and the provision of a (taxpayer funded) surrogate for the victim's theoretical civil remedy against the offender. More recently some states have questioned the value of compensation payments akin to those available in civil proceedings, preferring to redirect public funds to the immediate amelioration of the victim's losses. This questioning has become sharper as states seek to cut their expenditure in the interests of sovereign debt deficit reduction.

The scope of 'a criminal injury'

National victim compensation schemes universally apply to victims of violent crime; in the United States in 2010/11 the majority 'were victims of assault, homicide, and child abuse (including sexual and physical abuse)' (Office for Victims of Crime 2011, p. 8). By article 1 the European Directive applies to 'violent intentional crime' and as the Commission noted in its report, all respondent member states confirmed that their schemes covered this category of victims (Commission of the European Communities 2009, pp. 8–9).[27] Opinions differ on the value of specifying what constitutes a 'violent crime'. Many schemes, including those in Australia, the European Union and the United States, do no more than give examples of crimes that they typically cover. The British scheme, for example, simply provides that a crime of violence is a crime which involves 'a physical attack', which in limited circumstances may include 'an animal attack', or 'a threat against a person, causing fear of immediate violence in circumstances which would cause a person of reasonable firmness to be put in such fear'. In the United States 'violent crime' expressly extends to federal crime and to injuries on tribal lands or military premises. Open phrases can result in uncertain application; which can be remedied, at the risk of over- or under-inclusion, by reference, as in British Columbia and Ontario, to 'prescribed offences' in the Canadian Criminal Code. In addition to those who might be regarded as the primary victim of a crime of violence, a majority of the European Union's member states' schemes extend to injuries sustained by secondary victims; that is, persons who themselves suffer (typically mental) injury on seeing a (closely) related direct victim sustain a criminal injury. This is not to be confused with claims by persons who are responsible for the welfare and claim on behalf of the primary victim, or who in the case of a homicide are the victim's dependants (or survivors). Where secondary victims sustain criminal injuries they are, of themselves, eligible victims under these schemes.

In addition to offences of personal violence some schemes specifically include the injuries a person sustains when engaging in an act of law enforcement, whether they are good citizens going to the aid of the police or criminal justice employees whose actions go above and beyond the call of duty. Often these injuries will in any event be the result of a crime of violence, but as a corollary of the notion of civic trust such victims too may be singled out as deserving of financial recognition; their inclusion in some common law schemes being a legacy of their initial establishment.[28] Beyond the paradigm case of violence between strangers, a sensitive point of difference between national schemes has been their approach to domestic violence. Within the European Union such provision has traditionally been subsumed within the general definition of violent crime (Bochmann and Griesham 1999). But in response to concerns about fraud and the possibility of the award ending up in the offender's hands, claims arising from domestic violence are often subject to additional eligibility requirements; for example, that the offender be prosecuted or convicted,[29] requirements also to be found in the Australian states' schemes (Barrett-Mayering 2010). These considerations largely describe the former position in the United States, but in enacting VOCA Congress insisted that to qualify for federal funding a state scheme was obliged to include victims of domestic violence; in 2010–11 around 30% per cent of all assault-related claims were of this origin. The OVC has a similar concern about benefitting the offender, but schemes must not deny these claimants solely because they share a residence with the offender or because they are members of the same family; though they may if the payment would substantially 'unjustly enrich' an offender. The United States' schemes are also distinctive in their coverage of injuries caused by drunk driving; this too is an OVC requirement, as not all schemes in the 1980s covered this offence. Where the offender is insured the schemes are not engaged; in contrast road traffic injuries in other common law countries and in the European Union are included only where the vehicle was itself being used as a weapon.

For reasons touched on earlier, national victim compensation schemes do not extend to victims of property crime. A robbery victim may be compensated for the mental trauma of being threatened with a firearm, *a fortiori* if the weapon is used against him/her, but not for the stolen property. Nor is a victim of burglary or criminal damage to her house compensable for the trauma caused by those crimes against property, though in many United States' schemes he/she may be eligible for a single 'crime-scene clean up' payment; for example, California (US$1,000), Texas (US$750) and New Jersey (US$4,000). The federal rules do not prohibit compensation for property offences but they do prohibit the use of federal funds to pay for them (Office for Victims of Crime 2001); very few states will compensate them from their own funds. But in common with schemes in Australia, Canada and the European Union, federal funds can be used, in the words of the British scheme, to pay for 'property or equipment, which was relied on by the applicant as a physical aid and which was lost or damaged as a result of the incident giving rise to the injury'. The loss of or damage to such items as spectacles and medical and dental prostheses may indeed not be thought of at all as crimes against 'property', but, given their purpose, as offences against the person who relies upon them. Interestingly, VOCA funding in the United States also requires schemes to cover costs relating to physical injury or death that might be involved in crimes involving damage to religious property, especially when racially motivated; but this does not extend to the property damage itself. The Final Guidelines emphasize that priority under VOCA continues to be coverage for victims of violent crime (Office for Victims of Crime 2001).

Eligibility: innocent, blameless victims

One of the fundamental policy questions to be answered in the creation of any crime victim compensation scheme is how it deals with victims who, by virtue of their personal characteristics or conduct resemble, or have been, offenders. This is a conceptual problem because the differentiation between 'offenders' and 'victims' is confounded by the complexities inherent in individual and societal responses to suffering. Persons who suffer harm or injury are not 'victims' in and of themselves, but as a result of complex social and forensic interactions which label them so (Miers 2000). It is also factually problematic because the reality of criminal victimization is that many victims have also been offenders and that in particular incidents it may be a matter of chance as to which of two protagonists the criminal justice process subsequently labels the 'victim'. Both of these problems challenge what has often been the political motivation underpinning these schemes: to compensate 'innocent', 'blameless' or, as Nils Christie (1986) famously coined them, 'ideal' victims. These are stereotypically children, the elderly and the law abiding, whose lives are disrupted by stereotypically predatory, young, male offenders. These stereotypes are just that, but they play a powerful role in populist demands for 'justice' for victims of crime, a role that is accentuated where the scheme is funded by the taxpayer.

Almost without exception, criminal injury compensation schemes will either exclude altogether or reduce any compensation that might be payable to victims who in some way contributed to the incident in which their injuries were sustained. The NACVCB's brochure, which relates to all of the United States' schemes, provides that the victim must 'not have committed a criminal act or some substantially wrongful act that caused or contributed to the crime'.[30] Article 7 of the European Commission's minimum standards for national compensation schemes provides that 'member states may reduce or refuse compensation on grounds of the behaviour of the applicant in direct relation to the event that caused the injury or death'; and the review of the 2004 Directive found that with two exceptions (Latvia and Slovakia), all member states did so provide (Matrix Insight 2008a, p. 43). Similarly, all of the schemes in the Australian states and territories require that 'the victim's conduct before and at the time of the offence did not contribute to their injury' (Barrett-Mayering 2010, p. 8), while the substance of the Ontario legislation, 'in determining whether to make an order for compensation and the amount thereof, the Board shall have regard to all relevant circumstances, including any behaviour of the victim that may have directly or indirectly contributed to his or her injury or death' is typical of the Canadian schemes.

Much more contentious is the question whether 'a life of crime' should also result in the refusal or reduction of a claim where the injury is wholly unconnected with that life. Here the European Commission's minimum standards are silent, although it is clear from its language that article 7 is not to be read as extending to cases of this sort, but is to be confined to the notion of contributory negligence, a basic principle of tort law that depends on causation. By contrast paragraph 3 of article 8 of the Council of Europe's Convention provides that 'compensation may also be reduced or refused if an award or a full award would be contrary to a sense of justice or to public policy (*ordre public*)' (Council of Europe 1983a). The 2008 analysis of twenty-four member states' schemes found that only six answered the question 'does your scheme provide that a claimant who has a criminal record may be refused compensation or receive a reduced amount?' in the affirmative (Matrix Insight 2008a, p. 44). This minority view is seen also in the United States, where of the fifty-three current schemes, six provide for mandatory and three for discretionary exclusion of victims with criminal records.[31] A review of schemes in Australia and Canada suggests that, like the majority, claim rejection or reduction in an award is limited to cases in which the victim contributed to or was committing an offence at the time of the incident causing the injury.[32]

Good citizens also co-operate with the police, the prosecuting authorities and their state's compensation authority, so all schemes provide that failure to meet these eligibility requirements may result in claim rejection or reduction. But they also recognize that in the circumstances of the particular crime, notably sexual assault, or of the particular victim, notably children, it may be inappropriate to insist on strict adherence, for example, to reporting requirements. Almost all of the United States' schemes specify a reporting period, typically within seventy-two hours of the incident. By contrast, schemes in Australia, Canada and some member states of the European Union prefer the narrative requirement, 'within a reasonable time', 'as soon as reasonably practicable', or 'without delay'; but whether time-specific or narrative, schemes can provide, in the words of the revised scheme introduced in Great Britain in 2012, that 'particular account will be taken of: (a) the age and capacity of the applicant at the date of the incident; and (b) whether the effect of the incident on the applicant was such that it could not reasonably have been reported earlier'. Insistence on the victim's compliance with these reporting requirements is necessary primarily because no scheme requires the offender to have been convicted of an offence arising from the violent incident; indeed, it will often be the case that the offender is unidentified. What schemes will require is credible, that is, on the balance of probabilities, independent evidence of the incident and the injury, perhaps via a witness, and certainly by reference to police and medical records. Thereafter they will also expect the victim to co-operate in the police or prosecuting authorities' investigation, on pain of claim rejection or reduction in any award. The subsequent application for compensation is also subject to a limitation period, typically one to three years after the incident; but here too, as in the case of late-discovered child sexual abuse, a scheme may waive this requirement or, as in the Australian states, run the limitation period from the victim's eighteenth birthday.

Compensable losses and injuries

Broadly speaking, victim compensation schemes distinguish actual losses arising from the injury from payments for the injury itself, a distinction that reflects what in common law jurisdictions constitute respectively special and general damages, and in civil law, material and immaterial losses. All schemes compensate those victims who survive the crime of violence and, in cases of homicide, their dependants; but there is wide variation between them in respect of the particular losses and injuries that will be compensated, their methods of assessment and of the level of awards.

Under the category of 'losses', the vast majority of schemes reimburse reasonable medical expenses where free public health provision does not already cover them. In the United States this and the costs of mental health counselling for crime victims are conditions of federal funding (Office for Victims of Crime 2001), which, with dental treatment constitute more than 50% per cent of all payments (Office for Victims of Crime 2011, p. 8). Similarly, all of the Australian states and territories cover medical and counselling expenses (Barrett-Mayering 2010, p. 4), as do a majority of the Canadian provinces.[33] Unlike the Council of Europe, which stated that 'compensation shall cover' medical and hospitalization expenses (Council of Europe 1983a, para.4), the European Union's 2004 Directive does not specify what is to be included as 'material' losses. It does this for the same underlying reason that informs its entire approach to the assessment of compensation: to respect and reflect national laws. But article 12(2) does require national schemes to provide 'fair and appropriate compensation', which the European Commission's research confirmed did in most cases cover medical expenses (Commission of the European Communities 2009, p. 9; Matrix Insight 2008a, p. 48). Because of the availability of free health care, the British scheme does not compensate medical expenses unless the injuries are long-term or disabling, when, in common with a number of schemes in Australia, Canada and other European Union member states, awards may be made to cover, for example, adaptations to the victim's home, the provision of additional care, or rehabilitation (Matrix Insight 2008a, p. 49). In the United States awards for such 'special expenses' are not a condition of federal funding, but awards for building modification and equipment to accommodate physical disabilities resulting from a compensable crime may be made from VOCA funds.

The second principal loss the victim may experience is loss of earnings and earning capacity. Here VOCA funding mandates payments for lost wages, as do all Australian states and territories (Barrett-Mayering 2010, p. 4). Of the twenty-five member states that responded to the European Commission's research project, twenty-two covered loss of earnings, and of these eighteen provided additional compensation for future loss; four did not compensate for either loss (Matrix Insight 2008a, p. 49). There is also a mixed picture in Canada, reflecting the differing approaches its provinces have adopted: British Columbia and Ontario cover both loss of earnings and earning capacity; New Brunswick and Nova Scotia do not. A fundamental policy question that arises in connection with awards for these losses is whether schemes should fund victims who were, prior to the injury, high earners. The Council of Europe's Explanatory Report on the 1983 Convention noted that compensation for the losses and injuries stipulated by a national scheme in compliance with article 4 were 'to be calculated by the State paying the compensation according to the scales normally applied for social security or private insurance or according to normal practice under civil law' (Council of Europe 1983b, para.28). But recognizing that where a scheme is funded by the taxpayer it may be thought objectionable that high earners should be compensated at public expense, article 7 provides: 'Compensation may be reduced or refused on account of the applicant's financial situation.' As the Explanatory Report comments, 'since compensation of the victim from public funds is an act of social solidarity, it may be unnecessary [to compensate lost earnings] where the victim or his dependants are plainly comfortably off' (Council of Europe 1983b, para.32). One of the ways in which limits may be set is, as has always been the case in the British scheme,[34] to cap the *rate* at which loss of earnings is calculated. But the most common is to cap the *amount* that is payable. This can, in turn, be achieved either by imposing a maximum on any award for the loss of (future) earnings, and/or by imposing a maximum on the total award, including any other compensated losses or injuries. About one half of European Union member states specifically limit loss of earnings awards, but almost all impose an upper limit on the total payable award (Matrix Insight 2008a, pp. 50–51). In the United States all schemes impose a limit on the total award that may be made, and nearly every state has limits below the maximum on some specific expenses, including lost wages;[35] a similar picture exists in the Australian schemes,[36] while those Canadian schemes that cover loss of earnings rely on an overall maximum, with the exception of Ontario which also imposes a specific limit.

Where the criminal injury is fatal, it appears that all schemes reimburse funeral expenses; in the United States this is a condition of federal funding. But provision for what is likely to be the dependants' principal financial loss, the loss of dependency on or support from the victim's income, is not universal, and where it is covered there are considerable differences in the levels of payment. Within the European Union fifteen of the twenty-three member states that responded to the review of the 2004 Directive compensate for loss of dependency, and as noted above they all impose limits on payments either for this loss or for all compensable losses. The Australian schemes that cover loss of dependency similarly impose financial or other limits,[37] as do some Canadian schemes;[38] while in an echo of the British scheme Manitoba and Quebec apply a cap on the rate at which the victim's loss of earnings is to be assessed.[39] VOCA funding requires payments for loss of support; here too there are many variations, though they are all subject to the state's own overall upper limit.[40]

Whether it provides compensation for the injury itself has historically depended on the state's conception of the place that its scheme should occupy along the continuum between a welfare function and the provision of a (taxpayer funded) surrogate for the victim's theoretical civil remedy against the offender. The paradigm of the civil remedy surrogate has been the British scheme which, until 1995, compensated surviving victims' pain and suffering largely according to the principles applicable at common law. In part because it was now considered inappropriate that public funds should compensate on the same basis as judicial decisions fixing financial responsibility on insured defendants, and in part for reasons of financial exigency, a new, statutory scheme was introduced in 1996. This provides for payment to be made on the basis of a tariff of awards that groups together injuries of comparable severity to which a financial value is attached; the minimum level is £1,000 and the maximum for a single injury, even after the major restructuring in 2012, remains £250,000 (Miers 2013). When they were first introduced, the Canadian common law schemes also resembled the surrogate model (Burns 1992); subject in each case to a financial limit; this remains the case in Alberta (CAN$110,000), Ontario (CAN$25,000), Prince Edward Island (CAN$15,000) and New Brunswick (CAN$1,000), the schemes in British Columbia and Saskatchewan now being confined to special damages.[41] All of the Australian jurisdictions provide awards for elements of non-financial loss, though the range of compensable injuries varies. In its table of compensable injuries to which standard amounts of compensation are prescribed (minimum AUS$2,400, maximum AUS$50,000), the New South Wales scheme resembles the British tariff model. A variant is a connotative definition of the compensable injuries, as those that involve 'extremely severe injury' (Australian Capital Territory) or have a 'significant adverse effect' on the victim (Queensland, Victoria), again with corresponding tariff values subject to financial limits of AUS$50,000 and AUS$10,000 respectively for the most severe or significant injuries (Barrett-Mayering 2010, pp. 6–7). Finally, some Australian states simply provide that limited awards may be made for pain and suffering.[42]

Within the civil law tradition 'immaterial loss' contemplates injuries to a person's body, health, liberty or other personal rights for which financial redress may be sought. This may be undertaken either via civil proceedings against the offender or by means of the claimant's formal status as a party to the criminal proceedings against the offender, at the conclusion of which, if convicted, the offender may be ordered to pay compensation. As noted, the 2004 Directive requires national schemes to provide 'fair and appropriate' compensation, but does not define its content. As the European Commission's research found, all but two of its respondents considered that their schemes did meet this requirement, although there was inevitably a wide range of understanding among them. A number indicated that payments for 'immaterial loss' were made in accordance with a tariff based on such criteria as days lost through sickness or a hierarchy of injury categories, at levels reflecting social security legislation for equivalent injuries, or that provided the same levels of compensation for all claimants, though it was not clear whether this meant all claimants for criminal injury compensation or claimants for all other kinds of injury, such as medical negligence or road traffic injuries (Matrix Insight 2008a, pp. 44–47). In any event, as noted earlier, the vast majority of schemes impose a maximum amount of compensation that can be paid to an individual claimant.

The compensation function

As the preceding paragraphs indicate, a state's conception of the compensation function its criminal injury scheme is to perform is reflected in its focus and in the financial limits that it imposes. It is also the case that, in part for reasons of financial exigency, states have come to reconsider where that focus should lie.

In stark contrast with the position in the European Union and in other common law countries, only two of the United States' schemes compensate for pain and suffering, a defining element of the civil remedy against the offender, and only then to a very limited extent: Hawaii (maximum of US$2,000), and Tennessee, for sexual offences only, with a maximum of US$3,000.[43] There is no mention of compensation for general damages in the VOCA funding arrangements, nor, in the case of fatal criminal injuries, is there any compensation for bereavement in favour of the victim's close family or dependants. This is typically a fixed sum, commonly found in the European Union's schemes (Matrix Insight 2008a, p. 50),[44] but interestingly, only in some of those other common law jurisdictions that adopted the civil remedy model.[45] In the case of the United States these omissions reflect the fact that having no universal state or federal social insurance provision, its victim compensation schemes focused on the actual, the 'hard' costs of crime (medical and dental bills, etc.). The original state-level schemes thus performed a welfare function (Edelhertz and Geis 1974), which in turn became the federal conception of victim compensation under VOCA. Some make provision for replacement services for work that the victim is unable to perform because of the injury (primarily child-care and housekeeping) and for rehabilitation, which may include physical therapy and/or job therapy, but these are essentially welfare functions performed in the absence of free public access to such services. Whether 'Obamacare' will prompt any reconsideration of state schemes' compensation function remains to be seen.

By 1983 all of the Australian states and territories had enacted schemes that, while imposing upper limits, provided compensation for special, and elements of general, damages. But like Great Britain, the financial pressures occasioned by both the level of awards and the schemes' administrative costs drove a number to introduce tariffs or to make substantial reductions in their scope and compensation levels.[46] These retrenchments were accompanied by greater emphasis on recovery from the offender (Freckelton 2001),[47] while many of the present arrangements were stated in the context of new and more comprehensive legislative provision for victim services. In Canada, too, fiscal considerations prompted changes that were also the product of a change in policy. This was that there were more effective responses to the here-and-now of victimization than delayed compensation. Compensation schemes that seek to stand in for the offender, even where there are upper limits on awards that would be inapplicable in a civil action, inevitably suffer from many of its disadvantages. Delay (encouraging compensation neurosis), complexity in the calculation of awards and the generation of unrealistic expectations about their amount are long-standing issues. Such schemes also perpetuate a more profound philosophy: that postponed awards (however hard the scheme's administrators seek to decide claims quickly) are an appropriate response to personal victimization. In 1996 Victoria and in 2002 British Columbia shifted the focus of their schemes from financial compensation to benefits targeted to victims' immediate needs, such as crime scene clean-up and vouchers for travel to work or psychiatric counselling, the Nova Scotia scheme being limited entirely to such counselling.

Perhaps the most radical recent change has been the revisions to the British scheme made in 2012. In an earlier consultation the Home Office had proposed that victims of 'non-serious' crimes would no longer be the recipients of state compensation, but would instead be eligible for a 'menu' of services to be delivered by Victim Care Units. This menu would comprise two elements, the first being the provision of emotional support, to include counselling; the second addressing more immediate needs, such as hardship payments, vouchers for taxis to work where the injury left the victim unable to drive, personal alarms and target hardening the victim's house following a burglary (Home Office 2005, pp. 27–28; Miers 2006). Published shortly after the London terrorist bombings in July 2005, there was no further action, but the urgency of national deficit reduction has since then prompted radical surgery. The 2012 scheme has eliminated the lowest and revalued downwards a middle range of tariff bands, excluding perhaps half of the number of hitherto successful claimants, focusing instead on those victims sustaining serious and disabling injuries. It has also reset the rate at which loss of earnings and dependency will be calculated to statutory sick pay, thus bringing crime victims in line with any other victim of any other disabling injury. As the scheme retains some elements of a civil remedy (notably an award for bereavement in fatal cases) and retains the same tariff values for the most serious injuries, this new model may be conceived as a form of enhanced social welfare (Miers 2013).[48]

Whether the state conceives that its scheme should do no more than perform a welfare function or should contemplate a broader notion of social justice that adopts some elements of what the victim could receive in a civil action for damages, all schemes require the deduction of any publicly funded benefits to which the victim, or in fatal cases, the dependants, are entitled. It is axiomatic that any compensation that the victim or the dependants recover from the offender, for example by means of a court order on conviction, must be deducted; and it may be that the benefits that they receive under private insurance may also fall to be deducted in full. In the European Union all but one member state answered affirmatively the question whether their scheme 'made deductions to the value of compensation paid due to other payments received by the claimant to compensate them' (Matrix Insight 2008a, p. 54). While they display important differences in their scope, all of the Canadian schemes require any provincial or federal collateral benefits to be taken into account, as do those in Australia. In the United States the 'payer of last resort' injunction is explicit – the Office for Crime Victims (2001) states that:

When a victim is eligible to receive benefits from a federal program such as Veterans' benefits, Medicare, and Social Security Disability or federally financed state or local program, such as Medicaid the state compensation program shall not use VOCA funds to pay costs that another federal or federally financed program covers.

The differences between a welfare and a civil remedy (or elements thereof) function are seen also in the financial limits on awards, although for all states there will inevitably be budgetary limitations. Taken as a whole, the United States' schemes, which are constrained by both state and federal funding,[49] cover the same major types of loss (but not the injury itself) as do the civil remedy models. But the maximum benefits are generally very low even by comparison with the 2012 revisions to the British scheme, which range from £1,000 (US$1,600) for the least to £250,000 (US$400,000) for the most serious, single injury, with a maximum of £500,000 (US$800,000) for the total award.[50] The majority of awards in the United States have a US$25,000 limit, in a range between US$10,000 and US$50,000; a few states have higher maxima for 'catastrophic' injuries, though these too show considerable variation.[51] Its schemes thus present a very different financial picture to that in Great Britain, clearly revealed by their respective expenditure figures. As noted earlier, in the two fiscal years 2009 and 2010 the total of payments made by all schemes in the United States was, in broad terms, US$921 million to some 329,000 claimants (average US$2,800; Office for Victims of Crime 2011, p. 8). In the same period, the British scheme made payments of around £490 million (US$784 million) to some 61,330 claimants (average £8,000; CICA 2010, 2011). A very crude comparison shows that if the number of awards in the United States bore the same ratio to its population as its population does to that of Great Britain (5:1), the annual total would be closer to 825,000 claimants, at an annual cost of US$2,301 million (£1,386 million). I have not attempted here to draw any comparisons with the position across the European Union. The picture in terms of the numbers of victims of recorded crimes of violence and resulting claims, together with the intricacies of member states' national compensation schemes, makes such an exercise exceedingly difficult and too complex for this chapter.[52]

A right to compensation

To say that victims have a 'right' to a named (beneficial) provision is to say that they have an enforceable expectation that where their circumstances fall within the factual scope of a rule having legal force an agent of the state will in turn have the authority and the obligation to apply the rule's provision to them. It is plainly the case in civil and common law that victims have a right to be compensated by those who cause them personal injury, and that the courts (or other judicial bodies) have both the authority and the obligation to enforce that right where the offender's liability is determined according to law. And it is worth remarking that here, unlike the case of imposing a fine upon conviction, the civil court has no duty to consider the impact of the order for damages on the offender, who may, in consequence, be bankrupted. What then should be the role of the state where the offender is unknown or impecunious? As we saw earlier, though many states have enacted criminal injury schemes funded by the taxpayer or by financial penalties or surcharges imposed on convicted offenders, none has accepted that this provision follows from a legal duty upon the state to arrange for the compensation of crime victims from public funds. Where the question has been raised, states have emphatically rejected any notion that they are (vicariously) responsible in law for the offender's behaviour, whether because, for example, of reductions in police resources or the failure of their criminal justice systems to reduce reoffending.

The introduction to this chapter suggested that one interpretation of a state's motivation behind the introduction of a victim compensation scheme was to respond to popular criticism of liberal criminal or penal justice policies; and this arguably remains the case (Spalek 2006, ch.2; and see the policy background to the changes to the British scheme, Miers 2013). In its review of its member states' provision of compensation for acts of terrorism, the United Nations commented (United Nations 2011, p. 53):

> It should be noted that many legal systems have statutory provisions concerning the rights of victims. This is the case, for example, in Canada and the United States, where there is also a civil society movement endeavouring to obtain constitutional rights for victims. In adversarial models, in particular, where the equality of arms between prosecution and the defence is of central significance, victim participation is limited in order to secure respect for the rights of the accused, which are often of constitutional rank, in conformity with international standards.

Some commentators are indeed wary of efforts to 'equalize' procedural rights for victims at the expense of defendants' long-established criminal justice rights (Ashworth 2000; and see discussion in Hall 2009, ch.2). But the allocation of public funds to the compensation of crime victims hardly threatens any inequalities between them; indeed, as many commentators (and especially the cynics) have observed, the enactment of such schemes may help to neutralize opposition to liberal policies (Goodey 2005, ch.5; Kirchengast 2006, ch.9). This is a process that in earlier writing I have characterized as the politicization of deserving or innocent victims (Miers 2000).

Whereas the earliest common law schemes were enacted alongside other legislative efforts to address criminal justice concerns, some of the revisions introduced in Australia and a majority of those now in force in Canada were explicitly made in the context of the wider provision of victim services. Their incorporation into this provision can also be construed as a further concomitant of the notion of 'civic trust': that the state's failure reliably to meet citizens' reasonable expectations for the prevention of crime requires not just monetary recognition but active steps to assist them to deal with its consequences. In terms of popular demands that offenders should be required to make reparation for their offences, for example by strengthening the sentencing court's power to order the offender to pay compensation to the victim, this provision has even greater potency where its funding is drawn in whole or part from victim surcharges or more general financial penalties imposed on offenders. As we have seen, these penalties constitute the tax base for VOCA funding of the United States' schemes, as is also the case with the Canadian provincial schemes.[53] In 2012 the British government increased the scope and levels of the victim's surcharge levied against convicted offenders, but there is no equivalent in the 2012 Directive.[54]

We may therefore say that where they fall within the terms of an enacted scheme, victims have a 'right' to be compensated as a matter of the positive law. The central question then is, compensation for what? Debates about victims' rights largely centre on three matters: the scope of the factual circumstances set out in the relevant rule, the scope of the benefit to which the eligible victim is entitled and the consequences of the agent's failure to apply the rule according to law (see generally Doak 2007; Hall 2009, 2010). For example, in the instance of decisions taken by public prosecutors as to the charge to be preferred against an offender, there will be debate about the nature and timing of any information to be given to the victim (or possibly to the victim's family), the opportunity, if any, and scope of any consultation about the charge, and so on. Similar issues arise in the case of victim impact statements: when and in what circumstances are such statements permitted and what cognizance must the court give to them? And as consumers of these and other services (Rock 2004, ch.4), what remedies do victims enjoy where the prosecutor, court or other criminal justice agency fail to meet their obligations? As we have seen, in the case of criminal injury compensation these debates centre on the questions who is to be regarded as an eligible victim of what kinds of criminal injuries, for what range of economic and non-economic losses, and to what level will eligible victims be compensated? Underpinning the answers, which should include some appeal or review mechanism should the agency fail to apply the scheme to eligible claims, these schemes are publicly funded, hypothecated from criminal fines and penalties or directly from general taxation. Accordingly (a) their scope is to be informed by broader considerations generated by public and governmental ambitions for the criminal justice system, and (b) they are subject to the same process for determining its value for money as is any other publicly funded social policy. These considerations may severely limit how these substantive questions are to be answered. A victim may well have a legally enforceable right to benefit from compensation, but in some cases it will be a right to very little.

Annex: legislative instruments

Australia

Federal

Social Security Amendment (Supporting Australian Victims of Terrorism Overseas) Act 2012 (22 July 2012, No. 106).
www.comlaw.gov.au/Details/C2012A00106

State

NEW SOUTH WALES

Victims Support and Rehabilitation Act 1996
www.austlii.edu.au/au/legis/nsw/consol_act/vsara1996372/

SOUTH AUSTRALIA

Victims of Crime Act 2001
www.legislation.sa.gov.au/LZ/C/A/Victims%20of%20Crime%20Act%202001.aspx

TASMANIA

Victims of Crime Assistance Act 1976
www.austlii.edu.au/au/legis/tas/consol_act/vocaa1976271/

VICTORIA

Victims of Crime Assistance Act 1996 No. 81 of 1996
www.austlii.edu.au/au/legis/vic/consol_act/vocaa1996271/

WESTERN AUSTRALIA

Criminal Injuries Compensation Act 2003
www.austlii.edu.au/au/legis/wa/consol_act/cica2003321/

Canada

Federal

Justice for Victims of Terrorism Act S.C. 2012, c. 1, s. 2
http://laws-lois.justice.gc.ca/eng/acts/J-2.5/page-1.html
On Canada generally see Department of Justice Canada
www.justice.gc.ca/eng/pi/pcvi-cpcv/prov.html

Provincial

ALBERTA

Victims of Crime Act of 1997 Revised Statutes of Alberta 2000 Chapter V-3
www.qp.alberta.ca/documents/Acts/v03.pdf

BRITISH COLUMBIA

British Columbia (Criminal Injury Compensation Act [RSBC 1996] Chapter 85) superseded by the Crime Victim Assistance Act [SBC 2001] ch 38
www.bclaws.ca/EPLibraries/bclaws_new/document/ID/freeside/00_01038_01
Crime Victim Assistance Act, Crime Victim Assistance (General) Regulation
www.bclaws.ca/EPLibraries/bclaws_new/document/ID/freeside/10_161_2002

MANITOBA

The Victims' Bill of Rights, CCSM c V55
www.canlii.org/en/mb/laws/stat/ccsm-c-v55/latest/ccsm-c-v55.html
The Victims' Bill of Rights Amendment Act (Denying Compensation to Offenders and Other Amendments) S.M.2010, c. 45
http://web2.gov.mb.ca/laws/statutes/2010/c04510e.php

NEW BRUNSWICK

Victims Services Act, SNB 1987, c V-2.1
www.canlii.org/en/nb/laws/stat/snb-1987-c-v-2.1/latest/snb-1987-c-v-2.1.html

NOVA SCOTIA

Victims' Rights and Services Act Chapter 14 of the Acts of 1989
http://nslegislature.ca/legc/statutes/victims.htm

ONTARIO

Compensation for Victims of Crime Act R.S.O. 1990, ch C.24
www.e-laws.gov.on.ca/html/statutes/english/elaws_statutes_90c24_e.htm

PRINCE EDWARD ISLAND

Chapter V-3.1 Victims of Crime Act 1989
www.gov.pe.ca/law/statutes/pdf/v-03_1.pdf

QUEBEC

Crime Victim Compensation Act 1971, c. 18
www2.publicationsduquebec.gouv.qc.ca/dynamicSearch/telecharge.php?type=2&file=/I_6/I6_A.htm

An Act to promote good citizenship 1977, chapter C-20
www2.publicationsduquebec.gouv.qc.ca/dynamicSearch/telecharge.
php?type=2&file=/C_20/C20_A.html
Worker's Compensation Act 1985
www2.publicationsduquebec.gouv.qc.ca/dynamicSearch/telecharge.
php?type=2&file=/A_3/A3_A.html

SASKATCHEWAN

Criminal Injuries Compensation Act RSS 1978 c C47; superseded by the The Victims of Crime Act 1995
www.qp.gov.sk.ca/documents/English/Statutes/Statutes/V6-011.pdf

European Union

Council Directive 2004/80/EC of 29 April 2004 relating to compensation to crime victims

Member States

SPAIN

Victims of Terrorism Solidarity Act 1999, No. 32/1999 of October 8 1999, amended in 2000 and 2003, and Royal Decree No. 288/2003 of March 7 2003

UNITED KINGDOM

Victims of Overseas Terrorism Compensation Scheme (Crime and Security Act 2010, sections 47–54)

GREAT BRITAIN

The Criminal Injuries Compensation Scheme 2012
www.justice.gov.uk/downloads/victims-and-witnesses/cic-a/am-i-eligible/criminal-injuries-comp-scheme-2012.pdf

NORTHERN IRELAND

Criminal Injuries to Persons (Compensation) (N.I.) Act 1968; repealed and replaced by the Northern Ireland Criminal Injuries Compensation Scheme 2012. The Criminal Damage (Compensation) (Northern Ireland) Order 1977 No. 1247 (N.I. 14)

United States of America

Federal

Air Transport Safety and System Stabilisation Act 2001, SEC. 403
International Terrorism Victim Expense Reimbursement Program

State

ARKANSAS

The Arkansas Crime Victims Reparations Program
www.ag.arkansas.gov/crime_safety_crime_victims_reparations.html

CALIFORNIA

California Victim Compensation and Government Claims Board
www.vcgcb.ca.gov/

FLORIDA

Florida Division of Victim Services and Criminal Justice Programs
myfloridalegal.com/victims

LOUISIANA

Louisiana Crime Victims Reparations Board
www.lcle.state.la.us/programs/cvr.asp

MISSISSIPPI

Mississippi Crime Victim Compensation Division
www.ago.state.ms.us/index.php/sections/victims/victim_compensation

MISSOURI

Missouri Crime Victims' Compensation Program
www.dps.mo.gov/dir/programs/cvc/

NEW JERSEY

Victims of Crime Compensation Office
www.nj.gov/oag/njvictims/index.html

NORTH CAROLINA

North Carolina Crime Victims Compensation Division
https://www.nccrimecontrol.org/index2.cfm?a=000003,002144,000016

OHIO

Ohio Office of the Attorney General Crime Victim Services
www.ohioattorneygeneral.gov/Victim

RHODE ISLAND

Rhode Island Crime Victim Compensation Program
www.treasury.ri.gov/divisions/crimevictim/

TEXAS

Texas Crime Victims Compensation Program, Victim Services Division
https://www.oag.state.tx.us/victims/about_comp.shtml

WASHINGTON

Washington State Crime Victim Compensation Program
www.lni.wa.gov/claimsins/crimevictims/default.asp

Notes

1 I am grateful to Dan Eddy of the National Association of Crime Victim Compensation Boards for his helpful advice on the position in the United States of America; any errors are mine.
2 In its Directory of International Crime Victim Compensation Programs 2005 the US Department of Justice's Office for Crime Victims identified thirty-six countries as having compensation programmes (Office for Victims of Crime 2005). These were principally to be found in North America and Europe. There were none in South America (except Colombia) or the Caribbean (except Trinidad and Tobago); none in Africa; none in the Near East (except Israel); and a small number in East Asia and the Pacific (Australia, Hong Kong, Japan, New Zealand, Philippines, Republic of Korea and Taiwan).
3 Article 9 of the European Council's Framework Decision of 15 March 2001 on the standing of victims in criminal proceedings provided for 'a right to compensation in the course of criminal proceedings', though it was not explicit about the type of compensation (financial and/or otherwise) which offenders should be encouraged to provide, save that it should be 'adequate' (European Union 2001). The Framework Decision was replaced in 2012 by a Directive establishing minimum standards on the rights, support and protection of victims of crime (European Commission 2012). Of relevance here are Articles 4.4(e), which includes the right of victims to receive information on 'how and under what conditions they can access compensation' (which could include state compensation), and 16, which outlines the right of victims to receive compensation from the offender in the course of criminal proceedings; though this does no more than is stated in Article 9 of the 2001 Framework Decision.
4 This required the establishment of arrangements by which victims could apply through their own national compensation scheme ('the Assisting Authority'), which was then obliged to transmit that application to the scheme in the country in which the crime took place (the 'Deciding Authority'), which was in turn obliged to determine the application and communicate the outcome to the Assisting Authority, finally contacting the applicant.

5 This drive to convergence in the provision of Europe-wide crime victim compensation can also be seen in the development of restorative justice (Miers and Willemsens 2004; Miers and Aertsen 2012); and see article 12 of the 2012 Directive.
6 The research was conducted by Matrix Insight, which submitted its two reports (Empirical and Synthesis) in December 2008 (Matrix Insight 2008a, 2008b).
7 The contractor is GHK in partnership with Milieu Ltd and von Freyhold Vial & Partner Consultants (GHK 2013).
8 Austria, Belgium, Denmark, Finland, France, Germany, Ireland, Luxembourg, Netherlands, Portugal, Spain, Sweden, and the United Kingdom (which comprises two schemes: one for Great Britain and one for Northern Ireland).
9 These include victim assistance and victim/witness assistance programmes, which in turn include advice on restitution orders and on victims' right to make oral and written victim impact statements at an offender's sentencing. The allocation of funds as between these and the state compensation programmes is determined by a spending formula; see Office for Victims of Crime, www.ojp.usdoj.gov/ovc/pubs/crimevictimsfundfs/intro.html#vc
10 France is an exception. Under a private sector service levy system, le Fonds de Garantie des victimes d'actes de Terrorisme et d'autres Infractions (FGTI), manages a Criminal Injuries Compensation scheme to assist victims of terrorism and other offences. This fund (FGTI) raises revenue from a levy on property insurance of 3.3 euros (£2.87) per insurance contract (in 2004). FGTI pays compensation which has been set according to requirements/criteria set by the Compensation Commission for Victims of Offences (CIVI) which is part of each county court.
11 'As of August 2010, the Fund balance had reached over four billion dollars and includes deposits from federal criminal fines, forfeited bail bonds, penalties, and special assessments collected by US Attorneys' Offices, federal US courts, and the Federal Bureau of Prisons. Federal revenues deposited into the Fund also come from gifts, donations, and bequests by private parties, as provided by an amendment to VOCA through the USA PATRIOT Act in 2001 that went into effect in 2002. In the period 2002–2010, over US$300 thousand dollars were deposited into the Fund through this provision'; see Office for Victims of Crime www.ojp.usdoj.gov/ovc/about/victimsfund.html.
12 www.nacvcb.org/ The NACVCB's purpose is 'to provide leadership, professional development, and collaborative opportunities to our members to strengthen their capacity to improve services to crime victims and survivors'. It organizes training and other events to support the states' boards' officials, and publishes an informative Crime Victim Compensation Quarterly. Its Program Directory helpfully summarizes the key features of all of the United States' schemes to a common template.
13 The European Judicial Atlas on Civil Matters aims to catalogue national schemes, but for a number of member states the relevant information is not available; http://ec.europa.eu/justice_home/judicialatlascivil/html/cv_information_en.htm?countrySession=2&.
14 Law enforcement and judicial procedures typically confer more extensive powers of search and seizure, and of arrest and detention of suspects, than those that routinely apply to crime of violence. See generally Letschert and Ammerlaan (2010).
15 For much of the twentieth century, compensation in Northern Ireland was payable via a civil court procedure to the victims of collective violence, the awards levied on the police authority. This was a legacy of arrangements from the previous century whose purpose was to place the responsibility for the financial consequences of unlawful assemblies and riots, to both persons and property, on the community within which the offenders were assumed to live. These arrangements were replaced in 1968 by a statutory version of the Scheme then operating in Great Britain and was applicable to any victim of violent crime; see now the Northern Ireland Criminal Injuries Compensation Scheme 2012, managed by the Northern Ireland Compensation Agency; www.dojni.

gov.uk/compensation-agency. This Agency also administers the 1977 Northern Ireland legislation providing compensation for property damage caused by acts of terrorism ('riot and unlawful assembly'). In England and Wales the Riot (Damages) Act 1886 fixed financial responsibility on the police for damage caused by riot in their authority's area. Still good law, claims in the region of £100 million arising from the riots in England in August 2011 are, in difficult economic times, unwelcome. See Koch (2004) for an overview of the role of tort law and of insurance in compensating property damage caused by terrorism.
16 The legislation provides that the state will fund the medical treatment of those suffering physical or psychological injury as a result of a terrorist attack or, in case of death, financial aid to the closest relatives of the person. When it sentenced the surviving terrorists responsible for the March 2004 Madrid train bombings, the court ordered them to pay their victims E900,000 each, but recognized at once that the payment would in practice be made under the 1999 Act.
17 See generally United Nations (2011), para.68: 'For the purpose of compensation, a number of States have followed a model for victims of acts of terrorism along the lines of existing models of compensation for military and civilian victims of war. This may be regarded as a consequence of the more general duty of States to protect individuals on their territories, as well as a recognition of the value of the involuntary sacrifice of victims on behalf of the State, which is the most frequent target of terrorist acts.'
18 The lump sum is 5,000 New Israeli Shekels (£850); later, and if the need arises, they may qualify for extra NIS 30.000 (£5,000) to reimburse death-related expenses. I am grateful to Dr Uri Yanay for drawing my attention to this development.
19 There is, however, substantial doubt as to whether the survivors would have been able to establish liability as a matter of law (Diller 2004; Sebok 2004).
20 See Holt (2003–04); Alexander (2004); Goldscheid (2004); Issachoroff and Mansfield (2006). See also Grey (2005–06) for an instructive comparison between this Fund and the schemes in Israel and Great Britain then in force.
21 The Fund paid out more than US$7 billion dollars to surviving victims and families of those who died, with payments to families averaging over US$2 million.
22 These payments have covered medical and evacuation support, consular assistance and assistance with funeral costs and other expenses.
23 The victim of a terrorist act committed in Canada may be eligible for compensation from an existing provincial or territorial programme if it is determined that the act is a crime committed within that province or territory and the victim meets that programme's other eligibility criteria. An interesting development is the 2012 federal legislation by which 'any person that has suffered loss or damage in or outside Canada on or after January 1 1985 as a result of an act or omission that is, or had it been committed in Canada would be, punishable under Part II.1 of the Criminal Code, may, in any court of competent jurisdiction, bring an action to recover an amount equal to the loss or damage proved to have been suffered by the person'.
24 Being readily insurable, victim compensation schemes normally exclude criminal damage to or the theft of property. In addition, the extent of such losses and the indirect costs of checking for fraudulent claims are insurmountable objections to their inclusion; but compare the position concerning property loss caused by acts of terrorism; see text above.
25 This is explicit in the particular cases of sexual offences and homicide compensated under the British scheme. Here, the Home Office argued, the public finds sexual offences 'especially repugnant' and the circumstances of homicide 'particularly horrific and the trauma to the victim's family [...] severe'. A financial award 'is society's way of acknowledging the harm that has been done to the victim as a representative of

the community' (Home Office 2005, pp. 14, 21). While making substantial cuts in the levels of compensation, the 2012 Scheme maintains the established levels for physical and sexual abuse of children and adults (see Miers 2013).

26 (1989) ECR 195.
27 The notable exception is Italy, which covers only victims of organized crime and extortion.
28 In Canada, for example, see schemes in British Columbia, Manitoba, Ontario and Quebec.
29 The European Commission's analysis of the 2004 Directive was not in a position to capture data on injuries arising from domestic violence (Matrix Insight 2008a, p. 37). Compare the position under the European Convention on Human Rights (Hasselbacher 2010), and under article 30 of the Council of Europe's convention on domestic violence: 'Adequate State compensation shall be awarded to those who have sustained serious bodily injury or impairment of health, to the extent that the damage is not covered by other sources such as the perpetrator, insurance or State-funded health and social provisions. This does not preclude Parties from claiming redress for compensation awarded from the perpetrator, as long as due regard is paid to the victim's safety' (Council of Europe 2011).
30 www.nacvcb.org/index.asp?bid=14; 'Crime victim compensation: an Overview. Case No. 93,701, *Greg and Linda Fisher Appellants v Kansas Crime Victims Compensation Board* exemplifies the approach taken by the United States' schemes. The Kansas Supreme Court, relying heavily on similar rulings in other states that a compensation programme must find some causal or contributory connection between the victim's behavior and the victimization, rather than rely solely on the victim's illegal behavior for denial, held that the Kansas Board had wrongly denied compensation to a 15-year-old driver whose blood alcohol level exceeded the legal limit when he was killed by a drunk driver, there being no causal connection between his drunkenness and his victimization.'
31 Arkansas, Mississippi, Missouri, North Carolina, Ohio and Washington (mandatory), and Florida, Louisiana and Rhode Island (discretionary); the details of the nature of the criminal record vary.
32 Manitoba has since 1998 provided that compensation payable to a victim of crime may be denied or reduced if the victim has been involved in prescribed illegal activity in the five years preceding the claim.
33 The Criminal Injuries Counselling Program in Nova Scotia is limited to the offer to pay for professional counselling for victims of violent crimes. The Financial Benefits Program of Alberta does not provide compensation for any costs or losses, which it expects victims to pursue as a civil action against the offender, but pays a single lump sum assessed on a point system, where a victim's injuries are given a certain number of points based on the severity of their physical and mental injuries.
34 Until the 2012 revision, this was one and one half times average weekly earnings; from 2012 it is now fixed at the universal rate for statutory sick pay.
35 These limits vary widely. For individual state details see the NACVCB's Program Directory www.nacvcb.org/index.asp?sid=5,
36 New South Wales: AUS$10,000; South Australia: AUS$50,000; Victoria: AUS$20,000.
37 New South Wales: AUS$50,000; South Australia: AUS$50,000; Victoria: loss during a period of up to two years after the occurrence of the act of violence.
38 Alberta: CAN$12,500; Ontario: CAN$25,000.
39 Quebec: compensation is at a rate not exceeding 150% of the deceased's income; Manitoba: the rate is 55% to a maximum of CAN$25,000 a year.

40 Texas: a maximum of US$500 a week; Illinois: US$1,000 a month; California: no more than five years' loss of support; Pennsylvania: US$20,000 but in any event not to exceed average industrial earnings.
41 Neither Manitoba nor Quebec has provided compensation for general damages.
42 South Australia: AUS$50,000; Tasmania: AUS$50,000; Western Australia: AUS$75,000.
43 Rhode Island did but abandoned this provision as the benefit became too expensive, creating a ten-year claims backlog.
44 The British scheme pays £11,000 for one 'qualifying claimant' or £5,500 each for more than one.
45 British Columbia: provision for 'bereavement leave' from employment; Quebec: the parents of a minor child who dies as a result of crime are eligible to receive CAN$2,000; South Australia: a payment not exceeding AUS$10,000 may be made for 'grief'; Western Australia: a close relative may be made an award for mental or nervous shock.
46 In contrast, Western Australia continues to cover both pain and suffering and loss of enjoyment of life while also increasing in 2003 the maximum award payable to AUS$75,000 from AUS$50,000.
47 Victoria: excluding pain and suffering the 1996 Act provided that the court may make an order against the offender for such compensation (in 2000 there was a partial reinstatement to a limit of AUS$7,500); Tasmania: financial assistance is available to enable victims to sue their offenders.
48 None of these changes was, however, as radical a departure from the offender surrogate model as occurred in New Zealand, which established its scheme in 1963 but replaced it in 1972 when enacting its omnibus no-fault scheme.
49 'In FYs 2009 and 2010, as the number of claims grew and revenue sources were reduced, state programs continued to face the challenge of finding sufficient funding to reimburse crime victims for expenses related to their victimization' (Office for Victims of Crime 2011, p. 8).
50 At the time of writing the pound sterling is worth 1.60 US dollars.
51 Arkansas: US$25,000, from a US$10,000 base figure; New Jersey: US$60,000 and US$25,000; Texas: US$125,000 and US$50,000.
52 See the tentative analysis in GHK (2013).
53 The Canadian Federal Government funds its Department of Justice's Victims of Crime Initiative but has no responsibility for the provincial or territorial compensation schemes.
54 But see the press release by Viviane Reding Vice-President of the European Commission, EU Justice Commissioner Putting Victims first – Better protection and support for victims of crime Conference 'Victims of Crime in the EU – The post-Lisbon legislative agenda' Trier 9 June 2011 (Speech 11/424 09/06/11). 'Let me stress that the present package of minimum rules is just a first step to address victims' rights. We will continue to examine key issues relating to victims, for instance by improving the application of the 2004 Directive on compensation for crime victims and studying the provision of legal aid to victims. I also want to look at other ideas, such as victims surcharge fines or offender compensation or restitution schemes to ensure that victims across Europe obtain a fair compensation to the crime that was inflicted on them. Next year I will therefore come up with a second package of measures to ensure that we develop a sustained effort in strengthening the rights of the victims of crime.'

Bibliography

Alexander, J., 2004. Procedural design and terror victim compensation. De Paul Law Review, 53, pp. 627–718.

Ashworth, A., 2000. Victims' rights, defendants' rights and criminal procedure. In: A. Crawford and J. Goodey, eds, Integrating a victim perspective in criminal justice. Aldershot: Ashgate, pp. 185–206.

Barrett-Mayering, I., 2010. Victim compensation and domestic violence: a national overview. Sydney: Australian Domestic and Family Violence Clearinghouse, Stakeholder Paper 8. January 2010.

Bochmann, C. and Griesham, K.-W., 1999. Compensation practices of states of the European Union connected to crimes against women. HEUNI Paper No.12. Helsinki, Finland: The European Institute for Crime Prevention and Control, affiliated with the United Nations.

Buck, K., 2005. State compensation to crime victims and the principle of social solidarity. European Journal of Crime, Criminal Law and Criminal Justice, 13(2), pp. 148–178.

Burns, P., 1992. Criminal injuries compensation: social remedy or political palliative for victims of crime? 2nd edition. Woburn: Butterworth-Heinemann.

Christie, N., 1986. The ideal victim. In: E. Fattah, ed., From crime policy to victim policy. London: Macmillan, pp. 1–17.

CICA., 2010. Criminal Injuries Compensation Authority. Annual Report and Accounts 2009/10. London: The Stationery Office, HC 115. Available at: www.justice.gov.uk/downloads/publications/corporate-reports/cica/Annual-report-and-accounts-09-10.pdf [Accessed 8 March 2013].

CICA., 2011. Criminal Injuries Compensation Authority. Annual Report and Accounts 2010/11. London: The Stationery Office, HC 1246. Available at: www.justice.gov.uk/downloads/publications/corporate-reports/cica/cica-annual-report-2010-11.pdf [Accessed 8 March 2013].

CICA., 2012. Criminal Injuries Compensation Authority. Annual Report and Accounts 2011/12. London: The Stationery Office, HC 296. Available at: www.justice.gov.uk/downloads/publications/corporate-reports/cica/cica-annual-report-2011-12.pdf [Accessed 8 March 2013].

Commission of the European Communities, 2001. Compensation to crime victims. Brussels, 28.09.2001 COM(2001) 536 final. Available at: http://eur-lex.europa.eu/LexUriServ/site/en/com/2001/com2001_0536en01.pdf [Accessed 8 March 2013].

Commission of the European Communities, 2009. Report from the Commission to the Council, the European Parliament and the European Economic and Social Committee on the application of Council Directive 2004/80/EC relating to compensation to crime victims. SEC(2009) 495. Brussels, 20.4.2009. COM(2009) 170 final. Available at: http://ec.europa.eu/civiljustice/news/docs/report_compensation_crime_victim_en.pdf [Accessed 8 March 2013].

Council of Europe, 1983a. European Convention on the Compensation of Victims of Violent Crimes. European Treaty Series No 116 agreed on 24 November 1984 and into force on 1 February 1998. Available at: www.conventions.coe.int/Treaty/Commun/QueVoulezVous.asp?NT=116&CM=8&DF=08/03/2013&CL=ENG [Accessed 8 March 2013].

Council of Europe, 1983b. European Convention on the Compensation of Victims of Violent Crimes (European Treaty Series No 116 agreed on 24 November 1984 and into force on 1 February 1998). Explanatory Report. Available at: www.conventions.coe.int/Treaty/Commun/QueVoulezVous.asp?NT=116&CM=8&DF=08/03/2013&CL=ENG [Accessed 8 March 2013].

Council of Europe, 2005. Human rights and the fight against terrorism: The Council of Europe Guidelines, adopted by the Committee of Ministers on 11 July 2002. Available at: www.echr.coe.int/NR/rdonlyres/176C046F-C0E6-423C-A039-F66D90CC6031/0/LignesDirectrices_EN.pdf [Accessed 8 March 2013].

Council of Europe, 2011. Convention on preventing and combating violence against women and domestic violence. Istanbul 11.05.2011. Council of Europe Treaty Series No. 210. Available at: www.conventions.coe.int/Treaty/Commun/QueVoulezVous.asp?NT=210&CM=8&DF=08/03/2013&CL=ENG [Accessed 8 March 2013].

de Greiff, P., 2006. Justice and reparations. In: P. de Greiff, ed., The handbook of reparations. Oxford: Oxford University Press, pp. 451–477.

Doak, J., 2007. Victim's rights, human rights and criminal justice: reconceiving the role of third parties. Oxford: Hart Publishing.

Diller, M., 2004. Tort law and social welfare principles in the Victim Compensation Fund. De Paul Law Review, 53, pp. 719–768.

Edelhertz, H. and Geis, G., 1974. Public compensation to victims of crime. Massachusetts: Lexington: Praeger.

Elias, R., 1983. Victims of the system. New Brunswick: Transaction Press.

European Commission, 2009. Report from the Commission to the Council, the European Parliament and the European Economic and Social Committee on the application of Council Directive 2004/80/EC relating to compensation to crime victims. SEC(2009) 495. Brussels, 20.4.2009. COM(2009) 170 final. Available at: http://ec.europa.eu/civiljustice/news/docs/report_compensation_crime_victim_en.pdf {Accessed 8 March 2013].

European Commission, 2011. Communication from the Commission to the European Parliament, the Council, the European Economic and Social Committee and the Committee of the Regions. Strengthening victims' rights in the EU {SEC(2011) 580 final}{SEC(2011) 581 final}. Brussels, 18.5.2011 COM(2011) 274 final. Available at: http://ec.europa.eu/justice/policies/criminal/victims/docs/com_2011_274_en.pdf [Accessed 8 March 2013].

European Commission, 2012. Directive 2012/29/EU of the European Parliament and of the Council of 25 October 2012 establishing minimum standards on the rights, support and protection of victims of crime, and replacing Council Framework Decision 2001/220/JHA. Available at: http://eur-lex.europa.eu/smartapi/cgi/sga_doc?smartapi!celexplus!prod!CELEXnumdoc&lg=EN&numdoc=32012L0029 [Accessed 8 March 2013].

European Union, 2001. Council Framework Decision 2001/220/JHA of 15 March 2001 on the standing of victims in criminal proceedings, OJ L 082/1 22 March 2001. Available at: http://eur-lex.europa.eu/smartapi/cgi/sga_doc?smartapi!celexapi!prod!CELEXnumdoc&lg=EN&numdoc=32001F0220&model=guichett [Accessed 8 March 2013].

European Union, 2004. Council Directive 2004/80/EC of 29 April 2004 relating to compensation to crime victims, OJEU L. 261/15, 06/08/2004. Available at: http://eur-lex.europa.eu/LexUriServ/LexUriServ.do?uri=OJ:L:2004:261:0015:0018:en:PDF [Accessed 8 March 2013].

European Union, 2011. Council of the European Union. Resolution of the Council of 10 June 2011 on a roadmap for strengthening the rights and protection of victims, in particular in criminal proceedings (2011/C 187/01). OJEU 28/6/11. C 187/1. Available at: http://eur-lex.europa.eu/LexUriServ/LexUriServ.do?uri=OJ:C:2011:187:0001:0005:EN:PDF [Accessed 8 March 2013].

Freckelton, I., 2001. Criminal injuries compensation: law, practice and policy. Sydney: the Lawbook Company.

GHK., 2013. Preparatory study for an impact assessment on future EU measures relating to compensation to crime victims. Final Report to DG Justice. August 2013. London: 67 Clerkenwell Road, London, EC1R 5BL.

Goldscheid, J., 2004. Crime victim compensation in a post 9/11 world. Tulane Law Review, 79, pp. 166–233.

Goodey, J., 2005. Victims and victimology: research, policy and practice. London: Pearson Education.

Greer, D., ed., 1996. Compensating crime victims: a European survey. Freiburg: MaxPlanck-Institut.

Grey, B., 2005–06. Homeland security and federal relief: a proposal for a permanent compensation system for domestic terrorist victims. New York University J. Legis. & Pub. Policy, 9, pp. 663–750.

Hall, M., 2009. Victims of crime: policy and process in criminal justice. Cullompton: Willan Publishing.

Hall, M., 2010. Victims and policy making: a comparative perspective. Cullompton: Willan Publishing.

Hasselbacher, L., 2010. State obligations regarding domestic violence: the European Court of Human Rights, due diligence, and international legal minimums of protection. Northwestern University Journal of International Human Rights, 8, pp. 190–215.

Holt, E., 2003–04. The September 11 victim compensation fund: legislative justice sui generis. New York University Annual Survey of American Law, 59, pp. 513–562.

Home Office, 2005. Rebuilding lives: supporting victims of crime. London: The Stationery Office, Cm 6705. Available at: www.official-documents.gov.uk/document/cm67/6705/6705.pdf [Accessed 8 March 2013].

Issachoroff, S. and Mansfield, A., 2006. Compensation for the victims of September 11. In: P de Grieff, ed., The handbook of reparations. Oxford: Oxford University Press, pp. 284–320.

Kirchengast, T., 2006. The victim in criminal law and justice. Basingstoke: Palgrave Macmillan.

Koch, B., 2004. Terrorism, tort law and insurance. London: Springer Verlag.

Letschert, R. and Ammerlaan, K., 2010. Compensation and reparation for victims of terrorism. In: R. Letschert, A. Pemberton and I. Staiger, eds, Assisting victims of terrorism: towards a European standard of justice. London: Springer, pp. 215–266.

Matravers, M., 2010. The victim, the state, and civil society. In: A. Bottoms and J. Roberts, eds, Hearing the victim. Cullompton: Willan Publishing. Ch.1.

Matrix Insight, 2008a. European Commission Directorate – General justice, freedom & security, analysis of the application of Directive 2004/80/EC relating to compensation to crime victims, Synthesis Report 12 December 2008. Available at: http://ec.europa.eu/civiljustice/publications/docs/study_application_directive_compensation_synthesis_report_en.pdf [Accessed 8 March 2013].

Matrix Insight, 2008b. European Commission Directorate – General justice, freedom & security, analysis of the application of Directive 2004/80/EC relating to compensation to crime victims, Empirical Report 12 December 2008. Available at: http://ec.europa.eu/justice/criminal/files/2008_comp_study_empirical_report_en.pdf [Accessed 8 March 2013].

Mikaelsson, J. and Wergens, A., 2001. Repairing the irreparable. Umea: The Crime Victim Compensation and Support Authority, Swedish Ministry of Justice.

Miers, D., 2000. Taking the law into their own hands: victims as offenders. In: A. Crawford and J. Goodey, eds, Integrating a victim perspective within criminal justice. Aldershot: Ashgate, pp. 77–95.

Miers, D., 2006. Rebuilding lives: operational and policy issues in the compensation of victims of violent and terrorist crimes. Criminal Law Review, pp. 695–721.

Miers, D., 2007. Looking beyond England and Wales: the development of criminal injuries compensation. In: S. Walklate, ed., Handbook of victims and victimology. Cullompton: Willan Publishing, pp. 337–362

Miers, D., 2013. Compensating deserving victims of violent crime: the criminal injuries compensation scheme 2012. Legal Studies, DOI: 10.1111/lest.12013.

Miers, D. and Willemsens, J., eds, 2004. Mapping restorative justice: developments in 25 European countries. Leuven: The European Forum for Victim–Offender Mediation and Restorative Justice.

Miers, D. and Aertsen, I., eds, 2012. Regulating restorative justice: a comparative study of legislative provision in European countries. Frankfurt am Main: Verlag für Polizeiwissenschaft.

Ministry of Justice, 2012a. Arrangements for making ex-gratia payments to certain victims of terrorism in respect of designated acts committed outside the UK. Available at: www.justice.gov.uk/downloads/victims-and-witnesses/cic-a/victims-overseas-terrorism/vots-ex-gratia-scheme.pdf [Accessed 8 March 2013].

Ministry of Justice, 2012b. A guide to the Victims of Overseas Terrorism Compensation Scheme 2012. London: Criminal Injuries Compensation Authority. Available at: www.justice.gov.uk/downloads/victims-and-witnesses/cic-a/victims-overseas-terrorism/victim-of-overseas-terrorism-scheme-guide-2012.pdf [Accessed 8 March 2013].

Ministry of Justice, 2012c. Getting it right for victims and witnesses: the Government response. London: The Stationery Office, Cm 8397. Available at: https://consult.justice.gov.uk/.../a-gov-response-getting-right-victims [Accessed 8 March 2013].

Office for Victims of Crime, 2001. Department of Justice, Office for Victims of Crime [OJP(OVC)–1319] Victims of Crime Act Victim Compensation Grant Program, Final Guidelines. Federal Register, 66(95), Wednesday, May 16, 2001 / Notices. Available at: www.ojp.usdoj.gov/ovc/voca/pdftxt/voca_guidelines2001.pdf [Accessed 8 March 2013].

Office for Victims of Crime, 2005. Directory of International Crime Victim Compensation Programs 2004–2005. US Department of Justice. Available at: www.ncjrs.gov/ovc_archives/reports/intdir2005/welcome.html [Accessed 8 March 2013].

Office for Victims of Crime. 2011. Rising to the challenge: A new era in victim services. OVC 2011 Report to the Nation. Available at: www.ojp.usdoj.gov/ovc/pubs/reporttonation2011/ReporttoNation2011.pdf [Accessed 8 March 2013].

President's Task Force on Victims of Crime, Final Report, 1982. Available at: www.ojp.usdoj.gov/ovc/publications/presdntstskforcrprt/87299.pdf [Accessed 8 March 2013].

Rock, P., 2004. Constructing victims' rights. Oxford: Oxford University Press.
Sebok, A., 2004. What's law got to do with it? Designing compensation schemes in the shadow of the tort system. De Paul Law Review, 53, pp. 501–526.
Shapo, M., 2005. Compensation for victims of terrorism. Dobbs Ferry: Oceana Publications.
Sommer, H., 2003. Providing compensation for harm caused by terrorism: lessons learned in the Israeli experience. Indiana Law Review, 36, pp. 335–365.
Spalek, B., 2006. Crime victims: theory, policy and practice. London: Palgrave Macmillan.
United Nations, 2011. The criminal justice response to support victims of acts of terrorism. Vienna: United Nations Office on Drugs and Crime. Available at: www.un.org/en/terrorism/ctitf/pdfs/victims_rights_e-book_en.pdf [Accessed 8 March 2013].
Yanay, U., 2004. A tough life for victims: crime victims and the Israeli justice system. Social Security, Special English Edition, 7, pp. 115–138. Available at: http://scholar.google.co.uk/scholar?q=A+tough+life+for+victims%3A+crime+victims+and+the+Israeli+justice+system.+&btnG=&hl=en&as_sdt=0%2C5 [Accessed 8 March 2013].
Yanay, U. and Gal, T., 2010. Lobbying for rights: crime victims in Israel. In: G. Shoham, P. Knepper and M. Kett, eds, International handbook of victimology. Boca Raton: Taylor & Francis, pp. 373–396.

Chapter 7

Legal protection and assistance for victims of human trafficking in the United States
A harm reduction approach

Xin Ren

Introduction

Human trafficking is a form of modern-day slavery, a crime against human rights and dignity. It involves an act of recruiting, transporting, transferring, harbouring or receiving a person through a use of force, threat, coercion or other means, for the purpose of sexual and/or labour exploitation (United Nations Office of Drug Control (UNODC) 2013). The most recent estimate by the International Labour Organization from open sources suggests that at least 20.9 million people – men, women and children – are in forced labour even though it is still difficult to know exactly how many of these victims are resulted from trafficking. For a conservative estimate, some 2.5 million people are trafficked for labour and sexual exploitation in the world (United Nations Global Initiative to Fight Human Trafficking (UN.GIFT) 2010). Women, children and migrant workers are the most vulnerable groups who often fall into the hands of traffickers, in their own countries and/or abroad. Women count for 55 to 60 per cent of victims in those detected human trafficking cases while children make up 27 per cent of total victims (17 per cent girls and 10 per cent boys); adult males make up the remaining 14 per cent of the total victim population (UNODC 2012a). Although developing countries and regions are accountable for contributing a large number of victims to global human trafficking, 'every country in the world is affected by trafficking, whether as a country of origin, transit or destination for victims' (UNODC 2013, p. 27).

Since the adoption of the United Nations Protocol to Prevent, Suppress, and Punish Trafficking in Persons, Especially Women and Children (UN 2000a, The UN Trafficking Protocol thereafter) and the United Nations Protocol against the Smuggling of Migrants by Land, Sea, and Air (UN 2000b, The UN Smuggling Protocol thereafter), much progress has been made in preventing trafficking, detecting and prosecuting traffickers, and rescuing and assisting victims of human trafficking in the world. A global campaign against human trafficking was launched and has since transcended the traditional definition of human trafficking that puts an emphasis on moving, transporting or trafficking victims from one place to another, to the criminal acts of fraud, violence, exploitation, and abuse of trafficked victims. To recognize the importance of protecting human rights and human dignity of victims, a *harm reduction approach* is reshaping the global war against human trafficking by developing *victim protection-centred* national laws, enforcement strategies and victim assistance plans. This chapter outlines legal instruments developed in the United States at the federal and state level to identify victims, prosecute traffickers and qualify victims and their families for various federally and state sponsored assistance programmes that help victims to recover and reintegrate back to a normal life. It also provides an examination of these legal protections and assistance programmes available for rescued victims of human trafficking.

Common misconceptions about human trafficking

Due to the victims' behaviour in crime reports and the prioritized enforcement of law against human trafficking, there are many public misperceptions about the definition, nature and extent of human trafficking, and the characteristics of victims and victimization. Below are some common misconceptions about trafficking in human beings.

- Human trafficking requires crossing national or international borders.
- Crime of trafficking in persons must involve moving victims from one location to another.
- Trafficking only involves foreign nationals, not US citizens.
- It is not illegal if a person consents to being trafficked.
- You can consent to labour exploitation, domestic servitude or slave type of work.
- If someone is paid by his/her employer, he or she cannot be victim of human trafficking.
- Sending victims home is the best solution for victim assistance/services.

These misconceptions not only represent general public's reluctant attitude towards victims of human trafficking but also hinder law enforcement's efforts in rescuing and assisting victims of human trafficking. Since the enactment of Trafficking Victims Protection Act in 2001, national statistical data compiled by the USDOJ on human trafficking have shown that human trafficking is not just a problem that only involves foreigners but also many American citizens, especially children and young women who were born and grew up in the United States.

Current trends of trafficking in persons in the United States

According to the US Department of Justice 2011 report, the Task Forces on Human Trafficking (a total of forty-two regional Task Forces) opened investigation on a total of 2,515 suspected incidents of human trafficking cases between January 2008 and June 2010. A total of 389 human trafficking cases were confirmed, involving 488 offenders and 527 victims. Of those victims 90 per cent of victims were female and 10 per cent male. Comparing sex trafficking with labour trafficking, eight in ten cases investigated were sex trafficking, while one in ten cases was labour trafficking. For gender distribution of victims, an overwhelming majority of victims in sex trafficking were female (96 per cent) versus only 68 per cent of victims in labour trafficking. Victims in sex trafficking seem also younger (13 per cent were twenty-five or older) while victims tended to be older in labour trafficking (68 per cent were twenty-five or older). For victims' ethnic/racial background, white (26 per cent) and black (40 per cent) were more likely to be victims of sex trafficking, while Hispanic (63 per cent) and Asian (17 per cent) were more likely to be victims of labour trafficking. Although most incidents involved allegations of sex trafficking, 350 incidents involved allegations of labour trafficking in unregulated industries (e.g. drug sales, forced begging or roadside sales) and/or more commercial industries (e.g. hair salons, hotels and bars). Four-fifths of victims in confirmed commercial sex trafficking were US citizens (83 per cent), while the majority of victims in confirmed labour trafficking were undocumented aliens (67 per cent) and qualified aliens (28 per cent).[1] In most confirmed human trafficking cases, male suspects counted for 82 per cent. For sex trafficking cases 62 per cent of suspects were black, while 48 per cent of suspects in labour trafficking were Hispanic. Due to the statutory mandates, federal agencies are more likely to lead in labour trafficking investigations (29 per cent) while the overwhelming majority of sex trafficking investigations (93 per cent) are led by local law enforcement agencies (Banks and Kyckelhahn 2011).

The most recent statistics from the US Department of Homeland Security (USDHS) provide additional data on the human trafficking cases investigated by the Homeland Security Investigations (HSI). Table 7.1 compares the numbers of human trafficking cases investigated by HIS between 2011 and 2012. Although the data do not separate sex trafficking and labour trafficking cases, the characteristics reported by the USDOJ data, it is clear that federal agencies take the lead in more labour trafficking cases than in sex trafficking cases. Another noteworthy characteristic is that though the investigation outcome (indictment and conviction) has continuously improved, with increased numbers of successful indictments and convictions, the total value of assets seized in investigations has sharply declined by 45 per cent in 2012 from the previous year: it averaged US$2,845 per case in 2011 and US$1,262 per case in 2012. Speculatively, most trafficking cases in 2012 do not involve large illicit business establishments that have huge profits and assets.

Understanding the legal framework of human trafficking

The UN Trafficking Protocol (2000) and the UN Smuggling Protocol (2003), as two of three supplemental legal instruments to the United Nations Convention against Transnational Organized Crime[2] (The UN Palermo Convention thereafter), are the two main international instruments in fighting against global human trafficking. The UN Trafficking Protocol is the first global legally binding instrument with an agreed definition of trafficking in persons. The intention of this definition is to facilitate convergence in national approaches with regard to the establishment of domestic

Table 7.1 Human trafficking cases investigated by HSI in 2011 and 2012

Case status	2011	2012	Percentage change
Cases initiated	722	894	+24
Arrested	938	967	+3
Indictments	444	559	+26
Convictions	271	381	+4
Seizure of assets	US$2,054,459	US$1,128,553	-45

Source: HSI, USDHS, 2013, from a presentation made by an HIS agent on 8 February 2013.

criminalization of human trafficking that would support effective international cooperation in investigating and prosecuting cases of human trafficking and protect and assist the victims of human trafficking with full respect for their human rights (UNODC 2012b). According to the UN *Trafficking Protocol*, article 3*(a)*:

> Trafficking in persons (TIP) shall mean the recruitment, transportation, transfer, harbouring or receipt of persons, by means of the threat or use of force or other forms of coercion, of abduction, of fraud, of deception, of the abuse of power or of a position of vulnerability or of the giving or receiving of payments or benefits to achieve the consent of a person having control over another person, for the purpose of exploitation. Exploitation shall include, at a minimum, the exploitation of the prostitution of others or other forms of sexual exploitation, forced labour or services, slavery or practices similar to slavery, servitude or the removal of organs.
>
> (UN.GIFT 2010, p. 2)

The UN definition clearly lays out the legal foundation for individual state parties to promulgate their own national law against human trafficking. The definition identifies three legal material elements in recognizing prosecutable crime of trafficking in persons: *process* to obtain a human being, *means* to control a human being and *goals* to profit from exploitation and abuse of persons. Figure 7.1 illustrates the legal elements in identifying a crime of trafficking in persons.[3]

When a condition from each category is met, the result is a crime of trafficking in persons. The legal community seems to have the consensus that for adults, if any of those illegal means is used to profit from a victim, the victim's consent is irrelevant. For children, the consent is irrelevant if any of these illegal means is used to control a child for purpose of making profit by exploiting a child.

Responding to the UN Palermo Convention against Transnational Organized Crime and the UN Trafficking Protocol, the US Congress quickly enacted the Trafficking

PROCESS	MEANS	GOALS
Recruiting	Threat	**Profit from**
or	Or	
Transporting	Force	Prostitution
or	Or	or
Transferring	Coercion	Sexual Exploitation
or	Or	or
Harbouring	Abduction	Forced Labour
or	Or	or
Receiving	Fraud	Servitude
	Or	or
	Deception	Slavery
	Or	or
	Abuse of Power	Organ Removal

Figure 7.1 The legal elements in identifying a crime of trafficking in persons

Victims Protection Act (TVPA) in 2000. TVPA emphasizes three 'Ps' (Prevention, Prosecution and Protection) and defines human trafficking as the recruitment, harbouring, transportation, provision or obtaining of a person for one of three purposes:

- labour or services, through the use of force, fraud, or coercion for the purposes of subjection to involuntary servitude, peonage, debt bondage or slavery;
- a commercial sex act through the use of force, fraud or coercion;
- any commercial sex act, if the person is under eighteen years of age, regardless of whether any form of coercion is involved.

TVPA also provides protection to trafficked persons through immigration relief and other benefits, authorizes the US Department of State to compile data and release annual reports on an individual country's condition of trafficking in persons, and establishes interagency task forces to monitor and combat trafficking in persons (GovTrack 2000).

The Trafficking Victims Protection Reauthorization Act of 2005 (TVPRA 2005) further requires the US Department of Justice to publish a biennial report on the scope and characteristics of human trafficking in the US, by using available data from individual states and local authorities. As part of an effort to meet these congressional mandates, the Bureau of Justice Statistics (BJS), in partnership with the Bureau of Justice Assistance (BJA), Northeastern University (NEU) and the Urban Institute (UI) developed the Human Trafficking Reporting System (HTRS). The HTRS is a crime incident-based reporting system that collects human trafficking data from forty-two regional Task Forces which cover 25 per cent of the US residential population. To be confirmed as human trafficking: 1) The case must have led to an arrest and been subsequently confirmed by law enforcement, or 2) The victims in the case must a) have had a 'continuing presence' requested on their behalf, or b) have received an endorsement for a T-Visa or U-Visa application.[4]

In 2008, when TVPA was reauthorized by the Congress, additional new crimes relating to trafficking in persons were incorporated into the federal statutes. These new offences are:

- 18 USC § 1351: Fraud in Foreign Labour Contracting: 'Whoever knowingly and with intent to defraud recruits, solicits or hires a person outside the United States for purposes of employment in the United States by means of materially false or fraudulent pretenses, representations or promises regarding that employment shall be fined under this title or imprisoned for not more than 5 years, or both.'
- 18 USC § 1593A: Benefiting Financially from Peonage, Slavery, and Trafficking in Persons: 'Whoever knowingly benefits, financially or by receiving anything of value, from participation in a venture which has engaged in any act in violation of section 1581(a) 1592, or 1595(a) [18 USCS § 1581(a) 1592, or 1595(a)], knowing or in reckless disregard of the fact that the venture has engaged in such violation, shall be fined under this title or imprisoned in the same manner as a completed violation of such section.'
- 18 USC § § 1583-84, Enticement into slavery stipulates that anyone who kidnaps or carries away any other person, with the intent that such other person be sold into involuntary servitude, or held as a slave; entices, persuades, or induces any other person to go on board any vessel or to any other place with the intent that he or she may be made or held as a slave, or sent out of the country to be so made or held; or sale into involuntary servitude, or obstructs, or attempts to obstruct, or in any way interferes with or prevents the enforcement of this law is subject to criminal fine and/or imprisonment up to twenty years.
- 18 USC § §1591-92 Sex trafficking of children has expanded to include 'reckless disregard' of force, fraud or coercion, and minor's age. In regards to minor's age, no actual knowledge of minor age is required for prosecution. The defendant just needs 'reasonable opportunity to observe' the victim's age; and 18 USC § 1594 Trafficking Conspiracy.

Besides these enhanced federal statutes, a new jurisdiction called *extra-territorial jurisdiction* was introduced under TVPRA of 2008. In addition to any domestic or extra-territorial jurisdiction otherwise provided by law, the courts of the United States now have extra-territorial jurisdiction over any offence (or any attempt or conspiracy to commit an offence) under sections 18 USCS § 1581, 1583, 1584, 1589, 1590, or 1591 if (1) an alleged offender is a national of the United States or an alien lawfully admitted for permanent residence (as those terms are defined in section 101 of the Immigration and Nationality Act (8 U.S.C. 1101)); or (2) an alleged offender is present in the United States, irrespective of the nationality of the alleged offender.

When the TVPA was reintroduced in 2011 for reauthorization (TVPRA 2011),[5] additional terms and conditions were added to the penalty expansion against sex offenders. These terms are: 1) limit or restrict the passport of a sex offender to one year; and 2) revoke the passport of a person convicted of a sex crime in a court of competent jurisdiction in foreign countries. To effectively combat labour trafficking, the TVPRA of 2011 also included additional provisions: 1) to expand Labor Department's responsibility in identifying goods produced by forced and child labour in foreign countries and company/business/contractor used forced or child labour to produce those goods; 2) to recommend that the Peace Corps joins the Interagency Task Force; 3) to require the Department of Defense to designate a director on anti-trafficking policies; and 4) expand protection and assistance for victims of trafficking in persons (GovTrack 2011). The TVPRA 2013 also puts a new focus on human trafficking by targeting those countries where children are trafficked or abused for exploitation such as using child labour for exported goods or using child soldiers in civil or domestic wars. The TVPRA 2013 renews critical federal anti-trafficking programmes, provides invaluable resources for the provision of specialized services for survivors of human trafficking, grants prosecutors new tools to go after the traffickers who exploit others and enhances partnerships with focus countries to protect children and prevent child trafficking.

Individual state responses to human trafficking

Responding to TVPA legislation at the federal level, individual states also enacted state laws to combat trafficking in persons. As of 31 July 2012, all fifty states have passed Criminal Anti-Trafficking Laws, with forty-eight states passing criminal statutes against sex trafficking and all fifty establishing labour trafficking laws (Polaris Project 2012). West Virginia became the forty-ninth State to pass anti-trafficking legislation following Ohio in March 2010 and Massachusetts in November 2010. Recently, the Polaris Project, a non-profit NGO based in Washington DC devoted to fighting against human trafficking, developed a state law rating system (ten categories) with four tiers that can be scored between zero and eleven points to measure the comprehensiveness of anti-trafficking laws in individual states. On the basis of this rating, as of 31 July 2013, thirty-two states are now rated in Tier 1 (7–11 points), up from twenty-one states in 2012. Washington and New Jersey received perfect scores (11 points), meaning they have most comprehensive anti-trafficking laws that fulfil all ten categories (see Figure 7.2). The ten categories used in rating comprehensiveness of anti-trafficking laws are ranged from targeted sex and labour trafficking to law enforcement training and to protection of minors of sex trafficking and exploitation.

Typology of victims of human trafficking

Traditionally, victims of human trafficking are often categorized according to the final disposing outcomes at the end of the trafficking process or by the exploitation types (such as victims of sex trafficking, labour trafficking or organ trafficking).

Improvements in State Laws: 2011

Figure 7.2 Polaris Project (2013): 2013 State ratings on human trafficking laws.

Source: Polaris Project 2013; available at: www.polarisproject.org/what-we-do/policy-advocacy/national-policy/state-ratings-on-human-trafficking-laws/2013-state-ratings-on-human-trafficking-laws [Accessed 28 February 2014].

However, in reality, trafficking victims often have a dual status before the law. On the one hand, they may have been victims of trafficking in persons; on the other hand they are often illegal aliens who entered the country unlawfully without proper documentation and/or have criminal status (for example, they may be prostitutes[6], drug offenders or juvenile delinquents). For instance, many international migrant workers illegally cross international borders and unlawfully enter a country without proper or legal documentation such as a passport and a visa. Under the immigration law in any given country, these migrant workers are often viewed as illegal aliens who have violated immigration and border control laws, even though they may have been subjected to sex or labour exploitation and abuse in the hands of traffickers or smugglers. Their illegal or criminal status often makes it almost impossible for them to consider themselves as victims of crime and thus they are reluctant to report their victimization to the authorities. Their dual legal status also may make local law enforcement officers less willing to help them in case of a reported abuse. Furthermore, for those victims whose legal status is not in question because of their legitimate citizenship, the dual status of victims may also exist in the situation where victims may be involved in prostitution or drug crime. Typically, those traditionally labelled as juvenile delinquents or runaway children under the family welfare and child protection law may also potentially be victims of human trafficking when they are lured, controlled, trafficked and exploited by adult pimp-traffickers. To provide effective protection for victims of human trafficking for harm reduction purposes[7], it is critical to recognize the dual legal status of victims in trafficking cases and go beyond victims' illegal status to see their suffering, their victimization and the grave violation of their human rights and human dignity. The harm reduction approach is vital in facilitating effective identification of victims, criminal investigations and prosecutions, and in providing timely needed assistance to these victims.

By recognizing the foremost importance of victims' suffering and the grave violation of their human rights, the typology of victims of human trafficking can be categorized into the following two large groups:

1. US immigrants with non-US nationality:
   - Immigrants with legal documentation/status: students with an F-1 visa; immigrants with a work permit; immigrants married to a US citizen; immigrants with a legal status of refugee; and immigrants with permanent resident status.
   - Illegal immigrants: entered country legally but overstayed their legal status; entered country illegally with legal documents; entered country illegally without legal documents; and seasonal/migrant workers from neighbouring countries.
2. Non-immigrants (US citizens): runaway children (run away because of trouble at home or because they are lured away by deception outside of the family); juvenile delinquents (prostitution, drug crime, other crime); street/homeless children; mentally ill persons; drug addicts; and sex workers.

The dual status of many victims in human trafficking often creates confusion and difficulty in identifying victims in the criminal investigation process. Victims sometimes may be reluctant to report victimization or refuse to cooperate with the authorities, because they are aware of their illegal status in the country and are afraid of arrest and detention for deportation. There are a number of other reasons why victims may not be able or refuse to help with the identification process: total illiteracy; severe mental retardation or psychological trauma; language barriers; fear of the police; lack of nationality/citizenship (stateless people); or, as noted earlier, simply because they wish to avoid identification in order to stall or avoid the deportation process. In countries with victims' protection-centred laws against trafficking in persons, law enforcement, prosecution and court systems emphasize protection and assistance to enhance the success rates of prosecution and conviction, while in other countries with offenders-centred anti-trafficking laws, the government agencies often concentrate on deportation and repatriation, by arresting, detaining and confining victims in detention centres for identification purposes, without any other assistance and services for victims. The victims' illegal alien status supersedes their victim status. For those domestic victims with dual status before the law, their fate is often no better than their international counterparts. For instance, when underage prostitutes, young drug offenders or child street beggars are arrested by police, they are simply booked as juvenile offenders or runaway children by police even though a little detailed interview will reveal that those young children were actually recruited and were being controlled by pimps-traffickers, and are victims of human trafficking.

Human trafficking is often entangled with the phenomenon of international migration as a result of the gaps in economic development among countries/regions in the world (ILO 2012). Although international migration is not the same as transnational trafficking in persons, traffickers do strive to prey on those vulnerable groups among migrating workers such as women, children and stateless people, those who live in poverty in mountainous or isolated regions, those uneducated, unskilled, and socially and economically marginalized for various discriminations when millions of migrant workers are riding the influx of international migration (Tullao et al. 2007). When the legitimate channel or venue of migration is not available to (or is limited for) those who lack social capital and resources, this provides attractive opportunities for traffickers/smugglers to help them chase the same dream shared by millions of migrant workers. Some migrant workers may even have paid their way to illegally enter a country in hope of finding a job or better economic opportunity. When they are abused at the hands of traffickers, a false perception that the victims have seemingly precipitated their own victimization and thus are partially responsible for their own victimization is created. To emphasize the harm reduction, the victims' suffering should be the overriding principle in identifying victims of human trafficking, regardless how they got into the trafficking situation in the first place.

Human trafficking survivors' needs and assistance available under TVPA

Legal protection for victims of human trafficking covers a wide range of assistance programmes and services. Victims are entitled to: privacy; information; legal representation; a hearing in court; medical assistance; compensation for damage/injury; social assistance; employment; and they may also seek residence, return home, and reunify with their families.

Because the survivors of human trafficking are likely to suffer serious physical, psychological and/or sexual abuse at the hand of traffickers, an extensive network of culturally and linguistically appropriate service providers are required to meet their urgent and acute needs. These include:

- language assistance during intake interviews, police investigations and testimony in court;
- housing assistance for temporary shelter or permanent residence;
- food and clothing for the immediately needy family;
- medical care (both emergency and long-term care) and health education;
- mental health care for emotional and psychological trauma;
- legal aid for immigration and legal representation in various legal proceedings;
- safety planning for victims and their families;
- training for independent living and working skills, job placement/employment; and
- human rights education.

The services/assistances available to victims of human trafficking in the United States can be considered under five headings: immigration relief, benefits and services, civil remedies, legal aid and assistance, and the Equal Employment Opportunity Commission (EEOC).

Immigration relief

Survivors of trafficking in persons can receive immigration relief, provided by the TVPA, for temporary or permanent stays in the US if they meet the condition that they agree to assist the authorities in their criminal investigation and/or prosecution. In an effort to eliminate further delays, facilitate criminal investigations and assist victims in obtaining the legal status intended by the US Congress in the 'Victims of Trafficking and Violence Protection Act' (VTVPA),[8] a number of immigration reliefs are made available for victims of human trafficking and certain criminal activities. The forms of relief specific to TIP victims include: temporary relief through continued presence; the possibility of adjusting status to become a legal permanent resident through T-Visa or U-visa; and family parole for minor victims of TIP.

Continued Presence is defined by the US Immigration and Customs Enforcement (USICE 2012) as:

> a temporary immigration status provided to individuals identified by law enforcement as victims of human trafficking. This status allows victims of human trafficking to remain in the US temporarily during the ongoing investigation of human trafficking-related crimes committed against them.

Continued Presence is initially granted for one year and may be renewed in one-year increments. It is authorized under the provisions of section 107(c)(3) of the TVPA, which has since been reauthorized, and is codified at 22 U.S.C. § 7105(c)(3). Initially, only federal law enforcement agents can request a Continued Presence status for a trafficking survivor to receive this benefit in the United States. However, Continued Presence eligibility was greatly expanded when TVPA was reauthorized in 2008. TVPRA of 2008 stipulates that:

> Law Enforcement shall take measures to protect the safety of trafficking victims including taking measures to protect their family members; Continued Presence shall be extended if the individual has filed a civil action under Section 18 USC §1595 until the action is concluded; materials about Continued Presence for state and local law enforcement will be developed and distributed.

The T non-immigrant status (T-Visa) was created by the US Congress in TVPA (2000) to create a set of non-immigrant visas for those who are or have been victims of human trafficking, protect victims of human trafficking, and allow victims to remain in the United States to assist in an investigation or prosecution of human trafficking. It enables certain victims of human trafficking to live and work in the US for up to four years. Victims can petition to have spouses and children accompany them; they may receive government benefits, including cash assistance for eight months; and they may apply for the Green Card (Permanent Residence status). Meeting all of the following criteria may qualify a person for a T-Visa:

- is or has been victim of severe form of trafficking in persons;
- is present in US, American Samoa, Northern Marianas on account of trafficking;
- has complied with reasonable requests for assistance in investigation or prosecution of acts of trafficking (children under eighteen do not need to meet this criterion but do need to have proof of age);
- would suffer extreme hardship involving unusual and severe harm upon removal from the US.

With regard to the requirement of assisting in investigation and prosecution, the Violence Against Women Act (VAWA) 2005 made changes to the original mandate in TVPA by including provisions that law enforcement cooperation is not required for trafficking victims whose physical or psychological trauma impedes their ability to cooperate with law enforcement. Evidence of physical trauma suffered can be provided through forensic photographs of bruises and injuries, police reports, medical reports and affidavits by witnesses. Evidence of psychological trauma suffered can be provided through medical reports or affidavits by medical personnel.

The U-nonimmigrant status and U-Visa classification was originally created in 2000 with the passage of VAWA. It allows a battered immigrant victim to petition for legal status in the United States without having to rely on an abusive spouse who is a US citizen or legal permanent resident, or parents, or children to sponsor their petition. For many immigrant victims of domestic violence, the abusers who are US citizens or lawful permanent resident family members may threaten to withhold their sponsorship as a means to continuously control and abuse victims. The purpose of the U-Nonimmigrant status or U-Visa is to allow victims the opportunity to 'self-petition' or seek legal immigration status without sponsors while they help law enforcement agencies investigate and prosecute cases of domestic violence, sexual assault, human trafficking and other crimes, as well as offer to protect victims of such crimes. This classification provides immigration opportunity to victims of qualified criminal activities (see list below) who suffered substantial physical or mental abuse as a result and who have been, are being or likely to be helpful to law enforcement. Under the revised VAWA, U-Visa applicants no longer have to show that they would face extreme hardship and they are also allowed to apply for permanent residence from outside the US, if they can demonstrate that they were the victims of domestic violence in the US (USDHS 2009).

The qualifying criminal activities for T-Visa or U-Visa are not defined in the same ways. For a T-Visa, 'Severe forms of trafficking in persons' means:

A   sex trafficking in which a commercial sex act is induced by force, fraud, or coercion, or in which the person induced to perform such act has not attained 18 years of age; or
B   the recruitment, harbouring, transportation, provision, or obtaining of a person for labour or services, through the use of force, fraud, or coercion for the purpose of subjection to involuntary servitude, peonage, debt bondage, or slavery.

For a U-Visa, 'qualifying criminal activity' is defined by statute to be:

Activity involving one or more of the following or any similar activity in violation of Federal, State, or local criminal law:

Rape; torture; trafficking; incest; domestic violence; sexual assault; abusive sexual contact; prostitution; sexual exploitation; female genital mutilation; being held hostage; peonage; involuntary servitude; slave trade; kidnapping; abduction; unlawful criminal restraint; false imprisonment; blackmail; extortion; manslaughter; murder; felonious assault; witness tampering; obstruction of justice; perjury; or attempt, conspiracy, or solicitation to commit any of the above mentioned crimes.

Advanced Parole for family members is the third immigration relief under TVPRA 2005. Under 8 USC §1229(b)(6), law enforcement agencies may submit written requests for advanced parole for family members of trafficked persons. Advanced Parole may be extended until final determination of the T-visa application for victims under twenty-one: the spouse, child, parent, or unmarried sibling under eighteen can be included. For victims who are twenty-one or older, only the spouse or child can be included. All victims are encompassed irrespective of age, and so is a parent or sibling if the law enforcement agency determines them to be in present danger of retaliation as a result of either the victim's escape from a severe form of trafficking or because of their cooperation with law enforcement.

Benefits and services [9]

Under TVPA, victims are eligible to receive benefits and services from multiple sources with a *federal certification*. Certification allows victims of trafficking who are non-US citizens to be eligible for a special non-immigrant status that confers certain benefits and services under any federal or state programme or activity to the same extent as a refugee. Certification provides victims of trafficking with the necessary documentation to be eligible to receive benefits and services that they may need to rebuild their lives while remaining in the United States. Victims of trafficking who are US citizens do not need to be certified in this way because they may already be eligible for many benefits. Victims of a severe form of trafficking who have been certified by the Department of Health and Human Services are eligible for benefits to the same extent as refugees:

a   Federal and state public assistance benefits, such as Refugee Cash and Medical Assistance, Temporary Assistance for Needy Families (TANF), Medicaid, Supplemental Security Income (SSI), and Food Stamps; and
b   Refugee self-sufficiency Matching Grant Program and other ORR (Office of Refugee Resettlement) discretionary grant programmes and ORR discretionary grant benefits programmes for victims of trafficking.

At the State level, for example, the California Department of Social Services provides: Refugee Cash Assistance (limited to eight months for state-funded services, eligibility begins from date of the application for the benefits); Refugee Social Services (available for sixty months from the date of application for benefits); Food Stamps; CALWORKs (limited to a five-year period for adults: aid begins the date of application); Cash Assistance Program for Immigrants (CAPI); Employment Social Services; In-Home Supportive Services (IHSS) Programs (Personal Care Services Program (PCSP), IHSS Plus Waiver and IHSS Residual Program); State of California Department of Health and Human Services (Refugee medical assistance, Medi-Cal, Healthy Families Program).

Civil remedies

On 19 December 2003, when TVPA was reauthorized by Congress, provision was made for a private right of action for trafficked persons to seek civil remedy by holding his/her abusive spouse, employer, traffickers accountable for the injuries and damages. Civil litigation against perpetrators/abusers in human trafficking is a powerful tool to support victims in pursuing civil litigations against traffickers/abusers for civil compensation and serves as a disincentive to deter potential traffickers/abusive employers from financially exploiting victims in the future (Kim and Werner 2005). It may be the only means by which victims of trafficking can be 'made whole' again to recover and resume a normal life.[10]

Legal aid and assistance

'Helping trafficking victims access legal avenues to justice, restitution, and other compensation for their suffering is a key element of any effective victim protection strategy' (US Department of State 2009, p. 1), and this is particularly true when addressing the needs of foreign and disadvantaged victims who are not familiar with laws, customs, rights, and procedures and lack the financial resources needed to fund representation by private attorneys in the various legal proceedings they often encounter. One way in which the State helps is to provide legal aid attorneys to represent victims in civil litigation, criminal proceedings, immigration petition and protection of minors.

Civil litigation includes litigation against employers, traffickers or buyers of a person; applications for immigration reliefs such as a petition for T- or U-visa and unification of family; and the dissolving of a marriage or obtaining a marriage licence (this will include such issues as child custody, support and visitation rights; property division; spousal support; return home; obtaining of legal travel documents; and financial assistance for travel). Criminal proceedings include the following:

- advise victims of their rights, options, consequences of criminal trial and prosecutions;
- represent victims in criminal investigation and prosecution process;
- represent victims in restitution settlements;
- notify victims upon release of offenders;
- advise and represent victims in applying for the victim compensation fund.

Compensation for civil damages includes compensatory damages, punitive damages, nominal damages, injunctive and other equitable relief, liquidated damages, statutory damages, pre-judgement interest, attorney fees and costs, and the Assembly Bill 22 in Legislature of the State of California (AB22) provides for damages if human trafficking is proven.

Equal Employment Opportunity Commission

The EEOC, a federal law enforcement agency, was created under the 1964 Civil Rights Act to investigate claims of discrimination in workplace and to work out settlements between worker and employer/company in judicial proceedings. It consists of a five-member Commission, a General Council and more than fifty offices located nationwide in fifteen districts. The EEOC was also given authority in 1972 to sue employers in federal court on behalf of employees, including illegal alien workers, for violation of federal statutes. All financial compensation recovered from EEOC lawsuits goes to victims. Under the federal mandates, the EEOC is responsible for enforcing the following four laws: Title VII of the Civil Rights Act of 1964; Equal Pay Act of 1963; Age Discrimination in Employment Act of 1967; and Americans with Disabilities Act of 1990.

In recent years, the EEOC has joined other law enforcement agencies to become a powerhouse in fighting against human trafficking, especially labour trafficking. It represents victims against abusive employers in labour trafficking cases in civil courts for the following wrongdoings: denial of benefits; withholding wages; confiscation of ID/legal documents; sexual harassment in the workplace; sexual assault and rape of domestic or farm workers (legal or illegal); physical abuse or emotional abuse; sex discrimination in the workplace; and forcible performance of illegal acts in the course of employment.

Trafficking cases often involve discrimination on the basis of national origin or race. Even when employees are legally brought into this country, employers may discriminate on the basis of national origin or race through the use of force, fraud or coercion. This discrimination may include harassment and setting different terms and conditions of employment. It also may include retaliation against workers for exercising their rights under the anti-discrimination laws, by threatening them with or subjecting them to suspension from work, deportation, physical harm or fraud. In trafficking cases, it is not unusual for employers to maintain segregated jobs, pay unequal wages or deduct unreasonable amounts from pay. Many labour trafficking cases also involve sexual harassment, exploitation, and sexual assault or rape. Trafficked women are sometimes sexually assaulted or subjected to other severe sexual harassment. The EEOC is the federal agency charged with preventing, investigating and remedying sex discrimination, including sexual harassment and sexual exploitation (EEOC 2011a).

In recent years, the EEOC has successfully sued several large corporations for alleged discrimination in labour trafficking cases. In 2006, Federal District Court Judge Claire V. Eagan in a seventy-one-page decision following two earlier trials ordered John Pickle Co. to pay US$1.24 million compensation to fifty-two foreign workers in a labour trafficking case. The EEOC's lawsuit was joined with a related civil action which had been filed by the workers on their own behalf, alleging false imprisonment, minimum wage violations under the Fair Labour Standards Act (FLSA), deceit and intentional infliction of emotional distress.[11] The total damages awarded by the Court addressed the claims in both the government's suit and the private action. In the same year, the EEOC also settled a civil litigation against Trans Bay Steel Inc. for an estimated US$1 million in total monetary relief and compensation for forty-eight welders of Thai descent who were discriminated against and exploited due to their national origin.[12] In 2011, in what was then its largest human trafficking case in agriculture, the EEOC filed lawsuits in Hawaii and Washington against Global Horizons Inc., a Beverly Hills-based farm labour contractor, and eight farms. The EEOC contended that Global Horizons engaged in a pattern or practice of national origin and race discrimination, harassment and retaliation, when it trafficked over two hundred Thai male victims to farms in Hawaii and Washington where they were subjected to severe abuse[13] (EEOC 2011b).

Conclusions

It is clear that human trafficking is an emerging human rights issue in the twenty-first century. The real issue of harm behind trafficking, transporting or moving human beings across national or international borders is not about trafficking per se but about the slavery, exploitation and abuse of human rights and human dignity that it involves. As President Obama stated recently '…[it human trafficking] ought to concern every nation because it endangers public health and fuels violence and organized crime… It is barbaric and it is evil, and it has no place in a civilized world' (Human Trafficking Watch 2013). For public health, community safety and society's wellbeing, prevention and protection policies must focus on reducing harm for victims of human trafficking, especially in the post-rescue stage. Victims have suffered tremendous physical, sexual and psychological abuse and have survived incredible ordeals at the hands of abusers and traffickers. To help them recover and resume a normal life, relocating them in a safe and secure environment, and reuniting them with their family members is the most effective and humanitarian strategy for successful criminal investigation and prosecution in any civilized country.

Notes

1 'Qualified aliens' include (Sec 431): Legal permanent residents, asylees, refugees, aliens paroled into the US for at least one year, aliens whose deportations are being withheld, aliens granted conditional entry (prior to April 1, 1980), battered alien spouses, battered alien children, the alien parents of battered children, alien children of battered parents who fit certain criteria, Cuban/Haitian entrants, and victims of a severe form of trafficking (US Department of Health and Human Services: 2009. See http://aspe.hhs.gov/hsp/immigration/restrictions-sum.shtml#sec1).
2 The Convention was adopted by General Assembly resolution 55/25 of 15 November 2000 and entered into force in 2003.The third instrument of the Convention is the Protocol against the Illicit Manufacturing of and Trafficking in Firearms.
3 There is ongoing debate on whether commercial and illegal adoption of children or trafficking for forced marriage should be recognized as a form of human trafficking and be included in this definition chart. Those crimes are more prevalent in developing countries than in the industrialized world. For further information, visit the ILO and IOM websites for more discussion and details.
4 Under the TVPA mandate, federal statutes (US Code, Title 18) have incorporated the following provisions in regard to crime of trafficking in persons: 118 U.S.C. § 1581 Peonage (Debt Bondage); 18 U.S.C. § 1583 Enticement into slavery; 18 U.S.C. § 1584 Sale into Involuntary Servitude; 18 U.S.C. § 1589 Forced Labor; 18 U.S.C. § 1590 Trafficking Into Servitude; 18 U.S.C. § 1591 Sex Trafficking; 18 U.S.C. § 1593A Benefiting Financially from Peonage, Slavery, and Trafficking in Persons; 18 U.S.C. § 1351 Fraud in Foreign Labor Contracting; 18 U.S.C. § 1592 Falsified or Fraudulent Documents.
5 This bill (S. 1301 (112th)) was originally introduced on 13 October 2011, in the 112th session of the US Congress, but was not enacted and was pending for reintroduction in 2012. The Bill was reintroduced to the Congress in 2012. Led by Senator Leahy, the TVPRA was reauthorized (P.L. 113-4). On 7 March 2013, President Obama signed this bill into law.
6 Prostitution is illegal in most States in the US, as it is in the majority of countries in the world. Even in those countries where it is legal, engagement of an illegal alien in prostitution is nevertheless deemed illegal because of the alien's illegal status in the country.
7 Harm reduction is a set of practical strategies that help people reduce the negative consequences of drug use, alcoholism and mental illness by addressing the conditions of use and treatment. It was originally developed to deal with drug abuse in the community by emphasizing improving the quality of life, health and wellbeing of individuals and communities as the primary criteria for success (Single et al. 1997; International Harm Reduction Association 2010).
8 Victims of Trafficking and Violence Protection Act of 2000, Pub. L. No. 106-386 (Oct. 28 2000). Codified at INA §§ 101(a)(15)(T) 101(a)(15)(U) 214(n) 214(p) 245(l), and 245(m).
9 The information contained in this section was partially contributed by CAST (Coalition Against Slavery and Trafficking in Los Angeles).

10 The Trafficking Victims Protection Act of 2003 provides the explicit right to civil action under 8 USC § 1595 (TVPRA of 2008 – No action may be maintained under this section unless it is commenced not later than ten years after the cause of action arose; prior to 2003 – Implied rights of action under the Thirteenth Amendment and its enabling statute). California: AB 22 granted explicit right to civil action and treble damages: Fair Labor Standards Act, Alien Tort Claims Act, Migrant and Seasonal Agricultural Worker Protection Act, Title VII of the Civil Rights Act and Civil Rights Act of 1866 ('Section 1981').
11 *Chellen et al. and EEOC v. John Pickle Company, Inc.*, Case Number 02-CV-0085-CVE-FHM [Base File] and 02-CV-0979-CVE-FHM [Consolidated] in the US District Court for the Northern District of Oklahoma.
12 US EEOC v. Trans Bay Steel, Inc., Case Number CV 06-07766 CAS (JTLx).
13 The EEOC filed its lawsuit in the US District Court for the District of Hawaii *(EEOC v. Global Horizons, Inc. d/b/a Global Horizons Manpower, Inc., Captain Cook Coffee Company, Ltd et al.*, Case Number CV-11-00257-DAE-RLP) and the US District Court for the Eastern District of Washington *(EEOC v. Global Horizons, Inc. d/b/a Global Horizons Manpower, Inc., Green Acre Farms, Inc. et al.*, Case Number 2:11-cv-03045-EFS).

Bibliography

Banks, D. and Kyckelhahn, T., 2011. Characteristics of Suspected Human Trafficking Incidents, 2008–2010. Available at: www.bjs.gov/index.cfm?ty=pbdetail&iid=2372 [Accessed 15 January 2013].

Equal Employment Opportunity Commission (EEOC), 2011a. Human Trafficking and EEO Law. Available at: www.eeoc.gov/eeoc/interagency/trafficking.cfm [Accessed 10 April 2013].

Equal Employment Opportunity Commission (EEOC), 2011b. EEOC Files Its Largest Farm Worker Human Trafficking Suit Against Global Horizons, Farms. Available at: www.eeoc.gov/eeoc/newsroom/release/4-20-11b.cfm [Accessed 10 April 2013].

Homeland Security Investigation (HIS, USDHS), 2013. Human Trafficking Cases Investigated by Homeland Security Investigations. Presented at Human Trafficking Conference: Protecting Our Children. Sacramento, 8 February 2013.

GovTrack, 2000. Congress Bill-H.R. 3244 (106th): Victims of Trafficking and Violence Protection Act of 2000. Available at: www.govtrack.us/congress/bills/106/hr3244 [Accessed 20 December 2012].

GovTrack, 2011. Congress Bill-S. 1301 (112th): Trafficking Victims Protection Reauthorization Act of 2011. Available at: www.govtrack.us/congress/bills/112/s1301 [Accessed 5 March 2013].

Human Trafficking Watch, 2013. Barack Obama on Human Trafficking. In Human Trafficking Awareness. Available at: http://humantrafficwatch.wordpress.com/2013/02/07/7219/ [Accessed 7 February 2013].

International Harm Reduction Association, 2010. What is Harm Reduction? A position statement from the International Harm Reduction Association. Available at: www.ihra.net/files/2010/08/10/Briefing_What_is_HR_English.pdf [Accessed 3 March 2014].

ILO, 2012. A Global Alliance against Forced Labour and Trafficking in Persons: Key Achievements of the ILO's Special Action Programme to Combat Forced Labour and Trafficking in Persons, 2001–2011. Geneva: ILO.

Kim, K. and Werner, D., 2005. Civil Litigations on Behalf of Victims of Human Trafficking. Los Angeles: Legal Aid Foundation of Los Angeles.

Polaris Project, 2013. 2013 State Ratings on Human Trafficking laws. Available at: www.polarisproject.org/what-we-do/policy-advocacy/national-policy/state-ratings-on-human-trafficking-laws/2013-state-ratings-on-human-trafficking-laws [Accessed 28 Febuary 2014].

Tullao, T., Cortez M.A. and See, E., 2007. The Economic Impacts of International Migration: A Case Study on the Philippines. Center for Business and Economics Research and Development De La Salle University- Manila, Philippines.

United Nations, 2000a. Protocol to Prevent, Suppress and Punish Trafficking in Persons, Especially Women and Children, Supplementing the United Nations Convention against Transnational Organized Crime. Geneva: UN.

United Nations, 2000b. Protocol Against the Smuggling of Migrants by Land, Sea, and Air, Supplementing the United Nations Convention against Transnational Organized Crime. Available at: www.uncjin.org/Documents/Conventions/dcatoc/final_documents_2/convention_smug_eng.pdf [Accessed 5 March 2013].

United Nation Global Initiative to Fight Human Trafficking (UN.GIFT), 2010. Analysing the Business Model of Trafficking in Human Beings to Better Prevent the Crime. Vienna: UN.GIFT.

United Nations Office of Drug Control (UNODC), 2012a. Global Report on Trafficking in Persons-2012. Vienna: UNODC.

United Nations Office of Drug Control (UNODC), 2012b. United Nations Convention against Transnational Organized Crime and the Protocols Thereto: Sixth session of the Conference of the Parties to the United Nations Convention against Transnational Organized Crime, Vienna, 15–19 October 2012. Available at: www.unodc.org/unodc/en/treaties/CTOC/index.html [Accessed 8 February 2013].

United Nations Office of Drug Control (UNODC), 2013. Human Trafficking and Migrant Smuggling. Available at: www.unodc.org/unodc/en/human-trafficking/what-is-human-trafficking.html[Accessed 10 February 2013].

UNODC and UN.GIFT, 2009. Anti-Human Trafficking Manual for Criminal Justice Practitioners. Vienna: UNODC.

US Department of Homeland Securiy(USDHS), 2009. Improving the Process for Victims of Human Trafficking and Certain Criminal Activity: The T and U Visa, January 29, 2009. Office of the Citizenship and Immigration Services Ombudsman.

US Department of State, 2006. The Trafficking Victims Protection Reauthorization Act of 2005. Office to Monitor and Combat Trafficking in Persons: US Laws on Trafficking in Persons.

US Department of State, 2009. Legal Assistance for Trafficking Victims: Fact Sheet. Office of Monitor and Combat Trafficking in Persons: Democracy and Global Affairs.

US Immigration and Customs Enforcement (USICE), 2011. Victims of Human Trafficking: T Nonimmigrant Status. Available at: www.uscis.gov/portal/site/uscis/menuitem.eb1d4c2a3e5b9ac89243c6a7543f6d1a/?vgnextoid=02ed3e4d77d73210VgnVCM100000082ca60aRCRD&vgnextchannel=02ed3e4d77d73210VgnVCM100000082ca60aRCRD [Accessed 5 March 2013].

Single, E., Stockwell, T. and Plant, M.A., 1997. Alcohol: Minimising the Harm. Free Association Books Limited.

Part II
Transitional justice

Chapter 8

Victims, transitional justice and social reconstruction
Who is setting the agenda?

Harvey M. Weinstein

> ... what first appears as a hypothesis – with or without its implied alternatives, according to the level of sophistication – turns immediately usually after a few paragraphs, into a 'fact'. Which then gives birth to a whole string of similar non-facts, with the result that the purely speculative character of the whole enterprise is forgotten.
> (Hannah Arendt, *On Violence*, 1969, p. 6–7)

Introduction

In a post-conflict society, citizens are faced with two critical tasks – holding accountable those who committed human rights violations and rebuilding a trusting society dedicated to coexistence with former enemies. These two options may be pursued simultaneously or in sequence but each direction may have the untoward consequence of undermining the other's goals. In this chapter, I examine this tension as it is manifested around the needs of those who have suffered repression, torture, disappearances and mass violence. Victims occupy a special place in the lexicon of international justice; its Latin derivation connotes a sacrificial animal (Van Dijk 2009). Post-conflict justice attempts to assuage the sacrifice by securing punishment for the guilty and sometimes, reparations for the harmed. But what if a focus on retributive punishment means that a society may have greater difficulty in securing stability and peace? What if the focus on victimhood results in long-term negative consequences for those so labelled? Has the notion of universal norms for international criminal justice disempowered local communities in their efforts to achieve peace and the opportunity to rebuild their lives? Do truth commissions meet the needs of victims or are they primarily half-hearted efforts at state-building? And most importantly, are we wedded to disciplinary beliefs and structures that blind us to what is best for those who have lost the worlds they knew? Transitional justice attempts to address many of these questions in its efforts to respond to both victims and to the needs of a fractured society. I suggest that despite transitional justice's many accomplishments, this tension remains unresolved.

In examining the complex interaction of victim needs, transitional justice and social reconstruction, I want to emphasize three points: first, context matters. Although transitional justice strategies have evolved over time, the underlying premises about the value of retributive justice and the importance of revealing factual truth have not changed. These assumptions may make little sense across cultures and may be resisted. Second, transitional justice processes reinforce a sense of victimhood and entitlement that rarely is satisfied, leading to dashed expectations and the maintenance of negative attitudes towards those who have committed wrongs. Further, those who have suffered at the hands of an abusive regime may become lost in the politics of victimhood, discipline boundaries and political power plays. Finally, I argue that the global community has established transitional justice processes that may clash with the goal of rebuilding societies. If these societies do not undergo a social transformation towards pro-social behaviours, then most victims may remain victims – consigned to second-class status and excluded from access to the rights and privileges of full citizenship. An emphasis on legalism and the litigation of human rights abuses may lead to the untoward consequence of neglecting the goals of social reconstruction rather than contributing to its achievement.

Since the 1990s, the principal focus of transitional justice has been on judicial mechanisms and truth commissions. The rapid growth of a judicial approach to holding perpetrators legally accountable for their actions in violating international humanitarian law reached its zenith in 1998 when 120 countries adopted the Rome Statute that established a legal framework for the International Criminal Court. The court entered into force in 2002 when 60 countries ratified the statute (Bass 2000; Teitel 2003; Roht-Arriaza and Mariezcurrena 2006; Weinstein *et al.* 2010). The goal of an international tribunal (as with the legal system in general) is primarily to focus on individuals, to determine their innocence or guilt, and to sentence them accordingly. Such a court is top-down and is primarily perpetrator-centred.[1] Partially, in response to this, truth commissions that are victim-centred have evolved sometimes as stand-alone mechanisms, in conjunction with trials, domestic or international, associated with amnesties or as a prelude to trials. There is overlap in many goals of truth commissions and trials, e.g. in developing a record of 'truth' or in contributing to the development of historical memory, although how each mechanism does that or uses these findings differs.

As transitional justice mechanisms have evolved, what is expected of these processes has evolved as well. From a focus on individual accountability, practitioners, policymakers, diplomats and scholars have expanded the reach of transitional justice to include peace, reconciliation, development, governance, legal reform, economic reform, and women's rights – most of which are designed to produce democratic free market states governed by rule of law in which human rights are scrupulously observed. It is the transformation of institutions, a component of transitional justice, which has been the most difficult goal to achieve. The idea of social repair or social reconstruction seems intuitively to be a good idea. If a society has been fractured by violence and war, rebuilding its infrastructure – physical, political and social – seems like a worthwhile endeavour. Yet, as we have seen, time and again, elections do not bring democracy; rebuilding courthouses, providing computers, and training court personnel do not necessarily bring rule of law. Nor does rule of law necessarily means an end to human rights abuses. Restructuring the political system does not always mean the end of corruption or crony capitalism. While transitional justice programmes may lead to positive societal changes (Olsen *et al.* 2010), other reports raise questions about what these so-called positive effects of transitional justice mean on the ground.

This chapter is divided into five sections: first, I examine some of the critical perspectives on transitional justice, international norms and rule of law; second, I look at the debate around the effects of international intervention and transitional justice with reference to Bosnia and Herzegovina; third, I examine the role of victims and victimhood in relation to the discipline of victimology and the concept of social reconstruction; fourth, I summarize some of the studies that have examined victim attitudes to transitional justice – in particular, trials (domestic and international) and truth commissions; and finally I look at the association of trauma effects and trials. In the conclusion, I explore the dilemma raised by Hannah Arendt (quoted above) in relation to unfulfilled expectations and the limitations of unexamined assumptions.

Transitional justice, international norms and the 'rule of law'

The restoration of 'rule of law' has become the focus for those involved in the rebuilding of societies after periods of repression, mass violence and in so-called failed states. As legal scholar Rosa Ehrenreich Brooks describes the motivation for this emphasis, she notes that there is a confluence of interests – human rights advocates, business interests and security interests. Literally, millions of dollars have gone into funding these endeavours over the past two decades but as Brooks (2002–3, p. 2280) notes, '… promoting the rule of law has become a fundamentally imperialist enterprise in which foreign administrators backed by large armies govern societies that have been pronounced unready to take on the task of governing themselves'. Consequently, this legalist perspective results in a concerted effort to adopt and implement the more procedural aspects of change such as the writing of a new constitution, judicial reform and training of judges and prosecutors, penal reform, police training and reform. Institutional change involves the dismantling or rearrangement of state structures; this is usually directed from above or by internationals from outside the country. Thomas Carothers of the Carnegie Endowment for International Peace (1998) describes the difficulty in achieving rule of law in that the formal aspects are easy to achieve; however, putting it into practice is far more problematic. While both Brooks and Carothers acknowledge the need for rule of law, they are realists and acknowledge that too much has been expected of its success in rebuilding societies. Why is this?

The answer is clear: there exists a fundamental gap between achieving formal structural change and the will to change among those most affected. There are many constituencies to consider, including those in power who do not cede it willingly, those who see new opportunities for personal gain and those who see themselves as powerless to influence the policies that might improve their opportunities and freedoms. The law functions because a society's values espouse the protections that rule of law can offer. As Brooks (2002–3, p. 2285) notes, '... creating the rule of law is most fundamentally an issue of norm creation'. And further,'... the rule of law is a culture, yet the human-rights-law and foreign-policy communities know very little – and manifest little curiosity – about the complex processes by which cultures are created and changed'. Rosemary Nagy (2008, p. 278) touches on similar points in a critical reflection on transitional justice by emphasizing that transitional justice 'has been heavily influenced by that "international legalist paradigm", which focuses on generating elite and mass compliance with international humanitarian norms'.

There are two potential problems here: first, that externally imposed solutions based on values that differ from those that underpin a society's attitudes, behaviours and history will be extremely difficult to implement; second, that the focus of transitional justice on retributive approaches narrows the lens to that of perpetrators and victims; to guilt and innocence of individuals and away from the social norms and policies that allowed human rights abuses to develop and be sustained. The idea of transition further reinforces the idea of 'now' and 'then' (Nagy 2008, p. 280) and ignores societal continuities that are a far greater challenge to influence. Carothers (2002) raises the critical question of whether the idea of transition is even viable or useful and suggests that it is time to end the 'transition paradigm'. Bronwyn Leebaw (2011) in her analysis of two approaches – human rights legalism and restorative justice – notes how they share the premise that the crime represents a deviation from community norms and thus the focus on individual victims and perpetrators is reasonable. However, this leads to a depoliticization of transitional justice. That is, the legalistic focus tends to downplay the systematic or ingrained societal contributions to the history of abuse. While holding perpetrators accountable has value, of course, an opportunity to influence the character of a society, i.e. norm change, may be lost.

I suggest in this chapter that the influence of rule of law is overplayed and that both the huge sums of money spent as well as the timing and processes of implementation are based more on assumptions than evidence. As Brooks (2002–3, p. 2298) notes, in quoting the work of social psychologist Tom Tyler and criminologist Raymond Paternoster 'moral beliefs were more central to decisions about whether to break the law than assessments of the likelihood and seriousness of punishment'. Again, societal values come into play: '... when people already believe law matters, it will matter; when people think law doesn't matter, it never can, and it is unclear how to go from the latter state to the former' (p. 2301). While common belief holds that law prevents violence, Brooks presents a cogent argument that this is only true when a society has collectively accepted that rule of law represents its shared values. If this is so, then the challenge is how to inculcate these beliefs in a society where repression, violence and mass atrocity permeate its history.

David Gray (2010, p. 55) examines these issues from the perspective that transitional justice is 'extraordinary justice' and that 'what distinguishes pre-transitional abuses from ordinary crime is the role played by an abusive paradigm'. He defines this as 'a combination of social norms, law, and institutional practice that utilizes a bipolar logic to justify targeted violence'. That is, it reflects a societal definition of who is in and who is out. This paradigm emerges when there is a collapse of 'the overlapping network of associations and oppositions that restricts violence and violent impulses in stable regimes'. The task then is to reconstitute this network and the question is how transitional justice processes can contribute to this process of social reconstruction. Ordinary criminal justice – individual victims and perpetrators – in domestic courtrooms, usually does not address these kinds of questions. If the end result of the abusive paradigm is that members of the ostracized or excluded group lose their full privileges of participation in society's institutions, then transitional justice must include measures to restore them to full membership in the community and be recognized for their loss of status. This implies societal change with attention to social and economic rights and distributive justice.

The characteristic focus of transitional justice processes has been either exclusively or primarily on violations of civil and political rights. However, consider the argument of Louise Arbour, then UN High Commissioner for Human Rights (Arbour 2006, pp. 4–5):

> Given transitional justice's additional objective of bringing about social transformation that will prevent a resurgence of conflict, (it is perhaps) even more effective to attack the sources of legitimate grievances that, if unaddressed, are likely to fuel the next conflagration.

She further highlights the tension between a focus on the individual and an appropriate response to the collective. 'We need to be clear,' she states, 'that reparations to individual victims will never substitute for more broad based and longer term socio-economic policies that aim to address and prevent widespread inequalities and discrimination' (p. 12). While acknowledging the needs of those who have suffered, High Commissioner Arbour recognized that social transformation of a society is fundamental to social reconstruction – not secondary and not left to others to achieve but part and parcel of the transitional justice response.

Transitional justice on the ground – Bosnia and Herzegovina in 2011

Given the questions raised about the limits of retributive justice and the need for change in social norms to achieve long-term social reconstruction, it is instructive to examine the impact of transitional justice in Bosnia-Herzegovina, with an almost twenty-year history of exposure to the work of the International Criminal Tribunal for the Former Yugoslavia (ICTY) and the War Crimes Chamber in the Criminal Division of the State Court. In both cases, retributive justice is the model. The concept paper prepared for the ICTY Global Legacy Conference (November 2011) details its achievements: the conference goal was to 'explore the impact of the Tribunal's work on international humanitarian law and international criminal procedure as well as the potential of its jurisprudence to shape the future of global justice and the advancement of human rights' (Introduction). Its focus, many would say appropriately, was on its legacy in advancing jurisprudence in this area.

Missing in the concept paper is an examination of the legacy of the ICTY with respect to the social reconstruction of Bosnia-Herzegovina. If social transformation does in fact require change in societal norms, then it seems unreasonable to expect any court to achieve this goal. However, given the context in which the Court was established and the expectations raised for its contributions to peace and reconciliation, we should, some twenty years later, offer a perspective on whether the court has contributed or influenced change in that direction. What we find is that, despite differences in research methodologies and disciplinary proclivities, the contribution of transitional justice is not straightforward. Further, given the important dimension of time, it is exceedingly difficult to parse out the influence of transitional justice from the conflating factors of security, refugee return, peace and cross-ethnic coexistence.

Legal scholar Diane Orentlicher's important study of the impact of the ICTY in Bosnia reaffirms the complexity of social transformation and the difficulty in assessing how much an international tribunal has influenced that process. She writes (Orentlicher 2010, p. 19) that Bosnia has 'seen only limited progress' towards the goal of seeing the ICTY influence war criminals, bystanders and beneficiaries to acknowledge their roles, condemn the crimes and express remorse. As the Berkeley Human Rights Centre found in its 2000 and 2002 surveys (Stover and Weinstein 2004), she reports that 'leaders of all three major ethnic groups have treated convicted war criminals from their own ethnic group as war heroes. And most Bosnians experience justice through an ethnic lens'. However, she further notes 'many Bosnians believe that the ICTY's unassailable conclusions are a form of justice in themselves'. This is a critical finding in that it may reflect both the strength and weakness of an international tribunal. Orentlicher (2010, p. 99) writes:

> While many of our interlocutors in Bosnia are discouraged that 'three versions of the truth' persist fourteen years after Dayton, we did not interview anyone who concluded that the ICTY was for that reason a failure. Instead, many believe that disappointments in this regard make the Tribunal's role in establishing facts all the more important.

Although the Berkeley group found that over a two-year period these attitudes changed for some, the fact they persist so many years later suggests that the contribution of the law to attitude change is considerably less than one might hope.

Several practitioners and scholars have advanced a more optimistic view of Bosnia's success as a socially transformed state. Political analyst Gerald Knaus frames the successes as the 'return of over one million persons and refugees throughout all of Bosnia... the large-scale restitution of assets ... (and) the almost complete demilitarization of post war Bosnia' (Stewart and Knaus 2011, p. 119). Bosnians do live together with no serious inter-ethnic violence; there has been some school integration and a multi-ethnic police force. Knaus suggests that the establishment of the ICTY was a critical factor in Bosnia's success, although he situates it in the midst of a remarkable number of other factors that could just as easily account for the changes. Political scientist Lara Nettelfield (2010a, p. 15) also argues that the ICTY 'contributed to positive democratic development inside Bosnia... because it played a role in the creation of new post war identities based on rule of law and participation'. She suggests that it changed narratives about the past, promoted positive attitudes towards justice and accountability, and promoted an important growth in civil society.[2] Her study on attitudes towards the ICTY among soldiers of the Armed Forces of Bosnia and Herzegovina (BiH) (Nettelfield 2010b) suggests that many believed the Court had contributed to aspects of democratization, although Bosnian Serbs were less positive on most of the variables, such as whether the ICTY was a credible institution. There was, however, agreement on the question of whether those who commit war crimes should be brought to justice – a finding replicated by other studies.

And yet, is this the whole picture? Other writers find the situation to be far more complex on the ground, in the lived existence of those who confront the aftermath of the conflict more than fifteen years post-Dayton.[3] Political scientist Janine Natalya Clark (2009, p. 464) in a large qualitative study of 'ordinary' people found that none of the claims made by many who supported the establishment of the ICTY – that it would reduce the need for revenge, individualize guilt, establish a historical record and promote reconciliation – were supported by the interviews except perhaps, the first, where there is evidence for criminal justice as the most acceptable response to war crimes and crimes against humanity. The question of 'whose truth?' persists, as does denial and an ethnic lens in war narratives. She notes (Clark 2009, p. 475) that: 'what exists is a negative rather than a positive peace. It is peace "only as the absence of war" and not peace as the "harmonious ordering of differences". Extreme mistrust persists.'

Other studies suggest that Bosnian attitudes towards war crimes trials are ambivalent at best. Journalist and former spokesperson for the ICTY and the Outreach Section of the Court of BiH, Refik Hodzic, completed an interview study of victims' perspectives of war crimes trials in the municipality of Prijedor in the Republika Srpska where mass killings, rapes, torture, concentration camps and ethnic cleansing stained the history of the town forever. This rich compilation of victim narratives reveals great disappointment and frustrated expectations for what legal justice might have brought. Hodzic (2010, p. 118) writes:

... victims today do not have great – or in many cases any – expectations that war crimes trials will bring, or are capable of bringing, about the transformation of the social environment in which they live... most victims appear to have gone full circle from the trauma of the crimes committed against them, through the hope and high expectations of comprehensive justice, and, ultimately, to resignation and apathy that have arisen in part from disappointed expectations.

Victims, victimology and social reconstruction

The United Nations 1985 Declaration of Basic Principles of Justice for Victims of Crime and Abuse of Power raises two concerns in its conception and wording. First, its introduction states 'Cognizant that millions of people throughout the world suffer harm as a result of crime and abuse of power...'. This phrasing that lumps together ordinary crimes and abuse of power masks the very different problems that must be addressed when that abuse is promulgated by the state. Second, the Declaration notes that it '... is designed to assist Governments (and the international community)'. While it encourages states to legislate against human rights abuse, prohibits such practices as secret places of detention and encourages states to develop channels for victims to communicate, much of the Declaration is focused on criminal justice and does not lay out in the same detail the measures needed to acknowledge the needs of those who have been abused by state practices or indeed, non-state actors in a situation of mass violence or conflict.

The Declaration, which often is cited in the victimology literature, reinforces my view that victimology as a field has not focused sufficiently on those who are the recipients of human rights abuse. The 2005 Basic Principles on the Right to a Remedy and Reparations for Victims of Gross Violations of International Human Rights Law and Serious Violations of International Humanitarian Law addressed the omission of more specific guidelines to state abuse. However, with its focus on violations of international human rights and international humanitarian law, the legal paradigm became firmly entrenched in how states and the international community should respond to these violations. In these so-called van Boven-Bassiouni Principles, issues of social repair are limited to institutional transformation defined in such terms as the courts, the military, intelligence services, protection for certain professions, etc. The larger questions of distributive justice are ignored.

It would seem then that, just as conceptions of international criminal justice have emerged out of the idea of 'ordinary justice', views of how to respond to survivors of mass violence mimic the responses to 'ordinary crime', i.e. a legal response. Historically, the field of victimology has embraced this perspective.

Criminologist Ezzat Fattah (2000, p. 18) defines victimology as 'the scientific study of crime victims'. He describes the evolution of victimology in four important areas – first, data gathering; second, legislation to promote victim rights;

third, state compensation, offender restitution and victim–offender mediation programmes; and finally, a widespread though variable growth in victim services including psychotherapy. There is debate in the field about whether victimology has been sidetracked into an advocacy role (Cressey 1992; Elias 1994). Of even more concern is the question of whether this advocacy position has, in Fattah's words (2000, p. 25), 'helped to reinforce primitive vengeful reactions to crime and provided much needed ammunition to conservative politicians thus enabling them to implement their punitive agenda'. One example of this would be California's 'Three Strikes' law.[4] Elias (1994, p. 5) reinforces this view by asking whether the field is too heavily influenced by a law-and-order mentality or 'right realism'. From this perspective, crimes result from 'individual choices, not social conditions'. This belief echoes the views of those who see transitional justice primarily in terms of holding individuals accountable and paying less attention to the economic, social and cultural factors that usually underlie the repression or mass conflict that led to human rights abuses.

The retributive justice view is based partially on the idea that victims want justice and that the legal system is established to channel individual acts of vengeance into a system where the state supplies the remedy. But do we know what victims want or only what some of them want? And how much are attitudes determined by societal expectations influenced both politically and by media representations? Elias offers both case studies and other documentation to suggest that revenge and punishment may not be the most desired outcome for many victims. The New Zealand Department of Justice in a 1996 report finds that crime victims 'are no more punitive than non-victims' (Ch. 4.2) They quote Boers and Sessar (1991) who found in a quantitative study in Germany that ordinary people accepted restitution instead of punishment for hypothetical minor crimes. This was not the case for legal professionals. The New Zealand report recapitulates these findings.

Another dimension to how victims are viewed lies in the social construction of 'victimhood' and the societal elements that have converged to sustain the notion of the passive, helpless victim who requires legal intervention, political advocacy and punishment of victimizers. The process is similar to that described by psychiatrist Arthur Kleinman (quoted in Shoeb 2006, p. 6) who argued that survivors of traumatic experience must exchange stories of trauma for 'physical resources at their new place of refuge'. Victimologist Jan Van Dijk (2009) describes the bargain that takes place between society and those who have been victimized: in return for acknowledgement and various forms of support, victims will forsake their right to revenge. In his study of victims, he describes three themes that emerge from their narratives. These themes include manifestations of resilience, core feelings of anger and revenge fantasies, and post-traumatic altruism – the desire to channel their responses into positive interventions on behalf of those who have been victimized. However, society does not appear to accept these emerging strengths or any evidence of autonomy. Surprisingly, what often is seen is what Van Dijk (2009, p. 18) terms 'reactive victim scapegoating' – the victim is rejected if the dependent role is not acted out. Rather than building upon these core strengths and using the residual anger as a motivation, Western society turns victims into traumatized patients who require trauma treatment and a traumatic therapeutic victimology that leads to retributive punishment. As we will see, for survivors of mass violence, this approach often leads to significant disappointment. The victimology approach may, in fact, reinforce an essentialized notion of victimhood, often stripping them of any sense of agency – labelled a victim, living a new identity and trapped in the past.[5] Nils Christie (2010) also cautions about the untoward consequences of this approach and Fattah (2000, p. 38) is even more vehement: '… victimization is a normal and natural occurrence, a fact of life'. It should not be portrayed 'as a pathological and abnormal phenomenon'. Further, he argues that:

> the victim lobby has adamantly rejected any claim, even when supported by irrefutable evidence, that the roles of victim and victimizer are interchangeable and that much violence is the outcome of dynamic and explosive interactions rather than deliberate and unilateral actions of a flawed perpetrator's personality.

However, legal justice holds individuals accountable. There are perpetrators and there are victims. In mass violence, the line between the two is frequently blurred – perhaps, even more so than in ordinary crimes but the legal process follows the same route.

Thus we see a confluence of several movements – the victims' rights lobby, the therapist-trauma lobby and those who believe in the need and primacy of legal justice. The untoward consequences of the labelling of victims and the stripping away of their sense of efficacy are not usually considered.

In the rebuilding of states after mass violence and human rights abuses, a critical dilemma has emerged. If there is an emphasis on individual acts – usually of those in command positions – most of those who acted to inflict suffering will return to their homes and neighbourhoods and live among those who were victimized. Secondly, if the emphasis is primarily on punishment, will that be sufficient for victims? If as a consequence of trial decisions or truth commissions or peace treaties the idea of reparations or restitution for victims is promoted, then we must confront such questions as: What kinds of reparations? To whom should they go? Should they be symbolic or material? Should they be directed at individual victims and their families or should they be offered to victimized communities? These questions have important implications for transitional justice and the rebuilding of destroyed societies, especially if there is a goal of societal norm change – an objective that presents a challenge not only for retributive justice but also for the other mechanisms of transitional justice. We then must ask the question of what those victimized want after their homes have been destroyed, their loved ones missing, maimed or killed, their communities (physical and social) laid waste, and their futures, often in refugee camps or other countries, in doubt? We have a veritable army of 'experts' across fields as diverse as psychology, development, law, political science, diplomacy, military strategy, humanitarian assistance – but in all these, do the voices of those most affected receive a reasonable hearing?

Victims' attitudes towards transitional justice

The dilemma of how to assess the needs of survivors of mass violence confronts transitional justice researchers with the strengths and limitations of different data-gathering methodologies. Policymakers can base decisions on the traditional process of interviewing survivors or witnesses, a method followed by most human rights organizations and indeed, the method used in crime investigation, or they can develop population-based surveys that may offer a wider base of information.

Beginning in 1999 in the countries of the former Yugoslavia and Rwanda, the Human Rights Centre at the University of California, Berkeley initiated epidemiological surveys across randomly selected populations in an attempt to elucidate systemic patterns of human rights abuses as well as attitudes and beliefs about justice and reconciliation (Pham *et al.* 2004; Stover and Weinstein 2004; Pham *et al.* 2005; Pham *et al.* 2007; Vinck *et al.* 2008; Pham *et al.* 2009; Vinck *et al.* 2009; Pham and Vinck 2010; Vinck *et al.* 2011). As we have described elsewhere (Weinstein *et al.* 2010, p. 38), surveys allow us to

> examine broad patterns of experiences, attitudes and responses across geographic and socioeconomic boundaries; second, to look at the influence of demographic differences; third, to look at important associations of factors that may influence attitudes; and finally, to minimize biases that that may distort our understanding of events by random selection of respondents.

Over the next decade, these studies were implemented in Uganda, the Democratic Republic of Congo, Central African Republic, Cambodia and Liberia. While I focus here on the survey work, we also have employed qualitative methods such as interviews, focus groups and ethnographic studies, e.g. in Iraq shortly after the invasion where an interview study of a 'representative' sample was our most reasonable option (International Centre for Transitional Justice and Human Rights Centre 2004). Our studies suggest that multiple types of data-gathering methods will assure the most valid information on these attitudes.

While these surveys have examined attitudes towards justice, reconciliation, need for services, ethnic distance and other attitudes, in this chapter I focus specifically on how these survivors view the place of justice in social reconstruction. A review of the Human Rights Centre studies over the past decade[6] suggests that one cannot take for granted that all victims want legal justice. A great many factors are associated with these attitudes, such as exposure to trauma, socioeconomic status and education, prior life experience with members of the opposing group, belief in the national judicial system, knowledge of the international system of criminal justice, security status, cultural beliefs and practices and group identity. The responses may vary also with how a question is asked and the interpretation of findings needs to take this into account. For example, if the question is asked about what are the important priorities after mass violence, very few people choose justice. Thus, in Northern Uganda in 2005, less than 1 per cent of the sampled population reported that justice was an immediate need or concern (as opposed to peace at 31 per cent and food at 33 per cent). An interesting finding that emerged from the 2005 Uganda study was that those respondents who reported symptoms of post-traumatic stress disorder (PTSD) and depression were more likely to favour violent over nonviolent means to end the conflict. This may lend credence to Van Dijk's notion of the role of anger in those who have been victimized but raises concerns about how victims might perceive judicial mechanisms in which they are primarily observers or witnesses.

In a repeat survey in 2007, only 3 per cent listed justice as the top priority. However, if questions are asked specifically about accountability, over two-thirds of respondents believed it important to hold accountable those who committed violence. When asked which mechanisms would be most appropriate 29 per cent chose the International Criminal Court and 28 per cent the Ugandan courts. However, 20 per cent chose amnesties. To further complicate our understanding, when asked about how to prevent further conflict, 33 per cent of respondents chose the option of pardoning the leaders of the Lord's Resistance Army (LRA) and 20 per cent suggested forgiveness of the LRA leaders. Only 9 per cent selected accountability. In 2005, when asked whether they would accept amnesty if that were the road to peace, overall support was 71 per cent. Responses to these kinds of questions varied with geographic location, ethnic group and exposure to trauma but not always in the expected direction e.g. those who had been exposed to at least one of eleven traumatic events were more likely to support amnesty. In a third study in 2010 after the violence had subsided and displaced people were returning to the homes, priorities were food, agricultural assistance, education and health. The percentage who saw accountability and the need for trials as a high priority had dropped to 10 per cent or less. A 2008 study in Eastern Democratic Republic of Congo also found that when peace and security have not been achieved and basic needs are not met, only 2 per cent listed justice as a priority, 2 per cent prioritized arrests of perpetrators and 1 per cent described punishment as an important immediate action. Only 10 per cent thought that justice should be a priority for the government. However, as we have seen elsewhere, when asked specifically about accountability, more than 80 per cent of respondents felt it important to hold perpetrators accountable and an equal percentage saw accountability as necessary for peace. Similar findings were found in the Central African Republic, Liberia and Cambodia.

Other scholars have utilized surveys to unpack attitudes towards transitional justice. Their findings illustrate how our assumptions do not lead to clear-cut conclusions. Political scientists David Backer and Anu Kulkarni examined attitudes towards amnesty in five African countries and found that the majority of the victims supported amnesties (Backer 2009). This was associated with awareness that prosecutions would be problematic for the stability and peace in the state. Most felt that amnesties were unfair but were willing to accept limited amnesties if perpetrators performed actions related to restorative justice e.g. apologies or truth. Given the prevailing norm that amnesty provisions reinforce impunity and undermine rule of law, these finding are striking.

Finally, in Burundi, political scientist Cyrus Samii (2010) carried out another examination of transitional justice. In this 2007 survey, Samii found that in an ethnically divided society after peace was declared and before any transitional justice measures were instituted, support for retributive justice and punishment as well as truth-seeking appears to be lower than expected by policymakers, legal scholars and diplomats. The most common preference was for conditional forgiveness associated with a preference to forget the past. Samii suggests that political gain may be sufficient compensation for those who have been previously abused leading to avoidance of mechanisms designed to seek truth or punishment that might undermine those gains. His conclusions raise questions about the widely held assumptions of what victims want.

In summary, these quantitative studies indicate that the international community cannot continue to assume that current transitional justice mechanisms – trials and truth commissions in particular – lead clearly and unambiguously to a satisfactory response to the needs of those who have suffered. All the studies find that victim attitudes vary as a function of geography and war exposure, ethnic group identity, education, trauma, political pressures, historical context, and cultural ways of dealing with conflict and trauma especially place-based mechanisms, socioeconomic needs and security concerns. Context is critical.

Two books (Hinton 2010; Shaw *et al.* 2010) illustrate the value of deep qualitative analysis in piecing together the pieces of the puzzle to understand victim needs, by offering anthropological perspectives on transitional justice and local cultures in many countries across the world such as Peru, Guatemala, Burundi, Uganda and Timor Leste. Many use what Tim Kelsall (2009, p. 19) calls an 'anthropolitical perspective' to analyse these local perceptions and effects. Cyrus Samii's quantitative findings in Burundi are substantiated by the qualitative study of Nee and Uvin in Burundi (Shaw *et al.* 2010). They draw on three sources of data – a 2006 interview study on attitudes towards justice and reconciliation among 53 individuals in two communes selected for different trajectories of social reconstruction; a more open-ended study of 152 individuals in the same communes; and finally, another open-ended, nine-month study that included 238 interviews in these communes plus additional sites. Their overall finding is that the majority of Burundians across ethnic groups prefer to be silent – to forget. Most (with the exception of those in a large refugee camp years after peace was declared) have little desire for prosecutions or a truth commission. There appears to be little faith in judicial responses to injustice coinciding with a societal norm of letting-go and forgetting as a survival mechanism. As noted in the surveys previously described, Burundians appear to value security more than justice. Nee and Uvin (2010, p. 181) report that their study refutes the dominant assumption made by those who advocate transitional justice – 'that "the people" want western style justice' but are blocked by the elites. These findings corroborate those of Samii, who used a very different methodology and illustrated the value of combined methods in assessing victim needs.

Trauma, therapeutic justice, therapeutic victimology and social reconstruction

Fattah (2000, p. 41) decries the dangers of so-called 'victim therapy' and predicts its demise. He critiques the 'huge army of therapists' and suggests that the natural healing powers of human beings are obviated by these treatments. As I have described, the subjective experience of a victimhood mentality and the process of societal labelling often converge to change social identity from that of an active participant with agency to that of passive, dependent and helpless sufferer. Thus, trauma therapists constitute another advocacy group that influences how victims are seen and I argue that this emphasis on trauma with its individual focus inhibits social reconstruction.

In order for social reconstruction of a post-conflict society to occur, there clearly needs to be some shift in how individuals, communities and formerly warring groups perceive each other. Further, in order for social bonds to be constructed, a process for rehumanizing the stereotyped 'others' must be put into place (Kelman 1973; Halpern and Weinstein 2004). What this process is, or whether any outside or superimposed mechanism can be effective in influencing its rate or depth remains an open question. I suggest, however, that the disproportionate emphasis on legal and truth-seeking mechanisms that primarily are backward-looking and have characterized the response of the international community over the past twenty-five years may be steering us away from more localized, culture-congruent measures that may be less retributive and forward-directed. I argue here that the emphasis on responding to individual acts of violence and holding individuals accountable is a narrow perspective that limits the opportunities for social repair. Further, the universal prescriptions of international law promoted by the human rights community may be neither understood nor appreciated by those affected by violence (Kelsall 2009). While I support the idea that victims should receive reparations, the nature of those and the level at which such reparations should be directed – individual or community, tangible or symbolic, monetary or facilitative of autonomy and independence – exemplifies a concern that directly implicates the area of victimology.

Joan and Arthur Kleinman have challenged our conceptions of human suffering by describing how our affection for trauma narratives reduces 'complicated stories, based in real events... to a core cultural image of *victimization*' (Kleinman and Kleinman 1996, p. 9). They focus on how the medical profession transforms social experience into disease pathology. They note further: 'The person who undergoes torture first becomes a victim, an image of innocence and passivity, who cannot represent himself, who must be represented.' For medical professionals this representation comes in the form of a disease to be treated – post-traumatic stress disorder (PTSD). While I cannot in this chapter explore the vagaries of the debates both within the professions of psychiatry and psychology and between disciplines (e.g. anthropology and the therapeutic professions) about the validity of the PTSD diagnosis (Young 1995; Spitzer *et al.* 2008), my concern here is on how the concept of victimization is used in ways that may inhibit the processes of rehumanization and social repair in post-conflict societies. Here the appropriation of 'representation' occurs when legal professionals and the human rights community translate social suffering into a tort or crime that demands restitution or reparation. Lost in translation are the issues of distributive justice – the social, economic and cultural rights concerns – that may underlie the events that led to repression and/or violence. The word 'social' has an important meaning in considering social suffering and suggests that a broader lens on what constitutes social suffering and how to alleviate its effects requires attention to social forms of intervention. The focus on war crimes and crimes against humanity, while obviously of great import, may do very little to allow people to move beyond their societally sanctioned roles as victims. In fact, the process may have the untoward consequence of leaving them stuck – mired in the passive, dependent role of supplicant. As Kleinman (1997, p. 319) notes: 'this process of appropriation silences the collective authenticity of their own voices and denies their agency while redefining their needs away from demand for basic reforms of fundamental rights'. And what of truth commissions – are they not established to give voice to victims? I suggest that here as well, appropriation occurs, sometimes by government, sometimes by the international community, often by non-governmental organizations. The politics of transitional justice reflect powerful incentives on the part of its participants. Those incentives may not always be in the best interests of those who have suffered.

Didier Fassin (2009) in his exploration of 'the empire of trauma' describes how the focus on trauma actually obliterates lived experiences, especially in terms of what preceded the traumatic event (e.g. state oppression or the effects of extreme poverty). The simplistic condensation of the concept may obscure the realities of what the individual has experienced but may still be used by sufferers as a way of gaining a tangible form of acknowledgement that is socially supported. Thus, society makes judgements about who is the legitimate victim based on a variety of factors such as the validity of the claim, their social group, etc. This leads to some differentiation in how the idea of trauma is used, such as to argue for compensation or reparations or to find the truth as in truth commissions or court testimony and finally, for certification as in UN status as a refugee. In a post-conflict situation, where the roles of victim and perpetrator are so often blurred, some will be seen as the real suffers of trauma, others not. We constantly make these decisions that then send the sufferer on one path or another. As Kleinman (1997, p. 321) points out, social suffering '... is a professional discourse that organizes forms of suffering into as bureaucratic categories and objects of technical intervention'. He then elaborates: '... suffering is social, not only because social force breaks networks and bodies but also because social institutions respond with assistance to certain categories of sufferers while denying others or treating them with bureaucratic indifference'. These concerns are applicable in evaluating the contribution of transitional justice interventions to the rebuilding of societies – a social goal.

One additional assumption underlies the concept of therapeutic justice and what I term, therapeutic victimology. It is often stated that trials bring relief to victims, and that combating impunity is a necessary precondition for victims and thus, communities to 'heal'. Psychiatrist Metin Basoglu and colleagues, in a matched control group study of some 1,300 survivors of wartime atrocities in ex-Yugoslavia, found no evidence for this claim. They (Basoglu et al. 2005, p. 580) found that 'PTSD and depression in war survivors appear to be independent of sense of injustice arising from perceived lack of redress for trauma'. Further, they found that insecurity and loss of control over their lives were more closely associated with these symptoms. Therefore they note that if impunity is defined as leading to ongoing threat, then retributive justice might be seen as helpful at the level of community. Basoglu (2011) later clarified these findings:

> ... various other forms of redress, such as investigation of human rights violations, punishment of perpetrators, disclosure of the truth, public recognition of crimes..., public apology by the State, ... monetary and non-monetary compensation, restitution, and satisfaction are not likely to facilitate recovery from trauma in the absence of (specific)... psychological interventions.

Most survivors prefer interventions that restore social and economic recovery. However, Basoglu notes that for those with psychological symptoms, there is very little evidence for the effectiveness of most treatments for torture rehabilitation other than those designed to restore control over their lives to those affected. His studies cast doubt on the therapeutic justice model and raise questions about the generalizability of the therapeutic victimology model as well.

Conclusion

There are many stakeholders in the domestic and international arenas that firmly believe that they know how to respond when societies deconstruct. The agenda for post-conflict response has been set primarily at the international level by diplomats, political scientists, legal scholars and practitioners, military strategists, international non-governmental organizations, human rights groups, victim advocates and victims' rights groups. Still we see no definitive roadway that delineates the steps that might be helpful.

In this chapter, I have argued that context is critical; that transitional justice is limited in its capacity to promote social reconstruction; that those who have suffered may be re-victimized by the very processes designed to respond to their needs; and that the social transformation of a country requires processes that create pro-social norms and values.[7] Transitional justice, as currently understood, does not address those processes. Indeed, many would say that it should not.

It is not my purpose to denigrate the role that transitional justice – in particular, trials and truth commissions – can play in the rebuilding of fractured societies. Each of the traditional components of transitional justice may in concert offer some steps towards coexistence and stability. However, I do question the claims made for the effectiveness of each one and for the larger claims that suggest they lead to reconciliation, closure and the development of new and peaceful societal norms. Further, the assumptions that establishing rule of law (based on a Western view), as the primary step that will lead to all good things to follow has not been demonstrated conclusively. The drive to combat impunity through retributive justice also does not bear up under scrutiny. Just as the death penalty has not been shown to end homicide so are there no data to support the notion that trials decrease the likelihood of the next ethnic cleansing or genocide. What trials can do is to institutionalize a society's values of what behaviours will be acceptable. We are left, however, with the question of whether the universalization of the human rights regime generalizes a view of how to respond to behaviour that is based on assumptions that are not relevant in all societies.

The value of truth commissions may be contextually related as well. Not all societies want to remember and, as Shaw (2005, p. 1) has pointed out in Sierra Leone, not all societies want to articulate their experiences verbally and in public, preferring instead a 'forgive and forget' approach. Other components of transitional justice such as memorialization or lustration may have consequences when used for political gain or manipulation. My focus in this chapter is on untoward consequences – the 'side-effects' of direct intervention.

I have suggested then that retributive justice with its focus on individual perpetrators may undermine the drive towards social stability. As we have seen in the case of Bosnia, there has been little in the way of social reconstruction at the local level. The transformation of social norms remains the most significant challenge in post-conflict societies. We need to utilize what is known about norm creation at a population level in order to achieve this kind of change. Understanding and working within local cultures in collaboration with those affected is a first step. The gap between the establishment of democratic structures and democratic beliefs and behaviours can be very wide. The question remains as to whether a society prefers democracy with all its messiness or chooses a kind of order that may feel more secure but is associated with some constraints on its freedoms. How open is the global community to variation in justice and governance?

Further, I raise concerns about how those affected by mass violence may find themselves at the mercy of well-meaning advocates who espouse different strategies for 'healing' their pain. Both victimology and transitional justice practitioners have developed approaches that purport to provide justice, acknowledgement and treatment for victims which, it is hypothesized, then contribute to the rebuilding of fractured societies. These approaches often lead to untoward consequences such as the development of a 'victimization' identity characterized by passivity and dependence and disappointed survivors of conflict who become disillusioned by the inability of judicial mechanisms to punish sufficient numbers of perpetrators or that offer plea bargains or short sentences. While there is some evidence at a state level that combinations of trials, amnesties, and truth commissions (a 'justice balance') can lead to stronger democracies and human rights protections after repression and mass violence (Olsen *et al.* 2010), this chapter addresses the more immediate effects of these mechanisms at the level of individuals, communities and the quotidian nature of social reconstruction. I do not argue against these processes but caution against the conceptual creep that suggests their ability to achieve more than what they actually are capable of delivering. They are based on assumptions that have become almost factual – sets of beliefs that are insufficiently challenged. As Hannah Arendt describes in the quotation that began this chapter, 'the purely speculative nature of the whole enterprise in forgotten'. Perhaps if we stand back and revisit our goals, drop preconceived notions and listen to those most affected – in their communities, with their own language, understandings and rituals, we will become more effective in assisting those who have suffered while, at the same time, confront our own blind spots in theory and practice. If those invested in peace building and social repair learn to work with the language and in the traditions of post-conflict communities, then social transformation and value change may be possible. The emphasis on universal notions, heartily endorsed by human right groups and the United Nations, has heightened awareness of the gap between the global and the local. This is an opportune time to move beyond lip service and address this gap.

Notes

1 In recognition of this limitation, the International Criminal Court provides for victims to participate in a very circumscribed manner (i.e. not as witnesses) at the discretion of the Court. The Extraordinary Chambers in the Courts of Cambodia (ECCC) provide for the participation of 'civil parties' but here as well, participation has run into difficulty and increasingly has been constrained.
2 In contrast to Nettelfield, Jamie Rowen found that attempts to establish a regional commission in the countries of ex-Yugoslavia through the formation of an NGO network, the Coalition for RECOM (regional commission for truth-seeking about war crimes and other serious human rights violations committed in the recent past), or CoRECOM, foundered in BiH on persistent mistrust viewed through an ethnic lens that sabotaged the process. See Rowen (2012).
3 The 1995 Dayton Accord, signed near Dayton, Ohio by the presidents of Bosnia and Herzegovina, Croatia, and Serbia ended the 1992-95 Bosnian war by offering a General Framework for Peace.
4 California's draconian 1994 Three Strikes Law required that people with third felonies, even if minor, be imprisoned for life. In 2012, a referendum modified the law to assure that this would no longer be the case. Available at: <www.slate.com/articles/news_and_politics/jurisprudence/2012/11/california_three_strikes_law_voters_wanted_to_reform_the_state_s_harsh_law.html> [Accessed 17 December 2012].
5 Clarke (2009, p. 237) argues that international justice promotes the idea of victim helplessness: 'institutions such as the International Criminal Court actually draw their

power from the imaginary of the victim, whose liberation is possible only through suffering; the victim figure thus remains both central and marginal to the process'. She further notes '... the power to end violence exists more in its construction of justice than in its potentiality'.

6 The earliest studies in Rwanda, Uganda and the Balkans (2002–2005) were succeeded by a series of surveys in Congo, Liberia, Central African Republic, and Cambodia, carried out as part of the Initiative on Vulnerable Populations at the Human Rights Center led by Phuong Pham and Patrick Vinck and associated colleagues. Detailed reports and methodology can be found on the website of the Human Rights Centre at the University of California, Berkeley at: www.hrcberkeley.edu.

7 Prosocial behaviour is a term used in psychology defined as actions that benefit other people or society as a whole (Twenge et al. 2007). Available at: http://216.22.10.76/wiki/Prosocial_Behavior [Accessed on 4 January 2012].

Bibliography

Arbour, L., 2006. Economic and Social Justice For Societies in Transition. Centre For Human Rights and Justice Working Paper Number 10. NYU School of Law. Second Annual Transitional Justice Lecture Oct. 25.

Arendt, H., 1969. On Violence. San Diego, New York, London: Harcourt Brace & Company.

Backer, D., 2009. The Layers of Amnesty: Evidence from Surveys of Victims in Five African Countries. Global Studies Review, 5(3), October 22. Available at: www.globality-gmu.net/archives/1742 [Accessed 16 July 2012].

Basoglu, M., 2011. Prevention of Torture and Rehabilitation of Survivors – Review of the UN Committee against Torture Working Document on Article 14: Convention against Torture and other Cruel, Inhuman or Degrading Treatment or Punishment. In Metin Basoglu's Blog: Mass Trauma, Human Rights and Mental Health. July 29. Available at: http://metinbasoglu.wordpress.com [Accessed 10 January 2012].

Basoglu, M., Livanou, M., Crnobarić, C., Franciskovic, T., Suljić, E., Durić, D. and Vranesić, M., 2005. Psychiatric and Cognitive Effects of War in Former Yugoslavia: Association of Lack of Redress for Trauma and Posttraumatic Stress Reactions. JAMA, 294(5), pp. 580–590.

Bass, G., 2000. Stay the Hand of Vengeance: The Politics of War Crimes Tribunals. Princeton: Princeton University Press.

Boers, K. and Sessar, K., 1991. Do people really want punishment? On the Relationship between Acceptance of Restitution, Needs for Punishment, and Fear of Crime. In: K. Sessar and H.J. Kerner, eds, Development in Crime and Crime Control Research. New York: Springer, pp. 126–149.

Brooks, R.E., 2002–3. The New Imperialism: Violence, Norms and the 'Rule of Law'. Michigan Law Review, 101, pp. 2275–2340.

Carothers, T., 1998. The Rule of Law Revival. Foreign Affairs, 77(1), pp. 95–106.

Carothers, T., 2002. The End of the Transition Paradigm. Journal of Democracy, 13(1), pp. 5–21.

Christie, N., 2010. Victim Movements at a Crossroad. Punishment & Society, 12, pp. 115–122.

Clark, J.N., 2009. The Limits of Retributive Justice. Journal of International Criminal Justice, 7(3), pp. 463–487.

Clarke, K.M., 2009. Fictions of Justice: The International Criminal Court and the Challenge of Legal Pluralism in Sub-Saharan Africa. New York: Cambridge University Press.
Cressey, D.R., 1992. Research Implications of Conflicting Conceptions of Victimology. In: E.A. Fattah, ed., Towards a Critical Victimology. New York: St. Martin's Press, pp. 57–73.
Elias, R., 1994. Has Victimology Outlived Its Usefulness? Critical Criminology, 6(1), pp. 4–25.
Fassin, D., 2009. The Empire of Trauma: An Inquiry into the Condition of Victimhood. Princeton/Oxford: Princeton University Press.
Fattah, E., 2000. Victimology: Past, Present and Future. Criminologie, 33(1), pp. 17–46.
Gray, D., 2010. Extraordinary Justice. Alabama Law Review, 62(1), pp. 55–109.
Halpern, J. and Weinstein, H.M., 2004. Rehumanizing the Other: Empathy and Reconciliation. Human Rights Quarterly, 26(3), pp. 561–583.
Hinton, A.L., ed., 2010. Transitional Justice: Global Mechanisms and Local Realities after Genocide and Mass Violence. New Brunswick: Rutgers University Press.
Hodzic, R., 2010. Living the Legacy of Mass Atrocities: Victims' Perspectives on War Crimes Trials. Journal of International Criminal Justice, 8, pp. 113–136.
ICTY Global Legacy Concept Paper, 2011, November 15–16. The Hague.
International Centre for Transitional Justice and Human Rights Centre, University of California, Berkeley, 2004. Iraqi Voices: Attitudes Toward Transitional Justice and Social Reconstruction. New York. Available at: www.ictj.org/sites/default/files/ICTJ-Iraq-Voices-Reconstruction-2004-English.pdf [Accessed 16 July 2012].
Kelman, H.C., 1973. Violence Without Moral Restraint: Reflections on the Dehumanization of Victims and Victimizers. Journal of Social Issues, 29(1), pp. 25–61.
Kelsall, T., 2009. Culture Under Cross-Examination: International Justice and the Special Court for Sierra Leone. Cambridge: Cambridge University Press.
Kleinman, A., 1995. Writing at the Margin: Discourse between Anthropology and Medicine. Berkeley: University of California Press. Quoted in Marwa H. Shoeb, The Trauma Story: A Qualitative and Quantitative Exploration of Iraqi Survivors Experience. Master's thesis, University of California, Berkeley, 2006. On file with author.
Kleinman, A. and Kleinman, J., 1991. Suffering and Its Professional Transformation: Toward An Ethnography of Interpersonal Experience. Culture, Medicine and Psychiatry, 15(3), pp. 275–301.
Kleinman, A. and Kleinman, J., 1996. The Appeal of Experience, The Dismay of Images: Cultural Appropriations of Suffering in our Times. Daedalus, 123(1), pp. 1–23.
Kleinman, A., 1997. 'Everything That Really Matters': Social Suffering, Subjectivity, and the Remaking of Human Experience in a Disordering World. Harvard Theological Review 90(3), pp. 315–335.
Leebaw, B., 2011. Judging State-Sponsored Violence, Imagining Political Change. Cambridge: Cambridge University Press.
Nagy, R., 2008. Transitional Justice as Global Project: Critical Reflections. Third World Quarterly, 29(2), pp. 275–289.
Nee, A. and Uvin, P., 2010. Silence and Dialogue: Burundians' Alternatives to Transitional Justice. In: R. Shaw, L. Waldorf, with P. Hazan, eds, Localizing Transitional Justice: Interventions and Priorities After Mass Violence. Stanford: Stanford University Press, pp. 157–182.

Nettelfield, L., 2010a. Courting Democracy in Bosnia and Herzegovina: The Hague Tribunal's Impact in a Postwar State. Cambridge: Cambridge University Press.

Nettelfield, L., 2010b. From the Battlefield to the Barracks: The ICTY and the Bosnian Armed Forces (AFBiH). International Journal of Transitional Justice, 4(1), pp. 87–109.

New Zealand Ministry of Justice, 1996. Public Attitudes Towards Restorative Justice. In Restorative justice: A Discussion Paper: Ch. 4. Available at: www.justice.govt.nz/publications-archival/1996/restorative-justice-a-discussion-paper-1996 [Accessed 16 July2012].

Olsen. T.D., Payne, L.A. and Reiter, A.G., 2010. Transitional Justice in Balance: Comparing Processes, Weighing Efficacy. Washington: United States Institute of Peace.

Orentlicher, D.F., 2010. That Someone Guilty Be Punished: The Impact of the ICTY in Bosnia. New York: Open Society Justice Initiative and the International Centre for Transitional Justice.

Pham, P. and Vinck, P., 2010. Transitioning to Peace: A Population-based Survey on Attitudes About Social Reconstruction and Justice in Northern Uganda. Berkeley: Human Rights Centre. Available at: www.law.berkeley.edu/11979.htm [Accessed 16 July 2012].

Pham, P., Weinstein, H.M. and Longman, T., 2004. Trauma and PTSD Symptoms in Rwanda: Implications for Attitudes Toward Justice and Reconciliation. JAMA, 292(5), pp. 602–612.

Pham, P., Vinck, P., Wierda, M., Stover, E. and di Giovanni, A., 2005. Forgotten Voices. A Population-based Survey on Attitudes About Peace and Justice in Northern Uganda. New York and Berkeley: International Centre for Transitional Justice and Human Rights Centre, UC Berkeley. Available at: www.law.berkeley.edu/11979.htm [Accessed 16 July 2012].

Pham, P., Vinck, P., Stover, E., Moss, A., Wierda, M. and Bailey, R., 2007. When the War Ends: Northern Uganda. New York, NY and Berkeley: International Centre for Transitional Justice, Human Rights Center, UC Berkeley, and Payson Centre for International Development. Available at: www.law.berkeley.edu/11979.htm [Accessed 16 July 2012].

Pham, P., Vinck, P., Stover, E., Balthazard, M. and Hean, S., 2009. So We Will Never Forget. A Population-based Survey on Attitudes About Social Reconstruction and the Extraordinary Chambers in the Courts of Cambodia. Berkeley: Human Rights Center. Available at: www.law.berkeley.edu/11979.htm [Accessed 16 July 2012].

Pham, P., Vinck, P., Blathazard, M. and Hean, S., 2011. After the First Trial: A Population-based Survey on Knowledge and Perceptions of Justice and the ECCC. Berkeley: Human Rights Centre. Available at: www.law.berkeley.edu/11979.htm [Accessed 16 July 2012].

Roht-Arriaza, N. and Mariezcurrena, J., 2006. Transitional Justice in the Twenty-First Century: Beyond Truth versus Justice. Cambridge: Cambridge University Press.

Rowen, J., 2012. Mobilizing Truth: Agenda Setting in a Transnational Social Movement. Law and Social Inquiry 37(3), pp. 686–718.

Samii, C., 2010. Who Wants to Forgive and Forget? Transitional Justice Preferences in Post-war Burundi. Journal of Peace Research 50(2), pp. 219–233. Available at: www.nyaapor.org/pdfs/samii_forgive_forget101206.pdf [Accessed 11 January 2011].

Shaw, R., 2005. Rethinking Truth and Reconciliation Commissions: Lessons from Sierra Leone. Special Report, 130. Washington: United States Institute of Peace.

Shaw, R., Waldorf, L., with Hazan, P., eds, 2010. Localizing Transitional Justice: Interventions and Priorities After Mass Violence. Stanford: Stanford University Press.

Shoeb, M.H., 2006. The Trauma Story: A Qualitative and Quantitative Exploration of Iraqi Survivors Experience. Master's thesis, University of California, Berkeley. On file with author.

Spitzer, R., Rosen, G. and Lillienfeld, S., 2008. Revisiting the Institute of Medicine Report on the Validity of Posttraumatic Stress Disorder. Comprehensive Psychiatry, 49(4), pp. 319–320.

Stewart, R. and Knaus, G., 2011. Can Intervention Work? New York: W.W. Norton and Company.

Stover, E. and Weinstein, H.M., 2004. My Neighbour, My Enemy: Justice and Community in the Aftermath of Mass Atrocity. Cambridge: Cambridge University Press.

Teitel, R.G., 2003. Transitional Justice Genealogy. Harvard Human Rights Journal, 16, pp. 69–94.

Twenge, J.M., Baumeister, R.F., de Wall, C.N., Ciaroco, N.J. and Bartels, J.M., 2007. Social Exclusion Decreases Prosocial Behavior. Journal of Personality and Social Psychology, 92(1), pp. 56–66.

Van Dijk, J., 2009. Free The Victim: A Critique of the Western Conception of Victimhood. International Review of Victimology, 16, pp. 1–33.

Vinck, P. and Pham, P., 2010. Building Peace, Seeking Justice: A Population-based Survey on Attitudes about Accountability and Social Reconstruction in the Central African Republic. Berkeley: Human Rights Centre. Available at: www.law.berkeley.edu/11979.htm [Accessed 16 July 2012].

Vinck, P., Pham, P. and Kreutzer, T., 2011. Talking Peace: A Population-based Survey on Attitudes About Security, Dispute Resolution and Post-Conflict Reconstruction in Liberia. Berkeley: Human Rights Centre. Available at: www.law.berkeley.edu/11979.htm [Accessed 16 July 2012].

Vinck, P., Pham, P., Baldo, S. and Shigekane, R., 2008. Living With Fear: A Population-based Survey on Attitudes About Peace, Justice and Social Reconstruction in Eastern Democratic Republic of Congo. Berkeley, New York, New Orleans: International Center for Transitional Justice, Human Rights Centre, UC Berkeley, and Payson Center for International Development. Available at: www.law.berkeley.edu/11979.htm [Accessed 16 July 2012].

Vinck, P., Pham, P., Stover, E. and Weinstein, H.M., 2009. Exposure to War Crimes and Implications for Peace Building in Northern Uganda. JAMA, 298(5), pp. 543–554.

Weinstein, H.M., Fletcher, L., Vinck, P. and Pham, P., 2010. Stay the Hand of Justice. In: R. Shaw, L. Waldorf. with P. Hazan, eds, Localizing Transitional Justice. Stanford: Stanford University Press, pp. 27–48.

Young, A., 1995. The Harmony of Illusions: Inventing Post-traumatic Stress Disorder. Princeton: Princeton University Press.

Chapter 9

Integral justice for victims

Rama Mani

Toda obscuridad contiene un punta di luz.
'All darkness contains a point of light.'
Vera Schiller de Kohn, refugee and survivor of Nazi invasion
(Schiller de Kohn 2006, p. 28)

Introduction: treating victims as latent heroes

Victims of political violations or personal tragedy carry within themselves the seed of the hero/heroine: they carry the potential not only to live meaningful lives again, but also to become agents of transformation in their societies.

Generally, we associate victimisation with feelings of hopelessness and apathy. Victims often live in constant fear that what victimised them before could happen again, at any time; that their perpetrators may reappear on their doorstep. When victims do not experience a full sense of justice and reintegration, some may turn their frustration against themselves, becoming depressed and apathetic. Some may transmit their trauma wordlessly to successive generations. Some may direct their vengeance at others and become aggressors in their turn. They may strike out against those they hold responsible for their plight, or, if they are powerless to access their real or presumed perpetrators, they may oppress those around them. In all these cases, victims are neither able to live fulfilling lives nor to give the best of themselves to society. They get trapped in endlessly perpetuated cycles of violence and victimisation.

Yet, in innumerable cases, victims emerge stronger from their trauma. They are able to free themselves from their prior identities, context and stories, and uncover unfathomed layers of their true being. There, they tap into a power greater than themselves, and are transformed. In the depths of darkness, they find their inner fire and become guiding lights for society.

Great leaders are born from such experiences. Such leaders highlight a different paradigm of leadership, rooted in inner power rather than brute force (Elworthy 1996). Nelson Mandela epitomises such leadership. Rising above the expectable feelings of revenge and score-settling that might goad them, such leaders, like

Mandela, make inner peace with themselves, their societies and even with their perpetrators. Simone Veil, who survived both Auschwitz and the death march to Birkenau, became France's first female minister of state and first woman president of the European Parliament. She was shaped by her life-threatening experience and she remains committed to commemorating the Shoah, but is not captive to it. She has championed diverse causes, including women's, workers and immigrants' rights, in her political and personal capacity.

Great artists are also honed by such experiences. An example is Aleksandr Solzhenitsyn. He survived the horrors of the Soviet gulag, and found an inner faith that enabled him to use his literary gifts to speak out against injustice in all its forms. He highlighted the responsibility of artists towards society in his remarkable Nobel lecture:

> ... the artist has merely to be more keenly aware than others of the harmony of the world, of the beauty and ugliness of the human contribution to it, and to communicate this acutely to his fellow-men. And in misfortune, and even at the depths of existence – in destitution, in prison, in sickness – his sense of stable harmony never deserts him.
>
> (Solzhenitsyn 1970)

Such voices speak at once personally of their own suffering, collectively of fellow victims, and universally of the human condition. They transcend their personal pain to shape collective consciousness.

Scholars and visionaries emerge from such tribulations. Their anguish enables them to understand the kernel of suffering, penetrate the mysteries of human nature, and discover the deeper purpose of existence. Eminent psychiatrist Victor Frankl, who survived Nazi concentration camps, observes poignantly, 'even the hapless victim of a hopeless situation ... may turn a personal tragedy into a triumph' (Frankl 2006, p. 146).

Simone Veil, Nelson Mandela, Aleksandr Solzhenitsyn, Victor Frankl and thousands of less well-known individuals in diverse countries have transitioned from victimisation to transformation; from nursing their wounds to nurturing humankind. Those who make this journey become the conscience of humankind. They awaken victims, perpetrators and bystanders alike to higher awareness, break vicious cycles of violence and victimisation, and sow harmony in society. Such heroic examples proliferate throughout the world, although they are often little known beyond their communities and spheres of influence; one such is Vera Schiller de Kohn.

Vera Schiller de Kohn escaped Prague after the Nazi invasion with her husband and his family, and became a refugee in Ecuador. War's horrors and homesickness persisted and made her depressively suicidal. At the age of forty-five, she abandoned her family in the hope of returning to her European homeland. By chance this woman, a Jew, met and became the student of German psychotherapist and Zen master Karlfried Graf Dürckheim. Over three years, her old victim identity died as her universal Self was born.[1] She returned to Quito with a new sense of purpose, and founded the Centre for Integral Development, becoming a national icon in Ecuador. Until her hundredth birthday in March 2012, she continued to counsel and heal patients, direct her centre, train indigenous villagers in psychology and lecture at universities in Ecuador and around the world. She died peacefully in June 2012. Vera transformed her paralysing victimisation into an enlightened life of contribution to humanity. She says: 'Suffering and tragedies are a part of life... And overcoming them is inherent to the process of growth' (Schiller de Kohn 2006, p. 27).[2]

Every individual victim, whatever their cause of personal or collective victimisation, is a potential Nelson Mandela or Vera Kohn. What each one needs is the space, support and opportunity to transform. Each victim is different; his or her individual circumstances are unlike anyone else's. Yet, each of them can overcome suffering and transform their victimisation to fulfil their innate potential, as Vera did.

Two core arguments

This chapter makes two core arguments. First, an appropriate approach to victimology and transitional justice must treat each 'victim' as an incipient 'hero' or 'heroine' in the making. That is, it must regard each victim as much more than 'just' a victim, frozen in their victim identity and trapped forever in their victimisation. Instead, it must treat each victim as a whole human being with the inherent potential to resume a meaningful life and contribute richly to society. Second, the kind of justice that is required to enable this 'victim' to make the transition and complete the transformation from victimhood to 'hero-hood' is 'Integral Justice'.

Integral justice offers a more holistic approach to the transformation of victimisation than transitional justice as it is pursued today. Integral justice builds on both the lessons of transitional justice and the findings of victimology, but also reaches beyond these two fields to integrate the dimensions of culture, ecology and spirituality. Each victim is unique and each one's experience of victimisation and journey towards healing, wholeness and reintegration will be singular and differentiated. Yet, if victims are assisted by these two factors – a changed and empowering attitude towards them as heroes-in-the-making, and a changed and holistic approach to justice itself – it is much more likely that they will be able to undertake and complete the transformation into who they really are and can be: powerful and inspiring lights in their societies.

Genesis and expansion of transitional justice

While this chapter seeks to contribute to both the fields of victimology and transitional justice (TJ), it situates itself particularly in the praxis of the latter and makes specific reference to the experiences and lessons of TJ.

Transitional justice emerged in the early 1990s with the paradigmatic cases of South Africa, former Yugoslavia and Rwanda, drawing on earlier experiences since the Second World War (Kritz 1995).[3] TJ is linked to criminal justice and prioritises accountability, but also offers other mechanisms to meet victims' rights (Minow 1998; Teitel 2000; Balint 2011; Schabas 2012). Truth commissions or 'truth and reconciliation commissions' (TRCs), are highly popular, but have both advantages and limitations (Hayner 2001/2011; Borer 2006). Vetting to remove egregious offenders from public service, institutional and rule of law reform, individual and collective reparations, and commemoration, are all additional accepted mechanisms of TJ for victims.

TJ has expanded and matured rapidly in theory and practice. TJ practitioners have continually undertaken new experiments in the field while TJ scholars have embarked on new avenues of research and analysis. While TJ is now accepted as an essential element of post-conflict peacemaking and peace-building processes, there has often been a clash between the global and local levels – between global standards, expectations and mechanisms and local realities, needs and cultures (Hinton 2011). Scholars have developed detailed databases to analyse transitional justice processes in different countries and have subjected these diverse mechanisms to the test to evaluate their efficacy (Olson et al. 2010). Much to their credit, scholars have also begun to examine and evaluate self-critically the successes, failures and lessons of transitional justice.[4] Despite some shortcomings of transitional justice, which we examine below, it is important to acknowledge first TJ's valuable contribution to victims' rights.

Limitations of traditional criminal justice for victims

Before venturing further, it first must be clarified that the approach of integral justice proposed here does not by any means imply abandoning the pursuit of criminal justice; it is still essential to ensure accountability for perpetrators, and obtaining whatever reparation can be afforded for victims. These are the hard-won gains of international and domestic law and should not be lost or squandered. To the degree that political will can be stretched through citizen pressure and to the extent that financial and logistical constraints will allow them, accountability and reparation must be pursued with determination. However, certain limitations of criminal justice in providing justice to victims must be recognised.

First, victims' rights and the pursuit of justice still remain subject to the whims of politicians. Victorious political leaders ultimately decide whether or not justice will be pursued at all, how and with what means. When political leaders or their close allies believe they will gain from justice processes, they adopt them; when they fear personal damage, they avoid justice processes.

Second, criminal justice is costly. Even when political elites support justice measures, the process depends on the largesse of donors. If international funders see an interest in justice, the money is forthcoming; often it is not or it is inadequate. Furthermore, expensive trials are conducted at the expense of similar amounts of money being spent on reparation or assistance to victims. Millions of dollars are spent simply working around the machinations of wily lawyers who defend perpetrators and seek loopholes to escape justice or reduce the severity of sentences.

Third, the judicial system and its laws, even its best-intentioned dimensions like human rights and humanitarian law, are man-made inventions. Justice systems and laws are subject to all the fallibilities of their human creators. We have not yet found adequate means to 'punish' perpetrators in ways that might enable them to genuinely repent, reform and eschew repetition of their crimes. Even the best national and international justice systems are victims of bureaucracy; they are costly, slow and not entirely accessible to the powerless. Even the best penitentiaries are not conducive to the transformation of prisoners so that they might truly repent, be deterred from recurrence and hope to return to society as contributing citizens. The benefit of legal processes for victims and societies is somewhat questionable.

Fourth, even if trials or truth commissions are conducted and their outcome is as 'satisfactory' as possible, this can only produce a measure of relief, but will not in itself enable the victim to overcome trauma and live a productive, harmonious life. Judicial remedies are useful but inadequate to effect transformation in victims. Much more is needed. Psycho-social healing has been one helpful response, albeit inadequate due to the sheer scale of needs, especially in cases of mass victimisation. A holistic approach to victims is essential.

Fifth and finally, once victims undergo transformation, they may view justice differently. They may no longer see justice as a simplistic question of right and wrong. They may realise that what they seek is not the incarceration and privation of their perpetrator, but the awakening of his/her conscience to a full awareness of the harm he/she caused. They may hope for a self-realisation that will propel perpetrators to a process of expiation and transformation to underpin genuine efforts to undo harm and instead serve society. Transformed victims may then prefer means of justice that go beyond the legal remedies provided by current judicial and penal systems and proffer deeper satisfaction.

The lacunae of 'transitional' justice

The profound injustices perpetrated during conflicts or periods of repression do not cease the day the conflict officially terminates. Injustices very often precede the outbreak of violent conflict, and long outlive their end. Transitional justice steps in at the time of transition from war to peace, dictatorship to democracy or repression to liberation, as an attempt to redress and reverse these injustices. TJ is intended and designed as a short-term measure to respond to a specific need that overwhelms the means of normal judicial procedures. However, the persistence of historical injustices experienced by certain populations signals that TJ may often be inadequate to break cycles of victimisation.

The Aboriginals who arrived on the Australian continent 40,000 years ago and preserved an unbroken oral record of their history, culture and legends and traditions over this period are a vivid example. So too are the Native Americans of the United States of America and Canada, the Mayas of Guatemala, the Quechua and other indigenous peoples of Peru, the Dalits and Adivasis of India. These original inhabitants were progressively stripped of their lands, cultures, languages and lifestyles; they were deprived of their power and identity. Despite piecemeal redress undertaken by governments, such as public apologies, memorials, partial restitution, reservations, quotas and enabling legislation, their profound sense of injustice and marginalisation is still transmitted inter-generationally and continues to affect current lives. The political measures undertaken in each case, but they do not significantly obliterate the depth of the injustice.

In South Africa, the persistent penury of black South Africans despite the success of the TRC suggests that conventional TJ measures cannot efface injustice and end victimisation. Many blacks still live in the same squalid huts in the same segregated townships they were forced into by the apartheid regime. Neither the political, legal and economic, nor the piecemeal cultural measures have succeeded in making them feel a sense of participation and belonging within a genuinely inclusive society. Even today, decades after the ostensible end of conflict, victims' groups remain frozen in their victim identity, with a profound sense that their needs and rights have been inadequately understood or met, as far afield as Israel, Peru and South Africa.

What is missing? Why do neither politico-legal measures such as trials and TRCs, or restitution and reservations, nor occasionally attempted social and cultural reconciliatory measures such as memorials, fully heal the festering wounds of injustice and help victims transcend their suffering? Many scholars have examined some of the shortcoming of transitional justice processes (Duggan 2010). Elsewhere, I have put forward my own critiques, pointing out that the two favoured and most often implemented transitional justice mechanisms, trials and truth commissions, tend in practice to deepen divisions between perpetrators and victims, while transitional justice claims to seek reconciliation, and peace-building requires civic inclusion and national unity (Mani 2007). This is why I have argued that transitional justice, focusing on war crimes and violations, has to be expanded to also address rule of law on the one hand and distributive justice and development on the other (Mani 2002, 2008). I had also proposed and developed the concept of 'reparative justice' as a more appropriate expression of transitional justice, as it is more inclusive, flexible, tailor-made, multi-pronged and culturally sensitive (Mani 2002, 2005). Restorative justice attempted likewise to deepen the praxis of 'transitional' justice, but remains 'a deeply contested concept', with its theorists and practitioners divided between its 'three different but overlapping conceptions: the *encounter* conception, the *reparative* conception and the *transformative* conception (Johnstone and Van Ness 2007).

The experience of the interim years suggests that even reparative justice and the three-pronged approach of transitional, legal and distributive justice I had earlier advocated, fall short, as they neither address the whole victim nor the whole social reality they belong to. These lacunae, despite the commendable expansion of TJ and advances of restorative justice in recent years, have brought me to the more holistic concept of integral justice.

The integral approach to justice

Integral justice acknowledges and builds on the valuable contributions of victimology and TJ. Both fields have taken giant strides in advancing victims' rights, especially in the past two decades, after long periods of neglect of and political antipathy towards victims. Integral justice builds on both and goes a stage beyond. It steps from the outside to the inside. Most approaches provide external assistance to victims: meeting their physical and material deprivation, their demands for justice and reparation, or their medical complaints. In some cases they may respond partially to the needs for psycho-social support – a first step towards the multiple invisible and often unstated needs of victims. What is required beyond these externally-oriented approaches is an 'integral' approach that taps the tacit, invisible and internal layers of victims' diverse and multiple needs. This alone can break through the shell of suffering and free the human being trapped within.

An integral approach is one that looks at the whole human being before and long after their trauma, beyond their outer identity. It recognises and honours but transcends the victim's current state of disempowerment. It is not merely concerned with the impact of the trauma on the victim and on filling their material needs or meting justice for that immediate act. It is concerned with what might happen thereafter: with the innate potential of the human being as a whole.

The integral approach depends for its insights not only on society, politics and law, but also on culture and aesthetics, nature and spirituality. It stems from the realisation that the only way to understand what is missing and what would make justice whole is to start with the actual suffering that injustice imposes on its victims and explore questions like: what do they demand overtly and what do they crave covertly, deep within the silence of their hearts? While their immediate needs are understandably material, political and legal, their deepest unvoiced needs are cultural, ethical, ecological and spiritual.

Integral justice is a more satisfactory response to the needs of 'transitional' justice generally, because it understands that the anguish caused by injustice is experienced at several levels at once, some of which are visible, explicit and tangible and some of which are invisible, inexplicit and difficult to access or assess. Conventional transitional justice measures respond to the explicit levels, to the articulated demands of victims, the mandate of the law and the political will of governments. The invisible, tacit levels are often too sensitive to name, articulate and translate into specific demands, and, therefore, remain unrecognised.

Each layer of injustice, visible or invisible, needs to be addressed. Remedial measures at one level may not satisfy the needs and feelings experienced at another, deeper level. Over the passage of time, the visible layers often lose the sharpness and prominence they had in the immediate aftermath, while the tacit layers, so long unspoken, become more important for the victims. Yet they often remain under the surface, because there is no accepted language to articulate them, nor the institutions and mechanisms to respond to them. An 'integral' approach to justice offers a holistic response to the needs of victims and societies for the injustices associated with war, violence and all forms of oppression and tyranny by helping to make explicit that which has so far been implicit, and thus, overlooked.

The nature and characteristics of 'integral' justice

The idea of an 'integral' approach is gaining ground in diverse fields due to growing dissatisfaction with compartmentalised, mono-disciplinary and sectarian responses. The trans-disciplinary scholar Ken Wilber (2007, pp. 17–18), who developed the integral approach through his numerous books, explains:

> An integral approach ensures that you are utilising the full range of resources for any situation, with the greater likelihood of success… An integral approach allows you to see both yourself and the world around you in more comprehensive and effective ways.

Ken Wilber's many books, particularly *Integral Vision*, *Integral Spirituality* and *Integral Psychology*, build on his particular version of the integral model. The integral approach has now burgeoned in different fields. Alexander Schieffer and Ronnie Lessem, for example, have developed their own integral 'four worlds' perspective. Their integral framework integrates the cultural perspectives of the north, south, east, west and centre, providing an inclusive global lens. The concept and framework of 'integral justice' I propose here does not use the frameworks proposed by Wilber, Schieffer and Lessem, or other scholars. It simply shares their understanding that for most critical issues of our time, a mono-disciplinary, technical response will not suffice. This is particularly the case for justice after violent conflict.

An integral approach is fundamentally *trans-border, trans-cultural and trans-disciplinary*. As humans we are complex beings. We are not only social or political animals, but also emotional, cultural, psychological, spiritual, natural and physical, creative beings, with complex and changing needs and evolving levels of consciousness. It is essential therefore, that justice transcends borders, penetrates and understands cultures, and combines disciplines to provide satisfactory responses to the injustice suffered by victims and the wounds inflicted upon society as a whole as a consequence.

The 'Integral' in integral justice lends the term two defining characteristics. First it is *holistic and inter-related*, such that each of the parts reinforces all the others and the whole is more than the sum of its parts. Second, it is *incremental and integrative*:

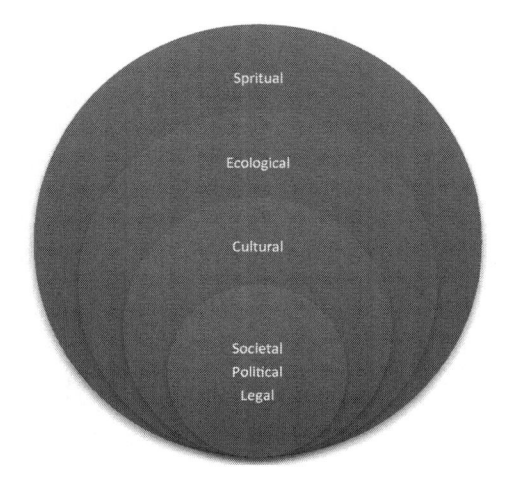

Figure 9.1 Dimensions of Integral Justice.

each successive dimension of justice builds upon, stretches beyond, but integrates the previous dimensions. Nothing is lost in evolution. Each dimension incorporates the previous ones and thus benefits from all their experience and learning. It is not just neo-Darwinian evolution based on the 'survival of the fittest', that presumes the extinction of the less fit. On the contrary, it is co-evolution, which enables the unfolding of full potential, capacity and consciousness, so that nothing and nobody gets 'stuck' at any one stage.

Integral justice comprises five deepening dimensions: *the politico-legal, the societal, the cultural, the ecological and the spiritual.* It is crucial to understand that *each successive level does not deny, reduce, or in any way diminish the previous level, but rather gives it full space and expression, while embedding it within a wider framework.*

This can be envisioned two dimensionally as concentric circles where the societal, political and legal are encompassed and embedded within the wider cultural, ecological and spiritual dimensions.

This structure of integral justice can also be envisioned three-dimensionally as a conical iceberg, whose broad circular base unseen under the frozen waters is the spiritual and whose successive levels rise up, above the subterranean level, to expose the visible dimensions of societal and politico-legal justice. This helps us understand that the visible levels stand upon the shoulders of and build upon the wider and deeper invisible dimensions. We can now appreciate that while politico-legal and societal justice mechanisms are the most apparent and frequently implemented, they actually stand on the deeper ground of cultural, ecological and spiritual justice; they are the visible part of a larger indivisible whole.

The integral framework proposed by Lessem and Schieffer is not irrelevant to our concerns here. It seeks dynamic balance between the four cardinal directions that represent the four geographic and cultural regions of the world, as well as the four human faculties (heart, spirit, mind and body) that need to be integrated at the centre for transformation to occur.

> A sustainable 'integral' society... would have found dynamic balance between its 'Southern' environmental or animate sector encompassing nature and community; its 'Eastern' civic sector encompassing culture and spirituality; its 'Northern' public sector encompassing governance, science and technology; its 'Western' private sector encompassing finance and enterprise; and finally its moral centre, encompassing religion and humanity.
> (Lessem and Schieffer 2010, p.xxi)

While they use this framework in the context of economics, to argue for a more culturally inclusive and integrated global economy, we could apply this insight to justice. Justice can no longer be treated as 'only' a governance issue, requiring the political will of leaders to take remedial action and the judicial or quasi-judicial measures that might ensue. This is only the first step, albeit essential. This must be followed by the social, cultural and ecological, and finally anchored in the spiritual dimension to have lasting impact. In the spiritual ground, all dimensions find integration and completion within the larger reality of our individual and inter-dependent existence within the cosmos.

The integral justice approach does not require the conventional political, legal and societal measures of transitional justice to change or expand dramatically to encompass the newly identified invisible dimensions of cultural, ecological and spiritual justice. Rather, it suggests that politico-legal and societal justice measures will be more effective if they are fully cognizant of these deeper dimensions on which they are founded, and are designed and implemented accordingly. Further, they will be most effective if designed and implemented with the input of informed and transformed victim representatives.

The integral justice framework works best, therefore, when each dimension is fully aware of the other dimensions and builds this knowledge and understanding into specific measures. For example, trials of perpetrators and their sentences will have greater impact if they take into consideration the relevant customary laws and traditional practices of punishment for similar crimes utilised by affected populations. A government apology will provide greater solace to victims if it is cognizant of their cultural values and the deeper ethical damage or spiritual pain experienced by victims beyond material loss. In integral justice, each part addressed is treated as belonging to the interconnected and interdependent whole, which it is impacted by and which it impacts in turn. With this integrated approach, integral justice is much more likely to meet victims' needs and build just societies without some of the unintended negative ramifications that TJ has had in the past.

Five dimensions of integral justice

Here the five dimensions are described briefly, to reveal both their distinctness and interconnectedness.

Politico-legal justice

The first level of political and legal justice is what we are most familiar with in victimology and transitional justice. It includes any measure taken by the political establishment or passed through the state's legal system. It starts with the demand and lobbying for justice made to political decision makers in transitional situations and the decisions they take. It includes trials to establish accountability and reverse impunity, through national tribunals, *ad hoc* international tribunals, hybrid or mixed courts. It also includes amnesties. Human rights lawyers and TJ experts are becoming adept in crafting conditional amnesties, as in South Africa and Guatemala, which are more politically and socially acceptable than past impunity. Officially established national or international truth commissions, or truth and reconciliation commissions, also fall within this category. Vetting of state officials to remove egregious offenders from public office is another common measure. Likewise official state apologies, commemoration and compensation undertaken by the government and processed through courts of law would also fall in this category, although they partially overlap with societal measures in their ramifications.

Societal justice

Societal justice includes those measures taken at the societal level without necessarily bearing the official stamp of the government, parliament or judiciary, that lie beyond the scope of politico-legal justice measures described above. There may sometimes be a slight overlap in some measures. For instance, the state may adopt the principle of revising textbooks to present a more nuanced and inclusive view of history, but leave implementation to university chancellors or school boards. Alternatively, the state may agree to undertake commemoration, but turn to civil society representatives to determine its nature and form in consultation with victims. Societal measures may also mirror or replicate the politico-legal measures when these are not forthcoming or inadequate.

An example is Guatemala's Recovery of Historical Memory (REMHI) established by the Catholic Church to complement the perceived inadequacy of the mandate and access accorded to the official Truth commission. In El Salvador, an NGO coalition conducted in-depth investigations of human rights abuses and handed its report to the Ad Hoc Commission that investigated abuses by army officers, and removed those found guilty. Similar human rights monitoring and investigation of abuses by civil society organisations have been very important in numerous countries including the Democratic Republic of the Congo (DRC) and Peru. These civic processes often feed into and shape official political processes at national and international level, as they did in El Salvador, DRC, Peru and more recently Sri Lanka.[5] The work of both civil society organisations and the media in bringing to light war crimes committed in the final stages of the Sri Lankan war have been instrumental in creating the pressure that led to the establishment of both the UN High Level Panel and the Sri Lankan Government's Lessons Learned Commission. It was again this public pressure that led to the adoption of the UN human Rights Council Resolution on Accountability in Sri Lanka in March 2012.

Beyond such measures that feed into official processes lies a whole range of independent civic and societal initiatives that aim to address the pain of injustice within the society in various ways. They may undertake commemorations in diverse ways, create bridges of reconciliation or dialogue between opposing groups, provide psycho-social support for victims and help reunite divided families, or even support perpetrators in rehabilitation. Many such initiatives are innovative and sometimes have an even greater impact on individuals and communities than official politico-legal measures. This is especially so if they are designed and implemented by victims themselves or by concerned persons who seek to fulfil the needs of victims and the wider society.

Cultural justice

The third dimension, cultural justice, goes a step deeper than the two previous levels. Anchoring itself within the culture in which violations occurred, cultural justice seeks to understand and integrate the complexities of cultural values, beliefs, practices and traditions and their deep imprint on people, when responding to injustices. It seeks to address and heal, for example, old wounds of cultural ethnocide that often accompany political injustice. It attempts to regenerate the decimated cultural fabric and build bridges between once-divided cultural groups. Culture includes art, religion, traditions, myths and other cultural practices that give meaning and grounding to societies that have been uprooted and eroded by violence and injustice. Elsewhere, I have argued why transitional justice is incomplete if it does not integrate culture and I have outlined what culture represents and what cultural justice would consist of. To summarise:

> As with all other social fields – religion, politics, economics– there has been the ubiquitous tendency for certain actors to seize authority and manipulate cultural rules and practices to their benefit – thus leading to the erroneous belief that culture itself is violence-prone. At its depth, culture is the contrary – it is the ever-adaptive *terra-firma* that gives each community and nation its specific meaning, its unique identity, and thus its vital energy to determine its own future. It remains a repository of the accumulated wisdom of each society from ancient times, despite social periods of dilution or stagnation, and human attempts at manipulation, domination or oppression. This is why it is

incomplete to exclude culture from any endeavour to restore justice within society, as it neglects a fundamental and defining component of how the society's members see themselves, and how they wish to deal with their recent past and shape their own future.
(Mani 2011a, p. 548)

While it is essential today to integrate cultural justice meaningfully within the ambit of 'transitional' justice, it is important to spell out exactly how this should be done and what it would involve. This is necessary to avert or minimise the risk of culture being misused by opportunists to foment division or discrimination – as often happens during conflict – rather than to foster justice and peace. Implementing cultural justice would consist of three component parts.

> First, its overall approach would be embedded within a nuanced understanding of the culture of the society in question: the core values, beliefs, traditions, expressions, manifestations that define and shape a particular society including its main variants; it would also consider their historical evolution and recent transmutations during conflict. Second, it would design and adopt measures within its overall TJ strategy that take into account this specific cultural context and seek to restore justice in harmony with these cultural determinants, with due respect for universal human rights. Third, and importantly, while culture has often been seen to be oppressive and marginalising of women and minorities, cultural justice would specifically seek to redress these tendencies. It would do so not by pressure from outside, but by eliciting internal debate and seeking out reformist and enlightened local thinkers and actors within the culture who can bring about such positive change with public support.
> (Mani 2011a, p. 548)

In some recent cases, elements of cultural justice have been addressed, either through official state-mandated means or through civic or informal initiatives. The inclusion of the annex on religions and traditional practices in the Truth and Reconciliation Report of Liberia is one example. Addressing cultural justice needs to become much more widespread and 'systematic' – without becoming rigid or technical. Each culture and society will require an entirely differentiated, tailor-made and context-specific set of cultural justice measures which cannot simply be imported or replicated mechanically from elsewhere.

An important component of cultural justice is the powerful role played by art and creativity, which has indeed been recognised in some cases. Art serves the process of overcoming victimisation in several ways. It helps victims to express their deepest feelings. It goes beyond the artist's individual representation to speak for the larger victim community. It raises consciousness and alerts conscience within society. It deters repetition by vividly portraying horrors. It maintains a historical record, not with dates, facts and statistics but with indelible images, words, sounds and impressions that are forever engraved in memory. At its very best, when the artist is infused with spiritual inspiration, art can have a healing and even transforming effect not only on the victim or the observer, but even on the perpetrator (Mani 2011b, 2012). Solzhenitsyn alludes to this transformative power of art in his Nobel Lecture:

> Not everything assumes a name. Some things lead beyond words. Art inflames even a frozen, darkened soul to a high spiritual experience. Through art we are sometimes visited – dimly, briefly – by revelations such as cannot be produced by rational thinking.
> (Solzhenitsyn 1970)

While great care should be taken not to co-opt and instrumentalise art, deeper attention should be paid to its healing and transformational role for victims. Both cultural justice as a whole, and the role of art and creativity specifically, require a greater space in future.

Ecological justice

Ecological justice has been largely overlooked within transitional justice and it merits some attention now to understand why it is so important to integrate it. Archaic humans and surviving indigenous populations consider all of creation to be sacred: '(A)ll nature is capable of revealing itself as cosmic sacrality' (Eliade 1987, p. 12). Nature is not only intrinsically linked to politics, society, culture and spirituality but is actually their source. Culture, art and religions all emerged from nature. The desire to propitiate the elements and express gratitude for nature's bounty inspired the oldest religious and cultural practices and artistic expressions. It was from nature's laws, resources, and seasons that economy, society and politics in all societies emerged.

The reverence for and sense of unity with nature persisted for thousands of years, until barely 4,000 years ago. Nature was worshipped in the form of the Great Mother across most ancient cultures (Neumann 1963). Paintings and sculptures venerating the Mother Goddess or Nature are found in archaeological sites in India, Sumer and Egypt, as also in France, Spain, Germany, Greece and other European sites. They indicate that nature and goddess worship persisted in diverse civilisations from 20,000 BC until the later Bronze Age, with Crete being the last civilisation where it survived (Baring and Crawford 1991). Historians and archaeologists observe that only about 4,000 years ago new 'dominant' cultures and 'patriarchal' religions emerged and wiped out 30,000 to 40,000 unbroken years of these prior 'partnership' cultures based on feminine or matriarchal principles of egalitarianism, inclusion, cooperation and creativity (Eisler 1988). Historians note that alongside the many positive contributions of the newer Abrahamic religions of Judaism, Christianity and Islam that arose in this period, their negative side was their patriarchal rejection of the prior peaceful matriarchal traditions and their domination of both nature and the feminine (Arguelles 1975; Baring and Harvey 1996). For thousands of years, human societies around the world, with the exception of surviving traditional indigenous cultures, have been cut off from nature and lost their original sense of interdependence with and awe of creation. Nature has been dominated, exploited and destroyed, and the rich and deep ecological bonds between humans and their habitat have been severed.

The tragic experiences of Native Americans, Australian Aboriginals and so many other indigenous peoples around the world help us understand the depth of ecological injustice. Their profound sense of injustice stems not only from economic deprivation as their lands were stripped and their livelihoods destroyed. Nor only from political disempowerment as they become second class citizens in their own native lands. Their deepest suffering came from the injustice done by invading settlers to their precious earth. It came from the needless slaughter and extinction of flora, fauna and landscapes considered both sacred and invaluable to their livelihoods. The inexplicably violent and greedy behaviour of 'Wasichus' or whites suggested to Native Americans like the holy man Black Elk that, 'they had forgotten that the earth was their mother' (Neihardt 2008, p. 167).

This sense of violation felt by the earth's indigenous people is repeated over and over in today's violent conflicts, which very often destroy the natural habitat, and plunder natural resources egregiously. The Democratic Republic of Congo, Sierra Leone, Sudan, Afghanistan and Colombia are some examples of this widespread abuse of nature. In all violent conflicts today, innumerable innocent victims are forced to abandon their ancestral lands and beloved landscapes, leaving them to be plundered and destroyed when they flee, often never to return. The suffering of refugees and displaced persons arises not only from material loss or physical pain, but more deeply from this unplanned and involuntary estrangement from the land that was the birthplace and millennial home of their culture, spirituality and way of life.

Recently, UN agencies such as UNEP and the UN UNEP/OCHA Joint Unit for Environmental Emergencies have begun to address humanitarian and conflict-related environmental issues. While this is essential, it is grossly inadequate from the point of view of victimology and transitional justice. Technical and technological approaches and 'environmental science' may be partially able to reduce the devastation done to nature by war. However, these technical approaches to the environment do not recognise and thus cannot restore the broken ecological relationship between humans and nature. So far, transitional justice has overlooked the portion of victims' suffering that emerges from their brutal separation from their natural habitat and their sense of violation at seeing their honoured habitat being desecrated by invaders. It has not responded adequately to victims who endured not only the humiliation and plunder of their own bodies but also of their ancestral lands.

The spiritual and cultural bond that people feel to their land and the capacity of nature to heal the wounds of war were potently expressed by Nelson Mandela in his Presidential Inauguration Speech in 1994:

> To my compatriots, I have no hesitation in saying that each one of us is as intimately attached to the soil of this beautiful country as are the famous jacaranda trees of Pretoria and the mimosa trees of the bushveld. Each time one of us touches the soil of this land, we feel a sense of personal renewal. The national mood changes as the seasons change.
>
> We are moved by a sense of joy and exhilaration when the grass turns green and the flowers bloom. That spiritual and physical oneness we all share with this common homeland explains the depth of the pain we all carried in our hearts as we saw our country tear itself apart in terrible conflict…[6]

That his short Presidential inauguration speech accorded so much importance to nature shows how he understood that nature could heal the pain of violence and serve as a unifying force for all South Africans regardless of colour or political affiliation. This love for nature, Mandela recognised, was not merely physical, but also spiritual, underlying the deep connection between ecological, spiritual and cultural justice.

For many cultures in Africa, Australia and elsewhere, the burial places of their ancestors or the songlines of their mythic predecessors located in designated sacred places require regular ritual propitiation and safeguarding (Isaacs 2006). The sanctified spots where rituals are conducted and relics are worshipped or stored are secret and require specific maintenance. There are prescribed rituals for transferring ancestral remains or relics if a family or community is forced to relocate (Mbiti 1969; Mutwa 1998). Most war-affected populations flee in haste with no possibility of preserving their relics or respecting these rituals. Abandoning their ancestors' burial grounds, relics and holy sites causes them profound anguish and signifies a loss of their identity and power. However, they are rarely able to articulate such ecological and spiritual distress in ways that might be comprehensible to either environmentalists or transitional justice practitioners. These are some of the reasons why ecological justice must be integrated within transitional justice, so that victims' suffering can be more deeply comprehended and addressed.

Spiritual or metaphysical justice

Spiritual justice is the culminating dimension of integral justice. Spirituality is essentially concerned with the central themes of metaphysics, the ancient branch of philosophy that explored fundamental questions of being and the nature of the world and existence. It refers to those issues that are beyond matter. Larger scientific questions were examined as part of metaphysics till the development of the empirical scientific method in the nineteenth century, when it diverged from the philosophical method of reflection, debate and contemplation. Cutting edge scientific discoveries are revealing again that there are no clear frontiers between science and spirituality, as shown by eminent quantum and nuclear physicists such as David Bohm and Hans-Peter Duerr, and neuro-biologists such as Francesco

Varela. As Einstein tellingly observed, 'The fairest thing we can experience is the mysterious' (Einstein 2006, p. 7).

Just as the millennial philosophic debates on the nature and forms of justice appear nowhere in the consideration of transitional justice practice today, neither do metaphysical issues of being and the meaning of existence.[7] Spirituality addresses the core metaphysical issues examined by early philosophers in each part of the globe and in all cultures. This explains why many of these issues also surface in the philosophical treatises of all world religions and in theological debates. As the term spirituality is more widely used in the literature and in common parlance than metaphysics, it is the one used here for purposes of clarity.

While policymakers and scholars of peace, justice and security have begun to address issues of religion recently, the deeper philosophical realm of spirituality has not yet entered their consideration. So far, spirituality has fallen outside the remit of academic analysis generally, and in the study of peace-building and transitional justice specifically. Furthermore, spirituality has become the subject of apprehension and misunderstanding amongst academics. It is not considered a topic that merits serious attention or study. Consequently, it is important to explain what spirituality and spiritual justice mean to understand why they constitute the foundation for transitional justice specifically and peace-building generally. Scilla Elworthy (1996, p. 132) explains:[8]

> There is indeed a general confusion around the word 'spirituality'. For many people it is synonymous with religion, and yet in reality it is beyond religion. It is certainly far beyond any of the dogma involved in most religions; it has nothing to say about belonging to or believing in any set of ideas. Spirituality, to me is an aspect of the self – a capacity, a potential.

Spirituality is connected – but not reducible – to religion, as it goes beyond prescribed or organised religion. Nevertheless, it can be found and experienced in the essence of most religions: in that part that speaks not only to confirmed adherents, but rather to all humans. Spirituality encompasses the 'substance' or philosophic kernel and universal truths inherent in mainstream religions, but goes beyond the 'form' or institutional and ritualistic aspects and exclusive belief systems of religions. The essential difference between spirituality and religion is that the former is free of scripture and dogma, and does not impose any one belief system. Although spiritual justice intersects with culture and religion, it goes beyond their exclusiveness and consequent divisiveness to be inclusive and unifying. Thus, spirituality overlaps partially with culture. However, spirituality requires us to penetrate the external form of culture to arrive at the substance of its inner purpose. Spirituality lies in the deeper meaning of the symbols, rituals, scriptures and myths of diverse religions and cultures. Addressing religion and culture per se is not sufficient to comprehend spirituality and integrate spiritual justice.

Spirituality is fundamentally about personal experience. It requires a commitment to personal evolution and consequently to collective wellbeing, rather than adherence to the specific belief system or ritual behaviour of a particular religion or culture. Philosopher Ken Wilber describes this as 'deep spirituality', which he describes thus: 'deep spirituality involves the *direct investigation of the experiential evidence disclosed in the higher stages of consciousness development*' (Wilber 2007, p. 77).

A defining characteristic of contemporary post-religious spirituality is increasing individual and collective consciousness and ecological awareness. 'Collective human consciousness and life on our planet are intrinsically linked' (Tolle 2005, p. 23). This indicates the second important overlap: between spiritual and ecological justice. Indeed, with rising consciousness, there is a return by modern day spiritual seekers to the sense of unity with nature, belonging to the earth, and loving protection for all beings that characterised indigenous communities and archaic humans. Indeed, it would not be remiss to refer to the spiritual and ecological dimensions together as Eco-Spirituality, as the globally emergent spirituality we are witnessing today is deeply embedded in reverence for the earth and concern with both ecological devastation and human suffering.

Spiritual and ecological justices are the culminating dimensions of integral justice and serve to lift victimology and transitional justice out of short-term and transitory time frames and beyond political and legal constraints. Spiritual justice is of central importance to victims and to the fields of victimology and transitional justice, because it shifts the locus and time frame beyond this material and ephemeral lifetime to highlight what is at once essential to human life and beyond human time and space. The spiritual dimension makes integral justice genuinely transformative, both individually and collectively.

Spirituality's relevance to victims: meaning and purpose

The specific relevance of spirituality to transitional justice and victimology arises principally from its central function of giving deeper meaning and purpose to life. Victimisation deprives victims of a sense of meaning, purpose and orientation. Spiritual justice helps them to find meaning at a much deeper level, despite and indeed through their suffering.

The yearning for deeper meaning and higher purpose is inherent to humans; it is universal and timeless. Great prophets and saints of diverse religious traditions have expressed this longing throughout the ages, although those who pursued this solitary path of higher purpose were often repudiated by mainstream institutionalised religions.

St Francis of Assisi, noted: 'We are all in mourning for the experience of our essence we knew and now miss' (Ladinsky 2002, p. 45). The twelfth-century Muslim saint Ibn 'Arabi (1995, p. 75), said:

> Everything is created to fulfil a need… That need comes from your essence the noble soul that the Lord blew into you. Always question yourself about the reason for your existence, the purpose of your creation.

> Do not spend the numbered breaths which you have been given to you just to wander around the face of this planet, without purpose, with actions of no consequence. Every action, every motion, must be for a divine purpose.

Religious traditions originally sought to provide humans with philosophical, ethical and psychological counsel to deal with life's challenges, to understand ourselves and evolve towards our higher purpose. They did so directly through scriptures or indirectly through myths, parables and embodied rituals. Over time, the philosophy, ethics and psychology of religions were diluted and replaced by static ritual observance, coercive morals and rigid socially-codified conduct devoid of their original meaning.

Spirituality is a return to this philosophical and psychological core. It seeks to go beyond prescribed moral conduct to the source of ethics. This is indeed the path that is often prescribed by realised beings but ignored by the masses that prefer the safer confines of religious ritual to the challenging pursuit philosophical insight and psychological depth. A stark example is provided in Hinduism. While the majority of Hindus devoutly perform a plethora of rituals prescribed in their holy books called the Vedas with unquestioning faith, the most sacred, ancient texts of Hindu philosophy, the Upanishads, written over 2,000 years ago, clearly point out: 'The rituals and sacrifices described in the Vedas deal with lower knowledge. The sages ignored these rituals (a)nd went in search of higher knowledge' (Easwaran 1987. p. 110).

The same is true in other religions, including Christianity. Writing in the perilous period of the Spanish inquisition, St. Theresa of Avila daringly observed: 'The child blames the external and focuses his energies there. The warrior conquers the realms within and becomes gifted' (Ladinsky 2002. p. 286). St. Theresa of Avila echoes the pre-eminent exponent of Tao philosophy in pre-Confucian China, Lao Tzu. Well before the fifth century BCE, the Tao Te Ching, attributed to Lao Tzu, observes:

> Knowing others is intelligence;
> Knowing yourself is true wisdom
> Mastering others is strength;
> Mastering yourself is true power.
>
> (Lao Tzu 1992, p. 33)

Ultimately, then, spirituality is the quest to first understand our human nature and then to rise above it to realise our universal nature. The Upanishads state:

> Those who depart from this world without knowing who they are or what they truly desire have no freedom here or hereafter.
> But those who leave here knowing who they are and what they truly desire have freedom everywhere, both in this world and in the next.
>
> (Easwaran 1987, pp. 191–192)

Spirituality is the response to this deep yearning for purpose and meaning, particularly in moments of despair within human life. While self-knowledge and self-realisation is important for all humans, it is particularly crucial to those who suffer deep victimisation and lose purpose and direction in life.

Integral justice as the catalyst for victims' transformation

The longing for deeper meaning becomes particularly strong in those who suffer profoundly. It is as if the distress caused by external events reawakens the inner yearning for our forgotten essence. Since the last century, survivors of terrible traumas such as the Nazi holocaust, world wars and civil wars have rediscovered this.

Karlfried Graf Dürckheim developed his psycho-spiritual therapy following his experiences in the first and second world wars. Demoted in his diplomatic career due to suspicions of his Jewish ancestry, he was nonetheless sent as a diplomat-scholar to Japan in 1938 by the Nazi government to investigate Zen Buddhism and spent eight years in this deepening pursuit. Captured in October 1945, by US troops following their occupation of Japan, his year and half as a prisoner in Sugamo prison was painful but transformative. On returning to Germany, he combined psychology with Zen Buddhism and the Christian theology of Meister Eckhart to develop what he called initiation therapy. The diplomat, one-time German nationalist and prisoner of war stated:

> The destiny of everything that lives is that it should unfold its nature to its maximum potential. ... Ultimately... we cannot escape from the fact that our wholeness and welfare depend on our fulfilling our inner mission and living from our essence.
>
> (von Dürckheim 2007, p. 3 8)

Viktor Frankl developed a new psychotherapeutic approach called 'logotherapy', based on 'man's search for meaning', following his survival from harrowing experiences in Nazi concentration camps. He notes that '... human life, under any circumstances, never ceases to have a meaning, and that this infinite meaning of life includes suffering and dying, privation and death...'. He goes on to explain:

> Life ultimately means taking the responsibility to find the right answer to its problems and to fulfill the tasks which it constantly sets for each individual. These tasks and therefore the meaning of life differ from man to man and from moment to moment. Thus it is impossible to define the meaning of life in a general way. (...) Life's tasks... form man's destiny, which is different and unique for each individual.
>
> (Frankl 2006, p. 83, p. 77)

The spiritual grounding of integral justice treats victims as whole human beings, and does not freeze them in time and space to the moment of their violation, and reduce them to 'only' victims condemned to live truncated lives ever after. It recognises the inherent potential within each individual. It strives to enable the victim to overcome suffering and realise this inherent potential in order to reconnect to life. In fact, integral justice recognises that underneath the terrible anguish of victims lies the seed of possibility.

Several spiritual philosophers emphasise that every event in our lives happens for a purpose: to teach us valuable lessons and enable us to grow in Self-knowledge. Suffering, particularly, offers a pathway to evolution. 'Every painful event contains in itself a seed of growth and liberation' (de Mello 1991, p. 156). This is neither to justify nor glorify suffering; it is neither to instrumentalise nor trivialise it. Frankl observes:

> I speak of tragic optimism, that is, an optimism in the face of tragedy and in view of the human potential which at its best always allows for: (1) turning suffering into a human achievement and accomplishment; (2) deriving from guilt the opportunity to change oneself for the better; and (3) deriving from life's transitoriness an incentive to take responsible action.
> (Frankl 2006, p. 138)

Victims are ready to receive the higher learning and awakening that often only comes forth after one has survived the experience of extreme personal torment. When one has not suffered personally, life becomes either an entertaining playground or an absorbing drama. Life is busy, but lacks meaning. Suffering disrupts the routine to act as a catalyst for transformation. Dürckheim observes:

> … without experiences that render life unbearable and make the hope of something new appear alluring and promising, there is no impulse towards inner change. (…) … shocks and catastrophes can occur which pierce the armor of a man's I and these can bring sudden enlightenment.
> (von Dürckheim 2007, pp. 89–90, p. 112)

Understandably, many victims are too devastated initially by their loss to be able to accept this opportunity. As victims, we even become attached to our suffering, and are loath to abandon our victim identity. Transcending victimisation is even experienced by many victims as a betrayal of those who did not survive.[9] Yet Jewish refugee Vera Schiller de Kohn indicates from her own experience why it is essential to break out of the prison of victim identification.

> Our thoughts lead us in interminable circles without exit… Our mind traps us in fixed ideas… Loss is a natural condition of life: we must drop, abandon, if the new is to appear… For the new to surge up, we must bury the old… The act of burying contains a profound secret that liberates and transforms.
> (Schiller de Kohn 2006, pp. 27–28)

Trauma can trap some victims indefinitely in victimisation and a conviction that unfairness and injustice have singled them out. However, deep suffering may alternatively crack the shell of their normal identity. The renowned Indian thinker Nisargadatta Maharaj noted, 'It is the person you believe yourself to be that suffers, not you' (Nisargadatta 2003, p. 495). This realisation may suddenly dawn upon victims. It may take them beyond their normal understanding of themselves to an insatiable curiosity about the purpose of life beyond material existence. Dürckheim described this breakthrough in war-affected victims precisely, and is cited as such by the philosopher Alan Watts in his book, *In my Own Way*.

> A great deal of my present work is in helping people who underwent great spiritual crisis during the war. We know, of course, that sometimes, in extreme circumstances, people have a natural satori or spiritual awakening when it appears that all is finished for them –and they accept it. This happened often in the war....
>
> There were three typical ways in which this crisis came about. You heard the whistle of a bomb falling straight at you, and you knew that this was quite certainly the end. You accepted it, and quite suddenly the whole universe made sense. All problems, all questions vanished, and you understood that there was no 'you' other than the eternal. But the bomb was a dud, and you lived to remember the experience...You were in a concentration camp, and you had been there so long that you were fully convinced that you would stay there for the rest of your life. Finally, you had to accept it, and in that moment you understood everything...You were a displaced refugee far from home. You had utterly lost your friends and relatives, your possessions, your job, your very identity, and saw no hope of regaining them. You accepted it, and suddenly you were light as a feather and as free as the air.
>
> (Watts 1972, p. 321)

Thus, at the right moment, victims experience this breakthrough and are transformed. The memory of their suffering remains, but is no longer a burden that stops them from living. Instead it makes them grow in self-knowledge, empathy and compassion. It clarifies to them the deeper purpose of their lives and imbues them with inner power to fulfil this vision. It liberates them to fulfil their highest potential, and reach beyond themselves to others. This is when the full transformative power and potential of integral justice, with its deepest roots in spirituality, can be realised. When integral justice, fully cognizant of and rooted in its consecutive layers of cultural, ecological and spiritual justice, is adopted and applied, it enables victims to reconnect to the larger purpose of existence, find new meaning in life and take their place again within their societies, *despite and through their suffering*.

Two final considerations concerning victims and perpetrators

Two last considerations merit underlining before concluding this chapter, one concerning victims and one concerning perpetrators.

First regarding victims, we must recognise that there is one underlying factor that traps victims in their victim identity and makes them reluctant to overcome it. As long as they are defined as 'victims' they bear moral weight and legal entitlement to rights. As 'victims', their state is legally obliged to meet their rights, failing which they may appeal to existing regional or international courts for redress. The International Criminal Court, for example, recognises victims' rights, particularly to reparation, which national legislation often overlooks. Victims may have the understandable fear that giving up their victim identity could deprive them of their moral status and legal entitlements. Recalcitrant states may indeed sideline victims' rights and demands for justice if they see 'victims' now acting as empowered citizens. Effectively victims get imprisoned in their disempowering identities because this is what our states, societies and we ourselves expect of them. It is essential to recognise and overcome this unspoken but debilitating presumption. Victims' rights must gain such authority that they simply cannot be neglected. However, victims must not be obliged to live eternally truncated lives and remain frozen in their trauma to meet our stereotypical expectations. We must work hand in hand with victims to both ensure they obtain their rights and transform their victimisation. The holistic approach of integral justice can be of support here to enable both.

The second concerns perpetrators. This integral justice approach and the possibility of transformation applies not only to victims but also to perpetrators. Certainly, several perpetrators are beyond reform. Many war criminals, such as Slobodan Milosevic and Charles Taylor, remain unrepentant even when confronted in the courtroom with evidence of their misdeeds. Yet, there are innumerable perpetrators who experience genuine remorse for their misdeeds, and wish to undo their wrongs and contribute to society. Earlier, we discussed the limitations of the conventional justice system. Rehabilitation of perpetrators remains polemical in theory and practice, notwithstanding advances in criminal justice systems (Ward and Maruna 2007). Especially in situations of mass violations with multiple victims and overstretched or dysfunctional legal systems, there are few avenues for genuine rehabilitation and transformation of perpetrators. There is also the fear that a 'soft' rehabilitative approach to perpetrators betrays victims.

Enabling the transformation of those perpetrators who are ripe for it does not need to be synonymous with impunity. Accountability is essential not only for victims but also for societal wellbeing and politico-legal governance. However, once victims effect their own transformation, they themselves might become more understanding and less intransigent. They may come to share Frankl's humble observation in the Nazi camps: 'No man should judge unless he asks himself in absolute honesty whether in a similar situation he might not have done the same' (Frankl 2006, p. 48).

They may begin to share Mahatma Gandhi's injunction to judge the deed and not the doer. As Gandhi said, 'Man and his deed are two distinct things. Whereas a good deed should call forth approbation and a wicked deed disapprobation, the doer of the deed, whether good or wicked, always deserves respect or pity, as the case may be' (Gandhi 1960, p. 33). As victims transform themselves and begin to view their perpetrators and their misdeeds through a different prism, they may prefer the redemption of their perpetrators so that they can serve society, to their execution or incarceration, which would serve no wider purpose.

Integral justice aspires to pursue both accountability for violations and transformation for perpetrators simultaneously, without trumping victims' rights. Thus, integral justice allows space for the transformation of both victims and perpetrators, so that both may find their higher purpose and contribute to society meaningfully.

Conclusion: the value of integral justice

In conclusion, integral justice deepens transitional justice and substantiates the field of victimology. It meets the complex and multi-layered needs of victims more holistically. It also builds more inclusive and integrated societies. Experience shows that politico-legal, societal and even cultural measures adopted to help victims are often sharply contested and prove deeply divisive. By anchoring justice more deeply within the ecological and spiritual dimensions, these divides can slowly be overcome, and inclusive and just societies can be built.

Integral justice provides an approach to transitional justice and victimology that is more constructive for victims by addressing and reintegrating all dimensions of their humanity and restoring their place within society. Furthermore, integral justice is more constructive for society as a whole, as it recognises that the entire society is deeply disintegrated and fragmented by violations, and that society as a whole needs to be revived and reintegrated.

Reintegrating societies, like reintegrating victims, requires us to start with the natural habitat of which they are a part and to restore ecological justice, so that affected people can once again connect with and be healed by the nature they grew up with. It requires reviving meaningfully the spiritual ground, the deep values and traditions that held individuals and their societies together. It requires reviving and re-crafting culture, replacing what has become decrepit with collectively acceptable constructs, for culture is fluid and needs adjustment after crises and violence. Only when it is thus placed within the crucible of spiritual, ecological and cultural justice will social and politico-legal justice have a firm foundation upon which to stand; only then will these measures take effect and be beneficial to victims and to society. Only then will we build together the wise and durable foundations of just peace. This is the contribution integral justice seeks to make.

Notes

1. The use of 'Self' with the capitalised S refers to the higher sense of being, to distinguish it from the small 'self' or ego entity. This usage is common in Hindu Vedantic philosophy, and is also used by several contemporary spiritual philosophers.
2. This draws as well on my personal interactions with Vera Schiller de Kohn between 2005 and 2012.
3. Transitional justice as a field of study and practice started, one might say, with the first comprehensive multi-volume publication, Transitional Justice edited by Neil Kritz in 1995. It has by now spawned an immense library of publications and attracted a growing field of scholars that addresses every aspect of TJ mentioned here.
4. I particularly recommend The International Journal of Transitional Justice published by OUP, headquartered in South Africa, for exposing case studies, critical analysis and evaluation of TJ from multiple perspectives and highlighting experience from the field and particularly for soliciting and supporting Southern viewpoints and scholarship.
5. To give one example, as an advisor on conflict for Oxfam GB in Africa, I was personally involved in a joint civil society process with other NGOs such as Human Rights Watch that led to the findings of local and international NGOs on war economies and the pillaging of resources in the DRC being reported confidentially to the UN Security Council under the format of the Arias formula meetings in 2000.
6. Nelson Mandela's full speech can be accessed at: http://db.nelsonmandela.org/speeches/pub_view.asp?pg=item&ItemID=NMS176&txtstr=inauguration [Accessed 7 February 2012]. All his other speeches are also archived at: www.nelsonmandela.org.
7. This is why I devoted a chapter of my book Beyond Retribution to examining philosophical conceptions and discussions of justice, as a necessary foundation for the praxis of current day transitional justice. It would be essential for theories of justice to inform practice, just as emerging practice of TJ should shape, inform and help evolve philosophical theorising of justice further.
8. Scilla Elworthy, founder of Oxford Research Group and Peace Direct, is a winner of the Niwano Peace Prize and was thrice nominated for the Nobel Peace Prize. Central to her peace work is shifting focus from physical power and brute force to inner power and spiritual resources.
9. Of relevance here is what the spiritual philosopher Eckhart Tolle describes as the individual and collective 'pain body'. He describes in detail the crippling effect this 'pain body' can have on our lives, if we don't recognise it, and give it up (Tolle 2005, pp. 129–185).

Bibliography

Ibn'Arabi (trans. Tosun Bayrak)., 1997. Divine Governance of the Human Kingdom. Louisville: Fons Vitae.
Arguelles, Jose, 1975. The Transformative Vision: Reflections on the Nature and History of Human Expression. London: Shambala.
Balint, J., 2011. Genocide, State Crime and the Law. Abingdon: Routledge.
Baring A. and Crawford, J., 1991. Myth of the Goddess: Evolution of an Image. London: Viking.
Baring, A. and Harvey, A., 1996. The Divine Feminine. Hants: Godsfield Press.
Borer, T.A., ed., 2006. Telling the Truths: Truth Telling and Peacebuilding in Post-Conflict Societies. Notre Dame: University of Notre Dame Press.
de Mello, A., 1991. The Way to Love, the Last Meditations of Anthony de Mello. London: Image Double Day.

Duggan, C., guest ed., 2010. Special issue: Transitional Justice on Trial – Evaluating its Impact. International Journal of Transitional Justice, 4(3).
Easwaran, E. trans., 1987. The Upanishads. Tomales CA: Nilgiri Press.
Einstein, E., 2006. The World as I See It. New York: Citadel.
Eisler, R., 1988. The Chalice and the Blade: Our History, Our Future. New York: HarperCollins.
Eliade, M., 1987. The Sacred and the Profane: the Nature of Religion. London: Harvest Harcourt.
Elworthy, S., 1996. Power and Sex. Shaftesbury: Element.
Frankl, V., 2006. Man's Search for Meaning. Boston: Beacon Press.
Gandhi, M., 1960. All Men are Brothers. Ahmedabad: Navjivan Trust.
Gopin, M., 2000. Between Eden and Armageddon: The Future of Religion, Violence and Peacemaking. Oxford: Oxford University Press.
Hayner, P., 2001/2011. Unspeakable Truths: Transitional Justice and the Challenge of Truth Commissions. New York: Routledge.
Hinton, A.L., ed., 2011. Transitional Justice: Global Mechanisms and Local Realities after Genocide and Mass Violence. Piscataway: Rutgers University Press.
Isaacs, J., 2006. Australian Dreaming: 40,000 years of Aboriginal History. Sydney: New Holland Publishing.
Johnstone, G. and Van Ness, D., eds, 2007. Handbook of Restorative Justice. Cullompton: Willan Publishing.
Kritz, N., ed., 1995. Transitional Justice. Washington DC: USIP.
Krog, A., 1998. Country of my Skull. Johannesburg: Random House.
Ladinsky, D., trans., 2002. Love Poems from God. New York: Penguin Compass.
Lao-Tzu., trans Mitchell, S., 1992. Tao Te Ching. New York: Harper Perennial.
Lessem, R. and Schieffer, A., 2010. Integral Research and Innovation: Transforming Enterprise and Society. London: Gower.
Lessem, R. and Schieffer, A., 2011. Integral Economics: Releasing the Economic Genius of Your Society. London: Gower.
Mani, R., 2002. Beyond Retribution: Seeking Justice in the Shadows of War. Cambridge: Polity/Blackwell 2002/2007.
Mani, R., 2005. Pursuing 'Reparative Justice' in the Aftermath of Violent Conflict. In: K. De Feyter, S. Parmentier, M. Bossuyt and P. Lemmens, eds, 2005. Out of the Ashes: Reparation for Victims of Gross and Systematic Human Rights Violations. Antwerp/Oxford: Intersentia, pp. 53–82.
Mani, R., 2007. Does Power trump Morality? Reconciliation or Transitional Justice? In: E. Hughes, W.A. Schabas and R. Thakur, eds, Atrocities and International Accountability: Beyond Transitional Justice. Tokyo: United Nations University Press, pp. 23–41.
Mani, R., 2008. Dilemmas of Expanding Transitional Justice, or Forging the Nexus between Transitional Justice and Development. Guest Editorial. Special issue on Transitional Justice and Development, International Journal of Transitional Justice (OUP), 2(3), pp. 253–265.
Mani, R., 2011a. Women, Art and Post-Conflict Justice. Journal of International Criminal Law, 11, pp. 543–560.
Mani, R., 2011b. Creation Amidst Destruction: Southern Aesthetics and R2P. In: R. Mani and T. Weiss, eds, Responsibility to Protect: Cultural Perspectives from the Global South. Abingdon: Routledge, pp. 96–130.

Mani, R., 2012. The Aesthetic and Ethic of Historical Justice Creation as Transformation and Integration. Keynote address at the International Conference on Historical Injustice, University of Swinburne, 14 February 2012.

Mbiti, J., 1969. African Religions and Philosophy. London: Heinemann.

Minow, M., 1998. Between Vengeance and Forgiveness. Boston: Beacon.

Mutwa, C., 1998. Indaba, My Children: African Tribal History, Legends, Customs and Religious Beliefs. Edinburgh: Payback Press.

Neihardt, J., 2008. Black Elk Speaks. Albany: SUNY Press.

Neumann, E., 1963/1967. The Great Mother: An Analysis of the Archetype. Princeton: Princeton University Press, Bollingen Series.

Nisargadatta, M., 2003. I Am That: Talks with Sri Nisargadatta Maharaj, translated by Maurice Frydman, 4th edition. Mumbai: Chetana Publishers.

Olson, T., Payne, L. and Reiter, A., 2010. Transitional Justice in Balance: Comparing Processes, Weighing Efficacy. Washington DC: USIP.

REHMI, Recovery of Historical Memory Project, 1999. Guatemala: Never Again – The Official Report of the Human Rights Office of the Archdiocese of Guatemala. New York: Orbis Books.

Schabas, W., 2012. Unimaginable Atrocities: Justice Politics and Rights at the War Crimes Tribunals. Oxford: Oxford University Press.

Schiller de Kohn, V., 2006. Terapia iniciatica: hacia el nucleo sagrada. Quito: Editoria Ecuador.

Solzhenitsyn, A. Nobel Lecture in Literature, 1970.Nobelprize.org.Nobel Media AB 2013. Available at: www.nobelprize.org/nobel_prizes/literature/laureates/1970/solzhenitsyn-lecture.html [Accessed 17 July, 2013].

Teitel, R., 2000. Transitional Justice. Oxford: OUP.

Tolle, E., 2005. A New Earth: Awakening to your Life's Purpose. London: Penguin.

Tutu, D., 1999. No Future Without Forgiveness. London: Image Double Day.

von Dürckheim, K., 2007. The Way of Transformation: Daily Life as Spiritual Practice. Sandpoint ID: Morning Light Press.

Ward, T. and Maruna, S., 2007. Rehabilitation: Beyond the Risk Paradigm. London: Routledge.

Watts, A., 1972. In My Own Way. Nowato: New World Library.

Wilber, K., 2000. Integral Psychology: Consciousness Spirit Psychology Therapy. Boston: Shambhala Publications.

Wilber, K., 2006. Integral Spirituality: A Startling New Role for Religion in the Modern and Post Modern World. Boston: Integral Books.

Wilber, K., 2007. Integral Vision. Boulder: Shambala.

Chapter 10

Repairing the impossible
Victimological approaches to international crimes

Rianne Letschert and Stephan Parmentier

Introduction

When it comes to mass victimization, every attempt to provide justice and reparation to victims is an extremely difficult task. After all, what would be a fitting punishment for the killing of thousands? Is it possible to adequately distinguish offenders, victims and bystanders in the chaos of a state in collapse? What does reparation mean for victims who have lost everything – their families, their homes, their possessions – and who either witnessed the cruellest forms of sadism or were themselves victims of such cruelty? These are just a few of the complex questions post-conflict societies are struggling with.

In societies going through a transition from violent conflict to democracy, recent history has shown that more and more attention is paid to reparative measures, particularly in Africa and Latin America. Various mechanisms and processes and other experiments have been set up, often in combination with one another, for example criminal trials[1] (de Brouwer and Heikkilä 2012), truth and reconciliation commissions, administrative reparation programmes and institutional reform. The ways in which a state tries to deal with the suffering that has befallen its population are heaped together under the term 'transitional justice', which also encompasses reparative measures.[2] From a victim's perspective, four concepts are important here: accountability, truth-telling, reparation and reconciliation (Parmentier 2003; Parmentier and Weitekamp 2007). Accountability means that the responsibility for past violations is individualized, acknowledged and also sanctioned in one way or another, whereby criminal prosecution is only one of the possible approaches. Truth-telling posits that the scale of the violence and their underlying causes are mapped and will become part of society's collective memory. Truth-telling also plays an important part on the micro-level, where it is phrased as the right to know: it gives survivors the opportunity to find out the truth about what happened to relatives who are missing or who have been killed.[3] Reparation focuses on taking material and/or immaterial or symbolic measures to acknowledge victims' individual or collective victimhood, and – as far as possible – to make amends for their suffering. Reconciliation is one of the most difficult concepts to define. It refers to the process of gaining common ground between former enemies and trying to prevent past events continuing to be sources of new conflict and new violence. Because of these concepts, some authors have suggested using the umbrella term 'reparative justice', i.e. justice aimed at repair in the broadest sense, as a more suitable alternative to 'transitional justice', which suggests that justice can only be pursued during the transition period (Danieli 2009; Letschert and Van Boven 2011).

In this chapter we intend to present a victimological approach to international crimes such as crimes against humanity, war crimes and genocide (the crimes also falling under the jurisdiction of the International Criminal Court) and our leading question is to analyse what is known about victims' needs in relation to reparation measures after such crimes. To address these issues, we will partly draw on the academic literature and partly refer to empirical studies in post-conflict societies. After sketching some general insights into victimology from the viewpoint of mass victimization, we discuss the main aspects relating to reparations for victims and the results of three field studies on compensation in particular. Throughout the chapter we highlight the many complexities that surround the topic of reparations for victims of international crimes, including the difficulties in determining what victims really want, taking into account that victims are not a homogenous group and the fact that needs change over time.

Victimology in the context of mass victimization

Despite the fact that victimologists have traditionally considered human rights violations to be an object of study and even the origin of victimology (Elias 1985; Van Dijk *et al.* 2007), it has to be admitted that subjects of war crimes, crimes against humanity and genocide have long received little to no attention in traditional victimology. Victimologists have traditionally studied the consequences of victimhood within the scope of conventional crimes, although it should also be noted that they are gradually studying a variety of research questions relating to the consequences of mass victimization resulting from conflict situations. However, it could rightfully be questioned whether their findings relating to conventional crimes are equally applicable to the context of mass victimization. Before we go further into the complexity surrounding reparation for victims, we will briefly outline the various ways in which situations of mass victimization pose a challenge for traditional victimology. We limit ourselves to a brief analysis of the types of measures that provide victims with certain rights in judicial procedures (and therefore have a legal basis) and of the psychological consequences of victimhood.

Measures for victims in judicial procedures

According to Groenhuijsen (2011) victimology focuses

> mainly on determining the nature and frequency of crimes committed, on how the victims concerned respond, the needs these victims have in the aftermath of an offence and on the question as to how the negative consequences of crimes can be restricted to a minimum.

Traditionally, the criminal justice system has played a major part in this and the focus has been on investigating possible ways to prevent secondary victimization (i.e. limiting the possible negative consequences of participating in criminal proceedings). In addition, there is a tendency to investigate whether elements of reparation could also be brought into criminal proceedings (i.e. elements promoting positive consequences). The focus on rights in criminal proceedings is also seen in international judicial instruments.

The 1985 UN Declaration entitled Basic Principles of Justice for Victims of Crime and Abuse of Power has seventeen articles that mainly focus on victimhood as the result of conventional crime. Victims, for instance, have the right to access mechanisms of justice, the right to participate in the trial and the right to receive financial compensation. A definition of victimhood is provided in Articles 1 and 2. It is important to note that the rights and principles stipulated in the Declaration apply both to direct victims and to certain indirect victims. The Declaration contains only four ambiguously formulated articles about the abuse of power by governments. The subsequently adopted UN Basic Principles and Guidelines on the Right to a Remedy and Reparation for Victims of Gross Violations of International Human Rights Law and Serious Violations of International Humanitarian Law (2005), hereafter referred to as the Reparation Principles (Shelton 2005) and the Rome Statute of the International Criminal Court (1998) have partly filled up this legal void. In spite of the fact that these instruments incorporate victim rights, implementing classic victim rights (such as the right to participate in the trial and the right to receive financial compensation) in practice turns out to be much more difficult in the context of massive human rights violations and international crimes (see further Letschert and Groenhuijsen 2011). Seen from the perspective of victims of international crimes, it is important to acknowledge the limitations of the criminal justice system and pay attention to adequate communication with victims about what criminal justice can and cannot offer. This is in part due to the specific problems that international crimes cause for criminal justice (for instance the often high number of victims), but also due to the victimological insight that the relationship between victims and criminal justice is always complicated (Pemberton *et al.* 2011).

Psychological impact of victimization

Another field of study for victimologists is the psychological consequences of victimization. It is important to examine whether the consequences of mass victimization have similar or different psychological effects on victims compared to those of conventional crimes. Several studies (particularly with regard to terrorism; for an overview, see Letschert *et al.* 2010) have shown that victims have very similar needs, regardless of whether they are victims of large-scale crime or of conventional crime. Generally, they respond in similar ways and, for instance, experience shock, anger, depression, guilt, fear and the desire to see the offenders punished (Winkel 2007). However, the impact of victims' experiences can be more extensive in some circumstances (Letschert *et al.* 2010; Letschert *et al.* 2011). Victims of group violence, for example, are not only concerned with their own safety, but also with the safety of family, friends, and other members of the group, and they often share the same horrible experiences. Group victimhood also has consequences for the circumstances in which victims can rebuild their lives. In many cases, the offenders are part of that context, sometimes as victims and offenders in the same period.

With regard to mass victimization resulting from international crimes, for many people victimization is not an isolated incident. Instead, multiple victimization occurs, in both direct and indirect ways. One and the same person may fall victim to multiple instances of gang rape, may be witness to the torture and/or death of one or more family members and may see the destruction of all his or her possessions. The book *The Men Who Killed Me* (De Brouwer *et al.* 2011) strikingly documents the testimonies of sexual assault victims in Rwanda. The testimonies reveal the duration, gravity and consequences of multiple victimization during war. Several studies have shown that the effect of multiple victimization can be cumulative, causing the trauma to have a different impact (Shaw 2001; Wemmers 2011). As a final example, the amount of physical and mental strength individuals possess and the way in which they themselves, as well as others, experience their vulnerability are part of their experiences relating to the crimes they have fallen victim to (Goodey 2005). Physical and mental strength influence the effect the crimes have on victims and affect the ways in which they can recover. This particularly plays a part in post-conflict situations, given the gravity of the violence, the absence of good medical and psycho-social care after the conflict is over, and the collapse of formal as well as informal social networks.

Access to reparation

As mentioned in the introduction, reparation focuses on taking material and/or immaterial or symbolic measures to acknowledge victims' individual or collective victimhood and – as far as possible – to make amends for the suffering they went through. The concept of reparation is by now also firmly embedded in international judicial and quasi-judicial instruments. The right to reparation has a substantive as well as a procedural part: the former concerns the obligation to award one or more forms of reparation, while the latter deals with the procedure to enforce this obligation.

Forms of reparation

In the 2005 Reparation Principles, the right to reparation is subdivided into five specific categories: (a) restitution, (b) compensation, (c) rehabilitation, (d) satisfaction and (e) guarantees for the prevention of a similar conflict arising in the future (De Feyter *et al.* 2005; Letschert and Van Boven 2011).

1. *Restitution*, an age-old legal concept, originates from the idea that victims are to be brought back into the position they were in before their rights were violated. This can be realized, for instance, through the restoration of citizenship, possessions or a job.
2. *Compensation* concerns the financial reimbursement for damage, including physical or emotional damage; loss of employment, education or other social benefits; and other forms of material damage.
3. *Rehabilitation* covers medical and psychological help, as well as legal and other social services.
4. *Satisfaction* is the broadest concept: it is concerned with making the truth public, provided that such a disclosure will not cause any more harm to or jeopardize the safety of victims, surviving relatives or others involved. Satisfaction can also mean looking for victims' remains and extending facilities for a dignified funeral or other ceremony in close consultation with the wishes of the surviving relatives. It can also entail organizing a memorial service or a tribute to the victims or expressing a public apologies, including an acknowledgement of the facts and an acceptance of responsibility. Finally, the concept of satisfaction can include legal and administrative sanctions for those responsible for the violations as well.
5. The fifth category of reparation encompasses *guarantees of non-repetition*, a euphemistic expression meaning all kinds of strategies and measures to avoid similar violent conflicts in the future. They include the fundamental reform of hard-core state institutions such as the police, the army and intelligence services, the judiciary, as well as soft-core bodies such as schools, health institutions, the media, etc. The hearts of many legislators or policymakers will sink when this list is presented to them. This is why there is a wide divide between the analytical force of these measures and their practical feasibility, not only when individual measures are concerned.

In sum, the proposed measures can be ordered in three categories. There are measures which take shape through *legal action*, for instance, participating in trials that on the one hand bring a form of recognition and on the other hand can provide a means to receive financial compensation. In addition, there are *symbolic measures* which can lead to the recognition of victimhood, for example a public apology or the establishment of a memorial day. The final category relates to *financial* measures that focus on compensation of the damage suffered. They can sometimes be enforced through legal action, but this is certainly not always the case. Financial reimbursements can also be granted through administrative reparation programmes by means of individual payments (lump sum or through pensions), compensation for school tuition or collective investments in community projects. Considering the massive suffering that victims of international crimes or gross human rights violations go through, no form of reparation will ever be able to meet the victims' many needs. Therefore, it must be concluded that all the above-mentioned measures are for a large part symbolic (Hamber 2001) and that repairing the gigantic harm of victims is in fact impossible.

Individual versus collective measures

In several academic contributions scholars have questioned whether the implementation of an individual right to reparation after mass victimization is *feasible* for the large group of victims. Seen from a purely pragmatic or politically realistic point of view, the answer would have to be no.[4] In the context of mass victimization, the restrictions of an unlimited individual right to reparation are abundantly clear. Of what use is such a right to a victim when it is obvious beforehand that enforcing this right in practice will be unfeasible? This will only strengthen the feeling of injustice brought about by the violent crimes, a process referred to in victimology as 'secondary victimization' (Orth 2002). However, since the first major human rights treaties were drafted, normative human rights legislation has considered the right to an effective individual legal remedy after violations of human rights to be one of the core rights. As Groenhuijsen (2011) argued: 'Any criminal act is a severe violation of the victim's human rights, on the basis whereof the victim is entitled to an effective remedy within current judicial procedure.'

But is this realistic within the context of mass victimization? It seems that states' options and ability to actually offer individual victims an effective remedy are extremely limited when violence was the rule rather than the exception (De Greiff 2006, p. 454; Tomuschat 2005). This is the case for reparation claims via human rights procedures in which the state is held responsible, as well as via criminal procedures in which an individual is ordered to pay compensation. An extra complication in this matter is the fact that international human rights legislation is characterized by an expansive normative framework but still lacks effective means of enforcement.

Within the international legal framework, the concept of collective reparation is less well-developed compared to reparation in individual cases. Yet some developments suggest that international law has embraced collective compensation (Dubinsky 2004; Roht-Arriaza 2004; Laplante 2007; Hofmann 2010; Rosenfeld 2010). The Inter-American Court of Human Rights case law has given an important impetus to its further elaboration.[5] The Rules of Procedure and Evidence of the International Criminal Court Statute also stipulate that the Court may award reparations 'on a collective basis' and, if possible, may also order an award for collective reparations through the Trust Fund (Rules 97 and 98, respectively). Additionally, several Truth and Reconciliation Commissions in the recent past have made recommendations towards collective reparations.[6] The most important aspect mentioned in this context is the country's economic reality.

An important issue that requires more research is the question of how individual needs relate to collective needs. Social psychologists have already pointed out that the psychological needs of individuals and society often widely diverge and are sometimes even incompatible. The way in which reparations are awarded will therefore have to take these needs into account (Hamber and Wilson 2002; Haldemann 2011). These psychologists have, for instance, drawn attention to the fact that individual needs are made subordinate to the demands of national unity and reconciliation; they also suggest that there may be many differences between the individual psychological processes and national processes such as those triggered by truth commissions. Hamber (2000, p. 10) also argues that 'although socio-economic development (social reconstruction) is necessary, the physical and psychological impact of violence has to be addressed directly and individually if we are ever to deal with the traumas of the past and prevent cycles of revenge from emerging'. At the same time, psychologists acknowledge that, in some respects, the two are closely linked, as is shown when victims have to speak publicly at, for example, Truth and Reconciliation Commission hearings.[7]

Judicial and non-judicial approaches

Arguably, international legal procedures (either criminal proceedings or before human rights courts) provide a suitable means to give a symbolic meaning to damages, while the compensation and reparation of acute and large-scale damage can be tackled more effectively and more efficiently by other means than the law, such as for instance through administrative reparation programmes (Groenhuijsen and Pemberton 2011; Letschert *et al.* 2011; Letschert and Van Boven 2011). Letschert and colleagues (2011) have encapsulated this position in a straightforward manner: 'Even more so than on the national level, justice is done if it is experienced as such.'

Not all institutions of international criminal justice may agree with this proposition. The Prosecutor for the International Criminal Court, in a press release entitled *ICC Cases an opportunity for communities in Ituri to come together and move forward*, stated on the occasion of the violence in Ituri, DR Congo, in 2008:

> Our mandate is justice, justice for the victims. The victims of Bogoro; the victims of crimes in Ituri; the victims in the DRC. This case, and each of our cases, is a message to victims of crimes worldwide, that perpetrators will be held accountable...This case and our other cases in the DRC are an opportunity for all the communities in this province torn by conflict, to come together.
>
> (ICC-OTP-20080627-PR332, Press Release)

Despite this position, it could be argued that people's expectations of non-judicial measures in providing justice and reparations are increasing and may overtake those offered by judicial bodies. It may suffice to have a closer look at the empirical surveys mentioned in the following paragraphs to substantiate this argument. Also the Trust Fund for Victims, which has been set up alongside the International Criminal Court, has generated higher expectations with victims than the judgements in the cases investigated by the International Criminal Court itself (see De Brouwer 2007). Apart from paying out the individually granted reparations, the Trust Fund also plays a more humanitarian role, in which it can collectively support affected communities in the reconstruction after conflict (www.trustfundforvictims.org). It should be noted, however, that the Trust Fund relies on voluntary contributions by donors and it remains to be seen whether it can meet the most urgent needs of victims of international crimes.

For the most part, it seems that victims' *individual* rights to compensation (reparation-as-a-right, Letschert and Van Boven 2011) can be achieved with more success through the implementation of other elements of reparative justice, both in the acute phase (emergency aid, legal aid, health care) as well as in the long run (aimed at economic and social development). Does this mean that the idea of reparation as a right should be completely abandoned? In our opinion, this would be going too far. The developments on the international level, particularly the creative and innovative interpretations by the Inter-American Court of Human Rights regarding the right to reparation, for groups as well, have set an important precedent for other international and national judicial bodies to build on. However, it seems important not to raise the expectations too high when large numbers of victims are involved and the relevant states face the immense challenge of having to rebuild a nation despite major financial shortcomings. In this context, the development of reparation is a complicated matter, especially when it also comprises the categorization of individuals and groups into victim groups or beneficiaries (see for more on this matter Letschert and Van Boven 2011). While the human rights discourse has placed high ambitions, it is equally important not to lose sight of reality and to take account of what is feasible.

Victim perspectives on reparation

How do victims themselves view reparation and what do they think about the balance between individual and collective measures? Asking these questions is also paying attention to the fact that the opinions of victims, and the population at large, are rarely taken into account in the case of international crimes. Most often, policies of post-conflict justice, including reparation policies, are designed and implemented by national and international elites in a 'top-down' manner, i.e. without due reference to the attitudes and needs of victims. Since the end of the twentieth century, more attention is paid to empirical studies conducted from a 'bottom-up' perspective, i.e. with the aim to highlight the opinions and attitudes of the population, and sometimes of victims specifically, in relation to post-conflict justice issues in general and reparations in particular.

In the following sections we focus on three cases from different continents: Bosnia/Serbia, Northern Uganda and Cambodia. While throughout these cases we focus primarily on the first two categories of reparations, namely restitution of property or material goods and monetary compensation, other forms of reparations will also be mentioned. This attention to empirical studies brings us in line with a transitional justice approach 'from below' (McEvoy and McGregor 2008). Before presenting the main findings, we mention two caveats that are congruent with important conclusions on the limitations of empirical research about transitional justice (Thoms *et al.* 2008). First of all, it is an illusion to think that victims constitute a homogenous group and therefore all have the same individual attitudes and needs. An analysis of empirical research into victims' expectations in post-conflict situations shows varying results, possibly because of the specific research methodology used and the paucity of comparative studies. Secondly, research has also shown that victims' attitudes and needs change over time, partly because respondents have unreliable recollections of the past and that any empirical findings should be treated with the highest degree of caution (Hamber 2009, among others).

Bosnia and Serbia

We first have a look at some salient findings based on our own research in Bosnia and Serbia (Parmentier *et al.* 2009; Parmentier *et al.*, 2014). Both countries belonged to the former Yugoslavia that was hit by a series of violent conflicts in early 1992, following the breakup of the mother country. Bosnia and Herzegovina plunged into a devastating war that lasted for almost four years and took an enormous toll on its population, infrastructure and cultural heritage. Many atrocities such as mass murders, extrajudicial executions, torture, rape, illegal detention, forced displacement, looting and destruction of religious and cultural sites are fairly well documented, though responsibilities for them continue to be contested. While most of the armed conflict during the Yugoslav war took place outside the borders of today's Serbia, its population also encountered victimization on its own territory or in relation to Serbian groups in other parts of the former Yugoslavia. The Dayton Peace Agreements signed in December 1995 put an end to the war.

In 2006 and 2007 a research team from the University of Leuven conducted a self-administered quantitative survey on the territory of Bosnia and Serbia respectively (Parmentier, *et al.* 2009; Parmentier *et al.* 2014). The general aim of the survey was to inquire about the attitudes and opinions of individuals about the process of dealing with the past (or transitional justice), with a particular focus on the 'possibilities' (or opportunities) and the potential of a restorative approach to such process. The same methodology was used in both countries:

a   creating an instrument of data-gathering, namely a printed questionnaire with a total of thirty-eight questions, all of them closed or semi-closed with only one open question on the meaning of reconciliation;
b   determining an adequate sampling method: given the absence of a population census in Bosnia and Serbia since before the war and the impossibility of creating an accurate national representative sample, we opted instead for a 'quota sampling method'. This implied dividing the target population into subgroups or strata according to the criteria of particular interest;
c   collecting the data through the distribution of the questionnaire: in Bosnia students of the Faculty of Criminal Justice Sciences, University of Sarajevo,

distributed the questionnaires in their home towns or villages and retrieved them after a few days, leading to 855 questionnaires returned from a total number of 900 distributed; in Serbia the questionnaires were distributed by members of nineteen Serbian NGOs who belong to the Association Joint Action for Truth and Reconciliation, each of them with diverse target groups; of the total number of 1,200 questionnaires distributed 922 were returned duly filled; and

d   analysing the data gathered: a mask was created using SPSS software, all data were entered and several levels of analysis were performed, including univariate, bivariate and multivariate analyses, factor analysis, cluster analysis and tests of the reliability of scales.

The questions about restitution and monetary compensation were asked under the heading of the accountability for the perpetrators of the harm done 'to you' (meaning the victims). In the case of Bosnia (Parmentier *et al.* 2009):

- 80 per cent of the respondents gave priority to restitution (return of property and material goods) and to confession alike;
- 70 per cent of the respondents agreed/strongly agreed with prosecution in courts in Bosnia;
- 68 per cent thought perpetrators should apologize;
- 66 per cent thought they should be obliged to pay compensation to the victims;
- 62 per cent thought they should do community work when compensation or restitution would not be possible;
- 61 per cent thought they should be prosecuted in a court outside of Bosnia; and
- 59 per cent thought only those with highest responsibility should be prosecuted.

In the case of Serbia, the results were strikingly similar, despite the very different nature of the conflict and the types of harm (Parmentier *et al.* 2014):

- 84 per cent favoured confession by the perpetrator;
- 82 per cent favoured restitution of property and material goods;
- 75 per cent thought perpetrators should apologize;
- 69 per cent thought they should be obliged to pay compensation to the victims;
- 66 per cent thought they should do community work when compensation or restitution would not be possible;
- 63 per cent thought prosecution should take place in a criminal court in one of the countries of former Yugoslavia;
- 63 per cent thought only those with highest responsibility should be prosecuted; and
- 58 per cent thought prosecution should take place in a criminal court outside of former Yugoslavia.

These results suggest that at least two-thirds of the respondents in both countries expressed an interest for measures of restitution and monetary compensation and that they favoured material measures (restitution and compensation) and symbolic measures (confessions and apologies) over any other (e.g. criminal prosecutions).

Northern Uganda

Similar fieldwork was undertaken in several African countries by the International Centre for Transitional Justice (New York) and the Human Rights Center at Berkeley School of Law (University of California). We limit ourselves here to their studies on Northern Uganda in 2005 and 2007 (Pham *et al.* 2005; Pham *et al.* 2007). This region has fallen prey to two decades of violent conflict with the Lord's Resistance Army (LRA) fighting against the Ugandan government and applying extreme brutality against the people of the region. Countless civilians were mutilated and tens of thousands of children and adults were abducted to serve as soldiers and sex slaves for the commanders. Because it was unable to beat the LRA in a military way or even to bring it to the negotiation table, the Ugandan government in December 2003 decided to refer the situation in Northern Uganda to the International Criminal Court in order to conduct investigations and issue indictments against some LRA commanders. This decision and the ensuing indictments by the Court sparked huge and at times fierce debates in Uganda and in the international community. The situation in Northern Uganda dramatically changed in late 2005 with the withdrawal of the LRA forces from Uganda into other countries of the Central African region and in the summer of 2006 the peace talks between the LRA and the government started and finally led to a joint agreement in June 2007.

The empirical researches were aimed at measuring the exposure to violence and the opinions and attitudes of the population about specific transitional justice mechanisms, as well as to understand these opinions in more depth and to assess the needs of the population. For this purpose, the first study of 2005 entailed interviews with slightly more than 2,500 respondents from four districts in Northern Uganda, using random sampling methods to obtain a representative overview of the situation. The face-to-face interviews were conducted by a wide number of teams of trained interviewers in April and May 2005, using a structured questionnaire. In 2007, after the negotiations between the government and the LRA and in a changed political situation, more or less the same research team decided to conduct a follow-up study in Northern Uganda, using the same research methods with more than 2,800 respondents.

It is interesting to compare the results of the surveys with respect to reparation measures and particularly restitution and monetary compensation. In the 2005 survey, the respondents were asked to define human rights, peace and justice (Pham *et al.* 2005). Within the latter category, an overall 31 per cent defined justice as trials and an overall 18 per cent viewed it as reconciliation (in both cases with considerable differences across the four main districts in the region). Compensation was listed by no more than 8 per cent of the respondents, but this figure was identical across the districts. In the 2007 study conducted around the end of the hostilities, around 70 per cent of the respondents indicated that those responsible for the crimes should be held accountable (Pham *et al.* 2007). Much more emphasis than before was put on mechanisms for truth-seeking about the crimes of the past and on reparations to victims. As to the latter, the majority of respondents answered that they would prefer direct compensation, in the form of monetary compensation (52 per cent), food (9 per cent) or cattle (8 per cent), while apologies, justice and reconciliation were each deemed important by 10 per cent of respondents and memorial sites were preferred by 59 per cent of respondents. These new findings led the researchers to recommend that the government and the international community should promote the national dialogue for truth-seeking in Northern Uganda and set up a reparations programme for victims. It should be noted that none of the surveys asked about the restitution of property or other material goods, which is quite remarkable in view of the categories contained in the United Nations Basic Principles and Guidelines that were adopted in 2005 after long discussions.

Cambodia

The third example is from Cambodia: between 1975 and 1979 an estimated 1.7 million people passed away as a result of oppressive policies implemented by the Khmer Rouge regime under the leadership of Pol Pot (Pham *et al.* 2009). Its philosophy was based on agriculture and total collectivism and the country was completely sealed off from the outside world. The Khmer Rouge regime first instilled a climate of terror and violence upon the population and then deported many people to the countryside and detention centres all over the country where the vast majority of them were killed or died from starvation, disease, etc. In 1979 the Vietnamese army invaded the country and the Pol Pot regime collapsed. After the Vietnamese withdrawal and the signing of the Paris Peace Agreement in 1991, a decade of negotiations between the new government and the United Nations started. It resulted in the establishment of the Extraordinary Chambers in the Courts of Cambodia (ECCC) to try the crimes of the Khmer Rouge regime. This court in fact constitutes a hybrid system with a mix of national and international judges and operating under the civil law system. The ECCC can only propose collective reparations (De Brouwer and Heikkilä 2012).

In September 2008 the Human Rights Centre of the University of California, Berkeley, conducted a first population-based survey in Cambodia to measure public awareness of the ECCC and capture attitudes about the Khmer Rouge regime and the desire for justice and reparations for past crimes (Pham *et al.* 2009). Respondents were randomly selected among all adult residents of Cambodia by means of a four-stage cluster sampling strategy to ensure that the final sample was representative. Face-to-face interviews were conducted in an anonymous manner with about 1,000 individuals by means of a structured questionnaire. The data collection process took place in partnership with the Center for Advanced Study, a Cambodia-based non-profit research organization. A follow-up survey was conducted in December 2010, a couple of months after the ECCC rendered its first judgement in the case of Duch, who was sentenced for crimes against humanity and grave breaches of the 1949 Geneva Conventions (Pham *et al.* 2011). Likewise, about 1,000 Cambodians were interviewed to measure their awareness of the ECCC and their attitudes to justice and reparations. The results of both surveys should therefore be seen against a specific background: the ECCC deals with crimes that took place in the 1970s, i.e. more than thirty-five years ago; and at least 25 per cent of all respondents were born after the fall of the Khmer Rouge regime.

The 2009 survey (Pham *et al.* 2009) revealed that:

- a majority of respondents (88 per cent) said (symbolic) reparations should accrue to victims of the Khmer Rouge;
- 68 per cent said that these should be provided to the community as a whole;
- over 53 per cent said that such measures should be in a form that would benefit the Cambodians' daily lives and should include:
  ○ social services (20 per cent)
  ○ infrastructure development (15 per cent)
  ○ economic development programmes (12 per cent)
  ○ housing and land (5 per cent).

One important observation arising from this survey was pointed out by Pham *et al.* (2009, p. 4–6):

> most respondents said it was more important for the country to focus on problems Cambodians face in their daily lives than on the crimes committed by the Khmer Rouge. This suggests that the ECCC must find ways to ground its activities in the current concerns and needs of the population.

The follow-up survey of 2011 recorded very similar results (Pham *et al.* 2011):

- 83 per cent (2008:76 per cent) of the respondents emphasized that, even though justice is important, their priorities lie with the realization of basic needs;
- 63 per cent (2008: 53 per cent) of victims would have preferred that the money to fund the ECCC had been spent on something else; although the vast majority of respondents believed that the ECCC would:
  ○ correctly address the crimes committed by the Red Khmer (84 per cent)
  ○ rebuild trust in Cambodia (82 per cent)
  ○ help promote national reconciliation (82 per cent)
  ○ bring justice for the victims of the Khmer Rouge regime (76 per cent).
- The results on reparations were similar to the 2008 results in that the vast majority of respondents (91 per cent) stressed symbolic reparations (47 per cent: building memorials; 34 per cent: public ceremonies) and three out of

four (73 per cent) said they preferred community reparations. Other results on reparations were that:
- 33 per cent of the respondents recommended social services (such as health care and education);
- 25 per cent wanted monetary compensation and/or agricultural support; and
- 14 per cent wanted the government to build infrastructure for the affected communities.

Conclusions

While victimology has traditionally paid substantive attention to victims of conventional or common crimes and the consequences of their victimhood, recent years have witnessed an increasing interest in victims of war crimes, crimes against humanity and genocide. The psychological and social consequences of their victimization, as well as the legal strategies to provide information, assistance and reparation, have become the object of new and promising research. In the case of international crimes even more attention is paid to the implications of victimization for the wider context of the community and society at large.

In this chapter we have focused on one crucial aspect of victimization and its consequences, namely reparations for victims who have suffered tremendous and unthinkable harm in the course of wars, violent conflicts, genocide and other cruel circumstances. The concept of reparation is by now firmly embedded in international judicial and quasi-judicial instruments, and the individual right to reparation for victims encompasses a substantive as well as a procedural part. Despite the legal consequences that they may entail, it seems that judicial procedures awarding individual reparation orders to victims are not always considered by victims to be the most effective. In some cases, victims may be drawn to non-judicial bodies that offer them concrete services, such as the Trust Fund for Victims. Arguably, a balanced mix between judicial and non-judicial measures is crucial to give effect to the right of reparation for victims of international crimes.

The debate about reparations for victims has been strongly dominated by top-down policies designed and implemented by national and international elites. The attitudes and opinions of victims themselves and the affected populations at large have rarely been taken into account. But several empirical researches have captured the viewpoints and expectations of common people, many of them victims of international crimes. For the most part, they relate to quantitative surveys with representative samples of the populations affected, although very few apply exactly the same methodologies and instruments, which makes hard comparisons in time and space extremely difficult. Moreover, people and victims in particular do not constitute a homogenous group and therefore may have very different individual attitudes and needs, which tend to change over time. Our concise overview of three such cases, Bosnia/Serbia, Northern Uganda and Cambodia, has revealed the many issues that play in a post-conflict justice context – and sometimes while the violent conflict is still ongoing. Despite the caution to be applied, it is possible to derive from the data a strong interest in reparations, sometimes more materially or financially oriented, at other times very symbolic and sometimes more geared towards providing services for communities rather than individuals. Whatever the outcome of such surveys, they do provide us with important insights about people's views and therefore constitute important sources of information for policymakers on how to address the tremendous harm and far-reaching consequences of international crimes, which in reality, can never be fully repaired.

Notes

1 For instance, the International Criminal Tribunal for the Former Yugoslavia, the International Criminal Tribunal for Rwanda, the Special Court for Sierra Leone, the Extraordinary Chambers in the Courts of Cambodia.
2 The renowned International Center for Transitional Justice defines transitional justice as referring 'to the set of judicial and non-judicial measures that have been implemented by different countries in order to redress the legacies of massive human rights abuses'. See www.ictj.org
3 As incorporated in the UN Convention on the Protection of All Persons from Enforced Disappearances, which took effect on 23 December 2010 (Article 24.2).
4 United Nations reports also note the large amount of discretionary power of governments: 'While, under international law, gross violations of human rights and serious violations of international humanitarian law give rise to a right to reparation for victims, implying a duty on the State to make reparations, implementing this right and corresponding duty is in essence a matter of domestic law and policy. In this respect, national Governments possess a good deal of discretion and flexibility' (UNHCHR 2008, p. 14).
5 IACtHR, Case of the Moiwana Community v. Surinam, Judgment of 15 June 2005, para. 194: 'Given that the victims of the present case are members of the N'duka culture, this Tribunal considers that the individual reparations to be awarded must be supplemented by communal measures; said reparations will be granted to the community as a whole.' See also IACtHR, Case of the Mayagna (Sumo) Awas Tingi Community v. Nicaragua, Judgment of 31 August 2001. For more detailed references, see International Law Association, The Hague Conference, Reparation for Victims of Armed Conflict, including a Draft Declaration of International Law Principles on Reparation for Victims of Armed Conflict 2010; available at: www.ila-hq.org/en/committees/index.cfm/cid/1018.
6 Peruvian Truth and Reconciliation Commission, Plan of Integral Reparations (PIR), June 2003, para. 3.6, available at: www.cverdad.org.pe; Guatemala, Memory of Silence, Report of the Commission for Historical Clarification, Recommendations, III, para. 10, available at: http://shr.aaas.org/guatemala/ceh/report/english/toc.html; Final Report of the Truth and Reconciliation Commission of Sierra Leone, Vol. 2, Chapter 4, Reparations, para. 27, available at: www.sierra-leone.org/TRCDocuments.html; Chega!, Report of the Commission for Reception, Truth and Reconciliation in Timor-Leste (CAVR), available at: www.cavr-timorleste.org/en/chegaReport.htm.
7 Both academic literature and publications aimed at the general public often feature claims regarding the positive influence of post-conflict processes on victims' psyches. For these claims, empirical evidence is often lacking (Doak 2011, p. 269).

Bibliography

de Brouwer, A. and Heikkilä, M., 2012. The victims' role in international criminal proceedings: participation, protection, reparation and assistance. In: G. Sluiter, H. Friman, S. Linton, S. Vasiliev and S. Zappalà, eds, International criminal procedure: towards the codification of general rules and principles. Oxford: Oxford University Press.

Danieli, Y., 2009. Massive trauma and the healing role of reparative justice. Journal of Traumatic Stress, 22(5), pp. 351–357.

De Brouwer, A., 2007. Reparation to Victims of Sexual Violence: Possibilities at the International Criminal Court and at the Trust Fund for Victims and Their Families. Leiden Journal of International Law 20, 207–237.

De Brouwer, A., Chu, S.K.H. and Muscati, S., 2011. The men who killed me. Nijmegen: Wolf Legal Publishers.

De Feyter, K., Parmentier, S., Bossuyt, M. and Lemmens, P., eds, 2005. Out of the ashes. reparation for victims of gross and systematic human rights violations. Antwerp/Oxford: Intersentia Publishers.

De Greiff, P., ed., 2006. The handbook of reparations. Oxford: Oxford University Press.

Doak, J., 2011. The therapeutic dimension of transitional justice: Emotional repair and victim satisfaction in international trials and truth commissions. International Criminal Law Review, 11, pp. 263–298.

Dubinsky, P., 2004. Justice for the collective: the limits of the human rights class action, 102 Michigan L.Rev., pp. 1152–1190.

Elias, R., 1985. Transcending our social reality of victimization: toward a new victimology of human rights. Victimology, 10 (1/4), pp. 6–25.

Goodey, J., 2005. Victims and victimology: research, policy and practice. Harlow: Pearson Education.

Groenhuijsen, M.S., 2011. Toegang tot het strafrecht: Een slachtofferperspectief. Delikt en Delinkwent, 41(3), pp. 209–219.

Groenhuijsen, M.S. and Pemberton, A., 2011. Genocide, war crimes and crimes against humanity: a victimological perspective. In: R.M. Letschert, R. Haveman, A. de Brouwer and A. Pemberton, eds, Victimological approaches to international crimes: Africa. Antwerp: Intersentia, pp. 9–34.

Haldemann, F. 2011. Drawing the line: Amnesty, truth commissions and collective denial. In: R.M. Letschert, R.H. Haveman, A. de Brouwer and A. Pemberton, eds, Victimological approaches to international crimes: Africa. Antwerp: Intersentia, pp. 265–288.

Hamber, B., 2001. Does the Truth Heal? A Psychological Perspective on Political Strategies for Dealing with the Legacy of Political Violence. In: Biggar, N., ed., Burying the Past. Making Peace and Doing Justice after Civil Conflict. Washington DC: Georgetown University Press, pp. 131–148.

Hamber, B. 2009., Transforming societies after political violence: truth, reconciliation, and mental health. Heidelberg: Springer.

Hamber, B. and Wilson, R., 2002. Symbolic closure through memory, reparation and revenge in post-conflict societies. Journal of Human Rights, 1(1), pp. 35–53.

Hofmann, R., 2010. Reparations for victims of armed conflicts. Report to the ILA Hague Conference 2010. Available at: www.ila-hq.org/en/committees/index.cfm/cid/1018 [Accessed 15 November 2013].

Laplante, L.J., 2007. On the indivisibility of rights: truth commissions, reparations, and the right to development. Yale Hum. Rts & Dev. L.J., 10, pp. 141–177.

Letschert, R.M., 2010. Protecting and empowering victims of international crimes through the human security concept – A new challenge for victimologists? Available at: http://ssrn.com/abstract=1594250 [Accessed 15 January 2014].

Letschert, R.M. and van Boven, T., 2011. Providing reparation in situations of mass victimization: Key challenges involved. In: R.M. Letschert, R. Haveman, A. de Brouwer and A. Pemberton, eds, Victimological Approaches to International Crimes: Africa. Antwerp: Intersentia, pp. 153–184.

Letschert, R.M. and Groenhuijsen, M.S., 2011. Global governance and global crime: Do victims fall inbetween? In: R.M. Letschert and J.J.M. van Dijk, eds, The new faces of victimhood. Houten: Springer, pp. 15–40.

Letschert, R.M., Staiger, I. and Pemberton, A., eds, 2011. Assistance to victims of terrorism: Towards a European standard of justice. Dordrecht: Springer.

Letschert, R.M., Haveman, R.H., de Brouwer, A. and Pemberton., A., eds, 2011. Victimological approaches to international crimes: Africa. Antwerp: Intersentia.

McEvoy, K. and McGregor, L., 2008. Transitional justice from below: An agenda for research, policy and praxis. In: K. McEvoy and L. McGregor, eds, Transitional justice from below: grassroots activism and the struggle for change. London/Oxford: Hart Publishing, pp. 1–14.

Orth, U. 2002., Secondary victimization of crime victims by criminal proceedings. Social Justice Research, 15(4), pp. 313–325.

Parmentier, S., 2003. Global justice in the aftermath of mass violence. the role of the international criminal court in dealing with political crimes. International Annals of Criminology, 41(1-2), pp. 203–224.

Parmentier, S. and Weitekamp. E., 2007. Political crimes and serious violations of human rights: towards a criminology of international crimes. In: S. Parmentier and E. Weitekamp, eds, Crime and human rights. Series in Sociology of Crime, Law and Deviance, vol. 9, pp. 109–144. Amsterdam/Oxford: Elsevier/JAI Press.

Parmentier, S., Valiñas, M. and Weitekamp, E., 2009. How to repair the harm after violent conflict in Bosnia? Results of a population-based survey. Netherlands Quarterly of Human Rights, 27(1), pp. 27–44.

Parmentier, S., Rauschenbach, M. and Weitekamp, E., 2014. Repairing the harm of victims after violent conflict: Empirical findings from Serbia. Special Issue on Celebrating the 20th Anniversary, edited by J. Shapland and J. Sloan, 20(1) International Review of Victimology, 20(1), pp. 85–99.

Pemberton, A., Letschert, R.M., de Brouwer, A.L.M. and Haveman, R., 2011. Een victimologisch perspectief op het internationale strafrecht. Tijdschrift voor Criminologie, 53(4), pp. 74–88.

Pham, P., Vinck, P. Balthazard, M., Hean S. and Stover, E., 2009. So we will never forget. a population-based survey on attitudes about social reconstruction and the Extraordinary Chambers in the Courts of Cambodia. Berkeley: Human Rights Centre, University of California.

Pham, P., Vinck, P. Balthazard, M. and Hean S., 2011. After the first trial. A population-based survey on knowledge and perceptions of justice and the Extraordinary Chambers in the Courts of Cambodia. Berkeley: Human Rights Centre, University of California.

Pham, P., Vinck, P., Wierda, M., Stover, E. and di Giovanni, A., 2005. Forgotten voices. a population-based survey on attitudes about peace and justice in Northern Uganda. New York/Berkeley: International Centre for Transitional Justice/Human Rights Centre, University of California.

Pham, P., Vinck, P., Stover, E., Moss, A., Wierda, M. and Bailey, R., 2007. When the war ends. A population-based survey on attitudes about peace, justice, and social reconstruction in Northern Uganda, New York/Berkeley/New Orleans: International Centre for Transitional Justice/Human Rights Centre, University of California, Berkeley/Payson Centre for International Development, Tulane University.

Rombouts, H. and Parmentier, S., 2009. The International Criminal Court and its trust fund are coming of age: towards a process approach for the reparation of victims. Special Issue on Victim Reparation and the International Criminal Court, edited by J.-A. Wemmers, International Review of Victimology, 16(2), pp. 149–182.

Rosenfeld, F., 2010. Collective reparation for victims of armed conflict. International Review of the Red Cross, 92(879), pp. 731–746.

Roth-Arriaza, N., 2004. Reparations decisions and dilemmas. Hastings International & Comparative Law Review, 27, pp. 157–219.

Shaw, M., 2001. Time heals all wounds? In: G. Farrell and K. Pease, eds, Repeat victimization. Crime Prevention Studies, volume 12. Monsey: Criminal Justice Press, pp. 218–233.

Shelton, D., 2005. The United Nations Principles and Guidelines on Reparations: Context and Contents. In: K. De Feyter, S. Parmentier, M. Bossuyt and P. Lemmens, eds, 2005. Out of the ashes. Reparation for victims of gross and systematic human rights violations. Antwerp/Oxford: Intersentia Publishers, pp. 11–33.

Thoms, O., Ron, J. and Paris, R., 2008. The effects of transitional justice mechanisms. A summary of empirical research findings and implications for analysts and practitioners. Ottawa: Centre for International Policy Studies, University of Ottawa.

Tomuschat, C., 2005. Darfur, compensation for the victims. 3 J. Int'l Crim. Just. 579.

United Nations, General Assembly, 2005. Basic principles and guidelines on the right to a remedy and reparation for victims of gross violations of international human rights law and serious violations of international humanitarian law, 24 October 2005, A/C.3/60/L.24.

UN, High Commissioner for Human Rights 2008. Rule-of-law tools for post-conflict states; reparations programs. HR/PUB/08/1.

van Dijk, J.J.M., Groenhuijsen, M.S. and Winkel, F.W., 2007. Victimologie. Voorgeschiedenis en stand van zaken. Justitiële Verkenningen, 33(3), Victimologie, Slachtofferschap en Samenleving.

Wemmers, J., 2011. Victims' need for justice: Individual versus collective Justice. In: R. Letschert, R. Haverman, A. De Brouwer and A. Pemberton, eds, Victimological approaches to international crimes: Africa. Antwerp: Intersentia, pp. 145–152.

Winkel, F.W., 2007. Post traumatic anger. Missing link in the wheel of misfortune. Rede uitgesproken bij het aanvaarden van het ambt van hoogleraar aan de Universiteit van Tilburg, 17 oktober 2007.

Chapter 11
Transitional justice and the victims
A special focus on the case of Chile

José Zalaquett

Introduction

This chapter focuses on the transitional justice policies adopted by Chile after the country's return to democratic rule in 1990, following nearly seventeen years of military dictatorship. The case of Chile is widely regarded as one of the richest and most important experiences in transitional justice in the Americas and beyond. Thus, an analysis of this case may help to shed light on many critical transitional justice issues.

Transitional justice and the evolving notion of victim

Political change towards democratic rule in Latin America in the 1980s and 1990s

Transitional justice started to be shaped around the political transitions to democracy in South America from the early 1980 onward. The first of these was the Argentinean transition, which began in December of 1983. The term of art 'transition to democracy' preceded by nearly a decade that of 'transitional justice'.[1] It was first coined from the perspective of political science in the mid-1980s (O'Donnell *et al.* 1986). Transition to democracy was understood then as an interval between the demise of an authoritarian regime and the installation of a democratic one in its stead. What the authors had in mind was the process of revaluation of the democratic idea and the end of the military dictatorships regimes in Latin America which, by the time they were writing, had already occurred in Argentina and Uruguay. That process coincided with the beginning of the dissolution of the Soviet system and of the Cold War. It spread later on to Central and Eastern Europe, Africa, Central America, South East Asia and the Middle East. The initial development of this concept of transition to democracy has been well described by Mainwaring (1989).

Although there were European examples of political change from an authoritarian regime to democracy before the Argentinean transition – Greece, in 1974; Spain, in 1975; and Portugal, in the period 1976–78 – it was the end of the military regime in Argentina, in December of 1983, following the defeat of the armed forces of that nation by the British forces in the Falkland war of 1982, that spearheaded international concern over the need to address a legacy of past abuses.

Transitional justice as the ethics for a time of political reconstruction

We are reminded by Max Weber (2004), that different realms of life call for specific moral norms. Such prescriptions are not necessarily weaker or stronger than the equivalent rules which are appropriate for other spheres. Also, they may all derive from some superior norm, but their more specific content ought to fit the particulars of a given realm, be it that of family relations, commercial transactions or political life. It may be added that the domain of democratic political ethics is governed by distinct moral norms that depend on the time or moment to which they apply: a foundational time, a time of sustainable life of the democratic system, a time of utter breakdown of the social contract or a time of reconstruction. For the first three of these 'times', there have been norms, doctrines and practical precedents, widely agreed upon, which go back to the eighteen century and have continued to be produced since that period.

For the foundational time of a republic, there are theories of moral philosophy, the precedent of liberal revolutions, and constitutional theory. For the time of the sustainable life of a democracy, among other relevant norms, one may count the guarantees for individual rights, the notions of the rule of law and public accountability, and the electoral systems that allow for the will of the people to manifest itself. For the time of breakdown of a nation's order the norms of International Humanitarian Law and of emergency rule may be applicable. Yet, for the period of democratic reconstruction, there was no set of generally agreed upon principles until the development of transitional justice. The fact that this field is young may account for the attention it has received in the last three decades in political and academic circles worldwide and for the intensity of the debates it elicits.

Certainly, there were significant precedents of what is now termed transitional justice before the 1980s. Yet it was with the Argentinean transition to democracy that the international political and academic community took notice of the need for the development of principles to address a legacy of past State crimes. In certain cases – certainly, those of Argentina, Uruguay and Chile – political transition meant indeed a process of democratic re-foundation. Yet most political changes occurring in subsequent years marked the beginning of a novel democratic *construction*, rather than a re-foundation.

Evolution of the transitional justice field

Following the first South American experiences that started in the 1980s, the transitional justice agenda expanded to encompass a variety of situations: attempts at the fresh foundation of a proper democratic regime, rather than at restoring a defunct democracy (El Salvador, Guatemala); political change that ended a regime of institutionalized discrimination (South Africa); the disintegration of a State (former Yugoslavia); an ongoing civil war (Uganda, Sierra Leone) or the coexisting of internal armed conflict and a functioning democracy (Colombia); reforms to increase respect for human rights, without changing the regime into a democracy (Morocco); situations in which a peaceful or armed revolution has brought to an end a dictatorial regime, but the respective nation has no traditions of democratic rule in living memory (Central and Eastern Europe, starting in the late 1980s; Egypt and Tunisia, starting in 2011). Most new cases add to the existing typology.

The centrality of the figure of the 'victim' in transitional justice

The notion of 'victim' certainly precedes the development of transitional justice. Yet as this field has been evolving, the figure of the victim has acquired a particular centrality. Truth commissions have accounted for their fate; memorials have been erected to honour them; official declarations of acknowledgement of past crimes focus on the dignity of the victims and the determination not to let such atrocities reoccur; reparations have been established; specialized institutions have been created to provide for rehabilitation for victims of torture. Even in the field criminal justice, which focuses mostly on the alleged perpetrator, novel concepts have emerged, such as the 'rights' to truth and to justice. The United Nations notion of victim is as follows:

> Victims are persons who individually or collectively suffered harm, including physical or mental injury, emotional suffering, economic loss or substantial impairment of their fundamental rights, through acts or omissions that constitute gross violations of international human rights law or serious violations of international humanitarian law. Where appropriate, and in accordance with domestic law, the term 'victim' also includes the immediate family or dependants of the direct victim or persons who have suffered harm in intervening to assist victims in distress or to prevent victimization.[2]

Victims may, then, be individual or collective; direct or indirect. In the following sections the experience of Chile is analysed so as to critically examine the previously mentioned developments, and comparative references are made.

The victims of human rights violations in Chile

The repressive practices of the military dictatorship (1973–1990)

The Chilean armed forces overthrew the government of Salvador Allende on 11 September 1973. In the climate of the 1960s, Latin America's younger generations tended to embrace radical politics, shifting the political balance towards the left. In Chile, a coalition of left-wing parties was instrumental to the electoral victory of Allende in 1970. Following the 1973 coup d'état, the Chilean armed forces ruled for sixteen and a half years, before handing over power to an elected civilian candidate, on 11 March 1990.

During their time in power, the Armed Forces, led by General Augusto Pinochet, dissolved the Chilean Parliament, banned elections, outlawed political parties and unions, subjected Chilean universities to military tutelage, closed down independent media and declared emergency rule. In short, they controlled the country and stifled all dissent.

The Chilean dictatorship became notorious, worldwide, for the massive human rights violations it perpetrated. The total toll of documented individual victims of various forms of human rights violations in Chile, a country that by 2012 has just under seventeen million people, is as follows:

a people who lost their lives (including political killings and forced disappearances): 3,189;[3]
b people who suffered from political imprisonment: 37,050;[4]
c victims of torture: the Chilean truth commissions found that torture was systematically practiced against political prisoners;
d political exiles: around 20,000 persons were officially banned from the country and a much higher number sought refuge abroad;
e people who lost their jobs as civil servants or employees of State-related corporations for political reasons: there is an official list of 157,094[5] which includes thousands of cases wrongly characterized as victims;
f people who lost their jobs in the private sector of the economy: an unknown number;
g academics fired from their university positions: about 3,000;
h university students expelled: certainly many times more than the number of academics who lost their jobs.

In addition, the whole population of Chile suffered from a suspension of its civil and political rights. These restrictions were accepted by the supporters of the military regime, many of whom felt they benefitted, as a trade-off, from political tranquillity, economic gain or both.

Assistance to the victims of human rights violations

On 6 October 1973, just a few weeks after the coup d'état, a religious coalition made of the Catholic Church, five other Christian denominations and the Great Rabbi of Chile, formed the Committee of Cooperation for Peace in Chile (known as Peace Committee), a human rights body charged with providing legal material and moral assistance to the victims of human rights violation. In January of 1976, under pressure from General Pinochet, the Archbishop of Santiago, Cardinal Raúl

Silva Henríquez, dissolved this committee and created in its stead the Vicariate of Solidarity, an organ of the Archdiocese of Santiago. The Vicariate continued its activities until the end of the military regime and it functioned for two more years following the recovery of the democracy in Chile, providing documentation to the National Truth and Reconciliation Commission created in May of 1990. It wound down its operations in 1992.

Years after the birth of the Vicariate of Solidarity other human rights organizations were created in Chile, although the Peace Committee and the Vicariate remained the largest and the ones most sought after by the victims and their relatives. The work of these two organizations was manifold. Central to their efforts was to provide legal aid to the relatives of people imprisoned or subjected to forced disappearances, through the presentation of habeas corpus writs[6] and other legal actions in thousands of cases. These actions were to no avail from a judicial standpoint, but they had significant indirect consequences, for several reasons:

a   the relatives of the victims felt supported if a lawyer was acting on their case;
b   the habeas corpus petitions could give a clue as to the intentions of the political police regarding the prisoner in question – if they responded to the queries of the courts saying that no such person was detained, it meant that probably the person was killed already or that they intended to kill him/her, whereas if they acknowledged the detention but attempted to justify it, it indicated that they would not kill the prisoner;
c   to give up the legal actions would have meant abandoning the arena of justice;
d   it was expected that the cumulative effect of so many thousands of petitions would end up by persuading some judges or politicians that human rights violations were indeed taking place, and this did indeed happen with a few of them;
e   gathering testimonies and documentation contemporary to the facts had a special documentary value and could in the future prove of great importance. In fact, in 1990 such records were made available to the National Truth and Reconciliation Commission.

Other lines of work of the above mentioned organizations included processing information about human rights violations and communicating them to church leaders in Chile, to the correspondents of foreign media visiting the country, to non-governmental human rights organizations and to UN and OAS (Organisation of American States) human rights bodies; seeking asylum in foreign embassies accredited to Chile for people being persecuted and eventually helping them to relocate in another country; providing legal assistance to workers arbitrarily dismissed from their jobs; and helping unemployed people to organize small economic ventures.

Associations of victims or their families

Starting in 1975, under the umbrella of the Peace Committee, and later on the Vicariate of Solidarity, relatives of victims of forced disappearances formed an organization called Asociación de Familiares de Detenidos Desaparecidos. It has functioned to this day, organizing protests, initiating legal actions to try to find the truth concerning the fate met by the relatives' loved ones and/or the disposal of their remains, seeking for justice to be meted out and promoting human rights. Later, similar organizations were created by relatives of victims (or by victims themselves) of political killings, imprisonment, torture or loss of jobs for political reasons.

During the late phase of the dictatorship, institutions dealing with the rehabilitation of victims were created in Chile. Particularly worthy of note are the Instituto de Salud Mental y Derechos Humanos (ILAS), which focuses on psychotherapy for victims and La Fundación Protección a la Infancia Dañada por los Estados de Emergencia (PIDEE), devoted to assisting children. They continue to be active, now with a larger mandate.

The polarized stand concerning the victims

Opponents to the military regime, in Chile and the world, knew of the massive human rights violations it committed. The *de facto* military authorities and their supporters denied them, although harsh political repression was for them an essential tool to fight an insidious internal enemy. The military indoctrinated their rank and file personnel, making them believe that the victims were less than human ('humanoids' was the term used by Admiral José Toribio Medina, the head of the Chilean Navy and a member of the Military Junta): people without principles, terrorists... Demonization of people who are considered 'internal enemies' has been common to many authoritarian regimes as a way of assuaging the possible scruples of the men in uniform who were ordered to kill or torture them.

Transitional justice policies in Chile and their focus on victims

The Southern Cone's transitions to democracy

The Argentinean transition, in 1983, followed the defeat of that country by Britain in the Falklands war, in 1992. By contrast, in Uruguay and Chile transition was prompted by electoral defeat. In November of 1980, Uruguayan military rulers held a referendum on a new Constitution. They lost. That electoral defeat led to negotiations with civilian politicians and, four years later, to the election of President Julio María Sanguinetti. In October of 1988, the Chilean Military Junta called a yes-no plebiscite on the continuation of General Pinochet as president. The 'no' option won. A year later a competitive presidential election was organized. Patricio Aylwin, leader of the opposition, was elected and inaugurated on 11 March 1990.

President Aylwin faced the restrictions inherent to the fact that the political forces he represented had defeated the military regime at the ballot-box and within the framework of rules of the game set by that government. They included the fact that a Constitution passed in 1980 by the military dictatorship allowed General Pinochet to remain as commander in chief of the Chilean Army until 1998. Given this, President Aylwin promised that concerning human rights abuses he would deliver 'the whole truth and justice to the extent that it is possible'. This formulation gave ground to criticism, in Chile and abroad. Probably the choice of words was infelicitous. Yet political development in subsequent years have proved that after the revelation of the truth about human rights violations, the scope for more transitional justice measures was expanding with time.

Since Patricio Aylwin was inaugurated more than six years later than Argentina's Raúl Alfonsín, and more than five years after Uruguay's civilian president, Raúl Sanguinetti, took over power, he could draw lessons from the transitional policies undertaken by these countries. Argentina had taken energetic measures, including creating a first Truth Commission with a mandate to cover the whole period of authoritarian government in that country (1974–1983). Uruguay, where the transition was negotiated with the military, had not done much. President Aylwin followed a middle ground between these examples. He started by establishing a Truth Commission. Twenty two years later, much has happened in Chile concerning transitional justice. True, a lot has yet to be achieved. Notwithstanding that, by comparison with the forty or so examples of transitional justice policies (or lack thereof) of many countries since the 1980s, it may be asserted that Argentina and Chile are the two countries that have gone the furthest concerning truth-telling, memory preservation, acknowledgement, reparations, criminal justice and even institutional reform. In the case of Argentina the transitional justice process has been marked by positive steps alternating with drawbacks[7]. In the case of Chile, the transitional justice process has instead gone, since 1990, through a gradual expansion, with a couple of periods of stagnation. By the time of concluding this text (January 2013), both countries exhibit significant advances in most aspects of their respective transitional justice processes.

The revelation of the truth concerning past human rights violations

One of the most visible measures adopted as part of transitional justice policies has been the establishing of Truth Commissions. The first widely known and effective truth Commission was the Argentinean National Commission on the Disappearance of Persons (known as CONADEP, its acronym in Spanish), created in December of 1983. The rationale of practice of forced disappearances that was developed systematically in Chile by the Dirección de Inteligencia Nacional (DINA) and then applied at a much larger scale in Argentina during the period 1976–80, was to get rid of people considered dangerous and unredeemable, while at the same time avoiding the bad image that would result from their outright execution.[8]

People who supported the military regimes in Argentina and Chile (not a small percentage) did not believe – or they needed not to believe, so as not to have a bad conscience – that their leaders were responsible for such heinous crimes, or else they thought the violations they committed were much smaller in scale, and at any rate justified as a lesser evil. Thus, both the Argentinean CONADEP and the Chilean Truth and Reconciliation Commission (1990–91) focused on revealing the truth about grave human rights violations that resulted in loss of life and which remained secret or denied by the former dictatorial rulers. For the objective of reconstructing the broken democratic system, it was critical to produce a credible official document about the truth of the human rights violations of the past that no one in good faith could ignore or deny. That explains why in both countries the respective truth commissions worked (for nine months each) in chambers, in order to write a solid report, that was subsequently broadly disseminated. Had they held public hearings during the course of their investigations, much acrimonious social debate would have likely ensued, making it improbable that a report could have been produced that met with widespread acceptance.

The situation was quite different regarding the Truth and Reconciliation commissions in South Africa (1995–98) and in Peru (2001–3). They held public hearings which were broadcast by radio and television. In those countries there was not much doubt about the ruthlessness of the apartheid regime (South Africa) or about the fact that many crimes had been committed both by Shining Path and other guerrilla groups, and by the State forces fighting them. The hearings held by the truth commissions of these two countries had the purpose of giving a public voice to the victims. The process of truth gathering was, thus, as important as the actual final report by each of these truth commissions or perhaps more so.

Nearly three decades after CONADEP was created, there have been dozens of examples of truth commissions in countries in different corners of the world (Hayner 2010). They cover a wide range of organizational modes, mandates, methodology, resources. The quality and credibility of their reports vary greatly. A minority of them may be considered reasonably successful in their task of truth-telling. In an even smaller number of cases, the truth commission's work was followed eventually by serious efforts in the areas of memory preservation, acknowledgement, reparations, criminal justice for the gravest crimes and institutional reform. The cases of Argentina and Chile belong in that small number.

In certain countries, the truth-telling process, reasonably well done as it might have been, was intended by the national authorities to close the traumatic chapter in the nation's history, rather than to open the way for further transitional justice measures.[9]

Accounting for individual victims: the question of figures

Truth commissions have dealt with the accounting of victims in different ways. CONADEP, the Argentinean commission, produced a two-volume report in

September of 1984. The second volume consisted of a printout of 8,961 names of individuals 'disappeared'. The list was compiled from different lists elaborated by human rights organizations.

Later on, a figure of 30,000 people subjected to forced disappearance in Argentina has been claimed by the Mothers of Plaza de Mayo. Anyone publicly disputing that figure may become suspect of belittling the Argentinean tragedy. Thus, visiting foreign journalist and Argentinean human rights practitioners refrain from doing so, even if they know that such figure is much inflated. Needless to say, one person disappeared is one too many. Also, crimes against humanity are such regardless of a precise body count. Yet if reference to figures of victims is to be made at all, rigorousness is of the essence. It could well be that the real toll of victims is greater than the one given by the CONADEP report but certainly the total of 30,000 is too high. More accurate figures await future research endeavours.

Perhaps one key factor accounting for the fact that CONADEP could just publish a printout of names, without describing the circumstances in which the individuals were abducted, was the fact that the hierarchy of the Argentinean Catholic Church did not take action to protect human rights during that country's military dictatorship. In South and Central America, the Catholic Church and other religious denominations were often the only independent institutions allowed to function under the respective military dictatorships. Where the Churches or key Church leaders decided to work for the protection of human rights, as in Sao Paulo (Brazil) and Chile, in South America or El Salvador, in Central America, a measure of relief to the victims and their families could be provided, and the gathering of relevant information was more complete. Where the Church hierarchy did not or could not take action, as in Argentina, Uruguay or Guatemala, victims and their families were left to fend for themselves. In the initial and harsher years of the 1976–1983 Argentinean dictatorship, work on behalf of victims rested mostly on the valiant action of the relatives of some of them. Although a few civil society human rights organizations existed in those early years, they could not systematically document human rights violations.

Given that Chile had Church-supported human rights organizations from the beginning of the dictatorial rule, the work of the 1990–1991 Truth and Reconciliation Commission could account for the circumstances in which fatal victims were killed or abducted. Thus, the total toll of 3,189 fatal victims during the period 1973–1990 documented by the Chilean Truth and Reconciliation Commission and its successor commissions is widely accepted in Chile, with minimal variations.

The Salvadoran Truth Commission is an example of a truth-telling organ that investigated and reported a number of emblematic or illustrative cases. This commission published the names of the State agents and guerrilla fighters it deemed responsible for them. In an Annex it published the list of cases of killings, disappearances and other gross abuses that it came to know of. In this case, the sheer number of actual victims[10] probably prevented the Truth Commission from carrying out an exhaustive accounting.

The Peruvian commission gave two overall figures. It stated that it received information on 23,969 people killed or disappeared during the period 1980–2000. It added that in many regions documentation was sorely lacking. Thus, using statistical methods, it estimated the total number of fatal victims of guerrilla fighters or of State security forces to reach the number of 69,280 people or 2.9 times the number of cases brought to its attention. Sound as this extrapolation may have been, it was the target of criticism by certain opinion makers in Peru.

True, erroneous and false claims to victimhood

The widespread belief that victims do not lie largely bears out in reality. They do not need to. Even more, they are often reticent to tell their stories in any detail, out of self-restraint, shame or reluctance to relive painful episodes. The key point, of course, is how to determine who is a victim in the first place.

Needless to say, the status of certified victim carries with it much legitimacy as well as material entitlements. Because of that, next to the true victims there often are many people who in good faith believe that their plight fits a given legal definition of victim. Others may know or suspect that they do not qualify as victims but they feel that they did suffer much on other accounts during the period of authoritarian rule and they ought to have some redress, whatever the manner of obtaining it. And there are those who plainly take advantage of legal gaps or loose proceedings to claim a status of victim they do not deserve.

In Chile, the Truth and Reconciliation Commission (1990–1) as well as the Commission on Political Imprisonment and Torture (2003–5, re-opened in 2011) received many more applications than they accepted. Perhaps most of the unsuccessful applications were presented in good faith. It is generally considered that the work of these commissions was rigorous. However, the loose laws and administrative mechanisms set up to determine the victims of arbitrary dismissal from State-related bodies and corporations (*exonerados politicos*), as discussed later, allowed for many thousands of wrong or fabricated claims to go through without much vetting.[11]

Memory preservation

In recent years there has been an upsurge of monuments, plaques, inscriptions and many other ways of commemorating and honouring the victims of human rights violations and war crimes in many countries. An international Coalition of Sites of Conscience was created in 1999.

In Chile, a wall of names with inscriptions listing all the fatal victims reported by the Truth and Reconciliation Commission and its follow-up commissions was built in the General Cemetery. Memorials including lists of names of fatal victims have also been erected in centres of secret detention, torture and death; in sites where clandestine tombs have been discovered and in places where opponents to the military regime were found dead. In many union halls, professional guilds' headquarters, schools and other such places within the Chilean territory, plaques or monoliths bearing the names of associates who were victimized are often found. A similar profusion of memorials is found in Argentina and in other countries. In Chile, a Museum of Memory and Human Rights was inaugurated in 2010. It is owned by a non-profit foundation. and receives funds from the State.

Acknowledgement

Individual acknowledgement of criminal guilt may not, of course be forced. The South African Truth and Reconciliation Commission was legally empowered to grant amnesty to perpetrators of politically motivated crimes who declared the full truth of what happened. They were entitled to legal representation in the respective proceedings. By 1997 some 7,116 people had applied to receive this amnesty. About two thirds of the applications were rejected. In Chile and elsewhere there have been guilty pleas before the courts in some cases. Or else, some perpetrators have admitted to their responsibility after being convicted or because they were prompted by remorse even if they were never prosecuted; sometimes these admissions took place decades following the actual events.

The acknowledgement of institutional responsibility for policies or directives ordering criminal acts is of paramount importance in the process of founding or rebuilding a broken society. Such admissions, whether by the military, political parties, Churches or other institutions, help to rectify the evil doctrine once espoused, whether explicitly or tacitly, by the organization, to affirm the values that were transgressed and to recognize the dignity of the victims. Further, it opens the way for a political agreement about the need to provide for reparations by law.

It is important that such acknowledgement is done in a manner that represents the institution in question. In Chile, after President Aylwin announced to the nation the findings of the Truth and Reconciliation Commission on 4 March 1991, political parties and social organizations acknowledged that truth (many of them with strong reservations and caveats, but they did). Nevertheless, General Pinochet openly rejected the report on behalf of the Army and no frank acknowledgement came from the other branches of the armed forces either. Eight years later, once General Pinochet, by then retired from the command of the Army, was under house arrest in London, facing an extradition request from a Spanish Judge, the Chilean government agreed with the Chilean armed forces, then under the command of a new generation of military men, to create a Round Table Discussion (*Mesa de Diálogo*) on human rights. This panel gathered together high-ranking officials, human rights lawyers, religious leaders and academics. Its final statement, issued in June of 2000, acknowledged the human rights violations committed during the military government in Chile. Although many deemed that acknowledgement to be not sufficiently categorical, it did open the way to further pronouncements by military leaders culminating, in 2003 with a document signed by the then Army Chief, General Cheyre, titled 'Never Again' (*Nunca Más*), an expression that evokes the determination not to let the Holocaust happen again and that has powerful symbolic connotations in transitional justice milieux. Actually, days prior to the release of the report by the National Commission on Political Imprisonment and Torture, in 2004, Chilean military commanders rushed to acknowledge it, even before they could know its content.

In Argentina, in 1995, General Martín Balza, then the Army Commander, acknowledged by means of a television appearance the human rights violations committed during the 1976–1983 military dictatorship. He amplified this acknowledgement later on. Honest as it was, this admission was more personal than institutional and he was spurned and isolated by his military comrades, both retired and in active service.

Reparations

A major landmark on reparations for human rights abuses was the study produced in 1993 by the Special Rapporteur on this topic for the Sub-commission on Prevention of Discrimination and Protection of Minorities of the United Nations' Commission on Human Rights (van Boven 1993). On the basis of this document, the General Assembly of the United Nations adopted, in 2005, a resolution proclaiming basic principles applicable to reparations.[12] Several additional studies were later published on the topic of reparations (de Greiff 2006; Nash 2009).

Reparations may consist of: (a) restitution, whenever it is possible to restore the victim to the original situation; (b) compensation for assessable damage; (c) rehabilitation; (d) satisfaction, including public apologies, truth, justice and measures aimed at restoring the victim's dignity; and (e) guarantees of non repetition, which comprise a variety of preventive measures and institutional reform. Reparations may also be individual or collective, material or symbolic.

Reparations, including preventive measures and some institutional reform, have been made the main aspect of the transitional justice policies of Morocco. The Truth Commission of this country, called the Equity and Reconciliation commission (2004–2005) laid the ground for such reparative measures.

Chile and Argentina are among the countries which have provided for a whole range of reparations. In Argentina, a number of laws established compensations for victims of political imprisonment; for relatives of people subjected to forced disappearances; for people born of a mother who was in detention and whose real identity was supplanted; and for military personnel who suffered from reprisals for refusing to join the coup d'état. Many measures of reparation have been applied in Chile (Lira and Loveman 2005), as listed below.

a   *Relatives of fatal victims (killed or 'disappeared')*: a pension for the closest relatives; scholarships for the victims' children; health services; dispensation of military service for the victims' children and grandchildren; allocation of State funds for memorials. These reparations were enacted by law 19.123 of 1992 and law 19.980 of 2004.

b   *Political imprisonment and torture:* laws 19.992 of 2004 and law 20.405 of 2009 provided a pension for the victims, plus health, educational and housing benefits, and dispensation of military service for their children.
c   *People dismissed from their State-related jobs for political reasons (exonerados politicos)*: law 19.234 of 1993 and law 19.582 of 1998 instituted either pensions or the coverage of gaps in their pension plans' deposits.
d   *Exiled people who returned to Chile*: law 18,894 of 1990, law 19.074 of 1991 and law 19.128 of 1992 granted such people exemption from customs duties and other facilities for their reinsertion in the country.
e   *Law 19.568 of 1998 ordered restitution (or compensation) of property* from political parties, trade unions and other organizations that had been confiscated by the military regime, as well as giving back their jobs in State universities or civil service to some people dismissed for political reasons during the military dictatorship.
f   *Symbolic measures* were implemented, mostly those mentioned earlier.
g   *Prevention and guarantees of non repetition:* Chile has ratified most international human rights conventions, reinforced the principle of human rights protection in its Constitution, amended some laws and created some relevant State organizations. Among the later are the Consejo para la Transparencia, established by law 20.285 of 2008, which must oversee the implementation of the right of access to public information, and the National Institute of Human Rights. Some defective laws have yet to be amended or repealed, the creation of an office of Ombudsman is still pending and the incorporation of human rights in educational programmes is sorely lacking.

Justice

Criminal justice is commonly the most arduous of transitional justice tasks in cases where the perpetrators of political crimes are still a force to be reckoned with. On the other hand, where they have been completely defeated by feat of arms, there is a strong possibility of a non-impartial 'victor's justice'. This is a reminder that in practice transitional justice's policies may be better or worse but hardly optimal.

The Statute of Rome of 1998 that established the International Criminal Court reiterates the principle of the 1968 Convention on the Non-Applicability of Statutory Limitations to War Crimes and Crimes against Humanity.[13] Other than for these egregious crimes, measures of amnesty and forgiveness are not prohibited. However, the philosophy of transitional justice requests that if such measures are to be granted to less than enormous crimes, they must be consistent with the purpose of building or reconstructing a just society following a traumatic national period (Zalaquett 1999). Nowadays many human rights activists espouse the view that criminal justice must be meted out for human rights violations, whether or not they may be characterized legally as war crimes or crimes against humanity, and regardless of other considerations.

As to the relationship between the rights of victims and criminal justice, three developments must be noted, particularly in the Americas. In countries such as Argentina and Chile there has been a considerable increase in the numbers of criminal investigations, proceedings and convictions. In March 2012 the Chief Justice of Chile's Supreme Court revealed that there were 1,268 judicial investigations still open concerning human rights violations. A study conducted by the Universidad Diego Portales' Human Rights Centre reported that by the end of 2009 there had been 185 people convicted for human rights violations by criminal courts, of whom 59 were still serving their penalties. This result has been made possible by the persistent action of human rights lawyers and organizations of relatives of victims; by the truth-telling policies that contributed to an increased social awareness concerning past State crimes and about the moral hierarchy of human rights; and by the changing composition of the Chilean judiciary through a natural process of generational renewal over the years.

There is also a greater sensitivity about the rights of the victims of human rights violation, even among judges. Yet the articulation of such rights has been effected mostly by international courts. In the Inter-American Court's judgement of 25 November 2000 in the Bámaca Velázquez v. Guatemala case, it is read, in paragraph 197, that:

> ... as a result of the disappearance of Bámaca Velásquez, the State violated the right to the truth of the next of kin of the victim and of society as a whole. In this respect, the [Inter-American] Commission [of Human Rights] declared that the right to the truth has a collective nature, which includes the right of society to 'have accesses to essential information for the development of democratic systems', and a particular nature, as the right of the victims' next of kin to know what happened to their loved ones, which permits a form of reparation. The Inter-American Court has established the obligation of the State to investigate the facts while there is uncertainty about the fate of the person who has disappeared, and the need to provide a simple and prompt recourse in the case, with due guarantees. Following this interpretation, the Commission stated that this is a right of society and that it is emerging as a principle of international law under the dynamic interpretation of human rights treaties and, specifically, Articles 1(1) 8 25 and 13 of the American Convention.

Judge Cançado Trindade and Judge Salgado Pesantes wrote separate opinions elaborating on the right to truth. The Inter-American Court has also pronounced on a right of the victims to justice. In its 2001 judgement on the case Barrios Altos v. Peru, it stated that:

> The so-called self-amnesties are, in sum, an inadmissible offence against the right to truth and the right to justice (starting with the very access to justice). They are manifestly incompatible with the general – indissociable

– obligations of the States Parties to the American Convention to respect and to ensure respect for the human rights protected by it....

Reconciliation

Further to the Chilean Truth and Reconciliation Commission other truth commissions have adopted the same name, notably those of South Africa, Peru, Liberia and Canada. The inclusion of the word 'reconciliation' in the name of the Chilean Commission was meant to suggest that the ultimate purpose of the truth-revealing exercise was to advance towards the aim of having a reconciled society, after an extremely divisive period when gross human rights violations were committed. High-minded as this intention may be, it has been subject to criticism.[14] It is pointed out that the word 'reconciliation' has religious overtones. It has been said also that reconciliation is not quantifiable – as truth-telling, memorials, compensation or criminal justice are – and it is therefore imponderable, a kind of 'Northern star' to guide navigation.[15]

Reconciliation at the individual level, between a given victim and his or her victimizer, is a personal matter, which no public policy may address. Social reconciliation, on the other hand, may be understood as the reconstruction of a broken social contract; or as the attainment of a state in society where the recurrence of past atrocities is deemed unthinkable; or as a cultural development in society that leads everyone to recognize his or her opponents not as enemies but as adversaries who are entitled to the enjoyment of human rights; or as a situation that permits former victims to relate to their former perpetrators from a position of psychological and personal safety.

Conclusions

The young field of transitional justice represents an attempt to deal with a moment of political ethics that until the 1980s had not been systematically addressed – that of the reconstruction of a society following a period of breakdown marked by human rights violations and/or war crimes. Largely because of its relative newness, this field has attracted much political and academic attention as well as controversy. In good measure, transitional justice is rooted in the modern notion of human rights and its main focus on the dignity and inalienable rights of all persons. This helps to explain why, although its ultimate purpose is to build or rebuild a sustainable, just political system on the wreck left by conflict and inhuman practices, its main focus is on the victims of such criminal acts. All aspects of transitional justice – truth-telling, memory preservation, acknowledgement, reparations, criminal justice and the purported superior objective of national reconciliation – may be examined from the standpoint of the victims' needs and rights. The traditional notions of victim has thus, acquired new connotations within the framework of transitional justice.

The case of Chile over the period 1990–2012, one of the richest national experiences in transitional justice, illustrates the main lessons and dilemmas that this field presents in relationship to its central focus on victims. Other national experiences similarly illuminate the many complexities of transitional justice.

As a general conclusion it may be said that much conceptual, legal, moral and practical progress has been made with regards to the protection of victims of gross State abuse. Yet as with most human endeavours, this progress follows at times a meandering course. The necessary emphasis on moral imperatives does lead at times to unyielding propositions; unavoidable political considerations and debates may be unduly disregarded in the name of high-minded principles; the righteousness of the cause of tending to the victims has sometimes resulted in a relaxation of fact-finding standards and in exaggerated claims and even fraudulent ones.

Law and jurisprudence at the national and international levels change fast in their move forward regarding truth-telling, justice and the concern for victims. This is mostly a salutary development. Yet, it must be refined and consolidated in the time ahead so as to make transitional justice claims not only morally right but legally and intellectually stronger.

Notes

1 In the view of this author the expression 'transitional justice', although widely accepted, is not entirely appropriate. It was first proposed in the early 1990s by Professor Ruti Teitel, from the New York School of Law, who has so titled her book on this topic (Teitel 2000). Later on it was adopted and disseminated by the publication of an influential three-volume compilation of theories, legal norms and cases (Kritz 1995), and subsequently by the creation of the International Center of Transitional Justice, in 2001, the prime non-governmental organization dealing with this issue. The term 'transitional justice' may give raise to some confusion: it may suggest that justice itself is transient; further, it may lead to the belief that the sole or paramount purpose of transitional policies is to mete out criminal justice. Of course, justice is of prime importance when addressing a legacy of State atrocities, but the expression 'transitional justice', does not encompass truth-telling, memory preservation, acknowledgement and reparations, in addition to justice. Granted, it is hard to convey all these desirable connotations in one brief term; probably that fact has contributed to the current broad acceptance of 'transitional justice'.

2 Point V.8 of the Basic Principles and Guidelines on the Right to a Remedy and Reparation for Victims of Gross Violations of International Human Rights Law and Serious Violations of International Humanitarian Law. General Assembly Resolution 60/147 of 16 December 2005.

3 The report of the Comisión Nacional de Verdad y Reconciliación (nicknamed The Rettig Commission), issued in February of 1991 accounted for 2,279 fatal victims. The report of its successor Corporación Nacional de Reparación y Reconciliación, published in 1996, added 899 victims. Another 17 victims were added by a report of the reopened Valech Commission (see Note 4 below) issued in 2011. On the other hand, since 1991 it has become known that six cases had been wrongly characterized as victims.

4 The Report of the Comisión de Prisión Política y Tortura (nicknamed The Valech Commission), issued in 2004, listed 27,255 victims of political imprisonment. This commis-

sion was reopened in 2011 and charged with reviewing new applications of the Rettig Commission as well (see Note 3 above). As to victims of political imprisonment, the 2011 report added 9,795 cases.
5 The website of the office of the Chilean Ministry of the Interior in charge of the programme to compensate this category of victims (www.oep.gov.cl) has been on maintenance, throughout the year 2012. The author obtained this figure by calling the said office.
6 Habeas corpus writs (in Chile known as "recursos de amparo") are legal petitions addressed to a High Court to correct an illegal detention or to put an end to it.
7 Before relinquishing power, the fourth and last Argentinean military junta to rule the country since 1976, passed, in September of 1983, an amnesty law. This law was declared null by law 23.040, in December of the same year, under the elected government of Raúl Alfonsín. In February of 1984 another law was enacted providing that the State crimes perpetrated by the military would be tried by the Supreme Council of the Armed Forces. Predictably, this Council did not indict the military leaders. The trial moved then to the (civilian) Federal Court of Appeals which convicted several former military junta members. Later, President Alfonsín, under military pressure, had two laws approved to prevent more trials of the military: the so-called Full Stop Law (Ley de Punto Final) of December 1986 and a Due Obedience Law in June 1987. In 1989, president Menem issued several decrees pardoning many people, including the convicted military junta members and guerrilla fighters. In August 2003, the Argentinean Senate annulled the Full Stop Law and the Due Obedience Law of 1987. In July of 2007 the Argentinean Supreme Court declared unconstitutional the decrees of pardon issued by President Menem in 1989.
8 The Chilean newspaper *El Mercurio* reported on page A8 of its edition of 14 April 2012, that that very day a book titled *Disposición Final*, by the journalist Ceferino Reato, was being launched in Argentina. In it, Jorge Rafael Videla, former leader of the Argentinean military junta, is reported to have acknowledged that the Argentinean military killed some 7,000 to 8,000 civilians and that 'it was necessary that this was done in a secret way, so that the society did not know of it'.
9 In the view of this author, such was the case with the truth commissions of El Salvador and Guatemala. In Morocco, the truth commission was meant to identify victims who would benefit from reparations and these reparations were intended to 'close the chapter'.
10 The most repeated estimate is 70,000 although a fully substantiated estimate also awaits future research.
11 The Chilean government announced that having reviewed 50,000 files of people certified as *exonerados politicos*, 18.7% of more than 157,000 showed as 'anomalies'. See newspaper El Mercurio of 8 April 2012, page C2. The figure is disputed but not the fact that very many applicants were wrongly certified.
12 General Assembly resolution 60/147 of 16 December 2005.
13 Following the definition of the Crime of Aggression that had been postponed by the Statute of Rome, at the Kampala Conference of 2010, the non-applicability of statutory limitations extends to this crime as well.
14 An account of this criticism may be found in Daniel Philpott's 'Religion, Reconciliation, and Transitional Justice: The State of the Field' Social Science Research Council working paper of 17 October 2007.
15 This metaphor was used by Chilean professor Agustín Squella in an unpublished conference given in Santiago, in 1996.
16 In addition to the bibliography detailed in this section, the author has drawn from his own memories of the described events, his personal diary and his private papers.

Bibliography[16]

de Greiff, P., 2006. The Handbook of Reparations. New York: Oxford University Press.
Hayner, P., 2010. Unspeakable Truths, 2nd edition. New York: Routledge, Inter-American Institute of Human Rights, 1999. Truth and Justice: In Search of Reconciliation in Suriname. San José. IIDH.
Lira, E, and Loveman, B., 2005. Políticas de Reparación. Chile 1990–2004. Santiago: LOM ediciones.
Mainwaring, S., 1989. Transitions to Democracy and Democratic Consolidation: Theoretical and Comparative Issues. Working paper No. 130. South Bend: The Hellen Kellog Institute for International Studies.
Nash, C., 2009. Las Reparaciones ante la Corte Interamericana de Derechos Humanos (1988–2007), 2nd edition. Santiago. Centro de Derechos Humanos, Facultad de Derecho, Universidad de Chile.
O'Donnell, G., Schmitter, P. and Whitehead, L., 1986. Transitions from Authoritarian Rule: Prospects for Democracy. Baltimore: Johns Hopkins University Press.
Philpott, D., 2012. Just and Unjust Peace. An Ethic of Political Reconciliation. New York: Oxford University Press.
Quinn, J., 2010. The Politics of Acknowledgement. Truth Commissions in Uganda and Haiti. Vancouver: UBC Press.
Rosenberg, T., 1991. Children of Cain. Violence and the Violent in Latin America. New York: W. Morrow and Co.
van Boven, T., 1993. Study Concerning the Right to Restitution, Compensation and Rehabilitation for Victims of Gross Violations of Human Rights and Fundamental Freedoms. U.N. document E/CN.4/sub.2/1993/8, Truth Commissions: A Comparative Assessment, 1996. Cambridge: Human Rights Program, Harvard Law School.
Weber M., 2004. The Vocation Lectures. 'Science as a Vocation', 'Politics as a vocation'. Indianapolis: Hackett Pub Co.
Zalaquett, José, 1999. Truth, Justice and Reconciliation: Lessons for the International Community. In: Cynthia Arnson, ed., Comparative Peace Processes in Latin America. Woodrow Wilson Center Press/Stanford University Press.

Truth Commission reports

Argentina: Nunca Más. Informe de la Comisión Nacional de Desaparición de Personas. (revised version). Buenos Aires. Eudeba, 2006.
Chile: Report of the Chilean National Commission on Truth and Reconciliation. 2 vols. Notre Dame, IN. Center for Civil & Human Rights. 1993.
Chile: Informe de la Comisión Nacional sobre Prisión Política y Tortura. Santiago. La Nación, 2004.
Colombia: Comisión Nacional de Reparación y Reconciliación. Recomendación de Criterios de Reparación y de Proporcionalidad Restaurativa. Bogotá. CNRR, 2007.
El Salvador: Informe de la Comisión de la Verdad para El Salvador. 3 vols. N.p. 1993.
Guatemala: Nunca Más. Guatemala, Guatemala: ODHAG, 1998.
Honduras: Informe de la Comisión de la Verdad y La Reconciliación. 2 vols. San José. Editorama, 2011.

Marruecos: La Verdad, la Equidad y la Reconciliación. Coquimbo, Chile: Centro Mohammed VI, 2009.
Panama: La Labor de la Comisión de la Verdad. Informe Especial. Panama. Comisión de la Verdad de Panama, 2002.
Peru: Informe Final de la Comisión de la Verdad y Reconciliación. 5 vols. Lima. IDEHPUCP, 2008.
South Africa: Truth and Reconciliation Commission of South Africa. 5 vols. Cape Town. CTP Book Printers, 1998.

Additional references

Aspen Institute, 1989. State Crimes. Punishment or Pardon. Queenstown, MD. Aspen.
Centro Internacional para la Justicia Transicional, 2003. Ensayos sobre Justicia Transicional. New York: ICTJ.
Cohen, S., 2001. States of Denial. Cambridge: Polity Press.
Dyzenhaus, D., 1998. Judging the Judges, Judging Ourselves. Truth, Reconciliation and the Apartheid Legal Order. Oxford: Hart Publishing,
Forsberg, T, and Teivanen, T., 1998. The Role of Truth Commissions in Conflict Resolution and Human Rights Promotion. Finnish Institute of International Affairs Working Papers 10.
Fundación Social, 2005. Compilación de Instrumentos Internacionales, doctrina y Jurisprudencia Sobre Justicia, Verdad y Reparación. Bogotá, Colombia: Geminis.
Gray, D., 2010. A No-excuse Approach to Transitional Justice: Reparations as Tools of Extraordinary Justice. Washington University Law Review, 87(5). pp. 1043–1103.
Hayner, P., 2008. Verdades Innombrables. Mexico City: EFE.
Kritz, N., 1995. Transitional Justice. Washington: US Institute of Peace.
Minow, M., 1999. Between Vengeance and Forgiveness. Boston: Beacon Press.
Rettberg, A., 2005. Entre el Perdón y el Paredón. Preguntas y Dilemas de la Justicia Transicional. Bogotá: Ed. Uniandes.
Rosenberg, T., 1995. The Haunted Land. Facing Europe's Ghosts After Communism. New York: Random House.
Rott-Arriaza, N., 1999. Human Rights in Political Transitions: Gettysburg to Bosnia, New York: Zone Books.
Stratmann, H., 1999. Excusas por la Verdad. Desapariciones y las Consecuencias. Amsterdam: HOM.
Teitel, R., 2000. Transitional Justice. New York: Oxford University Press.
Walling, C. and Waltz, S., 2011. Human Rights, From Practice to Policy. Ann Arbor, MI. U. of Michigan.

Chapter 12

The Transitional Justice Imaginary
Uncle San, Aunty Yan and victim participation at the Khmer Rouge Tribunal

Alexander Laban Hinton[1]

Uncle San, a Cambodian villager in his mid-sixties, is living suspended in time. He is caught in a state of traumatic dysfunction, unable to escape from a violent past that afflicts him with nightmares. He is like many other rural Cambodians of his generation and, through metonymy, could even be seen as a symbol of Cambodia itself. Who is Uncle San? He is a figment of the transitional justice imaginary.

More specifically, Uncle San is the protagonist in a thirty-four page booklet entitled 'Uncle San, Aunty Yan, and the KRT [Khmer Rouge Tribunal]', the pages of which are divided (on the left-hand pages) by visual representations accompanied (on the right-hand pages) by explanatory text. It was produced in 2008 by the Khmer Institute of Democracy (KID), a non-governmental organisation in Cambodia conducting outreach for the Khmer Rouge Tribunal (KRT), officially known as 'The Extraordinary Chambers in the Courts of Cambodia' (ECCC).

After several years of negotiation, this UN-backed hybrid court was established in 2003 to try the surviving leaders of the Khmer Rouge. Upon taking power in Cambodia on 17 April 1975, this group of Maoist-inspired revolutionaries set out to launch a 'Super Great Leap Forward' that would outdo all other communist revolutions, even that of their close socialist ally, China. By the time of its downfall on 6 January 1979, the policies the Khmer Rouge implemented, ranging from collectivisation and forced labour to increasingly frequent purges of suspected enemies, had resulted in the death of perhaps 1.7 to 2.2 million of Cambodia's 8 million inhabitants, almost a quarter of the population, due to starvation, overwork, malnutrition or execution (see Kiernan 1996; Chandler 1999; Hinton 2005).

The ECCC, whose mandate is to try the 'senior leaders' and those 'most responsible' for the atrocities that took place during this period, began operation in 2006. The court includes international and Cambodian officials in all major offices, including co-lawyers, co-prosecutors and co-judges.[2] It is one of a number of 'hybrid' tribunals established in the 2000s (other hybrid tribunals include those of Kosovo, Sierra Leone, Timor Leste, and Lebanon) to offset some of the problems that emerged with the *ad hoc* tribunals of the 1990s (the International Criminal Tribunal for the former Yugoslavia and Rwanda), particularly in terms of cost, duration and proximity to the populations involved in given conflicts.

Hybrid tribunals, like their ad hoc counterparts and other modes of redress such as truth and reconciliations commissions, are often referred to as transitional justice mechanisms. The field of transitional justice emerged in the late 1980s and early 1990s as the Cold War was ending and a number of places, ranging from Southern Cone states to Eastern European countries, were grappling with recent violent pasts while seeking a way forward, in what was often referred to as 'democratic transition'.

The term 'transitional justice' emerged in the post-Cold War 'new world order', as criminal tribunals, truth and reconciliation commissions, memorialisation and reparation efforts, and institutional reforms, emerged as favoured mechanisms for providing some sort of redress and sense of justice that would enable these countries under transition to move from troubled pasts to better futures.[3] Such transitional justice mechanisms directly grapple with the legacies of the past and are often said to have a preventative dimension, diminishing the potential for the recurrence of violence and seeking to 'combat impunity', promote the 'rule of law', reveal 'the truth' and educate the larger populace.

The Transitional Justice Imaginary

In this chapter I argue that such transitional justice mechanisms are frequently characterised by a particular social imaginary, one that is manifest in the booklet 'Uncle San, Aunty Yan and the Khmer Rouge Tribunal'. By social imaginary, I refer to an imagining manifest in a set of interrelated discourses, practices, and institutional forms that help generate a sense of shared belonging among a group of people – in this case the transitional justice community (which is itself is part of the larger 'international community') in the broadest sense. This definition draws from Benedict Anderson's (2006) notion of imagined communities as well as related theorisations of the social imaginary, especially that of Charles Taylor (2004; see also Castoriadis 1987), while also being more slightly inflected by notions of fantasy, misdirection, or, in its strongest form, false consciousness of a non-Marxist sort. Such imaginaries may be gleaned from a variety of sources, ranging from ritual practices to myths and, as in this case, stories.

'Uncle San, Aunty Yan, and the KRT' is one such story in which this transitional justice imaginary is condensed. While not the only imaginary circulating and variable across contexts, the transitional justice imaginary is widespread and implicit in much of what is said and done within transitional justice domains like the KRT. At its core, the transitional justice imaginary revolves around the imagined transformation of post-conflict societies from a negatively marked spatiotemporal modality of being to a positively valued future, with the transitional justice mechanism serving as the vehicle of change. In this imaginary, the past is constructed as one of contamination, violence, savagery, authoritarianism and backwardness, while the future contains the opposite qualities (purity, peace and reconciliation, civilisation, democracy and progress). In contrast to the oft-heard truth claims associated with such transitional justice mechanisms, this highly normative construction erases the very critical historical and sociocultural complexities that are supposed to be unpacked even as it posits an oversimplified 'good' of the liberal democratic society and rights-bearing subject.

Accordingly, the transitional justice imaginary is normative (i.e. it is associated with certain truth claims and moral-laden assumptions), performative (i.e. through its enactment, people constitute an imagined community) and productive (i.e. the imaginary produces certain subject positions and types of being). The imaginary is also characterised by a particular temporality, what I have called 'transitional justice time' (Hinton 2013) premised on a value-laden pre-post state of conflict and teleological movement between them. In the transitional justice imaginary, time is linear and progressive.

Transitional justice imaginary is not monolithic and varies across localities and individuals. Nevertheless, I would argue that it can be found in most transitional justice contexts, including the KRT, as the members of the 'international community' and local elites constitute themselves through the assertion of a transitional justice imaginary – one that may differ significantly from local vernaculars.[4]

More specifically, implicit within transitional justice time is a highly normative concept of past and present. Violent pasts are delimited and narrowed, erasing historical complexities and suggesting an essentialised notion of regressive being, epitomised by phrases such as 'failed states' or indexical registers equating a country with violence and death (for example, the frequent juxtaposing of countries like Cambodia next to images of skulls). This foreshortened vision of the authoritarian past is set against an imagined liberal democratic future, with transitional justice as the mechanism of teleological change. This splitting of past and future, mediated by a liminal present, is linked to a series of binary oppositions, such as contamination/purity, savagery/civilisation, authoritarian/democratic, and so forth. Within this timescape, people like Uncle San, and the larger group of Cambodians victims for whom he stands, are imagined in certain sorts of ways.

Finally, the transitional justice imaginary is also what we might call 'redactic' (Hinton 2013), a missing third piece in the oft-heard binary that juxtaposes legalism against the didactic dimensions of transitional justice. Both legalism and didactic narratives involve redacting, an editing out. The term redact is etymologically related to the Latin *redigere*, which means 'to drive or send back, return, to ring back, restore, to convert, reduce, to bring (into a condition), to bring (under a category), to bring into line'. This term nicely captures several dimensions of the work of the transitional justice imaginary, which involves a 'bringing into line' of thought and agency, a 'reduction' of complexity into a more manageable form, a 'driving back' of messiness and complexity that may upset the narrative in-the-making, a 'conversion' of subjectivity, and an 'editing out' of unwanted historical pasts and local experience and practices that do not jive with normative assumptions being asserted.

Uncle San and the Transitional Justice Imaginary

Uncle San lives within the transitional justice imaginary and moves through its spatiotemporal horizons. The first line of the booklet delimits a temporal horizon of the past, as the introductory note (p. 2) explains:

> The Khmer Rouge Regime is generally recognised as the time between 17 April 1975 and 6 January 1979. This was a time in Cambodian history where the Communist Party of Kampuchea held control over the entire country and committed many crimes against the Cambodian people.

Here, at the very start of the booklet, time is immediately constructed in three interlinked ways. First, in terms of periodicity, time is placed within a delimited period 17 April 1975 to 6 January 1979, or the period of Khmer Rouge rule in Cambodia. This interval is then coloured in two ways. On the one hand, it constitutes a juridical frame, or what is called the temporal jurisdiction of the court. On the other hand, this interval is marked as one of criminality as a criminal act ('many crimes') has been committed by a perpetrator (the Communist Party of Kampuchea) against a victim ('against the Cambodian people'). There is no room in this temporal horizon for ambiguity; there are perpetrators and victims and nothing in between. Transitional justice time does not cope well with 'grey zones'. This delimitation of time is further bound by a spatial framing, as the crimes take place in a particular national space, as opposed to a geopolitical space that is thereby erased, suggesting the problem was solely internal to Cambodia.

The booklet provides a quick overview of what happened in this spatiotemporal context through the eyes of Uncle San, a moustached Cambodian villager who wears a chequered yellow Cambodian scarf slung over his right shoulder. 'Hello, my name is San,' his story begins. 'I am 64 years of age... I have lived in this village since I was young, but during the Khmer Rouge Regime I was forced to live in another area' (p. 4). The accompanying graphic shows Uncle San sitting cross-legged on a table-like platform telling several of his fellow villagers about his forcible eviction. The importance of his experience is emphasised by the attentiveness of those gathered around, including two young children, as he tells his story.

Uncle San's experiences could be those of any Cambodian village survivor. Indeed, the Director of the KID told me that they selected the names Uncle San and Aunty Yan because they were 'common names among [the] rural population … very poor, grassroots type of names'.[5] Individual difference is thereby compressed as Uncle San's experiences could be those of any rural Cambodian survivor. The image asserts Uncle San's everyman status – he stands as an emblem of the Cambodian survivor-victim and, through metonymy, of Cambodia itself.

And he, and Cambodia by extension, exists in a deeply troubled state, one that suggests a lack and failure ('a failed state'). On page 5 of the booklet, Uncle San dozes fitfully in a hammock, dreaming about the Khmer Rouge past, which is represented by four recollections: his stealing a crab and the Khmer Rouge torching a village, menacing two Buddhist monks being forcibly disrobed, and executing a man who looks like Uncle San in a mass grave filled with skulls. As in earlier shots, all of the characters resemble the moustached Uncle San. He is everyone and yet no one. He tells us on p. 6:

> During the Khmer Rouge Regime, I was forced to plant rice all day long. Once, I took a crab from the field and was beaten for doing so. I remember the mistreatment of monks, hard work, poor food, tortures, and killings. When it was over and I went back to my village, my home was destroyed. What makes me most sad is that all of my family members were killed. Since then, I have bad dreams every night about what happened.

In the next frame, Uncle San sits chatting with Aunty Yan and some other villagers in a rustic, traditional village space, one that lacks signs of modernity (for example, electricity, cars, motorcycles, industry, upscale commodities). 'Usually,' Uncle San tells us in the accompanying text, 'I try not to think about the past by spending my time planting rice, going to the pagoda, and chatting with my neighbours.' Aunty Yan, it turns out, is a childhood friend who also lost her family during the Khmer Rouge regime and with whom Uncle San often shares meals or drinks tea.

If time is partly one of criminality in the booklet, it also suggests a pre-existing stasis. Perpetrators bear the impurity of their act, an unchanging stigma marking them as nefarious. Victims, in turn, remain wounded and unhealed, awaiting rescue. Thus Uncle San reveals, 'Since then, I have had bad dreams every night about what happened' and he tries 'not to think about the past' by keeping busy. This spatiotemporal freezing is indexed grammatically, as the temporal marker, 'since then' (*chap teang pi pel nuh mok*) frame the pronoun 'I' (*khnom*). Uncle San, and, as the everyman, by implication all Cambodian victims of the Khmer Rouge, lives suspended in a past of traumatic experience, which persists, unchanging, through a set of symptoms, including re-experiences (flashbacks, bad dreams and nightmares), avoidance behaviours (trying 'not to think about the past'), and, as the frowning photo of him in the hammock suggests, hyper arousal (difficulty sleeping and feeling tense).[6]

Indeed, there is a direct relationship between transitional justice time and one of the subject positions produced by the transitional justice imaginary, that of 'the trauma victim'. We could even speak of a sort of pop-psychology 'trauma imaginary' that overlaps with the transitional justice imaginary. In this trauma imaginary, individuals are viewed as existing in a state of regressive dysfunction, trapped by the seeds of past trauma. These 'seeds' manifest themselves through the aforementioned set of symptoms (the 'shoots' of the trauma 'seeds'). The trauma victim is more or less helpless until saved.

Within the transitional justice imaginary, the helpers are a legion of psychosocial specialists who treat trauma victims in post-conflict situation. But the transitional justice mechanism itself is depicted as constituting a form of treatment, evident in the frequent assertion that transitional justice mechanisms will help the society 'heal'. The post-conflict society is metonymically represented by the 'trauma victim', frozen in a regressive, impure, backward 'pre-' state until liberated by transitional justice and its practitioners, who launch it forward to a pure, progressive, liberal democratic state through a given form of 'treatment', the transitional justice mechanism (mirrored by the healing of the trauma victim through engagement with transitional justice practitioners and practices, especially the mechanisms in question).

On pages 9–10 of the booklet, this past and present of transitional justice time come sharply into focus. The left-side graphic shows a split scene of Uncle San lighting incense and praying for the spirits of the dead juxtaposed with an Aunty Yan speech bubble as she hails him to come to a 'special meeting about the Khmer Rouge… in our village' being conducted by a 'Citizen Advisor' from the KID, the non-governmental organisation that produced the booklet to use in its tribunal outreach activities.

Here we see transitional justice time in motion, as Uncle San moves from his frozen, backward states (performing ineffective 'traditional' practices incapable of healing his trauma) to an active, progressive, civilised state (engaging with the court, which has the potential to heal the traumatic wounds that have afflicted him for so long). In this context, civil society practitioners serve as the mediators of transformation as they bring the court to the villages that are so distant from it, a practice aptly termed, as noted above, 'outreach'. The court reaches out and provides its healing touch to even those living in the remote countryside with the help of organisations like KID.

Particularly during the early phases of the court, which started operation in mid-2006, a number of these organisations served as intermediaries between the court and the population. Many of these intermediary organisations had been established during or soon after the 1993 UN-sponsored elections in Cambodia to promote human rights, law and democracy. Over time, each developed particular areas of focus and distinct mechanisms to fulfil their missions.

KID, for example, was established on 6 October 1992, just prior to the UN-backed elections, by a group of Cambodian-Americans and Ambassador Julio Jeldres, an advisor to and official biographer of King Norodom Sihanouk.[7] KID's homepage states that the NGO's mission is 'to foster democratic values in Cambodian society by maintaining a neutral political position'. To this end, KID 'carries out a number of activities to promote a liberal democratic order as determined by the 1991 Paris Peace Agreement, based on a multi-party liberal democracy system, on human rights, and the respect of law as stipulated in the Constitution'.[8]

This mission is reflected in KID's Khmer Rouge Tribunal outreach programme, which began in November 2005 and involved tens of thousands of villagers in seven provinces. It was carried out with the goal of 'eliminating Cambodia's culture of impunity, ensuring respect for the rule of law, and facilitating people's participation in the tribunal process'.[9] KID's 184 'citizen advisors', comprising respected and more educated villagers such as teachers, stand at the heart of this and other KID initiatives. Inspired by the citizen advisors created in Britain during World War II, KID's citizen advisors seek to help and inform 'local people in remote areas, where there is a poor knowledge of democracy and limited respect for human rights' and thereby 'promote understanding of the law and its administration, how to prevent and resolve conflict, and how to promote peace in the community'.[10]

Starting in 2007, KID's citizen advisors were tasked with conducting outreach workshops with groups of 25–30 people in different villages.[11] The sessions provided a basic explanation of what the tribunal was and how it operated as well as how victims might become involved. Indeed, the citizen advisor also assisted those who were interested in filling out applications to become civil parties, complainants or witnesses at the tribunal. Prior to the start of this initiative, KID's outreach team had begun to develop a variety of outreach materials, ranging from a flip chart and films to several explanatory booklets, including *Uncle San, Aunty Yan, and the Khmer Rouge Tribunal*.

In the speech bubble juxtaposed with the image of Uncle San praying to the spirits of his ancestors, an 'interested' and 'curious' Uncle San is hailed, like the reader of the booklet, to participate in a KID outreach session. Standing in front of a European Union and an ECCC poster affixed to a wooden beam, a KID citizen advisor reads from one of the KID outreach booklets to twenty villagers. Uncle San relates how, 'at the meeting, KID's CA [Citizen Advisor] described the Khmer Rouge Trials,' about which the villagers had never before heard. He learns that the tribunal is located in the capital of Cambodia, Phnom Penh, and is composed of international and national staff.

The citizen advisor also tells Uncle San and his fellow villagers how the United Nations and the Cambodian government reached an agreement to hold the tribunal in 2003 in order to 'to seek justice, national reconciliation, stability, peace, and security in Cambodia' (p. 12). A graphic shows the Cambodian and UN officials in suits signing the agreement. No one in this frame looks like Uncle San. Here we meet transitional justice time head on as we jump from the Khmer Rouge period (1975–1979) to the origin of the transitional justice mechanism in 2003. Uncle San, the Cambodian everyman who is locked in a static, traumatised, primitive and savage time of the past, steps into the progressive, healing, developed and civilised time of the present transitional justice moment. What happened prior to 1975 and between 1979 and 2003 is flattened and erased[12] a temporal erasure that is one of the hallmarks of dichotomous transitional justice time.

In other words, transitional justice time de-historicises in contrast to the truth claim with which it is often associated. We learn nothing of the origins or the immediate aftermaths of the conflict, such as the Vietnam War or the geopolitical politics that helped civil war until the late 1990s. After being toppled in early 1979, the former genocidaires were rearmed by the US, China, Thailand and others – and even given Cambodia's seat at the United Nations. Uncle San does not occupy this time. There is just the Khmer Rouge period and then the 2003 agreement. Without it, there is no progression, just stasis. Uncle San, like the 'failed' state of Cambodia, is frozen in time until this moment, in which he is remade. Despite the oft-heard claims that the KRT will reveal 'the truth', transitional justice time involves erasures, as a broader understanding of Cambodian society, history and geopolitics, factors that provide the critical backdrop and aftermath of the genocide, disappear from sight, diminishing understanding and producing an eclipsed truth.

In the next frame, Uncle San and Aunty Yan are seen sitting on a Cambodian platform bench in front of her cement house, which suggests somewhat greater wealth and status – and perhaps education – than Uncle San, who lives in a traditional wooden house. A radio hangs from a window. Uncle San holds a pen and looks expectantly towards her as they fill out forms. He states (p. 14):

> Aunty Yan knows more about the KRT than me because she listens to the radio every day. Aunty Yan taught me that the victims can submit a complaint to the court: She showed me the complaint form and taught me how to fill it out.

This scene suggests some of the key normative goods underlying the transitional justice imaginary, particularly freedom of choice and equality. On the one hand, Uncle San has the right and freedom to choose whether or not to participate in the tribunal. He asserts this liberal subjectivity by stating, 'I think I want to [become a complainant]!' On the other hand, the positions of Uncle San and Aunty Yan reverse traditional village gender norms, where the man would normally be assumed to speak from the position of authority.

The KID project officer who was in charge of developing the booklet told me that the picture was drawn this way because 'we have a human rights project. Here it is the influence of the human rights concept of gender'. He stated that they wanted to combat the notion that 'women don't know anything in the grassroots [level]' and to teach people 'to not look down on the women in the community, but to show that every person has the same rights and dignity'. This focus on gender equality can also be seen in the legal proceedings, where gender-based crimes, such as sexual violence and forced marriages, have been foregrounded.

The page concludes with Uncle San stating, 'Aunty Yan and I also want to take a trip to the ECCC.' Most of the remainder of the booklet describes their journey and experiences there. Their mode of transportation is a sleek, modern bus with an ECCC logo on the side. The project officer explained that the bus was meant to reflect the 'international standards' of the court. It can also be read as a vehicle of transformation, as the UN symbolically 'conveys' Uncle San from the regressive past as he 'enters' the domain of transitional justice. He will leave transformed.

Here we find a spatiotemporal progression that mirrors the transformation of consciousness taking place. Uncle San's position of stasis is first destabilised by the KID village outreach programme, which 'hails' him towards the transitional justice imaginary. There, he begins to learn the outlines of this vision, manifest in discussions about the court and its operations. He is invited to become a part of the process, first by considering becoming a complainant ('I think I want to') and then, through the bus ride, directly entering into the spatiotemporal zone of the court, thereby 'leaving behind' the 'static' and 'less developed' village. All of this could readily be viewed through the anthropological lens of a rite of passage, in which Uncle San passes through a threshold, boarding the 'international standards' bus and crossing the gates of the court (behind which, in the booklet, stands the courtroom building, which is modern yet looks almost royal with towering Khmer spires in the background) and is transformed through ritual activities (legal procedure in the broadest sense) in this liminal space.

Uncle San and Aunty Yan next attend a court session, where they are 'given headphones to listen', an act that could be read as a symbolic exercise of the new identity in the making, as 'modern' transitional justice language and procedure is 'translated' into the Cambodian context. Everyone, Uncle San notes, is 'interested' (p. 20). Such translation is never straightforward, as the global flows of transitional justice meet the local realities on the ground. Thus, Uncle San says that he 'didn't understand who was being accused of being criminals'. This question mirrors a key concern of many Cambodians who, like Uncle San, have trouble understanding why the immediate killers of their friends and family are not being tried.

Aunty Yan, who is situated as the voice of the court here and elsewhere (perhaps in part because she embodies the normative good of transitional justice through assertion of gender equality), explains that the court will 'only try the senior leaders of the Khmer Rouge and those most responsible for committing serious crimes during the Khmer Rouge Regime'. To try lower level cadre, she tells him, would jeopardise the court's goal of helping Cambodians achieve 'justice, national reconciliation, peace, and security' (p. 22). The opposite graphic makes this clear, as it crosses out an arrow pointing towards a Khmer Rouge cadre executing a person at a killing field in favour of a frame that shows a cadre telling his subordinates: 'Comrades, you must smash [our] enemies completely.' This frame exchange portrays the process of calibration that takes place in transitional justice contexts, as local understandings and concerns must be brought into some sort of functional consonance with those of the mechanisms in place and vice versa (though almost invariably the local is normatively expected to adapt to the more 'developed' international norms, as illustrated by the continual privileging and emphasis on 'international standards' at the court).

The next graphic shifts perspective from one of without, in which Uncle San and Aunty Yan sit in the visitor's gallery looking into the glass-enclosed courtroom, to one of within, as if the viewer has directly become part of the process itself. Each party in the court is labelled (witness, accused, judges, prosecution, etc.), with the largest label appearing above the heads of a group of 'regular' Cambodians designated as 'civil parties'. Aunty Yan explains that a 'civil party is a victim who submitted an application to the court and was accepted by the judges. They directly take part in the trials or take part though their representatives.' Here, through participation (first in the outreach session and then in the court itself), we see Uncle San going through a steady transformation into an active juridical subject.

This transformation begins to be solidified on the next page, when Uncle San goes, now alone, to see the head of the court's victims unit, who tells him that he can become a civil party if 'I fill out the form and the judges accept my application based on several conditions of the law. If I am a civil party, I have the right to participate in all of the court proceedings, plus a right to request collective and moral reparations' (p. 26).

Indeed, civil parties in Cambodia enjoy almost full procedural rights in the proceedings, including the right to sit in the courtroom and to be represented by their own lawyers, who support the prosecution. Such civil party participation at the KRT, which is enabled by Cambodian civil law, empowers the victims more than perhaps any other international tribunal in the world. But the contours of Uncle San's new-found subjectivity are further refined, as he is constituted as a participatory, rights-bearing victim, who is entitled to redress like the civil parties sitting in the courtroom. This status is ritually affirmed by the filling out of an application, which requires a reframing the past and the applicants subjectivity in juridical terms.

On the trip home, Aunty Yan asks Uncle San if the Khmer Rouge might harm them if they participate in the trial. Uncle San reassures her, noting that the Khmer Rouge held power long ago and that head of the Victims Unit had told him protection was available if there were a strong risk. The court here is depicted as patron and protector, an image that resonates with Cambodian notions of moral ties but also suggests the hierarchical position of the court as an entity that provides assistance to 'needy' Cambodia, a role that again erases the history of geopolitical interference in Cambodia and suggests the country's 'lack'. The court offers protection to the almost childlike Uncle San, much as a parent protects a child from danger. Indeed, Uncle San is depicted in childlike terms throughout much of the booklet, even as he 'matures' into a more 'developed' form of being.

The day after their trip to the KRT, Uncle San and Aunty Yan are depicted discussing the tribunal with several of their fellow villagers. They have become like emissaries of the court – a manifestation of the longed-for 'multiplier effect' that one often hears mentioned in the outreach community – as they inform other villagers about what they saw and learned. The entry of this information into the consciousness of the other villagers is illustrated by a series of five thought bubbles in the graphic: a convicted criminal being led to jail, the scales of justice, the court itself, a well, and a stupa – images that contrast strongly with the images of Khmer Rouge violence that preoccupied Uncle San at the start of the booklet. 'We talked a long time about the KRT and the future of Cambodia,' Uncle San tell us. 'We agreed that the establishment of the KRT is very good to seek justice for victims. The trials can find truth and give us relief (*sabay chhet*) from the past.'

Here we find another manifestation of the normative dimension of the transitional justice imaginary: the notion that such mechanisms will deliver a set of goods such as truth, healing, moral reparation and societal transformation. These normative goods thereby connected to the end point of the teleology driving transitional justice time towards a longed-for state of progress and development.

Conclusion

This seemingly simple booklet, so popular that apparently the court considered purchasing the rights to it, can be read in many ways. On the most obvious level, it provides an overview of the reasons for and structure of the court with a particular focus on victims' participation. In this sense it echoes, in a very general sense, much of the outreach message that the KRT and various intermediary organisations have been attempting to convey.

As such, it may also be read as a token of the court that symbolises and condenses its larger meanings. Most broadly, I want to argue that the booklet is productive in two senses. First, the booklet embodies notions of transitional justice that are central to the larger functioning and legitimisation of the court itself and are part of a larger transitional justice imaginary. This imaginary, as I have written elsewhere (Hinton 2010b), suggests a teleology of a movement from a contaminated pre-state (of regressive savagery, violence, chaos, anarchy, etc.) to a purified post-state of a modern liberal democratic order (associated with what is civilised, peaceful, ordered, progressive, etc.), with the transitional justice mechanism – in this case the tribunal – serving as the mechanism of change.

This schema is directly manifest in the booklet. It begins with a coding of Cambodia as a place of violence, savagery and regression, as Uncle San recalls the horrors of the Khmer Rouge. He himself embodies the regression, as he is plagued by dark memories of the past. He is a traumatised victim, childlike, an incomplete, not fully functioning being. Like Cambodia, he needs help to move forward.

The court is the vehicle of this transition. Indeed, the slogan of the court is 'Moving Forward through Justice'. The end state of the transition, as we are told several times, is stated in its basic goals: justice, reconciliation, peace, truth and relief. The court itself signifies Cambodia's lack, manifesting the modernity it has not achieved. Uncle San notes the technology at the court even as the graphic images, such as the bus frame, suggest the sleek, modern, high-tech nature of the court

This mechanism already suggests the end, the post-state of modernity to be achieved. At the end of the process, Cambodia will attain what it lacks. Thus, after their visit to the court, Uncle San, Aunty Yan and their neighbours discuss not just the court but the future of their country, the post-state. The accompanying graphics contains a picture of the court as part of a series of interlinked images that suggest this better future: criminals (who lived freely because of a 'culture of impunity' and a lack of 'the rule of law') are taken to jail as justice is upheld; the scales of justice balanced; a stupa symbolising peace for the dead and reparations for the living; and a well signifying reparation, development, social justice and repair. Once again, at the end, Uncle San himself embodies the new state of progress as he, like Cambodia, is healed and democratised by the process. He then sleeps through the night like a young child who has finally stepped forward into a blissful new stage of development.

And symbolically Uncle San is not the same. His very being has been transformed as he becomes (at least it is suggested) a modern liberal, rights-bearing subject who is healed through the process. Indeed, he now lives in a new world of modernity. The last graphic shows Uncle San sleeping in his hammock near a thatched house.

In contrast to the initial hammock frame in which a frowning Uncle San is plagued by the nightmares of the past, the last graphic shows him sleeping comfortably in his hammock, a slight smile on his face as he dreams of a new Cambodia with electricity, fancy wooden houses, and even a factory in the distance. The accompanying caption reads, 'Then… I slept the whole night with no bad dreams' (p. 34). Uncle San, like Cambodia, is imagined as purified, renewed and remade through the mechanism of the court as he passes through transitional justice time.

The KID project leader, who worked with an art student to design all of the graphics, was explicit about the message of this last frame, 'Here, Uncle San, after his participation, a long walk and journey, comes [back] to his own house. He can now close his eyes peacefully, and he [dreams of] a peaceful situation and happiness.' Flipping back forth between the initial graphic of Uncle San's 'bad dreams' and his dream on the last page, he explained:

> This one [the first page] is tragedy, bad things, the [last page has] good things… birds and trees… kids who go to school in peace. The villagers have jobs [and] there is no mistreatment of monks. … And you can see [that the village] now has electricity… Normally only the rich have money to buy wood tile [houses]. So [this page] means that there is prosperity… no famine… [and] where we have factories, [we have] development.

The project leader explained that the meaning of the booklet was that people would live 'peacefully after participating in the court process. This is the real output we would like to explain to the grassroots. That is your benefit.' Uncle San, he continued, is a changed man, who no longer has psychological syndromes or bad dreams. 'We let the reader conclude that the court changed him because of his participation.' The factory, in turn, symbolised economic development in a rural landscape that normally lacks such industry. The people imagined in Uncle San's new dream bubble 'go to the factory to produce the final product [that is sold on the] market. That is the development process'.

Here the KID team leader explicitly describes the end point of transitional justice time: a liberal democratic order occupied by the functional, rights-bearing individual, capitalism and, of course, the qualities that supposedly come with it: peace, happiness and progress.

With Uncle San, the reader journeys through the transitional justice imaginary. Our minds, like his, become filled new thoughts and images, symbolically depicted by the thought bubble graphics. And like him, the reader symbolically passes through a transformative rite of passage and produces a new state of being. This imaginary asserts specific sorts of time (a transitional justice time characterised by temporal erasure, a teleology, and the instantiation of a series of pre- and post-state binaries), subjectivity (liberal, democratic, rights-bearing, juridical beings such as lawyers, civil parties and even defendants whose fair-trial rights are frequently invoked) and moral economies of justice (the 'gift' of the international community and the sorts of normative goods it bestows, such as peace, reconciliation, healing, truth, justice). In this imaginary, even as the transitional society emerges, it achieves a still-fragile status of 'newly emerging democracy', one that is not on par with the implicitly 'mature' democratic governments and institutions – who are part of the 'international community' constituted in the transitional justice imaginary – that help guide the transition.

To seek to unpack the assumptions of transitional justice is not to simply dismiss it. It is to engage in a 'critical transitional justice studies' (Hinton 2010b) that allows us to recognise the gaps within and shadows behind that which is assumed and naturalised. In particular, this imaginary has a tendency to erase historical and sociocultural complexities, ones that are directly relevant to the presumed normative goods of 'truth', 'prevention', and 'understanding the past' that are so often asserted in transitional justice rhetorics. Even for a strong supporter of transitional justice initiatives, such understanding is crucial, for it suggests alternative ways in which such mechanisms for dealing with the legacies of the past might unfold. To ignore such critical thinking is to risk remaining, like Uncle San, caught, unknowing, in the webs of the transitional justice imaginary.

Notes

1 The material in this chapter, which is a revised version of Hinton (2013), is based on an ongoing ethnographic research project on the Khmer Rouge Tribunal that extends from the court itself to rural villages. This research has been supported by grants from the United States Institute of Peace and the Rutgers Research Council. The original essay was written while I was in residence as a Member of the Institute for Advanced Study at Princeton (2011–12). In addition to thanking these institutions for their support, I'd like to thank Nicole Cooley, Deborah Meyersen, Annie Pohlman and the editors for their thoughtful comments and suggestions.
2 A 'supermajority' of judges is required for conviction, thereby ensuring that at least one foreign judge must join in any decision made by the Pre-Trial Chamber (4 out of 5 judges), Trial Chamber (4 out of 5 judges), or Supreme Court Chamber (5 out of 7 judges), each of which has a majority of Cambodia jurists.
3 On the origins and history of transitional justice, see Arthur (2009), Hinton (2010a) and Teitel (2003). On the components of transitional justice from a practitioner side, see

the website of the International Center for Transitional Justice (http://ictj.org/about/transitional-justice, accessed 8 November 2011).
4 An examination of this issue is beyond the scope of this chapter but is addressed in the book on the tribunal that I am writing.
5 Interview with Chhaya Hang, 23 June 2011.
6 On the symptoms of PTSD, see http://www.nimh.nih.gov/health/publications/post-traumatic-stress-disorder-ptsd/what-are-the-symptoms-of-ptsd.shtml, accessed 3 November 2011. The booklet seems to assume a Western biomedical model of post-traumatic stress disorder symptomology as opposed to local idioms of distress that are found in Cambodian villages (see Hinton *et al.* 2010).
7 The Khmer Institute of Democracy homepage, http://www3.online.com.kh/users/kid/index.htm, accessed 3 November 2011.
8 Ibid.
9 'Outreach Activities', Khmer Institute of Democracy, http://www.khmerrough.com/pdf/OutreachActivities.pdf, accessed 3 November 2011.
10 'Proto-Ombudsman Program (Citizen advisor Project)', Khmer Institute for Democracy, http://www3.online.com.kh/users/kid/program.htm, accessed 3 November 2011.
11 'Citizen Advisor Training and Outreach', Khmer Institute of Democracy, http://www.khmerrough.com/citizen.htm, accessed 3 November 2011.
12 For an overview of some of the events that took place during this period, see Fawthrop and Jarvis (2004).

Bibliography

Anderson, B., 2006. Imagined Communities: Reflections on the Origin and Spread of Nationalism. New York: Verso.
Arthur, P., 2009. How 'Transitions' Reshaped Human Rights: A Conceptual History of Transitional Justice, Human Rights Quarterly, 31(2), pp. 321–367.
Castoriadis, C., 1987. The Imaginary Institution of Society. Cambridge: MIT Press.
Chandler, D.P., 1999. Voices from S-21: Terror and History in Pol Pot's Secret Prison. Berkeley: University of California Press.
Fawthrop, T. and Jarvis, H., 2004. Getting Away with Genocide: Cambodia's Long Struggle Against the Khmer Rouge. London: Pluto.
Hinton, A.L., 2005. Why Did They Kill? Cambodia in the Shadow of Genocide. Berkeley: University of California Press.
Hinton, A.L., ed., 2010a. Transitional Justice: Global Mechanisms and Local Realities after Genocide and Mass Violence. Piscataway: Rutgers University Press.
Hinton, A.L., 2010b. Introduction: Toward an Anthropology of Transitional Justice. In: A.L. Hinton, ed., 2011. Transitional Justice: Global Mechanisms and Local Realities after Genocide and Mass Atrocity. Piscataway: Rutgers University Press, pp. 1–22.
Hinton, A.L., 2013. Transitional Justice Time: Uncle San, Aunty Yan, and Outreach at the Khmer Rouge Tribunal. In: D. Meyersen and A. Pohlman, eds, Genocide and Mass Atrocities in Asia: Legacies and Prevention. New York: Routledge Press, pp. 86–99.
Hinton, D., Hinton, A.L., Eng, K-T. and Choung, S., 2010, PTSD Severity and Key Idioms of Distress among Rural Cambodians: The Results of a Needs Assessment. In: B. Van Schaack, D. Reicherter and Y. Chhang, eds, 2011. Cambodia's Hidden Scars: Trauma Psychology in the Wake of the Khmer Rouge, An edited Volume on Cambodia's Mental Health. Phnom Penh: Documentation Center of Cambodia, pp. 47–68.

Khmer Institute of Democracy, 2008. Uncle San, Aunty Yan, and the KRT. Khmer Institute of Democracy. Phnom Penh, Cambodia.

Kiernan, B., 1996. The Pol Pot Regime: Race, Power, and Genocide in Cambodia under the Khmer Rouge, 1975–79. New Haven: Yale University Press.

Taylor, C., 2004. Modern Social Imaginaries. Durham: Duke University Press.

Teitel, R.G., 2003. Transitional Justice Genealogy. Harvard Human Rights Journal, 16, pp. 69–94.

Part III

Trauma, resilience and justice

Chapter 13

Perceived control over traumatic events

Is it always adaptive?

Patricia Frazier

Introduction

This chapter provides an overview of my research programme on the relations between perceived control and adjustment to traumatic events, including victimisation. I will begin with a review of some early research on attributions and then describe a new model of perceived control and the development of a new measure of perceived control. I will then review some findings regarding whether the relations between control and adjustment differ as a function of characteristics of the person or event. Finally, I will describe an online intervention we are developing that is designed to increase perceived control over stressful and traumatic events.

Because I am only reviewing one aspect of my research, I would like to put it in the context of my broader research programme. On the broadest level, my research is concerned with stressful and traumatic life events. I have done research on the prevalence of traumatic life events in community (Anders *et al.* 2011) and college (e.g. Frazier *et al.* 2009; Anders *et al.* 2012) samples and on the effects of trauma exposure. This includes research on Post Traumatic Stress Disorder (PTSD) (Frazier *et al.* 2011) as well as post-traumatic growth (Frazier *et al.* 2009). In our most recent work we are also using latent class growth analyses to identify different patterns of change in symptoms over time following traumatic events (Frankfurt *et al.* 2012; Frankfurt *et al.* 2012). I have also carried out research on factors associated with trauma recovery, such as the type of trauma experienced (Anders *et al.* 2011) and various psychosocial factors that are associated with victim recovery (e.g. Frazier *et al.* 2005). Finally, my recent research also involves developing and testing interventions for trauma survivors, particularly online interventions, as described below.

I am particularly interested in online interventions because trauma survivors can access them without stigma, they are convenient, they are less expensive than face-to-face treatments to administer, and because research shows that they can be quite effective (e.g. Barak *et al.* 2008). Along with various students and colleagues, I am conducting three ongoing intervention studies. One involves testing the efficacy of brief video-based coping skills and relaxation interventions for sexual assault survivors. This intervention has previously been found to be effective (Acierno *et al.* 2003) and we are attempting to replicate those findings. I am also part of another research team that is conducting an online expressive writing intervention for returning veterans based on the work of James Pennebaker (2004). Finally, my students and I are developing and testing an intervention to increase perceived control over traumatic events. Research on that intervention is reviewed below.

Perceived control and adjustment to trauma

Overview

As mentioned, one aspect of my work focuses on identifying factors associated with trauma recovery, particularly factors that can facilitate adjustment. My work has focused on psychosocial factors that are amenable to change through psychosocial interventions, such as social support, coping strategies and in particular perceived control.

I have focused on perceived control because it is a very important construct in theories of the development of PTSD. Specifically, several theories (e.g. Foa *et al.* 1992; Ehlers and Clark 2000) propose that uncontrollable events are more likely to lead to PTSD than are controllable events. In fact, Foa and colleagues argued that the perceived uncontrollability of traumatic events is so important that it should be incorporated into the definition of traumatic events in diagnostic manuals such as the Diagnostic and Statistical Manual of Mental Disorders (DSM) (American Psychiatric Association 2000). It also is important to point out that perceived uncontrollability is thought to be more important than objective uncontrollability (Foa *et al.* 1992). Two people can experience the same event and one can see it as controllable and the other as uncontrollable; it is this perception that is important.

This theory is based on animal research showing that ongoing exposure to uncontrollable stressors, such as electric shocks, causes greater fear responses over time than exposure to controllable stressors (Foa *et al.* 1992). However, many human traumas are discrete events rather than ongoing. For example, sudden bereavement and sexual assault are discrete events. Certainly, some traumas involve ongoing abuse but many do not. Whether events are ongoing or not, is it better for people to perceive traumas as controllable? For example, if my spouse or child died, or if I was assaulted, would I be less distressed if I perceived that trauma as controllable or preventable? Would that make me feel better? This is the question I have been interested in over the past several years.

Early research on attributions

In my initial research on control, I addressed this question about the role of control in adjustment to trauma by testing Janoff-Bulman's (1979) influential theory regarding the role of behavioural and characterological self-blame in adjustment to rape. In this theory, behavioural self-blame involves blaming a rape on specific controllable behaviours. For example, a victim who is engaging in behavioural self-blame might say: 'If I had not gone to that party, I would not have been raped.' Characterological self-blame, on the other hand, involves blaming the rape on uncontrollable factors. For example, a victim might say: 'I am just the victim type. These things always happen to me.' So, she is blaming herself but not something about herself that she can change or control.

According to Janoff-Bulman's (1979) theory, behavioural self-blame is adaptive because it is associated with the belief that future rapes can be avoided. So, if a victim says to herself, 'If I had not gone to that party, I would not have been raped' she can also say to herself that she will not go to parties like that again and thus can avoid the same thing happening again. According to this theory, that will provide a sense of control and facilitate adjustment. Characterological self-blame is not hypothesised to lead to the same sense of control and thus is not thought to be adaptive. I was particularly interested in testing this theory because it is contrary to clinical approaches for working with victims that actively discourage all types of self-blame. That is, victim advocates often are trained to tell victims that it was not their fault, that they are not to blame. Thus, we have a theory telling us that self-blame can be good and clinical practice dictating the opposite approach.

I conducted three studies testing Janoff-Bulman's (1979) theory on three different samples of women who had been raped. The first was a study of female rape victims who were seen in a hospital-based rape crisis programme one week post-rape (Frazier 1990). The second was a longitudinal study at the same rape crisis centre with women who had recently been sexually assaulted (Frazier 2000). The third was a study of female college students who had been raped an average of eight years previously (Frazier and Schauben 1994). With these samples we were attempting to replicate findings across different types of samples and time frames post-assault.

In all three studies, the results failed to support Janoff-Bulman's (1979) model. For example, both behavioural and characterological self-blame were consistently associated with more distress. In fact, victims may have difficulty separating the two types of self-blame because it is difficult to blame one's behaviour *without also* blaming one's self for being the type of person who engages in that behaviour. Thus, this theoretical distinction did not translate well to the real world. In addition, victims who engaged in more behavioural self-blame were not more likely to believe that they could avoid being raped in the future. This was the key aspect of Janoff-Bulman's (1979) theory – that behavioural self-blame is adaptive because it is associated with a sense of future control.

Another interesting finding was that all types of attributions were associated with more distress. That is, victims who blamed the rapist more and who blamed society more also reported more distress, as did victims who reported more often thinking about 'why' the rape occurred. This is important because many theories have focused on which types of attributions are more helpful than others. However, our data suggested that it might not be productive to try to find a particular attribution that is helpful but rather it might be better to shift the focus away from attributions about the event.

Development of the temporal model of control

Before we drew the broad conclusions that we should move away from the focus on specific types of attributions, we needed to acknowledge that although rape is a common – and very distressing – event and very worthy of study, the relations we found studying sexual assault may not generalise to other events. This led us to move beyond theories developed specifically to explain adjustment to rape to a broader review of the literature on control and adjustment to stress (Frazier *et al.* 2002). In reviewing this literature, we realised, first, that there are many constructs related to control. In fact, in an excellent review, Skinner (1996) noted that there are more than a hundred control-related constructs that differ along several dimensions. In our review of the broader literature on perceived control and adjustment to stress, one dimension that stood out for us was the temporal dimension. This dimension stood out because, as illustrated below, different forms of control that differ along the temporal dimension appeared to be differentially related to adjustment. Although Skinner mentioned this dimension, it had not at that point been strongly emphasised in the literature.

Thus, based on our broad review of the literature, we developed a temporal model of control over stress and trauma. In other words, perceptions of control have a temporal dimension and can be focused on the past, the future or the present. *Past control* focuses on the question: 'Could I have prevented the event from occurring? Did I have control over the fact that the event occurred?' It involves focusing on the past and the cause of the event. *Future control* involves perceptions about personal control over the event occurring again in the future. 'Can I keep it from happening again?' This distinction between the past and the future was part of Janoff-Bulman's (1979) theory about behavioural and characterological self-blame. Behavioural self-blame involves past control which was hypothesised to be associated with future control. However, as mentioned, this hypothesis was not supported. One aspect of control that was not part of Janoff-Bulman's (1979) model and was not really explicit in the literature at all when we carried out our review (Frazier *et al.* 2002) was *present control*. In our review, we located several studies that included measures related to aspects of stressors or traumas that were controllable in the present. These involved control over illness symptoms, control over medical care and treatment, and control over the recovery process. As these terms suggest, this form of control was often measured in the context of coping with a medical condition or illness.

This temporal dimension is important because, in our review, these three different aspects of control had very different relations with measures of adjustment to stress and trauma (Frazier *et al.* 2002). For example, past control was either unassociated with or positively associated with distress. That is, the more individuals believed that they had control over the event occurring in the past the more distress they reported. This is contrary to the theoretical assumption that controllable events are less distressing, if control is defined in terms of control over the cause of the event in the past. In the literature review carried out by Frazier *et al.* (2002), the relations between measures of future control and distress were mixed and depended on the extent to which the event actually was controllable in the future. If an event definitely was not controllable (e.g. a sudden bereavement), the belief that that event could be prevented in the future was associated with more distress. In essence, it is not helpful to try to control events over which we clearly do not have control. Finally, various measures of present control – such as control over the recovery process – were consistently related to less distress and the relations were more robust. Present control was the only type of control associated with less distress because we do have more control over the present than the past or the future. Thus, the model that we developed after reviewing the literature was one in which different forms of control have different relations with adjustment, which is in contrast to the typical assumption in the literature that 'control is good'. The next step was to actually test the model.

Initial test of the temporal model

We first tested our temporal model in a longitudinal study of 171 rape victims seen for a sexual assault examination in the same hospital emergency room where we did our previous studies (Frazier 2003). Participants completed measures of past control including behavioural self-blame and blaming the rapist, present control which was operationalised in terms of control over the recovery process and future control which was here assessed in terms of taking precautions to try to prevent a future assault. Distress was assessed in terms of symptoms of depression, anxiety and hostility using the Brief Symptom Inventory (Derogatis 1993).

The results of this study supported our temporal model. Across time, and across distress measures, past control was associated with more distress, future control was unassociated with distress, and present control was consistently related to less distress, with medium to large effects.

We replicated these findings regarding present control in a community sample of 135 women who had been raped an average of sixteen years previously (Frazier *et al.* 2004). Present control was related to less distress, with almost the same effect size as in the previous study. In the same study, present control was the only factor related to less distress in a sample of 159 bereaved women.

In this research in which we were conducting the initial tests of the temporal model, we created face valid measures of past, present and future control but we had not gone through an extensive process to create and validate the scores on those measures. In other research on the relations between perceived control and adjustment to trauma, researchers had often used 1-item measures to assess control. One item is not typically considered to be adequate to measure a psychological construct (Brewer *et al.* 2007). If measures had more than one item, the items often combined past, present and future control. This is problematic given that, as described above, these different aspects of control have very different relations with adjustment. Measures also were often designed to assess control within the context of a specific event. Such measures cannot be used to compare the relations between control and adjustment across events. Surprisingly, despite the importance of control to theories of the development of PTSD (e.g. Foa *et al.* 1992), there was at that time no general measure that could be used to assess perceived past, present and future control across events. There are many measures of social support and of coping but no measure of perceived control over trauma that assesses the three aspects of control in our temporal model.

Development of a measure of perceived control

Thus, the next goal of our research programme was to develop such a measure, which we call the Perceived Control Over Stressful Events Scale (PCOSES) (Frazier *et al.* 2011). Much of the measure development work was done with undergraduate students, some of whom have experienced very severe traumas (see e.g. Frazier *et al.* 2009).

We have conducted approximately nine studies involving about 5,000 students to develop the PCOSES. In these studies, students describe past or ongoing stressors or traumas they have experienced and complete the PCOSES with regard to these events, and complete measures of distress and of related constructs that we use to establish the validity of scores on our measure (see Frazier *et al.* 2011 for more details). A sample item for past control is 'I could have done something to prevent this event from happening'. A sample item for present control is 'How I deal with this event now is under my control'. And a sample item for the future control subscale is 'I can do things to make sure I will not experience a similar event in the future'. A new subscale that assesses the likelihood that an event will happen again in the future has also been developed (Frazier *et al.* 2012).

One important question is whether scores on the PCOSES were related to important outcomes, such as distress. The answer to that question is 'Yes'. However, as predicted, the relations differed depending on the type of control. Individuals who felt that they could have controlled the event in the past or could prevent it from happening in the future tended to report more distress. In contrast, present control was consistently associated with less distress; present control at one point predicted less distress at a later point; and in prospective studies, individuals who reported more control over present aspects of the trauma reported less increase in distress from pre to post-trauma. Together, the three PCOSES subscales explained up to one-third of the variability in distress, a significant amount (Frazier *et al.* 2011).

Another important question was whether our event-specific measure of control predicted distress beyond other factors that we know predict distress. Again, the answer was 'Yes'. Our measure predicted distress beyond general perceptions of control (such as measures of mastery and self-efficacy), coping strategies that involve either approaching or avoiding problems, social support from friends and family, the personality trait of neuroticism which involves being more reactive to stress, and the number of prior traumatic events experienced (Frazier *et al.* 2011; Frazier *et al.* 2012). Of all of these measures, present control has the strongest relations with distress and is one of the few factors associated with better adjustment.

Summary

In summary, with regard to past control, the data do not support models of PTSD based on animal research that assume that controllable events are less distressing if by control we mean control over the event occurring. Most human traumas are not controllable and focusing on how they could have been controlled or prevented in the past does not seem to be helpful. Future control also is generally associated with more distress because it is not helpful to try to control things that really are not controllable. For example, people who have experienced a sudden death and think that they can prevent it from happening again actually report more distress. This may be because they are engaging in strategies to try to prevent the event that really are not going to help. Future control may be more adaptive for events that are more controllable. For example, in one of our studies, students who felt that they had more control over how they would do on an upcoming examination did have better subsequent grades on that exam (Frazier *et al.* 2011). Although examinations are not a major trauma, this study illustrates the point that the relation between future control and outcomes may depend on the actual controllability of the event. Finally, one way to maintain a sense of control in the face of trauma is to focus on what we *can* actually control in the present – how we react to the event and how we think and feel about the event. In every study we have carried out, present control is consistently related to better adjustment and it is one of the few things we have studied that is associated with *better* adjustment. This is important because we know a lot more about factors that hinder adjustment than about factors that facilitate adjustment.

Developing an intervention to increase present control

Because present control seems to be helpful, we thought that it would be a good target for interventions. Before we tried to develop an intervention to increase present control, we first wanted to assess whether there were situations in which present control was unhelpful.

Is present control ever unhelpful?

Specifically, we examined whether there were differences in the relations between present control and distress as a function of gender, race and type of event in samples of university students. We did not expect any differences because we predicted that present control generally would be helpful for men and women, for different racial groups and in the context of different kinds of events.

These analyses suggested that present control was related to fewer PTSD symptoms for both men and women and across different racial groups (white, Asian American and African American). The relationship between present control and lower distress was smaller among the African American group but the difference between groups was not significant. With regard to type of event, we compared two common events – sudden bereavement and sexual violence. In both cases, present control was related to less distress. Thus, in these analyses, we did not find any situations in which present control was associated with more distress.

Description of intervention

The next step in our research programme was to develop and test an online intervention specifically designed to increase present control in the face of stress. As mentioned, we used an online format to increase accessibility and reduce the stigma associated with help-seeking. Because this is a new intervention, we wanted to test it first with college students before testing it with more severely traumatised groups. However, it also is true that students are not immune from stress and trauma. We first carried out two pilot studies to make sure the intervention had some benefit, which it did, particularly in terms of increasing present control. We also used data from the pilot studies to refine the intervention before testing it in a larger study.

The intervention contained four web modules that each took ten to twelve minutes to complete. Each one followed a similar format. First, participants saw a video of me talking about the research findings on a particular topic (see below). Second, they saw a narrated presentation with examples from participants in our pilot studies. Then they did an activity in which they applied the topic to their own lives. They did the first three modules every other day and then after the third module they spent one week practising present control by completing three stress logs. These logs asked participants to write down what has been causing them stress, what aspects of these stressors were out of their control, what aspects of these stressors were controllable and what actions they could take to feel better. Finally, after one week of practice they completed the fourth module online.

The topics of the four modules were: (1) stress and its effects; (2) different aspects of control and the benefits of present control; (3) problem solving around implementing present control; and (4) moving forward. The last module was designed to help students keep practising present control and incorporated motivational interviewing techniques.

Methods

We had three conditions in this study to which participants were randomised. The first condition was the present control intervention just described with the four web modules and three stress logs (present control). The second condition was that same intervention but with supportive feedback to the participants about their stress logs (present control plus feedback). We added this condition based on research suggesting that self-help programmes that contain some support from a counsellor are more effective (e.g. Richards and Richardson 2012). The third condition was the first stress module without any information about present control and no feedback (stress information only).

We randomised about 100 people to each group. We selected people who scored lower (below 3) on our measure of present control because in our pilot studies it appeared that some people really did not need the intervention because they already had the skill we were trying to teach (see below for details). Our sample was a typical college student sample; primarily female, white and 18–21 years old.

To assess the effectiveness of the intervention, participants completed various outcome measures before and immediately following the intervention and then three weeks later. The outcome measures included present control (assessed using the present control subscale of the PCOSES) (Frazier *et al.* 2011), general self-efficacy (General Self-Efficacy Scale) (Schwarzer and Jerusalem 1995), perceived stress (Perceived Stress Scale) (Cohen *et al.* 1983) and depression, anxiety and stress symptoms (DASS-21) (Lovibond and Lovibond 1995).

Results

Attrition

Before presenting the results of the analyses assessing the effectiveness of the intervention, it is important to present data on attrition. Online interventions can be quite effective if people complete them, but often they do not (Richards and Richardson 2012). A few weeks before the intervention about 400 students completed our prescreening measure of present control. Of those, about 300 scored less than 3 on our present control scale and were randomly assigned to one of our three conditions. Of those in the two active intervention conditions, about 60 per cent to 70 per cent completed at least two stress logs and all four modules. In other words 30–40 per cent signed up for the study but never began the intervention. Of those who actually began the intervention 85–90 per cent completed at least two logs and all four modules. Thus, we had very good retention in the study for those who actually started the interventions.

Intervention effectiveness

Intervention effectiveness was examined by assessing change from pre-intervention to the three week follow-up in the three groups using paired t-tests. Participants in both intervention conditions (present control and present control + feedback) had significant and large increases in present control from pre-intervention to three weeks post-intervention. The intervention groups also reported significant increases in general self-efficacy that were medium in size. The general self-efficacy measure assessed perceived control over life events more broadly whereas the PCOSES assessed perceived control over a specific stressor. The group that only received information on stress did not increase in present control or general self-efficacy.

The two present control intervention groups also reported significant and medium-sized decreases in perceived stress and in symptoms of depression, anxiety and stress from pre-intervention to the three week follow-up. Stress symptoms included things like nervous tension, difficulty relaxing and irritability whereas perceived stress referred to the perception of stress (e.g. coping with all the things you had to do). There were no pre to post-intervention differences for the stress-information only comparison group on any of these measures.

Two other findings are of note. First, differences were bigger at follow-up than immediately following the intervention. Thus, the effects of the intervention – rather than diminishing – seemed to increase over time. Second, the intervention condition in which participants were provided with feedback on their stress logs was slightly more effective than the intervention condition that did not provide feedback.

The effectiveness of the intervention also can be assessed indirectly by looking at the stress logs to see if participants' stress levels seemed to be going down and if their stressors were being resolved. The following are some examples that concerned relationship stressors: 'I have let go of the other person's behaviour.' 'I have definitely stopped worrying about how he feels. I've told him how I feel, and I can't control how he feels about it.' 'Since I talked to my boyfriend, I've spent less energy worrying about our relationship and I am able to expend my energy elsewhere.' These examples illustrated that participants did appear to have learned skills in identifying what they can and cannot control and to focus on the things they can.

In summary, there were significant changes from pre-intervention to three week follow-up on all six outcome measures in both present control intervention groups. Interestingly, the effects were even bigger at follow-up than they were immediately after the intervention. Combining across measures, the effect size was medium, or about one-half of a standard deviation of change. The effects were slightly bigger in the group that got feedback. The feedback took about eight hours across all participants and the entire intervention.

Conclusion

Despite prevailing theories that controllable events are less distressing, our research suggests that the only aspect of control that is consistently associated with less distress is present control. Thus, we have developed a very brief intervention that has been shown to increase present control and reduce distress. Our intervention is certainly less comprehensive than many online interventions but it is also much shorter and it teaches one specific skill that can be very useful. Participants also have responded well to it. In addition, at least in college students, those who start the intervention are very likely to finish it.

We are continuing to revise and expand the intervention both in terms of content and production values and adapt it for use in specific groups. For example, in terms of production values we recreated the video modules using a professional recording studio. We have tested this revised intervention at a local community college that serves a more diverse student body and again found the intervention to be effective in increasing present control and decreasing distress. We have also created a new module that teaches mindfulness skills and are testing whether the addition of that module increases the effectiveness of our intervention. Finally, we are developing a new version of our intervention that is specifically geared towards medical patients with voice disorders who may find it difficult to participate in traditional talk therapies.

Bibliography

Acierno, R., Resnick, H., Flood, A. and Holmes, M., 2003. An acute post-rape intervention to prevent substance use and abuse. Addictive Behaviors, 28(9), pp. 1701–1715.

American Psychiatric Association, 2000. Diagnostic and statistical manual of mental disorders, text revision, 4th edition. Washington: Author.

Anders, S.L., Frazier, P.A. and Frankfurt, S.B., 2011. Variations in Criterion A and PTSD rates in a community sample of women. Journal of Anxiety Disorders, 25, pp. 176–84.

Anders, S., Frazier, P. and Shallcross, S., 2012. Prevalence and effects of life event exposure among undergraduate and community college students. Journal of Counselling Psychology, 59, pp. 449–457.

Barak, A., Hen, L., Boniel-Nissim, M. and Shapira, N., 2008. A comprehensive review and a meta-analysis of the effectiveness of internet-based psychotherapeutic interventions. Journal of Technology in Human Services, 26(2-4), pp. 109–160.

Brewer, N.T., Chapman, G.B., Gibbons, F.X., Gerrard, M., McCaul, K.D. and Weinstein, N.D., 2007. Meta-analysis of the relationship between risk perception and health behavior: The example of vaccination. Health Psychology, 26, pp. 136–45.

Cohen, S., Kamarck, T. and Mermelstein, R., 1983. A global measure of perceived stress. Journal of Health and Social Behavior, 24, pp. 386–396.

Derogatis, L., 1993. Manual for the Brief Symptom Inventory. Minneapolis: National Computer Systems.

Ehlers, A. and Clark, D., 2000. A cognitive model of posttraumatic stress disorder. Behaviour Research and Therapy, 38, pp. 319–345.

Foa, E.B., Zinbarg, R. and Rothbaum, B.O., 1992. Uncontrollability and unpredictability in posttraumatic stress disorder: An animal model. Psychological Bulletin, 112, pp. 218–238.

Frankfurt, S., Frazier, P. and Howard, K., 2012. Identifying posttrauma outcome trajectories prospectively using Latent Class Growth Analysis (LCGA). Poster presented at the 14th International Symposium, World Society of Victimology. The Netherlands: The Hague.

Frankfurt, S., Frazier, P., Syed, M. and Jung, K.R., 2012. Methods for identifying individual differences in patterns of change over time: A primer. Manuscript submitted for publication.

Frazier, P., 1990. Victim attributions and post-rape trauma. Journal of Personality and Social Psychology, 59, pp. 298–304.

Frazier, P., 2000. The role of attributions and perceived control in recovery from rape. Journal of Personal and Interpersonal Loss, 5, pp. 203–225. Reprinted in: J. H. Harvey and B.G. Pauwels, eds, 2000. Post traumatic stress theory, research, and application. Philadelphia: Bruner/Mazel.

Frazier, P., 2003. Perceived control and distress following sexual assault: A longitudinal test of a new model. Journal of Personality and Social Psychology, 84, pp. 1257–1269.

Frazier, P., Anders, S., Perera, S., Tomich, P., Tennen, H., Park, C. and Tashiro, T., 2009. Traumatic events among undergraduate students: Prevalence and associated symptoms. Journal of Counselling Psychology, 56, pp. 450–460.

Frazier, P., Anders, S., Shallcross, S., Keenan, N., Perera, S., Howard, K. and Hintz, S., 2012. Further development of the temporal model of control. Journal of Counselling Psychology, 59, pp. 623–630.

Frazier, P., Berman, M. and Steward, J., 2002. Perceived control and posttraumatic distress: A temporal model. Applied and Preventive Psychology, 10, pp. 207–223.

Frazier, P., Gavian, M., Hirai, R., Park, C., Tennen, H., Tomich, P. and Tashiro, T., 2011. Prospective predictors of PTSD symptoms: Direct and mediated relations. Psychological Trauma: Theory, Research, Practice, and Policy, 3, pp. 27–36.

Frazier, P., Keenan, N., Anders, S., Perera, S., Shallcross, S. and Hintz, S., 2011. Past, present, and future control and adjustment to stressful life events. Journal of Personality and Social Psychology, 100, pp. 749–765.

Frazier, P., Mortensen, H. and Steward, J., 2005. Coping strategies as mediators of the relations among perceived control and distress in sexual assault survivors. Journal of Counselling Psychology, 52, pp. 267–278.

Frazier, P. and Schauben, L., 1994. Stressful life events and psychological adjustment among female college students. Measurement and Evaluation in Counselling and Development, 27, pp. 280–292.

Frazier, P., Steward, J. and Mortensen, H., 2004. Perceived control and adjustment to trauma: A comparison across events. Journal of Social and Clinical Psychology, 23, pp. 303–324.

Frazier, P., Tennen, H., Gavian, M., Park, C., Tomich, P. and Tashiro, T., 2009. Does self-reported post-traumatic growth reflect genuine positive change? Psychological Science, 20, pp. 912–919.

Janoff-Bulman, R., 1979. Characterological versus behavioral self-blame: Inquiries into depression and rape. Journal of Personality and Social Psychology, 37, pp. 1798–1809.

Lovibond, P.F. and Lovibond, S.H., 1995. The structure of negative emotional states: Comparison of the Depression Anxiety Stress Scales (DASS) with the Beck Depression and Anxiety Inventories. Behaviour Research and Therapy, 33, pp. 335–343.

Pennebaker, J., 2004. Writing to heal: A guided journal for recovering from trauma and emotional upheaval. Oakland: New Harbinger.

Richards, D. and Richardson, T., 2012. Computer-based psychological treatments for depression: A systematic review and meta-analysis. Clinical Psychology Review, 32, pp. 329–342.

Schwarzer, R. and Jerusalem, M., 1995. Generalized Self-Efficacy scale. In: J. Weinman, S. Wright and M. Johnston, eds, 1995. Measures in health psychology: A user's portfolio. Causal and control beliefs. WindsorK: NFER-NELSON, pp. 5–37.

Skinner, E.A., 1996. A guide to constructs of control. Journal of Personality and Social Psychology, 71, pp. 549–570.

Chapter 14

Procedural justice for victims of crime
Are victim impact statements and victim–offender mediation rising to the challenge?

Tinneke Van Camp and Vicky De Mesmaecker

Introduction

Upon disclosure of a crime to the police, victims concede control over how to respond to the offence to judicial authorities. Meanwhile, regaining control over one's life and over the consequences of victimization is instrumental to victims' recovery (Herman 1997). Consequently, when victims delegate control over the offence to the judicial authorities, this does not imply they do not feel a need for involvement in subsequent proceedings (Wemmers 2002). Participation has in fact been found to be fundamental to victims' perceptions of the fairness of the criminal justice system. This association can be explained by procedural justice theory.

The objective of this chapter is to describe the procedural justice framework and present it as a particular way to look at the interests of victims of crime in the criminal justice system. The procedural justice model was developed and is being advanced by social psychologists exploring the perceived fairness of conflict resolution in a wide array of social conflicts. Whereas early procedural justice research was mainly concerned with workplace conflicts and civil litigations, more recently studies have been conducted with regard to fairness assessment in criminal law proceedings, some of which address perceptions of fairness by victims of crime. Findings suggest that procedural justice matters to victims (e.g. Wemmers 1996).

In this contribution, we first briefly outline victim concerns in the criminal justice system. This is followed by a description of the procedural justice model. Finally, we examine two particular forms of victim participation – victim impact statements (VIS) and victim–offender mediation (VOM) – and their potential for compliance with procedural justice requirements.

Meeting victim concerns

Victims of crime have multiple concerns in the aftermath of a crime (Strang 2002; Wemmers 2003; Goodey 2005). These can be classified in two categories: those that follow directly from the victimization experience and those that ensue from the encounter with the criminal justice system. The response to these concerns has been subject to change over the last decades.

Victim concerns in the aftermath of victimization

Individuals falling victim to a crime can suffer a number of psychological consequences, which include but are not limited to fear, anxiety, humiliation and feelings of powerlessness (Maguire 1991). The impact of such suffering on victims' lives leads to a number of particular concerns. Examples are the concern that the police respond to the offence quickly and do their utmost to recover stolen goods and apprehend suspects (De Mesmaecker 2011; Karmen 2012), the concern for practical and emotional support and social recognition of the victimization experience (Shapland *et al.* 1985; Wemmers 2003; Lemonne and Vanfraechem 2010; Bolívar 2012a), the concern for material and emotional restoration (Strang 2002; Strang and Sherman 2003) and the concern for the offender to be held accountable for his act (Poulson 2003; De Mesmaecker 2011; Bolívar 2012a) – which may but does not necessarily imply a concern for some form of punishment (De Mesmaecker 2011; Van Camp 2011).[1]

Another category of concerns comprises those that result from being confronted with the criminal justice system. Such confrontation gives rise to specific interests relating to how the criminal authorities handle the case. A number of those relate to opportunities for involvement in the criminal proceedings. Victims have repeatedly expressed the wish to be informed about the progress of their case and their rights as a victim by the criminal authorities (Wemmers 1995, 1999; Strang 2002; De Mesmaecker 2011). They have furthermore expressed great interest in having their voice heard and be recognized and in being allowed to participate in the criminal proceedings in an active manner (Shapland *et al.* 1985; Strang 2002). Other concerns relate to the interaction with the criminal authorities: to receive a respectful and fair treatment figures high on victims' priority list (Wemmers 1996; Strang 2002).

Responding to victim concerns

The first studies investigating the concerns of those affected by crime (for an extensive overview of these studies and their results, see Maguire 1991) focused mainly on concerns of the first type. While the direct impact of victimization on victims' psychological well-being remains an important field of study (see e.g. Hanson *et al.* 2010; Kunst *et al.* 2013) more recently, the second category of concerns has attracted much scholarly attention too. With this development came an evolution in thinking about the key actors that could respond to victim concerns. Before the 1970s, victims were mainly dependent on their community of care for relief and alleviation of their suffering.[2] Obviously, victims' communities of care continue to constitute an important source of emotional support (Davis *et al.* 1999; Bolívar 2012b), but other actors have been added to the range of 'service-providers'. In the 1970s, the first victim support and victim (-witness) assistance services were established (Fattah 2000; Burgess *et al.* 2010).

But most importantly in light of our discussion, in the 1970s and 1980s academics uncovered the fact that victims also expect the criminal authorities to take their concerns into account while the criminal justice process is taking its course. Empirical research on this matter is connected with a growing literature on therapeutic jurisprudence (e.g. Wexler and Winick 1991). Researchers in the field of therapeutic jurisprudence investigate the impact of law, legal rules, legal actors and justice systems on people's psychological functioning, mental health and psychological well-being (Wexler and Winick 1991; Wexler 1993; Winick 1997; Erez *et al.* 2011). Many have looked at victim participation in criminal proceedings from this perspective, arguing that victims may reap great benefits from participation in their case because the sense of active involvement may aid their emotional recovery process (Wemmers 2008). However, certain conditions apply in order to ensure that participation is therapeutic and not anti-therapeutic (Wemmers 2008).[3] One such condition is procedural fairness.

Looking at victim interests through a procedural justice lens

The procedural justice model

Procedural justice theory derives from the seminal work by John Thibaut and Laurens Walker, who in the 1970s published the results of a series of laboratory studies set up to examine participants' preferences for different dispute resolution procedures, for example arbitration, autocratic decision making, or mediation (Thibaut and Walker 1975). They demonstrated that perceptions of fairness are not only associated with the fairness of the outcome, but also with how this outcome is reached, and that outcome and procedure independently affect overall fairness assessments. Moreover, participants in their experiments consistently displayed a preference for dispute resolution procedures that allowed them a certain degree of process control or 'voice'. For example, they preferred those procedures offering the conflicting parties opportunities for presenting their views and evidence supporting their argument to those that did not. Thibaut and Walker understood participants' interest in process control to be instrumental: in their view, litigants value process control or 'voice' because it may help them to get the decision maker to take a decision that is favourable to them.

Thibaut and Walker's observations inspired multiple studies on the issue; two ground-breaking studies in this respect were those by Tyler (1987) and Lind *et al.* (1990). Both showed that litigants value the opportunity to address the decision maker and state their case regardless of whether doing so actually influences the decision. Tyler *et al.* (1985) called this the 'value-expressive' effect of voice, which they contrasted with the instrumental importance of voice. Tyler (1987) hypothesized that the reason why people heavily value opportunities for voicing their opinion in the course of dispute resolution procedures is that (not) being offered to do so affects their self-esteem. This stance incited research on so-called non-instrumental or relational concerns that play a role in justice judgements (Lind and Tyler 1988; Tyler 1989, 1990; Tyler and Lind 1992). Multiple studies empirically supported the idea that fairness matters to litigants because being treated in an unfair manner by an authority figure suggests that one is not a valuable member of the societal group that the authority represents (Tyler et al. 1996; Tyler and Blader 2003).

Lind and Van den Bos (2002) uncovered a third reason why procedural fairness matters in demonstrating that perceived procedural justice is particularly important when disputants are facing uncertainty. They identified two sources of uncertainty: informational (or environmental) and personal uncertainty. The first source is related to the notion that disputants need information to assess conflict resolution procedures. Unfortunately, in practice, process and/or outcome related information can be unclear or incomplete (Lind and Van den Bos 2002; Van den Bos 2009). Research revealed that under circumstances of informational uncertainty, the impact of procedural fairness on the overall appreciation of an intervention is more important than under conditions of informational certainty (Lind and Van den Bos 2002). Several empirical studies have demonstrated that in addition to informational uncertainty, personal uncertainty impacts fairness assessment. Personal uncertainty is described by Van den Bos (2009) as the aversive feeling that results from doubt, lack of control or instability in views of the self and/or the world as a consequence of certain unpleasant events or contextual factors. It intensifies the impact of voice and procedural fairness on the overall fairness assessment of a certain intervention (De Cremer and Sedikides 2005; Van den Bos et al. 2008; Van Hiel et al. 2008). Uncertainty is an uncomfortable and disconcerting feeling that people wish to eliminate or at least reduce and they seem to do so by focusing on the fairness with which their conflict is being handled (Van den Bos et al. 2008). As such, managing uncertainty presents itself as a justice motive (Lind and Van den Bos 2002), in addition to the relational justice motive that is apparent in Lind and Tyler's model of procedural justice (1988; see also De Cremer and Blader (2006), Hollander-Blumoff and Tyler (2008) and Kazemi and Törnblom (2008)).

Three categories of non-instrumental or relational concerns have been identified that are commonly regarded as the antecedents of perceptions of procedural fairness among litigants. The first is voice. Voice was defined by Folger (1977) as the opportunity for parties involved in a conflict to participate in decision making procedures concerning their conflict and to express their views throughout the procedure. Wemmers (1996), who conducted one of the first studies to explore the significance of procedural justice for victims of crime, highlights that actually being heard by the decision maker is an important aspect of voice. Not only does being able to express oneself matter, but so also does the impression that one was heard by the decision maker (see also Tyler 1987). The other two antecedents of procedural fairness are the quality (or fairness) of treatment and the quality (or fairness) of the decision making process (Tyler and Blader 2000, 2003; Tyler and Huo 2002; Blader and Tyler 2003a, 2003b). Judgements of the quality of treatment depend on litigants' perceptions of whether they have been treated with dignity and respect by the legal authorities, whether the authorities have shown concern for their needs and whether their rights have been acknowledged. Judgements on the quality of the decision making process are determined by people's views on whether the decision maker bases its decision on accurate and truthful information, eliminating every possible ground of partiality or discrimination, and behaves in an honest way.

Throughout the years, research on procedural justice in different cultures has shown that these antecedents apply in a consistent way across cultures (see e.g. Lind *et al.* 1994, 1997; Sugawara and Huo 1994; Ohbuchi *et al.* 2005) and matter independently of demographic characteristics such as gender, education or age (Tyler 1988, 1994).

Why procedural justice matters to victims of crime

Empirical studies on procedural justice have focused largely on workplace conflicts, civil law conflicts or group dilemmas, but procedural justice researchers have also taken an interest in perceptions of the fairness in dealing with criminal offences (e.g. Tyler and Wakslak 2004) as well as in general interpersonal conflict resolution methods (e.g. Mikula 1993). The framework has also been applied to victim experiences and satisfaction with criminal justice proceedings (Wemmers *et al.* 1995; Wemmers 1996, 2010; Malsch and Carrière 1999; Wemmers and Cyr 2006a; Bradford 2011). Procedural justice has, for instance, been associated with victim empowerment[4] (Cyr and Wemmers 2011) and absence of secondary victimization (Orth 2002). In other words, findings in this regard indicate that procedural justice matters to victims of crime, the reason for which is twofold.

First, victims value procedural justice because being allowed voice, a fair treatment and fair decision making affirm their standing in the group (Wemmers *et al.* 1995). Through involvement, victims are not primarily looking to influence judicial decisions in their case (Wemmers 1996); instead it offers them assurance that they are being taken into consideration and are deserving of fair treatment. In other words, procedural justice does not serve an instrumental purpose, but a normative one (Wemmers *et al.* 1995), as is explained in the relational model of procedural justice presented by Lind and Tyler (1988). Put differently, procedural justice matters because victims are looking for recognition.

Second, victims can experience a loss of control as a consequence of victimization. Victims have experienced an adverse event, which can be destabilizing. Recovery then requires that they regain control (Herman 1997). One such form of control could be to have insight into what is going on and how the police and judicial actors are dealing with their complaint. A lack of such information has been found to be an obstacle to empowerment (Cyr and Wemmers 2011). The criminal justice system can be intimidating to victims and is experienced as complex and non-transparent (Lemonne and Vanfraechem 2010), despite many legal initiatives to support victims throughout criminal proceedings. Also, a complaint passes through different services and through the hands of different judicial actors before a final judicial decision is taken. Only when victims have sufficient and transparent information about, for instance, the different investigatory and prosecutorial actions taken in their case, as well as about the timing and results of these actions, do they learn that their case is being taken seriously and what is expected of them in the process (Goodey 2005). Information and involvement allow first-hand insight into the proceedings and enable victims to assess whether their complaint is being dealt with in a fair manner. If they are certain they are being treated fairly, confidence in the criminal justice system increases (Wemmers 1996). In other words, the importance of procedural justice for victims of crime could theoretically also be related to managing uncertainty, although this has, to our knowledge, not been empirically verified as such.

Accounting for procedural justice in practice

After having established that procedural justice matters to victims of crime, we will move onto how it can be delivered. In what follows, we examine the potential for compliance of two particular forms of victim participation, VIS and VOM, with procedural justice antecedents.

Victim impact statements

A good number of common law jurisdictions and some civil law jurisdictions have enacted provisions giving (certain categories of) victims the right to submit a VIS.[5] A VIS is a written or oral statement in which the victim of a crime describes the physical, material, psychological and social harm he/she suffered as a result of the crime (Erez 1991, 1999). In some jurisdictions, the victim may include his or her opinion on the sentence to be imposed on the offender(s), which may be taken into account by the court in the sentencing phase of the trial.[6] The VIS is added to the case file for the judge, the prosecutor and the defendant and his/her lawyers to read; in many jurisdictions victims are also allowed to read aloud their VIS in court during the trial.

VIS, as Clarke et al. (2003, p. 4) put it, allow victims to 'personalize' the crime. By way of a VIS, victims can provide personal input in the criminal procedure that is otherwise extremely rational and not particularly receptive to the personal views and concerns of victims (Joutsen 1994). This stands in stark contrast to a situation in which victims depend on the prosecutor to convey their suffering to the court and the defendant (Karmen 2012), since the 'transformation of lay events in judicial ones' (Messmer 1997, p. 137) implies the simplification of typically complex and emotional events. VIS, then, potentially serve an important communicative function (Roberts and Erez 2004; Szmania and Gracyalny 2006; Roberts 2009).

The VIS has been a controversial instrument from the very start, since it heralded a fundamentally different role for victims within the criminal justice system and introduced emotions in the legal sphere. After a period in which victim rights were largely limited to service rights such as a right to information or support, the VIS invited – and continues to invite – quite some sceptical and critical responses, which relate in particular to the effect of the introduction of victim statements on sentence severity and on defendants' rights (see e.g. Bandes 1996; Ashworth 2000). Empirical evidence has consistently countered such criticism, invariably demonstrating that the introduction of VIS had no significant impact on aggregate sentencing practices and that VIS do not infringe upon the rights of the defendant (Roberts 2009).

In this chapter, however, we are concerned with the way the right to submit a victim statement affects victims of crime. Based on a review of studies on this topic, Roberts (2009) concludes that empirical findings demonstrate that the majority of victims who submitted a victim statement benefited from the experience, felt better after submitting the statement, would do so again and would recommend other victims to file a VIS (see e.g. Leverick *et al.* 2007; see also Lens *et al.* 2010). Meanwhile, victims have also reported a number of problems regarding the procedure of filing a victim statement (for an overview see De Mesmaecker 2012), which warrants a careful examination of the instrument. In this chapter we explore the potential of VIS to enhance perceptions of procedural justice. Note that the daily practice and legal provisions on VIS vary across countries and jurisdictions, which puts limits to our analysis. But despite the great variation in VIS schemes and implementation practices, a number of commonalities and trends can be detected.

Voice

Above, we defined 'voice' as consisting of two aspects: the opportunity to express one's views about the conflict to the decision maker (Folger 1977), and the impression that one was heard (Wemmers 1996). The first aspect of voice, namely to present one's views, is precisely what VIS aim to facilitate. Principally, VIS have been introduced to allow victims to express their concerns to the court, providing the court with information about the nature and seriousness of the crime that may be useful when meting out the sentence (Erez 1991). As such, VIS offer victims the opportunity to have their voice heard and their concerns recorded. Victims have in addition been found to value the VIS particularly as an important tool for communicating the impact of the crime to the offender and the general public (Kool *et al.* 2002; Szmania and Gracyalny 2006; Lens *et al.* 2010; Roberts and Manikis 2011). Nevertheless, two limitations seem to exist with regard to the degree to which VIS comply with this first aspect of voice; these are associated with the extent to which victims are in fact free to express their views through VIS.

First, throughout a number of studies victims have been found to express dissatisfaction about the limitations put on the content of VIS in many jurisdictions, denouncing in particular the prohibitions on expressing their opinion about sentencing (see e.g. Hoyle *et al.* 1998; Graham *et al.* 2004; Lens *et al.* 2010) or on talking about the offence itself (Lens *et al.* 2010). Also, in some jurisdictions, for example New-Zealand, England and Wales and a number of American states (for more details, see De Mesmaecker 2012; on England and Wales' specific regulations see Roberts and Manikis 2013), VIS are prepared by justice officials. In such cases, the statement may not accurately reflect the harm experienced by the victim. Though some research reports victims being satisfied about the way the official had completed their statement (Lens *et al.* 2010), other studies suggest that victims may feel that their concerns and views have not been correctly recorded by the official writing their statement (e.g. Kool *et al.* 2002; Graham *et al.* 2004).

The second limitation to expressing one's views through a VIS is related to the nature of the criminal proceedings in which VIS are being implemented, in particular to the fact that communication in courtrooms is restrained. Courtroom communication is meant to fit a predefined procedure and to take place within what Strang (2004, p. 101) calls the 'bounds of civility' of the courtroom, which may limit personal accounts of the crime (Messmer 1997; Englebrecht 2008). For instance, victims participating in a study by Englebrecht (2008) said they experienced limitations regarding the type of language they were allowed to use in court. Attorneys, judges and victim advocates asked victims for example not to use any derogatory or inflammatory language towards the defendant, which made some victims feel they could not fully express their emotions. One needs to also consider that not all victims are allowed to read their statement in court during the sentencing hearing – in England and Wales in particular, victims are only afforded a right to a written statement (Roberts and Manikis 2013). The restriction to a written statement could hamper victim voice and as such limit the communicative value of the VIS.

With respect to the compliance of VIS with the second aspect of voice, that is, the feeling that one was heard by the decision maker, we need to consider research on the question of whether judges convey signs of having read and understood the VIS to victims. One of the few studies that examined how often judges directly address victims present during court hearings was conducted by Roberts and Edgar (2006) in Canada. The exact question judges were asked was: 'Do you ever address the victim directly in delivering oral reasons for sentence?' A little under two-thirds of the judges participating in the study said they 'often' or 'sometimes' address the victim directly on this occasion. Lens *et al.* (2010) report that in the Netherlands in two thirds of the cases either the judge or the prosecutor refers to the victim statement during the trial, and that victims are usually satisfied with the attention paid to their statement by the judge. Obviously not all victims are present at sentencing hearings. As for written comments providing recognition of the VIS, which is important to victims absent from the trial, Erez and Rogers' (1999) Australian study is relevant. They quote judges as saying they refer to the VIS in their sentencing remarks whenever possible. These are all positive findings with a view to the development of perceptions of procedural justice, though research on this point is as yet rather limited.

In conclusion, VIS seem useful vehicles for communication by victims to their offender and to the judge, yet a number of limitations exist as well. These are related to the rigid nature of court proceedings within which VIS are implemented and the regulations regarding what victims are allowed to include in their statements. These limitations are not easily remedied as they need to be balanced against other rationalities of the criminal proceedings. Yet two clear recommendations for good practice result from our analysis. The first recommendation is for judges to systematically try to incorporate a reference to the VIS in their sentencing comments or during the sentencing hearing. When judges publicly acknowledge that the VIS was read and heard, they could positively impact victims' perceptions of having had a chance for voice. The second is to ensure that victims who do not wish to completely relinquish control over the content of their statement to a professional are indeed permitted to write their statement in person, meanwhile still making sure that assistance by a victim advocate or another professional is available to them. As we will see below, such assistance is greatly valued.

The quality of treatment

In a number of countries that grant victims the right to submit a VIS, victims write their statements by themselves; in other countries, another person is in charge of preparing it (Erez 1999). Those victims who write their VIS themselves, however, may be assisted throughout this process by professionals. These are usually victim support workers (e.g. in the Netherlands)[7] or victim advocates (e.g. in the United States, see Szmania and Gracyalny 2006); in the United States, prosecutors too are involved in the process of completing a VIS (see Englebrecht 2008). Hence, when discussing whether the procedure of filing a VIS may contribute to perceptions of qualitative treatment, one must differentiate between those victims who complete their statements on standard forms in the privacy of their homes and those who are assisted by professionals.

As for those victims who receive help or support from victim services when submitting a VIS, we may refer to a Belgian qualitative study on victims' experiences with victim services showing that victims tend to be very satisfied with the support delivered by victim services, including the support received when filing a VIS (Lemonne and Vanfraechem 2010). Furthermore, Bradford (2011) found contact with victim services to be linked to more favourable views of the fairness of the criminal justice system. High quality treatment by victim support workers assisting victims in the process of filing a VIS may, then, enhance perceptions of procedural justice. The same is true for those victims who have regular contact with the prosecutor during the preparation of the VIS, though, to our knowledge, this seems to be applicable exclusively to the United States and much depends on the quality of the interpersonal contact with the prosecutor (Englebrecht 2008).

If assistance of victim support services or prosecutors is absent, however, victims may experience little interpersonal contact with any of the officials involved in the administration of justice. This does not necessarily imply that such victims have no ground on which to judge the quality of the treatment they receive. Leferink and Vos (2008) and Lens *et al.* (2010), for example, found the Dutch victims participating in their studies saying that the mere existence of the opportunity of participating in the criminal procedure by means of a VIS gave them a feeling of being acknowledged and being taken seriously. The opportunity to orally submit one's statement to court too contributed to these victims feeling acknowledged and having the impression that they had been taken seriously (Lens *et al.* 2010). However, in Canada, Wemmers and Cyr (2006b) did not find that VIS satisfied victims' need for recognition. Hence, we are faced with mixed evidence concerning the degree to which perceptions of qualitative treatment may proceed from the mere existence of a legal provision on VIS.

The contradictory nature of these findings may be due to variations in actual practice and implementation of VIS schemes. Future research should therefore compare different VIS schemes to validate the impact of (absence of) interpersonal contact on victims' perceptions of qualitative treatment. An important task to be taken up by such research is to compare fairness assessments by victims who were assisted when writing their VIS with fairness assessments by those who had no access to such assistance.

The quality of decision making

Allegedly, victims who file a VIS perceive this to be a contribution to the quality of decision making. Indeed the opportunity to describe the harm sustained as a result of the crime in a statement that is added to the case file may alleviate the concern that victims' views are less prominently present in trials than offenders' views and that offenders have more rights than victims. This concern was voiced by the victims interviewed by Englebrecht (2011); they indeed tended to compare their position in the process to the defendant's. Having the right to file a VIS, then, may enhance the victim's perception of equal treatment of all parties and impartiality of the decision maker.

Meanwhile, studies on VIS also demonstrate that many victims feel that their statement was not taken into account by the judge in his decision. Only 29 per cent of the victims participating in Roberts and Manikis' (2011) England and Wales study thought their statement had been fully taken into account; an additional 28 per cent felt their statement had been taken into account 'to some extent'. The other victims either did not know whether their statement had been taken into account (14 per cent) or had the feeling it had not (18 per cent). Similar results come from the Dutch study of Lens *et al.* (2010): although victims were convinced that their VIS would assist the judge in making a decision, when asked whether they thought their statement had actually impacted the case outcome or whether they thought the judge had taken their statement into account when deciding on the sentence, they were less optimistic. Englebrecht (2008) too reported that many of the victims participating in her US study had the impression that their statement actually had little impact on the outcome of the case, which caused frustration and disappointment.

In conclusion, the analysis shows a clear pattern. The concerns about VIS outlined above seem to be related to its implementation rather than to the instrument itself. It seems in fact that VIS have great potential for enhancing perceptions of procedural justice, yet the way VIS are implemented shows flaws that prevent this potential from being fulfilled completely (see also Crawford (2000, p. 290) who speaks of an 'implementation failure' and Walklate (2012, p. 113), who identified an 'implementation gap'). Based on procedural justice theory, we argue that including verbal acknowledgement of the concerns voiced in a VIS and interpersonal contact in all the VIS schemes could enhance perceptions of procedural fairness.

Victim–offender mediation

Another particular form of victim participation is the restorative justice practice of victim–offender mediation (VOM). Restorative justice is about facilitating active involvement of victim and offender in the settlement of the conflict, bringing about communication between them and working towards a settlement of the conflict that satisfies all (Van Ness 1997; Zehr and Mika 1998; Wemmers 2002; Strang and Sherman 2003; Umbreit *et al.* 2006). VOM, the most commonly implemented restorative practice worldwide (Umbreit 1994a; Vanfraechem and Aertsen 2010), involves the voluntary participation of the victim and offender of a particular offence. Both parties are assisted by a trained mediator who conducts shuttle mediation (i.e. travels between victim and offender to facilitate indirect communication between the parties) and possibly a face-to-face meeting (Groenhuijsen 2000; Umbreit *et al.* 2004). Whereas VIS is implemented within the criminal justice system, VOM rather operates in the margins of the criminal justice system, either as a complementary or diversionary procedure.

Numerous evaluative and comparative studies offer encouraging indications as to the satisfaction with and beneficial impact of restorative justice felt by victims of various types of crime (including property crime and crime against a person; see Wemmers and Canuto (2002), Poulson (2003), and Sherman and Strang (2007)). Findings from evaluative studies on the benefits of restorative interventions, such as VOM, for victims of crime who agreed to participate, are consistently positive, even more consistently so than data on the impact of these interventions for offenders (such as reoffending; see Sherman and Strang (2007)). On the basis of a meta-analysis of evaluative findings on restorative practices and their benefits for victims, Sherman and Strang (2007) conclude that restorative justice outperforms the criminal justice proceedings on various accounts. Victim satisfaction, for example, is generally very high (Sherman and Strang 2007; Shapland et al. 2011). Victims who participate in VOM are also more likely to get compensation in comparison to victims who only follow the criminal justice proceedings (Braithwaite 1999; Latimer et al. 2005). Furthermore, they are more likely to believe that the offender has been held accountable (Poulson 2003; Sherman and Strang 2007) than victims who only went through the criminal justice proceedings. VOM has been associated with a healing or therapeutic impact on victims (Wemmers and Cyr 2005; Shapland et al. 2007; Rugge and Scott 2009) and with reduced levels of fear and anger (Strang et al. 2006) and reduced symptoms of PTSD (Angel 2008). Moreover, victim-participants would recommend VOM to other victims (Sherman and Strang 2007).

Yet VOM is not for everyone. Based on their review of empirical studies on victim experiences with restorative justice, Wemmers and Canuto (2002) conclude that a minority of victim-participants report a negative impact, such as increased stress, following participation on a restorative intervention. Daly (2004) warns restorative justice proponents for being overly optimistic and highlights the need for having realistic expectations as to what can be expected of restorative justice for victims of crime. However, the negative impact on victims' well-being could, according to Wemmers (2009), be averted with a better selection of cases referred to VOM. Also Daly (2004) emphasizes that traditional criminal justice proceedings are more likely to cause secondary stress than restorative procedures do.

While the evidence in favour of offering restorative justice to victims is abundant, data giving insight into why exactly victims benefit from restorative justice is only sparsely available (Sherman and Strang 2007; Vanfraechem and Aertsen 2010). Vanfraechem and Aertsen, therefore, urge researchers to explore factors that mediate and influence victim appreciation of restorative justice, including perceived fairness. The emphasis in VOM on involvement of the affected parties, indeed, infers that it holds a great potential to comply with procedural justice (Aertsen 2004; Braithwaite 2006; Shapland et al. 2006). A few studies explore the significance of procedural justice determinants for victim appreciation of VOM and offer empirical support for this assumption. The findings of our own qualitative studies further advance this idea (De Mesmaecker 2011; Van Camp 2011). We interviewed victims of violent and property crime in Belgium and Canada who participated in VOM and learned that appreciation of VOM is related to the different antecedents of procedural fairness.

Voice

There are considerable indications that voice is a prominent contributing factor to the appreciation of VOM. Early evaluative studies under the supervision of Umbreit (1989, 1994b) in the USA and a more recent study by Shapland et al. (2011) in England and Wales reveal that VOM is appreciated by victim-participants for the opportunity it offers to express themselves and contribute to the search for a solution. The opportunity to communicate with the offender, either directly in a face-to-face meeting or indirectly through shuttle mediation, seems to serve multiple expressive needs victims experience, that is, to describe the multiple consequences of victimization to the offender, to raise victim awareness and to express emotions to the offender (ranging from anger and sadness to forgiveness; see Van Camp (2011) and Van Camp and Wemmers (2013)). In addition, victims appreciate having the choice between meeting the offender face-to-face or limiting the intervention to shuttle mediation and making arrangements as to the topics to address and which to avoid with the offender (Van Camp 2011). As such, VOM complies with the elements that have been associated with 'voice' by pioneers of procedural justice research such as Folger (1977), that is, the opportunity to participate and present one's views.

Moreover, Wemmers and Cyr (2004 2006b), who applied the procedural justice model to victims' perceptions of VOM in Canada, found that victims also had a strong sense of having been heard and their concerns taken into account. Hence, VOM also responds to the need to be heard, which Wemmers (1996) found to be significantly associated with perceived justice. Victims find it liberating to express their concerns and feelings and to be heard by the offender (Wemmers and Canuto 2002; Sherman and Strang 2007; De Mesmaecker 2011; Shapland *et al.* 2011; Van Camp 2011). According to Shapland *et al.* (2011), it is such interpersonal communication that victims who agreed to participate in a restorative intervention, including VOM, were looking for when accepting the offer. Messmer (1997), who conducted a study on victim–offender interactions in VOM, found that for the parties involved in mediation to develop mutual understanding, communication about the conflict, including opportunities for responding to one another's interpretations, is key. Being witness to the offender's immediate responses and reactions to their story and being able to discuss these further is significant to victim appreciation of VOM (Sherman *et al.* 2005; Strang *et al.* 2006; Van Camp 2011).

In other words, VOM does not only facilitate the opportunity to speak and be heard, but offers a chance for dialogue, as such complying with and even going beyond the procedural justice model. Such a dialogue allows getting answers that are not provided in the judicial case file and trial and can only be retrieved directly from the offender. Since the dialogue between victim and offender in the context of VOM is confidential, the offender could be encouraged to be honest (Van Camp 2011). New understandings of the offence are important for victim recovery (Aertsen *et al.* 2011) and knowing the truth about what happened diminishes uncertainty and might enable victims to find closure (Shapland *et al.* 2007).

Nevertheless, the degree of involvement in restorative justice is substantial and communication with the offender might not appeal to all victims. While VIS is more of a one-time opportunity to express one's concerns, VOM represents a more active involvement and often includes multiple contacts with the mediator and offender. Consequently, mediators should interpret the readiness of victims with care, but should also avoid persuading (or dissuading) victims to participate

(Jacobson *et al.* 2012). Victims appreciate that they are not pressured into participation and that they can freely accept the offer of VOM or reinitiate it after an initial refusal (Umbreit *et al.* 2002).

The quality of treatment

VOM is associated with a perception of fair treatment by victim-participants (Shapland *et al.* 2011). The interaction with the mediator is found to be key in the appreciation of VOM (Pruitt *et al.* 1993; Umbreit 1994b; Umbreit *et al.* 2006; Shapland *et al.* 2007). Commonly, VOM starts with an individual meeting with the mediator (in which the mediator explores the willingness to participate) and is followed by shuttle mediation (in which the mediator travels between victim and offender to transfer messages, possibly leading up to a face-to-face meeting). Interaction between the mediator and the victim is therefore inherent to the restorative practice of VOM. Whereas VIS schemes do not by default imply interpersonal contact with a victim advocate or another professional actor, interpersonal contact is implied in VOM.

Moreover, the individual meetings with the mediator offer opportunities to provide participants with information about the procedure and possible outcomes. Such information is associated with increased victim satisfaction with VOM (Strang and Sherman 2003; De Mesmaecker 2011; Wemmers and Raymond 2011). In general, being provided with clear and complete information about an intervention increases perceptions of fairness (Van den Bos 2009). Victims indeed perceive the restorative procedure as transparent and comprehensive, which seems to contribute to their satisfaction (Van Camp and Wemmers 2013). In their interactions with the victim and offender, the mediators can get a feel for what the victim and offender wish to ultimately get out of the intervention and prepare the procedure and each of the participants accordingly. Consequently, in their interaction with the mediator, victims are supported in developing realistic expectations about the process, outcome and the offender's motives to participate (Van Camp and Wemmers 2013). As such, uncertainty about the process and possible outcome can be attenuated through interaction with the mediator.

In addition to the quality of the treatment by the mediator, the attitude of the offender also matters. In her qualitative study, Van Camp (2011) found that victims, who felt that the offender respected them for participating in VOM or for what they communicated to the offender, associate this with a sense of recognition and validation. Another particular element of victim appreciation with VOM is the opportunity to hold the offender accountable and for the offender to accept responsibility and recognize the consequences of victimization (Umbreit 1989; Strang *et al.* 2006; Shapland *et al.* 2007). The comparative studies on restorative justice reviewed by Poulson (2003) reveal that victims are five times more likely to feel that the offender was held accountable in VOM than in court proceedings. Wemmers and Cyr (2005) note that an offender is required to accept responsibility for the crime in order to participate in VOM. This condition could hence be conducive to the victim-participants' perception of recognition. In terms of the procedural justice model, recognition confirms to victims that they are valued members of society. Respect and fair treatment matter because they represent recognition, and recognition is restorative.

The quality of decision making

Another distinctive determinant of procedural justice is the quality of decision making and the neutrality of the decision maker. VOM, however, is a bilateral procedure and allows victim and offender to work out an agreement (Wemmers 2002), both in its diversionary set-up or as a complementary procedure to the criminal proceedings. The mediator is a facilitator and does not impose any decisions. As such, strictly speaking, the decision making within VOM does not belong to an authority, but to the victim and offender. While victims are generally more interested in process control than decision control (Wemmers 1996), the way a VOM progresses might make the decision control implied by VOM more manageable. The mediator guides the victim and offender towards a solution through a process of preparation and shuttle mediation. De Mesmaecker (2011) and Van Camp (2011) both found that victim-participants appreciate the capacity of mediators, in their role as facilitator, to remain neutral throughout this process and this contributes to the appreciation of VOM. Mediators assist both parties equally in their communication and respect both parties' choices for involvement. The mediator works with the victim and offender in individual meetings for as long as needed and as long as the parties are willing. VOM is, therefore, not a one-shot deal meeting, but an intensively and cautiously prepared communication. As such, despite the bilateral nature of VOM, 'victims find mediation fair because it offers them recognition and respect through consultation, not because it allows them to make demands' (Wemmers and Cyr 2006b, p. 123).

The decision control implied by the bilateral nature of VOM seems also more acceptable because VOM is perceived as an informal procedure, as opposed to the highly formal proceedings in the criminal justice system, including VIS (Shapland *et al.* 2006; Van Camp 2011). Victim-participants in VOM seem willing to accept informal decision control and are still looking for the offender to be held formally accountable and to have a third party maintain final decision making power (Van Camp 2011). As such, victims seem to support the idea that restorative justice and the criminal justice system can function independently (Van Camp and Wemmers, 2013).

Conclusion

While victimologists are clear on victim concerns and what victims are looking for in the criminal justice system, there is much debate on how to meet those concerns. This is true especially for the victims' concern for involvement in the criminal proceedings. Different forms of victim participation have been introduced to respond to this need. In this chapter we have looked into the degree to which two specific forms of victim participation in criminal justice, VIS and VOM, comply with one particular condition, procedural justice.

Our review suggests that, on the one hand, for VIS to achieve their full potential of enhancing victims' perceptions of procedural justice they should be accompanied by interpersonal contact in the form of assistance in completing the form and by clear acknowledgement of the victims' concerns expressed in the VIS by the judicial officials. The lack of interpersonal contact with the decision maker and the other party as well as the formality of the courtroom context in which they are used can lead to VIS not fully meeting the different procedural justice requirements. VOM, on the other hand, seems to apply the procedural justice model particularly well. With its attention to the parties' voices, interactional quality and transparency, it provides victims with the recognition they are looking for. Good interpersonal contact with the mediator is key. Such interpersonal contact is inherent in the concept of VOM, as opposed to filing a VIS, which is not automatically accompanied by support from a victim advocate. Moreover, VOM, as opposed to VIS, encourages the expression of emotions and direct interaction between victim and offender. Nonetheless, not every victim is interested in VOM and attention should be paid to ensure that other forms of victim participation are also in place to award victims a procedurally fair treatment.

Notes

1 Regarding this concern for punishment of the offender, note that victims are not generally vindictive or retributive. It is a misapprehension that victims expressing a concern for the offender to be held accountable want to see the offender suffer. In fact, research shows that, first, victims have very nuanced and deliberated opinions on the sentence to be imposed on their offender, and, second, the reason victims want the offender to be held accountable often relates to their concern for acknowledgement and for offender rehabilitation (Umbreit 1989; Sprott and Doob 1997; De Mesmaecker 2011; Van Camp 2011; Bolívar 2012a). Furthermore, victims do not seem to feel a need to decide on the sentence (Wemmers and Cyr 2004; De Mesmaecker 2011).
2 The term 'community of care', used mainly in restorative justice literature, points to individuals with whom victims have a meaningful personal relationship (McCold 2004).
3 Although therapeutic jurisprudence literature has left the term 'therapeutic' rather vague and different views exist on what it means exactly, Winick (1997, p. 192), one of the founders of therapeutic jurisprudence literature, has conceptualized it broadly as 'anything that enhances the psychological well-being of the individual'. The therapeutic jurisprudence literature is based on the viewpoint that traditional legal paternalism is anti-therapeutic, that is, it may negatively affect litigants' well-being, and instead stresses the importance of individual autonomy in legal procedures. On the definition of 'therapeutic', see Winick (1997).
4 For their study, Cyr and Wemmers (2011) adopted the definition of empowerment developed by Rappaport (1987, p. 122), which states that empowerment is 'a process, a mechanism by which people, organizations, and communities gain mastery over their affairs'.
5 The United States, Canada, Australia and New Zealand were among the first to enact laws allowing victims to file a VIS, which they did throughout the 1980s. A second

wave of countries that introduced VIS legislation includes England and Wales, South Africa, the Netherlands, Malaysia and Japan – all these countries introduced VIS after the millennium.
6 Victim Statements of Opinion, as the type of victim statements that include victims' opinions on sentencing are called, are only used in bifurcated trial systems. They are not submitted to the court unless the defendant has been found guilty. To our knowledge, none of the unitary trial systems that afford victims the right to submit a victim statement allows victims to include their opinions on sentencing.
7 See www.slachtofferhulp.nl/Algemeen/Strafproces/Spreekrecht/.

Bibliography

Aertsen, I., 2004. Slachtoffer-daderbemiddeling: een onderzoek naar de ontwikkeling van een herstelgerichte strafrechtsbedeling. Leuven: Universitaire Pers Leuven.

Aertsen, I., Bolívar, D., De Mesmaecker, V. and Lauwers, N., 2011. Restorative justice and the active victim: exploring the concept of empowerment. Temida, Journal of Victimization, Human Rights and Gender, 14(1), pp. 5–19.

Angel, C., 2008. Crime victims meet their offenders: Testing the impact of restorative justice conferences on victims' post-traumatic stress symptoms. Presentation at the XV World Congress of the International Society for Criminology, Barcelona, 20–25 July 2008.

Ashworth, A., 2000. Victims' rights, defendants' rights and criminal procedure. In: A. Crawford and J. Goodey, eds, Integrating a victim perspective within criminal justice. Aldershot: Ashgate Darthmouth, pp. 85–204.

Bandes, S., 1996. Empathy, narrative, and victim impact statements. University of Chicago Law Review, 63(2), pp. 361–412.

Blader, S.L. and Tyler, T.R., 2003a. A four-component model of procedural justice: Defining the meaning of a 'fair' process. Personality and Social Psychology Bulletin, 29(6), pp. 747–758.

Blader, S.L. and Tyler, T.R., 2003b. What constitutes fairness in work settings? A four-component model of procedural justice. Human Resource Management Review, 13(1), pp. 107–126.

Bolívar, D., 2012a. Victim–offender mediation and victims' restoration: a victimological study in the context of restorative justice. Doctoral dissertation. Leuven: KU Leuven.

Bolívar, D., 2012b. Community of care from a victim-perspective: a qualitative study. Contemporary Justice Review, 15(1), pp. 17–37.

Bradford, B., 2011. Voice, neutrality and respect: Use of Victim Support services, procedural fairness and confidence in the criminal justice system. Criminology and Criminal Justice, 11(4), pp. 345–366.

Braithwaite, J., 1999. Restorative justice: Assessing optimistic and pessimistic accounts. Crime and Justice, 25(1), pp. 1–127.

Braithwaite, J., 2006. Doing justice intelligently in civil society. Journal of Social Issues, 62(2), pp. 393–409.

Burgess, A.W., Regehr, C. and Roberts, A.R., 2010. Victimology: Theories and applications. Sudbury: Jones and Bartlett Publishers.

Clarke, D., Davis, L. and Booyens, K., 2003. A silver era for victims of crime: reassessing the role that victim impact statements can play in improving victim involvement in criminal justice procedures. Acta Criminologica, 16(2), pp. 43–56.

Crawford, A., 2000. Salient themes towards a victim perspective and the limitations of restorative justice: Some concluding comments. In: A. Crawford and J. Goodey, eds, Integrating a victim perspective within criminal justice. Aldershot: Ashgate Darthmouth, pp. 285–311.

Cyr, K. and Wemmers, J.-A., 2011. *Empowerment* des victimes d'actes criminels. Criminologie, 44(2), pp. 125–155.

Daly, K., 2004. A Tale of Two Studies: Restorative Justice from a Victim's Perspective. Chapter prepared for E. Elliott and R. Gordon, eds, 2005. Restorative Justice: Emerging Issues in Practice and Evaluation. Cullompton: Willan Publishing. Available online at: www.griffith.edu.au/__data/assets/pdf_file/0009/50310/kdaly_part2_paper7.pdf

Davis, R.C., Lurigio, A.J. and Skogan, W.G., 1999. Services for victims: a market research study. International Review of Victimology, 6(2), pp. 101–115.

De Cremer, D. and Blader, S.L., 2006. Why do people care about procedural fairness? The importance of belongingness in responding and attending to procedures. European Journal of Social Psychology, 36(2), pp. 211–228.

De Cremer, D. and Sedikides, C., 2005. Self-uncertainty and responsiveness to procedural justice. Journal of Experimental Social Psychology, 41(2), pp. 157–173.

De Mesmaecker, V., 2011. Perceptions of justice and fairness in criminal proceedings and restorative encounters: Extending theories of procedural justice. Doctoral dissertation. Leuven: KU Leuven.

De Mesmaecker, V., 2012. Antidotes to injustice? Victim statements' impact on victims' sense of security. International Review of Victimology, 18(2), pp. 133–153.

Englebrecht, C.M., 2008. The victim impact statement: an analysis of its content, function, and meaning within the criminal justice system. Doctoral dissertation. Albany: State University of New York.

Englebrecht, C.M., 2011. The struggle for 'ownership of conflict': An exploration of victim participation and voice in the criminal justice system. Criminal Justice Review, 36(2), pp. 129–151.

Erez, E., 1991. Victim impact statements. Trends and Issues in Crime and Criminal Justice, 33, pp. 1–8.

Erez, E., 1999. Who's afraid of the big bad victim? Victim Impact Statements as victim empowerment and enhancement of justice. Criminal Law Review, pp. 545–556.

Erez, E., Kilchling, M. and Wemmers, J.-A., eds, 2011. Therapeutic jurisprudence and victim participation in criminal justice: international perspectives. Durham: Carolina Academic Press.

Erez, E. and Rogers, L., 1999. Victim impact statements and sentencing outcomes and processes. The perspectives of legal professionals. British Journal of Criminology, 39(2), pp. 216–239.

Fattah, E., 2000. Victimology: past, present and future. Criminologie, 33(1), pp. 17–46.

Folger, R., 1977. Distributive and procedural justice: combined impact of 'voice' and improvement on experienced inequity. Journal of Personality and Social Psychology, 35(2), pp. 108–119.

Goodey, J., 2005. Victims and victimology: Research, policy and practice. Harlow: Pearson Education Limited.

Graham, J., Woodfield, K., Tibble, M. and Kitchen, S., 2004. Testaments of harm: a qualitative evaluation of the Victim Personal Statements scheme. London: National Centre for Social Research.

Groenhuijsen, M.S., 2000. Victim–offender mediation: legal and procedural safeguards. Experiments and legislation in some European jurisdictions. In: The European Forum for Victim–Offender Mediation and Restorative Justice, ed., Victim–Offender Mediation in Europe. Leuven: Leuven University Press, pp. 69–83.

Hanson, R.F., Sawyer, G.K., Begle, A.M. and Hubel, G.S., 2010. The impact of crime victimization on quality of life. Journal of Traumatic Stress, 23(2), pp. 189–197.

Herman, J.L., 1997. Trauma and recovery. The aftermath of violence – from domestic abuse to political terror. New York: Basic Books.

Hollander-Blumoff, R. and Tyler, T.R., 2008. Procedural justice in negotiation: Procedural fairness, outcome acceptance, and integrative potential. Law & Social Inquiry, 33(2), pp. 473–500.

Hoyle, C., Cape, E., Morgan, R. and Sanders, A., 1998. Evaluation of the 'One Stop Shop' and victim statement pilot projects. London: Home Office.

Jacobson, M., Wahlin, L. and Andersson, T., 2012. Victim–offender mediation in Sweden: Is the victim better off? International Review of Victimology, 18(3), pp. 229–249.

Joutsen, M., 1994. Victim participation in proceedings and sentencing in Europe. International Review of Victimology, 3(1-2), pp. 57–67.

Karmen, A., 2012. Crime victims. An introduction to victimology. Belmont: Wadsworth.

Kazemi, A. and Törnblom, K., 2008. Social psychology of justice: Origins, central issues, recent developments, and future directions. Nordic Psychology, 60(3), pp. 209–234.

Kool, R., Moerings, M. and Zandbergen, W., 2002. Recht op schrift. Evaluatie projecten Schriftelijke slachtofferverklaring. Deventer: Kluwer.

Kunst, M.J.J., Rutten, S. and Knijf, E., 2013. Satisfaction with the initial police response and development of posttraumatic stress disorder symptoms in victims of domestic burglary. Journal of Traumatic Stress, 26(1), pp. 1–9.

Latimer, J., Dowden, C. and Muise, D., 2005. The effectiveness of restorative justice practices: a meta-analysis. The Prison Journal, 85(2), pp. 127–144.

Leferink, S.B.L. and Vos, K.H., 2008. Spreekrecht en schriftelijke slachtofferverklaring: recht of kans? Utrecht: Victim Support Netherlands.

Lemonne, A. and Vanfraechem, I., 2010. Evaluatie van de voorzieningen ten behoeve van slachtoffers van inbreuken: de belangrijkste bevindingen. In: I. Vanfraechem, A. Lemonne and C. Vanneste, eds, Wanneer het systeem de slachtoffers ontmoet. Eerste resultaten van een evaluatieonderzoek aangaande slachtofferbeleid. Gent: Academia Press, pp. 13–118.

Lens, K., Pemberton, A. and Groenhuijsen, M., 2010. Het spreekrecht in Nederland: een bijdrage aan het emotioneel herstel van slachtoffers? Tilburg: INTERVICT/PrismaPrint Tilburg.

Leverick, F., Chalmers, J. and Duff, P., 2007. An evaluation of the pilot victim statement schemes in Scotland. Edinburgh: Scottish Executive.

Lind, E.A., Huo, Y.J. and Tyler, T.R., 1994. And justice for all: ethnicity, gender, and preferences for dispute resolution procedures. Law and Human Behavior, 18(3), pp. 269–290.

Lind, E.A., Kanfer, R. and Earley, P.C., 1990. Voice, control, and procedural justice: Instrumental and noninstrumental concerns in fairness judgments. Journal of Personality and Social Psychology, 59(5), pp. 952–959.

Lind, E.A. and Tyler, T., 1988. The social psychology of procedural justice. New York: Plenum Press.

Lind, E.A., Tyler, T.R. and Huo, Y.J., 1997. Procedural context and culture: Variation in the antecedents of procedural justice judgments. Journal of Personality and Social Psychology, 73(4), pp. 767–780.

Lind, E.A. and Van den Bos, K., 2002. When fairness works: toward a general theory of uncertainty management. Research in Organizational Behavior, 24, pp. 181–223.

Maguire, M., 1991. The needs and rights of victims of crime. Crime and Justice, 14(1), pp. 363–433.

Malsch, M. and Carrière, R., 1999. Victims' wishes for compensation: the immaterial aspect. Journal of Criminal Justice, 27(3), pp. 239–247.

McCold, P., 2004. What is the role of community in restorative justice theory and practice? In: H. Zehr and B. Toews, eds, Critical issues in restorative justice. Monsey: Criminal Justice Press, pp. 155–172.

Messmer, H., 1997. Features of procedural fairness: communication in decision-making about diversion and victim–offender mediation. In: K.F. Röhl and S. Machura, eds, Procedural justice. Aldershot: Ashgate Darthmouth, pp. 137–160.

Mikula, G., 1993. On the experience of injustice. European Review of Social Psychology, 4(1), pp. 223–244.

Ohbuchi, K., Sugawara, I., Teshigahara, K. and Imazai, K., 2005. Procedural justice and the assessment of civil justice in Japan. Law & Society Review, 39(4), pp. 875–892.

Orth, U., 2002. Secondary victimization of crime victims by criminal proceedings. Social Justice Research, 15(4), pp. 313–325.

Poulson, B., 2003. A third voice: A review of empirical research on the psychological outcomes of restorative justice. Utah Law Review, 15(1), pp. 167–203.

Pruitt, D.G., Peirce, R.S., McGillicuddy, N.B., Welton, G.L. and Castrianno, L.M., 1993. Long-term success in mediation. Law and Human Behavior, 17(3), pp. 313–330.

Rappaport, J., 1987. Terms of empowerment/exemplars of prevention: Toward a theory for community psychology. American Journal of Community Psychology, 15(2), pp. 121–148.

Roberts, J., 2009. Listening to the crime victim: evaluating victim input at sentencing and parole. Crime and Justice, 38(1), pp. 347–412.

Roberts, J. and Edgar, A., 2006. Victim Impact Statements at sentencing: judicial experiences and perceptions. Ottawa: Department of Justice Canada.

Roberts, J. and Erez, E., 2004. Communication in sentencing: exploring the expressive function of victim impact statements. International Review of Victimology, 10(3), pp. 223–244.

Roberts, J. and Manikis, M., 2011. Victim Personal Statements at sentencing: A review of the empirical research. London: Office of the Commissioner for Victims and Witnesses of England and Wales.

Roberts, J. and Manikis, M., 2013. Victim personal statements in England and Wales: latest (and last) trends from the Witness and Victim Experience Survey. Criminology and Criminal Justice, 13(3), pp. 245–261.

Rugge, T. and Scott, T.-L., 2009. Restorative justice's impact on participants' psychological and physical health. Ottawa: Public Safety Canada.

Shapland, J., Atkinson, A., Atkinson, H., Chapman, B., Dignan, J., Howes, M., Johnstone, J., Robinson, G. and Sorsby, A., 2007. Restorative justice: the views of victims and offenders. The third report from the evaluation of three schemes. London: Ministry of Justice Research Series.

Shapland, J., Atkinson, A., Atkinson, H., Colledge, E., Dignan, J., Howes, M., Johnstone, J., Robinson, G. and Sorsby, A., 2006. Situating restorative justice within criminal justice. Theoretical Criminology, 10(4), pp. 505–532.

Shapland, J., Robinson, G. and Sorsby, A., 2011. Restorative justice in practice. London: Routledge.

Shapland, J., Willmore, J. and Duff, P., 1985. Victims in the criminal justice system. Brookfield: Avebury Publishing Co.

Sherman, L.W. and Strang, H., 2007. Restorative justice: The evidence. London: Smith Institute.

Sherman, L., Strang, H., Angel, C., Woods, D., Barnes, G., Bennett, S. and Inkpen, N., 2005. Effects of face-to-face restorative justice on victims of crime in four randomized, controlled trials. Journal of Experimental Criminology, 1(3), pp. 367–395.

Sprott, J.B. and Doob, A.N., 1997. Fear, victimization, and attitudes to sentencing, the courts, and the police. Canadian Journal of Criminology, 39(3), pp. 275–291.

Strang, H., 2002. Repair or revenge. Victims and restorative justice. Oxford: Clarendon Press.

Strang, H., 2004. Is restorative justice imposing its agenda on victims? In: H. Zehr and B. Toews, eds, Critical issues in restorative justice. Monsey: Criminal Justice Press, pp. 95–105.

Strang, H. and Sherman, L., 2003. Repairing the harm: Victims and restorative justice. Utah Law Review, 15(1), pp. 15–42.

Strang, H., Sherman, L., Angel, C.M., Woods, D.J., Bennett, S., Newbury-Birch, D. and Inkpen, N., 2006. Victim evaluations of face-to-face restorative justice conferences: A quasi-experimental analysis. Journal of Social Issues, 62(2), pp. 281–306.

Sugawara, I. and Huo, Y.J., 1994. Disputes in Japan: a cross-cultural test of the procedural justice model. Social Justice Research, 7(2), pp. 129–144.

Szmania, S.J. and Gracyalny, M.L., 2006. Addressing the court, the offender, and the community: a communication analysis of victim impact statements in a non-capital sentencing hearing. International Review of Victimology, 13(3), pp. 231–249.

Thibaut, J. and Walker, L., 1975. Procedural justice. A psychological analysis. New Jersey: Lawrence Erlbaum Associates.

Tyler, T.R., 1987. Conditions leading to value-expressive effects in judgments of procedural justice: A test of four models. Journal of Personality and Social Psychology, 52(2), pp. 333–344.

Tyler, T., 1988. What is procedural justice?: Criteria used by citizens to assess the fairness of legal procedures. Law & Society Review, 22(1), pp. 103–135.

Tyler, T.R., 1989. The psychology of procedural justice: A test of the group-value model. Journal of Personality and Social Psychology, 57(5), pp. 830–838.

Tyler, T.R., 1990. Why people obey the law. Princeton: Princeton University Press.

Tyler, T.R., 1994. Psychological models of the justice motive: Antecedents of distributive and procedural justice. Journal of Personality and Social Psychology, 67(5), pp. 850–863.

Tyler, T.R. and Lind, E.A., 1992. A relational model of authority in groups. In: M.P. Zanna, ed., Advances in Experimental Social Psychology, vol. 25. London: Academic Press, pp. 115–191.

Tyler, T. R. and Blader, S., 2000. Cooperation in groups: Procedural justice, social identity, and behavioral engagement. London: CRC Press.

Tyler, T.R. and Huo, Y.J., 2002. Trust in the law: Encouraging public cooperation with the police and courts. New York: Russell Sage Foundation.

Tyler, T.R. and Blader, S.L., 2003. The group engagement model: Procedural justice, social identity, and cooperative behavior. Personality and Social Psychology Review, 7(4), pp. 349–361.

Tyler, T.R. and Wakslak, C.J., 2004. Profiling and police legitimacy: Procedural justice, attributions of motive, and acceptance of police authority. Criminology, 42(2), pp. 253–281.

Tyler, T.R., Rasinski, K.A. and Spodick, N., 1985. Influence of voice on satisfaction with leaders: Exploring the meaning of process control. Journal of Personality and Social Psychology, 48(1), pp. 72–81.

Tyler, T., Degoey, P. and Smith, H., 1996. Understanding why the justice of group procedures matters: A test of the psychological dynamics of the group-value model. Journal of Personality and Social Psychology, 70(5), pp. 913–930.

Umbreit, M.S., 1989. Crime victims seeking fairness, not revenge: Towards restorative justice. Federal Probation, 53(3), pp. 52–57.

Umbreit, M.S., 1994a. Victim meets offender. The impact of restorative justice and mediation. Monsey: Criminal Justice Press.

Umbreit, M.S., 1994b. Victim empowerment through mediation: The impact of victim offender mediation in four cities. Perspectives, Special Issue, pp. 25–30.

Umbreit, M.S., Coates, R.B. and Vos, B., 2002. The impact of restorative justice conferencing: A review of 63 empirical studies in 5 countries. Minnesota: Center for Restorative Justice & Peacemaking.

Umbreit, M.S., Coates, R.B. and Vos, B., 2004. Victim–offender mediation: Three decades of practice and research. Conflict Resolution Quarterly, 22(1-2), pp. 279–303.

Umbreit, M.S, Vos, B., Coates, R.B. and Armour, M.P., 2006. Victims of severe violence in mediated dialogue with offender: the impact of the first multi-site study in the US International Review of Victimology, 13(1), pp. 27–48.

Van Camp, T., 2011. Is there more to restorative justice than mere compliance to procedural justice? A qualitative reflection from the victims' point of view. Doctoral dissertation. Montreal: Université de Montréal.

Van Camp, T. and Wemmers, J.-A., 2013. Victim satisfaction with restorative justice: More than simply procedural justice. International Review of Victimology. 19, pp. 117–143.

Van den Bos, K., 2009. Making sense of life: The existential self trying to deal with personal uncertainty. Psychological Inquiry: An International Journal for the Advancement of Psychological Theory, 20(4), pp. 197–217.

Van den Bos, K., Ham, J., Lind, E.A., Simonis, M., Van Essen, W.J. and Rijpkema, M., 2008. Justice and the human alarm system: The impact of exclamation points and flashing lights on the justice judgment process. Journal of Experimental Social Psychology, 44(2), pp. 201–219.

Van Hiel, A., De Cremer, D. and Stouten, J., 2008. The personality basis of justice: The five-factor model as an integrative model of personality and procedural fairness effects on cooperation. European Journal of Personality, 22(6), pp. 519–539.

Van Ness, D., 1997. Legislating for restorative justice. Paper presented at Drafting Juvenile Justice Legislation: An International Workshop, Cape Town, South Africa, 4–6 November 1997.

Vanfraechem, I. and Aertsen, I., 2010. Empirical research on restorative justice in Europe: perspectives. In: I. Vanfraechem, I. Aertsen and J. Willemsens, eds, Restorative Justice Realities. Empirical Research in a European Context. The Hague: Eleven International Publishing, pp. 267–279.

Walklate, S., 2012. Courting compassion: Victims, policy, and the question of justice. The Howard Journal, 51(2), pp. 109–121.

Wemmers, J.-A., 1995. Victims in the Dutch criminal justice system: the effects of treatment on victims' attitudes and compliance. International Review of Victimology, 3(4), pp. 323–341.

Wemmers, J.-A., 1996. Victims in the criminal justice system. Amsterdam: Kugler Publications.

Wemmers, J.-A., 1999. Victim notification and public support for the criminal justice system. International Review of Victimology, 6(3), pp. 167–178.

Wemmers, J.-A., 2002. Restorative justice. The choice between bilateral decision- making power and third party intervention. In: B. Williams, ed., Reparation and Victim-Focused Social Work. London: Jessica Kingsley Publishers, pp. 34–44.

Wemmers, J.-A., 2003. Introduction à la victimologie. Montréal: Les Presses de l'Université de Montréal.

Wemmers, J.-A., 2008. Victim Participation and Therapeutic Jurisprudence. Victims and Offenders, 3(2-3), pp. 165–191.

Wemmers, J.-A., 2009. Where do they belong? Giving victims a place in the criminal justice process. Criminal Law Forum, 20(4), pp. 395–416.

Wemmers, J.-A., 2010. The meaning of justice for victims. In: P. Knepper, S. Shoham and M. Kett, eds, International Handbook of Victimology. Florida: Taylor and Francis Group, pp. 27–43.

Wemmers, J.-A. and Canuto, M., 2002. Expériences, attentes et perceptions des victims à l'égard de la justice réparatrice: Analyse documentaire critique. Ottawa: Ministère de la Justice Canada.

Wemmers, J.-A. and Cyr, K., 2004. Victims' perspectives on restorative justice: How much involvement are victims looking for? International Review of Victimology, 11(2/3), pp. 259–274.

Wemmers, J.-A. and Cyr, K., 2005. Can mediation be therapeutic for crime victims? An evaluation of victims' experiences in mediation with young offenders. Canadian Journal of Criminology and Criminal Justice, 47(3), pp. 527–544.

Wemmers, J.-A. and Cyr, K., 2006a. Les besoins des victimes dans le système de justice criminelle. Montréal: Centre international de criminologie comparée.

Wemmers, J.-A. and Cyr, K., 2006b. What fairness means to crime victims: a social psychological perspective on victim–offender mediation. Applied Psychology in Criminal Justice, 2(2), pp. 102–128.

Wemmers, J.-A. and Raymond, E., 2011. La justice et les victimes: l'importance de l'information pour les victimes. Criminologie, 44(2), pp. 157–169.

Wemmers, J.-A., Van der Leeden, R. and Steensma, H., 1995. What is procedural justice: Criteria used by Dutch victims to assess the fairness of criminal justice procedures. Social Justice Research, 8(4), pp. 329- 350.

Wexler, D.B., 1993. Therapeutic jurisprudence and the criminal courts. William & Mary Law Review, 35(1), pp. 279–299.

Wexler, D.B. and Winick, B.J., 1991. Essays in therapeutic jurisprudence. Durham: Carolina Academic Press.

Winick, B.J., 1997. The jurisprudence of therapeutic jurisprudence. Psychology, Public Policy, and Law, 3(1), pp. 184–206

Zehr, H. and Mika, H., 1998. Fundamental concepts of restorative justice. Contemporary Justice Review, 1(1), pp. 47–55.

Chapter 15

Delivering justice to child victims of crime

Navigating the support and criminal justice systems

Ilse Vande Walle

Introduction

Each year thousands of children[1] become victims of crime and violence. Sometimes these are very severe cases; sometimes they are less so. But in all cases, we see that children are left affected by what happens to them. Research reveals that young people are at a much greater risk of becoming victims of crime than the general population, with the figures indicating that young people run twice the risk of becoming victims than the population in general (Victim Support Scotland 2011).

In the last years, a lot has changed for child victims. They have become increasingly visible in public policy. The recent EU Directive establishing minimum standards on the rights, support and protection of victims of crime of the 25 October 2012 specifically singles out child victims as a group needing specific attention 'due to their vulnerability to secondary and repeat victimization, to intimidation and to retaliation'.[2] A flurry of cross-national projects within the European arena has sought to improve both the legislative (for instance the CURE-project)[3] and the practical assistance to child victims (for instance the MUSAS-project).[4] Beyond Europe, the United Nations has also seen fit to shine the spotlight on child victims, culminating in the adoption in 2005 of the Guidelines on Justice for Child Victims and Witnesses of Crime.

However, too often many young victims are still forgotten. They are not seen by adults, and/or their reactions and needs are misunderstood and/or taken for granted. This chapter specifically focuses on the ways in which child victim's needs, desires and experiences are misjudged by adults and other caretakers. It is an abridged summary of the findings of research we conducted into child victim's experiences with the aftermath of crime in Flanders (Belgium), which culminated in the book *'Ik krijg het moeilijk uit mijn hoofd'* ('It is difficult to get it out of my head', Vande Walle and Willems 2013).

The chapter considers the consequences child victims experience in the aftermath of crime and the way in which this is similar and different from adult victims. This is followed by a similar analysis of the child victims' needs for support and assistance. Throughout the chapter representative quotes of the respondents in the interviews are provided as illustration of the phenomena discussed.

The impact of a crime on children

The consequences of victimization by crime can be viewed on a number of domains, which are often difficult to distinguish from each other (e.g. Letschert *et al.* 2010). For the purpose of this chapter, we divide the consequences into six different categories, five of which also apply to adult victims: psychological and emotional consequences, physical consequences, financial and material consequences, social and behavioural consequences, and legal consequences. To this list we add a sixth category that is more relevantly idiosyncratic to the experience of child victims, namely neuropsychological consequences.

Psychological and emotional consequences

Every child reacts differently during and after a crime. One child will panic. Another child will cry. Another child will become angry. Yet another child will freeze. And there is also a category of children who react as if nothing had happened and who just continue with whatever they were doing (Alisic 2012). Like adults, children will display stress reactions after becoming a victim of a crime (e.g. Ehlers and Clark 2000). With some children this may be more severe than with others. And in most cases these reactions will disappear by themselves. A large number of children will recover in a natural way, with the help of their own social network.

Stress reactions that children display after a criminal event can be divided into three different categories (Eland *et al.* 2000; Alisic 2011). First there are symptoms of re-experiencing the event. At unexpected moments, memories of the traumatic event will resurface. Those memories are re-experienced in conjunction with severe anxiety. This can be so severe that the experience is felt to be re-lived. It is as if the traumatic event happens all over again. Mostly, re-experiencing takes the shape of individual images appearing to the victim; namely those images that are most vivid to the child. This may not be the most frightening and/or threatening moment of the event. It might be, for example, a mother's last words to her child before she dies. Re-experiencing events in this way often happens in very quiet moments, for instance when the child is alone for a moment in a class or when he or she goes to bed; indeed, it often coincides with nightmares. Apart from these types of experience, children can also have other kinds of anxiety-filled dreams. Children may also repeatedly play out or draw what happened to them.

Second, victims display avoidance in behaviour and thoughts of reminders of the traumatic event. Patterns of re-experiencing are often interspersed with periods of attempting to avoid reminders of the trauma. In these cases the child will avoid people, things and places that remind him or her of what happened. Another way in which children avoid memories of the trauma is through a general numbing of their emotions and reactions. They may not wish to play anymore. They may be generally uninterested in things around them. Or they may lose an interest in things that formerly interested them, such as sports or music.

Finally there are symptoms of increased arousal. The child is very alert and often anxious. He or she displays a sense of imminent danger. This can result in difficulties sleeping, which in turn may cause fatigue, anger, stubbornness, difficulty concentrating and other psychosomatic problems.

These experiences are common to adult victims too. But, in the case of children and youngsters, the following reactions appear to be more prevalent than in adult victims (Alisic 2011):

- *Feelings of guilt*: Children may think that their own behaviour caused the crime to occur. These feelings of guilt may also result from magical thinking, in that the behaviour appears in reality to be unrelated to the event. For example, a child might feel that the quarrel he/she had with his/her sibling – including shouting that he/she never wanted to see the sibling again – was in some way the cause of the sibling's death shortly after the argument.
- *Regressive behaviour*: Children might retreat to an earlier phase of development. For instance they might start sucking their thumb again or wetting their bed.
- *Separation anxiety*: The experience might reduce the extent to which a victim can stand to be separated from their parents. This separation anxiety can result in tantrums and extreme distress when their parents are leaving or have left. Children might display extreme clinging behaviour.
- *Reckless behaviour*: In adolescents in particular the traumatic experience might give rise to reckless and risky behaviour, including abuse of drugs and alcohol, dangerous physical activities and sexual behaviour. For many adolescents this can be traced to their cognitions in the aftermath of crime that 'the worst has happened, and nothing can happen to me now'.

In addition to the stress reactions described above, children also experience a whole range of emotions such as anxiety and/or anger. They may feel lonely, helpless or misunderstood. Or, they may blame themselves or feel a strong emotional inclination to exact revenge. Becoming a victim of crime coincides with a loss of trust. This may be loss of trust in themselves, the direct environment, society at large and, in the most general sense, the assumption of a safe and just world (e.g. Janoff-Bulman 1992). For children and youngsters this can result in a radical change in their view and expectations of the future.

Like in the case of adults, for the majority of the children the symptoms will decrease or disappear after a few weeks. But not for all children: a minority develop a psychological disorder. The most common disorder after becoming a victim of a traumatic event is Post Traumatic Stress Disorder (PTSD). The development of PTSD is linked to risk factors and protective factors. Those factors are related to the event, the child, the family of the child and to the environment (e.g. Beer and de Roos 2012). The age and developmental level of the victim also play a role in the recovery after a trauma (Salmon and Richard 2002). There are a lot of similarities in the way in which children of different age groups recover after a crime, but there are also differences between children in different age groups, which are largely a function of the differential interaction between the traumatic complaints and the particular development tasks at various ages (Beer and de Roos 2012). Most stress-reactions of children are similar across different cultures: inter-individual differences outweigh the inter-cultural differences. But, nevertheless, there can be cultural differences in the way traumatic events are interpreted; in the way the feelings associated with trauma are put to words and play; and the interpretation of appropriate behaviour in the aftermath of trauma. Awareness of the possibility of 'lost in translation' of trauma is therefore an important element of support and assistance in cross-cultural or multi-cultural settings (Alisic 2012).

Children and youngsters, who are confronted with a sudden, traumatic loss of someone close to them, may also develop traumatic grief. In these cases, children have to deal with both trauma and loss (Cohen *et al.* 2006).

In general terms, the traumatic reactions associated with the experience of multiple traumatic events are similar to those associated with a single trauma. But other factors are also relevant. For example, abuse of power by caregivers in dependent relationships and the associated loss of trust and damage to feelings of attachment in particular, are very important (e.g. Muller *et al.* 2000). The continuous experience of stress for children exposed to chronic trauma, for example through violence in the family or in the neighbourhood, may impact the child's overall physiology. Those children may have PTSD but are often (mis)-diagnosed with Attention Deficit Hyperactivity Disorder (ADHD) as similar symptoms comprise both diagnoses (e.g. Henrichs and Bogaerts 2012). Of course, not all children diagnosed with ADHD have stress reactions or PTSD, but it is important to make the correct assessment, as the etiology of the two disorders display relevant differences. Stress-related symptoms and behaviour can be diagnosed with just a simple question asked of the child, such as: 'What is the worst thing that has happened to you in your life?' or 'Since the last time I saw you, has anything really scary or upsetting happened to you?'[5] Or if the child is too young, the parents can be asked if something happened to their child (Mannarino and Cohen 2011).

Physical consequences

Victims can suffer physical consequences that are directly caused by the crime. For example, this may happen where they have been physically assaulted or otherwise injured. In addition, in cases of sexual abuse the physical consequences might also take the form of sexually transmitted diseases and/or pregnancy (see Holmes *et al.* 1996).

The psychological stress reactions mentioned above might also manifest themselves in physical symptoms. These often include excessive tiredness (due to the heightened arousal) and psychosomatic complaints such as stomach aches, digestive problems and headaches. Many of these latter complaints are regularly misinterpreted (Alisic 2012), either as 'growing pains' or attributed to another source. This is particularly true if the child is not able to verbally express the source of his/her anguish.

Financial and material consequences

For children as well as adults, crimes can have financial and material consequences (e.g. Mulder 2013). Again, these can include direct consequences of the crime, as in the case where the child's property is damaged or stolen. In addition, it is important to realize that property that to adult eyes may be of negligible value, like a bike or a mobile phone, may be very important to the child.

In addition, this includes more indirect consequences, such as loss of income to the parent, costs associated with seeking psychological help or navigating the criminal justice system. Mostly, these sorts of indirect consequences are borne – in the first instance – by the parents but, even so, they may have knock-on effects for the child.

Social and behavioural consequences

Crime can have very significant social and behavioural consequences for child victims. Again, these can be direct – the theft of a mobile phone may mean a child cannot reach his or her friends until it is replaced. Child victims also frequently engage in avoidance behaviour, which may have a significant effect on their lifestyle. These types of changes are not always fully understood by adults. Sometimes, adults may think the changes simply reflect the development phase of the child, and not realize it is a specific response to the crime. The youngsters we interviewed mentioned the following (Vande Walle and Willems 2012):

> After a youngster of 15 was raped, she locked herself in her room, didn't go out with friends anymore, her parents thought this was normal, and just part of adolescence.

In addition the impact of crime may influence the child's parents: giving the appearance of having a 'different' parent. This can also have social consequences for the child.

> Since my little brother died, my mummy is totally different. She always was a nice mummy. And she still is, of course. A lot of friends used to come over, she used to go with us on day trips from school. She does not do

this anymore. I always try to be quiet in the house. I never talk about nice things. And, certainly, I never ask for friends to come over any more.

One of the most striking findings in the literature is that victimization increases the risk of renewed victimization (Farrell 2001). Indeed, studies have found that the best predictor of future victimization is past victimization – holding true for all types of crimes from property crimes to rape and sexual assault. In addition studies show that young people, if they do not adequately cope with the consequences of crime, may turn to crime themselves, not only when they are an adult but also as a youngster. The link between victimization and offending does exist and the link works in both directions, i.e. victimization predicts offending and vice versa. A particularly strong link has been found to exist between offending and victimization in relation to violent crime (for an overview see Lahlah 2013; see also National Center for Victims of Crime 2002; Smith 2004; Owen and Sweeting 2007).

Legal consequences

Although young people are more likely to become victims of crime than adults, they are less likely to report being victimized. The reasons for this include not knowing how to make such a report, or not trusting authority; thinking that what has happened is normal and not worth reporting; and fearing reprisals from perpetrators they know.[6]

Young people who do report being victimized are confronted with the criminal justice system. It is a well-known fact that the criminal justice process is not always sensitive to the needs of child victims (e.g. Capone 2013). This is the case even though child victims have been identified as a vulnerable group of victims in the legislation of many states, and that in recent years there has been much legislative activity concerning some categories of child victims, for example child victims of human trafficking.[7]

Two studies in Scotland (Smith 2004; Victim Support Scotland 2011) concluded that being a witness can be extremely stressful and re-traumatizing, both before and during the trial.

Neuropsychological consequences

The human brain is complex (e.g. Perry 1999, 2001; Crone 2008) and consists of tens of billions of neurons, which are connected with a large number of other neurons. What is most special about these types of cells is that they have the ability to form networks and communicate. Everything that a human being does or experiences is associated with some sort of brain activity. The brain's structure is more or less complete by the fourth month of conception. The only thing that happens after that is it expands and becomes more inter-connected. A good part of this development happens after the birth of the child, in the first years of life.

A critical concept related to memory and brain plasticity is the differential plasticity of different brain systems at different stages of development. There are specific periods when the brain is very flexible. This period is the perfect time for the brain to make connections. But if the connections are not made in this period, it is difficult for this to happen later. Accordingly either a lack of stimulation or damage at this time can have very significant negative effects. Thus, it is not surprising that traumatic events may alter brain functions. These alterations may manifest themselves as changes in emotional behaviour and emotional functioning and, in some chronic cases, may contribute to structural changes observable in the brain (Cohen *et al.* 2006).

Needs of children, victims of a crime

The consequences of victimization by crime lead to a number of different needs. In this section we discuss the main needs that we ascertained from our interviews and also discuss the bearing that these needs have on the role of parents and other caregivers in the support of child victims of crime.

Need to express themselves

Although young people are more likely to become victims of crime than adults, they are less likely to report being victimized, the main avenue through which adult victims receive support.[8] Young people give different reasons for not reporting (Victim Support Scotland 2011). They may minimize what has happened, often not recognizing it as a serious event and/or constituting a crime, instead perceiving it as something that 'just happens', as a normal part of being young. They may be too anxious about the consequences of reporting. This includes fear of the perpetrator(s); fear of getting into trouble; fear of not being believed; and fear of being stigmatized by peers. They may also mistrust adults, think that nothing will be done about their situation or be unaware of available support and/or lack of access to support.

If children do inform someone of what has happened, it is more likely to be their parents, a teacher or their peers, than the authorities. But even in this case, children can stay silent for months or years. This can be the cause of great regret.

> I think it's impossible not to tell anyone what happened. I didn't tell anyone for four months, until someone made an anonymous phone call about it to the director at school. Then I didn't want to deny it anymore. Of course I was scared of the reactions of my parents and other persons. But I was also very relieved that I could finally tell it to someone. Afterwards I think it was so stupid of me not to tell anyone for such a long time. That period, I think, was the most difficult time of my life.
>
> (Girl 15, victim of rape)

Children need to express themselves. But this expression takes different forms compared to that of adults, who normally express themselves through conversation.

Children may also adopt this method: talking to someone else about their experiences and feelings is considered a key protective factor preventing the pathway from victimization to offending (see also Owen and Sweeting 2007).

> I didn't want to talk about it. But one moment it was all too much. I always thought: if I don't talk about it, it will all turn out well. But after a while I noticed that it was not working. Hiding your feelings doesn't work. You just have to talk and express your feeling now and then.
> (Girl 17, victim of a robbery)

But for some children other modes of expression may be preferable. It can be very hard for children to talk about what has happened. Instead they might prefer to express themselves by drawing, writing or listening to music.

> It depends what kind of person you are. If the person is like me and doesn't want to talk, then you have to look for distraction. Like for me, my guitar. But if the person is social and likes to talk, than it's better to talk. But don't talk with just anyone; talk with someone who understands you.
> (Boy 17, whose mother had been murdered)

> I write letters to the offender. Letters which I will never send. Letters in which I say how sad and angry I feel.
> (Girl 11, whose little sister has been sexually abused)

Need for time and space to recover

It is important for children to have the feeling that there is time and space to recover, when they need it, and a person who will give them time and understands them.

> My mum supported me very well. She always said: 'If there is something, just come to me.' If she could do something, she would have dropped her job to support me.
> (Girl 15, victim of sexual assault)

> The teacher was there for me. She said: 'Just tell me when it's difficult, and then you can go out for a moment.' I found that a very good idea. So every time I had a moment when it was difficult, I told her.
> (Girl 11, whose sister has been sexually abused by her uncle)

Need for structure and routine

Children need safety to recover. Structure and routine can offer safety after a crime happens (Alisic 2012). For one thing, crime often has a disruptive effect on the family and the daily life of a child. The daily structure and routine often disappears or changes. Children are allowed to miss school, can sleep in bed with their parents. But children want to move forward with their lives. They do not always want to think about what happened. They need places where they can be themselves, where they – albeit temporarily – can forget what happened. That is why it is important to restore structure and routine in a child's life as soon as possible: normal bedtime, attending school, sports, hobbies and other leisure activities.

After a crime it is difficult to maintain the same rules and boundaries as before. It is easy to spoil a child and while, of course, this is not a problem in the immediate aftermath, in the longer run it should be avoided. Structure and boundaries offer important vehicles for support to children. It is often impossible to immediately erect the same structure as before, because the child may not be able to concentrate or may have difficulty sleeping. Requirements may be relaxed for a while and return to normal routines should proceed in gradual stages. This offers children the space to recover in a safe environment.

> The teacher was very nice after it happened. I was also allowed to do more than other children in the class. Sometimes, when it was difficult for me to concentrate, I looked outside and that was ok for the teacher, even though we are normally not allowed to do so. I also didn't have to do homework. In the beginning that was nice. But after a while it annoyed me because other children started to give comments on it. So I said to the teacher I also wanted to do homework, just like the others.
> (Girl 10, after the sudden death of her father)

> Every day my mum was talking about it. It was very difficult. We never talked about something else. It drove me mad. It was just too much.
> (Girl 11, whose younger sister had been sexually abused)

> I try not to treat her differently. Of course, you do that in the beginning. You just feel guilty the whole time. You can't think all the time: 'It's so difficult for my child.' You need boundaries and I also give boundaries. She also has to tidy up her room and listen. Of course it's terrible what happened, but life goes on.
> (Mother of a 10-year-old girl, victim of sexual abuse)

> The worst thing for me was I couldn't go on with my life. The day after, I wanted to get out of bed and go back to school, go back to football. But that was not possible and for me that was the most difficult thing. The moment I could play football again was a real relief. It's a way to think about something else. That you can forget for a moment what happened.
> (Boy 16, victim of stabbing)

> I play volleyball. There they know what happened, but not how I feel. And that's great for me. It's nice to have a place where life just goes on.
> (Girl 17, victim of robbery)

Need to focus on positive things

After a crime many children report that, besides all the negative feelings and consequences, there are also positive developments. It is also important to focus on these positive developments.

> When I was younger, I got bullied at school. It was also very hard for me to enjoy nice things in life. I could be very difficult. What happened to me was terrible. But I always thought: 'You want to get me down.' It took me a lot of energy, and sometimes it was very hard. But I succeeded in coping with this. It's still difficult sometimes, but I learned to enjoy nice things in life. I have more fun. And think I'm just much stronger now towards the less nice things in life.
>
> (Girl 15, victim of rape)

> Before it happened we, my parents and my sister, didn't do that much together. For example, we never had dinner together. First I ate, then my sister, then my mum and dad. But since it happened we always have dinner together. We sit together and eat together, and we talk more to each other. It's just much cosier now.
>
> (Boy 13, victim of violence)

In the academic literature, the term Post Traumatic Growth (PTG) is used. PTG is the experience of positive change that occurs as a result of the struggle with highly challenging life crises (Alisic 2011). The change may take place in three domains (Salter and Stallard 2004; Tedeschi and Calhoun 2004; Alisic 2011):

- *Perception of self*: e.g. considering oneself no longer as a victim, but as a survivor.
- *Interpersonal relationships*: e.g. becoming closer to relatives and friends.
- *Philosophy of life*: e.g. a change of life priorities, an appreciation of life generally, and an appreciation of the smaller things in life, and of spiritual development.

Until recently it was questioned if children experienced PTG. But studies of young victims of a traffic crash (Salter and Stallard 2004), young survivors of a hurricane and an epidemiological study of primary schoolchildren in the Netherlands (Alisic 2011) showed that children, like adults, may display PTG after becoming the victim of a traumatic event. The studies also revealed that PTG can co-exist with PTSD. PTSD does not prevent children from positive experiences post-event.

Children need positive reinforcement. Giving them compliments for signs of progress helps them through the often difficult steps that the recovery process entails. Understanding the challenges in this process and showing approval of the child's access in overcoming the obstacles to recovery are important protective strategies.

People don't have to say: 'Oh, it's so terrible.' It's better that they react in a positive way. Like saying: 'Wow, you are doing well, I see an improvement!' and showing that there are also nice things in life.

(Girl 11, after the sudden death of her father)

Need for awareness of the child's recovery process

Recovering from the consequences of crime can be a lengthy and gradual process. Sometimes a child may feel fully recovered at one point and then subsequently feel worse, for reasons that can be linked or unrelated to the event.

It is important to give children time and space to come to terms with the event and not to interfere with the natural healing process of a child. Most victims, including child victims, will recover by themselves, with the help of their own social network. But, at the same time, it is important to keep a watchful eye on signals of problems in the healing process. These might signal the development of PTSD (Sijbrandij 2009).

I thought I was OK. For a long time I didn't think of the event anymore. But when I heard he would be released from prison, it started again. The sleepless nights, the anxiety. I wonder how long it will take now to recover from it.

(Girl 17, victim of robbery)

It's every time we get back from holiday. Then our 10-year-old daughter has a very difficult time again. For a week she sleeps very badly, is very anxious, doesn't want to do anything on her own anymore. The first time I was very surprised when I saw it. Now, we are prepared. We know now after every holiday, there are some difficult days ahead.

(Mother of daughter and son of 8, victims of a robbery)

As mentioned above, the fact that children are still developing means that long-lasting post-traumatic complaints can have additional consequences on emotional, cognitive and social levels (Cohen *et al.* 2006). When symptoms do not decrease after a few weeks or when symptoms are very severe, it is very important to keep a close eye on the child.

It is even recommended to screen for PTSD and other possible disorders, in order to know when to offer appropriate support or even therapy. In recent years, some self-report instruments have been developed. The most widely used self-report instruments in research and clinical settings are the Children's Impact of Event Instrument, the Child Post Traumatic Stress Reaction Index and the Child PTSD Symptom Scale (see National Institute for Clinical Excellence 2005). Several of these instruments have been translated into different languages. For children who are too young to complete the self-report instruments, parent-report versions of the questionnaires can be used instead. As well as these, there is also the Paediatric Emotional Distress Scale (PEDS) instrument (see Saylor *et al.* 1999).

The recommended therapies for treatment of PTSD are the Trauma Focused Cognitive Behaviour Therapy (TF-CBT) and Eye Movement Desensitization and Reprocessing (EMDR) (e.g. NICE 2005; Cohen *et al.* 2006). These two therapies are equally effective and can be used for children and youngsters. When children suffer from traumatic grief it is important to provide them with combined trauma and grief focused treatment so that they will not have long-lasting PTSD symptoms and can at last move forward in beginning to resolve the typical tasks of grieving (Cohen *et al.* 2006). Apart from these main treatments, many others exist. Many of them are based on trauma focused cognitive behaviour therapy, and apart from the children, the parents will also be involved. Research suggests that in therapy focus has to lie on what happened, methods the child can use to handle stress reactions and support of the parents (Alisic 2012).

Need to talk to someone supportive

Even when children recover fully from crime, they mention that talking to someone supportive is very important. Of the young people who answered the questionnaires for the 'Hoodie or Goodie?' report, 70 per cent thought one-to-one support with a trained adult would be helpful to them (Owen and Sweeting 2007). For child victims it is important to talk to someone who is impartial and who has a non-authoritarian approach; who can give practical advice and information based on the needs of the child; who does not pressure the child but allows them to follow their own tempo to cope with what happened; who discusses with them what will be told to their parents; and who can refer to other support if necessary. The children and youngsters we interviewed ourselves also focused on the importance of 'their' Victim Support worker.

> When I went to Victim Support, that was really my hour. An hour for myself, where I could talk about the things that were difficult for me with someone who really understood me.
>
> (Girl 10, victim of sexual abuse)

Need for assistance in navigating the criminal justice procedure

The criminal justice process following victimization involves parents to a larger degree than children. But even then, children want to know what is happening and want to be involved. They want to know what the police will do after they have heard them. They have questions about the offender. They want to know whether they will have to go to court and what consequences this can have. For both parents and children, this is a new world, one for which they cannot rely on prior experience. Information and support are very important to familiarize them with the criminal justice process. Children have to know what their rights are and they need support, from the moment they go to the police until even after the trial.

Owen and Sweeting (2007) show that a positive attitude towards the police decreases the chances of offending after victimization. Adequate support from the police aids children's recovery. It offers them trust in the police, the justice system and in themselves. Unfortunately the first experience with the police is not always positive. This causes increased feelings of guilt, self-blame and an increased distrust towards the whole justice system. Often children regret reporting the crime. Our interviews with children and youngsters also revealed the significance of adequate support from the police.

> After a few months I told my mother what happened. She accompanied me to the police. The policewoman explained to me that what he did was a crime. She explained it was not my fault. A man of 38 is not allowed to do something like that with a 14-year-old girl. The night after we went to the police was the first night I slept well for months.
> (Girl 14, victim of rape)

> After my mobile was stolen, I went to the police. They said they couldn't do that much. When I said it's possible to trace a mobile via the satellite, they answered that this is something they would think of if I had been murdered. I regret so much I went to the police. I felt so stupid. My friend already told me the police wouldn't do anything and that I should better buy a knife.
> (Boy 13, victim of violent theft)

> On the way home from school, suddenly, a man pulled me from my bike. He was old, I was quicker and could escape. I immediately went to the police with my mother. But they just didn't believe me. I said I could describe him in detail but they were not interested. I have no idea what will happen now.
> (Girl 15, victim of sexual assault)

Assistance throughout the criminal justice process is also important. The questions of children and also their rights in the criminal justice procedure can change. Someone has to be there to keep an eye on this. An example of a programme which intends to achieve these goals is the Case Manager Project of Victim Support the Netherlands (Van Wijk *et al.* 2012). Key notions involve maintaining contact with victims of severe crimes and relatives of murder over a very long period, if possible by the same person, to inform them of any developments in the criminal process.

> When I was 7, I read in the newspaper my father was murdered. My mother told me it was true but that was the last and only time we talked about what happened. This is now 10 years ago. After that we never talked about it any more. For a long time I didn't think of it. But since about a year ago I really want to know. A few months ago I looked up on the internet some information about the case. I found something and I also found the names of the persons who murdered my father. I know they are out of prison, I looked up and found

their addresses. I thought of paying them a visit and asking them what happened, as my mum will never tell.

(Boy 17, whose father was murdered)

Importance of support from parents and other important caregivers

Long-term support from the direct environment of the child often plays a very important role after children have been victims of crime. This may be the most important factor in the recovery of a child (Alisic 2011). When children are well supported by their parents and other significant figures the chance decreases that they develop long-lasting PTSD symptoms. In addition, research reveals that sufficient support from the direct environment decreases the risk of offending behaviour on the part of victims (Owen and Sweeting 2007).

Importance of support from the parents

The reaction of the child's parents shortly after the event is a key factor. The extent to which the parents are able to support their child is a main determinant. The crime not only has an impact on the child, but also on other members of the family, both parents and siblings.

Parents' own problems may negatively impact their ability to offer support. This applies to pre-existing problems (relationship distress, financial difficulties) as well as the impact of the crime itself, particularly when they have developed severe traumatic stress symptoms as a consequence. And, even in cases where the parents did not directly experience the event, they may still feel powerless and anxious and can, as a result, suffer similar symptoms of traumatic stress as their child (e.g. Eland *et al.* 2000).

Young children are strongly affected by the reactions of their parents. When the parents cope well, young children usually do so as well. But if the parents are severely affected, young children are likely to follow this trajectory too. Scheeringa and Zeanah (2001) developed a model for 'Relational PTSD'. They describe three different types of parental responses which influence children's stress symptoms:

- *The withdrawn/unresponsive/unavailable parent*: Parents can be so involved with coping with their own trauma and reactions that this prevents them from attending to their children's needs;
- *The overprotective/constricting parent*: Parents want to protect their children. In many cases after a traumatic event, when parents have stress reactions themselves, they may also become over-protective, wanting to shield their offspring from the horrors they are experiencing themselves;
- *The frightening/endangering/re-enacting parent*: Parents may repetitively pressure the child to reiterate the details of the event: this might be due to

their own anxiety and need to know the facts of what happened, or because they believe that is to the benefit of the children to speak and emote about their experiences This constant reliving of the traumatic sequence of events may hamper the child's recovery.

A clear example of overprotection was visible in our interviews:

> A 17-year-old boy, whose father had been murdered 10 years ago, still doesn't know what happened. Even now his mother, other relatives and family think the truth would hurt him, that it's better to shelter him from the facts.

Not only with young children, but also in the cases of older children and adolescents, a clear link exists between the reactions of the parents and development of PTSD symptoms in the child. For instance a study of Cambodian children and parents who were refugees from the Khmer Rouge regime revealed the link between parents and children's PTSD. When parents did not meet the criteria for full-blown PTSD 12.9 per cent of their adolescent children did; one parent with PTSD increased this percentage to 21 per cent, while both parents with PTSD meant that 41.2 per cent of adolescent children had PTSD (Sack *et al.* 1995).

Moreover, research in the Netherlands found that responsive parenting after trauma was a central element in the recovery of children. Key issues in this regard are parents' attempts to follow their child's own pace of recovery while providing structure and guidance when necessary, and/or seeking help to do this. In addition, the parents felt that their capacity to be responsive was influenced by their own level of distress, in line with the results discussed above (Alisic 2011).

In our interviews with children and youngsters, we asked them who their most important supporting figure was. In almost all cases they answered 'my parents'. Significantly, the parents of adolescents we interviewed often did not recognize their importance for their children. The reason for this discrepancy may be that youngsters find their parents very important but that this does not imply that it translates into a need to talk to them extensively about the youngster's experience. Taking an example from adolescence, a girl of fifteen, a victim of rape, says:

> My parents support me the most. My mother is just there. She does not ask anything. My father protects me and arranges a lot of practical things. I like it more if they do not ask me about the event. Why? I don't know. I think I just don't want to burden them with it. I only talk with my friends. Yes, they may ask how I am. That's not a problem.

The mother of the same girl says:

> I don't think I support my daughter well. I do not think I am very important to her in the coping process. To begin with I asked how she was, but she never answered. Now I don't ask anymore. I think her friends are most important for her.

Importance of school

The interviewed children report that besides their parents, teachers and other representatives of schools are also important in helping them cope with their experience. School offers structure and routine to children. And after a crime, children will often rely on their teacher, tell the teacher their story and are often very happy that in turn they are given space in school to cope with what happened. Teachers are also often the first to notice the child's problems.

> The teacher was the first one, apart from the people in my family, to whom I told what happened. She thought it was very brave I told it to her. She even said at the parents evening that it was very brave that I told her everything, including the things I found most difficult.
> (Girl 11, whose little sister has been sexually abused)

> It was great from the school, they told me I didn't have to do my exams. If I could have done them, of course I would have finished them, but it was just impossible. I couldn't concentrate. And also going home after an exam would have been too difficult, because that was the moment of the burglary.
> (Girl 17, victim of a violent burglary)

Supporting child victims is not always easy for teachers. A lot of teachers struggle with this issue. Teachers have to strike a balance between the needs of the child who has been the victim of a crime or another traumatic event, the needs of other children in the class and their own needs, including their needs to acquire skills and knowledge to cope with a child after such an event (Alisic 2011). They often question where their role ends and where the role of a social worker and a psychologist starts. When schools and teachers explicitly consider post-trauma support (e.g. signalling serious coping problems and informing children about available mental health care facilities) to be part of their duty, this probably positively influences a child's well-being.

Importance of friends and other peers

In general, peers are very important for children and youngsters and this is particularly true following criminal victimization. The way in which peers feature in a child's life varies with age. Young children have an egocentric view of friendships. Friends are there to play with or have fun with. When children are involved in a crime or another traumatic event, they will often involve their friends in replaying the event. For older children and adolescents, friendships are more mutual relationships and are based on trust. Youngsters look to each other for the recognition and support that is so important for them (Crone 2008). When youngsters are confronted with a crime or a sudden death, they will talk with each other more than with their parents. But sometimes there can be problems. Sometimes youngsters are disappointed in the reactions of friends as they may be totally different to what they expected. This can make them feel misunderstood and lonely. That is why it can be important for youngsters to talk to peers who have had similar experiences. Friends may also exert a negative influence on youngsters (Owen and Sweeting 2007).

> I tell most to my friends. I also have a diary. Only my friends can read it.
> (Girl 15, victim of rape)

> I know I have a very hard time. But I don't need help. My friends help me. And that's enough for me.
> (Boy 17, after his father was killed)

> My friend told me going to the police would not make any difference. He advised me to buy a knife. That this would be better.
> (Boy 13, victim of a robbery)

> I know my friends are there for me, but they don't really understand me. In the beginning I could tell them a lot and they really listened. But now they go on with their lives and with their own things. Which are not so interesting for me any more, since what happened. Yes, I try to be with them and involved with the things they are doing. But it's just not my thing any more. Sometimes I'm very, very lonely. That's why I think it's really good to talk and mail with someone who has been through the same as me. That person would really understand.
> (Girl 14, victim of rape)

Importance of cuddly toys and animals

What also stood out in the interviews we conducted with children and youngsters was the importance of pets for adolescents. Pets are often one of the most important support figures. On the one hand they offer structure: they need to be cared for, they need to be taken for a walk, etc. And, on the other hand, adolescents have the feeling they are always available to listen and offer support.

> She listens, that's what I think. Of course I'm not sure of it. When I cry she is very quiet and normally she's a very active dog, like her mistress I think. If I say: 'Come on, it's not the moment', then she looks at me, with her sad eyes. She makes me so happy. I don't know, if I didn't have her, how I would be now, if I still would be here. We go out for a walk every day. Next to our house is a grass field. There she can run, I really enjoy that. I run with her and play with her. That really helped me. The man who did this to me knows my dog is very important to me. I'm very afraid that when he gets out of prison

> he will do something to her. That's why I go to the dog training school with her; to teach her that she can't take anything from a stranger.
>
> (Girl 15, victim of rape)

> I like it most to be with my animals. I have rabbits, a cat and a dog. When I didn't feel well, I just wanted to be with them. Because animals are so important, I'm studying now to become an animal keeper.
>
> (Girl 17, victim of a robbery)

Young children, on the other hand focus on the importance of cuddly toys (see also Alisic 2011).

> If another child should also have thieves with guns in his house, the day after I would lend him all my cuddly toys for the night. I know they would make him feel better!
>
> (Boy 6, victim of burglary)

How should adults support children?

For a lot of adults, being confronted with child victims is a very difficult issue. Children's reactions vary widely and so do their needs. Just like a lot of child-victims are resilient, a lot of adults are good support givers. Basing support on the needs of a child is essential (Alisic 2011). On the basis of our research we find the following three key principles: children need to be taken seriously; children do not what to be pressured; and children need encouragement.

Children need to be taken seriously

Adults have an inclination to want to protect children and youngsters from what happened. But when children become a victim of a crime, their direct or indirect involvement means that this is not possible, despite what adults may wish. Children also want to be involved. They want to know what is happening and to be consulted in matters that have direct bearing on their situation. They have a real earnest need for information and consultation.

Information must be given at the level appropriate to the child and in a language the child understands. The first thing is to give the child basic information. It is not necessary to give the child too many details. After that, it is important to answer the child's questions, which can sometimes be very confronting and it is not always easy for adults to give clear answers or explanations to a child.

> I read in the newspaper my father was murdered. Everyone told me it was an accident. I'm very angry about this.
>
> (Boy 7, after his father was killed)

Apart from information about the facts, psycho-education – information and education about possible reactions and experiences that the child may have as a consequence of their victimization (see de Eland *et al.* 2000) – can be important, both for the child and for the adult. But it is very important that psycho-education is given upon request, when a need to know more about psychological consequences is apparent and that it is offered with specific reference to the person's questions. General psycho-education is not beneficial and may even increase the victim's fear and anxiety.

> I thought everything was ok with my daughter, until someone told me what the problems of a victim can be. From that moment on, I have prepared myself, as I know the problems still have to come.
> (Mother of a 10 year old child, victim of a robbery)

Children need to be consulted if steps are taken that might impact them. They are the best source to ascertain their needs, and are able to express these.

> The headmaster told the teachers what happened. But every time he came to me to let me know to whom he was going to tell and he asked me first if it was OK for me.
> (Girl 17, victim of a robbery)

> I didn't go to court myself. My parents went, also a friend and my brother and sister have been. They gave me the choice. I didn't have the need to go and see the offenders. I would have found that too difficult
> (Boy 16, victim of stabbing)

Children do not want to be pressured

It's important to follow the child's pace of recovery. Sometimes children are focused on what happened and want to discuss it, but at other times they prefer to attend to other things in their lives and do not want to think or talk about the event.

> It's nice that my parents ask me how I feel. But I prefer they don't ask it too often. When they ask it too much, it's not nice any more. In the beginning it was sometimes too often. But then I just didn't answer any more and I think they noticed I didn't want to talk about it. Sometimes you just need peace.
> (Boy 13, victim of a robbery)

Children need encouragement

After a crime, children often become hesitant. Activities that they performed without any doubt or anxiety before the crime become large obstacles which they find themselves unable to overcome. Adults can play a significant role in helping children overcome their new anxieties. Encouraging children to rediscover their confidence in their own abilities will often require a step-by-step gradual approach.[9]

> Entering our house for the first time was most difficult. My mother supported me very well. She really pushed me inside the house. If she hadn't done that I think I would have stayed in front of the door for a few hours, hesitating to go in. Luckily my mother pushed me. It's good to get a boost but by someone you love and trust.
> (Girl 17, victim of a violent burglary)

Final remarks

Much has changed for the better for young victims of crime in recent years. There can be no doubt about this. But even so, they are still a vulnerable group. This vulnerability concerns first the added impact of victimization for child victims, in the sense of its possible interference with the child's development. In this chapter we have highlighted neuropsychological consequences, but also noted that the insufficient attention to child victims' recovery will in turn lead to them to become offenders themselves.

The vulnerability of child victims also expresses itself in their invisibility, even though their risk of victimization is (much) larger than that of adults. They rarely report victimization to the authorities and often the adult world will remain oblivious of the crimes that befall children and adolescents.

Finally both invisible and visible child victims are often misunderstood. One of the reasons for their decreased visibility is the fact that their reactions can be attributed to other causes, but even if it is apparent that a child has suffered crime, more care is needed to understand their experiences. Parents and other caregivers are prone to apply incorrect heuristics to the situation of victims of crime, sometimes as a consequence of their own anxiety and trauma. An important avenue therefore for improving the plight of child victims of crimes is to attempt to gain a better understanding of what they are going through.

Notes

1 'Children' here includes young children, primary school children and adolescents.
2 See Directive 2012/29/EU of the European Parliament and the Council of 25 October 2012, establishing minimum standards on the rights, protection and support of victims of crime, article 22, section 4 (see also Wheldon and Ezendam, this volume).
3 See www.brottsoffermyndigheten.se/Filer/B%C3%B6cker/Child%20victims%20in%20the%20Union,%20CURE.pdf [Accessed 15 July 2013].
4 See www.apav.pt/musas/musas2.html [Accessed 15 July 2013].
5 Carrion V. G., www.1–800-therapist.com/news-article/mental-health-issues-common-victims-childhood-trauma [Accessed 15 July 2013].
6 HM Government, 2008. Youth Crime action plan. Good Practice for Supporting Young Victims of Crime.

7 The Crime Victim Compensation and Support Authority Sweden, 2010. Child Victims in the Union-Rights and Empowerment (CURE). A Report of the CURE project 2009–2010.
8 HM Government, 2008 Youth Crime action plan. Good Practice for Supporting Young Victims of Crime.
9 An analogy may be drawn here to the graduated process of most cognitive therapies in the aftermath of victimization and trauma, e.g. Foa and Rothbaum (1998).

Bibliography

Alisic, E., 2011. Children and trauma. A broad exposure and recovery. PhD thesis. Utrecht: University of Utrecht.
Alisic, E., 2012. Kinderen ondersteunen na trauma. The Hague: Boom.
Beer, R. and de Roos, C., 2012. Diagnostiek van getraumatiseerde kinderen en adolescenten. In: E. Vermetten, R.J. Kleber and O. van der Hart,eds, Handboek posttraumatische stress stoornissen. Utrecht: the Netherlands. Tijdstroom, pp. 365–382.
Capone, F., 2013. Is anybody playing? The right to reparation for child victims of armed conflict. PhD thesis. Tilburg: Tilburg University.
Cohen J.A., Mannarino A.P. and Deblinger E., 2006.Treating trauma and grief in children and adolescents. New York: The Guildford Press.
Crone, E., 2008. Het puberende Brein. Over de ontwikkeling van de hersenen in de unieke periode van de adolescentie. Amsterdam: Bert Bakker.
de Eland, J., De Roos, C. and Kleber, R.J., 2000. Kind en trauma. Een opvangprogramma. The Hague: Swets and Zeitlinger Publishers.
Ehlers, A. and Clark, D.M., 2000. A cognitive model of posttraumatic stress disorder. Behavior Research and Therapy, 38, pp. 319–345.
Farrell, G., 2001. Repeat victimisation. Monsey: Criminal Justice Press.
Foa, E.B. and Rothbaum, B.O., 1998. Treating the trauma of rape: Cognitive-behavioral therapy for PTSD. New York: Guildford.
Henrichs, J. and Bogaerts, S., 2012. Correlates of posttraumatic stress disorder in forensic psychiatric outpatients in the Netherlands. Journal of Traumatic Stress, 25(3), pp. 315–322.
Holmes, M.M. Resnick, H.S., Kilpatrick, D.G. and Best, C.L., 1996. Rape-related pregnancy: Estimates and descriptive characteristics from a national sample of women. American Journal of Obstetrics and Gynaecology, 175(2), pp. 320–324.
Janoff-Bulman, R. (1992). Shattered assumptions. New York: Free Press.
Lahlah, A., 2013. Invisible victims? Ethnic differences in the risk of juvenile (violent) offending of Dutch and Moroccan-Dutch adolescent boys. Ridderkerk: Ridderprint.
Letschert, R.M., Staiger, I. and Pemberton, A., eds, 2010. Assisting victims of terrorism. Towards a European standard of justice. Dordrecht: Springer.
Mannarino, A.P. and Cohen, J.A., 2011. Traumatic loss in children and adolescents. Journal of Child and Adolescent Trauma, 4(1), pp. 22–33.
Mulder, J.D.W.E., 2013. Compensation: the victims' perspective. PhD thesis. Tilburg University. Nijmegen: Wolf Publishing.
Muller, R.T., Sicoli, L.A. and Lemieux, K.E., 2000. Relationship between attachment style and posttraumatic stress symptomatology among adults who report the experience of childhood abuse. Journal of Traumatic Stress, 13(2), pp. 321–332.

National Institute for Clinical Excellence, 2005. Post traumatic stress disorder; the management of PTSD in adults and children in primary and secondary care. Leicester: Gaskell and the British Psychological Society.

Owen, R. and Sweeting, A., 2007. Hoodie and Goodie. The link between violent victimization and offending in young people. London: Victim Support.

Perry, B.D., 1999. Memories of fear: How the brain stores and retrieves physiologic states, feelings, behaviors and thoughts from traumatic events. The Child Trauma Academy. Available at: www.ChildTrauma.org [Accessed 15 September 2013].

Perry, B.D., 2001. The neurodevelopmental impact of violence in childhood. In: D. Schetky and E. Benedek, eds, Textbook of child and adolescent forensic psychiatry. Washington: American Psychiatric Press, pp. 221–238.

Sack, W.H., Clarke, G. and Seeley, J., 1995. Posttraumatic stress disorder across two generations of Cambodian refugees. Journal of the American Academy of Child and Adolescent Psychiatry, 34, pp. 1160–1166.

Salmon, K. and Richard, A.B., 2002. Posttraumatic stress disorder in children. The influence of developmental factors. Clinical Psychology Review, 22, pp. 163–188.

Salter, E. and Stallard, P., 2004. Posttraumatic growth in child survivors of a road traffic accident. Journal of Traumatic Stress, 17(4), pp. 335–340.

Saylor, C.F., Swenson, C., Reynolds S. and Taylor, M., 1999. The Pediatric Emotional Distress Scale: A brief screening measure for young children exposed to traumatic events. Journal of Clinical Child Psychology, 28(1), pp. 70–81.

Scheeringa, M.S. and Zeanah, C.H., 2001. A relational perspective on PTSD in early childhood. Journal of Traumatic Stress. 14(4), pp. 799–815.

Sijbrandij, M., 2009. To debrief or not to debrief. Het effect van opvang van slachtoffers van schokkende gebeurtenissen. Goed recht, 25 jaar Slachtofferhulp Nederland.

Smith, D., 2004. The link between victimization and offending. Edinburgh: The University of Edinburgh, Centre for Law and Society.

Tedeschi, R.G. and Calhoun, L.G., 2004. Posttraumatic growth: Conceptual foundation and empirical evidence. Psychological Inquiry, 15(1), pp. 1–18.

The National Centre for Victims of Crime. 2002. Our vulnerable teenagers. Their victimization, its consequences, and direction for prevention and intervention. Washington DC: NCVC.

Vande Walle, I. and Willems, L., 2013. 'Ik krijg het niet uit mijn hoofd'. Getuigenissen van kinderen en jongeren na een misdrijf of een plotseling overlijden. Antwerp: Witsand.

Van Wijk, A., Van Leiden, I. and Ferwerda, H., 2012. Case management levensdelicten. Arnhem: Beke Advies.

Victim Support Scotland, 2011. Young victims of crime project. Scoping a national service model for supporting young victims of crime in Scotland.

Chapter 16

ETA terrorism victims' experience with restorative encounters in Spain

Gema Varona

Introduction

The text for this chapter draws on my previous work on restorative justice with respect to terrorist victimization in Spain committed by ETA.[1] I intend to extend the conclusions reached with an eye to translation to other contexts. To this end a critical victimological approach is adopted (Walklate 1990). In this view victims are citizens first, something the terrorist attack has denied.[2] Their identity is not shaped fully by their victimization. Professionals working with victims and/or victims issues should avoid – consciously or unconsciously – 'colonizing' their identity by the victimization or de-victimization process. Victimization and de-victimization processes cannot be understood solely as a *result*, but as plural, complex and multi-dimensional dynamics (Larizgoitia *et al.* 2009), in which the factor of time is particularly important. In addition, by considering the interrelation between individual, interpersonal and structural dimensions of vulnerability and protection, this opens up the possibility to study the fact of unequal distribution of recovery and restoration elements in society.

I follow Wilkinson and Pickett (2011, p. 15), when they argue that: 'What holds them all in place, like the mortar between bricks, and gives each society its particular character, is the subjective collective beliefs and behaviour of the people in that society.' Within that framework I have opted for a qualitative study of different victimization narratives, case studies and media discourses reflecting personal, political and social interests or concerns. Sources used in previous studies will be reinterpreted.[3]

The chapter is structured as follows. I will first introduce the history of restorative encounters with former ETA-terrorists in Spain. Then I will consider the main victims' associations' criticism of these encounters, which has also been voiced by many offenders. I will try to understand this criticism in relation to the conceptions of justice of these stakeholders and how this is in turn related to the wider context. Finally, before drawing conclusions, I will systematize relevant points learnt from the social, political and scientific debate in order to consider restorative factors in processes of de-victimization, including resilience, recovery and future reconciliation.

A brief history of restorative encounters with former ETA Terrorists

On 20 October 2011, after fifty years of activity, the terrorist organization ETA declared a definitive cease-fire demanding a 'fair and democratic solution to the decades-old conflict'.[4] According to the Victims of Terrorism Foundation, ETA has killed 829 people, including military staff, policemen, politicians, journalists, professors, judges, prosecutors, businessmen and ordinary people, some of them children.[5] Analysis of ETA activity by year (Table 16.1a) and by status, gender and location of victimization (Table 16.1b) is shown below.

ETA was founded at the end of Franco's dictatorship. Most fatalities and casualties occurred in the subsequent democratic period, when the Basque Country gained considerable autonomy within Spain and legitimate expectations of independence through peaceful means (de la Cuesta and Varona 2012).[6] ETA has caused much physical and emotional harm over a protracted period of time, inside and outside the Basque Country. More research is needed to evaluate the direct, indirect and diffuse victimization that took place. This should include the impact and interactions of personal, material and political harms experienced by different generations in

Table 16.1 (a) Numbers of ETA fatal victims over time (total 829 fatalities)

Year	Fatalities	Year	Fatalities	Year	Fatalities	Year	Fatalities
1968	2	1979	76	1990	25	2001	15
1969	1	1980	92	1991	46	2002	5
1970	0	1981	30	1992	26	2003	3
1971	0	1982	37	1993	14	2004	0
1972	1	1983	32	1994	12	2005	0
1973	6	1984	32	1995	15	2006	2
1974	19	1985	37	1996	5	2007	2
1975	16	1986	43	1997	13	2008	4
1976	17	1987	52	1998	6	2009	3
1977	10	1988	21	1999	0	2010	1
1978	66	1989	19	2000	23		

Source: Interior Ministry and Terrorism Victims' Foundation

Table 16.1 (b) ETA fatalities by status, gender and location of victimization[a]

Status	No.
Civilians (including 4 persons belonging to the penitentiary staff, 2 prosecutors, 1 judge, 4 magistrates and 3 journalists)	343 (including 23 minors)
Members of security forces	486
of whom:	
Civil Guard	203
National Police	146
Spanish Army	98
Local Police	24
Basque Autonomous Police	13
Catalonian Autonomous Police	1
French National Gendarmerie	1

TOTAL: 829 people killed (59 were women; 551 were killed in the Basque Country)

Source: Interior Ministry, www.interior.gob.es/prensa-3/balances-e-informes-21/ultimas-victimas-mortales-de-eta-cuadros-estadisticos-630?locale=es.

Note

a For a study with more variables, see Alonso et al. (2010, pp. 1210–1232). Cf. the suffering map and the memory map in the official web of the Victims of Terrorism Office of the Basque Government (www.interior.ejgv.euskadi.net/o11aWar/o11aIndex3.jsp?pageId=-617760275&ID_NAVEGACION=0). See also the special report on public policies towards victims of terrorism by the Basque Ombudsman (www.ararteko.net/RecursosWeb/DOCUMENTOS/1/1_1684_3.pdf).

diverse ways and different contexts. A particular characteristic of ETA actions was the constant atmosphere of threat and coercion.[7]

According to data of the Spanish Ministry of the Interior, at the end of 2012 there were only about fifty active ETA terrorists, but hundreds more have avoided capture, arrest and prosecution. Around 500 perpetrators of ETA crimes are currently incarcerated in Spanish prisons and one hundred in French prisons.[8] To large segments of the Basque population, they are considered *political prisoners* – as victims themselves, of the Spanish and French states, of police abuse of power and of counter-terrorism.

Restorative encounters between former ETA terrorists and their victims started in 2011. The initiative came from repentant ex-terrorists of the so called *via Nanclares*.[9] In a literature workshop within prison, they expressed the wish to meet their direct or indirect victims to ask for forgiveness.[10] The project was based on cooperation between Penitentiary Institutions of the Spanish interior ministry and the Office for Terrorism Victims of the Basque government. Both agencies were controlled by the socialist party at that time. In November 2011, the right wing *Partido Popular* won the general election and the restorative project was put on hold for several months.

On 30 April 2012, the interior ministry presented its own rehabilitation programme for prisoners sentenced for terrorism or organized crime. This programme dedicates four paragraphs to so-called *encounters to repair victims*.[11] The programme deals not only with restorative encounters, but also with broader issues. It tries to provide a match between the location of the offenders' prison and their former place of residence.[12] In order to do so the offender must publicly reject violence and severe connections to ETA. According to the current programme, the aim of 'encounters with victims to repair victims' is to facilitate a procedure in which victims – who wish to – may offer forgiveness to those convicted persons who are willing to ask for it.[13] A request for forgiveness from the victims – which does not imply that they will be forgiven – is required from inmates sentenced for terrorism or organized crime in order for them to be placed in so-called 'third degree' prisons, as the last stage of prison with a more open regime (art. 72. 6 of the Organic General Penitentiary Act) and in order to obtain a favourable final prognosis report before conditional release (art. 90 of the Penal Code). Thus, meetings are designed to satisfy this legal requirement.

Victims – those directly harmed or their relatives – should request the encounter. Correspondingly, prisoners asking for forgiveness should be the direct offenders or co-offenders of the crime in question. The brief text of the interior ministry programme also states that encounters should be sufficiently prepared to avoid causing secondary victimization. In addition, victimological reparation should be considered an essential part of the offender's rehabilitation. It is emphasized that, among victimization reparation mechanisms, those addressing material and moral harms are important. Prison treatment team members should evaluate participants' progress and document observations and conclusions for inclusion in the offender's file.

Due to a lack of consensus on policy towards terrorism, the encounters were conducted discreetly. No official evaluation has been made public, although the promoters collaborated with several penal law professors interested in restorative justice. By September 2011, organizers decided to inform the public of the existence of these encounters. Written and video interviews with some participating victims, offenders and coordinators were provided to media outlets.[14]

By this time, eleven encounters had taken place.[15] All encounters were conducted face to face, except one held by mail. The purpose of the encounters was to aid victims' recovery and victimizers' rehabilitation through the possibilities of forgiveness in a wide sense.[16] Often victims were relatives of a homicide victim and informed the offenders they could not forgive them in strict terms: the one who could do so had passed away. Nevertheless, most people participating in these encounters were positive about the offenders' expressions of remorse and their will to try to alleviate an irreparable harm.

After the publication of the interior ministry programme in April 2012, the occurrence of two additional encounters has been made public. However, these encounters were denounced by the original promoters as lacking key restorative features. They criticized the interior ministry for giving victims the initiative, fearing secondary victimization would result if offenders refused to participate. In addition they were wary that encounters would proceed without guaranteeing victims' restorative attitude and without using trained facilitators.[17]

Most victims' associations expressed their opposition to the encounters and to the plan of the ministry of the interior as a whole. Even though organizers made it clear that no penitentiary benefits followed encounters, many victims felt the plan amounted to a kind of 'soft' justice, and even impunity. Moreover, they stated that talking about forgiveness was an additional burden, one which should have been the prerogative of the deceased in any case.

Criticism has come from ETA prisoners as well, in line with the *abertzale left*.[18] They believe that only amnesties and general pardons, as mechanisms of transitional justice, will offer solutions to the *political conflict* while these individual solutions based on forgiveness instead amount to humiliation. In similar vein is the petition to recast the Basque Parliament commission on 'peace and living together' as a 'truth commission'.[19]

Victims' anxiety following the end of ETA

Victims' associations have played a key role in the history of ETA victimization. Mostly created by widows, the associations defended victims when no one else did. This pioneering and illuminating role regarding the lack of a social and political answers to grave victimization merits enduring recognition. However, the associations who are demanding a public role must also be prepared for the possibility of public criticism. Moreover the associations do not always sufficiently recognize two basic facts: the plurality of victims[20] and the multitude of victims who do not belong to any association or victims' group at all.

For this very reason it is difficult to explore victims' reactions to restorative encounters. On the basis of previous research, the hypothesis in this section is that many victims fear that restorative encounters with former ETA-terrorists will usher in impunity.[21] Many associations have already expressed their fear of both juridical and historical impunity (see Guiding Principles for a model on the End of the ETA without Impunity, 2010). Another hypothesis is that perceptions of both forms of impunity are very much related, while feelings of historical impunity have been underestimated in the process of recovery and restoration.

Diverse promises of material and symbolic justice to concerned stakeholders should be considered. By stakeholders I mean direct, indirect, vicarious, diffuse and hidden victims; offenders; legal professions[22]; political parties; media; and society. In particular, I will explore victims' fears and responses to them in three formal or theoretical systems or models: the current Spanish criminal justice system; the transitional justice model; and the so-called comprehensive law model.[23] This last model embraces elements of procedural justice, therapeutic jurisprudence and restorative justice.[24] Finally, proposals for hybrid models will be discussed.

Current Spanish legal system

The most relevant document in this field, produced by the main victims' associations, is the Guiding Principles for a Model of the End of ETA without Impunity (December 2010). It relies on the promises of a strict understanding of the formal rule of law, the assumption of the victory of the legitimate side to judge unjustifiable crimes and the efficacy of the judicial system to do so while also responding to victims' needs.

Most legal professionals and the public understand impunity as the lack of punishment. The origin and expression of victims' fear of impunity can be traced to the secondary victimization and social indifference they suffered for many years. There is also the experience of previous amnesties and pardons to ETA members in the 1970s and 1980s. Victims' fears make them suspicious of judges and the penitentiary administration regarding any change in the length of incarceration due to different interpretations of the law. Most public opinion within and outside the Basque Country reveals support for prisoners' true rehabilitation, but not for amnesties.[25]

The fact is that penalties for the most serious crimes have increased since 2003. However, the most valuable institutional responses might be found in the specific and integral protection and assistance legislation for terrorism victims at the regional and state levels.[26]

Transitional justice model

Some scholars, nationalist politicians and the *abertzale left*, support a transitional justice model.[27] As Williams and Nagy (2012, pp. 2–3) explain, the term *transitional justice* appears in the last decades of the twentieth century 'to denote a distinct field of political-legal practice and of scholarly inquiry'. The transitional justice toolkit comprises the removal and disqualification of public officials, international and/or domestic criminal trials, amnesties, pardons, truth commissions and reparations or compensation.[28]

Academic work on transitional justice reveals the complexity of the matter within and outside the Basque Country.[29] On the one hand transitional justice is just a new academic and activist name to describe periods of historical change in the aftermath of gross violations of human rights. On the other hand it includes the study of the different justice mechanisms to be applied in those historical periods of change.

Part of the theoretical and empirical work on transitional justice seeks to establish criteria to evaluate those mechanisms in policy, law and practice. The problem is that criteria for such an evaluation are not always grounded in international human rights, in their limitations and interdependence, but in practical or political concerns regarding the balance of justice with peace. What some experts consider adequate in some contexts varies from others. This is probably due to particularities of the context itself, but also to the different criteria of evaluation and the different definitions of conflict, peace, justice and the relation of these concepts to the democratic and humane rule of law. By humane I mean the consciousness that any transitional justice decision affects concrete human beings who have suffered a severe injustice. This is how the humanity principle should work in theory, even recognizing its complex and political dimensions in practice.[30]

In the case of today's Basque Country, transitional justice amounts to promises of a cessation of hostilities, but at the cost of lenient punishment for offenders.[31] Although each transitional context is unique, the situation in the Basque Country comprises neither a transition from an authoritarian regime to democracy nor a civil war/large scale conflict. It is true that transitional justice mechanisms have been applied to 'post-conflict situations', although the latter concept is quite ambiguous. It is also true that, since the South Africa Truth and Reconciliation Commission, restorative approaches in relation to a more victim-centred transitional justice have been explored.[32]

For the *abertzale left*, some political parties and legal professions in the Basque Country,[33] the transition context applies because both terrorist acts *and* abuses of power took place. Regarding extra limitations of state power, the *abertzale left* mentions criminal procedural law provisions allowing incommunicado detention linked to allegations of torture;[34] penal and penitentiary provisions hardening prison sentences; penitentiary jurisprudence to lengthen prison sentences;[35] and penitentiary policy on dispersion of prisoners. Moreover they recall the Act on Political Parties[36] and legal provisions that outlawed several newspapers on suspicion of collaboration in the financing of terrorism. In their interpretation of these policies and legislation, this means continuous and systematic violations of human rights by the Spanish state – extended to the French state as well.

The Basque parliament recently commissioned different studies of abuses of power, although this did not amount to the acknowledgement of the existence of two antagonistic violent sections in society. The Office for Terrorism Victims (2008) published a report on the violence of 'uncontrolled' groups, the extreme right and the Group of Anti-Terrorist Liberation (GAL).[37] Between 1975 and 1989, according to this report, 66 fatalities and 63 casualties and one kidnapping were the result of 74 terrorist acts committed by GAL, Spanish Basque Battalion, Triple A, and Anti-ETA Groups (GAE). The victims have been increasingly included into the Spanish legislation on terrorism victims' compensation schemes.[38]

There are about twenty cases with unknown offenders and many cases have not resulted in a sentence. Laura Martín, widow of a man murdered by GAL, laments that she did not have access to judicial truth through a sentence. She would have been satisfied with an institutional acknowledgement in the form of a public declaration recognizing the crimes committed by GAL.[39] She stated:

> We, victims of GAL, cannot claim our condition of innocent victims if we are not capable of condemning all terrorist attacks committed by ETA (...) Some people want to use me to justify ETA crimes, while others justify my husband's death as a reaction to ETA.
>
> (El Diario Vasco 25 July 1997)

In 2010, the Office of Human Rights of the Basque government published a report on victims of human rights violations and unjust suffering in a context of political motivation.[40] The first result of this report was the enactment of a Decree on reparation for victimization suffered between 1960 and 1978.[41] This has provoked criticism by several political parties and victims' associations that this amounts to justifying terrorism and reducing the guilt of the perpetrators. The ruling socialist party, supported by other political groups, explained that many of those victims were not related to ETA in any way.

Transitional justice appeals to the *abertzale left* because of the so-called internationalization of conflict in the sense of macro and neutral peace-building negotiations where amnesties might be possible. Juridical and historical impunity come together in what is perceived by victims to be an affront: the *abertzale left*'s demand of global and immediate responses for ETA prisoners; its resistance in acknowledging its accountability; and the pretence to look to the future and imposing a story of compensation of faults and guilt, even before an ETA declaration of disarmament and dissolution.

As the sister of a murdered man stated:

> Victimizers aspire to impunity, to manipulate the truth, to tell another story, so that they don't have to condemn what happened. Then, is it not too soon to talk about reconciliation? (...) There are over-sweet discourses, but I want to have a relationship with my victimizer neither of co-responsibility nor of bitterness. I don't see offenders with a right attitude. On the contrary they see themselves as victims and heroes... They killed my brother... They killed a lot of my friends, one after another.
>
> (Pagazartundúa 2011)

Part of the problem with transitional mechanisms such as amnesties and pardons is the Spanish past experience. They were already granted for ETA terrorists during the 1970s and 1980s. Beyond the legality debate on current possibilities of amnesties in Spain, previous legislation on individual pardons for any kind of crime should be rethought to include a victim participation approach so that a more humane and inclusive rule of law respecting human rights is guaranteed.[42] It does not appear coherent to appeal to international human rights in order to evaluate past wrongs and not to evaluate (transitional, restorative or ordinary) justice mechanisms themselves.

Comprehensive law models

In a procedural justice model, victims' justice needs are not only a function of the process results, but also of the process itself. This includes listening to victims; having regard for their opinion; showing them respect and support; and granting them trust in the competence of those controlling the process.[43] Perceptions of procedural justice have a positive impact on victims' recovery, healing and empowerment (Strang *et al.* 2008).

More and more in Spain, with specific central and regional legislation and offices for victims of terrorism, aspects of procedural justice are increasingly regarded by the penal system. There are still some aspects relevant to victims that are not considered at all by that system, although they would not imply a limitation of offenders' fundamental rights. As an example, consider victims' interest in facing victimizers. In 2011, after giving her testimony during trial, one homicide widow turned back and looked at the defendant. She was ordered by the judge to leave the courtroom. Later, she declared that it was very important for her to be able to do it. That gesture relieved her.[44]

Procedural justice is closely connected to therapeutic jurisprudence. According to Zawisza (2012, p. 5), therapeutic jurisprudence 'is an approach to the law and legal systems that focuses on the law's impact on the emotional life' and psychological and physical well-being. In this field, it has been applied to globalized emotional effects of terrorism.[45]

In a therapeutic jurisprudence model, forgiveness and other healing processes should be questioned. According to a facilitator of the first restorative encounters with ETA ex-terrorists: 'Participating victims are satisfied with sincere repentance. Forgiveness helps them to achieve closure in their mourning process… Victims and victimizers win, but victims will receive the primary emotional benefit.'[46] However, as will be discussed in next section, demands of forgiveness might entail secondary victimization.

Restorative justice promises due regard to victims' rights and needs as related to those of offenders and to community support and interests. In this sense, harms and perhaps relationships can be restored.[47] It might open new roles for victims' reparation in innovative terms; for offenders' active responsibility; and for community concerns and solidarity.

In the case of restorative justice, victims fear privatization and therapeutization of justice. They are afraid that the public dimension of terrorist's crimes and the rule of law will be neglected. In their opinion, de-legitimizing terrorism should be a priority.[48] In a restorative justice model, multi-dimensionality of harms and the condition of irreparability should be considered.

For victims participating in a restorative encounter with a former ETA prisoner, just recognizing the harm done does not amount to much because the harm is an obvious fact, even though former terrorists should acknowledge this. One such victim, Professor Iñaki García Arrizabalaga [49] said:

> Forgiveness should not be understood as humiliating, because it is just the contrary, a revolutionary thing... to see the human suffering they caused and to recognize that violence is not the way... I don't criticize his political options, but the means he used.

The victimizer he met told him that he knew he caused irreparable harms and wished he was his direct victim, but that, in any case, he wanted to request forgiveness for his membership of ETA:

> It really struck me. It was the first time a terrorist asked me for forgiveness... I made sure before that he would not do this expecting penitentiary benefits. I didn't want to be a useful fool... But he needed to do it from a human perspective.

He thinks that when victimizers argue that the terrorist's environment annuls their individual will, they are exposed:

> They have a pending reflection... I am not saying that their explanations are not sincere, but they are too easy. They should think why they couldn't rebel against it. If we talk about environments, we just talk of diffuse responsibilities for which no one seems accountable. It is more difficult to say 'I am responsible for entering this world; it is a personal decision for which I am accountable.' Of course, from a human point of view, it is understandable to try to derive part of that responsibility.

Finally he thinks about the person he found in that former terrorist:

> It might hurt some people to hear me say that it is good to discover the human side of a terrorist, but I think so... I could not forgive him because he killed other people, not my father, but I think he felt better after talking to me and so did I.

Some victims were suspicious of the encounters due to their emphasis on secrecy and the fact that offenders and penitentiary staff initiated them. In addition the aims of the programme were not clear to all victims. In the case of one victim, she was informed by the media that her sister's killer wanted to meet her.[50]

Victims' testimonies also provided evidence of contradictory perceptions of restorative justice.[51] Participating victims underlined that it was a personal decision, but when they described the encounter they did not maintain this view.

Societal concerns were highlighted, such as contributing to the offender's rehabilitation; living together in the future and even reconciliation as key individual and community prevention factors.[52]

Hybrid models adequate to different terrorist contexts

The United Nations Office on Drugs and Crime (2011) has recognized the need to give terrorism victims a voice within the justice system. This includes individualized responses to counteract de-personalization and further development of principles regarding reparation. Equal treatment for all terrorism victims should be developed hand in hand with personalized assistance within a criminal justice response geared to supporting victims.[53]

In this sense, restorative forums might help manage justice demands where rational and emotional elements cannot be separated:

> Moral feelings should be controlled so that senses are not cheated. But that control cannot be done sacrificing feelings... *Making suffering talk is the condition for all truth,* as Adorno stated. Truth is neither impartial nor impassive. It is not partisan either.[54]
>
> (Reyes 2011, pp. 25, 300)

Hybrid models considering the rule of law in current criminal justice systems, together with aspects of transitional justice, procedural justice and therapeutic jurisprudence and elements of restorative justice, could be useful and satisfying for some victims.

An example is the so-called Glencree Initiative, where victims of different terrorist acts in the Basque Country convened during several years to discuss the universality of human suffering, while recognizing the relevance of context (Iniciativa Glencree 2012). This group work was promoted by the Office of Terrorism Victims and developed by experts on victims' recovery. We can also consider the possibility of truth commissions for terrorist crimes without trial or without sentenced offenders, where the offender was granted amnesty or pardon, and for hidden victimization (see Figure 16.1).

Research perspectives on restorative justice

For the theoretical purposes of this section, *resilience* is defined as the mixture of resistance and flexibility in confronting adversity or victimization. *Recovery* refers mainly to victims' psychological and physical well-being, to go on with normal life. In this sense, resilience factors might be included within recovery processes. *Restoration* is a broader concept: in the forms and dimensions of harm it recognizes, and in its inclusion of accountability.[55] It means bringing together reparation to victims (by recovery, memory, truth, dignity and justice), offenders'

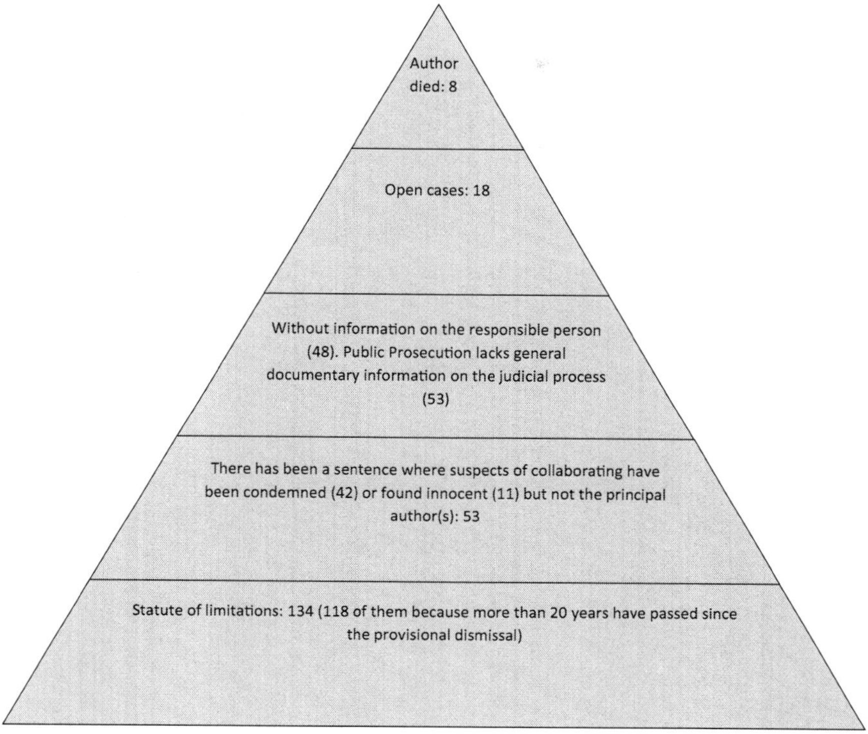
Author
died: 8
Open cases: 18
Without information on the responsible person (48). Public Prosecution lacks general documentary information on the judicial process (53)
There has been a sentence where suspects of collaborating have been condemned (42) or found innocent (11) but not the principal author(s): 53
Statute of limitations: 134 (118 of them because more than 20 years have passed since the provisional dismissal)

Figure 16.1: ETA killings without condemned main offender[a]

Source: Observatory against Impunity and National Court Prosecution Office, El País 2011, December 27). Available at: www.fundacionvt.org/images/fvt/notasprensa/Informe_de_asesinatos_de_ETA_sin_resolver.pdf [Accessed 1 September 2012].

Note

a Total number of ETA murdered victims without a condemned main offender: 314.

accountability and rehabilitation, while acknowledging the role that the criminal justice system plays.

In other works, my colleagues and I have listed some recovery and restorative factors supporting the process of de-victimization for terrorism in Spain (Varona *et al.* 2009).[56] Although it is difficult to establish a linear explanation of how these factors interact for each concerned person, some seem more important than others in the case of ETA victims. These factors should be evaluated with both victimological and legal, political and social criteria. A full overview of the factors of the individual interpersonal and contextual factors is shown in Table 16.2. In different degrees and depending on each victim, all these factors affect attitudes towards punitiveness and restorative encounters.

Here I will focus on two crucial aspects for the encounters held in the Basque Country: the response to indirect and diffuse victimization, and the private and public meaning of forgiveness and reparation. Both are related to restorative encounters' aims and access requirements and limitations.

Indirect and diffuse victimization

There are at least two reasons supporting participation of *vicarious* or *subrogated* victims and offenders. The first is the nature of terrorism itself, which uses the attack on the direct victims as means to achieve diffuse or collective victimization of the society as a whole.[57] Moreover, even if offenders belong to different squads, they receive orders from the same organization. Beyond the strict conception of criminal liability, they are collectively responsible for actions committed in the name of ETA. The second reason is that if victims want to meet with an offender and he declines, access to restorative justice will be contingent upon one offender's will. These victims might benefit from an encounter with other offenders.

On the new requirement by the 2012 interior ministry rehabilitation programme of meeting *direct* offenders or co-operators of caused victimization, one of the victims who participated in the earlier encounters declared: 'I made him responsible for the death of my father as he was part of the terrorist organization.' He found comfort in the conversation and left satisfied with the experience. He underlined that it was not about being too soft or vengeful. He had an interest in raising the offender's awareness of the real and deep victimization suffered by his family. In this sense he thought that the experience was hard for the victimizer. This victim perceived a person who was 'destroyed, repentant and very sincere. The offender did not have a clue of what victims have gone through.' In the case of facing the directly responsible terrorist, this victim thought it must be 'more complicated knowing that that finger pressed the trigger'.[58]

A former terrorist – incarcerated for twenty years for a car bomb in 1992 which caused three fatalities and twenty-one casualties – asked to meet the father of one of the deceased. In the end this was not possible because the father declined. The prisoner considered this negative answer to the encounter as natural and very respectful. According to him, after meeting another victim:

> I did that and I knew one day I should face it... I did that but I have never known who the victims were... I remember being very nervous... What struck me was the lack of hate on the part of the victim I met... But also his strength to keep going and how they remember everything, every detail... When I was involved with it, I saw victims as something impersonal, but when you meet them and they relate their suffering to you, from human being to human being, that is the reality. There is no greater suffering than that. When you listen to a victim you ask yourself: 'What have we done?' Until I talked face to face to a victim, I was not fully aware of many things. Of how many people are like that,

Table 16.2 Recovery and restorative factors in the process of de-victimization for terrorism in Spain

Individual level	Interpersonal level	Contextual (socioeconomic/political/institutional) level
• being a direct or indirect victim (partner parents, brothers, sisters and others); • perception of recognition and acknowledgement; • severity of crime as a subjective dimension; • perception of juridical and/or historical injustice; • emotional balance and character; • having suffered revictimization and/or secondary victimization; • religious beliefs or spirituality; • political ideology; • trust in institutions; • education; • socioeconomic status; • occupation.	• moving to another neighbourhood or town and living in or outside the Basque Country after the attack; • support by partner and by different family members; • professional support; • having a family of their own at the moment of the terrorist attack or later; • belonging to a victims' association; • helping other victims; • being helped by other victims; • participation in social and community life; • experiencing forgiveness; having received material and symbolic reparation by the offender or being asked for apologies (through restorative encounters or others); • memory acts in honour of victims in their town or city.	• end of terrorism (announcement of ceasefire/dissolution); • political consensus; • delegitimization of terrorism in education; • guarantees of cessation of terrorist acts; • public acknowledgement; • prisoners' collaboration with justice; • material and symbolic reparation programmes • public programs on memory and history; • the passage of time; • information and transparency regarding victims' and victimisers' policies; • being fairly treated • main offenders being brought to trial; • the existence of institutional processes of stating truth and accountability when trial is not possible; • severity of offender's penalty; • offender/s sentenced to keep distance regarding victims; • having received physical/mental health care and compensation over time; • existence of an institutional infrastructure to favour being asked for apologies; • religious institutions support; • strength of the victims' lobby; • strength of the prisoners' lobby. ...

> with so much suffering... And I have taken part in that. When I entered prison I thought: 'What have I done?' (...) I think terrorists participating in violence for many years never sleep well, but questioning it means renouncing your own life... Awareness comes with time. It is not something that happens from one day to another, there are different steps and it takes a lot of time.[59]

Victims and victimizers have recognized the difficulties for repentant former terrorists because they and their families might be under pressure from ETA and the *abertzale left*. According to another participating victim:[60]

> I am in favour of talking, negotiating is another thing... One day, all these people will be out of prison. If they are repentant, it will be better. Without more hate... ETA must dissolve; prisoners have to serve their sentences. But, what is wrong with these encounters? That one asking you for sincere forgiveness, should be listened to? My faith teaches me this... I asked him why he was sitting in front of me. He told me he wanted to apologize and showed a deep remorse. He told me one day he would have to tell his own children and that he could not sleep.

Regarding reparation of social harms, a victim whose father was murdered in 1980 points out how victims were previously identified and stigmatized, particularly in small towns: 'I said that rumours, people talking, killed him. I think that the one talking and the one shooting are both accountable.'[61]

Where participatory mechanisms of restorative justice are considered as a reaction to diffuse victimization, the time factor is important.[62] Here circles and conferences can be envisaged[63] so that relatives, friends, and professionals and social agents supporting victims and victimizers might participate and assure the community link in the restoration process. This offers the opportunity for personal, interpersonal and social harms to be taken into account simultaneously. In any case, within the specific Basque context, the meaning of that community link should be scrutinized with the aim of ensuring that citizens' democracy based on human rights prevails over authoritarian forms of relationships. At the same time, the central role of victims in the justice response should be guaranteed, although this does not mean excluding other actors' contributions.

The potentialities and limits of forgiveness

Elsewhere I have argued that the main objective of restorative encounters should not be forgiveness, but material and symbolic reparation and restoration (Varona 2012a). Forgiveness, in its private, interpersonal and public dimensions, is too ambitious and goes beyond what many victims and victimizers and their communities might acquiesce to. In fact, there are a few examples of victims of terrorism who had already forgiven the offender before they met.[64] Obviously, private and public acts of forgiveness should be welcomed whenever this is possible and fair.[65]

In relation to the forms of impunity feared by victims and restorative justice, there are different works on the connection between historical impunity and the value of forgiveness.[66] Beyond the current fashion of public contrition or apologies identified with sentimentality, examples described in Brooks (1999, p. 3) are 'a matrix of guilt and mourning, atonement and national revival'. From another perspective, Reyes (2011) explains the emergence of past consciousness as a cultural trend, originating in Holocaust studies. It increases victims' visibility and questions historical progress based on macro-level political-economic rationales to the neglect of concrete, individual human suffering.

As defined before, what is essential in restorative encounters is restoration as bringing together reparation to victims (including recovery, memory, truth, dignity and justice) and offenders' accountability. Victimizers might act as restoration agents by listening to victims; answering their questions; recognizing their dignity and their own accountability; trying to repair what is possible; engaging in memory projects for irreparable harms and in social prevention programmes.

Restoration is wider than forgiveness and allows stating the irreparable nature of many harms while avoiding secondary victimization to participating and non-participating victims of terrorism at the same time. This is so because it avoids placing the burden of forgiveness and future reconciliation upon them. Society and policymakers cannot stigmatize victims as 'good' or 'bad' (revengeful) just because they exercise their right to refuse participation in restorative encounters or, if they do, to decline to pardon offenders.[67]

In any case, due to the current Spanish legal provisions requiring forgiveness in the last phases of prison sentences for terrorism, its private, interpersonal and public dimensions over time should be clarified or at least acknowledged. According to Bernard Offen, Holocaust survivor:

> I have forgiven for what happened to *me*, for my own suffering. However, I cannot forgive for what others have suffered, for example, my family. I cannot forgive in their name. I think I reached forgiveness, and that is something that has allowed me to recover from the anger I felt. What happens is that I cannot avoid that that anger comes back from time to time. Then I have to forgive again.
>
> (El País, País Vasco 15 October 2011, p. 5)

In similar vein to the victims' associations *Guiding Principles for a Model on the end of ETA without Impunity*, the sister of Yoyes – a former terrorist who was killed by ETA in 1986, in front of her young child – declared: 'She was killed in a public manner, and that is the manner in which her offender should repent for his murder.'[68] Therefore, there should be a reinterpretation of the role of forgiveness in terms of restorative justice that goes beyond personal and therapeutic issues.

In relation to programme aims and access, international standards do not clarify whether beyond recognition of evident harm, offenders should not justify their behaviour in order to participate in restorative programmes.[69] That means that violence can never be justified as there is always a margin for individual free decision. In practice, due to the pluralities of the experience of victimization, flexibility to allow potentialities of the restorative process together with professional control to avoid secondary victimization should be promoted. Excuses might not be always regarded as justification[70] and encounters might be produced with victims willing to question that kind of justification or neutralization of accountability.[71] Beyond paternalism over victims, the facilitators' role and power are crucial at this point.

Concluding remarks

Restorative justice might offer something beyond dualism in the current legal analysis of terrorism. This mainstream analysis focuses on the balance between freedom and security. In peace theories on violent conflicts, it is expressed as the balance between justice and peace.

Restorative justice could promote the integration of diverse individual experiences without neglecting the macro and meso-level context. This chapter has focused on ETA cases, but restorative programmes can be conceived for victims of other terrorists in the Basque Country and for victims of other serious crimes, for instance torture.

Due to the influence of political ideology upon the concept of terrorism and terrorist victimization, restorative justice in this field has specific limits, but also potential. Victims have real reasons to be suspicious of restorative justice, but their qualms are also due to emotional elements grounded in a sense of historical impunity. For this reason among others, promoters of restorative justice should apply scientifically informed and transparent policies.

Experience with encounters between victims and offenders of serious crimes have been accumulating in the past decades in the USA, Canada, Australia and Europe. This experience reveals the potential for reparation and lack of secondary victimization.[72] Concrete experience of restorative processes in cases of terrorism can be found in Northern Ireland, Germany, Italy, Israel and Colombia. Most of these examples followed the cessation of terrorist activity and a process of self-criticism.[73]

This evidence tells us that restorative programmes can positively enrich social and institutional responses to victims of very serious crimes. This is only possible if participants' personal autonomy is respected and supported, not as a private process of recovery or return into society, but as a forum to express all dimensions of harms, including public and social harm.

In other work considering international standards (de la Cuesta and Varona 2012), we emphasized the following five critical issues in developing practical safeguards to minimize the risks of secondary victimization in relation to restorative encounters for terrorism victims: the extent of victims' and victimizers' will to participate and to repair and be repaired; the nature and control of facilitators' role and power; the diversity of harms produced in terrorist victimization (personal, material, social, political); the alternative avenues of restoration or responses to them; and the access to justice in relation to the rule of law in restorative processes.

In terms of human rights and participation, restorative justice might offer a better platform for a victim-centred response that simultaneously acknowledges the importance of offenders' reintegration in society and the interests of the community. This is possible if restorative justice is sufficiently integrated within the formal systems of criminal justice, health care and social work. The relevance of informal responses should also be articulated. In the context of Spanish criminal justice and the rule of law, the main actors' participation is not yet guaranteed. More risks appear in the macro-context of transitional justice. It is likely that victims consider political decisions on adopted transitional mechanisms as arbitrary and undermining their understanding of the rule of law.

Victims' right to restorative encounters might be envisaged within more general victims' rights to justice. According to international legislation and international doctrine, justice is understood as fulfilling legitimate expectations regarding state action to bring suspects to trial; to prosecute and sentence them according to democratic rule of law; to avoid secondary victimization; to have the right to a remedy; to be compensated; and to appeal.

Much confusion exists in today's Basque and Spanish political and public arenas on the meaning of restorative justice. Restorative justice should not be perceived to be swift, soft or simple. It cannot be solely identified with the technique of penal mediation because of its embrace of broader aims and its broader procedural arsenal (circles, conferencing and panels). It is not a general solution in all cases, nor is it always a success. And it cannot be a duty for victims or victimizers. It avoids secondary victimization without transforming justice into a private issue. It should not amount to a loss of juridical guarantees.[74] It is not mainly concerned with forgiveness, reconciliation or therapeutic outcomes.

Restorative justice has the potential to be a complex, dynamic and plural response to victimization within – but beyond – the rule of law that offers key roles to victims, victimizers and society. It provides willing victims and victimizers a space to meet and a way of communication in order to attempt to repair harms unjustly caused, including crimes without a known offender and/or under statute of limitations, amnesty or pardon.

The experience of injustice is subjective but conditioned by social context. One day ETA will disappear and many victims will continue living. Terrorism might end but the effects of its direct, indirect and diffuse victimization remain, even if some ETA prisoners ask for forgiveness. Offenders, victims, their families, friends and society have not come out unharmed by fifty years of terrorism. That harm belongs to all involved actors in diverse ways, although some have not recognized it yet. Accountability in reacting to human suffering allows harm to be a key element of balance between memory and justice.[75]

ETA's campaign of terrorist victimization is a story of endless suffering, but also a story of civic behaviour respecting the rule of law: as of yet no victim has taken revenge.[76] It is also a sad story, particularly for victims, because the supporters of ETA try to convince society to look towards the future, paving over the unjust past and subsequent accountability. However, it might be a challenging story as well, where lessons can be learned to alleviate the pain and to prevent its recurrence. Restorative encounters in this field will be particularly relevant if they are part of that multi-dimensional individual and collective storytelling and history.

Punishment is not the only remedy to counter injustice. Forms of severe punishment demanded by some victims of terrorism might not fulfil their rights and profound needs in relation to justice. Formal, informal, material, performance and symbolic responses to irreparable loss should be explored and conclusions expanded to other crimes.[77]

In the recovery process, individual, interpersonal and structural factors should be taken into account. That process has to come to terms with every individual victim's rights and needs, including social and institutional support; protection; psychological assistance; information; acknowledgement; respect; reparation; and justice. The legal system and the socio-political context condition the way victims express their justice-related needs. If that system only provides for the offenders' prosecution, trial and imprisonment, this will shape victims' expectations and demands. Subsequent failure to meet these goals will be felt by victims to be impunity. For irreparable harms it seems that what current formal justice offers to victims, when actually given according to democratic rule of law, does not fulfil their profound expectations. Reasons for this frustration go beyond the shortcomings of formal and substantial justice.

Remedies to historical injustice should be further studied. Here victims' testimonies in schools appear important.[78] The work of different people who have reacted to injustice should also be evoked. They were not indifferent and helped terrorism victims in different ways (as relatives, friends, neighbours, intellectuals). Reviews of research on Holocaust rescuers, by Zawisza (2012, p. 26), reveal that *universalistic caring* was the predominant value for helping: lack of indifference, beyond the values of justice, equality and respect. Remembering the support offered by these individuals might not be an easy task for many of us; we might find our own actions to support and assist to victims in the Basque Country to be left wanting.

Finally, within an ecological perspective, the relevance of places of victimization and de-victimization should be analysed by diverse sciences and ways of knowing, including art and photography.[79] Places where terrorist victimizations occurred serve as painful reminders to victims. The injustice they perceive in these environments remains invisible to others. We can conceive of restorative situational prevention of this particular form of secondary victimization. It can be focused on promoting democratic habitat elements in relation to social support that might impact positively on victims' vulnerabilities, resilience and recovery in the short, medium and long run.[80] In relation to community links, the interlocking Borromean rings can symbolize the strength and fragility of partnerships when one of the concerned agents fails to cooperate.[81] Future generations will judge whether historical progress or political aims at the cost of human lives have become more difficult to bear and the extent to which indifference towards injustice has been reduced.

Notes

1 See Varona (2009, 2012a, 2012b, in press 2014); Varona *et al.* (2009); de la Cuesta *et al.* (2011); and de la Cuesta and Varona (2012). ETA (*Euskadi ta Askatasuna – Basque Homeland and Freedom*) is a terrorist group – originally – promoting the independence of the Basque Country. Its view of the Basque Country can be described as a land currently unfairly divided into three Spanish provinces (Gipuzkoa, Bizkaia and Araba), Navarra and three French territories.

2 In this chapter a strict concept of terrorism victims is used, based upon Spanish legislation. For example, fatalities incurred in the commission of terrorism are not considered victims of terrorism. On internal legislation, see articles 3, 4, 5 and 17 of the 29/2011 Spanish Act on Acknowledgement and Integral Protection for Terrorism Victims; article 2.2 of the Basque 4/2008 Act on Acknowledgement and Reparation to Victims of Terrorism; and the Basque Decree 290/2010 on the Development of the Integral Assistance System to Terrorism Victims. On the international norms about the concept of terrorism victims, see, among others, paragraph 2 of the 1985 UN 40/34 Resolution on Basic Principles of Justice for Victims of Crime and Abuse of Power; article 1 of the 2012 EU Directive on victims' rights; paragraph 9 of the European Parliament Resolution of 15 June 2000 on the Commission communication on crime victims; art. 13 of the Council of Europe Convention on the prevention of terrorism (2005); and paragraph 2.3 of the Ministers Committee of the Council of Europe Recommendation (2006) 8 on assistance to victims.

3 All quoted testimonies and texts in Spanish are free translations into English by the author.

4 As at 2014, ETA had still not announced its disarmament and dissolution.

5 Other associations lists and academic works show the number of ETA fatal victims as ten, twenty or more higher in total; see Alonso *et al.* (2010).

6 For a general understanding on ETA terrorist victimization based on testimonies and socio psychological, historical and/or political science analysis, see inter alia Cuesta (2000); Calle and Sánchez-Cuenca (2004); Pulgar (2004); Calleja and Sánchez-Cuenca (2006); Aulestia (2007); Villa (2007); Sánchez-Cuenca (2007, 2010); Larizgoitia *et al.* (2009); Varona *et al.* (2009); Arregi (2011); Cuesta Arzamendi *et al.* (2011); Martín-Peña *et al.* (2011); and Elorza (2006, 2011).

7 See Pagazartundúa (2006, 2011), sister of a murdered chief of police of a Basque town. Until November 2012, she worked as president of the Foundation for Terrorism Victims. On the social context of ETA terrorism, see Salaburu (2011) and Carrión (2008).

8 See http://graficos.lainformacion.com/policia-y-justicia/terrorismo/donde-estan-encarcelados-los-miembros-de-eta_jQ79imUtTrBzLcr9rjBfl1. See also www.etxerat.info/fitxategia_ikusi.php?id_fitxategia=3422 [Accessed 1 September 2012].

9 Started in 2006. These prisoners were expelled from ETA. Nanclares is the name of the Basque town where the prison was situated.

10 In 2007, during the first institutional act in honour of terrorism victims by the Basque Government, the Basque president apologized for the institutional and social abandonment of victims during many decades. This could be considered an example of state or institutional public apology that had an echo in the Basque and Spanish legislation on terrorism victims. Cf. in other contexts Lefranc (2004) and Aguilar (2008).
11 See the 2012 *Program to develop a penitentiary policy of individual rehabilitation within the legal framework* (Madrid, 30 April). Available at: www.interior.gob.es/press/programa-para-el-desarrollo-de-la-politica-penitenciaria-de-reinsercion-individual-en-el-marco-de-la-ley-13712?locale=es [Accessed 1 September 2012].
12 A much-questioned policy of dispersion of prisoners to different Spanish penitentiary institutions in order to facilitate desistance started in 1989. On rehabilitation, negotiation and peace policies regarding ETA terrorism, see Escrivá (2006); Fonseca (2006); Cuerda (2007); Campo (2007); and Fernández and Romo (2012).
13 Forgiveness is studied from different scientific perspectives and has different meanings. On its subjective dimension, see inter alia Williamson and Gonzalez (2007) and Antonuccio and Jackson (2009). On its group effects, see Worthington *et al.* (2000). On its public dimension, see Van Stokkom *et al.* (2012) and Wohl *et al.* (2008). On the relation of justice and forgiveness, see Short (2011). On the timeless dimension of forgiveness, see Malcolm (2008). On public opinion and forgiveness, see Freedman and Chang (2010). On memory and forgiveness, from a philosophical point of view, see Valcárcel (2011). From the standpoint of ethics, see Murithi (2009). On self-forgiveness from women's perspective, see Baker (2008). On forgiveness in South African Truth and Reconciliation Commission, see Kaminer *et al.* (2001). On reconciliation, see Finkelstein (2011). On violent offenders, see Day *et al.* (2008). Basque authors like Professor Beristain (2007) had approached this debate within ETA terrorism from a religious and victimological point of view. Cf. Buesa (2006).
14 See the documentary *El Perdón*. Available at: www.tv3.cat/30minuts/reportatges/1835/El-perdo [Accessed 1 February 2012].
15 Including one that involved the director of the Terrorism Victims Office of the Basque government with one member of the squad that killed her husband (*El Diario Vasco* 24 October 2012, p. 29).
16 On the knowledge of the desistance and rehabilitation experience of ex-terrorists, see González (1987) and Alcedo (1997); for the case of extreme left Anti-Fascist Resistance 1st of October Groups (GRAPO), see Novales (1989); on the study of judicial files and interviews with ETA prisoners and ex–prisoners, see Reinares (2001). On Northern Ireland see Alonso (2003). Cf., in general, Horgan (2006).
17 See *El Correo* 6 June 2012, p. 20. The coordinator of the original programme was criminal law professor and lawyer Xabier Etxebarria. Professor Julián Ríos also had an important role. Cf. the narrative of the experience from a facilitator's point of view, coming from Social Work, Olalde (2012). See also the reflections from a magistrate in Sáez Valcárcel (2011, 2012).
18 The *abertzale left* refers to a coalition of different political parties under the current name of *Bildu* that has condemned violence as a political tool, but agrees with most ETA political objectives. It is the political group that best supports the majority of ETA prisoners.
19 El Correo 26 October 2012, p. 27.
20 Cf. on the debate of some associations regarding future end of ETA terrorist violence, *El País* 10 November 2011. See also the documentary film in Spanish produced by the Foundation of Terrorism Victims. Available at: www.fundacionvt.org/index.php?option=com_content&task=view&id=865 [Accessed 1 September 2012].
21 Impunity is mostly identified with injustice. On the general concept of injustice, see Sen (2010). Here I follow Reyes Mate's (2011) reflections on injustice.
22 This is a field involving professionals of different areas such as constitutional, crimi-

nal, procedural and administrative law. On restorative justice and different stakeholders within the legal profession, see Shapland (2011).
23 Comprehensive law is understood as a movement that considers subjective and interpersonal dynamics of legal affairs. Practical examples of this movement are drug treatment and mental health courts. See Daicoff (2006).
24 In all these theories concepts such as reparation, forgiveness or recovery do not find a unanimous definition.
25 The term *amnesty* is not mentioned in the 1978 Spanish Constitution. As for the term *pardon*, in section 62 it is stated that it is incumbent upon the king 'i) to exercise the right of clemency in accordance with the law, which may not authorize *general* pardons'. Because of this provision most academic experts understand that amnesties are forbidden in the Spanish legal system. Popular initiative for submission of non-governmental bills is not allowed on the prerogative of pardon (section 87). The prerogative of pardon shall not apply to the criminal liability of the President and other members of the government (section 102). The granting of pardons is ruled by an old Act of 1870, modified in 1988 and 1995 where, inconsistently in today's human rights conception, most victims do not play any role. The granting of pardons has been criticized by different human rights activists as being a door for impunity for white-collar and abuse of power crimes. See the general study on the kind of crimes granted pardons since 2000 by Doval *et al.* (2011).
26 See note 2.
27 The case of Northern Ireland has always served as an example for the *abertzale left*. On Northern Ireland and transitional justice, see McEvoy and McGregor (2008) and McEvoy (2010).
28 On the debate on amnesties, see Mallinder (2008).
29 Cf. Vriezen (2012) on balancing the need of (re)-building the rule of law with the need to end human rights violations in the case of amnesties. On the development of specific victims' human rights, see Tomás Sánchez (2012). For the case of terrorism victims, see Letschert *et al.* (2010); and for victims of transnational crimes, see Letschert and van Dijk (2011). On human rights and restorative justice in general, see Skelton and Sekhonyane (2007).
30 Cf. Cuesta (2011) and Bourke (2011) in relation to the expanding concept of human rights.
31 On the relation of transitional and restorative justice from victims' point of view, see Díaz Colorado (2008).
32 See for example Clamp and Doak (2012).
33 It should not be forgotten that many victims were killed by ETA outside the Basque Country.
34 The European Court of Human Rights has condemned Spain on several occasions for not carrying out an effective investigation on alleged torture related to the detention of suspects of ETA terrorism. European Court judgements do not consider the actual existence of torture but they determine that the Spanish state violated art. 3 of the Convention due to the vulnerability context of the incommunicado detention regime. This violation is regarded in procedural terms.
35 This so-called *Parot* doctrine refers to the Supreme Court decision in 2006 ruling that the reduction of sentences in exchange for labour – according to the 1973 penal code in force when convicted – must be calculated on the total sentence and not on the maximum prison sentence of 30 years, as it was done until then.
36 According to that Act, in 2003 the *abertzale left*, then under the name of *Batasuna*, was made illegal. Later the European Court of Human Rights considered this illegalization consistent with the European Convention. The political party coming from the *abertzale left*, but separated from it then because it always denounced violence, *Aralar*, was not illegalized.

37 *Informe sobre víctimas del terrorismo practicado por grupos incontrolados, de extrema derecha y el GAL* (2008). Available at: www.interior.ejgv.euskadi.net/r42-440/es/contenidos/informacion/informacion_documentos_interes/es_document/adjuntos/informe%20final.pdf [Accessed 1 February 2012]. See information in English provided by the University of Maryland on GAL, acting until 1987. Available at: www.start.umd.edu/start/data_collections/tops/terrorist_organization_profile.asp?id=3933 [Accessed 1 February 2012]. It refers to the trial of several politicians and policemen and subsequent granting of pardons.
38 See mainly the Spanish 32/99 Act on Solidarity with Terrorism Victims.
39 El Diario Vasco 1 April 2009, p. 27.
40 *Víctimas de vulneraciones de derechos humanos y sufrimientos injustos producidos en un contexto de violencia de motivación política* (2010). Available at: www.interior.ejgv.euskadi.net/r42-victimas/es/contenidos/informacion/informacion_documentos_interes/es_document/documentos_interes.html [Accessed 1 February 2012].
41 See the Basque Decree 107/2012, of June 12, on declaration and reparation of victims of unjust sufferings consequence of human rights violations between 1960 and 1978, in the context of politically motivated violence experienced in the Basque Autonomous Community (*declaración y reparación de las víctimas de sufrimientos injustos como consecuencia de la vulneración de sus derechos humanos, producida entre los años 1960 y 1978 en el contexto de la violencia de motivación política vivida en la Comunidad Autónoma del País Vasco*). Available at: www.jusap.ejgv.euskadi.net/bopv2/datos/2012/06/1202804a.pdf [Accessed 1 September 2012]. It should be noticed that most of that period was under Franco's dictatorship.
42 On victim participation in therapeutic jurisprudence, see Erez *et al.* (2011).
43 See Lind and Tylor (1988); and Röhly and Machura (1997).
44 El País 5 November 2011, p. 24.
45 See Edgardo Rotman (2008). Cf. Wexler (2011).
46 El Mundo 22 January 2012, p. 11.
47 Here we consider the classical book by Zehr (1990), as well as the reintegrative shaming perspective within the republican theory of Braithwaite (1989). On most recent research results on the matter, see inter alia Vanfraechem and Aertsen (2010). Cf. Walker (1999). On its meaning in criminal procedure, see Gyökös and Lany (2010). On its real impact and limitations, see Daly (2002).
48 On the concept of de-legitimation of terrorism, see Fundación Fernando Buesa (2011).
49 One such victim was University professor Iñaki García Arrizabalaga (see some of his declarations in *El Diario Vasco* 4 December 2011, p. 40; *El País* 26 September 2011, pp. 12–13; *El País Domingo* 18 December 2011, p. 6; *El Mundo* 22 January 2012, p. 11). Anti-capitalist Autonomous Commando Units, separated from the ETA, kidnapped and murdered his father, a representative of the Spanish Telephone Company, in 1980. García Arrizabalaga was then 19 years old. He has kept contact with the offender after the encounter.
50 El País 27 February 2012, p. 19.
51 On the meaning of the encounters, see Lozano *et al.* (2011).
52 El País 25 September 2011, p. 10.
53 On assistance to victims and its relation to the criminal justice system, see Hagemann *et al.* (2009).
54 For a further debate on truth and justice, see, among others, Park (2010).
55 On the meaning of restoration to victims, see Bolivar (2012).
56 Beristain questioned the concept of de-victimization, developed in Spain in the psychological arena (2007). He linked it to a more structural macro-victimization where many harms are irreparable and some indirect victims (relatives of the murdered person) feel they have the duty to remember the injustice so it might have a positive sense in order

57 On the methodological difficulties to assess diffuse victimization, see Martin-Peña et al. (2011).

to avoid further injustices in the future. We can relate this to previous considerations on the perspective of critical victimology.
57 On the methodological difficulties to assess diffuse victimization, see Martin-Peña et al. (2011).
58 Josu Elespe (*El Diario Vasco* 24 December 2011, pp. 39–40). His father, a socialist politician in a Basque town, was shot while he was in a bar in 2001.
59 Iñaki Rekarte, in *El Diario Vasco* 31 December 2011, p. 42.
60 María del Carmen Hernández, widow of a popular politician murdered by ETA in a Basque town in 2000. She continues to visit a psychologist once a month. When her husband was killed, one neighbour told her: 'Now they killed him, before that they just didn't let him live.' Regarding the pictures of ETA prisoners on the walls of some buildings of her town, she said: 'The mayor says those pictures don't harm anybody. They do harm me' (*El Mundo* 22 January 2012, p. 10).
61 Antonio Domínguez, whose father, a gravedigger in a small town, was murdered in 1980 (this testimony appears in the documentary film by Iñaki Arteta, *Voces sin libertad*).
62 Different circles in time with different aims (sentencing and reparation; support and accountability; healing and reconciliation, as well as prevention of (re)victimization).
63 On their significance and impact, see Blad and van Lieshout (2010); Walker and Greening (2011); Zinsstag and Vanfraechem (2012); and Guardiola (2012). About the relation of circles with the good lives theory, see Willis and Ward (2010). On responses based on supported accountability, see Jones (2008).
64 Jo Berry in Northern Ireland and one ETA victim mentioned in the documentary film *El Perdón* (2012). As part of a recovery process, sometimes results related to religious beliefs, one person can forgive even if the responsible one doesn't ask for it. At the same time, being forgiven doesn't mean that offender can forgive himself. This expresses the complexity of private, interpersonal and public dimensions of forgiveness. On self-forgiveness, see Holmgren (2002) and Umbreit (2005).
65 On the international trend towards public apologies, see the volume edited by van Stokkom et al. (2012).
66 Victims' claims to avoid historical impunity is an interesting topic for further reflection. See Boerefijn et al. (2012).
67 This is something that former terrorists themselves have considered, as Adriana Faranda's case in Italy showed. On political and social pressure over victims to go to a psychologist or a priest rather than to a judge, and the difference between justice and revenge, see Savater (2012). Cf. for a broader debate on victims and revenge, Strang (2002); Rohne (2008); and Frankenberg (2010) on punitiveness. On the meaning of emotions in the criminal justice system, see Karstedt et al. (2011).
68 El País 27 February 2011, p. 19.
69 Spanish legislation on forgiveness in terrorist crimes doesn't clarify this.
70 Cf. Scott and Lyman (1968).
71 See the cases of Jo Berry and Iñaki Arrizabalaga.
72 On the possibilities of restorative justice and serious crimes, see among others, Vos and Umbreit (2000); Szmania (2006); Strang, Angel and Van Camp (2008); Peterson (2010); Van Droogenbroeck (2010); Romera (2011); van Camp and Wemmers (2011); Ríos et al. (2012). See also the work of the Centre *Restorative Justice & Peacemaking*. Available at: www.cehd.umn.edu/ssw/rjp/Training/default.asp [Accessed 1 February 2012].
73 See Jamieson (1989); Gastaminza (2007); González (2006, 2008); and Staiger (2010).
74 See Ferrajoli's guaranteeing model (1995). The legal system should limit private and public power, supporting the weakest part by conditioning all decision or act to the content of fundamental rights in an interdependent and indivisible conception.
75 See Jones (2008).

76 Out of 829 families who suffered the murder of a relative, only one person (a son) has attempted to revenge his father. Similarly, nobody out of about 16,000 injured and several kidnapped people attempted revenge.
77 On restorative justice and torture, see Schechtman (2005).
78 On a peace culture in the Basque Country, see Bilbao and Etxeberria (2005); Páez and Martín (2009); and Pérez (2010). Cf. on the relevance of historical archives, which could include evaluation of restorative encounters, Schubotz et al. (2011). On memory and history, see Etxeberria (2010).
79 Cf. Uribe (2011) who gives us some knowledge, relevant to victimology, coming from photography.
80 Cf. Vertigans (2011) on the concept of *affordance*. About its relation to group identity, see Eagly et al. (2010).
81 The Borromean rings are named after the coat of arms of the Borromeo family in fifteenth century Tuscany. In mathematical terms they consist of three circles which are interlinked.

Bibliography

Aguilar, P., 2008. Políticas de la memoria y memorias de la política. Madrid: Alianza.

Alcedo, M., 1997. Militar en ETA. Historias de vida y muerte. San Sebastián: Haranburu.

Alonso, R., 2003. Matar por Irlanda. El IRA y la lucha armada. Madrid: Alianza.

Alonso, R., Domínguez, F. and García Rey, M., 2010. Vidas rotas. Historia de los hombres, mujeres y niños víctimas de ETA. Madrid: Espasa.

Altuna, Á. and Ustarán, J., 2005. Justicia retributiva, justicia reparadora y reinserción activa, El Diario Vasco, 23 May, p. 16.

Antonuccio, D. and Jackson, R., 2009. The Science of Forgiveness. In: W. O'Donohue and S. R. Graybar, eds, Handbook of Contemporary Psychotherapy: Toward an Improved Understanding of Effective Psychotherapy. Thousand Oaks: Sage, ch. 11.

Arregi, J., 2011. El problema es la herencia. El Diario Vasco, 21 January 2011, p. 20.

Associations and Foundations of Victims of Terrorism, 2010. Principios rectores para un modelo de fin de ETA sin impunidad. Madrid, 23 November 2010.

Aulestia, K., 2007. A modo de introducción: ETA y su instinto de conservación. In Luces y sombras de la disolución de ETA político-militar. Vitoria-Gasteiz: Fundación Fernando Buesa/Aldaketa.

Baker, M. E., 2008. Self-forgiveness: An Empowering and Therapeutic Tool for Working with Women in Recovery. In: W. Malcolm, N. DeCourville and K. Belicki, eds, Women's Reflections on the Complexities of Forgiveness. New York: Routledge/Taylor & Francis Group, pp. 61–75.

Beristain, A., 2007. Víctimas del terrorismo. Nueva justicia, sanción y ética. Valencia: Tirant lo Blanch.

Beristain, C. and Rovira, D., 2000. Violencia, apoyo a las víctimas y reconstrucción social. Experiencias internacionales y el desafío vasco. Madrid: Fundamentos.

Bermúdez, G., 2006. Ley y reinserción en procesos de paz. In: El significado político de las víctimas del terrorismo: el valor del Estado de Derecho y de la ciudadanía. Vitoria–Gasteiz: Fundación Fernando Buesa.

Bilbao, G. and Etxeberria, X., 2005. La presencia de las víctimas del terrorismo en la educación para la paz en el País Vasco. Bilbao: Bakeaz.

Blad, J. and van Lieshout, J., 2010. Families Solving their Problems – Family Group Conferencing on Family Problems in the Netherlands. In: M. Gyokos and K. Lanyi, eds,

European Best Practices of Restorative Justice in the Criminal Procedure. Budapest: Justice Ministry.
Boerefijn, I., Henderson, L., Janse, R. and Weaver, R., eds, 2012. Human Rights and Conflict. Essays in Honour of Bas de Gaay Fortman. Antwerpen: Intersentia.
Bolivar, D., 2012. Victim–offender Mediation and Victim's Restoration: A Victimological Study in the Context of Restorative Justice. PhD-Thesis. Catholic University of KU Leuven.
Borg, M., Karlsson, B., Hesook, S.K and McCormack, B., 2012. Opening up for Many Voices in Knowledge Construction Forum: Qualitative Social Research, 13(1), p. 1. Available at: www.qualitative-research.net [Accessed 1 September 2012].
Bourke, J., 2005. Fear: A Cultural History. London: Virago.
Bourke, J., 2011. Are Women Animals?: Historical Reflections on What It Means To Be Human, 1791 to the Present. London: Virago.
Braithwaite, J., 1989. Crime, Shame and Reintegration. Cambridge: Cambridge University Press.
Brooks, R. L., ed., 1999. When Sorry Isn't Enough: The Controversy Over Apologies and Reparations for Human Injustice. New York: New York University Press.
Buesa, M., 2006. Víctimas del Terrorismo y políticas del perdón. Cuadernos de pensamiento político, abril/junio, pp. 9–22.
Calle, L. de la and Sanchez-Cuenca, I.S., 2004. La selección de víctimas de ETA, Revista Española de Ciencia Política, 10, pp. 53–79.
Calleja, J.M., 2006. Algo habrá hecho. Odio, muerte y miedo en Euskadi. Madrid: Espasa-Calpe.
Calleja, J.M. and Cuenca, I.S., 2006. La derrota de ETA. De la primera a la última víctima. Madrid: Adhara.
Campo, J.C., 2007. Terrorismo y mecanismos para el fin de la violencia. In: J.L. González Cussac, ed., Fuerzas armadas y seguridad pública: Consideraciones en torno al terrorismo y la inmigración. Castellón de la Plana: Universitat Jaume I.
Carrión, V., 2008. Microterrorismo, El Diario Vasco, 20 June 2008, pp. 26–27.
Clamp, K. and Doak, J., 2012. More than Words: Restorative Justice Concepts in Transitional Justice Settings. International Criminal Law Review, 12, pp. 339–369.
Coates, R., Umbreit, M., Vos, B. and Brown, K., 2002. Victim Offender Dialogue in Crimes of Severe Violence. A Multi-Site Study of Programs in Texas and Ohio. St. Paul: Center for Restorative Justice and Peacemaking, School of Social Work, University of Minnesota.
Cuerda, M. L., 2007. El Derecho penal ante el proceso de paz. In: J.L. González Cussac, ed., Fuerzas armadas y seguridad pública: Consideraciones en torno al terrorismo y la inmigración. Castellón de la Plana: Universitat Jaume I.
Cuesta, C., 2000. Contra el olvido. Testimonios de víctimas del terrorismo. Madrid: Temas de Hoy.
de la Cuesta, J.L., 2011. Actualidad del discurso penal ilustrado: El principio de humanidad. Address to the Real Sociedad Bascongada de los Amigos del País. In: Nuevos Extractos de la Real Sociedad Bascongada de los Amigos del País/Euskaleerriaren Adiskideen Elkartea, Suplement 19-G to its Bulletin. Donostia-San Sebastián, pp. 161–182.
de la Cuesta, J.L. and Varona, G., 2012. Restorative Justice with respect to Terrorist Victimization: Critical Issues and Practical Safeguards. Poster presented at the 14th International Symposium of the World Society of Victimology, The Hague.

de la Cuesta J.L., Varona, G., Mayordomo, V. and San Juan, C., 2011. Estudio exploratorio sobre la Propuesta de un diseño de un programa público de reparación que facilite el retorno de los familiares de personas asesinadas y heridas por la organización terrorista ETA, así como de las personas secuestradas, agredidas, coaccionadas, amenazadas y/o que hayan sufrido daños causados por dicha organización, que manifiesten la voluntad de regresar a Euskadi. Report to the Interior Department of the Basque Government. Donostia-San Sebastián: Instituto Vasco de Criminología/Kriminologiaren Euskal Institutoa.

Daicoff, S., 2006. The Comprehensive Law Movement: An Emerging Approach to Legal Problems. Scandinavian Studies in Law, 49, pp. 109–129.

Daly, K., 2002. Restorative Justice: The Real Story. Punishment and Society: The International Journal of Penology, 4, p. 55–79.

Day, A., Gerace, A., Wilson, C. and Howells, K., 2008. Promoting Forgiveness in Violent Offenders: A More Positive Approach to Offender Rehabilitation? Aggression and Violent Behavior, 13(3), pp. 195–200.

Díaz, F., 2008. La justicia transicional y la justicia restaurativa frente a las necesidades de las víctimas. Umbral Científico, 12, pp. 117–130. Available at: www.redalyc.org [Accessed 5 May 2011].

Doval, A., Blanco Cordero, I., Fernández-Pacheco Estrada, C., Viana Ballester, C. and Sandoval Coronado, J.C., 2011. Las concesiones de indultos en España (2000–2008). Revista Española de Investigación Criminológica, 9, pp. 1–27.

Eagly, A.H., Baron, R.M. and Hamilton, V.L., eds, 2010. The Social Psychology of Group Identity and Social Conflict: Theory, Application, and Practice. Washington: American Psychological Association.

Elorza, A., ed., 2006. La historia de ETA, 2nd edition. Madrid: Temas de Hoy.

Elorza, A., 2011. La estela del terror. El País, 25 August 2011, p. 25.

Erez, E., Kilchling, M. and Wemmers, J.-A., eds, 2011. Therapeutic Jurisprudence and Victim Participation in Justice: International Perspectives. Durham: Carolina Academic Press.

Escamilla, M., 2012. La mediación penal en España: Estado de la cuestión. In: Justicia restaurativa, mediación penal y penitenciaria: Un renovado impulso. Madrid: Reus, pp. 15–47.

Escrivá, Á., 2006. ETA. El camino de vuelta. Barcelona: Seix Barral.

Etxeberria, X., 2010. Historización de la memoria de las víctimas del terrorismo en el País Vasco. In: A. Rivera and C. Herreros, eds, Violencia política. Historia, memoria y víctimas. Madrid: Maia, pp. 287–316.

Etxebarria, X., 2012. Justicia restaurativa y fines del derecho penal. In: M. Escamilla and P. Álvarez, eds, Justicia restaurativa, mediación penal y penitenciaria: Un renovado impulso. Madrid: Reus, pp. 47–69.

Fernández, G. and Romo, R., 2012. ETA y la Ley de Amnistía de 1977. El Diario Vasco, 15 October 2012.

Ferrajoli, L., 1995. Derecho y razón. Teoría del garantismo penal. Madrid: Trotta.

Ferrajoli, L., 2011. Principia iuris, teoría del derecho y de la democracia, vol.1/2. Madrid: Trotta.

Finkelstein, R., 2011. The Adversarial System and the Search for Truth. Monash University Law Review, 37, p. 135.

Fonseca, C., 2006. Negociar con ETA. Del proceso de Argel de Felipe González a la paz dialogada de Rodríguez Zapatero. Madrid: Temas de Hoy.

Fraley, S., 2001. The Meaning of Reconciliation for Prisoners Serving Long Sentences. Contemporary Justice Review, 4(1), pp. 59–74.

Frankenberg, K.V., 2010. Reciprocity in Retaliation and Mediation as a Means of Social Control. In: A. Armsborst and D. Jensen, eds, Retaliation, Mediation and Punishment. Summary of Proceedings IMPRS REMEP Winter University 2009. Freiburg i. B: MPI.

Freedman, S. and Chang, W-C.R., 2010. An Analysis of a Sample of the General Population's Understanding of Forgiveness: Implications for Mental Health Counselors. Journal of Mental Health Counseling, 32(1), pp. 5–34.

Fundación Fernando Buesa, 2011. IV Encuentros: ¿Qué significa deslegitimar el terrorismo...? Vitoria-Gasteiz: Fundación Fernando Buesa.

Gastaminza, G., 2007. La reconciliación entre la hija de un diputado 'tory' y el militante del IRA que le asesinó. El País, 4 November 2007, p. 24.

González, D., 1987. Yoyes desde su ventana. Pamplona: J. Lasa, G. Katarain and J. Dorronsoro, eds.

González, E., 2006. Adriana Faranda. Ex dirigente de las Brigadas Rojas. El País, 26 November, pp. 8–9.

González, E., 2008. El momento de las golondrinas. El País Domingo, 23 November, p. 14.

Guardiola, M. J., ed., 2012. És el conferencing una peina útil per als programes de mediació a l'àmbit penal del Departament de Justícia? Barcelona: Generalitat de Catalunya. Departament de Justícia. Centre d'Estudis Jurídics i Formació Especialitzada.

Guiding Principles for a Model on the End of the ETA without Impunity, 2010. Foundation Document, Meeting of Associations and Foundations of Victims of Terrorism, 23 November. Available at: www.fundacionvt.org/images/fvt/documentos/GUIDING-PRINCIPLES-FOR-A-MODEL-ON-THE-END-OF-ETA-WITHOUT-IMPUNITY.pdf [Accessed 12 September 2012].

Gyökös, M. and Lány, K., eds, 2010. European Best Practices of Restorative Justice in the Criminal Procedure. Budapest: Ministry of Justice and Law Enforcement of the Republic of Hungary.

Hagemann, O., Schäfer, P. and S. Schmidt, S., 2009. Victimology, Victim Assistance and Criminal Justice Perspectives Shared by International Experts at the Inter-University Centre of Dubrovnik. Mönchengladbach: Fachhochschule Niederrhein Verlag.

Holmgren, M. R., 2002. Forgiveness and Self-forgiveness in Psychotherapy. In: S. Lamb and J.G. Murphy, eds, Before Forgiving: Cautionary Views of Forgiveness in Psychotherapy. New York: Oxford University Press, pp. 215–231.

Honneth, A., 1992. Integridad y desprecio. Isegoría, 5, pp. 78–92.

Horgan, J., 2006. Psicología del terrorismo. Cómo y por qué alguien se convierte en terrorista. Barcelona: Gedisa.

Infante, J., 2007. La autodisolución de ETA pm desde la intendencia jurídica. In: Luces y sombras de la disolución de ETA político-militar. Vitoria-Gasteiz: Fundación Fernando Buesa/Aldaketa, pp. 141–150.

Iniciativa Glencree, 2012. Iniciativa Glencree: Nuestra experiencia compartida. Donostia-San Sebastián. Available at: www.interior.ejgv.euskadi.net/r42-victimas/es/contenidos/informacion/informacion_documentos_interes/es_document/documentos_interes.html [Accessed 1 September 2012].

Jamieson, A., 1989. The Heart Attacked: Terrorism and Conflict in the Italian State. London: Marian Boyars.

Jones, J., 2008. Thinking with Stories of Suffering: Towards a Living Theory of Response-ability. Thesis presented at Bath University. Available at: www.actionresearch.net/living/jocelynjonesphd.shtml [Accessed 5 May 2011].
Kaminer, D., Stein, D.J., Mbanga, I. and Zungu-Dirwayi, N., 2001. The Truth and Reconciliation Commission in South Africa: Relation to Psychiatric Status and Forgiveness among Survivors of Human Rights Abuses. British Journal of Psychiatry, 178, pp. 373–377.
Karstedt, S., Loader, I. and Strang, H., eds, 2011. Emotions, Crime and Justice. Oxford: Hart.
Larizgoitia, I., Izarzugaza, I. and Markez, I., 2009. La noche de las víctimas. Investigación sobre el Impacto en la Salud de la Violencia Colectiva (ISAVIC) en el País Vasco. Bilbao: Fundación Fernando Buesa.
Lefranc, S., 2004. Políticas del perdón. Madrid: Cátedra.
Letschert, R. and van Dijk, J., eds, 2011. The New Faces of Victimhood. Globalization, Transnational Crimes and Victim Rights. New York: Springer.
Letschert, R., Staiger, I. and Pemberton, A., eds, 2010. Assisting Victims of Terrorism. Towards a European Standard of Justice. Dordrecht: Springer.
Lind, E.A. and Tyler, T., 1988. The Social Psychology of Procedural Justice. New York: Plenum.
Lozano, F. and Pérez, L., 2012. Mediación penitenciaria: Pasado, presente y ¿futuro? In: M. Escamilla and P. Álvarez, eds, Justicia restaurativa, mediación penal y penitenciaria: Un renovado impulso. Madrid: Reus, pp. 273–309.
Lozano, F., Sáez, C., Escamilla, M. and Santos, E., 2011. Encuentros entre víctimas y terroristas. El País, 14 October 2011.
Magallón, C., 2011. Justicia, memoria y reconciliación tras la violencia. publico.es, 24 October.
Malcolm, W., 2008. The Timeliness of Forgiveness Interventions. In: W. Malcolm, N. DeCourville and K. Belicki, eds, Women's Reflections on the Complexities of Forgiveness. New York: Routledge/Taylor & Francis Group, pp. 304–334.
Mallinder, L., 2008. Amnesty, Human Rights and Political Transitions. Building the Peace and Justice Divide. Oxford: Hart.
Marshall, C.D., 2007. Terrorism, Religious Violence and Restorative Justice. In: G. Johnstone and D.W. Van Ness, eds, Handbook of Restorative Justice. Portland: Willan Publishing, pp. 372–394.
Martin-Peña, J., Opotow, S. and Rodríguez-Carballeira, A., 2011. Amenazados y víctimas del entramado de ETA en Euskadi: Un estudio desde la teoría de la exclusión moral. Revista de Psicología Social, 26(2), pp. 177–190.
McEvoy, K., 2010. The Troubles with Truth. Transition, Reconciliation and Struggling with the Past in Northern Ireland. Cullompton: Willan Publishing.
McEvoy, K. and McGregor, L., eds, 2008. Transitional Justice from Below. London: Hart.
Murithi, T., 2009. The Ethics of Peacebuilding. Edinburgh Studies in World Ethics. Edinburgh: Edinburgh University Press.
Naqvi, Y., 2006. The Right to the Truth in International Law: Fact or Fiction? International Review of the Red Cross, 88(862), pp. 245–273.
Novales, F., 1989. El tazón de hierro. Memoria personal de un militante de los Grapo. Barcelona: Crítica.

Olalde, A.J., 2012. Encuentros restaurativos en victimización terrorista: la mirada práctica del trabajo social. Dissertation presented to the Mediation Master of the Social Work Faculty, University of Murcia (Spain).

Ordaz, P., 2001. Diálogo entre víctimas. Hablar de la paz y de la justicia. El País, País Vasco, 4 March, p. 4.

Paez, D. and Beristain, C., 2009. Superando la violencia colectiva y construyendo cultura de paz. Madrid: Fundamentos.

Paez, D. and Martin, C., 2009. Superando la violencia colectiva y construyendo cultura de paz. Madrid: Fundamentos.

Pagazartundúa, M., 2006. La doble victimación. In: El significado político de las víctimas del terrorismo: el valor del Estado de Derecho y de la ciudadanía. Fundación Fernando Buesa: Vitoria-Gasteiz, pp. 140–160.

Pagazaurtundúa, M., 2011. La práctica de la justicia victimal y el valor público del testimonio de las víctimas del terrorismo. Communication presented within the Encuentro Internacional en Homenaje al Prof. Antonio Beristain, Hacia una justicia victimal, Donostia-San Sebastián.

Park, G., 2010. Truth as Justice. Harvard International Review, 1 February. Available at: http://hir.harvard.edu/big-ideas/truth-as-justice?page=0,2 [Accessed 12 November 2013].

Pérez, J.A., 2010. La memoria de las víctimas del terrorismo en el País Vasco: Un proyecto en marcha. In: A. Rivera and C. Herreros, eds, Violencia política. Historia, memoria y víctimas. Madrid: Maia, pp. 338–352.

Peterson, M., 2010. Victim–Offender Dialogue in Crimes of Severe Violence. In: M. Umbreit and M. Peterson, eds, Restorative Justice Dialogue. An Essential Guide for Research and Practice. New York: Springer, pp. 211–239

Pulgar Gutiérrez, M.B., 2004. Víctimas del terrorismo. 1968–2004. Madrid: Dykinson.

Rees, L., 2008. Los verdugos y las víctimas. Barcelona: Crítica.

Reinares, F., 2001. Patriotas de la muerte. Quiénes han militado en ETA y por qué. Madrid: Taurus.

Reyes, M., 2008. Justicia de las víctimas. Terrorismo, memoria, reconciliación. Barcelona: Fundación Alternativas y Anthropos.

Reyes, M., 2011. Tratado de la injusticia. Barcelona: Anthropos.

Ríos, J.C., ed., 2008. La mediación penal y penitenciaria. Experiencias de diálogo en el sistema penal para la reducción de la violencia y el sufrimiento humano. Madrid: Colex.

Ríos, J.C. and Etxeberria, X., 2012. El valor de la palabra. Encuentros restaurativos entre víctimas y condenados, Razón y Fe. Available at: www.razonyfe.es/index.php/component/content/article/84 [Accessed 5 February 2012].

Ríos, J. Sáez, R., Etxeberria, X., Segovia, J. L., Piñeyroa, C., Olalde, A., Urkijo, T., Pascual, E., Fábrega, C., Francés, P., Gallego, M. and Castillo, E., 2012. Reflexiones sobre la viabilidad de instrumentos de justicia restaurativa en delitos graves. In Justicia restaurativa, mediación penal y penitenciaria: Un renovado impulso. Madrid: Reus, pp. 127–173.

Röhly, K.F. and Machura, S., 1997. Procedural Justice. Ashgate: Oñati International Institute for the Sociology of Law.

Rohne, H.C., 2008. Conceptualizing Punitiveness From A Victims' Perspective – Findings in the Context of the Al-Aqsa Intifada. In: H. Kury and T. N. Ferdinand, eds, International Perspectives on Punitivity. Bochum: Universitätsverlag Dr N. Brockmeyer. pp. 161–187.

Romera, C., 2011. Mediación penal: Mediando en conflictos violentos. In: H. Muñoz, ed., Mediación y resolución de conflictos: Técnicas y ámbitos. Madrid: Tecnos, ch. 28.

Rotman, E,. 2008. Therapeutic Jurisprudence and Terrorism, University of Miami Legal Studies Research Paper No. 2008-33. Available at: http://ssrn.com/abstract=1291868 or http://dx.doi.org/10.2139/ssrn.1291868 [Accessed 1 December 2012].

Sáez, R., 2011. Mediación penal. Reconciliación, perdón y delitos muy graves. La emergencia de las víctimas. Cuadernos Penales José María Lidón, 8, pp. 71–125.

Sáez, R., 2012. Notas sobre justicia restaurativa y delitos graves. Dialogando sobre 'las reflexiones' y su viabilidad. In: M. Escamilla and P. Álvarez, eds, Justicia restaurativa, mediación penal y penitenciaria: Un renovado impulso. Madrid: Reus, pp. 173–207.

Salaburu, P., 2011. La vergüenza de nuestro silencio. diariovasco.com, 13 December.

Sánchez, J.M., 2012. El renacer de la víctima y el reconocimiento de sus derechos en la Unión Europea. In: M. Escamilla and P. Álvarez, eds, Justicia restaurativa, mediación penal y penitenciaria: Un renovado impulso. Madrid: Reus, pp. 69–109.

Sánchez-Cuenca, I., 2007. The Dynamics Of Nationalist Terrorism: ETA and the IRA. Terrorism and Political Violence, 19(3), pp. 289–306.

Sánchez-Cuenca, I., 2010. La pervivencia del terrorismo de ETA. In: A. Rivera and C. Herreros, eds, Violencia política. Historia, memoria y víctimas. Madrid: Maia/Instituto Universitario de Historia Social 'Valentín de Foronda', pp. 207–234.

Savater, F., 2012. ¡Y lo llaman venganza! elpais.com, 28 June. Available at: http://elpais.com/elpais/2012/06/26/opinion/1340726255_368654.html [Accessed 1 December 2012].

Schechtman, L., 2005. Applications of Peacemaking Circles in Meeting the Mental Health Needs of Torture Survivors. Thesis presented at University of Denver. Available at: www.restorativejustice.org/10fulltext/schechtman-lisa.-applications-of-peacemaking-circles-in-meeting-the-mental-health-needs-of-torture-survivors/view [Accessed 1 September 2012].

Schubotz, D., Melaugh, M. and McLoughlin, P., 2011. Archiving Qualitative Data in the Context of a Society Coming out of Conflict: Some Lessons from Northern Ireland. Forum: Qualitative Social Research, 12(3). Available at: www.qualitative-research.net/ [Accessed 1 September 2012].

Scott, M. and Lyman, S., 1968. Accounts. American Sociological Review, 33(1), pp. 46–62.

Sen, A.K., 2010. La idea de la justicia. Madrid: Taurus.

Shapland, J., 2011. Restorative Justice and States' Uneasy Relationship with their Publics. In: A. Crawford, ed., International and Comparative Criminal Justice and Urban Governance. Convergence and Divergence in Global, National and Local Settings. Cambridge: Cambridge University Press, pp. 439–461.

Sherman, L.W. and Strang, H., 2007. Restorative Justice: The Evidence. London: The Smith Institute.

Short, C.l., 2011. No Forgiveness without Justice? Annual address of The Forgiveness Project. Available at: www.theforgivenessproject.com [Accessed 1 September 2012].

Skelton, A. and Sekhonyane, M., 2007. Human Rights and Restorative Justice. In: G. Johnstone and D.W. Van Ness, eds, Handbook of Restorative Justice. Portland: Willan Publishing, pp. 580–598.

Staiger, I., 2010. Restorative Justice and Victims of Terrorism. In: R. Letschert, I. Staiger and A. Pemberton, eds, Assisting Victims of Terrorism: Towards a European Standard of Justice. London-New York: Springer, pp. 267–339.

Strang, H., 2002. Repair or Revenge: Victims & Restorative Justice. Oxford: Oxford University Press.

Strang, H., Angel, C. and Van Camp, T., 2008. Restorative Justice and Victims of Serious Crimes. Communication presented at the XVth World Congress of the International Society of Criminology, Barcelona.

Szmania, S., 2006. Mediator's Communications in Victim Offender Mediation/Dialogue Involved Crimes of Severe Violence: An Analysis of Opening Statements. Conflict Resolution Quarterly, 24(1), pp. 111–127.

Umbreit, M., 2005. The Paradox of Forgiveness in Restorative Justice. In: L. Everette and Jr. Worthington, eds, The Handbook of Forgiveness. New York: Routledge, pp. 491–505.

United Nations Office on Drugs and Crime, 2011. The Criminal Justice Response to Support Victims of Acts of Terrorism. New York: United Nations.

Uriarte, T., 2005. Mirando atrás. Del proceso de Burgos a la amenaza permanente. Barcelona: Ediciones B.

Uribe, W., 2011. Allí donde ETA asesinó. Barcelona: Los libros del lince.

Valcárcel, A., 2011. La memoria y el perdón. Barcelona: Herder.

Van Camp, T. and Wemmers, J.-A., 2011. La justice réparatrice et les crimes graves. Criminologie, 44(2), pp. 171–198.

Van Droogenbroeck, B., 2010. Victim Offender Mediation in Severe Crimes in Belgium: What Victims Need and Offenders can Offer. In: M. Gyokos and K. Lanyi, eds, European Best Practices of Restorative Justice in the Criminal Procedure. Conference Publication. Budapest: Justice Ministry, pp. 230–235.

Van Stokkom, B., Doorn, N. and van Tongeren, P., eds, 2012. Public Forgiveness in Post-Conflict Contexts. Antwerpen: Intersentia.

Vanfraechem, I. and Aertsen, I., 2010. Empirical Research on Restorative Justice in Europe: Perspectives. In: I. Vanfraechem, I. Aertsen and J. Willemsens, eds, Restorative Justice Realities: Empirical Research in a European Context. The Hague: Eleven Publishing, pp. 267–278.

Varona Martínez, G., 2009. Evolución jurisprudencial en la interpretación de diversos aspectos de la ejecución de sentencias condenatorias en materia de terrorismo de ETA. In: J.L. de la Cuesta and I. Muñagorri, eds, Aplicación de la normativa antiterrorista.. Donostia-San Sebastián: Instituto Vasco de Criminología, ch. 3.

Varona Martínez, G., 2012a. Justicia restaurativa en supuestos de victimización terrorista: Hacia un sistema de garantías mediante el estudio criminológico de casos comparados. Eguzkilore. Cuaderno del Instituto Vasco de Criminología, 26, pp. 201–245.

Varona Martínez, G., 2012b. Sistema de indicadores en justicia restaurativa en supuestos de victimización terrorista: Buenas prácticas validadas en la normativa internacional a la luz de la investigación victimológica. In: Terrorismo, Víctimas y Justicia Victimal, report presented to the Interior Department of the Basque Government. Donostia-San Sebastián: Basque Institute of Criminology.

Varona Martínez, G., (in press) Restorative Processes in the Context of ETA Terrorist Victimisations. In: J. L. Moreno and H. Soleto, eds, Terrorism. Madrid: Carlos III.

Varona Martínez, G., 2013. The Meaning of Impunity: What Do Victims, Offenders and Society Think of Restorative Encounters in the Context of ETA Terrorism in Spain? Restorative Justice: An International Journal 1(2): 215–243.

Varona, G., Larmarca, I., Hernández, J., López de Foronda, F., Pagola, A. and Oca, N., 2009. Atención institucional a las víctimas del terrorismo en Euskadi. Vitoria-Gasteiz: Ararteko.

Vertigans, S., 2011. The Sociology of Terrorism. People, Places and Processes. London: Routledge.

Villa, I., 2007. SOS Víctima del terrorismo. Madrid: Pirámide.

Vos, B. and Umbreit, M.S., 2000. Homicide Survivors Meet the Offender Prior to Execution. Restorative Justice Through Dialogue. Homicide Studies, 4(1), pp. 63–87.

Vriezen, V., 2012. Amnesty Justified? The Need for a Case Approach in the Interest of Human Rights. Antwerp: Intersentia.

Walker, L. and Greening, R., 2011. Reentry & Transition Planning Circles for Incarcerated People. Honolulu: Hawai'i Friends of Justice & Civic Education.

Walker, P., 1999. Saying Sorry, Acting Sorry. The Sycamore Tree Project, a Model for Restorative Justice in Prison. The Prison Service Journal, 123, pp. 19–20.

Walklate, S., 1990. Researching Victims of Crime: Critical Victimology. Social Justice, 17, pp. 25–42.

Wexler, D.B., 2011. From Theory to Practice and Back Again in Therapeutic Jurisprudence: Now Comes the Hard Part. Monash University Law Review, 37. Available at: http://papers.ssrn.com/sol3/papers.cfm?abstract_id=1580129. [Accessed 13 September 2013].

Wilkinson, R. and Pickett, K., 2011. Foreword. In: D. Dorling, Injustice. Why social inequality persists. Bristol: The Policy Press, pp. xv–xvii.

Williams, M.S. and Nagy, R., 2012. Introduction. In: M.S. Williams, R. Nagy and J. Elster, eds, Transitional Justice. New York: New York University Press, pp. 1–31.

Williamson, I. and Gonzalez, M.H., 2007. The Subjective Experience of Forgiveness: Positive Construals of the Forgiveness Experience. Journal of Social and Clinical Psychology 26(4), pp. 407–446.

Willis, G.M. and Ward, T., 2010. Risk Management versus the Good Lives Model: The Construction of Better Lives and the Reduction of Harm. In: M. Dréan-Rivette and M. Evans, eds, Transnational Criminology Manual, volume 3. Nijmegen: Wolf Legal Publishing, pp. 763–781.

Wohl, M.J.A., DeShea, L. and Wahkinney, R.L., 2008. Looking Within: Measuring State Self-forgiveness and its Relationship to Psychological Well-being. Canadian Journal of Behavioural Science/Revue canadienne des sciences du comportement, 40(1), pp. 1–10.

Worthington, E.L., Jr., Sandage, S.J. and Berry, J.W., 2000. Group Interventions to Promote Forgiveness: What Researchers and Clinicians Ought to Know. In: M.E. McCullough, K.I. Pargament and C.E. Thoresen, eds, Forgiveness: Theory, Research, and Practice. New York: Guilford Press, pp. 228–254.

Zawisza, C.A., 2012. Sprawuj się (Do Good): Using the Experience of Holocaust Rescuers to Teach Public Service Values. University of Memphis Legal Studies Research Paper, No. 115. Available at: http://papers.ssrn.com/sol3/papers.cfm?abstract_id=2065469 [Accessed 1 October 2012].

Zehr, H., 1990. Changing Lenses: A New Focus for Crime and Justice. Ontario: Herald Press.

Zinsstag, E. and Vanfraechem, I., eds, 2012. Conferencing and Restorative Justice: Challenges, Developments and Debates. Oxford: Oxford University Press.

Chapter 17

Victims of corruption
A conceptual framework

Qingli Meng and Paul C. Friday

Introduction

Research on corruption shows that bribery not only stymies development, but also has an impact on health services, literacy rates and the environment. This chapter is an effort to conceptualize in detail how corruption victimizes the society as a whole, its institutions and individuals. When corruption is prosecuted, the victims and their needs are generally ignored. This chapter attempts to create a model of the impact of corruption that recognizes the different dimensions of corruption. Corruption may be incidental (bribes to junior public officials), sporadic (affects different/select aspects of government) or systemic/endemic (having a developmental impact). Corruption infringes the fundamental human rights to fair treatment, unbiased decision-making, and secure civil and political status. Corruption can cause individual damage, institutional damage, and social or societal damage. Damage can be tangible or abstract. Recognizing these dimensions can aid the process of recognizing the different needs of victims of corruption.

Extent of corruption

Corruption is considered a serious hindrance to a country's social, economic and political development. Its power undermines the rule of law and results in the inefficient distribution of scarce resources, the demoralization of political systems and the abrogation of respect for human rights (United Nations 2012a). Embezzlement and other forms of corruption are recognized as serious issues in many countries, yet it is extremely difficult to assess the extent of these corruption forms on a worldwide scale. A number of facts have emerged showing that bribery and corruption are especially widespread in developing countries.

According to Transparency International (2010), corruption is estimated to increase the cost of achieving the UN Millennium Development Goal on water and sanitation alone by US $48 billion, and poor families in Mexico spend an estimated one-fifth of their income on petty bribes where bribery in public services cost the economy 32 billion pesos (US$ 2.6 billion) in 2010.

The same source states that in Bangladesh 84 per cent of the households who had interacted with one or more different public and private service sectors or institutions have been victims of corruption in 2010 with 33 per cent of these Bangladeshi people experiencing corruption in healthcare services. In addition, Transparency International reports findings from a seven-country study in Africa – Ghana, Madagascar, Morocco, Niger, Senegal, Sierra Leone and Uganda. The study showed that 44 per cent of the parents surveyed had paid illegal fees for schools that were legally free for their children.

Corruption is not simply a developing country problem; it is a global challenge (Stapenhurst and Sedigh 1999). Those concerned now recognize that corruption is not a private matter between corrupted and corruptor, but something that may destroy and degrade whole economies and cultures (World Economic Forum 2012). Transparency International (2011) produces a Corruption Perceptions Index, which ranks countries/territories based on how corrupt their public sector is perceived to be. A country/territory's score indicates the perceived level of public sector corruption on a scale of 0–10, where 0 means that a country is perceived as highly corrupt and 10 means that a country is perceived as free from corruption. A country's rank indicates its position relative to the other countries/territories included in the index. A cursory review of the nations involved shows that corruption is pervasive, affecting developed and developing countries alike. The country perceived to have the lowest rate of corruption with a score of 9.5 is New Zealand (Transparency International 2011) followed by Denmark (9.4), Finland (9.4), Sweden (9.3) and Singapore (9.2). The United States ranks 24th (7.1); China is 22nd (7.2). Those perceived to be the most corrupt are Afghanistan (1.5), Myanmar (1.5), and Somalia (1.0).

Overall, Transparency International categorizes three levels of corruption. *High rate* corruption countries mainly include countries in Southeast Asia, the Middle East, Latin America and parts of Africa. The *medium rate* corruption countries include developed countries such as Germany, the United States, Austria, France, Belgium, Japan and South Africa. The *low rate* corruption countries include developed countries like Singapore, New Zealand, Denmark, Finland, Canada, Sweden, Australia, Switzerland, The Netherlands, Norway and the United Kingdom. The low rate countries appear to have an effective adherence to the rule of law, good monitoring mechanisms, and a 'well rounded citizenship' (Rose-Ackerman 2002; Treisman 2006).

Manifestation and costs of corruption

Given the differing moral standards, values and economic organization of developed and developing societies, what constitutes and is labelled as corruption and the forms corruption takes within these two different social and institutional systems are not identical (Kwong 1997). Cultural differences decide tolerances to corruption in various societies. The identification of what corruption is and what should be considered corruption is key to any significant anti-corruption effort. In the high gift-giving culture of China, corruption is often disguised by so-called gift-giving behaviours. So the unveiling process of gift-giving with the nature of corruption behaviour is one of the major tasks in anti-corruption measures. Depending upon its degree, form and dimensions, corruption can be grand or petty, infrequent or pervasive, complicated or simple, direct or indirect, bilateral or unilateral, open or secret, routine or non-routine.

Definitions of corruption vary, depending on scholarly perspectives. Nye (1989), who focuses on the individual actors, sees public official corruption as deviant behaviour from one's formal duty because of rent-seeking, which can be demonstrated via either private financial or status gains, or both, or the 'violation of rules against the exercise of certain types of private regarding influence' (Nye 1989, p. 966), including bribery, use of reward to pervert the judgement of a person in a position of trust; nepotism, bestowal of patronage by reason of ascriptive relationship rather than merit; and misappropriation of public resources.

Klitgaard (1991) takes a more institutional economic approach, defining corruption by a formula in which corruption equals monopoly plus discretion, minus accountability. Monopoly power is conducive to corruption (Rose-Ackerman 1978; Della Porta and Vannucci 1999; Della Porta and Rose-Ackerman 2002). Klitgaard (1991, p. 75) states that 'illicit behavior flourishes when agents have monopoly power over clients, when agents have great discretion, and when accountability of agents to the principal is weak'. Corruption is not only limited to the embezzlement of public funds but extends to nepotism, bribe taking, cutting corners, undue influence, favouritism, lack of due process, lack of morals and neglect of acceptable societal values.

The nature of corruption is both covert and consensual. Corruption is such a secretive process in most cases that it is difficult to expose. 'Unlike the situation with many other types of crime, corruption benefits people on both sides of the immediate equation—those paying bribes to gain favours, for example, and those receiving bribes—giving both an interest in secrecy' (Stapenhurst and Sedigh 1999, p. 106). In general, there seem to be no obvious or direct victims even though corruption has a negative impact on the image of society and causes tremendous social welfare loss. 'The victims—for example, taxpayers who are overcharged for public services, or honest business people who lose contracts because of corrupt procurement practices—do not usually know what has happened' (Stapenhurst and Sedigh 1999, p. 106).

In developing countries corruption has hampered national, social, economic and political progress (Lambsdorff 2005). In a recent survey of 150 high level officials from 60 third world countries the respondents ranked public sector corruption as the most severe obstacle confronting their development process (Gray and Kaufmann 1998). Public resources are allocated inefficiently, competent and honest citizens feel frustrated and the general population's level of distrust rises (United Nations 2001). As a consequence, productivity is lower, administrative efficiency is reduced and the legitimacy of political and economic order is undermined. The effectiveness of efforts on the part of developed countries to redress imbalances and foster development is also eroded: foreign aid disappears, projects are left incomplete and ultimately donors lose enthusiasm (Svensson 2000). Corruption in developing countries also impairs economic development by transferring large sums of money intended for aid and investment into corrupt officials' offshore bank accounts beyond reach of the nations in question (United Nations 2001).

This reverse flow of capital leads in turn to political and economic instability, poor infrastructure, education, health and other services and a general tendency to create or perpetuate low standards of living. 'In short, it increases wealth for the few at the expense of society as a whole, leaving the poor suffering the harshest consequences' (World Bank 2012a). Some of those effects can be found in developed countries as well, although here the government's ability to combat corruption is greater since corruption is less widespread and is concentrated in certain types of business/government enterprises such as international trade, construction and defence contracting.

Corruption is also enhanced by the presence of organized crime at the domestic and international levels (Griffith 1997; World Economic Forum 2003). Apart from the obvious incentives for organized criminal groups to launder and conceal their assets, various forms of corruption allow such groups to minimize the risks and maximize the benefits of their criminal activity. In the case of organized crime, corruption raises the danger of corrupt political and judicial practices (Buscaglia 2000) to the point that organized crime can 'capture the State by co-opting public institutions' (Buscaglia and van Dijk 2003, p. 9). Officials can be bribed to overlook and sometimes even participate in the smuggling of commodities ranging from narcotics to weapons and human trafficking. In any case, official corruption is an essential part of the growth of organized criminal activities.

While systemic and widespread corruption is often viewed as an individual crime problem where anti-corruption measures focus on deterrence and criminal and penal measures (Huther and Shah 2005), a broader perspective sees corruption as rooted in deeper social, cultural and economic factors and recognizes that those factors must also be addressed if the fight against corruption is to succeed (Aidt 2009). It is also recognized that the deleterious effects of corruption go far beyond harm to individual victims. Corruption represents a serious obstacle to enhancing economic growth and to improving the lives of the poorest segments of the population in developing countries and societies and economies in transition. Development agencies have come to understand that corruption not only erodes the actual delivery of aid and assistance, but undermines the fundamental goals of social and economic development itself.

This broader understanding of the nature of corruption has led those confronted with it to seek more broadly based counterstrategies, such as the implementation of operational social control mechanisms at the national and local levels. Reactive criminal justice measures are now supplemented by social and economic measures intended not only to deter corruption but also to prevent it. The recognition that public sector and private sector corruption are often simply two aspects of the same problem has led to strategies that involve not only public officials but also major domestic and multinational commercial enterprises, banks and financial institutions, other nongovernmental entities and, in many strategies, civil societies in general (Huther and Shah 2005). This broader perspective suggests that corruption manifests itself differently depending upon the structure and development level of a given society. It also suggests that corruption impacts (victimizes) both individuals and the society itself. The impact of corruption is not one-dimensional.

A conceptual framework

The idea that a corruption is a 'victimless crime' is inaccurate. It implies that corruption is merely a matter of morals or an individual's decision. The damage caused by corruption is both material (human and financial loss, for example) and also immaterial or more abstract (loss of trust and credibility, for example); it can also simultaneously affect individuals (bidders who lost in a procurement process tainted by corruption), identifiable groups of people (children of a specific school) and also members of a community (such as the citizens of a country). As suggested above, the victims of bribery are often those living in poverty in the developing world in countries rich in resources but dominated by corrupt governments. While the vast majority of these citizens remain very poor, their elected officials accumulate enormous personal wealth, taking millions in bribes from corporations looking to secure lucrative contracts. These are the victims of corruption: a poor man who dies because of lack of efficient and affordable health care; a poor woman who is malnourished, hopeless and is not sure of where the next meal will come from; and a woman who dies in childbirth because of lack of access to medical care. In addition, a child who dies because of neglect and millions of children who are denied a basic education, food and medical care are victims. It is clear that individuals are victims of corruption and, as has been noted above, corruption also has definite effects on the society itself.

What follows is an exploratory effort to conceptualize a victimology of corruption. It is simplistic to say that both individuals and the society itself can be victims of corruption. We attempt to explore in more detail exactly how corruption victimizes individuals and society by conceptualizing levels of victimization and how each level is affected by the ways corruption manifests itself. We do not view the categorizations as mutually exclusive but we offer them in an attempt to stimulate a more detailed discussion on the harm caused by corruption.

Levels of victimization

Individual behaviours, conforming or deviant, can be viewed as the product of individual, institutional and wider social structural factors (Friday 1988).

Individual behaviour is influenced not only by personal characteristics such as age, race, gender and personality but also by interaction with others within social institutions such as the family, school, religious and governmental institutions. These institutions are also part of wider structural contexts such as the political economy, degrees of urbanization and cultural factors that tend to transcend time and individual influence. These levels of analysis, structural, institutional and individual, help explain human behaviour and they can also be used to help explain the levels of victimization.

We argue that not only can the cause of corruption exist on these different levels but that the victims of corruption also fall on these levels. Individuals are victims of corruption but so too are the social institutions within which corruption occurs and, subsequently, the society itself can be considered a victim of corruption.

Structural level

Corruption has been tied to political, demographic and cultural or structural aspects of society. Societies have been classified according to their structural dynamics. Using subjective ratings, Treisman (2006) found that highly developed, long-established liberal democracies, with a free and wide-reaching press, a high proportion of women in government and a history of open trade are perceived as less corrupt while countries that depend on natural resources or have invasive business regulations and unpredictable inflation are perceived as more corrupt. Despite cultural and linguistic differences in Nigeria, one thing that most Nigerians will agree on, argues Uwakwe (2012), is the fact that corruption has eaten into the fabric of the country. He argues that the consensus is that corruption is so embedded in national life that everybody appears to have accepted it as part of doing business in or with Nigeria. Unfortunately, the culture of Nigeria has become synonymous with corruption, suggesting that the society itself has become victimized by widespread and pervasive corrupt practices. Corruption is not just the product of immediate material incentive, but is also influenced by cultural orientations that are acquired through socialization and a society's historical heritage (Sandholtz and Taagepera 2005).

Structural level victimization. Olaya *et al.* (2010), using a case study in Costa Rica, argue that corruption has an effect on the national economy (a structural factor) by reducing the investor's trust. Corruption also impedes economic growth, making the society a victim. With rampant corruption, foreign and domestic investment is discouraged because corruption destroys predictability and increases the cost of doing business. It increases the uncertainty and risk attached to investment and reduces incentives for entrepreneurs. This is supported by studies focusing on bilateral money transactions between 14 source and 45 host countries in 1990 and 1991, showing the significant negative impact of corruption on foreign direct investment (Wei 2000). Other research provides strong evidence that corruption lowers a country's attractiveness to international and domestic investors (Lambsdorff 2005).

This reduces capital accumulation and lowers capital investment. Also, the productivity of capital suffers from corruption.

Corruption has been shown to infringe on the fundamental human rights to fair treatment, unbiased decision-making, and secure civil and political status (Evans, n.d.). Corruption also undermines the ability of societies to develop through investment and aid. Mauro (1995) finds that in a sample of 67 countries, in all cases corruption impacts negatively on the ratio of investment to GDP.

Institutional level

All societies have norms and expectations which are learned through interaction within the family, in schools, in community organizations and peer groups (Tarrant 2002). Behaviour associated with these norms and expectations is also learned (Bandura 1989). This occurs as a result of the roles individuals learn to play. The institutional level theories explain crime as a function of the transmission of norms and values by the social institutions in a given society. Informal constraints come from socially transmitted information and are a part of the cultural heritage (North 2005), which can be defined as the 'transmission from one generation to the next, via teaching and imitation, of knowledge, values, and other factors that influence behavior' (Boyd and Richerson 1985, p. 2). Ngo (2008) argues that rent-creation and rent-seeking are difficult to eliminate because they have become institutionalized as the constitutive parts of economic governance.

Different societies have various degrees of tolerance towards certain deviant behaviours. The degree of tolerance depends on the socialization of behaviour through the cultural transmission of cultural precepts, differential association, and techniques of neutralizations (Lima and Friday 2005). The decline in the moral costs of corruption stimulates its further spread. Thus, institutions serve as the context within which the values of corruption are transmitted and they are also the victims of that same transmission.

Institutional victimization. Corruption consumes the very agencies that generate it. This is accomplished through socialization and socialized expectations. Institutions, such as the police or other governmental agencies can become corrupted, thereby negatively impacting the citizens they are expected to serve. There is strong evidence that corruption distorts government expenditure and reduces the quality of a wide variety of government services, such as public investment, health care, tax revenue, investment in education and environmental control (Mauro 1998). This corroborates the argument that large welfare losses result from corruption.

Individual level

While studying corruption, the individual actor, his self-concept, social role and definition of the situation are the main forces determining behaviour. Each of these – self-concept, social role and how one defines situations – are the product of the socialization that occurs at the institutional level. However, each individual is unique and one must also look at variances in exactly *how* an actor interprets the world around him or her. According to Margolis (1982) an individual possesses two utility functions: the usual self-interest preference function and the purely social/group interested preference function. This suggests that people act to fulfil both selfish, individual, egoistic interests as well as altruistic or collective interests. Applying this to corruption, 'Public servants may achieve mediocrity if they work strictly within the limit of the law; yet, in order to reach levels of excellence, they must include the essential values of humanism, solidarity and tolerance in that exercise' (Lima and Friday 2005, p. 440). Sugden (1986) maintains that a convention acquires moral force when almost everyone in the community follows it and it is in the interests of each individual that people with whom he or she deals follow the rule providing that the individual does too. This is a 'morality of cooperation' (Sugden 1986, p. 173). Corrupt officials, like most criminals, can find justifications for their deviant behaviour by adjusting the definitions of their actions and by explaining to themselves and others the lack of guilt of their actions in particular situations (Sykes and Matza 1957).

Individual victimization. In short, corruption victimizes people. The impact may be very direct when, for example, aid money is siphoned into private bank accounts or bribes distort public spending priorities, thereby denying individuals the aid they were meant to receive. The poor will also suffer indirectly when bribery structurally damages a whole economy and public services are reduced or eliminated. Those who are poor are most dependent on good public services, for they have few alternatives and they cannot afford, for example, private health care or schools (Evans, n.d.).

In summary, a better way of looking at the victims of corruption is to put victimization into a conceptual framework that includes three levels – *Individual* (people), *Institutional* (social institutions such as education, government agencies) and *Structural* (natural and economic resource distribution, environment and culture).

Manifestations of corruption

We have argued that corruption as a phenomenon is caused by factors on three levels of analysis: structural, institutional and individual, and that victims of corruption can be found at each of these levels. The extent and frequency of corruption varies across societies. It can be extensive or incidental. We argue, based in part on the glossary of corruption provided by U4,[1] that corruption can be *systemic* or endemic (as part of the fabric of the society and deep rooted). Corruption can also be *sporadic*, occurring irregularly and not threatening the mechanisms of control nor the economy as such. Being sporadic it is not crippling, but it can seriously undermine morale and sap the economy of resources. It is selective and appears in diverse segments of society. We add a third manifestation – *opportunistic* or incidental. In this instance corruption is unpredictable and occurs only when the opportunity presents itself to the corrupt official or person providing services.

Systemic corruption

Corruption is *systemic* or *endemic* when it is widespread throughout the society and where the population considers it as part of their cultural expectations: the corruption is an integrated and essential aspect of the economic, social and political system. Systemic corruption is not a special category of corrupt practice, but rather a situation in which the major institutions and processes of the state are routinely dominated and used by corrupt individuals and groups and in which most people have no alternatives to dealing with corrupt officials. According to U4 (2012), systemic corruption is corruption which is primarily due to weaknesses of social processes, i.e. it comes from a breakdown in the rules governing the interaction. Systemic corruption is when there are consistent, expected demands for bribes for normal regular services (Tanzi 1998). It is systemic when routine resources are scarce or strictly controlled and access to them requires under-the-table and even sometimes overt, additional payment to get goods through customs, or get telephone services or required permits. Corruption is systemic when applicants for driver's licenses, building permits and other routine documents have learned to expect a 'surcharge' from civil servants (Evans, n.d.). At a higher level, bribes are paid to win public contracts, to purchase political influence (Tanzi 1998), to sidestep safety inspections, to bypass bureaucratic red tape and to ensure that criminal activities are protected from interference by police and other criminal justice officials. All of these acts or expectations are known to the public; to be systemic, corruption must be perceived to be pervasive. Where institutions are weak, other contrasts may emerge: a weak state may be vulnerable to illicit private pressures, while weak property rights or civil societies might leave citizens vulnerable to official demands (Rock and Bonnett 2004).

Sporadic corruption

As stated, sporadic corruption occurs irregularly throughout the political economic system creating a degree of uncertainty as to its location and scale. For this reason it negatively affects development by siphoning critical economic resources into private hands (U4 2012). Sporadic corruption is selective but consistent, generally within specific agencies or departments (Johnston 2005). In many instances sporadic corruption is more closely tied to criminal activity rather than to routine, life-course requirements for goods or services as is more characteristic of systemic corruption. Sporadic corruption enables such things as drug and arms trafficking, gambling, money laundering and other illegal activity, including organized crime, to function (Griffith 1997). While a systemically corrupt society also enables some of these activities, sporadic corruption can exist in an otherwise corruption-free society.

These would be the mid-range corruption level countries identified by Transparency International (2010) and those societies which Hao and Johnston (1995) referred to as 'influence markets' with strong political and economic opportunities yet where some corruption is still evident.

Incidental/opportunistic corruption

Opportunistic corruption is the everyday small-scale, bureaucratic or petty corruption that takes place at the practical end of politics – where the public officials interact directly with the public (U4 2012). Incidental or opportunistic corruption is not part of the wider fabric of the society, nor is it organized. It is committed by individuals on an irregular basis, depending upon the situation or circumstances. Incidental corruption is often bribery in connection with the implementation of existing laws, rules and regulations, and usually involves modest sums of money (U4 2012); not all persons within a department or agency are 'on-the-take'; an example might be individual police officers taking bribes to 'look the other way'. Incidental corruption can be considered 'doing favours' – often for 'favours in return' that may not involve money transactions. Circumstances dictate the offering and accepting of bribes or other exchanges. Prenzler (2002, p. 14) illustrates the difference between sporadic and incidental corruption (although not using the same terminology) when he suggests that officers in licensing or vice squads are more likely to engage in organized (sporadic) corruption while traffic officers are more likely to engage in opportunistic corruption.

Victims of corruption

We have argued that corruption, like crime in general, has etiological roots on three levels of analysis: structural, institutional and individual. Social structural forces influence institutional socialization of individuals who bring their own individual experiences into the equation to determine offending. We have also argued that corruption as a phenomenon varies in intensity and pervasiveness across societies where it is endemic or systemic in some societies, sporadic in others and purely opportunistic in yet others.

The victims of corruption have been shown to be either individuals or the society itself. From the perspective of the victim, we would like to add one additional dimension, the dimension of tangibility. The victimization of corruption can be either tangible (material – human and financial loss) or intangible (immaterial or abstract, for example loss in trust and credibility). On the one hand, there is financial harm or harms for which the victim can receive measurable compensation and on the other hand there is harm or damage that is more abstract and hard to measure and which cannot be compensated for effectively, namely damage to a person, agency or country's reputation. This damage can be considered indirect, intangible or non-pecuniary damage.

Table 17.1 is a heuristic device we developed to illustrate our conceptual framework. On the basis of general knowledge within the literature referenced above and our own thoughts we offer a few examples of the nature of victimization within each intersection.

Structural-systemic corruption

The first intersection between the manifestation of corruption and level of victimization is structural-systemic. In societies where corruption is systemic and victimization is at the structural level, society is the primary victim. Victimization is both tangible and intangible.

When corruption has become endemic or systemic the structure of and social processes within that society are impacted. Public resources are allocated inefficiently. At this level the resources are generally natural resources such as oil, gas or coal that are basic to the economic wealth of a country. The existence of an exploitable natural resource provides the opportunity for State authorities, both administrative and political, to obtain payments. Secondly, the general scarcity of public assets relative to demand, accompanied by policies of fixed official prices, creates opportunities for informal rationing through bribery (Dearden 2000).

Developing countries receive foreign aid to assist in development and the countries attempt to attract investors to maintain some balance of trade or commerce. The entire political economy of a country is at stake and corruption at this level has consequences for the country itself. If corruption is systemic/endemic the entire society is victimized both economically and politically (U4 2012). An example of the specific tangible victimization a society experiences from systemic corruption is the cutting off or disappearance of the foreign aid it receives (Wei 2000; Lambsdorff 2005) and the negative impact corruption has on Gross Domestic Product per capita (Mo 2001; Méon and Sekkat 2005). Welsh (2004) argues that the public is the victim in this sector when environmental safety is ignored, endangering the entire population, for the sake of individual profit.

The benefits from corruption are likely to accrue to the well-connected at the expense of the poor. The unequal distribution of wealth has led Guptae et al. (2002) to argue that corruption increases income inequality as measured by the Gini coefficient.[2] Gupta et al. (2002) argue that since corruption negatively affects economic growth, an increase in corruption is associated with lower income growth of the poor.

These are tangible victimizations. An intangible or more abstract example of the structural level victimization of systemic corruption is political instability (Mo 2001) that weakens the State's legitimization (Robinson 1998). Systemic corruption undermines the fundamental goals of social and economic development (Lambsdorff 2005) and perpetuates a culture of corruption. It is the ingrained culture of corruption that thwarts anti-corruption (Persson et al. 2012) and consequently a feature of this type of corruption is that it persists.

Table 17.1 Relationship of corruption manifestation and level of victimization – for illustrative purposes

How corruption manifests itself

	Systemic (Cultural)		Sporadic (Selective but consistent)		Incidental (Lower level participants)	
	Tangible	Intangible	Tangible	Intangible	Tangible	Intangible
Structural	Public resources are allocated inefficiently Foreign aid disappears Environmental safety may be compromised Creates great income disparity between rich and poor Lower GDP	Perpetuates a culture of corruption Undermines the fundamental goals of social and economic development Weakened State legitimization Political instability	Infrastructure (roads, bridges, buildings) of inferior quality	Undermines Rule of Law Loss in predict ability in doing business Undermines the value of honesty; reduced confidence in the system	NOT APPLICABLE	
Institutional	Poor education, health care and other services Public services on which the poor depend are starved of funds	Political and economic instability Good governance and good public financial mgt. lost Lost political credibility	Selective agency inefficiency – inefficient allocation of resources; lower productivity Opportunities for organized crime, drug/arms trafficking	Social trust, the trust and credibility of the institutions suffer Loss of State credibility Fundamental rights denied	Opportunities for select victimization by functionaries	Disrespect for the entire agency e.g. police
Individual	Low standards of living, poverty, high infant mortality Poor health from unclean water or other compromised resources	General population's level of distrust rises Competent and honest citizens feel frustrated	Economic costs transferred to individual Financial cost in proportion to income is great	Competent and honest citizens feel frustrated	Cost greater Frustration, anger	Unpredictability

LEVELS OF VICTIMIZATION

Structural-sporadic corruption

At the structural level society is also the victim when corruption is not endemic but is concentrated in specific domains. Victimization in this sector (structural-sporadic) is most often found in departments or agencies specifically involved with the allocation of resources (Lambsdorff 2005, p. 10). Lambsdorff (2005) suggests that those who allocate resources may have better opportunities to extract illegal income from large investment projects than from small contracts. Evans (n.d.) proposes that the process of public procurement gives wide scope for sporadic corruption (through paying bribes to secure contracts, overpriced contracts, insider dealing, claiming payment for goods which have not been delivered, etc.) He cites as an example (p. 11) that Tanzania gave a power contract to Malaysia under which the government would have been locked into buying electricity at 2.5 times the price available from another supplier.

Tangibly, therefore, such corruption is evidenced in specific domains of the corrupt agencies such as a poor infrastructure or poor quality public construction projects and overpriced public services. Development in specific areas is thereby thwarted.

It is more difficult to differentiate the intangible effects of sporadic from systematic corruption since both have similar effects on undermining morale and the value of honesty and predictability in business dealings. When the corruption is sporadic the public is never certain as to which segments of the system are corrupt and thus confidence in the system as a whole is reduced.

Institutional-systemic corruption

When corruption is systemic the impact is felt throughout the entire society. It was suggested above that at the structural level this involved malfeasance in the allocation of resources, victimizing the society as a whole. To consider systemic corruption at the *institutional level* we suggest that the resources involved are those that are directly consumed by the public *through* governmental institutions. The victims of corruption at this level are the institutions or agencies themselves. For example, according to Mauro (1998, p. 263) '... predatory behavior by corrupt politicians distorts the composition of government expenditure. Corruption is found to reduce government spending on education in a cross section of countries.' He also suggests that expenditures on health are also affected. These institutions do not get the resources needed for quality service delivery due to the diversion of those resources as a result of corruption. These are tangible victimizations. Looking at the systemic corruption-institutional level intersection, if corruption is systemic, all social institutions on which individuals rely are tangibly victimized, resulting in a poor education system, inadequate health services, inadequate sanitation, contaminated water, poor roads and, in general, a breakdown in any government-provided service where corruption exists.

The intangible victimization effect, as noted by the United Nations (2001), is that when public resources are allocated inefficiently, competent and honest citizens will feel frustrated and the general population's level of distrust rises. As a consequence, the legitimacy of the political and economic order is undermined.

The United Nations (2012b) also states that while economic development is stunted because foreign direct investment is discouraged (structural level victimization), small businesses within the country (institutional level) often find it impossible to overcome the 'start-up costs' required because of corruption and the added costs imposed to access institutional services. For example, corruption at this level was seen to reduce the credibility of politicians and political parties in Costa Rica and corruption was considered a reason for the increased the levels of abstentions in the election processes (Olaya et al. 2010). According to Olaya et al., there were other negative political ramifications as a result of corruption at this level. Their findings appear to be generalizable.

Institutional-sporadic corruption

Corruption victimization at the institutional level is not always pervasive; it can be located in specific institutions on which the public depends. This is corruption that affects, for example, a specific government department (Evans, n.d..); not all government departments or agencies are corrupt.

There have been some examples of institutional-sporadic corruption in developed countries. One example is the US government being accused of outsourcing many contracts without an open bid process. Hightower (2007) noted that:

> An analysis by the Times found that more than half of their outsourcing contracts are not open to competition. In essence, the Bushites choose the company and award the money without getting other bids. Prior to Bush, only 21 per cent of federal contracts were awarded on a no-bid basis.

Leigh and Evans (2006) reported in *The Guardian* that in the United Kingdom, the arms manufacturer BAE was being investigated for bribing Saudi officials to buy fighter planes. *The New York Times* has reported that Wal-Mart de Mexico was an aggressive and creative corrupter, offering large payoffs to get building permits where Mexican law otherwise prohibited such development (New York Times 2012).

International institutions, such as the United Nations and World Bank, have also come under criticism for corruption, ironically while presenting themselves to be in the forefront of fighting against corruption. The example with the UN was the oil for food scandal, where the headlines were about the corruption in the UN. But, it was not the UN as an organization per se that was institutionally victimized, but specifically the UN Security Council which was responsible for the monitoring the blockade and where the US received kickbacks for corrupt oil sales (Borger and Wilson 2005).

There is no discernible pattern to which departments are more (or less) likely to be corrupt, but when some departments are corrupt other departments become tainted, decreasing the efficiency of that particular agency and increasing insecurity on the part of the population. This has been noted in societies where the police, as an institution, has been considered corrupt (Prenzler 2002, 2009; Punch 2009). Other agencies and departments can be viewed the same way, resulting in selective agency inefficiency (tangible victimization) and the loss of trust and credibility of those institutions (intangible victimization). Ultimately, corruption of this type can lead to a loss of ability to govern adequately (Lambsdorff 2005).

With sporadic institutional corruption, particularly if it involves the police, comes the opportunity for organized crime to take hold. Drug and arms trafficking and other forms of illegal supply and demand for services increase when there is sporadic corruption (GAO 1998; Buscaglia and van Dijk 2003). The prime minister of Albania (ranked by the World Bank as the most corrupt country in Europe) has said that corruption within the police is in some cases 'at the centre of organised crime' (as cited in Evans n.d., p. 8). A police-organized crime connection increases the tangible costs to society as a whole and to individuals and families as they pay the consequences of organized crime operations. The affected institutions themselves are victims in an intangible way because of the reduction in the public's confidence and trust (La Porta et al. 1997).

Institutional-incidental corruption

Regardless of the efforts made to cleanse institutions of corruption, the likelihood exists that individuals within some institutions may take advantage of opportunities to be corrupt. This is small-scale and generally involves junior public officials, such as individual policemen or customs officers with high levels of discretion (Evans, n.d.; Myint 2000). Incidental corruption tangibly produces profound public alienation and distrust of the entire institution or department; it has little macro-economic cost, but it is often hard to curb. This has been termed the 'rotten apple' theory by the Knapp Commission in the US when it studied police corruption in the 1970s (Sherman 1974). This is opportunistic corruption within regulatory agencies where individuals have high levels of discretion without adequate accountability (Myint 2000; Buscaglia and van Dijk 2003). Intangibly, incidental corruption at the institutional level can result in disrespect for the institution or agency in which some individuals are perceived as being corrupt.

Individual-systemic corruption

Whether corruption is systemic, sporadic or incidental, individuals ultimately pay the price. Corruption increases wealth for a few at the expense of society as a whole (structural victimization), leaving the poor (individual victimization) suffering the harshest consequences (World Bank 2012a). The difference between the way corruption manifests itself and individual victimization is a matter of degree.

In societies characterized by systemic corruption there is a significant gap in income and resources, resulting in high levels of poverty and low standards of living (World Bank 2012b). The impact of corruption on health care and education is especially strong. Gupta *et al.* (2001) show that countries with high levels of corruption also have inefficient government services and low quality public health care. Using child and infant mortality as well as the percentage of low-birth weight babies out of total births as a proxy for the quality of public health care and using student drop-out rates as a proxy for the quality of public education, the authors found all these variables significantly related to levels of corruption. Child mortality rates in systemically corrupted countries are about one-third higher than in countries with low corruption; infant mortality rates and the percentage of low-birth weight babies are almost twice as high; and dropout rates are five times as high in countries with high levels of corruption (p. 139). Mauro (1998) found that government spending on education as a ratio to GDP is negatively and significantly correlated with corruption.

Other tangible victimizations at the individual level-systemic intersection are evidenced by the number of countries receiving vast amounts of foreign aid that never finds its way to fund the basic standards of living, clean water or adequate housing for which it was intended. From the broadest perspective, corruption distorts prices throughout the economy: the costs of bribes are passed onto the final consumer. Corruption creates delays in economic transactions and additional uncertainty (Dearden 2000). Myint (2000, p. 47) states that:

> the burden of corruption falls more heavily on the poor as they cannot afford to pay the required bribes to send their children to a decent school, to obtain proper health care, or to have adequate access to government provided services such as domestic water supply, electricity, sanitation and community waste disposal facilities.

Corruption also hurts the poor directly because 'it is an impediment to economic growth, reinforces inequality, distorts public expenditure allocation and through many other channels is an obstacle to poverty alleviation' (World Bank 2012b, p. 1).

Indirectly or intangibly, corruption has an impact on the individual's view of his/her society. Corruption distorts poor people's relationships with and trust for public officials, the police and people in authority who extort bribes from them (World Bank 2012b). There also develops a general distrust within the population that results in high levels of frustration.

Individual-sporadic corruption

Individuals are also the victims when corruption is sporadic since the costs of corruption are passed on to the individuals when they interact with the selected agencies or institutions where corruption continues to have a foothold. The difference between individual victimization that is systemic and individual victimization that is sporadic is merely a matter frequency. The tangible and intangible effects are the same for the individuals involved whether corruption is systemic or sporadic. The difference is whether they are victimized by all agencies or services or whether they are victimized by selective entities. If corruption is sporadic it may cost more to get electricity or a telephone, for example (Olaya *et al.* 2010), while there are no such 'surcharges' for other services.

The intangible victimization is related directly to the entity or agency that is corrupt. If a policeman or teacher takes advantage of his position to extract bribes it harms their reputation and relationship of trust, destroying social capital and decreasing moral standards (World Bank 2012b). Sporadic but unpredictable corruption leads to individual confusion, frustration and the loss of very limited resources. A governance and corruption survey in Cambodia revealed that lower income households on average spend 2.3 per cent of their income on bribes compared to 0.9 per cent for rich households (World Bank 2000).

Individual-incidental corruption

It has been noted above that corruption frequently takes place in societies where there is considerable discretion for public officials, limited accountability and little transparency in governmental operations. Incidental corruption will occur when individuals have considerable discretion and little accountability. It is not possible to devise rules and regulations that are watertight and foolproof and will take care of all contingencies that can arise in trying to control or direct an economic activity (Klitgaard 1991). Hence, some flexibility and discretionary powers will have to be given to administrators in interpreting and implementing rules. Individual police officers, individual customs agents, individual administrators may take advantage of their positions against unsuspecting individuals. There is uncertainty and unpredictability on the part of individuals who are the victims when corruption is incidental.

Synopsis and implications

Corruption is considered to be widespread but it varies significantly by country and it manifests itself differently. We have tried to conceptualize corruption in a way that enables better understanding of its impact; we have tried to present a victimology of corruption. Corruption can be systemic to a society and when it is there is widespread, consistent, predictable corruption throughout. This creates a recognized if not accepted culture of corruption. It was pointed out that corruption could also be sporadic but not culturally pervasive. That is, corruption can exist in some segments of a society and not in others. Victimization is different under these conditions, as it is if corruption is opportunistic or incidental.

The impact of corruption can be found on three levels of society – the structure and culture of the society itself, institutions within a society and above all, individuals. This chapter highlights the impact corruption has on each combination and permutation of corruption manifestation and level of impact.

This is a heuristic exercise that suggests that while some may place the blame of corruption on corrupt individuals, corruption is not possible if there is no institutional mechanism that makes it possible and that these institutions can, in fact, be victimized by the same corruption they help to generate. Corruption is not a matter of morals or the mere weakness of individuals in pursuit of personal gain. We have tried to show that it can be cultural and systemic, creating an expectation of corruption. The society itself is the victim of systemic corruption as critical institutions are compromised and trust is lost. Of course, individuals at the lowest economic levels suffer most directly.

We have highlighted a level of victimization not previously discussed: institutions. To reduce the victimization of corruption to individuals and society, the focus must be on the institutions that both enable it and which are also victimized by it. Only individuals within institutions that condone, enable or ignore corruption engage in corruption. Systemic corruption undermines all social institutions, including government. Poor education and health services are the result and both the society and individuals within that society are the victims. Good governance and good public financial management are lost when corruption is systemic. When corruption is sporadic in some institutions, organized crime is enabled and can flourish because critical institutions such as law and justice are compromised.

Our conceptualization of the dynamics and impact of corruption generates a few suggestions for controlling it and assisting all levels of victimization. The first is to correct the victimless misconception surrounding corruption. The primary focus, however, needs to be at the institutional level. The United Nations (2001, p. 8) offers the best set of recommendations: set basic democratic standards that include political accountability and pressures against corruption. Their suggestion to develop a strong civil society is seen as an important control on political corruption and each suggestion is at the institutional level including:

- free communications media
- public budget hearings;
- civil society control boards;
- public regulation commissions; and
- judicial monitoring systems.

Meng (2011, p. 185) makes a strong argument that corruption can be controlled by professionalizing the public institutional sector. She argues that the more formal the institution, the less corruption there is likely to be. She suggests that it is important to create an anti-corruption sub-culture (structural level) while at the institutional level the following can reduce the level of corruption:

- set salary commensurate with responsibility. There is somewhat less corruption where civil servants are paid better, compared with similarly qualified workers in the private sector (Van Rijckeghem and Weder 1997);
- increase the education level and the educational opportunities;
- upgrade and continue the education process and make the continuing education mandated;
- improve quality through the recruitment level;
- create professional standards and clearly define the requirements for jobs; and
- establish a special committee to implement the professional standard in a comprehensive and dynamic way.

Finally, Buscaglia and van Dijk (2003, p. 32) suggest that the following would help to address and prevent both corruption and organized crime:

- a reduction of poverty levels and an increase in salary levels for public employees, in order to hamper the uncontrolled growth of corruption, which tends to increase political instability, which in turn stimulates the penetration of the State by national criminal organizations or, worse, by transnational ones;
- a reduction in the incidence and dimension of informal markets that provide the economic input and output for organized crime;
- improvements in the distribution of income and wealth;
- a reduction of barriers to the international exchange of goods and services; and
- the adoption and more consistent application of financial regulations, which could be enforced by specialized supervisory state agencies responsible for financial investigations.

In sum we argue that corruption is not a victimless crime; individuals pay a direct financial price and there is an indirect increased loss of confidence in their government and society. The society itself is a victim at one level where the rule of law is subverted (United Nations 2012b), public participation is lost and resources are diverted to personal gain. Institutions within the society can also be the victims of corruption. Ultimately, individuals are clearly the victims and suffer because of the graft, bribery and embezzlement whether corruption is systemic, sporadic or incidental. Our conceptualization should help focus anti-corruption efforts where corruption victimization is often overlooked and yet where anti-corruption practices may be the most effective – the institutional level.

Notes

1 U4 Anti-corruption Resource Centre (U4) is a web-based resource centre for development practitioners who wish to effectively address corruption challenges in their work. Their aim is to provide users with relevant anti-corruption resources; including their own applied research, publications, a helpdesk service and online training. See: www.u4.no/
2 The Gini coefficient measures the inequality among values of a frequency distribution (Gini, 1936). It is commonly used as a measure of inequality of income or wealth.

Bibliography

Aidt, T.S., 2009. Corruption, institutions, and economic development. Oxford Review of Economic Policy, 25, pp. 271–291.
Bandura, A., 1989. Human agency in social cognitive theory. American Psychologist, 44, pp. 1175–1184.
Borger, J and Wilson, J., 2005. US backed illegal Iraqi oil deals. The Guardian Monday 16 May 2005. Available at: www.guardian.co.uk/world/2005/may/17/otherparties.iraq [Accessed 26 December 2012].
Boyd, R. and Richerson, P.J., 1985. Culture and the evolutionary process. Chicago: University of Chicago Press.
Buscaglia, E., 2000. Judicial corruption in developing countries: its causes and economic consequences. Essays in Public Policy. Stanford University: Hoover Institution Press, pp. 24–29.
Buscaglia, E. and van Dijk, J., 2003. Controlling organized crime and corruption in the public sector. Forum on Crime and Society, 3(1-2), pp. 3–32.
Dearden, S.J.H., 2000. Corruption and economic development. DSA European Development Policy Study Group Discussion Paper No. 18, October 2000.
Della Porta, D. and Vannucci, A., 1999. Corrupt exchanges: actors, resources, and mechanisms of political corruption. New York: Aldine de Gruyter.
Della Porta, D. and Rose-Ackerman, S. eds, 2002. Corrupt exchanges: empirical themes in the politics and political economy of corruption. Daden-Baden: Nomos.
Evans, B.R., n.d. The cost of corruption: a discussion paper on corruption, development and the poor. Teddington: Tear Fund.
Friday, P.C., 1988. A criminology of criminal justice: an effort toward theoretical integration. Journal of Contemporary Criminal Justice, 4, pp. 37–48.
GAO (Government Accounting Office), 1998. Information on drug related police corruption. Washington: US Government Accounting Office.
Gini, C., 1936. On the measure of concentration with special reference to income and statistics. Colorado College Publication, General Series No. 208, pp. 73–79. As cited by *Wikipedia* http://en.wikipedia.org/wiki/Gini_coefficient [Accessed 28 September 2012].
Gray, C.W. and Kaufmann, D., 1998. Corruption and development. Finance and Development, 35(1), p. 7.
Griffith, I.L., 1997. Narcotics arms trafficking, corruption and governance in the Caribbean. Journal of Money Laundering Control, 1-2, pp. 138–147.

Gupta, S., Davoodi, H. and Tiongson, E.R., 2001. Corruption and the provision of healthcare and education services. In: A.K. Jain, ed., The political economy of corruption. London: Routledge, pp. 111–141.

Gupta, S., Davoodi, H. and Alonso-Terme, R., 2002. Does corruption affect income inequality and poverty? Economics of Governance, 3, pp. 23–45.

Hao, Y. and Johnston, M., 1995. Reform at the crossroads: an analysis of Chinese corruption. Asian Perspective, 19(1), pp. 117–149.

Hightower, J., 2007. The Bushites have outsourced our government to their pals. The Hightower Lowdown.

Huntington, S.P., 1968. Political order in changing societies. New Haven: Yale University Press.

Huther, J. and Shah, A., 2005. Anti-corruption policies and programs: a framework for evaluation. World Bank Operations Evaluation Department. Available at: http://books.google.com/books?hl=en andlr= andid=v9biaVC1XHEC andoi=fnd andpg=PA17 anddq=anti-corruption+measures andots=CfSvOP6iJA andsig=kUoGjgpdktIAblHS9 RmXwFaEuqM#v=onepage andq=anti-corruption%20measures andf=false [Accessed 29 September 2012].

Johnston, M., 2005. Syndromes of corruption: wealth, power, and democracy. Cambridge: Cambridge University Press.

Klitgaard, R., 1991. Controlling corruption. Berkeley: University of California Press.

Kwong, J., 1997. The political economy of corruption in China. New York: M.E.Sharpe Armonk.

Lambsdorff, J.G., 2005. Consequences and causes of corruption – what do we know from a cross-section of countries? Volkswirtschaftliche Reihe der Passauer Diskussionspapiere. Diskussionsbeitrag Nr. V-34-05.

La Porta, R., Lopez-De-Silanes, F., Shleifer, A. and Vishny, R.W., 1997. Trust in large organizations. American Economic Review, Papers and Proceedings, CXXXVII (2), pp. 333–338.

Leigh, D. and Evans, R., 2006. National interest halts arms corruption inquiry. The Guardian Thursday 14 December. Available at: www.guardian.co.uk/uk/2006/dec/15/saudiarabia.armstrade [Accessed 26 December, 2012].

Lima, M. and Friday, P.C., 2005. Abuse of power: issues in theory and policy. In: E. Vetere and P. David, eds, Victims of crime: festschrift in honour of Irene Melup. Vienna: United Nations, pp. 435–449.

Margolis, H., 1982. Selfishness, altruism and rationality: a theory of social choice. Cambridge: Cambridge University Press.

Mauro, P., 1968. Corruption: causes, consequences, and agenda for further research. Finance and Development, pp. 11–14.

Mauro, P., 1995. Corruption and growth. Quarterly Journal of Economics, 110(3), pp. 681–712.

Mauro, P., 1998. Corruption and the composition of government expenditure. Journal of Public Economics, 69, pp. 263–279.

Meng, Q., 2011. On corruption-related crimes in transitional China – a panel data analysis from criminological and other multi-disciplinary perspectives. Charlotte: University of North Carolina-Charlotte.

Méon, P.-G. and Sekkat, K., 2005. Does corruption grease or sand the wheels of growth? Public Choice, 122, pp. 69–97.

Mo, P.H., 2001. Corruption and economic growth. Journal of Comparative Economics, 29, pp. 66–79.
Myint, U., 2000. Corruption: causes, consequences and cures. Asia-Pacific Development Journal, 7, pp. 33–58.
New York Times, 2012. The Bribery Aisle: How Wal-Mart got its way in Mexico. Available at: www.nytimes.com/2012/12/18/business/walmart-bribes-teotihuacan.html?emc=na [Accessed 12 December 2012].
Ngo, T-W., 2008. Rent-seeking and economic governance in the structural nexus of corruption in China. Crime Law Social Change, 49, pp. 27–44.
North, D.C., 2005. Institutions, institutional change and economic performance. political economy of institutions and decisions. Cambridge: University Press.
Nye, J.S., 1989. Political corruption: a cost-benefit analysis. In: A.J. Heidenheimer, M. Johnston and V. LeVine, eds, 2009. Political corruption: a handbook. New Brunswick: Transaction Publishers, pp. 963–984.
Olaya, J., Attisso, K. and Roth A., 2010. Repairing social damage out of corruption cases: opportunities and challenges as illustrated in the Alcatel case in Costa Rica. Available at: http://papers.ssrn.com/sol3/papers.cfm?abstract_id=1779834 [Accessed 15 September 2012].
Persson, A., Rothstein, B. and Teorell, J., 2012. Why anticorruption reforms fail—systemic corruption as a collective action problem. European Journal of Development Research, 10(2), pp. 1–14.
Prenzler, T., 2002. Corruption and reform: global trends and theoretical perspectives. In: T. Prenzler and J. Ransley, eds, Police reform: building integrity. Sydney: Hawkins Press pp. 3–22.
Prenzler, T., 2009. Police corruption: preventing misconduct and maintaining integrity. New York: CRC Publishers.
Punch, M., 2009. Police corruption: exploring police deviance and crime. New York: Willan Publishers.
Robinson, M., 1998. Corruption and development. New York: Frank Cass Publishers.
Rock, M.T. and Bonnett, H., 2004. The comparative politics of corruption: Accounting for the East Asian paradox in empirical studies of corruption, growth and investment. World Development, 32(6), pp. 999–1017.
Rose-Ackerman, S., 1978. Corruption: a study in political economy. New York: Academic Press.
Rose-Ackerman, S., 2002. When is corruption harmful? In: A.J. Heidenheimer and M. Johnston, eds, 2009. Political corruption: concepts and contexts, 3rd edition. New Brunswick: Transaction Publishers, pp. 353–371.
Sandholtz, W. and Taagepera, R., 2005. Corruption, culture, and communism. International Review of Sociology, 15, pp. 109–131.
Sherman, L., 1974. Police corruption: a sociological perspective. Garden City: Doubleday.
Stapenhurst, R. and Sedigh, S. J., 1999. Curbing corruption: toward a model for building national integrity. Washington: EDI Development Studies, the World Bank.
Sugden, R., 1986. The economics of rights, co-operation, and welfare. Oxford: Blackwell.
Svensson, J., 2000. Foreign aid and rent-seeking. Journal of International Economics, 51, pp. 437–461.
Sykes, G. and Matza D., 1957. Techniques of neutralization: A theory of delinquency. American Sociological Review, 22, pp. 664–670.

Tanzi, V., 1998. Corruption around the world: causes, consequences, scope, and cures. IMF Staff Papers, 45(4).
Tarrant, M., 2002. Adolescent peer groups and social identity. Social Development, 11, pp. 110–123.
Transparency International, 2010. MDG Report 2010. Available at: www.transparency.org.uk/corruption/statistics-and-quotes/cost-for-developing-countries [Accessed 9 September 2012].
Transparency International, 2011. Available at: http://cpi.transparency.org/cpi2011/results/ [Accessed 30 August 2012].
Treisman, D., 2006. What have we learned about the causes of corruption from ten years of cross-national empirical research? Los Angeles, CA: Department of Political Science, University of California, Los Angeles. Available at: Treisman@polisci.ucla.edu [Accessed 14 September 2012].
U4 Anti-corruption Resource Centre, 2012. Available at: www.u4.no/glossary/ [Accessed 22 September 2012].
United Nations. 2001. Empowering the victims of corruption through social control mechanisms, Vienna: United Nations.
United Nations, 2012a. Available at: https://www.unodc.org/unodc/en/corruption/index.html?ref=menuside [Accessed 9 September 2012].
United Nations, 2012b. Corruption prevention to foster small and medium-sized enterprise development, vol. II. Vienna: UNODCP.
Uwakwe, V., 2012. Socio marketing practices and corruption – a study of Nigerian nation, 23 March 2012. Available at: http://Hyattractions.Wordpress.Com/Author/Vallinks/ [Accessed 29 August 2012].
Van Rijckeghem, C. and Weder, B., 1997. Corruption and the rate of temptation: do low wages in the civil service cause corruption? IMF working paper 97/73. Washington: International Monetary Fund cited in P. Mauro, ed., 1968, Corruption: causes, consequences, and agenda for further research. Finance and Development, p. 12.
Wei, S.-J., 2000. How taxing is corruption on international investors? Review of Economics and Statistics, 82(1), pp. 1–11.
Welsh, H., 2004. Corruption, growth, and the environment: A cross-country analysis. Environment and Development Economics, 9, pp. 663–693.
World Bank, 2000. Cambodia: Governance and corruption diagnostic evidence from citizen, enterprise, and public official surveys. Available at: www-wds.worldbank.org/external/default/WDSContentServer/WDSP/IB/2004/09/23/000090341_20040923143650/Rendered/PDF/280190KH0Governance0and0corruption.pdf [Accessed 29 September 2012].
World Bank, 2012a. Costs and consequences of corruption. Available at: http://web.worldbank.org/WBSITE/EXTERNAL/TOPICS/EXTPUBLICSECTORANDGOVERNANCE/EXTANTICORRUPTION/0,,contentMDK:20221941~menuPK:1165474~pagePK:148956~piPK:216618~theSitePK:384455,00.html [Accessed 29 September, 2012].
World Bank, 2012b. Corruption, poverty and inequality. Available at: http://go.worldbank.org/6UZ4XEP700 [Accessed 26 December 2012].
World Economic Forum, 2003. Organized crime imposes cost on businesses. The Global Competitiveness Report 2002–2003. New York: Oxford University Press.
World Economic Forum, 2012. Global Risks, 2012, 7th Edition. Geneva, Switzerland: World Economic Forum. Available at: http://reports.weforum.org/global-risks-2012/ [Accessed 22 September 2012].

Chapter 18

Reconceptualizing sexual victimization and justice

Kathleen Daly

Introduction

The argument advanced here is based on two decades of researching and writing on victims' experiences in the aftermath of crime and their desires for justice. It reflects my interests to move across the fields of domestic and international criminal justice, to understand diverse contexts of sexual victimization and to consider the ways in which context matters for justice, from a victim's perspective. I wish to broaden the meanings of 'justice' for victims by identifying a wide range of justice mechanisms, both in law and civil society and to devise a robust method to assess and compare them. The Victimization and Justice Model presented here encapsulates these themes with three components: justice mechanisms, victimization contexts, and victims' justice needs (or interests). Sexual victimization is my focus, but the model has general applicability to serious crime.

I lodge the usual caveats about 'victims' (or a victimhood status). A victim status is not fixed, but socially constructed, mobilized and malleable (Rock 2002); and many prefer the term 'survivor'. Further, we know that there are blurred boundaries of victimization and offending (Daly 2010). Individuals have diverse experiences of victimization, diverse demands for justice and multiple goals for justice, which can change over time. There is no generic 'victim orientation' (Pemberton *et al.* 2007) and 'ideal' victims are in short supply (Christie 1986). These caveats can be stated more affirmatively. Victimization is a process, not a category or identity; likewise, justice is a process, not an event or intervention. At the same time, we require a word to refer to a person who has been victimized and 'victim' most readily comes to mind.

This chapter advances these arguments. First, government and civil society politics often eclipse the mantra of evidence-based policy in criminology and this problem is especially acute in addressing sexual victimization. I identify ways forward, but recognize that my proposals will be controversial to some readers. Second, the justice field needs a new way to depict and compare justice responses and I propose using the terms *conventional and innovative justice mechanisms*. The oppositional contrast of retributive and restorative justice was a 'catchy exposition' (Roche 2007, p. 87) in its early years, but it should now be set aside. We need a more sophisticated understanding of justice practices, not popular slogans. Relatedly, the elements discussed in justice practices (e.g. reparation, restoration, restitution, retribution and punishment) are defined and used differently, depending on the author; this must change if we are to build a scientific understanding of conventional and innovative justice mechanisms. Third, researchers specialize in one context of sexual victimization, but that context should be situated in a broader field of reference. I introduce the *Sexual Violence and Justice Matrix*, which arrays varied country contexts (developed and developing countries at peace and in conflict zones) and victimization-offending contexts (individual, institutional, organizational and collective) of violence. By giving attention to different contexts of victimization, we can build a more systematic and stronger empirical base on victimization and justice. Fourth, the justice field needs a better measure of victims' experiences of justice than vague notions of 'satisfaction' or the 'therapeutic effects' of justice activities. I introduce the construct of *victims' justice needs (or interests)*, which can be used to assess and compare conventional and innovative justice mechanisms from a victim's perspective. The construct also invites discussion and debate on normative questions of what victims should expect in a justice activity.

Political context

The Victimization and Justice Model identifies the main components in *the research problem*, which is to identify and compare justice mechanisms in responding to sexual victimization in diverse contexts of violence. However, the research problem sits in a contentious political field. I outline its contours in broad-brush terms with reference mainly to domestic contexts of criminal justice.

The response to rape and sexual violence seems to be contradictory: there is a *minimization* of sex offending and victimization, on the one hand, and *a demonization* of certain groups as 'sex offenders', on the other. Victims' rates of reporting these offences to the police are low (14 per cent, on average, in five common law jurisdictions from 1992 to the present; see Daly and Bouhours 2010, p. 572). Once reported, levels of attrition are high as a case moves from the police, to prosecution and court adjudication. Of those cases reported to the police, the conviction rate to any sexual offence is 12.5 per cent (1990 to 2005 data); but in an earlier period (1970 to 1989 data), it was higher (18 per cent) (Daly and Bouhours 2010, p. 597). Although an improved conviction rate should not be viewed as the only goal of rape law reform, its erosion over time in the jurisdictions studied suggests that we may have exhausted the potential of legal reform to effect significant change.[1]

At the same time, the 'sex offender' continues to attract a high degree of social outrage, exclusion and strong penal measures. This relatively small group has been convicted of or imprisoned for sex offences, or has been suspected (or convicted) of particular types of sex offences (e.g. serial offending against children by adults). Policies and practices vary by jurisdiction, but they include sex offender registries, community notification, preventive detention and GPS tracking. As McAlinden (2007, p. 21) suggests, 'the sex offender is demonised as a monster or fiend and is singled out above other dangerous offenders in society'.

Although seemingly contradictory, the minimization and demonization of sex offending are mutually reinforcing. Minimization occurs because most sex offending bears no relationship to the monstrous sex offender or to the less monstrous, but no less atypical 'real rape' (that is, between strangers in a public place, with visible injuries to a victim; see Estrich 1987); and because punitive penal measures are not appropriate for many forms of sex offending (McAlinden 2007). Demonization occurs because 'the sex offender' is a convenient scapegoat for social fears and vulnerabilities (Best 1990), which are amplified by sensational media stories about highly atypical cases (Thomas 2005; McAlinden 2007). Although scholars have analysed a societal obsession with 'the sex offender' and its negative effects on society and criminal justice (Simon 1998; Zimring 2004), few have observed how this phenomenon is linked to a minimization of sex offending and to debates over what should be done about it. For some, the way to address minimization is to 'get tougher' on sex offending by increasing the numbers of arrests, convictions and sentences.[2] The emphasis is on what I term *symbolic justice*: to send 'strong messages' to would-be offenders that sexual offending will not go unpunished and to vindicate victims by criminal justice responses. Others see the value of what I term *pragmatic justice* (Daly 2011), which relies on multiple pathways of formal and informal justice mechanisms, with an emphasis on victim participation.[3] This position recognizes that most victims will never see their case reach court and that non-stranger sexual offending will continue to face hurdles in a legal process, no matter how artful new legal language or procedures may be. The questions posed by Hudson (1998) and myself (Daly 2002a) more than a decade ago remain apt:

> How does one move away from punitive reactions, which – even when enforced – further brutalize perpetrators, without, by leniency of reaction, giving the impression that sexualized ... violence is acceptable behaviour?
> (Hudson 1998, p. 245)

> How do we treat harms as 'serious' without engaging in harsh forms of punishment or hyper-criminalization?
> (Daly 2002a, p. 62)

More recently, I have suggested these ways forward (Daly 2008, 2011; Daly and Bouhours 2010):

1 **Debate and clarify justice goals**. It is imperative to clarify the goals for socio-legal change: are they to increase arrests and convictions, impose more severe sentences, validate victims, deter would-be offenders or change people's behaviours and attitudes about gender and sexuality? For victim advocates and feminist scholars, these questions remain unsettled and contested. Those emphasizing

symbolic justice are concerned that hard-won gains from criminal law reform will be dissipated with 'more lenient' types of informal justice responses or apparently lighter sentences. Debate can be difficult because we lack a common metric to assess and compare justice mechanisms. I argue for a pragmatic justice position, which proposes the next four points.

2 **Focus on early stages.** For criminal justice responses, emphasize the early stages of the justice process, rather than the last stage of trial. For the period of time preceding or leading up to criminal justice responses, the early phase is crucial: it is when victims first disclose offences to people they know and perhaps then to authorities; and it is when suspects are first interviewed and investigations are conducted.

3 **Do not rely solely on criminalization and penal strategies.** Increasing criminalization and penalization will not help most victims. Greater attention should be given to responses that are more socially inclusive and re-integrative of offenders. Mechanisms should be considered to encourage more *admissions* to offending (only when it has occurred, of course) in legal or non-legal settings. Such admissions need not necessarily to be tied to *convictions* for sexual offences.

4 **Lift the bans on sexual offence eligibility for informal justice mechanisms.** Although informal justice mechanisms, such as conferences or mediation, are used in some jurisdictions for admitted youth and adult offenders (see Daly 2011, 2012), policymakers are wary of supporting them because they may appear to be 'too lenient'. However, the trade-off is not between a 'more' or 'less serious' response, but between any response or none at all. Careful introduction of justice mechanisms can be monitored and researched; and from this, an evidence base can be built.

5 **Identify a menu of options.** There should be a menu of options for victims, including those that do and do not articulate with criminal justice. Responses can run on multiple pathways, not just one pathway of formal criminal justice. Informal justice processes can occur in many socio-legal contexts (e.g. instead of reporting an offence; after charges are withdrawn by the police or prosecutor or dismissed in court; parallel with a court process, at sentence, post-sentence and post-release) and organizational contexts (e.g. government agencies and the non-government sector).

Other scholars have argued for using innovative responses to sexual violence (see for example Koss 2006; McAlinden 2007; Madsen 2008; Jülich 2010; Jülich *et al.* 2010; Naylor 2010; McDonald and Tinsley 2011; McGlynn 2011; Pali and Madsen 2011; McGlynn *et al.* 2012). This is encouraging, but a consideration of new justice ideas cannot be confined to just one context of violence (an individual hurting or harming another) in developed countries at peace.[4] With increasing attention to sexual victimization and justice in post-conflict societies, it is important that theory and research in domestic contexts inform developments in international or transitional contexts and vice versa (McEvoy 2007). The two are rarely analysed together (but see Waldman 2007; Boesten 2010), despite the recognition that the handling of rape cases in the International Criminal Court shows patterns similar to those in domestic courts (Mertus 2004).

The Victimization and Justice Model was developed to address the research problem, but it cannot easily alter the politics of rape and security, which range wildly between ignoring or doing nothing for most victims and ostracizing a small number of offenders. Victimology has a central role to play in challenging this situation by lowering the political heat, crossing the boundaries of domestic and international criminal justice and encouraging citizens and governments to think more deeply and constructively about the problem.

Victimization and Justice Model

Justice mechanisms

For some time, I have been critical of the oppositional contrast of retributive and restorative justice (Daly and Immarigeon 1998; Daly 2000, 2002b). This contrast has created obstacles for understanding what is and what could be optimal justice practices. Rather than review older arguments, however, I want to persuade you of the value of using new concepts.

I propose that we view *justice mechanisms* as residing on a continuum from conventional to innovative. The categories of conventional and innovative are overlapping; they are not mutually exclusive and can be combined in hybrid forms.[5] *Conventional* responses are concerned with improvements to evidence gathering, prosecution and trial, and support for victims in legal contexts. They may be part of a criminal justice system or work alongside of it. Most assume reliance on formal legality, with a focus on prosecution, trial, and sentencing. Other conventional responses include victim impact statements, specialist courts, civil litigation, state-based compensation or financial assistance, victim advocates and victim lawyers. *Innovative* responses may work alongside of or be integrated with criminal justice, be part of administrative procedures, or operate in civil society. They include mediated meetings or conferences of victims and offenders; informal justice mechanisms; truth-telling or truth-seeking; reparations packages having material elements (compensation, other forms of assistance) and symbolic elements (apologies, days of remembrance, and memorials); people's tribunals, documentary and street theatre and other types of art and activist projects in civil society.[6]

There are advantages to conceptualizing justice responses in this way. First, when viewing conventional and innovative responses as residing on a continuum, not as fixed or oppositional, we can recognize their dynamic quality, capacity for change, and interdependence. Second, we see that innovative responses are a broad set of justice mechanisms of which restorative justice is just one type. One reason why restorative justice is hard to define is that the term contains a diverse set of agendas, principles and practices: it is often used as an umbrella concept for any justice activity that is not a standard form of criminal justice. I am proposing that 'innovative justice' be used instead, as an umbrella concept, to contain a variety of *justice mechanisms*,[7] which may provide more openings for victim-defined participation and voice in justice activities. These may be part of a legal process, reside in civil society or be a combination of the two. I would emphasize that conventional mechanisms have equal importance and standing. Although prosecution and trial were not designed with victims' interests in mind, there have been improvements, particularly in providing some degree of participation for victims in a legal process. Conventional criminal justice cannot be disparaged as the 'bad' or 'punitive' justice, as often happens when restorative justice advocates compare retributive and restorative justice.[8] Rather, the theoretical and empirical tasks should be to determine the degree to which conventional and innovative justice mechanisms can address victims' justice needs or interests.

Key terms

If we are to build an empirically informed knowledge on conventional and innovative justice mechanisms and what they can (or cannot) achieve, we require some agreement on how to define and use key terms such as reparation, restoration, restitution and the like. Currently, there is no such agreement (see Daly and Proietti-Scifoni 2011).[9] Writers attribute different meanings to these terms, depending on their frame of reference and whether they are working in domestic or international criminal justice. The problem is even more acute in domestic criminal justice because the aim by some is to identify a new 'system' of justice. By contrast, in international criminal justice, a conventional mechanism of adjudication and punishment of offenders is a remedy distinct from that of reparation to victims. In an early collection on restorative justice in domestic settings, Harland (1996, p. 507) observed that the field should 'define and clarify the most essential aims and related mechanisms, beginning with restoration itself [but also] reconciliation, reparation to the community, mediation ... and so on'. His call for an authoritative glossary of key terms for domestic criminal justice has largely gone unanswered.

Those of us researching conventional and innovative justice mechanisms should reflect on the varied uses of key terms, within and across domestic and international criminal justice. Some translational work will be necessary because we are working in different contexts of victimization, with different types of justice mechanisms and legal conventions. An example of this endeavour is Clamp and Doak's (2012) analysis of the 'portability' of restorative justice to transitional justice contexts. What would be useful is an Oxford English Dictionary-style publication, which traces the development and evolution of key terms. Consistency for its own sake is not the goal. Rather, it is to build a solid and defensible theoretical and empirical literature, which requires shared understandings of the terms used.

Contexts of victimization

Most of us carry out research on victimization and justice with one context of victimization in mind. This is reasonable, but it is important to situate the work in a wider field of reference. I devised the Sexual Violence and Justice Matrix to array varied country contexts (developed, developing, at peace or conflict/post-conflict) and offending-victimization contexts of violence (Table 18.1). The three country categories reflect differing legal, economic and political capacities to respond to sexual victimization, along with differences in social organization and cohesion for countries in conflict or relative peace. The offending-victimization contexts are *individual* (row 1); *organizational* – i.e. a person using a position of organizational power (row 2); *institutional* – i.e. within a closed institution (row 3) or symbolically closed community (row 4); and *collective* – i.e. by loosely organized gangs or quasi-state combatants (row 5). The matrix identifies differing social relations and place elements, along with a broader political-economic context of violence.[10] Each cell identifies typical relations and places of victimization, along with the problems that victims face in seeking justice. Although not itemized, each cell may also use or have available differing types of justice mechanisms.

In general, one matrix cell – A1, an individual context in developed country at peace – dominates the landscape of thought. An individual context of violence is an individual hurting or harming another person outside an institution or without using a position of organizational power. If you are sexually victimized in an A1 context, the standard advice is to 'call the police' and mobilize criminal law and criminal justice, although, as we know, most victims do not do so.

In other contexts of sexual victimization, the situation is more difficult. I have in mind assaults in total institutions – for example detention centres, prisons, training schools, orphanages, military organizations (row 3); in racially or religiously segregated enclaves in urban areas or in remote indigenous settlements (row 4); and in war and conflict zones (column C). Reflect on being a victim in these contexts. What are your options? Calling the police and mobilizing criminal law may not be optimal, feasible or desirable. Our research of 19 major cases of institutional physical and sexual abuse of children in Australia and Canada (cell A3) shows that although some victims did make complaints to people in authority, including the police or government officials, no legal action was taken (Daly 2014). Their stories were ignored or disbelieved and investigations were dropped or did not result in laying charges. It took, on average, nearly 40 years for an official response to be initiated, using a conservative measure. Official reactions occurred after pressure was placed on governments or churches by victims' groups and the media, law suits against governments or churches and, at times, the charging or conviction of perpetrators.

In an Australian case that came to public attention in April 2012 in Melbourne, the clergy sexual abuse of young people was linked to higher than average rates of suicide. A Catholic Church Archbishop was quoted as saying that the '"great majority" of victims did not want to go to the police. ... Obviously the church has

Table 18.1 Sexual violence and justice matrix, A and C country contexts (B country contexts, developing country at peace, excluded)

Offending-victimization context of sexual violence	Country A Developed country at peace	Country C Conflict, post-conflict, or post-authoritarian regime
(1) Person acting alone	**A1** **Relations**: peer, familial, known, and (atypically) stranger relations **Place**: mainly residential **Problem**: must fit 'real rape' template (stranger relations, injury)	**C1** **Relations**: peer, familial, known, and (atypically) stranger relations **Place**: mainly residential **Problem**: must fit 'rape as weapon of war' template
(2) Person using position of organizational authority	**A2** **Relations**: religious, medical, or state official (e.g. clergy, doctor, police) and child/adult victim **Place**: residential and occupational **Problem**: trusted person or state official is the abuser	**C2** **Relations**: foreign peacekeepers, aid workers, and soldiers, in addition to A2 **Place**: residential and occupational **Problem**: legal jurisdiction, police or peacekeeper is the abuser, zero tolerance policy
(3) Person using position of organizational authority inside closed institutions (includes peer relations in institutions)	**A3** **Relations**: religious or state official having duty of care and child/adult victim **Place**: residential schools, prisons, detention centres, armed forces facilities **Problem**: trusted person or state official is the abuser, unable to escape, inmate code of silence	**C3** **Relations**: state official having duty of care and refugee/prisoner **Place**: refugee camps and detention centres, in addition to A3 **Problem**: official is the abuser, unable to escape, inmate code of silence
(4) Offending in symbolically closed communities	**A4** **Relations**: peer, familial, and known relations **Place**: remote communities or segregated urban enclaves **Problem**: fear and negative community consequences of disclosing; unable to escape	**C4** Limited documentation; but relations, place, and problem are likely similar to A4.
(5) Offending by loosely or well-organised groups	**A5** **Relations**: gangs, criminal enterprises, human trafficking groups **Place**: residential and occupational **Problem**: serious reprisals by offenders if reported, repatriation to home country	**C5** **Relations**: gangs, state or quasi-state combatants, militia, armed forces **Place**: everywhere **Problem**: scale of mass violence, civilian terror, no security presence, fear and negative consequences of disclosing

to ... walk with victims, but it is always to the extent to which they will let us, you see. That is the challenge' (McKenzie *et al.* 2012, p. 2).[11] If reporting offences to police authorities is not desirable or optimal for many (or most) victims, we should consider: what other justice options are available?[12]

Most research on sexual victimization and justice centres on cell A1, although more is emerging in C5 (collective contexts in countries in conflict or post-conflict) and, to a lesser degree, A2 (clergy abuse outside a total institution). Research and policy will improve when greater attention is paid to the specificity of victimization context and especially how context matters for justice from a victim's perspective. Otherwise, responses and justice practices generated from A1 contexts will be misapplied to other contexts. Here, the recent work by transitional justice scholars, who are calling for a better understanding of 'justice from below' is relevant (Lundy and McGovern 2008; McEvoy and McGregor 2008). Their research is challenging a 'top-down' rule of law perspective (i.e. international criminal law), which announces particular recommendations and unrealistic goals. The problem, in part, is that those victimized have few options, no voice and limited participation in justice agenda-setting; and in part, human rights advocates and organizations use a highly westernised individualized concept of crime and justice, with a focus on 'legalism' (Weinstein *et al.* 2010). Translating this into the vernacular of the Sexual Violence and Justice Matrix, justice responses that may be appropriate to an A1 individual context are being wrongly applied to C5.[13]

Victims' justice interests

For some time, I have been conducting research that seeks to compare conventional and innovative justice responses to sexual violence and to assess the merits of innovative justice responses, from a victim's perspective. For example, I have compared outcomes of youth sex offence cases that went to court and to conferences (Daly 2006) and presented case studies of the experiences of sexual assault victims who participated in conferences (Daly and Curtis-Fawley 2006). An important intervention was a critique of my research by Cossins (2008), who said that I did not provide sufficient evidence for my conclusion that conferences offered more for sexual assault victims than did court. In my response (Daly 2008), I said that Cossins had provided no evidence that court processes were better than conference processes from a victim's perspective. Our exchange reveals the state of 'debate' in the field: it was stalled because we did not have a common metric to compare justice mechanisms.

The problem is profound. We have no robust method of determining what is or is not an effective justice mechanism from a victim's perspective. We cannot assess the merits and limits of any one conventional or innovative mechanism nor can we make comparisons between them in a systematic way. There are some exceptions. For example, research carried out by the Justice Research Consortium randomly assigned burglary and robbery victims to court only or to court and a supplemental conference (Sherman *et al.* 2005; see also Shapland *et al.* 2011). This was a randomized field experiment, and it is one way to make comparisons. However, field experiments are expensive and have their own problems of sample selection bias.[14]

With some exceptions, research on conventional and innovative justice responses relies on general measures of victim *satisfaction* or with elements of *procedural justice* (e.g. being treated with respect, being listened to). For satisfaction, the dominant question in victim studies is: 'How satisfied were you ...?' or 'To what extent were you satisfied?' with a particular justice activity. This is despite the fact that most of us would say that the satisfaction variable is overly simplified, ambiguous and largely uninterpretable (Pemberton and Reynaers 2011, pp. 238–239).

Some researchers have used behavioural or psychological measures such as the frequency of apologies and their perceived sincerity by victims in court and supplemental conference practices (Sherman *et al.* 2005). These measures are more concrete than 'satisfaction', but they centre solely on the psychological benefits of justice activities for aiding victims' recovery from crime. Pemberton *et al.* (2007) have outlined several types of social-psychological measures to assess reductions in anxiety and anger for victims participating in restorative justice processes. Erez *et al.* (2011) have applied ideas from therapeutic jurisprudence to assess victims' experiences with criminal justice. In my view, therapeutic jurisprudence offers a limited range of options for victims: it centres on legal mechanisms and what legal actors do, and it uses satisfaction as a key measure. Furthermore, what is 'therapeutic' or 'anti-therapeutic' lacks specificity. For example, in Erez *et al.* (2011), the term 'therapeutic' refers to any activity that is 'helpful' for victims.

A radical reconceptualization is required. Rather than asking, 'are victims satisfied with a justice mechanism?', 'are they more satisfied with one than another?' or 'do they receive greater psychological or therapeutic benefits from one than another?', we should ask instead, *does a justice mechanism have the capacity to address one or more of victims' justice needs (or interests) and to what extent does it do so?* The construct of *victims' justice interests* contains some elements of procedural justice (i.e., aspects of participation and voice; see Tyler 1990; Wemmers 2010), but it encompasses more than respectful and fair treatment. It also includes validation, vindication and offender accountability. These five elements – participation, voice, validation, vindication and offender accountability – have been identified by others in the domestic criminal justice and transitional justice literatures as important to victims' sense of justice (e.g. Herman 2005; Koss 2006; Henry 2009; van der Merwe 2009; Auckland University of Technology Centre of Restorative Justice 2010; Backer 2012). My contribution is to give the construct greater weight and definitional precision, and to use it to assess and compare conventional and innovative justice mechanisms.

Contrary to those who focus on social-psychological effects of justice mechanisms, I believe that we should distinguish victims' justice needs (or interests) in a justice activity from *the effects* of that activity for changing psychological states (for example, for reducing victims' anger and fear or increasing self-esteem). It is important to separate these 'two logics' (van Stokkom 2011, pp. 209–211). A victim's justice need (or interest) is concerned with the legitimacy of a legal or justice element *in its own right*, independent of its emotional or psychological impact on a victim's well-being. This is where I am critical of therapeutic jurisprudence as applied to crime victims: it jumps too quickly to consider the consequences of law and justice activities without first asking, what principles or entitlements should we, as victims and citizens, expect from justice? Although I welcome research on the psychological impact of justice mechanisms, there needs to be prior consideration of what the optimal justice elements should be, from a victim's perspective.

The term 'victims' justice *needs*' is more often used in the literature (e.g. Koss 2006; van der Merwe 2009) than is justice *interests*. To me, *needs* connotes a psychological requirement, whereas *interests* connotes a victim's standing as a citizen in a justice activity, a connotation I prefer.[15] For now, I use the two interchangeably, although my preference leans to justice interests. The major elements of the construct are as follows.

1. **Participation**. Being informed of options and developments in one's case, including different types of justice mechanisms available; discussing ways to address offending and victimization in meetings with admitted offenders and others; and asking questions and receiving information about crimes (e.g. the location of bodies, the motivations for an admitted offender's actions).
2. **Voice**. Telling the story of what happened and its impact in a significant setting, where a victim/survivor can receive public recognition and acknowledegment. Voice is also termed truth-telling and can be related to participation in having a speaking or other type of physical presence in a justice process.
3. **Validation**. Affirming that the victim is believed (i.e. acknowledging that offending occurred and the victim was harmed) and is not blamed for or thought to be deserving of what happened. It reflects a victim's desire to be believed and to shift the weight of the accusation from their shoulders to others (family members, a wider social group, or legal officials). Admissions by a perpetrator, although perhaps desirable to a victim, may not be necessary to validate a victim's claim.
4. **Vindication**. Having two aspects of the vindication of the law (affirming *the act* was wrong, morally and legally) and the vindication of the victim (affirming *this perpetrator's actions* against the victim were wrong). It requires that others (family members, a wider social group, legal officials) do something to show that an act (or actions) were wrong by, for example, censuring the offence and affirming their solidarity with the victim. It can be expressed by symbolic and material forms of reparation (e.g. apologies, memorialization, financial assistance) and standard forms of state punishment.
5. **Offender accountability**. Requiring that certain individuals or entities 'give accounts' for their actions (Stenning 1995). It refers to perpetrators of offences taking active responsibility for the wrong caused, to give sincere expressions of regret and remorse, and to receive censure or sanction that may vindicate the law and a victim.

Victims' justice needs differ from survival or coping needs (e.g. for safety, food, housing, counselling), service needs (e.g. for information[16] and support) and violence prevention. All are relevant and some have greater priority than others, depending on the victimization context. For example, studies of severely disadvantaged groups in post-conflict societies show that for many survivors, food and housing are of more immediate importance than 'justice' (Robins 2011).[17] Likewise, in familial- or residential-based contexts of victimization, safety may be of more immediate importance.

'Victims' justice needs' (or interests), as defined here, is an emergent and untested construct. Members of my project team and I are operationalizing the meaning of each element in analyses that apply the construct to real cases and victims' experiences. As this work progresses, definitions of each element may require modification. However, the construct offers a promising way to assess and compare conventional and innovative justice responses to crime. We know that such responses have different aims, limits and potentials – a crucial, if overlooked, fact when efforts are made to compare their strengths and limits. For example, a conventional mechanism of the criminal trial was not designed primarily to address victim participation, voice or validation. In contrast, an innovative mechanism of mediated meetings or conferences of victims and admitted offenders was designed to enhance victim participation and voice, but it may be inadequate for addressing other justice needs.

There is more work to be done in applying the idea of victims' justice interests. My first step is to apply it retrospectively to data and cases I have already gathered to determine how to operationalize each of the elements. What I envision is that we can build a solid body of evidence about the strengths and limits of justice mechanisms because we have a common metric. In attempting to apply the idea, we may find that other elements should be added, or that other types of refinements are required. In doing so, we can engage in a normative discussion about the standing and interests of victims as citizens in justice activities. I have avoided the term 'victims' rights' for practical and political reasons. It gets caught up in a zero-sum game discussion of the entitlements of alleged offenders and victims in a legal process, and it invites conjecture on ways to balance these rights in an ideal justice 'system' (Cape 2004). My goal is more modest, at least initially: it is to address a problem I faced several years ago in the exchange between Cossins and myself on the relative merits of court and conference processes in responding to sexual violence. We could not engage in a meaningful debate because there was no common ground, no common metric. With the construct of victims' justice interests, we can begin to redress that problem.

Conclusion

In this chapter, I have called for a reconceptualization of sexual victimization and justice, working within and across domestic and international justice fields. I reiterate the key points. First, for politics, while we might wish that research evidence can trump ideology and prejudice, this is naïve for offences falling under the rubric of 'sex crime'. These offences are minimized or not addressed for most victims *and* they are demonized for a relatively small group of offenders. The political and media construction of sex offending and victimization has served to stymie discussion on rational and constructive change. Second, for research, we must get our conceptual house in order, as much as this is possible in light of working in new and expanding fields of knowledge. If we want to improve victims' standing and options in the aftermath of crime, we need a stronger evidence base. That requires a more coherent use of key concepts and more sound ways of depicting justice mechanisms that operate within, alongside or outside a legal process in civil society. Third, for research, we must respect the boundaries of domestic and international or transitional justice because each works in different victimization contexts and on different problems of justice for victims. For example, transitional justice is concerned with state building, economic development and social-political transformation whereas domestic criminal justice is not.[18] However, there are points of overlap in studies of sexual victimization in countries at peace and in conflict zones. Furthermore, we might imagine that a justice mechanism that is used in one context of victimization could be adapted to another context, which could, in turn, expand the repertoire of justice options for victims. Finally, for research and policy, it is time to say goodbye to 'satisfaction' as the measure of justice for victims. We can and must do better. I propose a new way to assess and compare justice mechanisms, which can further our research and understanding of victims' experiences in seeking justice. There is much work ahead.

Notes

1 Overall conviction rates declined in England and Wales, Canada and Australia, but not in the United States or Scotland; on average, rates range from 10 to 14 per cent (except Scotland, whose rates are 16 to 18 per cent). Research in civil law jurisdictions finds greater variability: from 4 and 8 per cent in Belgium and Portugal, respectively, to 18 and 23 per cent in Austria and Germany, respectively. These percentages are of 2004–2005 cases in a project headed by Lovett and Kelly (2009). By 'overall conviction rate', I mean the percentage of cases resulting in conviction (by plea or at trial) to any sexual offence of those reported to the police.
2 A 'get tough' stance is particularly focused on adults who sexually victimize children, 'as political parties vie for ever more punitive sanctions' (McAlinden 2007, p. 15).
3 McGlynn (2011, pp. 840–841) traces how these concerns unfolded in England and Wales in 2011 with a proposed sentencing discount for offenders who pleaded early to sex offences; she demonstrates the divisions among symbolic and pragmatic feminist positions, as I define them here.
4 The proposed ways forward, listed above, were written with this one context in mind; and they are likely to require revision for other contexts.
5 With respect to 'large-scale state-based conflict', Aertsen (2008, pp. 413–434) suggests that differing types of justice mechanisms – 'informal, formal, and in-between' – needed to be 'combined in a flexible way'. It is important that conceptual understandings of justice in both domestic and transitional justice contexts begin to appreciate the strengths of hybrid mechanisms.
6 These activities, although 'outside law', may use legal formats (e.g. popular tribunals, see Chinkin 2001). Examples of documentary theatre and art and activist projects are given in Buikema (2012) and Simić (2010), and are particularly visible in transitional justice contexts.

7 I am interested in identifying and researching *justice mechanisms*, not a 'justice system' or a 'type of justice' (e.g. transformative justice).
8 I would be less concerned if people used the terms 'conventional' and 'restorative' justice. My point is that it is inappropriate to characterize the entire apparatus of conventional criminal justice as 'retributive'; and in addition, retribution has value as a justice aim.
9 These ideas are developed in Daly and Proietti-Scifoni (2011) and glossed here. The problem is not that people do not define terms (although many do not), but rather that they seem to be unaware of how others have defined them or used them in empirical research.
10 The matrix's rows and columns could be expanded considerably (or sub-divided further) as researchers identify where their research sits in the matrix and how it is further inflected by differing cultural meanings.
11 There was mounting pressure from mid-2012 in Australia to address complaints of sexual abuse by clergy associated with Catholic and other churches in Victoria and New South Wales, which resulted in the Prime Minister's announcement on 12 November 2012 of her recommendation to create a Royal Commission. On 11 January 2013, the Governor-General issued Commonwealth Letters Patent for a Royal Commission into Institutional Responses to Child Sexual Abuse, appointing six commissioners and its terms of reference.
12 I am concerned with proposals for mandatory reporting of sexual abuse because this may not be desirable for many victims.
13 An example of misapplication is the common recommendation given by international NGOs to address sexual violence in developing countries in conflict or post-conflict. The advice is to use conventional forms of criminal justice, in particular, to implement international legal protocols and conventions, and to strengthen and enforce domestic criminal justice (Daly and Dalsgaard 2010).
14 An example is the Justice Research Consortium London Experiment (Sherman *et al.* 2005, p. 377). For each eligible case, an offender was first invited to participate; and if the offender agreed, then the victim in the case was invited. In the burglary experiment 59 per cent of victims consented to participate (from a set of 78 per cent of offenders who agreed to participate); and in the robbery experiment 52 per cent of victims consented to participate (from a set of 83 per cent of offenders). *Overall, then, 46 and 43 per cent, respectively, of victims in eligible burglary and robbery cases self-selected in the project.* The victims who opted in were then randomly assigned to participate in a supplemental conference (or not) pre-sentence. This protocol is undoubtedly appropriate from an ethical point of view. However, Sherman *et al.* (2005) then compare the orientations of this group of victims on such items as feeling 'forgiveness' towards an offender with the victims in the Re-Integrative Shaming Experiments (RISE). RISE victims had no choice to opt in (or not) to RISE because the process was entirely based on offender admissions before a random allocation of cases to a diversionary conference (or court). Thus, we might expect that the two groups of victims would be quite differently oriented towards the two types of justice activities, a fact that Sherman *et al.* (2005) do not consider.
15 My thanks to Robyn Holder, who suggested that justice 'interests' may be preferable to 'needs'.
16 Service needs for information can be distinguished from the role of information in victim participation in that the latter assumes a more active role for a victim to choose among several justice options.
17 Similar items have been proposed by transitional justice scholars (Backer 2012; Sonis, as summarised in van der Merwe 2009, p. 128). They consider not only victims' justice interests, but also societal reconstruction and transformation. Backer's 'justice index' has twelve elements: 'awareness/acknowledgment, voice, truth, admission/account-

ability, apology, liability/punishment, reparation, non-repetition, restoration, development, redistribution and transformation (socio-political)'. Sonis' 'justice scale' was developed to assess victims' views of the South African Truth and Reconciliation Commission; it has eight elements: 'voice, punishment, truth, accountability, acknowledgement, financial restitution, apology, and transformation'. Aertsen (2008, pp. 435–440) identifies these elements as important in responding to large-scale violent conflict: 'identity, dignity, truth, restoration, and justice'.

18 Of course, some argue that domestic criminal justice *should be* concerned with social and political transformation, with 'social justice' as the goal, but here I am comparing the standard aims and objectives of the two.

Bibliography

Aertsen, I., 2008. Racak, Mahane Yehuda and Nyabyondo: Restorative justice between the formal and the informal. In: I. Aertsen, J. Arsovska, H. Rohne, M. Valinas and K. Vanspauwen, eds, Restoring justice after large-scale violent conflicts: Kosovo, DR Congo and the Israeli-Palestinian case. Cullompton: Willan Publishing, pp. 413–443.

Auckland University of Technology (AUT) Restorative Justice Centre, 2010. Submission to the Ministry of Justice on the 'Victims of Crime' Consultation Document. Available at: www.restorativejustice.org/RJOB/Submission%20on%20Victims%20Rights.pdf [Accessed 27 Jan 2012].

Backer, D., 2012. Personal communication, 24 May 2012.

Best, J., 1990. Threatened children. Chicago: University of Chicago Press.

Boesten, J., 2010. Analyzing rape regimes at the interface of war and peace in Peru. International Journal of Transitional Justice, 4, pp. 110–129.

Buikema, R., 2012. Performing dialogical truth and transitional justice: The role of art in the becoming post-apartheid of South Africa. Memory Studies, 5, pp. 282–292.

Cape, E. ed., 2004. Reconciliable rights? Analyzing the tension between victims and defendants. London: Legal Action Group.

Chinkin, C., 2001. Women's International Tribunal on Japanese military sexual slavery. American Journal of International Law, 95, pp. 335–341.

Christie, N., 1986. The ideal victim. In: E. Fattah, ed., 1986. From crime policy to victim policy. Basingstoke: Macmillan, pp. 1–17.

Clamp, K. and Doak, J., 2012. More than words: restorative justice concepts in transitional justice settings. International Criminal Law Review, 12(3), pp. 339–360.

Cossins, A., 2008. Restorative justice and child sex offences: The theory and the practice. British Journal of Criminology, 48(3), pp. 359–378.

Daly, K., 2000. Revisiting the relationship between retributive and restorative justice. In: H. Strang and J. Braithwaite, eds, Restorative justice: Philosophy to practice. Aldershot: Ashgate/Dartmouth, pp. 33–54.

Daly, K., 2002a. Sexual assault and restorative justice. In: H. Strang and J. Braithwaite, eds, Restorative justice and family violence. Cambridge: Cambridge University Press, pp. 62–88.

Daly, K., 2002b. Restorative justice: The real story. Punishment and Society, 4(1), pp. 55–79.

Daly, K., 2006. Restorative justice and sexual assault: An archival study of court and conference cases. British Journal of Criminology, 46(2), pp. 334–356.

Daly, K., 2008. Setting the record straight and a call for radical change: A reply to Annie Cossins on restorative justice and child sex offenses. British Journal of Criminology, 48(4), pp. 557–566.
Daly, K., 2010. Feminist perspectives in criminology: A review with Gen Y in mind. In: E. McLaughlin and T. Newburn, eds, The SAGE handbook of criminological theory. London: Sage Publications, pp. 225–246.
Daly, K., 2011. Conventional and innovative justice responses to sexual violence. ACSSA Issues 12. Melbourne: Australian Centre for the Study of Sexual Assault, Australian Institute of Family Studies.
Daly, K., 2012. Conferences and gendered violence: Practices, politics, and evidence. In: I. Vanfraechem and E. Zinsstag, eds, Conferencing and restorative justice: Challenges, developments and debates. Oxford: Oxford University Press, pp. 117–135.
Daly, K., 2014. Redressing insitutional abuse of children. Basingstoke: Palgrave/Macmillan.
Daly, K. and Immarigeon, R., 1998. The past, present and future of restorative justice: some critical reflections. Contemporary Justice Review, 1(1), pp. 21–45.
Daly, K. and Curtis-Fawley, S., 2006. Restorative justice for victims of sexual assault. In: K. Heimer and C. Kruttschnitt, eds, Gender and crime: Patterns of victimization and offending. New York: New York University Press, pp. 230–265.
Daly, K. and Bouhours, B., 2010. Rape and attrition in the legal process: A comparative analysis of five countries. Crime and Justice: An Annual Review of Research, 39, pp. 565–650.
Daly, K. and Dalsgaard, S., 2010. Setting the agenda: How international NGO's respond to sexual violence against women. Australian and New Zealand Society of Criminology annual meeting. Alice Springs, September.
Daly, K. and Proietti-Scifoni, G., 2011. Reparation and restoration. In: M. Tonry, ed., Oxford Handbook of Crime and Criminal Justice. New York: Oxford University Press, pp. 207–253.
Erez, E., Kilching, M. and Wemmers, J., 2011. Therapeutic jurisprudence and victim participation in justice: An introduction. In: E. Erez, M. Kilching, and J. Wemmers, eds, Therapeutic jurisprudence and victim participation in justice: International perspectives. Durham: Carolina Academic Press, pp.ix-xix.
Estrich, S., 1987. Real rape. Cambridge: Harvard University Press.
Harland, A., 1996. Towards a restorative justice future. In: B. Galaway and J. Hudson, eds, Restorative justice: International perspectives. Monsey: Criminal Justice Press, pp. 505–516.
Henry, N., 2009. Witness to rape: The limits and potential of international war crimes trials for victims of wartime sexual violence. The International Journal of Transitional Justice, 3, pp. 114–34.
Herman, J., 2005. Justice from the victim's perspective. Violence Against Women, 11(5), pp. 571–602.
Hudson, B., 1998. Restorative justice: The challenges of sexual and racial violence. Journal of Law and Society, 25(2), pp. 237–256.
Jülich, S., 2010. Restorative justice and gendered violence in New Zealand: A glimmer of hope. In: J. Ptacek, ed., Restorative justice and violence against women. New York: Oxford University Press, pp. 239–254.

Jülich, S., Buttle, J., Cummins, C. and Freeborn, E., 2010. Project Restore: An exploratory study of restorative justice and sexual violence. Auckland University of Technology. Available at: http://aut.academia.edu/documents/0121/2233/The_Project_Restore_Report.pdf.

Koss, M., 2006. Restoring rape survivors: Justice, advocacy, and a call to action. Annals of the New York Academy of Sciences, 1087, pp. 206–234.

Lovett, J. and Kelly, L., 2009. Different systems, similar outcomes? Tracking attrition in reported rape cases across Europe, final report. London: Child and Woman Abuse Studies Unit, London Metropolitan University.

Lundy, P. and McGovern, M., 2008. Whose justice? Rethinking transitional justice from the bottom up. Journal of Law and Society, 35(2), pp. 265–292.

Madsen, K., 2008. From victim to action. Paper presented to the Associação Portuguesa de Apoio à Vítima (APAV) conference, Lisbon, July.

McAlinden, A., 2007. The shaming of sexual offenders: Risk, retribution and reintegration. Oxford: Hart Publishing.

McDonald, E. and Tinsley, Y., 2011. Rejecting one size fits all: Recommending a range of responses. In: E. McDonald and Y. Tinsley, eds, From real rape to real justice: Prosecuting rape in New Zealand. Wellington: Victoria University Press, pp. 377–438.

McEvoy, K., 2007. Beyond legalism: Towards a thicker understanding of transitional justice. Journal of Law and Society, 24(4), pp. 411–440.

McEvoy, K. and McGregor, L., eds, 2008. Transitional justice from below: Grassroots activism and the struggle for change. Oxford: Hart Publishing.

McGlynn, C., 2011. Feminism, rape and the search for justice. Oxford Journal of Legal Studies, 31(4), pp. 825–42.

McGlynn, C., Westmarland, N. and Godden, N., 2012. 'I just wanted him to hear me': Sexual violence and the possibilities of restorative justice. Journal of Law and Society, 39(2), pp. 213–240.

McKenzie, N., Baker, R. and Gordon, J., 2012. Inquiry looms as more suicides linked to sexual abuse by Catholic priests. The Age. Available at: www.theage.com.au/action/printArticle?id=3218093 [Accessed 19 Aug 2012].

Mertus, J., 2004. Shouting from the bottom of the well: The impact of international trials for wartime rape on women's agency. International Feminist Journal of Politics, 6(1), pp. 110–128.

Naylor, B., 2010. Effective justice for victims of sexual assault: Taking up the debate on alternative pathways. University of New South Wales Law Journal, 33(2), pp. 662–684.

Pali, B. and Madsen, K., 2011. Dangerous liaisons? A feminist and restorative approach to sexual assault. Temida, March, pp. 49–65.

Pemberton, A. and Reynaers, S., 2011. The controversial nature of victim participation: Therapeutic benefits in victim impact statements. In: E. Erez, M. Kilching, and J. Wemmers, eds, Therapeutic jurisprudence and victim participation in justice: International perspectives. Durham: Carolina Academic Press, pp. 229–248.

Pemberton, A., Winkel, F. and Groenhuijsen, M., 2007. Taking victims seriously in restorative justice. International Perspectives in Victimology, 3(1), pp. 4–13.

Robins, S., 2011. Towards victim-centred transitional justice: Understanding the needs of families of the disappeared in postconflict Nepal. The International Journal of Transitional Justice, 5, pp. 75–98.

Roche, D., 2007. Retribution and restorative justice. In: G. Johnstone and D. van Ness, eds, Handbook of restorative justice. Cullompton: Willan Publishing, pp. 75–90.

Rock, P., 2002. On becoming a victim. In: C. Hoyle and R. Young, eds, New visions of crime victims. Oxford: Hart Publishing, pp. 1–22.

Shapland, J., Robinson, G. and Sorsby, A., 2011. Restorative justice in practice: Evaluating what works for victims and offenders. London: Routledge.

Sherman, L., Strang, H., Angel, C., Woods, D., Barnes, G., Bennett, S. and Inkpen, N., 2005. Effects of face-to-face restorative justice on victims of crime in four randomized, controlled trials. Journal of Experimental Criminology, 1, pp. 367–395.

Simić, O., 2010. Breathing sense into women's lives shattered by war: Dah Theatre Belgrade. Law Text Culture, 14(1), pp. 117–132.

Simon, J., 1998. Managing the monstrous: Sex offenders and the new penology. Psychology, Public Policy, and Law, 4(1/2), pp. 452–467.

Stenning, P., 1995. Introduction. In: P.C. Stenning, ed., Accountability for criminal justice: Selected essays. Toronto: University of Toronto Press, pp. 3–14.

Thomas, T., 2005. Sex crime: Sex offending and society, 2nd edition. Cullompton: Willan Publishing.

Tyler, T., 1990. Why people obey the law: Procedural justice, legitimacy and compliance. New Haven: Yale University Press.

van der Merwe, H., 2009. Delivering justice during transition: Research challenges. In: H. van der Merwe, V. Baxter and A. Chapman, eds, Assessing the impact of transitional justice: Challenges for empirical research. Washington: United States Institute of Peace, pp. 115–142.

van Stokkom., 2011. Victims' needs, well-being and closure: Is revenge therapeutic? In: E. Erez, M. Kilching and J. Wemmers, eds, Therapeutic jurisprudence and victim participation in justice: International perspectives. Durham: Carolina Academic Press, pp. 207–227.

Waldman, E., 2007. Restorative justice and the pre-conditions for grace: Taking victim's needs seriously. Cardozo Journal of Conflict Resolution, 9, pp. 91–108.

Weinstein, H., Fletcher, L., Vinck, P. and Pham, P., 2010. Stay the hands of justice: Whose priorities take priority? In: R. Shaw and L. Waldorf, eds, Localizing transitional justice: Interventions and priorities after mass violence. California: Stanford University Press, pp. 27–48.

Wemmers, J., 2010. The meaning of justice for victims. In: S.G. Shoham, P. Knepper and M. Kett, eds, International handbook of victimology. Boca Raton: CRC Press, pp. 27–42.

Zimring, F., 2004. An American travesty: Legal responses to adolescent sex offending. Chicago: University of Chicago Press.

Index

9/11 attacks 110

Abdulaziz Al-Nasser, Nassir 91
abertzale left (leftist Basque parties) 326–7, 328–9, 336
acknowledgement of criminal guilt 238–9
activist victims 15, 18–19, 25
ADHD (Attention Deficit Hyperactivity Disorder) 303
advanced parole 152
Aertsen, I. 288
African victims of colonialism 89–95, 96–100
Alfonsín, Raúl 234
Alien Torts Claims Act (1789) 93
Allende, Salvador 230
'ambiguous wording' (of EU directives) 62
amnesties 162, 172–3, 178, 193
Anderson, Benedict 248
Antilla, Inkeri 17
anxiety 301–2, 306, 310, 313–14, 318–19
apartheid 93, 188, 235
appraisal respect 33–5, 36–7, 43, 44–5
'appropriation' 175
Arbour, Louise 165
Arendt, Hannah 161, 178
Argentina 228, 229, 233–6, 239
Arrizabalaga, Professor Iñaki García 331
art 194, 195–6
Artha Sastra (ancient Indian law) 72
Asociación de Familiares de Detenidos Desaparecidos (Chile) 233
attitude 34
'Aunty Yan' 247, 248, 250–1, 252, 254–6, 257
Australia 110–11, 117, 118, 119–20, 121, 124–5, 126
Aylwin, Patricio 233–4, 238

Backer, David 172–3
Bali bombing (2002) 110–11
Balza, General Martín 239
Bámaca Velázquez v. Guatemala (2000) 241
Barnard, Dianne Kohler 78
Barrios Altos v. Peru (2001) 241–2
Basoglu, Metin 176
Bayzler, Michael 92
Berkeley Human Rights Centre 166, 171, 220, 221
Blackstone, William 24
'blameless' victims 116–17
Boers, K. 169
Bohm, David 198
Bosnia-Herzegovina 165–8, 177, 218–20
Bottoms, A. 33
'bottom-up' victim perspectives 217
Bradford, B. 285
Brazil 69–70
bribery 355, 357, 358, 359, 362–5, 370–1
Brief Symptom Inventory 269
British Crime Survey (2010–2011) 14–15
Brooks, R. 163–4, 337
Brougham, Henry 25

Bunyoro people (Uganda) 94
Burundi 173–4
Buscaglia, E. 373

Cambodia 171, 221–3, 247–59, 314
Campbell, T. 18
Canada 111, 117, 118, 119–20, 121–2, 124–5, 126–8
Canuto, M. 288
Carmona, Teresa 75
Carnegie Endowment for International Peace (1998) 163
Carothers, Thomas 163–4
Case Manager Project (Netherlands) 312
Center for Advanced Study (Cambodia) 221–2
Central African Republic 171
Central American Court of Justice 95
Centre for Integral Development (Ecuador) 185
Cheyre, General 238
child mortality rates 370
child victims: and criminal justice systems 311–13; impact of crime on 301–6; legislation on 300; needs of 306–13; and PTSD 302–3, 309–11, 313–14; and risk of crime 300; and stress 301–4, 305, 310–11, 313–14; and trauma 301–3, 305–6, 309–11, 313–15, 319; and victim support services 311, 313–19; and victimization 300, 301, 305–7, 311–12, 315, 318, 319
Chile: and criminal justice 240–2; and development of transitional justice 228–30; human rights abuse victims 230–3, 234–7; and reparations 239–40; transitional justice study 228–30, 233–43
China 71, 82
Ching, Tao Te 201
Christie, Nils 116, 170
'civic trust' 112, 124–5
civil remedy surrogate system 114, 119–20
civil rights 68
Civil Rights Act (1964) 154
Clamp, K. 383

Clark, Janine Natalya 167
Clarke, D. 282
class 26
Code of Practice for Victims of Crime (2006) 21–2
collective reparations 215–16
colonialism: and human rights abuses 89–95, 96–100; and reparations for African victims 89–91, 92–5, 96–100; and slavery 91–2; and victims' rights in NICs 72, 74, 77, 78, 81
common law jurisdictions 23–4
compensable losses/injuries 117–20
compensation: characteristics of national schemes 113–25; and compensable losses/injuries 117–20; and compensation function 121–3; and 'criminal injury' 114–15; and criminal justice systems 105, 107, 109, 116, 124–5; and development of victims' rights 66, 67; and eligibility 116–17; and empathy 112; European Union provision 106–8, 112–13, 115–20, 122, 128; as form of reparation 214, 219–20, 221, 239, 240; justification for state schemes 111–13; and liberal ideology 105, 124; and offenders' rights 105, 116–17; and 'rebalancing' 105, 124; 'rights' to 123–5; and social justice 112–3, 122; and sympathy 112; and terrorism victims 105, 109–11, 122, 124; and trauma 115; and trust 112, 124–5; and victimization 105, 111, 116; and victims' rights in NICs 69, 70, 71, 73, 74–6, 79, 80, 81; and 'violent crime' 114–15; US provision 108–9, 112, 114–16, 118, 121, 122–3, 124, 125, 129–30; *see also* reparations
Compensation for Crime Victims (leaflet) 109
'compensation mechanisms' 71, 106–7, 113
'competitive grief' 14
CONADEP (Argentinean National Commission on the Disappearance of Persons) 234–6

constitutions 69, 70, 74–8, 79, 80
'continued presence' 150
Convention on the Compensation of Victims of Violent Crime (1983) 106, 107, 117, 118–19
Convention on the Non-Applicability of Statutory Limitations (1968) 240
conventional justice mechanisms 378, 382, 383, 386–7
corruption: conceptual framework 359–64; costs of 356–9; defining 357; in developing countries 357–8; extent of 355–6, 371–2; manifestation of 356–9, 362–4; and organized crime 358, 363, 369, 372, 373; reducing 372–3; and victimization 359–62, 364–72; as 'victimless crime' 359, 372, 373; victims of 364–71
Corruption Perceptions Index 356
Cossins, A. 386
Costa Rica 360
Council Directive 2004/80/EC (2004) 106–8, 113, 116, 118, 120
Council of Europe Recommendation (2006) 58
Cowan v Le Tresor Public (1989) 113
Criminal Injuries Compensation Authority 17, 23, 109
'criminal injury' 114–15
criminal justice systems: and access to information 281–2; and child victims 311–13; and compensation 105, 107, 109, 116, 124–5; and development of victims' rights 67; and ETA study 332, 333, 339; and EU action on victims' rights 52, 53–6, 59–61, 63–4; and integral justice 186–7; and procedural justice model 277; and respecting victims 33, 34, 40, 42–3; and sexual victimization 379–83; and transitional justice 240–2; and victim concerns 277–9, 281–2, 291; and victim impact statements 283–5, 292; and victim–offender mediation 287–8, 291, 292; and victimology 212; and victims' rights 11–12, 16–17, 19, 21, 24–6, 32; and victims' rights in NICs 71, 74, 78–9
Criminal Law (China, 1997) 71
Criminal Procedure Code (China, 1996) 71
critical victimology 14
cross-border cases 56–7, 60
CrPC (Criminal Procedure Code of India) 72–4
cuddly toy support figures (child victims) 316–17
cultural justice (dimension of integral justice) 191, 194–6
Cyr, K. 286, 289, 290

Daly, K. 288
Danegeld 19
Darwall, S. 33, 34
Dayton Peace Agreements (1995) 218
De Mesmaecker, V. 291
decision making procedures (procedural justice model) 279, 280–1, 286–7, 291
defining 'victims' 12–14, 230, 378
democracy 163, 228–9, 230, 252–3, 259
Democratic Republic of Congo 171, 172, 193, 216
demonization of 'sex offenders' 379–80, 390
devictimization 322, 333, 335, 340–1
diffuse victimization 334, 336
DINA (Dirección de Inteligencia Nacional) 234
disrespect 35–6
Doak, J. 383
domestic violence 20, 116
Domestic Violence, Victims and Crime Act (2004) 20, 21
Downes, David 17, 24
DSM (Diagnostic and Statistical Manual of Mental Disorders) 266
Duerr, Hans-Peter 198
Duff, Antony 41, 42
Dunn, Peter 19
'duty to understand' 33

Eagan, Judge Claire V. 155
Easwaran, E. 201

ECCC (Extraordinary Chambers in the Courts of Cambodia) 221–2, 247–8, 249, 253–4
Eckhart, Meister 202
ecological justice (dimension of integral justice) 191, 196–8
'Eco-Spirituality' 200
Edgar, A. 284
EEOC (Equal Employment Opportunity Commission) 150, 154–5
Einstein, Albert 199
El Salvador 193–4, 236
Elias, R. 112, 169
Elworthy, Scilla 199
'emancipation' of victims 32
EMDR (Eye Movement Desensitization and Reprocessing) 311
empathy: and compensation 112; and respecting victims 33, 37–8, 39, 40–1, 43, 45; and restorative justice 40–1; and victimization 40, 43, 45; and victims' rights 40–1, 45
'encounters to repair victims' 325–6, 334, 336
Englebrecht, C. 284
'equality of arms' 24
Erez, E. 285, 387
ETA (Euskadi Ta Askatasuna): and compensation 109; comprehensive law models 330–2; fatalities data 323–4, 333; and restorative justice 322, 323–6, 328, 330–41; and Spanish legal system 327; and transitional justice model 327–30; and victimization 322, 325, 326–7, 329–30, 333–6, 338–41
EU action on victims' rights: and criminal justice systems 52, 53–6, 59–61, 63–4; EU Directive (2011) 19, 51–2, 53–7, 58–64; Framework Decision (2001) 19, 51–3, 54, 55, 58, 62–4; Treaty of Lisbon (2007) 51, 53, 54; and victim support services 57–61
EU Directive on Victims' Rights (2011) 19, 51–2, 53–7, 58–64, 300

European Crime and Safety Survey (2005) 57
European Union compensation provision 106–8, 112–13, 115–20, 122, 128
Evans, B. 367
Evans, R. 368
'extraordinary justice' 165
extra-territorial jurisdiction 145

'failed states' 163, 249, 250, 254
fairness 279–81, 285–6, 287, 288, 290
false claims to victimhood 237
Farmer, Lindsay 24
Fassin, Didier 175
Fattah, Ezzat 168–9, 170, 174
federal certification 152–3
Federal-Provincial Task Force on Justice for Victims (Canada) 13, 19–20
feminism 11, 13, 14, 20, 380–1
FEMM Committee 54
financial/material consequences of crime (child victims) 304
FLSA (Fair Labour Standards Act) 155
Folger, R. 280, 289
forgiveness 173–4, 177, 325–6, 330–1, 336–8, 339
'four worlds' perspective 190, 192
Framework Decision on the Standing of Victims in Criminal Proceedings (2001) 19, 51–3, 54, 55, 58, 62–4
Francis of Assisi, Saint 200
Franco, Francisco 323
Frank, C. 79
Frankl, Victor 184, 202, 203, 205–6
Frazier, P. 269
Fry, Margery 67
future control 268–70
GAL (Group of Anti-Terrorist Liberation) 328–9
Gandhi, Mahatma 206
Garzón, Judge Baltasar 93
gender equality 254
genocide 91, 93, 99, 177, 211, 223, 254
German–Polish Convention (1922) 95–6
Ghafar, A. 75

Gini coefficient 365
Glencree Initiative (Spain) 332
Global Horizons Inc. (farm labour contractor) 155
Gottschalk, Marie 25
Graf Dürckheim, Karlfried 184, 202, 203, 204
Gray, David 165
Great Britain 109, 111, 112, 117, 118–20, 121–2, 125, 128
Groenhuijsen, M. 211, 215
guarantees of non-repetition 214, 239, 240
Guardian (newspaper) 368
Guatemala 193, 241
Guidelines on Justice for Child Victims and Witnesses of Crime (2005) 300
Guiding Principles for a Model of the End of ETA without Impunity (2010) 327
guilt, feelings of 302, 308, 312
Gupta, S. 365, 370
Gutto, S. 91

Hague Conventions 96, 98–9
Hao, Y. 364
'hard law' 51, 52, 53, 63
Harland, A. 383
harmfulness 33, 42–4
hate crime 13
Henríquez, Cardinal Raúl Silva 231–2
Herero people (Namibia) 94
'hero/heroine' status of victims 36, 44, 183–4, 185
Herrington, Lois 11
Hightower, J. 368
Hodzic, Refik 167–8
Holocaust 12, 202, 239, 337, 340
Holstein, J. 14
HSI (Homeland Security Investigations) 142, 143
HTRS (Human Trafficking Reporting System) 144–5
Hudson, B. 380
human rights abuses: accounting for victims 234–7; African victims of colonialism 89–95, 96–100; Chilean victims 230–3, 234–7; and human trafficking 140, 143, 148, 155; and mass victimization 211; and social reconstruction 163; and transitional justice 161, 162, 165, 168, 175; and victimology 211
Human Rights Act (1998) 20
Human Rights Watch (NGO) 76, 78
human trafficking: current US trends 141–2; data on 140, 141–2, 143; harm reduction approach 141; and human rights abuses 140, 143, 148, 155; and immigration 144, 147–9, 150–2; legal framework of 142–6; misconceptions surrounding 141; and slavery 140; state responses to 146, 147; survivors' assistance programmes 149–55; and trauma 151; typology of victims 146–9; UN protocols on 140, 142–4; victim protection approach 141
Hussin, N. 74, 75

Ibn 'Arabi 200–1
ICTY (International Criminal Tribunal for the Former Yugoslavia) 99, 165–7
'ideal' victims 116
ILAS (Instituto de Salud Mental y Derechos Humanos) 233
'imaginary' of transitional justice 247–59
imagined communities 248
'immaterial loss' 118, 120
immigration 144, 147–9, 150–2
implementation of EU directives 62–3
In my Own Way (book) 204
incidental corruption 362–3, 364, 366, 369, 371
India 71–4, 82
indirect victimization 334, 336
individual level victimization 361–2, 366, 369–71, 372
individual reparations 215–16
individual-incidental corruption 371
individual-sporadic corruption 371
industrial victims' rights 68
'innocent' victims 116–17, 124

innovative justice mechanisms 378, 382–3, 386–7
institutional level victimization 361, 366, 367–9, 372
institutional-incidental corruption 369
institutional-sporadic corruption 368–9
institutional-systemic corruption 367–8
integral justice: and criminal justice systems 186–7; dimensions of 191, 193–200; and 'hero/heroine' status of victims 185; nature/characteristics of 190–2; and perpetrators' transformation 205–6; and religion 194, 196, 199–201; and spirituality 198–204; and transformation of victims 202–4; and transitional justice 185–6, 189, 192, 193, 194–6, 200, 206; and trauma 183, 187, 189, 202, 204, 205; value of 189–90, 206; and victimization 185; and victimology 185, 189, 193, 200, 206; and victims' rights 205, 206
Integral Vision, Integral Spirituality and Integral Psychology (book) 190
International Centre for Transitional Justice (New York) 220
International Crime Victim Survey (2007) 54
International Criminal Court 162, 172, 205, 211, 215, 216–17
International Labour Organization 96, 140
International Prize Court (1907) 95
Israel 109–10
It is difficult to get it out of my head (book) 300

Janoff-Bulman, R. 266–7, 268
Jeldres, Julio 252
Jerin, R. 67
Jin, G. 71
John Pickle Co. (oil industry parts manufacturer) 155
Johnston, M. 364
Joutsen, Matti 13
just world theory 35–6
Justice Research Consortium 386

Khmer Rouge Regime (Cambodia) 221–2, 247, 250–6, 314
KID (Khmer Institute of Democracy) 247, 250, 252–3, 254–5, 258–9
Kleinman, Arthur 169, 174–6
Kleinman, Joan 174–5
Klitgaard, R. 357
Knapp Commission (US) 369
Knaus, Gerald 167
KRT (Khmer Rouge Tribunal) 247–8, 249, 253–6, 257
Kulkarni, Anu 172–3

Lambsdorff, J. 367
Lawrence, Stephen 20
lawyers 24
leadership 183–5
Leebaw, Bronwyn 164
Leferink, S. 286
legal aid 153–4
legal consequences of crime (child victims) 305
legalism 162, 163–4, 168–70, 174, 175
legislation protecting victims' rights: and criminal justice systems 52, 53–6, 59–61, 63–4; EU Directive (2011) 19, 51–2, 53–7, 58–64; Framework Decision (2001) 19, 51–3, 54, 55, 58, 62–4; Treaty of Lisbon (2007) 51, 53, 54; and victim support services 57–61
Leigh, D. 368
Lemert, Edwin 15
Lens, K. 284, 286, 287
Leopold II, King (Belgium) 91
Lessem, Ronnie 190, 192
Letschert, R. 216
liberal ideology 105, 124
Liberia 171, 195
Lind, E. 279, 280, 281
'logotherapy' 202
London bombings (2005) 109, 122
LRA (Lord's Resistance Army, Uganda) 172, 220

Maasai people (Kenya) 94
Maharaj, Nisargadatta 204
Mahidol, B. 79
Mainwaring, S. 228
'Maji Maji rebellion' 94
Malaysia 74–5, 82
Malimath Committee (India) 72
Mandela, Nelson 36, 183–4, 185, 197–8
Mani, R. 194–5
Manusmriti (ancient Indian law) 72
marginalisation of victims 11
Margolis, H. 361
'Martens Clause' (in Hague Conventions) 98–9
mass victimization: Bosnia-Herzegovina study 218–20; Cambodia study 221–3; psychological impact of 212–13; and reparations 210, 211, 212, 213–24; and reparative justice 210–11; Serbia study 218–20; and transitional justice 210–11; Uganda study 220–1; and victimology 211–13, 215, 223
'material loss' 118, 192, 197
Mau Mau people (Kenya) 94
Mauro, P. 361, 367, 370
McAlinden, A. 380
mediation 71, 169, 277, 287–91, 292
Medina, Admiral José Toribio 233
memory preservation 234, 235, 237–8
Meng, Q. 372–3
Messmer, H. 289
Mexico 75–6
Miers, D. 112
Mikaelsson, J. 106
Miller, G. 14
Milosevic, Slobodan 205
MoD (Ministry of Defence) 94
moralization gap 44
Myint, U. 370

Nagy, R. 164, 327
Nandi people (Uganda) 94
National Association of Crime Victim Compensation Boards (US) 109
National Commission on Political Imprisonment and Torture (Chile) 239
Nazism 93, 184, 202, 205–6
Nee, A. 173–4
Netherlands 63–4
Nettelfield, Lara 167
neuropsychological consequences of crime (child victims) 305–6, 319
'Never Again' (military document) 238–9
New York Times (newspaper) 368
NICs (newly industrialized countries): Brazil 69–70; China 71, 82; India 71–4, 82; Malaysia 74–5, 82; Mexico 75–6; Philippines 77–8, 81–2; South Africa 78–9, 82; Thailand 79, 82; Turkey 80; victims' rights in 68–82
Nigeria 360
non-bailable crimes 70
Northern Ireland 109
NOVA (National Organization for Victim Assistance) 15
Nozick, R. 43

OAS (Organisation of American States) 232
Obama, Barack 155
'Obamacare' 121
Offen, Bernard 337
offender accountability (victims' justice needs) 388
offenders' rights 105, 116–17, 124
Office for Terrorism Victims (Spain) 325, 328, 332
Oklahoma City bombings (1995) 110
Olaya, J. 360, 368
online interventions 265–6, 271–5
'ordinary justice' 168
Orentlicher, Diane 166
organized crime: and corruption 358, 363, 369, 372, 373; and ETA study 325; and human trafficking 142–4, 155; in NICs 75
OVC (Office for Victims of Crime) 108, 110, 115, 122–3

overprotection 313–14
Owen, R. 312

parental support (child victims) 313–14
Paris Peace Agreement (1991) 221, 252
Parker, L. 76
participation (victims' justice needs) 388
Partido Popular (Spanish political party) 325
past control 268–70
paternalism 39, 40
Paternoster, Raymond 164
PCOSES (Perceived Control Over Stressful Events Scale) 270, 273, 274
Peace Committee (Chile) 231–2
PEDS (Paediatric Emotional Distress Scale) 310
peer support (child victims) 315–6
Pemberton, A. 387
Pennebaker, James 266
perceived control over traumatic events: developing control 270–1; online interventions 265–6, 271–5; and present control 268–70, 271–5; and self-blame 266–7, 268, 269; and stress 268, 271, 272–4; temporal model of control 268–70
Peru 235, 237, 241–2
Pesantes, Judge Salgado 241
pets 316–17
Pham, P. 222
Philippines 77–8, 81–2
physical consequences of crime (child victims) 303–4, 318
Pickett, K. 322
PIDEE (La Fundación Protección a la Infancia Dañada por los Estados de Emergencia) 233
Pinochet, General Augusto 93, 231–2, 233–4, 238
Polaris Project (NGO) 146, 147
police investigations 61
political reconstruction 229
politico-legal justice (dimension of integral justice) 191, 193

positive focus (child victims) 309–10
Pot, Pol 221
Poulson, B. 290
pragmatic justice 380, 381
Prenzler, T. 364
present control 268–70, 271–5
private prosecutions 24–5
procedural justice: and decision making procedures 279, 280–1, 286–7, 291; and ETA study 327, 330, 332; quality of treatment 280–1, 285–6, 290–1; and sexual victimization 387–8; and victim concerns 279–82; and victim impact statements 277, 282–7, 292; and victimization 277, 281, 289; and victim–offender mediation 277, 287–91, 292; and 'voice' 279–80, 281, 283–5, 288–90
Property Tax and Compensation Fund Law (Israel) 110
psychological/emotional impact of victimization 212–13, 278, 301–3
PTG (Post Traumatic Growth) 309
PTSD (post-traumatic stress disorder): and child victims 302–3, 309–11, 313–14; and perceived control over traumatic events 265, 266, 270, 271, 272; and transitional justice 172, 175
public apologies 188, 192, 219, 221, 337

quality of treatment (procedural justice model) 280–1, 285–6, 290–1

racism 92–4
radical criminology 14
rape victims 266–8, 269–70, 380
'reactive victim scapegoating' 169–70
Reagan, Ronald 17, 67
'real rape' 380
'rebalancing' 105, 124
Rebuilding Lives: Supporting Victims of Crime (White Paper, 2005) 16
reckless behaviour 302
recognition respect 33–5, 36–7, 41, 43, 44–5

'recovered memory' 13
'recovery' 332
recovery process awareness (child victims) 310–11
recovery time/space (child victims) 307, 318
'redacted narratives' 249
Reeves, Helen 19
rehabilitation 214, 239, 325, 327, 332, 334, 336
Reiner, Robert 26
'relational PTSD' 313–14
religion 194, 196, 199–201
REMHI (Recovery of Historical Memory) 193
reparations: access to 213–17; and African victims of colonialism 89–91, 92–5, 96–100; Chilean study 239–40; collective measures 215–16; development of concept 95–6; and ETA study 325, 329, 330, 332, 334–7, 338, 340; forms of 213–15, 239–40; individual measures 215–16; judicial measures 216–17; and mass victimization 210, 211, 212, 213–24; non-judicial measures 216–17; and transitional justice 161, 165, 170, 239–40; victim perspectives on 217–23; *see also* compensation
reparative justice 188–9, 210–11, 217
'resilience' 332
respecting victims: and appraisal respect 33–5, 36–7, 43, 44–5; and criminal justice system 33, 34, 40, 42–3; defining 'respect' 32–3; and development of victims' rights 32; and disrespect 35–6; and empathy 33, 37–8, 39, 40–1, 43, 45; and harmfulness 33, 42–4; and recognition respect 33–5, 36–7, 41, 43, 44–5; and sentencing 43; and sympathy 33, 38–40, 43, 45; types of respect 33; and victimization 33–45; and wrongfulness 33, 41–5
restitution: and African victims of colonialism 96–7, 99; and development

of victims' rights 66, 67; as form of reparation 214, 219–20, 239; and victims' rights in NICs 71, 72, 74, 78, 79, 80
'restoration' 332
restorative justice: and African victims of colonialism 97; and development of victims' rights 66; and empathy 40–1; and ETA study 322, 323–6, 328, 330–41; and sexual victimization 378, 382, 383; and transitional justice 164; and victim–offender mediation 287–91, 292; and victims' rights in NICs 71, 79
retributive justice: and development of victims' rights 66; and sexual victimization 378, 382; and transitional justice 161, 162, 166, 169, 170, 177
Reyes, M. 337
Roberts, J. 283, 284
Rogers, L. 285
Rome Statute (1998) 162, 212, 240
rule of law 163–5
Rwanda 171, 213

Samburu people (Kenya) 94
Samii, Cyrus 173, 174
Samoei, Koitalel arap 94
Sanguinetti, Julio María 233
Sanguinetti, Raúl 234
'satisfaction' 214, 239, 387, 390
Schafer, S. 67
Scheeringa, M. 313–14
Schieffer, Alexander 190, 192
Schiller de Kohn, Vera 183, 184–5, 203
school support (child victims) 315
'secondary victimisation': and criminal justice systems 212, 215; and defining 'victims' 13; and development of victims' rights 11; and ETA study 325–6, 327, 330, 340–1; and victim identity 15; and victims' rights in NICs 78
self-blame 266–7, 268, 269
self-efficacy 270, 273, 274
self-expression (child victims) 306–7

September 11th Victim Compensation
    Fund 110
Serbia 218–20
Sessar, K. 169
'sex offenders' 379–80, 390
sexual victimization: and defining
    'victims' 378; and justice mechanisms
    378–9, 382–3, 386–8, 390; political
    context 379–82, 390; and Sexual
    Violence and Justice Matrix 379,
    384–6; and Victimization and Justice
    Model 378, 379, 382–90
Sexual Violence and Justice Matrix 379,
    384–6
Shapland, J. 288–9
Shapo, M. 110
Shaw, R. 177
Sherman, L. 40, 287–8
Shirk, D. 76
Sicilia, Javier 75
Sierra Leone 177
Sihanouk, King Norodom 252
Skinner, E. 268
slavery 91–2, 140
'social harm' 66–7, 336, 338
'social imaginary' 248
social justice 112–3, 122
social reconstruction: Bosnia-Herzegovina
    study 166–8, 177; and human rights
    abuses 163; and international norms
    165; and therapy 174–6; and transitional
    justice 162–3, 176–8; and victimology
    163,
    168–71; and victims' attitude studies 171
social/behavioural consequences of crime
    (child victims) 304–5
societal justice (dimension of integral
    justice) 191, 193–4
Solzhenitsyn, Aleksandr 184, 196
Sommer, H. 110
South Africa 78–9, 82, 235, 238
Spain 109; *see also* ETA (Euskadi Ta
    Askatasuna)
spiritual justice (dimension of integral
    justice) 191, 198–200

spirituality 198–204
sporadic corruption 362, 363–4, 366, 367,
    368–9, 371
Sri Lanka 194
Stockholm Programme (2010) 107
Strang, H. 40, 287–8
stress 268, 271, 272–4, 301–4, 305,
    310–11, 313–14
structural level victimization 360–1,
    365–7, 372
structural-sporadic corruption 367
structural-systemic corruption 365
structure/routine (child victims) 307–8
'Super Great Leap Forward' (Cambodia)
    247
'survivors' 12, 378
Sweeting, A. 312
symbolic justice 327, 380, 381
symbolic measures 210, 213–14, 220, 240
sympathy: and compensation 112; and
    respecting victims 33, 38–40, 43, 45;
    and victimization 38–40, 43, 45
systemic corruption 355, 358, 362, 363,
    365–6, 367–8, 370, 372

Taj Mahal Palace (Mumbai) 111
Task Force on Victims of Crime (1982) 11,
    15–16, 67, 108, 112
Task Force on Victims' Rights and the
    Justice System (1991) 14
Task Forces on Human Trafficking 141–2
Taylor, Charles 205, 248
temporal model of control 268–70
terrorism victims: and compensation 105,
    109–11, 122, 124; and ETA study 322,
    325–7, 329–30, 333–6, 338–41
TF-CBT (Trauma Focused Cognitive
    Behaviour Therapy) 311
Thailand 79, 82
The Men Who Killed Me (book) 213
therapeutic jurisprudence 40, 279, 330,
    332, 387, 388
'therapeutic justice/victimology' 176
Theresa of Avila, Saint 201
Thibaut, John 279

Thiruvalluvar 72
'Three Strikes' law 169
Tobolowsky, P. 66
'top-down' victim perspectives 217
Trafficking Victims Protection Act (2001) 141
Trans Bay Steel Inc. 155
transformation of victims 183–5, 202–4
transitional justice: accounting for victims 234–7; and amnesties 162, 172–3, 178, 193; attitude of victims 171–4; Bosnia-Herzegovina study 165–8, 177; and Cambodia study 247–59; Chilean study 228–43; and context 162; and criminal justice systems 240–2; and democracy 163, 228–9, 230, 252–3, 259; development of 228–30; and ETA study 327–30; and human rights abuses 161, 162, 165, 168, 175; 'imaginary' of 247–59; and integral justice 185–6, 189, 192, 193, 194–6, 200, 206; and international norms 163–5; judicial mechanisms of 162–3, 171–2, 173, 174, 175; 'lacunae' of 187–9; and legalism 162, 163–4, 168–70, 174, 175; and mass victimization 210–11; and memory preservation 234, 235, 237–8; normative dimension of 249, 254, 255, 257; and political reconstruction 229; and reconciliation 242; and reparations 239–40; and reparative justice 188–9; and retributive justice 161, 162, 166, 169, 170, 177; and rule of law 163–5; and sexual victimization 383, 386, 389; and social reconstruction 162–3, 176–8; tensions within 161–2, 177; and therapy 174–6; and trauma 163, 168, 169–70, 171–3, 174–6, 251–2; and trials 162–3, 167–8, 172–3, 176, 177–8; and truth commissions 161, 162, 163, 170, 173, 174, 175, 177–8, 186, 188; 'victim' figure within 230, 235–7; and 'victimhood' 161, 162, 163, 169–70, 174, 237; and victimology 163, 168–71, 176

Transparency International (NGO) 355–6, 364
trauma: and child victims 301–3, 305–6, 309–11, 313–15, 319; and compensation 115; developing control 270–1; and human trafficking 151; and integral justice 183, 187, 189, 202, 204, 205; online interventions 265–6, 271–5; perceived control over 265–75; and present control 268–70, 271–5; and rape victims 266–8, 269–70; and self-blame 266–7, 268, 269; temporal model of control 268–70; and transitional justice 163, 168, 169–70, 171–3, 174–6, 251–2; and victim identity 15; and victims' rights 15, 16
Treaty of Berlin (1878) 100
Treaty of Lisbon (2007) 51, 53, 54
Treaty of Versailles (1919) 95
Treisman, D. 360
trials: and EU action on victims' rights 56, 61–2; and integral justice 192; Khmer Rouge Tribunal 247–8, 249, 253–6, 257; and transitional justice 162–3, 167–8, 172–3, 176, 177–8; and victims' rights in NICs 72, 73, 74, 76–7, 78, 80
Trindade, Judge Cançado 241
trust 112, 124–5
Trust Fund for Victims 216–17, 223
truth commissions: and Chilean study 234–5, 236–7, 238, 242; and reparations 216–5; and transitional justice 161, 162, 163, 170, 173, 174, 175, 177–8, 186, 188
truth-telling 210
Turkey 80
T-Visa classification 150–2
TVPA (Trafficking Victims Protection Act, 2000) 143–4, 145–6, 149–53
TVPRA (Trafficking Victims Protection Reauthorization Act, 2005) 144, 146, 150, 152
Tyler, T. 164, 279–80, 281
Tzu, Lao 201

Index   407

Uganda 171, 172, 220–1
UN Declaration of Basic Principles of Justice for Victims of Crime and Abuse of Power (1985): and development of victims' rights 67–8; and EU action on victims' rights 57; and mass victimization 212; and nature of rights 19; and transitional justice 168; and victim identity 12–13; and victims' rights in NICs 71, 72–3
UN Palermo Convention 142, 143–4
UN Reparation Principles (2005) 168, 212, 213, 221, 239
UN Smuggling Protocol (2000) 140, 142
UN Trafficking Protocol (2000) 140, 142–4
uncertainty 280
'Uncle San, Aunty Yan, and the KRT' (booklet) 247, 248, 250–9
'Uncle San' 247, 248, 249, 250–9
uncontrollability 266–7
universalistic caring 340
Upanishads (ancient Hindu texts) 201
Uruguay 228, 229, 233–4
USA 108–9, 112, 114–16, 118, 121, 122–3, 124, 125, 129–30, 141–56
Uvin, P. 173–4
U-Visa classification 151–2
Uwakwe, V. 360

validation (victims' justice needs) 388
van Boven-Bassiouni Principles 168
Van Camp, T. 290, 291
Van den Bos, K. 280
Van Dijk, Jan 25, 169–70, 172, 373
Vanfraechem, I. 288
Varela, Francesco 198–9
Varna system (India) 72
VAWA (Violence Against Women Act, 2005) 151
Veil, Simone 184
Velásquez, Bámaca 241
via Nanclares (repentant ex-terrorists) 325
Vicariate of Solidarity (Chile) 232
Victim Care Units 122

Victim Compensation Act (Thailand, 2001) 79
victim concerns 277–82, 291
victim identity 14–16
Victim Support (England and Wales) 12, 15, 16
Victim Support (Europe) 19
Victim Support (Netherlands) 63, 312
victim support services: access to information 60; access to support 59; child victims 311, 313–19; and EU action on victims' rights 57–61; individual assessments 60; minimum service requirements 59–60; and procedural justice model 285–6; and victims' rights in NICs 69
'victim therapy' 174
Victim's Charter (South Africa) 78–9
'victimagogic programmes' 25
'victim-blaming' 17
'victimhood' 161, 162, 163, 169–70, 174, 237
victimization: and appraisal respect 33–5, 36–7, 43, 44–5; and child victims 300, 301, 305–7, 311–12, 315, 318, 319; and compensation 105, 111, 116; and corruption 359–62, 364–72; and empathy 40, 43, 45; and ETA study 322, 325, 326–7, 329–30, 333–6, 338–41; and harmfulness 42–4; and human trafficking 141, 147–8; and integral justice 185; levels of 359–62, 366, 372; mass *see* mass victimization; and perceived control over traumatic events 265; and procedural justice model 277, 281, 289; psychological/emotional impact of 212–13, 278, 301–3; and recognition respect 33–5, 36–7, 41, 43, 44–5; and respecting victims 33–45; sexual *see* sexual victimization; and sympathy 38–40, 43, 45; and terrorism 322, 325, 326–7, 329–32, 333–6, 338–41; and transformation of victims 183–5, 203–4; and transitional justice 169–70, 172, 174–5, 176–7; and victim

concerns 277–8, 281; and victim identity 15–16; and victims' rights in NICs 69, 73, 74, 78; and wrongfulness 41–5
Victimization and Justice Model 378, 379, 382–90
victimology: and criminal justice systems 212; and development of victims' rights 12; and integral justice 185, 189, 193, 200, 206; and mass victimization 211–13, 215, 223; and transitional justice 162, 168–71, 176
Victims Advisory Panel 16, 25
Victims of Crime Week (1987) 17
Victims of Crimes Bill (Philippines, 2010) 77
Victims of Hostile Action Law (Israel, 1970) 110
Victims' Code (2006) 21–2
'victims' justice needs' 388–90
victims' rights: and bipartisanism of lawyers 24; and class 26; and common law jurisdictions 23–4; and compensation *see* compensation; cost of 23; and crime figures 14–15; and Criminal Injuries Compensation Authority 17, 23; and criminal justice system 11–12, 16–17, 19, 21, 24–6, 32; and defining 'victims' 12–14; development of 11–12, 32, 66–8; eligibility of victims 16–18; and empathy 40–1, 45; EU action on *see* EU action on victims' rights; and feminism 11; and human trafficking *see* human trafficking; and integral justice 205, 206; legislation on *see* legislation protecting victims' rights; and marginalisation of victims 11; and nature of rights 18–20; in NICs 68–82; and private prosecutions 24–5; *realpolitik* of 20–6; and 'rebalancing' 105, 124; respecting victims *see* respecting victims; and restorative justice 330, 339; and trauma 15, 16; and

victim identity 14–16; and victimology 12; and Victims' Code (2006) 21–2
vindication (victims' justice needs) 388
'violent crime' 114–15
VIS (victim impact statements) 75, 277, 282–7, 292
VOCA (Victims of Crime Act, 1984) 108–9, 110, 115, 118, 121, 123, 125
'voice' 279–80, 281, 283–5, 288–90, 388
VOM (victim–offender mediation) 277, 287–91, 292
Von Hentig, Hans 67
Vos, K. 286
VTVPA (Victims of Trafficking and Violence Protection Act) 150

Waite, Terry 36
Walker, Laurens 279
Ware v. Hylton (1796) 95
Watts, Alan 204
WCAR (World Conference against Racism, 2001) 92
Weber, Max 229
Welsh, H. 365
Wemmers, J.-A. 280, 286, 288, 289, 290
Wendell-Holmes, Oliver 41
Wergens, A. 106
Wilber, Ken 190, 200
Wilkinson, R. 322
Williams, M. 327
Wispé, L. 38, 39
Witness Protection, Security and Benefits Act (Philippines, 1991) 77
World Society of Victimology Symposium (2003) 36
wrongfulness 33, 41–5

'yardstick of harm' 42, 43–4
'Yoyes' 337

Zawisza, C. 330
Zeanah, C. 313–14
Zheng, G. 71